ESSENTIAL UCC CONCEPTS

A SURVEY OF COMMERCIAL TRANSACTIONS

■ ■ ■

Candace M. Zierdt

Professor of Law
Stetson University College of Law

Kristen David Adams

Professor of Law
Stetson University College of Law

Juliet M. Moringiello

Commonwealth Professor of Business Law
Widener University Harrisburg School of Law

AMERICAN CASEBOOK SERIES®

WEST
ACADEMIC
PUBLISHING

American Casebook Series is a trademark registered in the U.S. Patent and Trademark Office.

© 2018 LEG, Inc. d/b/a West Academic
444 Cedar Street, Suite 700
St. Paul, MN 55101
1-877-888-1330

West, West Academic Publishing, and West Academic are trademarks of West Publishing Corporation, used under license.

Printed in the United States of America

ISBN: 978-1-62810-136-2

ACKNOWLEDGMENTS

Professors Adams and Zierdt gratefully acknowledge the support of Stetson University College of Law and the office of Faculty Support Services, especially Shannon Edgar and Jessica Zook. We also appreciate the excellent research assistance and work of Stetson students Jill Boyer and Danielle Dineen. In addition, Professor Adams thanks Jeff, Luke, and Allie Smith for their love and support. Professor Zierdt appreciates the research assistance provided by Stetson student Ahmed Mohamed. Additionally, she thanks Ginger and Holly for all their support. Professor Moringiello acknowledges the support of Dean Christian Johnson and Widener University Commonwealth Law School. She especially appreciates the assistance of faculty assistant Jeremy Wingert. In addition, Professor Moringiello thanks Matthew and Brendan for always keeping her on her toes.

SUMMARY OF CONTENTS

TABLE OF CONTENTS

———————

TABLE OF CASES

The principal cases are in bold type.

———————

TABLE OF STATUTES AND UNIFORM COMMERCIAL CODE SECTIONS

ESSENTIAL UCC CONCEPTS

CONCEPTS

A SURVEY OF COMMERCIAL TRANSACTIONS

INTRODUCTION

■ ■ ■

A. HISTORICAL CONTEXT AND THE UCC

This textbook introduces the Uniform Commercial Code ("UCC" or "Code") as well as earlier efforts to unify the commercial law of the United States. Complementary federal law is also mentioned from time to time, where relevant.

1. THE UCC: ITS ORIGINS AND AUTHORSHIP

The Uniform Commercial Code (as well as this casebook) purports to address the subject of "commercial transactions," and yet neither "commercial" nor "transaction" is a defined term within the Code. Instead, as **1–102** suggests, a commercial transaction, as that term is used in the UCC, is any matter that falls within one of the Code's ten substantive articles, which are briefly introduced below in Part C.

The UCC is not a product of any legislature or official government body, but rather is the result of a long-term collaboration between the Uniform Law Commission (ULC and formerly abbreviated as NCCUSL, for National Conference of Commissioners on Uniform State Laws) and the American Law Institute (ALI), both of which are private organizations. Because of this unique pedigree, the UCC is not law until it is adopted by a state legislature. The ALI and ULC came together on this project for the purpose of creating a uniform body of law to make commerce function more effectively, and to normalize expectations across jurisdictions so that a party in California, for example, can have some idea of what to expect while engaged in a commercial transaction with a party in Florida.

The ALI and ULC each have a distinct mission and means of selecting members. The purpose of the American Law Institute, as contained in its Certificate of Incorporation, is as follows:

> The particular business and objects of the society are educational, and are to promote the clarification and simplification of the law and its better adaptation to social needs, to secure the better administration of justice, and to encourage and carry on scholarly and scientific legal work.

ALI members, who are judges, lawyers, and law professors, are elected by an internal process. In addition, according to ALI Council Rules, the following classes of persons are recognized as ex-officio members:

The Chief Justice of the United States and the Associate Justices of the Supreme Court of the United States . . . ; The chief judge of the highest court of each State, of the District of Columbia, and of Puerto Rico, Guam, the U.S. Virgin Islands, American Samoa, and the Northern Mariana Islands; Chief Judges of the United States Courts of Appeals; The Attorney General and the Solicitor General of the United States; The Presidents of the National Conference of Commissioners on Uniform State Laws, the American, National, and Federal Bar Associations, and the Bar Association of each State and of the District of Columbia, Puerto Rico, Guam, the U.S. Virgin Islands, American Samoa, and the Northern Mariana Islands; and the dean of each law school that is a member of the Association of American Law Schools and the President of that Association.

The purpose of the ULC, as stated in its constitution, is as follows:

It is the purpose of the Conference to promote uniformity in the law among the several States on subjects as to which uniformity is desirable and practicable.

ULC Commissioners are appointed by the states independently of one another, and are typically chosen by the Governors of each state, although some are chosen by legislative directive. Each Commissioner must be a member of the bar of some state, although the organization's Constitution does not expressly require that Commissioners be admitted to the bar of the state selecting them for service in the Conference.

The first official UCC text was published in 1952. The Code project was not, however, the first attempt at preparing a uniform body of commercial law in the United States. In fact, the ULC had been engaged in uniform-law efforts since 1892 and had produced a number of Uniform Acts prior to the UCC, some of which were very successful. The following list of Uniform Acts predating the UCC is from the General Comment of National Conference of Commissioners on Uniform State Laws and the American Law Institute, which immediately precedes the text of the Code, and is modified to list the UCC Article that is most comparable to each:

Pre-UCC Uniform Law	Year	Comparable UCC Article
Uniform Negotiable Instruments Law	1896	Article 3: Negotiable Instruments
Uniform Warehouse Receipts Act	1906	Article 7: Documents of Title
Uniform Sales Act	1906	Article 2: Sales
Uniform Bills of Lading Act	1909	Article 7: Documents of Title

Uniform Stock Transfer Act	1909	Article 8: Investment Securities
Uniform Conditional Sales Act	1918	Article 9: Secured Transactions
Uniform Trust Receipts Act	1933	Article 9: Secured Transactions

In describing the importance of these previous Uniform Acts, the General Comment continues as follows:

> Two of these acts were adopted in every American State, and the remaining acts have had wide acceptance. Each of them has become a segment of the statutory law relating to commercial transactions. It has been recognized for some years that these acts needed substantial revision to keep them in step with modern commercial practices and to integrate each of them with the others.

It was the goal of the UCC to provide the needed revisions and integration referenced in the General Comment. As you read the Official Comments to the Code throughout your study of this material, note the reference to any "Prior Uniform Statutory Provision" that precedes the commentary to many Code provisions. As these references show, many UCC provisions incorporate content from previous Uniform Acts.

Even though the UCC was written by law professors, judges, and practicing lawyers, rather than legislators, *some version* of each Article has been passed into law in all 50 states, except for Louisiana, which never adopted Article 2 because the state's French civil-code heritage militated in favor of a different treatment of the law of contracts. Thus, the UCC project has been a tremendous success. The qualification "some version" is meant to countenance the way in which some states have chosen nonuniform enactments of the Code, as well as the way in which the Code has changed over time, as the discussion below of revisions will demonstrate. In addition to numerous amendments of the original nine Articles, two new Articles, 2A and 4A, were added in 1987 and 1989, respectively. Because of these additions and changes, the Code *as enacted* varies somewhat from state to state.

One important characteristic of the UCC is that many of its provisions are default terms; that is, parties can contract around many UCC standards if they so desire. Exceptions exist with regard to duties—like good faith, diligence, reasonableness, and care—that are deemed too important to be waived by private agreement. Even with regard to these exceptions, however, **1–302(b)** provides parties with some means of defining their obligations within reasonable parameters.

2. THE PURPOSE AND PHILOSOPHY OF THE UCC

This textbook is designed for a UCC survey course. Commercial law is a form of business law, and this book will demonstrate how each UCC Article covered shows up in common business transactions. Understanding the business context for the Code, as well as the drafters' philosophy of law, can help clarify why certain provisions are written as they are. Commercial law scholars have been particularly interested in studying the work of Professor Karl N. Llewellyn, who was the Code's Chief Reporter and principal architect.

1–103(a) sets forth the underlying purpose of the Code. This stated purpose shows that Professor Llewellyn was focused on making the Code a simple, clear, modern, and uniform product that would reflect the realities of business as transacted in the modern world. To that end, he recognized the important role of commercial practices, custom, and usages as well as private agreement.

Especially because the ALI and ULC must rely on state legislatures to adopt their work, their joint decision to create a Code that incorporates business norms as well as earlier, successful uniform codes of law was not only a reasonable choice, but probably also made an appreciable difference in the long-term success of the Code project.

3. UCC REVISIONS AND NONUNIFORM ENACTMENTS

That the Code may be revised when its drafters find a once-correct rule no longer useful or determine that a former enactment was ill-advised seems too obvious to merit further discussion. Because the Code revision process requires the action of state legislatures, the ULC and ALI revisions are undertaken only after considerable study and discussion. **1–103** Comment 1 shows how Code provisions can be construed broadly to address changes in the legal, technological, and business landscape without the need for constant revision. This type of construction has been regularly used with Article 2 because, despite 14 years of trying to revise it, Article 2 has not received a major overhaul since it was first promulgated in 1952.

Because neither the ALI nor ULC has any independent authority to make law, any revision faces the prospect that a certain number of states may choose not to enact the revision, or not to enact some portions of it. As you read this textbook, you might pause from time to time to examine whether your state has adopted the portion of the Code you are studying as written, or has made what is called a "nonuniform enactment," changing portions of the text to respond to local needs or interests.

B. SOURCES OF MODERN COMMERCIAL LAW

1–103(b) addresses the Code's relationship to other law. The UCC is not intended to be an exclusive statement of U.S. commercial law. Instead, the Code is to be understood as part of a larger domestic and international context. As you read through these materials, there will be times when you will be asked to consider bodies of law outside the UCC. For example, the law of agency—specifically, express, implied, and apparent authority—will help you to determine whether an agent has the authority to sign on a principal's behalf. Likewise, state law will dictate the highest rate of interest that can be lawfully charged, as well as when a contract is void rather than just voidable.

C. OVERVIEW OF THE UCC AND GUIDE TO ITS USE

The eleven articles of the UCC are briefly described as follows:

Article 1—General Provisions. As the name suggests, the provisions in Article 1 generally apply throughout the ten substantive Articles that follow.

Article 2—Sales. Article 2 is concerned with "transactions in goods" as that term is used in **2–102**, although the main focus for this book is on sales of goods in Article 2, which is narrower than "transactions." There was a serious attempt to revise Article 2 that began in the late 1980s and lasted 14 years. It was quite controversial and, as a result, Revised Article 2 has not been passed in any state.

Article 2A—Leases. Article 2A was first promulgated in the late 1980s. Although there have been attempts at subsequent revisions, they have not been successful.

Article 3—Negotiable Instruments. This material is sometimes called Commercial Paper. Together with Articles 4 and 4A, this body of law is also called Payment Systems. Negotiable Instruments law governs drafts (including checks) and promissory notes.

Article 4—Bank Deposits and Collections. Article 4 is concerned with the bank-collection process.

Articles 3 and 4 were revised in 1990 and 1991, respectively, and amended in 2002.

Article 4A—Funds Transfers. Article 4A addresses large funds transfers (sometimes called "wire transfers") between commercial entities.

Article 5—Letters of Credit. Letters of credit are an extremely important means of payment in international trade. This mechanism makes it possible for a seller to secure payment from an unfamiliar purchaser who may be halfway across the world, by guaranteeing payment through a third party.

Article 6—Bulk Sales. Historically, the bulk sale was a potential means of defrauding creditors. A fraudfeasor might acquire inventory on unsecured credit, sell it, and abscond with the proceeds without paying for the goods, thus thwarting the creditors who sold him the inventory. Article 6 addressed this problem by requiring certain purchasers of goods through bulk sales to provide the seller's creditors with notice of the sale before it took place. Recognizing that the requirements of Article 6 were onerous to purchasers, substantial reform making Article 9 security interests easier to obtain, coupled with remedies available under the Uniform Fraudulent Transfer Act, have resulted in the repeal of Article 6 in almost every jurisdiction.

Article 7—Documents of Title. Article 7 is primarily concerned with the law of bailment. This body of law establishes a standard means of establishing rights in goods either in storage or being transported from one location to another.

Article 8—Investment Securities. The Uniform Commercial Code, along with federal and other state law, provides part of the body of law relating to investment securities.

Article 9—Secured Transactions. Article 9 is the primary source of law governing sales, loans, and other credit agreements made with non-real-estate collateral. It was radically revised in 2001 and more modestly amended in 2010.

This book primarily focuses on Articles 2, 3, 4, and 9. Article 1 is mentioned to supply definitions and other general provisions where relevant, and Article 2A is discussed briefly in Chapters 1, 2, and 11. Articles 4A, 5, and 7 are introduced in Chapter 10. Investment securities, as that term is used in Article 8, are mentioned only in passing, and Article 6, having been repealed in most jurisdictions, is not discussed at all.

1. THE ARTICLES' RELATIONSHIP TO ONE ANOTHER

The various Articles of the UCC work in connection with one another, frequently within the context of a single transaction. Understanding these connections is crucial to a meaningful study of commercial law.

The following excerpt is taken from the General Comment of National Conference of Commissioners on Uniform State Laws and the American Law Institute, which immediately precedes the text of the Code. This excerpt provides some perspective on how the various Articles of the UCC fit together, as well as the way in which each topic represents some aspect of Commercial Transactions:

> The concept of the present Act is that "commercial transactions" is a single subject of the law, notwithstanding its many facets.

> A single transaction may very well involve a contract for sale, followed by a sale, the giving of a check or draft for a part of the

purchase price, and the acceptance of some form of security for the balance.

The check or draft may be negotiated and will ultimately pass through one or more banks for collection.

If the goods are shipped or stored, the subject matter of the sale may be covered by a bill of lading or warehouse receipt or both.

Or it may be that the entire transaction was made pursuant to a letter of credit either domestic or foreign.

Obviously, every phase of commerce involved is but a part of one transaction, namely, the sale of and payment for goods.

If, instead of goods in the ordinary sense, the transaction involved stocks or bonds, some of the phases of the transaction would obviously be different. Others would be the same. In addition, there are certain additional formalities incident to the transfer of stocks and bonds from one owner to another.

This Act purports to deal with all the phases which may ordinarily arise in the handling of a commercial transaction, from start to finish.

2. RECURRING THEMES IN THE CODE

As you study the UCC, you will notice certain, particularly important concepts that show up in various ways throughout the Code. One example is the Article 2 "good faith purchaser for value," who turns up in Article 3 bearing the name of "holder in due course," in Article 7 as a "holder by due negotiation," and in Article 8 as a "protected purchaser."

One of the pleasant results of the Code's continuity of themes, coupled with its consistent attention to business realities and preferences, is that students of commercial law often find themselves able to intuit the correct result in one area of the UCC, once they have become familiar with another. If one of the tests of good law is for it to be intuitive and consistent with societal norms, the Code's predictability may be one reason for its success.

3. READING THE CODE

Reading the Code can present a challenge, as many students find it grammatically awkward and sometimes difficult to follow in both its logic and its sentence constructions. Happily, there is assistance available. The ULC website provides "Act Summary" information for each Article, written in a conversational fashion, that gives insight into the drafters' priorities and intentions. Official comments provide the same function with regard to individual Code provisions. Although the comments are not part of the UCC text and are thus generally not enacted into law, they are a helpful research tool and a persuasive source regularly consulted by courts and litigants alike.

Finally, the Code's liberal use of internal cross-references can be a significant help in directing readers to definitions and other, related Code provisions. Becoming comfortable with the UCC itself, rather than resorting to this book (or any other text) as a primary source for explanation is a crucial skill for a commercial lawyer.

D. ARTICLE 1: THE BASELINE
FOR THE UCC

This section introduces the voluminous Article 1 definitions and the possibility that the parties to a transaction may depart from, or vary, the Code's provisions by agreement.

1. THE SCOPE OF ARTICLE 1

As **1–102** indicates, no transaction is governed by Article 1 unless it falls within the scope of one of the ten substantive Articles of the Code. Thus, there is no such thing as an Article 1 transaction. Instead, Article 1 can be thought of as a "helper" Article that supplements the substantive Articles of the Code that follow.

2. ARTICLE 1'S LENGTHY DEFINITIONS

This book makes reference to the definitions contained in Article 1 whenever they are relevant to the immediate context. In the meantime, note that one of the principal reasons to consult Article 1 is for definitions of key terms. Many of these are found in **1–201** through **1–206**. There are numerous defined terms under the Code, and Article 1 (especially **1–201**), as well as the first several sections of each subsequent Article, contains a wealth of definitions. Unless a more specific definition is presented within the text of each Article, Article 1's definitions apply throughout the Code. In case of conflict, however, a substantive Article's specific definitions trump the general Article 1 provisions, for purposes of that Article.

As you leave this introduction, stop to make sure that you are comfortable with the Code on a superficial level. You should have a sense of the philosophy and purpose of the Code, the historical context in which it was written, and its relationship with other domestic bodies of commercial law. You should also have a basic understanding of the subject of each of the UCC's ten substantive articles, an approach in mind for navigating the Code's text, and an idea of how Article 1 assists in this process.

CHAPTER 1

INTRODUCTION TO SALES LAW AND SCOPE

∎ ∎ ∎

A. INTRODUCTION

The first five chapters focus on the law relating to transactions in goods, an area of law governed by UCC Articles 2 and 2A, along with other state law, federal law, and an international treaty. Although Article 2 covers transactions in goods, our main focus is with the sale of goods. Article 2A deals with leases of goods.

Chapter 1 concerns scope issues and how to determine what laws might apply to various transactions. Chapter 2 focuses on the terms of an agreement covered by Article 2. Chapter 3 considers how and whether certain terms will be incorporated in an agreement. This includes rules relating to contract formation, boilerplate terms, the parol evidence rule, the statute of frauds, and title issues. Chapter 4 is primarily concerned with performance and what happens when parties do not perform as agreed. This includes studying the rules relating to rejection, acceptance, cure, revocation, and how to deal with goods that are damaged or lost during performance. Chapter 5 introduces the various rules relating to remedies for buyers and sellers. Chapter 5 also reviews how a party may be excused from a breach and when courts may refuse to enforce an entire contract or part of it through the doctrine of unconscionability.

This chapter focuses on transactions in goods and how the UCC rules impact and govern those transactions, especially Article 2. Additionally, this chapter will address a number of different laws that may apply to these transactions and interact with the UCC. In any transaction that appears to be governed by the UCC, especially Article 2, you may need to consider the impact of the following laws: UCC Article 2; UCC Article 2A; UCC Article 9; The United Nations Convention on Contracts for the International Sale of Goods (CISG); The Magnuson-Moss Warranty Act; and the common law. Deciding whether a law applies to a transaction is a scope issue. And, since more than one law may apply to a transaction it is necessary to determine:

(1) What law(s) might apply to a transaction,

(2) Whether more than one law applies, and

(3) If more than one law is applicable, does one preempt or enhance the other law?

There are many reasons why parties may want a particular law to govern a transaction. One common reason is the difference in the statute of limitations for UCC contracts as compared to other contracts (or causes of action such as torts) not governed by the UCC. Generally, the UCC statute of limitations for contracts for sales is shorter than the common law. **2–725**[1] provides that an action must be brought within 4 years from the time the cause of action accrued.[2] However, a state's statute of limitations for a general contract action is usually longer than 4 years, with some exceptions. For example, some states allow claims to be brought within 10 years and others require a case be brought within a shorter time, such as 3 years.[3]

Another reason why a party may want a certain law to apply or not apply relates to warranties—one of the most important set of default rules in Article 2. The common law tends to follow the pre-UCC rule of "caveat emptor," also known as "buyer beware." However, note some states have limited that rule and now allow implied warranties outside of the UCC, such as the implied warranty of habitability in non-commercial real estate rentals. A specific issue related to warranties that may cause a party to want to be in or outside the scope of Article 2 is privity. In the next chapter you will learn that Article 2 has expanded the concept of privity to allow third parties to sue a warrantor in certain situations, even though the third party is not a party to the original sales contract. This is in stark contrast to the common law rule that only allows parties to a contract to sue under the contract. Additionally, the federal Magnuson-Moss Warranty Act allows even more plaintiffs to sue for breach of warranty, notwithstanding they are not in privity with the warrantor.

1.   UCC ARTICLES 2 AND 2A

A common scope issue relates to the differences between a lease transaction and a sales transaction. There are valid reasons as to why a party desires to have a transaction drafted as a lease (governed by Article 2A) or a sale (governed by Article 2). Leases may include a variety of tax benefits for the lessee or a lessor that a sale does not, or they may have

---

[1]   This book omits the abbreviation for the UCC and section sign. Instead, when referring to particular UCC sections, it will just state the section number.

[2]   The time the cause of action accrues varies depending on whether the cause of action is for breach of warranty or another type of breach. *See* UCC § 2–725(2).

[3]   *See e.g.* R. I. GEN. LAWS § 9–1–13 (providing a 10-year statute of limitations, with minor exception); KY. REV. STAT. ANN. § 413.160 (providing a 10-year statute of limitations for a contract action), 735 ILL. COMP. STAT. 5/13–205–06 (providing a 10-year limitation for written contracts and a 5-year statute of limitations for unwritten contracts); ARIZ. REV. STAT. ANN. § 548(A)(1) (providing a 6-year statute of limitations for written contracts); OHIO REV. CODE ANN. § 2305.06 (providing an 8-year statute of limitations for breach of contract claims); D.C. CODE § 12–301(7) (providing a 3-year statute of limitation for a simple contract); MD. COURTS & JUD. PROC. CODE ANN. § 5–101 (providing a 3-year statute of limitations).

accounting implications for the lessee or lessor. As an example, bankruptcy courts treat leased property very differently from property owned by a debtor. Because a *lessor* "owns" the good being leased, instead of the *lessee*, a bankruptcy trustee does not have the same ability to acquire property leased by a debtor.

Additional differences exist between Articles 2 and 2A that may persuade a party to structure a transaction as a lease instead of a sale, or vice versa. For example, Article 2A permits the creation of a transaction called a "finance lease." A lessee in a non-consumer finance lease does not have the benefit of receiving any implied warranties from a lessor and the lessee must pay come "hell or high water" according to **2A–407**. For these reasons, it becomes critical whether a court interprets a transaction to be a lease or a sale. Another issue centers on the differences and interactions between sales, leases, and secured transactions. If a party thinks she agreed to a lease, however a court determines the transaction is not a true lease, but instead a disguised sale with some type of attempted security interest, then Article 9 and its more complicated rules on perfection may apply. Those rules will be covered in a later chapter.

2. UCC ARTICLE 2 AND THE CISG

UCC Article 2 applies to transactions in goods, but it overlaps with the CISG which also applies to sales of goods. The CISG is a federal treaty intended to cover the international sales of goods in commercial transactions. As of 2017, 87 countries have adopted the CISG, including many common trading partners of U.S. companies such as Canada, Mexico, China, France, Germany, and Japan, just to name a few. Because the CISG and UCC default rules differ significantly, it is important to determine whether the CISG or the UCC governs a transaction.

An example of a major difference is how both laws treat contract formation and the issue of boilerplate terms in a contract. You may recall the common law mirror image rule that you learned in your first-year contracts class. That rule states that an acceptance with different or additional terms cannot be an acceptance because it is not a mirror image of the offer. Article 2 completely rejects the common law mirror image rule and allows contracts to form even when an acceptance contains different or additional terms. However, the CISG takes a subjective approach to contract formation and does not completely reject the mirror image rule. Instead, it uses a modified approach.

3. MAGNUSON-MOSS WARRANTY ACT

One other federal law to consider in consumer sales transactions is the Magnuson-Moss Warranty Act. Because it is federal law, if Magnuson-Moss applies it overrides the UCC in a number of significant ways and supplements the UCC in other ways. Additionally, Magnuson-Moss permits a court to award a prevailing plaintiff reasonable costs and expenses, including attorney's fees, which the UCC does not. Another distinction is Magnuson-Moss' definition of consumer product. Though Magnuson-Moss only applies to consumer products, it contains a fairly broad definition, defining consumer product in terms of whether the product is *normally used* for personal, family, or household purposes, whereas the UCC defines a consumer in terms of how *the individual intends to use* the product—not how it is ordinarily used. *See* **1–201(b)(11)** and **15 U.S.C.A. § 2301(1)**.[4]

To understand this difference in definitions between the UCC and Magnuson-Moss, imagine Hunter Smith owns a restaurant and wants to buy a new car. Under Magnuson-Moss, it does not matter whether she wants to use the new car for her business or her family because regardless of her usage a car is *normally* used for personal, family, or household purposes. As such, the car would meet the definition of a consumer good and Magnuson-Moss would apply assuming the other jurisdictional requirements are met. However, under the UCC it may matter for what purpose Hunter intends to use the car. If Hunter plans to use it as a delivery vehicle for her restaurant, the UCC would not consider the car a consumer good. If, however, she planned to use it to transport her family, the car would be a consumer good under the UCC. There are other significant differences in the area of warranties that will be covered later in this book.

B. SCOPE

1. WHAT LAW WILL APPLY

When looking at a transaction, the first thing you should do is determine what law applies to that transaction. Since this book is about commercial law, the UCC is our starting point. The first five chapters focus mainly on Article 2, so we need to consider how to ascertain whether a transaction is within the scope of Article 2. The overarching question you want to ask is: Does the transaction fall within the scope of Article 2? **2–102** defines the scope of Article 2 by stating that it only applies to "transactions in goods" and it does not apply to contracts solely intended to operate as a security transaction (covered by Article 9). You will learn about secured transactions and the consequences of a failed lease in the last five chapters of this book.

That leads us to our first scope inquiry: Does the transaction involve "goods" as defined by the UCC? **2–105** defines a good as "all things (including specially manufactured goods) which are movable at the time of

---

[4] The rest of this book omits the full citation for Magnuson-Moss and the section sign. Instead, when referring to particular Magnuson-Moss sections, it will just state the section number from 15 U.S.C.A.

identification to the contract for sale other than the money in which the price is to be paid, investment securities (Article 8) and things in action." As a visual tool, it might be helpful to think about scope in terms of a linear chart—the first question on your chart will be whether the transaction involves goods. If the transaction does not involve goods, Article 2 will not apply. For example, Article 2 does not apply to a cause of action, real property, or services.

This inquiry may seem very cut and dry; however, many transactions include services as well as goods and different laws apply depending on the characterization of any given transaction. Because the UCC generally applies to goods and the common law applies to services, there needs to be a way to decide when the UCC governs. That brings us to our next inquiry: If the transaction does involve goods, does it also involve services? If the answer is yes, the contract is called a hybrid transaction.

2. HYBRID TRANSACTIONS

After determining that a contract involves a hybrid transaction for both goods and services, the next step requires an analysis of whether to apply the UCC or common law. **1–103** states that if an issue arises that the UCC default rules do not cover, the common law supplements the UCC, "unless displaced by the particular provisions." Additionally, if the UCC does not apply to a transaction, the common law (or other law or statute) may apply. However, the UCC does not state how to decide what law will apply to a hybrid transaction.

Consider the following situation. You own a large dog and you want your dog to be able to leave the house without always having to open the door for her, so you decide to buy a doggie door. After doing a little research you determine that you need to have a doggie door specially made because of the size of your dog, so you locate a contractor named Luke Smith who specializes in creating custom doggie doors for large dogs. You agree that Luke will visit your house to determine the best location for the door, create the necessary specifications, build the door with special locking and anti-theft devices so only your dog can use the door, and custom install the door in your home. How is this different from going to your local pet store and buying a pre-made door? You should realize that your purchase from Smith involves much more work on his part because it requires Smith to create a custom door to fit your dog's specifications. This includes buying the materials, designing the door, manufacturing the door, and installing it in your home. Because it involves both services (measuring the specifications, creating the design for the door, building the door, and installing it in your home) and the sale of a good, it is a hybrid transaction. The doggie door is a good under **2–105** because it is moveable after it has been manufactured.

Because the UCC does not state what law applies to hybrid transactions, we look to the common law. Courts have developed two different tests to apply when analyzing an issue in a hybrid contract: the Gravamen test and Predominant Purpose test. The majority of jurisdictions use the Predominant Purpose test. These tests also apply to leases that are hybrid transactions. Additionally, some commentators and courts have advocated for a more policy oriented approach to scope issues, particularly when determining whether warranties of quality or fitness are implied in hybrid agreements.[5]

The Gravamen test focuses on whether the problem lies with the good or service. If the problem is with the good, Article 2 applies to the entire transaction (even the service parts), but if the problem is with the service, then the UCC does not apply at all and the common law governs the whole transaction. Alternatively, the Predominant Purpose test focuses on the predominant reason why the parties entered into the transaction. The court in *Spectro Alloys Corp. v. Fire Brick Engineers Co., Inc.*, 52 F. Supp. 3d 918, 925 (2014) described the test this way:

> This test weighs whether the purpose of the contract is primarily the rendition of service, with goods incidentally involved (e.g. contract with an artist for a painting) or is a transaction for a sale of goods, with labor incidentally involved (e.g. installation of a water heater in a bathroom). (citations and quotations omitted) The courts consider several factors in determining a contract's predominant purpose, including, (1) the language of the contracts, (2) the relative value of the goods and services, and (3) the business of the seller.

If the predominant purpose was to acquire the good and the services were incidental, then Article 2 applies. If, however, the main reason for the transaction was to buy services, then the common law applies. Other factors that a court may consider when applying the predominant purpose test are the type of business involved, the reasons why the parties entered into the contract, and whether the contract contained separate pricing for the goods and services.

---

[5]   *See* Newmark v. Gimbal's Inc., 54 N.J. 585 (N.J. 1969).

The following chart may help you conceptualize potential scope issues for Article 2

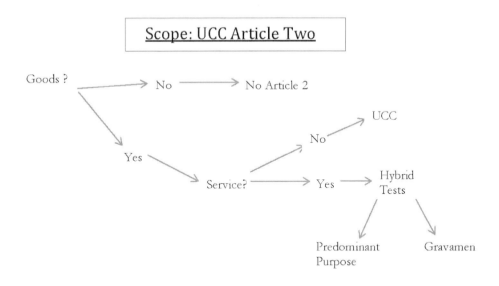

As you read the *Iler* case pay attention to the different arguments made by the parties. Why did the defendant want the UCC to govern the transaction? Look at the services provided and see if you can distinguish the services from the goods.

ILER GROUP, INC. V. DISCRETE WIRELESS, INC.

90 F. Supp.3d 1329 (N.D. Ga. 2015)

JONES, S.

This matter appears before the Court on Defendant's Motion to Dismiss Plaintiff's Complaint. For the following reasons, Defendant's Motion is **GRANTED, in part, and DENIED, in part**.

I.   FACTUAL AND PROCEDURAL BACKGROUND

* * *

On or about, July 11, 2006, Plaintiff and Defendant entered into a Dealer Agreement for the purchase of GPS tracking devices, resale of those devices, and provision of certain services related to commercial automobile fleet tracking. The agreement's initial term lasted three years, but the term automatically renewed on a month-to-month basis until either party provided written notice to terminate it. Pursuant to the agreement, Defendant granted Plaintiff, the "Dealer," the right to

(i)   purchase Products from Discrete Wireless and market, sell and distribute such Products to Customers located in and taking delivery within the Territory; (ii) market and sell the Services on behalf of Discrete Wireless as its sales representative; (iii) install the Products only for Customers; and (iv) provide First Level Support for the Products and the Services (collectively, the "Dealer Rights").

The agreement defines "Product" as "(I) a Unit; and (ii) any additional hardware products and related accessories that Discrete Wireless offers from time to time." 'Unit' means Discrete Wireless' vehicle mounted wireless vehicle tracking device and related antennae and cables . . . TTT Discrete Wireless may designate additional devices as a 'Unit' by providing written notice to Dealer."

After Plaintiff purchased Products from Defendant, Plaintiff would then execute a separate agreement with Customers for the resale of the Products. Plaintiff set the resale price and could set its own installation charges. Defendant would not activate a Unit—the GPS tracking device— however, unless Plaintiff first obtained a Service Order from the Customer. ("Prior to delivery or installation of a Unit to a Customer, Dealer shall obtain a Service Order (covering the Base Services for such Unit) that is fully executed by the authorized representative of Customer and Dealer shall deliver such fully executed Service Order to Discrete Wireless."). " 'Service Order' means Discrete Wireless' form of order TTT for the purchase of Services directly from Discrete Wireless and the terms and conditions included on Discrete Wireless' form of order."

It is important to understand the services offered to Customers under the Dealer Agreement—services provided either directly by Defendant or by Plaintiff on behalf of Defendant. "Service" is defined as "the Base Service and other services that Discrete Wireless offers Customers from time to time." " 'Base Service' means Discrete Wireless' GPS data collection and Internet-based vehicle tracking service that transmits GPS data approximately every five (5) minutes from the Unit to Discrete Wireless' Internet-based vehicle tracking solution." The agreement incorporates an attachment to define "First Level Support"—the support services Plaintiff was required to perform for Customers of Defendant. This support includes maintaining telephone support during business hours "for Customer questions and Customer issues with Products and Services[,]" providing Customer training on the Products and Services, managing the return of Products, providing "assistance with delivery and installation of any add-on features to the Products or Services[,]" maintaining Customer account records, and providing "all service calls for each of the Products and Services during the applicable Service Order Term."

Under the agreement, Defendant was required to pay Plaintiff a commission within forty-five days after the last day of each month. "The Commission payment includes full consideration to Dealer for providing First Level Support for those Units and the corresponding Base Services relating to a Service Order submitted by Dealer and accepted by Discrete Wireless." Plaintiff only received commissions for "Customer Base Service Fees received by Discrete Wireless during the Term *where the Customer Base Service Fees relate to a Service Order for at least a three (3) year term that was submitted by Dealer and accepted by Discrete Wireless.*" (emphasis added). In other words, Plaintiff received no commission unless Plaintiff secured a Customer for Defendant for a three-year term. Defendant had no obligation to pay Plaintiff a commission if a Service Order expired or was terminated, or if a Customer deactivated its Unit.

Plaintiff alleges, and Defendant does not deny, that on or around December 15, 2008, Defendant expressly told Plaintiff that "Mobitex network based devices TTT will no longer be eligible for Distributor commission after the November 2008 commission cycle." At that time, Plaintiff had been receiving "substantial ongoing commissions streaming from Mobitex network based devices." Plaintiff claims that this unilateral modification of the agreement amounted to a breach of contract by Defendant. Defendant made no commission payments to Plaintiff arising out of the Mobitex network based devices beginning with the December 2008 billing cycle through when Defendant provided notice to terminate the agreement on January 7, 2014.

After Defendant terminated the agreement, Plaintiff alleges Defendant "began sending emails and/or otherwise contacting [Plaintiff]'s Direct Bill Customers." "Direct Bill Customers" are not billed by Defendant for Service Orders procured by Plaintiff. These customers contract directly with Plaintiff for products and services, and Plaintiff, in turn, contracts with Defendant. Plaintiff incorporated one email in its complaint to illustrate the alleged contact Defendant made with Plaintiff's Direct Bill Customers. The email was sent by Mr. David Flores, an account manager for Defendant, to Ms. Diane Reynolds, who Plaintiff claims is a Direct Bill Customer representative for the City of Palm Coast, Florida. The email states,

> Ms. Reynolds,
>
> My name is David Flores with NexTraq[.] I am your new account manager. Here is my contact information. I extend to you an award winning level of account management in effort to exceed the experience you may have had with Fleetistics. If I may be of help please do not hesitate to reach out to me. Business as usual is all that's called for. Continue to use the same equipment and platform to manage your vehicles going forward. I look forward to speaking with you in the future.

. . . Plaintiff claims this "post-termination contact" is a violation of GUDTPA because it either "passes off the goods or services provided by [Plaintiff] to the Direct Bill Customers as the goods and services of [Defendant,]" or "causes the likelihood of confusion or of misunderstanding

18   INTRODUCTION TO SALES LAW AND SCOPE   CH. 1

as to the source, sponsorship, approval, or certification of goods or services[,]" or both. . . .

* * *

III. DISCUSSION

A. *Breach of Contract Claim*

Plaintiff alleges that Defendant breached the Dealer Agreement when it unilaterally stated it would no longer pay Plaintiff commissions on Mobitex GPS Units in December 2008. Defendant denies that it breached the agreement, but it bases its motion to dismiss this claim on a statute of limitations defense. Defendant argues that this contract is governed by Georgia's Uniform Commercial Code. ("UCC") which contains a four-year statute of limitations. *See* O.C.G.A. § 11–2–725(1) (2012) [**UCC 2–725**]. Because Defendant's alleged breach occurred, at the latest, in December 2008, Plaintiff's breach of contract claim is time barred because the complaint was filed on February 18, 2014, more than four years later. Plaintiff argues that the agreement is not for the sale of goods and thus not governed by Georgia's UCC. In Plaintiff's view, this is a services contract and was timely filed within the six-year statute of limitations for simple contracts in writing. *See* O.C.G.A. 9–3–24 (2012). Alternatively, Plaintiff argues, that even if the contract is subject to a four-year limitation, Defendant's failure to pay monthly commissions amounts to successive breaches, each of which begins a new statute of limitations. The Court, then, must determine whether the contract is governed by Georgia's UCC and when any alleged cause of action accrued.

1. *Governing Law*

Article 2 of the Georgia UCC applies to transactions involving the sale of goods. O.C.G.A. § 11–2–102 [**UCC 2–102**]. If a contract involves only the sale of goods, the UCC governs the contract. If a contract involves only the rendition of services, the UCC does not apply. "Difficulty arises in determining whether the UCC applies to a hybrid contract, i.e., a contract involving both goods and services." *J. Lee Gregory, Inc. v. Scandinavian House, L.P.,* 209 Ga. App. 285, 287, 433 S.E.2d 687, 689 (1993). "When the predominant element of a contract is the sale of goods, the contract is viewed as a sales contract and the UCC applies 'even though a substantial amount of service is to be rendered in installing the goods.' " If furnishing services is the predominant element of the contract, the UCC does not apply. The predominant purpose of a contract is "the thrust of the contract as it would exist in the minds of reasonable parties." The Georgia Court of Appeals recognized that "[w]hen presented with two elements of a contract, each absolutely necessary if the subject matter is to be of any significant value to the purchaser, it is a futile task to attempt to determine which component is 'more necessary.' " Therefore, to determine the predominant purpose is the surest "way to provide for predictable results in the face of a highly artificial classification system."

The contract between Plaintiff and Defendant involved both the sale of goods and the rendition of services. Plaintiff, in the first instance, purchased GPS tracking devices, or "Units," from Defendant and then resold them to Customers. The first service Plaintiff provided was the actual resale of Defendant's Units. Plaintiff then provided another service by procuring Service Orders from the Customers to whom it resold the goods. Under the agreement, Plaintiff could not resell the tracking devices to a Customer unless the Customer executed a Service Order with Defendant. Once Plaintiff made the resale and secured the Service Order, it then installed the devices on behalf of Defendant. Finally, Plaintiff provided First Level Support for Customers who purchased Defendant's products from Plaintiff.

Although Plaintiff may have provided a "substantial amount of service," the Court finds that the predominant purpose of the contract was the sale of goods. Plaintiff correctly states that three of its four "Dealer Rights" relate to services. But for the purchase and resale of Defendant's products, however, all of Plaintiff's services would be worthless. Regarding installation services, Georgia courts have found that installation of the goods sold does not amount to a predominantly service-based contract. The First Level Support provided by Plaintiff was limited to telephone support, Customer training, managing returns of the devices, maintaining Customer account records, and providing service calls. Every service encompassed within First Level Support related directly to Defendant's products that Plaintiff purchased from Defendant and then resold to Customers.

Plaintiff dedicates a significant amount of argument to the fact that it could not sell Defendant's tracking devices without first procuring a Service Order. Plaintiff claims this requirement demonstrates the service-based nature of the contract. This argument again misses the point. The Service Order details the "purchase of Services *directly from Discrete Wireless.*" Not only is this service provided directly by Defendant, the service is comprised of "Discrete Wireless' GPS data collection and Internet-based vehicle tracking service that transmits GPS data TTT *from the Unit* to Discrete Wireless' Internet-based vehicle tracking solution." Plaintiff's primary "service" is to resell the Unit it purchased from Defendant. The procurement of Service Orders for Defendant is incidental to the resale. There is no purpose to requiring a Service Order without the sale of a Unit. Moreover, without the Unit, as demonstrated in the definition of "Base Service," there would be no service to provide. In other words, if the Unit installed on the commercial automobiles did not collect GPS data and transmit that data to Defendant then "fleet tracking services" would be impossible.

Plaintiff further argues that the commission structure between the parties illustrates the predominately service-based nature of the agreement. The commission "includes full consideration to Dealer for providing First Level Support *for those Units and the corresponding Base Services* relating to a Service Order." "The Commission shall be limited to the Customer Base Service Fees received by Discrete Wireless during the Term where the Customer Base Service Fees relate to a Service Order for at least a three (3) year term that was submitted by Dealer and accepted by Discrete Wireless." " 'Customer Base Service Fee' means the monthly recurring fee *for the Base Services for each Unit* that is charged by Discrete Wireless to Customer." As explained, Plaintiff's procurement of a Service Order is incidental to the purchase and resale of the GPS tracking devices. First Level Support, while possibly a substantial service, is incidental to the purchase and resale of the Unit. The main service provided, Base Service, is provided directly by Defendant and tied directly to the products Plaintiff purchased and then resold. To illustrate, the Base Service itself primarily consists of the collection and transmission of data by the Unit. The agreement clearly links the commission payments to Customer Base Service Fees, which are monthly fees charged by Defendant to Customers "for the Base Services for each Unit." By limiting the commission payments to Customer Base Service Fees, the agreement effectively limits commissions to payments by Customers for use of the Unit and the substantial data it provides. The mere fact that the commission payments include consideration for First Level Support, services that are ancillary to the resale of goods yet provided solely by Plaintiff, does not change this result. Moreover, Defendant has no obligation to pay Plaintiff a commission on expired or terminated Service orders, or if a Customer deactivates a Unit. Thus, if a Customer discontinues using the GPS tracking device, the premise upon which a Service Order is founded, or deactivates the device, Plaintiff receives no further commissions. This is further evidence that the Unit, the goods purchased and resold, predominate over any services provided under the agreement.

To summarize, the predominant purpose of the agreement is the purchase and re-sale of goods, in this case, GPS tracking devices. All services provided by Plaintiff under the agreement are incidental to this primary purpose. Without the purchase and sale of a GPS tracking device, no "fleet tracking services" could be provided either by Plaintiff or Defendant. Therefore, the four-year statute of limitations under Georgia's UCC applies to Plaintiff's breach of contract claim. *See* O.C.G.A. § 11–2–725 [**UCC 2–725**].

* * *

3. UCC ARTICLE 2 OR 2A

Another scope issue arises when a transaction has been structured as a lease under Article 2A, but a court determines that it is really a disguised sale and consequently governed by Article 2. There are, of course, occasions where a transaction is clearly a lease and nobody would dispute it. For example, if you live in Pennsylvania and decide to go on vacation in California, you may not want to take the time to drive that far, so you decide to fly to your destination. After you arrive, you may want to rent a car, so you can visit places on your own time. To do so, you may lease a car from a national car rental company for the week or two you are visiting California. In those instances, it is rare to mistake that transaction for a disguised sale.

Consider a different example. Suppose that you start a food delivery business and you need refrigerated trucks for your business. You decide to lease instead of buy them because of the favorable tax consequences for leases. The trucks normally sell for $60,000. The transaction is structured as a lease with the following terms: You agree to pay $2,000 per month for the truck for three years, but at the end of the lease you have the option to buy the truck for $1,000. At the end of the lease, the truck will have a useful life of five more years and its fair market value will be $28,000. What would a rational businessperson do at the end of the lease? You should realize that you should certainly take the purchase option and buy the truck because you would be spending $1,000 to own a truck worth $28,000 and it would still have five more years of useful life. It would be crazy to do anything else! In that instance, a court would determine the "lease" was not a true lease but, instead, a disguised sale in the form of security interest. For the rest of this chapter, we will use the term "disguised sale" to describe this type of transaction.

You might wonder why that matters. For our purposes, there are two situations where it matters very much. One is where the lessee (you in this case) sells the goods to a third party and the second is when the lessee has too much debt, cannot pay her bills, and files for bankruptcy to try to alleviate some of the debt. Let's consider the ramifications of each one of these situations.

First, are you allowed to sell a good that has been leased to you? The answer depends on whether the transaction is a true lease or a disguised sale. If it is a lease, then you are not permitted to sell the good—you do not own the good, you do not have title to the good, and the true owner is usually the lessor. Although you have contracted to use the good, the lessor retains a reversionary interest in the leased good. If you sell that good, you are violating the rights of the lessor and you may be guilty of conversion. Further, the third party who purchased the good has no right to keep it because the true owner is the lessor. If, however, a court determines that your transaction was a disguised sale, then you owned the good, so you had the right to sell it and the third party likely will keep the good. You may be in breach of the "lease" contract but you would not be guilty of conversion. The lessor, who thought the transaction was a lease, does not have the ability to reclaim the goods and will be very unhappy with the attorney who structured the transaction in the wrong way. In that instance, a lessor's only recourse is to pursue you for breach of contract.

The second situation occurs when a lessee has too much debt and, as a result, tries to obtain some relief from the bankruptcy courts. The Bankruptcy Code is complex. You will learn a little more about bankruptcy when you study Article 9 later in this book. For now, you only need to understand that when a debtor files for bankruptcy the court appoints a trustee to gather all of the non-exempt property owned by the debtor, liquidate the property, and then distribute the proceeds to creditors depending on who has priority. If a transaction is a true lease, the trustee cannot treat the leased property in the same way as the property owned by the debtor. Because the lessor has a reversionary interest, the trustee will need to compensate the lessor before taking possession of leased goods. If, however, a court determines the transaction is a disguised sale, then the debtor owns that property and the trustee may be able to take it along with the rest of the debtor's non-exempt property. The trustee may sell that property and distribute the proceeds to the debtor's creditors according to the priority rules that you will learn about when you study secured transactions later in this course. Imagine how unhappy a lessor will be who thought she was leasing a good and then the court determines it was a sale, so the lessor no longer has a reversionary interest in the property. Without that reversionary interest, the lessor loses most, if not all, rights to retrieve the good.

How does a court determine whether a transaction is a lease or disguised sale? There are 2 tests. The first test to consider is a bright line statutory rule provided by the UCC. If the UCC's bright line rule applies, you should use it before applying the common law rules because a statute trumps the common law. This bright line rule is found in **1–203** entitled "Lease Distinguished From a Security Interest." For now, continue to think of a security interest in terms of a disguised sale. **1–203** will only provide an answer if the lease transaction contains a "no termination" clause or is found to not be subject to early termination. Beware however, just because a transaction says it has a termination clause does not necessarily mean a court will find that it is a true termination clause.

Assuming there is a valid no termination clause, the next step is to check the four bright line tests enumerated in **1–203(b)**. If one of the four subsections is satisfied, then the transaction is not a true lease under the bright line test and is instead considered a disguised sale and attempted security interest. However, the converse is not true. If the facts do not satisfy any of the four subsections that does not mean the transaction is a lease. Rather, the analysis must continue and the common law economic realities test should be applied next.

In the case of *In re Bailey*, 326 B.R. 156, 163–64 (W.D. Ark. 2005), the bankruptcy court considered whether a "lease" transaction for equipment was a true lease that kept the property from being included with the bankruptcy property owned by the debtor, or a security interest disguised as a sale. The "lease" had a clause that seemed to permit the lessee to terminate the lease. The court, however, found that just because a contract said it contained a termination clause did not mean it really permitted termination. Because of that finding the court applied **1–203** and found that the transaction was a disguised sale. The court proceeded to say:

> Applying this framework to the instant case, the Court finds that because the Debtor does not have a legal right to cease payments and walk away from the lease without liability for the deficiency, the Debtor does not have a right to terminate under the purported lease. According to the Addendum to each lease, the Debtor is liable for three months' lease payments if he chooses to 'bring back' the equipment. Lafayette's witness testified that if the Debtor terminates the lease, he is responsible for the remaining lease payments unless Lafayette is successful in re-leasing the equipment. Under either condition, the Debtor remains financially liable to the lessor for payments that become due after the termination date.

> The next step is to determine whether any of the four enumerated conditions listed in the statute apply. The Court finds that the fourth condition is applicable: the lessee has an option to become the owner of the goods for nominal additional consideration upon compliance with the lease agreement. In discussing nominal value, a leading treatise on the Uniform Commercial Code has stated that nominal value is determined by examining the parties' prediction, at the time of the contract, of the concluding value of the goods. The test is whether "the option price is so low that the lessee will certainly exercise it and will, in all plausible circumstances, leave no meaningful reversion for the lessor." James J. White & Robert S. Summers, 4 Uniform Commercial Code § 30–3 at 33 (5th ed. 2002).

> Even though there is no contractual obligation to exercise the option to purchase in this case, the Debtor has no other reasonable alternative. Lafayette's witness testified that at the expiration of the lease the tractors will be worth $15,000.00 each and he will sell them to the Debtor for their projected residual value of approximately $2230.00 and $2080.00. The purchase option in this case is 13% or 14% of what Lafayette estimates the fair market value will be when the lease expires. If the Debtor fails to

exercise the option, the Debtor will lose approximately $12,920.00 to $12,770.00 in equipment value (the estimated fair market value less the purchase price) for each tractor. If he does purchase the equipment, he pays only $2200.00 and $2080.00, much less than he will lose if the option is not exercised. Therefore, the additional consideration is nominal because it is less than the Debtor's reasonably predictable cost of performing under the lease but not exercising the option.

The first scenario in **1–203(b)** includes a situation where a lease term is equal to or greater than its remaining economic life. An example of this situation is a three-year lease where the remaining economic life of the good at the beginning of the lease is three years. In that case, the lease will expire at the end of the good's useful life and the transaction will be considered a disguised sale. You should understand why **1–203** views this as a disguised sale. It is because the "lessee" has no way to get out of the lease and, by the time the lease is finished, the goods are essentially worthless with no economic value left. In that case, the lessor has no reversionary interest. The next three sections of **1–203(b)** require the same analysis with the end result that if the lease requires a lessee to buy the good or to renew the lease for the rest of the good's economic life; or the lease contains an option to buy the good or lease the good for the rest of its economic life for optional or no consideration, then the transaction is a disguised sale and will be treated as such by the courts. If the goods were sold, the buyer may treat them as her own, hampered only by the contract.

What happens if **1–203** does not give a definitive answer or does not apply at all because there is a clause that allows a lessee to terminate the transaction? As mentioned above, it does not mean that the transaction is a lease. Instead, you must look to the common law for the next test which is called the economic realities test. The Supreme Court of Indiana in *Gibraltar Financing Corp. v. Prestige Equipment Corp.*, 949 N.E. 2d 314, 323 (Ind. 2011) stated the following:

> If a court finds that a transaction did not create a security interest per se, it must then "consider the economic reality of the transaction in order to determine . . . whether the transaction is more fairly characterized as a lease or a secured financing arrangement." *Duke Energy Royal, LLC v. Pillowtex Corp. (In re Pillowtex)*, 349 F.3d 711, 719 (3d Cir. 2003). Unfortunately, the U.C.C. does not provide any explicit test or methodology for assessing the economic reality of the transaction. As a result, the cases contain a plethora of formulations and approaches that we will briefly survey.

The majority of courts and commentators recite that the principal inquiry in this regard is " 'whether the lessor has retained a *meaningful reversionary interest* in the goods.' " *In re WorldCom,*

339 B.R. at 71 (emphasis in original) (citation omitted). However, again, the U.C.C. does not provide for assessing whether a lessor has retained a "meaningful reversionary interest." *In re QDS Components*, 292 B.R. at 341. Nevertheless, the *WorldCom* court explained the rationale for the "meaningful reversionary interest" test as follows:

> If the lessor does not possess a meaningful reversionary interest, the lessor has no interest in the economic value or remaining useful life of the goods, and therefore the lessor transferred title to the goods, in substance if not in form. In other words, the parties did not create a lease where the putative lessor does not have the interest, the entrepreneurial stake, in the goods that a true lessor would have.

The economic realities test is a two-part test that asks the following questions: (1) is there a reasonable likelihood that the good will return to the lessor; if yes, (2) when the good returns to the lessor, will it have some meaningful economic value? If the answer to either the first or second question is no, then the transaction is a disguised sale and will be governed by Articles 2 and 9. If the answer to the second question, in addition to the first one, is yes, then the transaction is a true lease because the good will return to the lessor while it still has some meaningful economic life and value. The main difference between a true lease and a disguised sale is that the lessor retains a reversionary interest in the good if it is a true lease.

Return to the example earlier in this chapter where you were starting your own food delivery business and wanted to lease several delivery trucks. In that example, the trucks had a fair market value of $60,000 when the "lease" began, they will have a fair market value of $28,000 at the end of 36 months, and they will have at least three years of economic life left. The transaction was structured as a lease with the following terms:

Rental term is for 36 months.

Rent is $2,000 per month, due at the first of every month.

The lease may not be terminated any time before the end of the 36 months.

At the end of the lease, lessee has the option to purchase each truck for $1,000.

Is this transaction a lease or a sale? Your analysis should start with the fact that this transaction contains a non-termination clause and that requires a consideration of the bright line rule in **1–203**. The next step in your analysis is to apply **1–203(b)(4)**. Is paying $1,000 for a truck valued at $28,000 nominal? To put it another way, would you be foolish not to buy the truck for $1,000? Most, if not all, courts would consider this to be nominal consideration. Would the economic realities test reach the same conclusion?

The above problem should help you understand how to analyze a transaction to determine whether it is a lease or a sale. Remember, that this matters for several reasons. If it is a lease, the lessee may not resell the good and, if the lessee files for bankruptcy, the property will be treated differently than if it was a disguised sale. Additionally, there may be tax and accounting reasons why a party wants a transaction structured as a lease instead of a sale. For example, leased goods may have certain tax deductions that owning goods does not have and the lessor, as the owner of the goods, may claim depreciation whereas the lessee will not have that option.

As you will see from the following case, it is not always easy to determine whether a transaction is a lease or a sale. The *Purdy* case shows how many judges can differ on the issues. You will revisit this case when you study secured transactions later in this class.

IN RE PURDY

763 F.3d 513 (6th Cir. 2014)

NELSON MOORE, K.

Between 2009 and 2012, Sunshine Heifers, LLC ("Sunshine") and Lee H. Purdy, a dairy farmer, entered into several "Dairy Cow Leases." Purdy received a total of 435 cows to milk, and, in exchange, he paid a monthly rent to Sunshine. Unfortunately, Purdy's dairy business faltered in 2012, and he petitioned for bankruptcy protection. When Purdy filed this petition, Sunshine moved to retake possession of the leased cattle. Citizens First Bank ("Citizens First"), however, had a perfected purchase money security interest in Purdy's equipment, farm products, and livestock, and it claimed that this perfected security interest gave Citizens First priority over Sunshine with regard to the 435 cattle. In particular, Citizens First argued that the "leases" between Sunshine and Purdy were disguised security agreements, that Purdy actually owned the cattle, and that the subsequently acquired livestock were covered by the bank's security interest. The bankruptcy court ruled in favor of Citizens First, finding that the leases were *per se* security agreements. Given that the terms of agreements expressly preserve Sunshine's ability to recover the cattle, we disagree, **REVERSE** the bankruptcy court's decision, and **REMAND** for further proceedings consistent with this opinion.

I. BACKGROUND

Purdy operated his dairy farm in Barren County, Kentucky. In 2008, he entered into a loan relationship with Citizens First, using his herd of dairy cattle as collateral. Purdy refinanced his loan on July 3, 2009, executing an "Agricultural Security Agreement" in exchange for additional principal in the amount of $417,570. As part of the security agreement, Purdy granted Citizens First a purchase money security interest in "all . . . Equipment, Farm Products, [and] Livestock (including all increase and supplies) . . . currently owned [or] hereafter acquired. . . ." Three days later, Citizens First perfected this purchase money security interest by filing a financing statement with the Kentucky Secretary of State. Purdy and Citizens Bank executed two similar security agreements in August 2010 and May 2012. Citizens First perfected these purchase money security interests as well.

Shortly after refinancing his loan with Citizens First in 2009, Purdy decided to increase the size of his dairy-cattle herd. He contacted Jeff Blevins of Sunshine regarding the prospect of leasing additional cattle. Sunshine was amenable to the idea, and on August 7, 2009, Purdy and Sunshine entered into the first of five contracts, three of which are relevant here: (1) a July 21, 2011 agreement, involving fifty head of cattle; (2) a July 14, 2012 agreement, rolling up two prior agreements and involving 285 head of cattle; and (3) another July 14, 2012 agreement, involving 100 head of cattle.

Each of these agreements is titled a "Dairy Cow Lease," and under their terms, Purdy received a total of 435 cattle for fifty months in exchange for a monthly rent. The agreements prohibited Purdy from terminating the leases, and Purdy agreed to "return the Cows, at [his] expense, to such place as Sunshine designate[d]" at the end of the lease term. Additionally, Purdy guaranteed "the net sales proceeds from the sale of the Cows . . . at the end of the Lease term [would] be [a set amount between $290 and $300] per head (the 'Guaranteed Residual Value')." Purdy further promised to maintain insurance on the cattle, to replace any cows that were culled from the herd, and to allow Sunshine the right to inspect the herd. When the parties signed these contracts, they also executed security agreements, and Sunshine filed financing statements with the Secretary of State.

In the dairy business, farmers must "cull" a portion of their herd every year, replacing older and less productive cows with younger, healthier ones. Many times, dairy farmers will replace the culled cows with their calves. Purdy, in contrast, sold off the calves of Sunshine's cows and purchased more mature replacements. This practice contravened the terms of the leases, but Sunshine was aware of Purdy's behavior and acquiesced in it. Nonetheless, the terms of the lease required Purdy to apply Sunshine's brand and a yellow ear tag to the original cows and their replacements. In contrast, Purdy applied a white ear tag to the cattle covered by Citizens First's security interest. By July 2012, Purdy had approximately 750 head of cattle on his farm. Of those cattle, 435 should have carried Sunshine's brand according to the terms of the leases.

In the fall of 2012, the price of cattle feed rose, and milk production became less profitable. Purdy responded by selling off cattle, including many bearing Sunshine's brand, at a faster rate. Unfortunately, Purdy could not keep his operation above water, and on November 29, 2012, he filed a voluntary petition for Chapter 12 bankruptcy relief, and the bankruptcy court issued an automatic stay, preventing the removal of assets from the farm. A week later, representatives of Citizens First and Sunshine inspected the 389 cattle still on the farm. Of the cows on the property, 289 had white ear tags (indicating that they were covered by Citizens First's security interest) and Sunshine's brand, 99 had only white ear tags, and one cow had neither a tag nor a brand. A short time later, another farmer returned forty-three cattle that had been taken in violation of the bankruptcy court's stay. Sunshine claimed that thirty-nine of those cattle bore Sunshine's brand.

* * *

On January 22, 2013, the bankruptcy court held a hearing on various motions. The dispute between Citizens First and Sunshine turned on whether the leases between Purdy and Sunshine were true leases or disguised security agreements. The bankruptcy court issued its decision on March 1, 2013, finding that

> The original term of the Lease was for 50 months. Clearly, 50 months is longer than the economic life of the goods [the cows]. Uncontradicted testimony indicated that a dairy herd is culled annually at an approximate rate of 30 percent. Within three years an entire herd is extremely likely to have been entirely replaced and certainly before the end of 50 months. Because [Purdy] met this term of the statute, the transaction is a *per se* security agreement and the Court's analysis ends here.

Consequently, the bankruptcy court determined that Citizens First's "prior perfected liens attach[ed] to all cows on [Purdy's] farm on the date the Petition was filed," and it denied Sunshine's motion to lift the stay. The bankruptcy court eventually granted Citizens First relief from the stay, however, and the bank foreclosed on the herd. Citizens First auctioned the cattle for $402,353.54, and the bankruptcy trustee awarded these proceeds to Citizens First, which applied them toward Purdy's outstanding debt.

* * *

III. ANALYSIS

The main question in this case is whether the agreements between Purdy and Sunshine are "true leases" or merely "security agreements." " 'A lease involves payment for the temporary possession, use and enjoyment of goods, with the expectation that the goods will be returned to the owner with some expected residual interest of value remaining at the end of the lease term. (Citation omitted.)'In contrast, a sale involves an unconditional transfer of absolute title to goods, while a security interest is only an inchoate interest contingent on default and limited to the remaining secured debt.'" If the agreements are true leases, then Sunshine has a reversionary interest in 435 head of cattle and is entitled to approximately $309,000 from the cattle auction. If the agreements represent the sale of the cattle and Sunshine's retention of a security interest, then Citizens First's perfected agricultural security interest trumps Sunshine's interest, and the bank keeps all of the proceeds from the cattle auction.

In deciding whether these "Dairy Cow Leases" are true leases or disguised security agreements, we look to the relevant state law.

Under Arizona law, "the facts of each case" dictate whether an agreement is a true lease or a security agreement, Ariz.Rev.Stat. § 47–1203(A) [**UCC 1–203(a)**], and our fact-sensitive analysis proceeds in two steps. First, we employ the Bright-Line Test. According to this test, "[a] transaction in the form of a lease creates a security interest if the consideration that the lessee is to pay the lessor for the right to possession and use of the goods is an obligation for the term of the lease and is not subject to termination by the lessee, and . . . [t]he original term of the lease is equal to or greater than the remaining economic life of the goods." § 47–1203(B) [**UCC 1–203(b)**]. If the lease runs longer than the economic life of the goods, then the lease is a *per se* security agreement. If the goods retain meaningful value after the lease expires, however, we move to the second step and " 'look at the specific facts of the case to determine whether the economics of the transaction suggest' " that the arrangement is a lease or a security interest. At all points in this analysis, the party challenging the leases bears the burden of proving that they are something else. . . .

A. Bright-Line Test

No one debates that Purdy lacked the ability to terminate the lease. The question is whether the lease term of fifty months exceeds the economic life of the cattle. The bankruptcy court fixated upon Purdy's testimony that he culled approximately thirty percent of the cattle each year, meaning that the entire herd would turn over in forty months. As a result, the bankruptcy court concluded that the lease term exceeded the economic life of the cattle that Sunshine initially gave Purdy and, therefore, that the lease was a *per se* security agreement. We disagree and hold that the bankruptcy court erred in its analysis of the cattle's economic life because the court focused upon the economic life of the individual cows originally leased to Purdy, instead of the life of the herd as required by the agreements.

According to the text of the agreements between Purdy and Sunshine, Purdy had a duty to return the same *number* of cattle to Sunshine that he originally leased, not the same cattle. ("Lessee hereby leases from Sunshine . . . the number of cows shown above ('the Cows'), each of which is identified by . . . Sunshine's brand and ear tag . . . , whether part of the Lease originally or a replacement."); ("Lessee shall maintain the number of Cows (as defined in the Lease) at all times."). It made little difference to Sunshine whether it received the exact same cows that it originally leased to Purdy; according to Blevins—Sunshine's owner—"the main thing is to maintain the leasehold, the integrity of the lease numbers. In line with this understanding, the agreements took into account industry practices, such as culling, by requiring Purdy to replace any unproductive cows that he sold. Sunshine protected its interest in the herd by inspecting Purdy's operation, requiring Purdy to carry insurance, and creating a "Residual Guaranty," which stated that the actual cattle returned would be worth at least a set amount (setting a minimum guaranteed price of $290 per head). Given these provisions and the testimony of the parties, it is clear to us that the relevant "good" is the herd of cattle, which has an economic life far greater than the lease term, and not the individual cows originally placed on Purdy's farm. Accordingly, we hold that the contracts flunk the Bright-Line Test and are not *per se* security agreements.

B.   Economics-of-the-Transaction Test

The precise contours of the economics-of-the-transaction test are rather unclear, but courts have largely focused upon two particular factors: (1) whether the lease contains a purchase option price that is nominal; and (2) "whether the lessee develops equity in the property, such that the only economically reasonable option for the lessee is to purchase the goods." The ultimate question for us, however, is whether Sunshine kept a meaningful reversionary interest in the herd. On the facts presented to us, we hold that Citizens First has also failed to carry its burden of establishing that the actual economics of the transactions indicate that the leases were disguised security agreements.

In this case, neither of the above-mentioned factors suggests that these agreements are something other than true leases because the contracts do not contain an option for Purdy to purchase the cattle at any price, let alone at a nominal one. In fact, the agreements explicitly state that Sunshine retains ownership in the cattle throughout the life of the lease and beyond. This lack of a purchase option distinguishes this case from others, in which the Ninth Circuit held that a purchase option highly favorable to the lessee converted a lease into a security agreement. Here, even if Purdy wanted to purchase the cattle at $300 per cow, there is nothing in the agreements that obligates Sunshine to sell to him. Sunshine could have retaken possession of its cows and leased them out to Purdy's competitor under the same terms, and there would have been nothing Purdy could have done under the agreement. In our view, this state of play is consistent with a lease.

Additionally, the fact that there is no purchase option also distinguishes this case from *In re Buehne Farms, Inc.,* 321 B.R. 239 (Bankr.S.D.Ill.2005), which the bankruptcy court relied upon heavily. In that case, the court was swayed by the fact that the purported leases allowed the lessee to purchase the cattle at the end of the lease for approximately $160 per cow. The court noted that the lessee had spent approximately $500,000 in rental payments over the life of the lease and that spending just six percent of that would give the lessee title to the cows. Considering that the lessee had spent significant money to replace culled cattle already, the *Buehne Farms* court reasoned that the lessee would be irrational not to exercise the purchase option. This situation indicated that the "rental payments" were actually installment payments and that the "purchase option" was really a cleverly disguised final payment. In stark contrast, Purdy's rental payments were just that—payments per a lease. Purdy had no legal right to purchase Sunshine's herd; there was no purchase option that he could exercise. Under the terms of the agreements, Purdy had to return the same number of cows that he originally leased in fair condition as indicated by the Residual Guaranty. At approximately $300 per cow, this herd had a minimum value of $130,500. It sold at auction for approximately $309,000. Ownership of this herd—in our view—is a significant asset, and thus, we hold that Sunshine retained a meaningful reversionary interest.

Finally, whether the parties adhered to the terms of these leases in all facets, in our view, is irrelevant to determining whether the agreements were true leases or disguised security agreements. Neither the bankruptcy court nor the parties have sufficiently explained the legal import of Purdy's culling practices or put forward any evidence that the parties altered the terms of the leases making them anything but what they proclaim to be. Moreover, Arizona Revised Statutes § 47–1203(C) [**UCC 1–203(c)**]clearly states that the fact that terms of the lease are unfavorable to the lessee, that the lessee assumes the risk of loss of the goods, or that the lease requires the lessee to maintain insurance on the goods is not alone grounds to find that a contract is a security agreement. As a result, we hold that Citizens First has not carried its burden of proving that the actual economics of the transaction demonstrate that the leases were security agreements.

IV. CONCLUSION

For the foregoing reasons, we conclude that Citizens First has failed to demonstrate that the "Dairy Cow Leases" were actually security agreements in disguise. Because the bankruptcy court found to the contrary, we **REVERSE** and **REMAND** to the bankruptcy court for further proceedings consistent with this opinion.

DRAIN, DISTRICT JUDGE, dissenting.

In this case, I respectfully disagree with the majority's decision on the application of the facts to the tests to be applied. I would affirm the bankruptcy court's decision finding that the transactions involved in this case were disguised security agreements as opposed to true leases.

A. Bright-Line Test

I agree with the bankruptcy court, and find *In re Buehne Farms* instructive. That case involved a dairy farmer/debtor who argued his fifty-month cattle leases were disguised as security agreements when his lessors motioned the bankruptcy court to extend the time for the debtor to assume or reject fifty month cattle leases. *In re Buehne*, 321 B.R. 239 at 240. The debtor obtained his cattle via two leases with third party buyers. The *Buehne Farms* leases are almost identical to Purdy's leases. The *In re Buehne* court found that the average dairy farmer culls at an annual rate of twenty to thirty percent and the debtor's cows had a forty-eight month economic life. The *In re Buehne Farms* court found the economic life of a dairy cow could range from thirty-six to sixty months.

Sunshine argues this case is distinguishable because the leases Purdy signed did not have purchase options. Although this is true, I find this case is instructive because it offers guidance on the economic life of dairy cows given a farmer's culling practices.

We review the bankruptcy court findings of fact under the clear-error standard. Under this standard, the reviewing court must ask whether the bankruptcy court's factual findings were erroneous.

The bankruptcy court in this case heard similar testimony about cull rates and the practices on the Purdy farm. The bankruptcy court determined that Purdy had a thirty percent cull rate. This rate causes nearly complete herd turnover after thirty-six months. I agree with the bankruptcy court's determination that the individual heads of cattle are the good at issue. Each head of cattle was a means of production rather than part of a unit. For Purdy, each cow was a sophisticated piece of equipment that produced a product; milk. The economic life of the individual heads of cattle would not last the term of the lease. Any cows on Purdy's farm at the end of the lease term would not be the original cows because he would have culled those cows from the herd. In fact, Purdy would have culled nearly all of the cattle from Lease 1 at the time of the petition. Thus, the agreements were for a period longer than the cows' economic value to Purdy. The lease and Sunshine's testimony speak to total herd maintenance over the lease term, but this was not important to the parties. The parties did not follow these provisions of the lease. This finding was within the economic life range used by the *In re Beuhne Farms* court who heard similar testimony regarding culling practices. I find no error in the bankruptcy court's factual finding of a thirty month culling rate. Therefore, I do not agree with the majority. Unlike the majority, I would hold the Bright-Line Test is met and the leases were *per se* security agreements.

B. Economic Realities of the Transaction

The majority finds that the leases fail the Bright-Line test. A lease agreement can fail the Bright-Line test, which is inevitable when the herd is the relevant good, and the court can still find that an agreement creates a security interest. It is my view that the economics of the transactions do not support a finding that the parties entered into lease agreements, and Citizens bore the burden of establishing the documents were not what they purported to be.

The UCC and its Arizona adaptation offer very little guidance to courts on how to analyze the economics of a transaction. A common factor courts use is whether the lessor has a reversionary interest in the leased goods or an option to purchase. Courts are not limited to these factors. In fact, by limiting itself to these factors, the court conducts a similar analysis to the Bight-Line test. Courts should focus on other relevant facts at the time of the agreements.

In re Phoenix Equipment Co. Inc. is distinguishable from this matter because it also involves a purchase option. The *In re Phoenix Equip. Co., Inc.* leases did not provide for an option in the language of the lease, but the court inferred the option by analyzing the parties' course of dealings. When the parties could not establish whether the purchase price on the option was nominal, the *In re Phoenix Equipment Co., Inc.* court focused on the structure and effect of the parties' transactions. The debtor needed capital in order to run his operation and entered into transactions in which he transferred title of equipment to his creditor in exchange for the capital. The court concluded the nature of the transactions showed that the debtor did not need a lease agreement, but needed capital to continue operating.

In the three relevant leases, third parties sold cattle to Purdy. Sunshine reimbursed Purdy for the cost of the cattle. Sunshine knew Purdy did not adhere to the replacement cattle provisions in its agreements, but chose to ignore his non-compliance. Sunshine was aware of Citizens' lien at the time it entered into the transactions and filed its statements. The facts of the case at the time of the transaction indicate that Purdy needed money to place cows on the farm. Sunshine, by the way it forwarded funds to Purdy, appears to have supplied Purdy with funds rather than the actual cattle. Sunshine received a lien on the cattle whose acquisition it financed. These facts indicate the parties entered into three financing transactions rather than three lease transactions.

* * *

. . . I would hold the economics of the transaction support a finding that the parties entered into security agreements for the cattle rather than leases.

For these reasons, I respectfully dissent and would affirm the bankruptcy court's decision.

* * *

---

4. CISG

The CISG is a treaty that the United States ratified effective January 1, 1988. Because it is federal law, it takes precedence over any state law, including the UCC. Since the CISG takes priority over the UCC, it is important to understand what transactions the CISG governs. Part 1, Chapter 1 of the CISG contains the main provisions regarding the scope of the law. The most basic requirement is that the transaction needs to be a sale of goods between parties who have places of business in two different countries, both of which have ratified the CISG. Please note that the CISG uses the term "states" throughout the law when it is referring to countries. Compare this to the scope section of the UCC; the CISG is narrower in that it only covers sales of goods whereas the UCC includes "transactions in goods." Additionally, the concept of subjective intent is much more important in the CISG than it is in the UCC or the common law of contracts.

There are two important CISG scope issues worth noting. The first issue relates to the knowledge of the parties at the time of the contract. This is important in terms of determining the internationality of the contract as well as the purpose of the contract. Read the following CISG Articles to see how the law considers subjective intent: **Article 1(2)**, **Article 2(a)**, and **Article 10**. You will see that **Articles 1** and **10** will not consider a transaction international unless the parties understood that they were dealing with parties with businesses in different countries or the contract or dealings between the parties showed that the parties had businesses in different countries.

The second important scope issue relates to the nature of the contract. The CISG governs international commercial contracts and specifically excludes consumer contracts in **Article 2**. However, like in the internationality of the transaction, whether the contract is consumer or commercial in nature depends on whether the seller knew or should have known that the goods were purchased for consumer use. If the seller did not know or had no reason to know the goods were being bought for consumer use the court will not exclude the transaction from CISG coverage. In later chapters, this book will point out some of the main differences between the UCC and the CISG.

5.   MAGNUSON-MOSS WARRANTY ACT

The Magnuson-Moss Warranty Act is very important with regard to UCC warranties, so it will be revisited in the chapter containing warranties. For now, it is important to understand the types of contracts within the law's scope. Magnuson-Moss only applies to contracts by consumers for consumer products. The definition of a consumer under Magnuson-Moss includes a buyer (other than for purposes of resale) of any consumer product and any person to whom a consumer product has been transferred during the duration of an implied or written warranty (or service contract). Additionally, if a warranty or state law allows a person other than the buyer of the consumer good to enforce the warranty that person may qualify as a consumer for Magnuson Moss purposes. **2301(3).** The law defines consumer products as "any tangible personal property which is distributed in commerce and which is normally used for personal, family, or household purposes. . . ." **2301(1).** Contrast the definition of a consumer product under Magnuson-Moss with the UCC's definition of consumer. Remember that the Magnuson-Moss definition is broader. Compare an owner of a pizza restaurant who buys a car to be used by her employees when making deliveries on takeout orders to a family who buys a car for family transportation. As mentioned earlier in this chapter, a car will be a consumer good under Magnuson-Moss's definition, even if it is purchased for a commercial purpose because nobody would dispute that a car is normally used for personal, family, or household purposes. However, that same car would not fall under the UCC's definition of a consumer good because the person buying it would not be buying the car primarily for personal, household, or family purposes. **1–201(b)(11).**

Another important scope issue relates to the ability of a consumer to sue under Magnuson Moss when the seller only gives an implied warranty and no written warranty. There is a disagreement among courts about whether Magnuson-Moss requires a written warranty before it will apply to implied warranties. Some courts determine that an implied warranty, without a written warranty, may be enough for jurisdiction under Magnuson-Moss as long as the other jurisdictional requirements are met. Two other requirements of Magnuson Moss are that a plaintiff must allow the person obligated under a warranty a reasonable opportunity to cure and, if a warrantor has established an informal dispute resolution procedure, the consumer needs to comply with that procedure before bringing a lawsuit. **2310(d)(1).** Lastly, Magnuson Moss provides a large incentive to encourage attorneys to take these cases by allowing a court to award a prevailing consumer costs and expenses, including attorneys' fees. Without this financial incentive, most attorneys would be very reluctant to handle these cases because they may involve inexpensive consumer products.

One last important reminder is to always research whether your state has enacted consumer protection laws. There may be a multitude of other laws that also cover the transaction depending on the type of transaction it is. For example, with a consumer transaction, individual states also may have some or all of the following laws: a consumer protection law such as the Song-Beverly Consumer Warranty Act in California, a lemon law, an unfair trade and deceptive practices act, and an anti-disclaimer statute that prohibits sellers from disclaiming warranties in certain types of consumer transactions. These consumer protection laws may either override or supplement the UCC.

6. COMPUTER INFORMATION AND SOFTWARE CONTRACTS

The UCC was drafted in the 1950s when computers were not the common household items that they are today. Most of the UCC Articles, with the exception of Article 2, have undergone major revisions in the past 60 years. Although the Uniform Law Commission attempted major revisions of Article 2 in the late 1990s and early 2000s, the Revised Article was so controversial that revision efforts failed in every state and in 2000 the Commission withdrew the proposed amendments. Consequently, courts have had to decide whether to try to apply Article 2 or other laws to software transactions and computer information. Additionally, the Uniform Law Commission and its drafting partners in the late 1990s drafted the Uniform Computer Information Transaction Act (UCITA). That law created a set of rules to govern areas such as software licenses and computer information. Unfortunately, there was a great deal of opposition to UCITA and only Virginia and Maryland successfully enacted the law. After the failure of revised Article 2 and UCITA, the American Law Institute (ALI), attempted another approach to software contracts in its Principles of the Law of Software Contracts. Although the Principles passed the ALI in 2009, it too was controversial and has not garnered much success. Consequently, the courts must decide whether to use Article 2 or the common law when litigation arises involving software contracts and computer information.

The following case should help you understand some of the issues courts struggle with when deciding whether the UCC applies to software contracts.

SMART ONLINE, INC. v. OPENSITE TECHNOLOGIES, INC.
No. 01 CVS 09604, 2003 WL 21555316 (N.C. June 17, 2003)

This Matter came before the undersigned on defendants' motion pursuant to Rule 12(b)(6) of the North Carolina Rules of Civil Procedure to dismiss Smart Online, Inc.'s ("Smart Online") claims in the Third Amended Complaint for breach of contract and breach of express warranty arising out of the version number of the computer software, and the allegation that Defendant OpenSite Technologies, Inc. ("OpenSite") verbally represented that the OpenSite software ("Software") could handle three to five thousand bids or transactions simultaneously. Defendants also ask the Court to dismiss plaintiff's claims for the following damages: (1) $145,000 paid to Dynamic Quest for implementation of the Software; (2) $1,935,900 paid to acquire Assets2Auction; (3) $1,817,000 paid to acquire e4close.com; (4) $3,823,000 in costs associated with expansion of Smart Online's business; and (5) additional damages based upon loss of revenue. Defendants have asked the Court to limit Smart Online's recoverable damages to $121,659, the amount plaintiff paid to license the software.

For the reasons set forth below, the Court GRANTS defendants' motion to dismiss the damage claims for the acquisition of Assets2Auction and e4close.com; and, at this stage, the Court DENIES defendants' remaining motions to dismiss plaintiff's claims.

* * *

I.   BACKGROUND AND PROCEDURAL HISTORY

This dispute arises out of Plaintiff Smart Online's licensing of Defendant OpenSite's software. Smart Online is an online provider of internet business applications. In March 2000, Smart Online and Defendant OpenSite entered into a software license agreement ("License Agreement") whereby Smart Online would utilize OpenSite's Software for its auction web site. In May 2000, Defendant Siebel Systems, Inc. ("Siebel") acquired OpenSite as a wholly owned subsidiary. Allegations regarding the promised capabilities of the Software form the heart of this dispute.

Smart Online filed this action in Wake County on August 7, 2001. In its complaint, Smart Online sought relief for breach of contract, breach of express warranty, breach of implied warranty of merchantability, breach of implied warranty of fitness for a particular purpose, civil conspiracy, unfair and deceptive trade practices, negligent misrepresentation and fraud. Plaintiff further sought punitive damages. Defendants filed a motion to dismiss on May 1, 2002, and on June 21, 2002 Smart Online moved to amend its complaint. The Court granted Smart Online's motion to file an amended complaint on June 26, 2002, at which time plaintiff filed its amended complaint. Defendants challenged the amended complaint under Rule 12(b)(6).

After a hearing, the Court entered an October 15, 2002 Order dismissing plaintiff's claims for breach of implied warranties of merchantability and fitness for a particular purpose; the Order limited contract damages and granted plaintiff thirty days to amend its complaint to address the particularity requirements for fraud, rescission and misrepresentation damages. Smart Online filed its Third Amended Complaint on November 14, 2002. Defendants filed a Rule 12(b)(6) motion directed to the Third Amended Complaint on December 12, 2002; plaintiff responded on December 23, 2002. The Court held oral arguments on March 13, 2003.

III. BREACH OF CONTRACT

Article 2 of the Uniform Commercial Code as adopted by North Carolina ("UCC") applies to "transactions in goods." N.C.G.S. § 25–2–102 (2002) [**UCC 2–102**]. The UCC defines goods as "all things (including specially manufactured goods) which are movable at the time of identification to the contract for sale other than the money in which the price is to be paid, investment securities (article 8) and things in action." N.C.G.S. § 25–2–105(1). [**UCC 2–105(1)**]

Where a contract is a mixed contract, in that it compasses both the sale of a good and the provision of services, our Court of Appeals has expressly adopted the "predominant factor" test to determine whether the UCC applies. [Citations omitted]. The predominant factor test states:

> [the] test for inclusion or exclusion is not whether [the sale of goods and the provision of services] are mixed, but, granting that they are mixed, whether their predominant factor, their thrust, their purpose, reasonably stated, is the rendition of service, with goods incidentally involved . . . or is a transaction of sale, with labor incidentally involved. . . .

Id. at *8–9 (quoting *Bonebrake*, 499 F.2d at 960) (alterations in original).

Courts have examined several factors under this test but have not found any one factor to be dispositive of the issue. Some of those factors include: "(1) the language of the contract, (2) the nature of the business of the supplier, and (3) the intrinsic worth of the materials." [Citations omitted].

Other jurisdictions have placed great weight on the language of the contract and the manner in which the contract was billed. . . .

* * *

North Carolina has not directly addressed the issue of whether the UCC should apply to a contract for software. Thus, this Court has looked to other jurisdictions for guidance. The case of *Advent Systems Limited v. Unisys Corp.*, 925 F.2d 670 (3rd Cir.1991) closely examined whether software could be considered a good or service. Advent produced an electronic document management system, a "process for transforming engineering drawings and similar documents into a computer data base." Unisys manufactured a variety of computers. Advent and Unisys executed two documents whereby Advent agreed to provide the software and hardware making up the document systems to be sold by Unisys in the United States. *Id.* Unisys began the process of restructuring and "decided it would be better served by developing its own document system and . . . told Advent their arrangement had ended." *Id.* Advent filed a claim in the United States District Court for the Eastern District of Pennsylvania alleging, *inter alia,* breach of contract. During pretrial proceedings, the District Court ruled that the UCC did not apply because the services aspect of the contract predominated. The jury awarded Advent $4,550,000 on the breach of contract claim. The Court of Appeals for the Third Circuit reversed and remanded the breach of contract claim after finding that the contract was subject to the UCC.

The Third Circuit analogized software to compact disc and music recordings. Its analysis is worth quoting at length here.

> Computer programs are the product of an intellectual process, but once implanted in a medium are widely distributed to computer owners. An analogy can be drawn to a compact disc recording of an orchestral rendition. The music is produced by the artistry of musicians and in itself is not a "good," but when transferred to a laser-readable disc becomes a readily merchantable commodity. Similarly, when a professor delivers a lecture, it is not a good, but, when transcribed as a book, it becomes a good.

> That a computer program may be copyrightable as intellectual property does not alter the fact that once in the form of a floppy disc or other medium, the program is tangible, movable and available in the marketplace. The fact that some programs may be tailored for specific purposes need not alter their status as "goods" because the Code definition includes "specially manufactured goods."

> * * *

> The relationship at issue here is a typical mixed goods and services arrangement. The services are not substantially different from those generally accompanying package sales of computer systems consisting of hardware and software.

The Court went on to point out the benefits and public policy concerns of applying the UCC to software transactions.

> Applying the U.C.C. to computer software transactions offers substantial benefits to litigants and the courts. The Code offers a uniform body of law on a wide range of questions likely to arise in computer software disputes: implied warranties, consequential damages, disclaimers of liability, the statutes of limitations, to name a few.

> The importance of software to the commercial world and the advantages to be gained by the uniformity inherent in the U.C.C. are strong policy arguments favoring inclusion. The contrary

arguments are not persuasive, and we hold that software is a "good" within the definition of the Code.

When addressing whether software should fall within the category of goods, the Court finds the public policy concerns outlined in *Advent* to be compelling. However, the Court is not prepared to find that there should be a blanket rule stating that all software is a good. In addition to the factors outlined above, a Court should consider additional factors such as the degree of development and customization necessary for a particular program or customer. As this is an issue of first impression in North Carolina, the Court turns to other jurisdictions for guidance.

At one end of the spectrum is a consumer who walks into the local electronics store, pulls a shrink-wrapped word processing program from the shelf, pays the cashier and goes home with it. Such a sale is very clearly one for a good. At the other end of the spectrum is a programmer that invents and develops new software for a particular customer. In that case, the contract is more like a services contract. [Citations omitted].

If that programmer were to then package the software and sell it to others, the analysis comes much closer to the sale of goods as to that transaction. Where programmers are selling preexisting software "albeit with custom modifications or upgrades to adapt it to the user's needs or equipment [and are paid] in a manner primarily reflecting sale of goods[,]" courts have been much more willing to find the contract falls under the UCC. [Citations omitted].

Although Smart Online and OpenSite have referred to themselves as licensee and licensor, there is some language within the Agreement that looks like UCC language. Paragraph 8.3 refers to the warranty as a "product warranty"; Exhibit A to their Agreement allows payment by "Purchase Order." However, the Court does not rely on this language in finding that this contract falls under the UCC. The Court finds the parties [sic] treatment and assumptions about their relationship to be compelling. They have treated the contract as though it were a contract for the sale of goods. All of Smart Online's complaints have defined OpenSite as a merchant "as such term is defined in N.C.G.S. 25–2–104." [**UCC 2–104**]. Defendants have responded by answering with UCC-based defenses, citing directly to the UCC. Indeed, all parties have crafted their briefs and argued as if the Software at issue is a good that falls within the purview of the UCC.

Furthermore, this transaction was more like *Pearl* than *Wharton*. Smart Online purchased a prepackaged product. The customization involved was not sufficient to create a services contract. This software was not developed for Smart Online's use. Smart Online searched for, and purchased, pre-existing software.

The payment terms of the agreement also indicate this was a sale for goods. Smart Online purchased "SUPPORTED AND CUSTOMIZED SOFTWARE." It paid upfront for a particular program coupled with fees for additional "Galleries" for the pre-existing program. Payments for the training, support and maintenance were not the predominant factor in the contract. [Citations omitted].

The Court finds that the Agreement was one for the sale of goods and that the UCC applies.

* * *

VI. CONCLUSION

For the foregoing reasons, the Court GRANTS defendants' motion to dismiss the damage claims for the acquisition of Assets2Auction and e4close.com and DENIES defendants' motions to dismiss plaintiff's claims for breach of contract and breach of express warranty. At this stage of the proceedings, the Court DENIES defendants' motions to disallow all tort-based damages incurred for the expansion of Smart Online's business and for additional damages based on loss of revenue. The Court further DENIES defendants' motion, based solely on the pleadings, to limit plaintiff's recoverable damages to the amount plaintiff paid to license the software. The issues may be more efficiently addressed at the summary judgment stage.

SO ORDERED, this the 17th day of June 2003.

PROBLEMS

1. Return to the transaction where you were purchasing the doggie door from Luke Smith and review those facts. (They are located in the section on hybrid contracts.) After you purchased the door from Luke, it began to have problems. It only opens automatically about 70% of the time and last night the door allowed a possum to come into your house, even though you were assured that nothing other than your dog could get through the doggie door because it is not supposed to open without recognizing the identity chip attached to your dog's collar. After animal control caught the possum, you verified it did not have any type of identity chip on it! Mr. Smith has not been forthcoming with a solution to the problem and seems to be ignoring you. As you consider your options, you know that it may make a difference whether the UCC or the common law governs your contract with Mr. Smith. Answer these preliminary questions:

    a. Why do you care whether the common law or the UCC applies to this transaction? See 2–313, 2–314, and 2–315.

42   INTRODUCTION TO SALES LAW AND SCOPE   CH. 1

b.   Does this transaction involve more than goods? Are services also a part of the transaction? If yes, what are the services and how will you determine whether the UCC or the common law will apply?

c.   After reading the warranty sections in Article 2, you realize it is important to you that the UCC governs your transaction. What do you have to show before the UCC will cover this transaction? Under the Gravamen test? Under the Predominant Purpose test? What would be the outcome with each test? See 2–102, 2–105, 2–104(1), 2–313, and 2–314.

After working through the analysis in the above problem, you should understand the importance of the UCC scope issue to any given transaction and that there might not always be a clear-cut answer to an issue.

2.   Read UCC 2–102, 2–105, and 2–107 and determine whether Article 2 will apply to the following transactions:

a.   A contract with a famous artist to paint a picture of your relatives.

b.   Sale of a standard poodle.

c.   Sale of a prefabricated home to be attached to the land.

d.   Sale of a home attached to the land.

e.   Purchase of a computer program to be downloaded from the Internet.

f.   Sale of oranges from an orange grove.

g.   A contract for a distributorship agreement where Allie Company (the distributor) contracts to distribute nautical products manufactured by Luke Company to retailers in the southeastern United States.

   i.   Would it make a difference to your answer if Allie Company was only paid by commission?

h.   Sale of a car.

i.   Sale of a right to collect damages on a tort claim.

j.   Sale of an insurance policy.

k.   Sale of natural gas.

l.   Sale of an ongoing business. Consider the following facts when making your determination:

MBH entered into a contract with Otte for the sale of Hallam Grain Co., a business that bought and sold grain, chemicals, and fertilizer. MBH agreed to sell Hallam Grain Co. to Otte as an ongoing business. The sales contract provided for the sale of real estate, buildings, fixtures, furniture, equipment, personal property, goodwill, inventory, and other assets associated with the said business. MBH also agreed to sell the name "Hallam Grain Co." to Otte and signed a covenant not to compete as part of the transaction. The contract provided for a purchase price of $430,000 and specified that the transaction was to be closed on or before October 15. The contract allocated the purchase price as follows:

Land	$10,000
Buildings	$170,000
Covenant not to compete	$100,000
All personal property, equipment, furniture and fixtures as reflected on attached Schedule "A"	$150,000
TOTAL	**$430,000**

Paragraph 5 of the contract provided for the sale of certain inventory items as follows:

Seller and Buyer further agree that, at the time of closing, Seller will sell, transfer, and convey to Buyer all remaining chemicals, grain, and fertilizer at a price not to exceed the sum of One Hundred Thousand Dollars ($100,000). Such sale is to be made after an inventory is taken by Seller and Buyer, of all such chemicals, grain, and fertilizer, after the close of business on the day preceding the date of closing.

m. Sale of a "smart home" system. The agreement included the purchase of the equipment and the following work:

1. Create independent zones of music throughout the house including 10 rooms and equipment to switch, power, and control the music system.

2. Lighting control system.

3. Network wiring for television, phone, music and computers throughout the home.

n. Sale of porcelain dental veneers by dentist to be put on the patient's teeth in the dentist office.

o. Sale of reading glasses from a drugstore.

p. Sale of reading glasses by an optometrist to correct astigmatism. Before the glasses can be created, the optometrist has to run special tests to diagnose the problem and determine the proper prescription.

q. Sale of a yacht by a yacht dealer.

3. Read 2A–103(1)(j) and 1–203 and determine whether the following transactions are true leases or sales with disguised security interest.

a. Marla Maples is the executive director of the National Rescued Greyhound Organization. This job requires that she drive to different parts of the country to pick up rescued greyhounds, transport them to new homes, and meet with local rescue groups. Marla wanted to buy a motor home so she could take her two large greyhounds, Athena and Jazz, with her as she traveled around the country. After a month long search, Marla could not find a suitable motor home. She needed a specially built motor home that could accommodate greyhounds. This required a longer home, specially built "doggie doors," and a high fence that could be detached while traveling and reattached when parked. Marla heard about Mars Mobile Vacation Home Builders from a friend. They produce custom made motor homes built for each individual buyer, so she decided to see if they could provide what she needed.

Marla met with Sam Spade, a salesman for Mars and explained her needs for the motor home to accommodate her dogs. When he told her the motor home would cost $100,000, Marla remarked that the price seemed quite high. Sam explained that the motor home was expensive because they had to create a special design for the doggie doors and fence as well as create new specifications for other parts of the home to accommodate her greyhounds. He also pointed out that $100,000 was not that expensive when you considered the fact that these homes lasted well over 20 years and retained about half their value after 10 years.

While discussing financing of the home, Sam expressed some doubt about whether Marla would be able to obtain adequate financing due to past and current debt problems. Sam suggested that she consider alternate financing in terms of a lease with an option to buy. Eventually, Marla opted to lease the motor home. The terms of the lease included the following:

(1)   Buyer will make a $5000 down payment, due upon signing the contract;

(2)   Marla's monthly payments will be $975 per month for ten years (total amount of monthly payments for the lease is $117,000);

(3)   Marla will have the option to buy the motor home at the end of the lease period for $20,000;

(4)   Marla is required to pay for all taxes and maintenance on the motor home; and

(5)   The lease may be terminated after the third year for a payment of $10,000, but if lessor is unable to release the property, Marla is responsible for the remainder of the payments.

b.   Same facts as (a.) except the agreement did not contain a termination clause.

c.   Same facts as (a.) except the option to buy the motor home was equal to the fair market value and there was a non-termination clause.

d.   Same facts as (a.) except the termination clause only required a payment of a restocking fee of $1,000, and the purchase price at the end of the lease was $1,000.

e.   Marhoefer Packing Co. negotiated with Robert Reiser & Co. for the acquisition of a Vemag Model 3007–1 Continuous Sausage Stuffer. The transaction was governed by a document entitled, "Lease Agreement." This agreement required Marhoefer to make 48 monthly payments of $665, with the first 9 payments (approximately $6000) to be paid upon execution of the lease. The other terms and conditions were as follows:

(1)   Any State or local taxes and/or excises are for the account of the Buyer.

(2)   The equipment shall at all times be located at:

Marhoefer Packing Co., Inc.
1500 North Elm & 13th Street
Muncie, Indiana

and shall not be removed from said location without the written consent of Robert Reiser & Co.

(3)   The equipment can only be used in conjunction with the manufacture of meat or similar products unless Robert Reiser & Co gives written consent.

(4)   The equipment will carry a ninety-day guarantee for workmanship and materials and shall be maintained and operated safely and carefully in conformity with the instructions issued by our operators and the maintenance manual. Service and repairs of the equipment after the ninety-day period will be subject to a reasonable and fair charge.

(5)   If, after due warning, our maintenance instructions should be violated repeatedly, Robert Reiser & Co. will have the right to cancel the lease contract on seven days notice and remove the said equipment. In that case, lease fees would be refunded pro rata.

(6)   It is mutually agreed that if lessee, Marhoefer Packing Co., Inc., violates any of the above conditions, defaulting in the payment of any lease charge hereunder, or if lessee shall become bankrupt, make or execute any assignment, or become party to any instrument or proceedings for the benefit of its creditors, Robert Reiser & Co. shall have the right at any time without trespass, to enter upon the premises and remove the aforesaid equipment, and if

removed, lessee agrees to pay Robert Reiser & Co. the total lease fees, including all installments due or to become due for the full unexpired term of this lease agreement and including the cost for removal of the equipment and counsel fees incurred in collecting sums due hereunder.

(7) It is agreed that the equipment shall remain personal property of Robert Reiser & Co. and retain its character as such no matter in what manner affixed or attached to the premises.

In a letter accompanying the lease, Reiser added two option provisions to the agreement. The first provided that, at the end of the four-year term, Marhoefer could purchase the stuffer for $9,968. In the alternative, it could elect to renew the lease for an additional four years at an annual rate of $2,990, payable in advance. At the conclusion of the second four-year term, Marhoefer would be allowed to purchase the stuffer for one dollar.

4.   Read 2301(1) and (3) from the Magnuson-Moss Federal Warranty Act and determine whether the transaction would qualify as one by a consumer and for a consumer product under the federal law.

a.   A contract with a famous artist to paint a picture of your relatives.

b.   Sale of a standard poodle.

c.   Sale of a prefabricated home to be attached to the land.

d.   Purchase of a computer program to be downloaded from the Internet.

e.   Sale of oranges from an orange grove to a grocery store.

f.   Sale of a car to be used for a business.

g.   Sale of porcelain dental veneers by dentist to be put on the patient's teeth in the dentist office.

h.   Sale of reading glasses from a drugstore.

i.   Sale of a yacht by a yacht dealer.

j.   Sale of a small airplane.

k.   Sale of an over the counter homeopathic remedy for children

l.   A pacemaker implanted by a heart surgeon

5.   Read CISG Articles 1 and 2 and determine whether the CISG would govern the following transactions (Canada is a party to the CISG):

a.   Sale of 50 cars by an Auto dealer in Canada to a car dealership in North Dakota.

b.   Sale of a car by an auto dealer in Canada to a family in North Dakota.

c.   Sale of a car by an auto dealer in Canada to the Stella Seed business in North Dakota. When Stella purchases the car from the auto dealer she intends to give it to her son so he can get back and forth to college.

    d.   Sale of an airplane from Boeing Corporation in Illinois to Black Palm industries in Winnipeg, Canada.

CHAPTER 2

THE DEFAULT RULES

▪ ▪ ▪

Now that you understand the importance of scope in answering the question of whether the UCC or other law governs a transaction, the next step is to consider the individual default rules contained in Article 2. You can, and I believe should, think of the default rules as a secondary scope issue. Not all default rules will apply to every contract and the parties have the power to contract around most of the default rules and occasionally they do, so it is important to determine which apply and which do not.

Articles 2 and 2A contain a series of default rules that may become part of any contract governed by UCC Article 2 or 2A if the parties have not already agreed on a term that covers the same issue as the default rule. How do courts determine whether to use the default rules? They do this through a process called "filling the gaps," which means when the parties have a dispute about their agreement or performance under their agreement that they cannot resolve and the agreement is silent about the issue, the court will turn to the appropriate UCC article to find a rule to fill the gap and supply the term.

To understand this process, read **2–308**. That default rule states where delivery should be made for a transaction "unless otherwise agreed." If nothing in the agreement covers who should deliver or pick up the goods, **2–308** would fill that gap and the agreement would require that the buyer pick-up the goods at her expense at the seller's place of business, assuming the seller had a place of business.

It is important to understand that parties have the ability to write themselves out of most, but not all, of the default rules. **1–302** explains that parties may vary from UCC terms by agreement but it clarifies that certain obligations such as good faith and reasonableness may not be disclaimed. For example, **2–302** allows a court to determine that a contract, or any part of that contract, is unconscionable (unconscionability will be addressed in Chapter 5. Upon a finding of unconscionability, a court may refuse to enforce a contract or limit the contract in other appropriate ways. Parties *do not* have the ability to circumvent this section by agreeing that they can enter into an unconscionable contract. There are other sections of the UCC that parties may not be able to avoid (other examples include **1–304** on the obligation of good faith and **2–318** on privity); however, for the majority of the UCC the parties have the power to control their own agreements and the default rules will not apply unless necessary.

A. THE AGREEMENT

Since the parties can contract around the default rules, before turning to the rules, you must always look initially at the agreement to determine whether a gap exists. The first place to look in the agreement is, of course, the words and terms of the contract itself. However, an agreement under Article 2 is larger than the face of the contract and may include terms that are not specified in a written contract.

The UCC operates under the assumption that agreements between parties are not usually static. In other words, the agreement incorporates additional terms that are not always written in a contract or agreed to orally during negotiations. Read **1–201(b)(3)**, which dictates how the code defines the agreement between the parties, and you will see that an agreement encompasses the totality of the bargain between the parties and is not limited solely to the contract. The totality of the bargain under this section also includes trade usage, course of performance, and course of dealing. You may have studied these terms in your contracts class; but as a refresher, these concepts relate to the behavior of the parties involved in past similar contracts, the ongoing performance in a current contract, and common behavior in an industry. To better familiarize yourself with these terms read **1–303**. If trade usage, course of performance, or course of dealing exist, they may be considered part of the agreement between the parties.

Since trade usage, course of performance, and course of dealing may be part of the agreement, what happens if they conflict with one another? What if the trade usage and course of performance for a specific agreement contradict one another? Further, what if the parties take the time to agree on certain terms and an express term of the contract conflicts with either trade usage, course of performance, or course of dealing? Which term prevails then? To answer these questions, read **1–303(e)**. That section states how to deal with instances like these. First, it says that if reasonably possible, we should read the express terms of the contract and trade usage, course of performance, and course of dealing as consistent with each other. If that is not possible, **1–303(e)** provides a hierarchy of terms: express terms prevail, then course of performance prevails over course of dealing, and finally course of dealing prevails over trade usage.

As an aside, answering these questions should illustrate how intuitive much of the UCC is. The UCC rules usually reflect how most people in business would contract, if they took the time to think about all of the terms they actually want to include in their contract. Unfortunately, many businesses do not have the time, or find it is not cost efficient to work out every term in a contract. In that situation, the UCC steps in and fills the gaps.

After confirming whether any relevant course of performance, course of dealing, and/or trade usage exist that should be made part of the contract, you have ascertained the agreement between the parties and can now turn to the default rules of Article 2. Remember, the default rules only apply if the agreement does not cover the issue addressed by the default rule, or if any of the terms in the agreement become unenforceable for some reason.

B. DEFAULT WARRANTY RULES

After identifying which terms are included in the agreement or contract, if you find there is a gap, then you can turn to the default rules. The next step requires you to consider which default rules, if any, become part of the contract. A thorough reading of Article 2 reveals that the drafters considered almost every essential term needed for a contract except for the issues of subject matter and quantity. The drafters even included a price term. *See* **2–305**. The remainder of this chapter will examine some of the most important default rules in Article 2, except for rules pertaining to remedies, which will be covered in Chapter 5.

The first group of default rules that stands out as extremely significant relates to warranties. We start by considering how warranties come into existence and attach to a sale, then turn to common defenses sellers use to avoid warranty protections. These defenses include disclaimers, privity, notice, and remedy limitations. Finally, we will briefly consider how the Magnuson-Moss Warranty Act, discussed in Chapter 1, changes the UCC default rules. Because Magnuson-Moss is federal law, you cannot fully understand UCC warranties and their impact without learning how Magnuson-Moss impacts state warranty law.

1. WARRANTY OF TITLE (2–312)

The warranty of title is not a warranty that relates to the quality of goods like the other warranties provided by Article 2. The warranty of title is much more basic. **2–312** implies in every contract, with very few exceptions, that goods sold to a buyer come with a good title free of any encumbrances. This warranty exists because without good title goods are worth very little, although you will learn in Chapter 3 that a voidable title may be transformed into good title if the proper requirements are met. In Chapter 6, however, you will see how the rules pertaining to transfer of title with goods are different than the rules governing negotiable instruments, under Article 3. Warranty of title is rarely disclaimed and a proper disclaimer of title is not a simple task. Further, the section that applies to disclaimers of warranties, **2–316**, may not be used to disclaim the warranty of title. The most important question that often arises relating to title is whether title passes from one party to another. That inquiry will be covered in chapter three.

2. EXPRESS WARRANTIES (2–313)

Under **2–313**, sellers may create express warranties. This section requires that a seller actually give a warranty as compared to implied warranties that exist because certain facts or situations occur. There are three different ways to establish an express warranty under **2–313** and none of them requires any type of formality, such as words like promise or guarantee. Simply stated, the three ways to create an express warranty are when a seller: 1) states a fact or promise about the goods that becomes part of the basis of the bargain, 2) describes the goods and it becomes part of the basis of the bargain, or 3) exhibits a sample or model that becomes part of the basis of the bargain.

A new concept introduced by **2–313** is the phrase "basis of the bargain." Unfortunately, the code does not define how something becomes part of the basis of the bargain. Reliance would show that a statement, model, or description was part of the basis of the bargain, however Comment 3 to **2–313** indicates that once a statement is made there is a presumption that it is part of the basis of the bargain. Comment 3 makes clear that reliance is not required for an express warranty to exist. To rebut the presumption in Comment 3 about the basis of the bargain, a seller needs clear affirmative proof that the statement, model, or description was not in fact part of the basis of the bargain. Although most courts have followed Comment 3 and held that no reliance is necessary for an express warranty to exist, a minority of courts still seem to feel more comfortable if a buyer shows that she relied on the facts, description, or sample to create the express warranty. Strictly following the UCC though, basis of the bargain is a rebuttable presumption.

3. IMPLIED WARRANTY OF MERCHANTABILITY (2–314)

Unless disclaimed, the implied warranty of merchantability exists in every sale of goods when the seller is a merchant who sells goods of the kind. Merchant is defined in **2–104**. Although it is not very clear from reading the statute, it is important to understand that there is more than one kind of merchant. The different kinds of merchants matter when deciding which default rules apply, especially the implied warranty of merchantability because that warranty requires a particular kind of merchant. Read **2–104(1)** and the Comments that follow. This is a good example of how the Comments can really help you understand the black letter law.

From your reading of the Comments in **2–104(1)**, you should see that the definition of merchant rests on the concept of a person in business, not just a person who sells things. Consider the differences between a law student, a lawyer, and a lawyer who owns a car dealership. A law student would not qualify as a merchant under **2–104** because she is not a professional in business. A lawyer, however, is a merchant simply by being a professional in business but she is not a merchant who sells goods of the kind. A lawyer who owns a car dealership qualifies as a special merchant under **2–104** because she sells goods of the kind, cars. The trick is being able to delineate between who is a merchant by the nature of their profession and who is a "special" kind of merchant who deals in the goods they sell. Is the buyer or seller a businessperson? If so, then that individual likely will be a merchant under the **2–104** definition. The default rules that apply to a general merchant, those defined under **2–104**, are more limited and only include certain sections that use the term merchants such as the contract formation rules and the statute of frauds. The implied warranty of merchantability requires the seller to be a special kind of merchant seller. To be a special merchant for the purposes of **2–314**, the seller needs to be in the business of regularly selling goods of a certain kind. For example, a car dealer is a merchant who sells goods of the kind—cars. So, if a car dealer sold you a car, then the implied warranty of merchantability would automatically attach to the transaction unless the seller disclaimed the warranty because the seller was a merchant who dealt in goods of the kind. However, if you bought a car from a lawyer who had never sold a car before, the implied warranty of merchantability would not attach to the sale even though a lawyer is a merchant by virtue of being a professional in business. Since the only requirement under **2–314** is that the merchant deals in "goods of that kind," the implied warranty of merchantability should exist in every sale by a merchant who sells goods she normally sells, unless it has been disclaimed.

After determining that the implied warranty of merchantability exists, the next step is to decide whether the warranty has been breached. A review of **2–314** cases reveals that the warranty standards are not particularly stringent and courts seem to indicate that merchantable goods only have to be "no worse than average." However, if the goods fall below average or certainly far below average then the seller has breached the implied warranty of merchantability. **2–314(2)** states the standards for merchantability. These standards include that the goods need to be fit for their ordinary purpose and should pass without objection in the trade under the contract description. If the contract is for a used car it will not be held to the same standard as a new car. Comment 7 to **2–314** states that a good indicator of the nature and scope of the warranty is the price paid for the good. Also, goods are judged by their ordinary purpose. Later in this chapter this will be compared to goods that are sold for a particular purpose.

It is important to remember that, although this warranty is strict liability, the breach must occur at the point of sale. That means that the goods must be defective when they are sold, as opposed to some event causing the defect after the goods have left the seller.

A seller has a number of possible defenses to a breach of warranty. In addition to causation, other defenses may include lack of notice under **2–607(3)**, lack of privity under **2–318**, or an effective disclaimer under **2–316**. All of these defenses will be discussed later in this chapter.

4. IMPLIED WARRANTY OF FITNESS FOR A PARTICULAR PURPOSE (2–315)

The implied warranty of fitness for a particular purpose ("implied warranty of fitness") does not require a merchant seller, general or special. Although this warranty is more likely seen in business-to-business transactions, any seller can give an implied warranty of fitness. **2–315** requires that: 1) the seller has reason to know of the buyer's particular purpose, 2) the seller either knows or has reason to know that the buyer is relying on the seller's skill or judgment to provide the appropriate goods, and 3) the buyer actually relies on the seller. This last requirement can be found in Comment 1.

Many people confuse the implied warranty of fitness with the implied warranty of merchantability. The difference between the two is that the merchantability warranty considers the *ordinary purpose* of a good, while the fitness warranty looks at whether the buyer has a *particular purpose* for purchasing the good. Some examples will help to illustrate the difference between the two warranties. If you went to a furniture store wanting to buy furniture that you could use in your home to sit on and put things on, you would be buying furniture for its ordinary purpose, not a particular purpose. However, if you go to a furniture store wanting to buy furniture that is weatherproof and can withstand the rains in your area because you plan to leave it outside, the buyer may want an implied fitness warranty because the purpose of needing weatherproof furniture is a particular purpose that may not apply to all furniture. But, the warranty only exists if the seller knows of the buyer's particular purpose of needing weatherproof furniture that can withstand the elements, the seller knows you are relying on her skills or judgment, and you rely on the seller by buying the goods after the seller directs you to furniture that can be used for that purpose.

Food is another good example. If you want to prepare a raw food meal, you should be very careful where you buy your ingredients because not all food may be fit for the particular purpose of eating raw, even though it may be fine for its ordinary purpose of being cooked and eaten. If you go to your local butcher or fishmonger and tell them you want to buy fish, beef, or pork to use in a raw food meal, they should sell you food fit for that particular purpose of being eaten raw. However, if you just tell them you need fish, beef, or pork, the butcher or fishmonger is not warranting that the food is of the quality to be eaten raw. It only has to be fit for its ordinary purpose of eating it cooked.

5. WARRANTIES FOR LEASES

Article 2A covers all the rules for leases, including warranties. 2A's warranties mostly mirror the Article 2 warranties previously discussed, with a few exceptions. First, Article 2A makes it clear that lessors in finance leases do not give implied warranties, **2A–212** and **2A–213**. Second, of course title is not transferred in a lease transaction; however, Article 2A contains a warranty that the goods being leased are free of any claim or interest in the goods that might interfere with the lessee's leasehold interest, **2A–211**.

C. BREACH OF WARRANTY DEFENSES

Sellers may have a number of defenses to a breach of warranty claim. This chapter specifically deals with three of them found in Article 2: 1) disclaimers, 2) notice, and 3) lack of privity. Other defenses to consider include the statute of limitations and, in some cases, assumption of the risk by a buyer. All of these defenses are cumulative.

A related concept is found in the remedy section of Article 2 which allows sellers to limit their liability and damages by limiting their remedies. **2–719** allows a seller to avoid certain default rules by providing exclusive remedies, such as limiting damages to repair and replacement of defective goods. Often, sellers are willing to stand behind their products and replace defective goods; however, they are concerned about being responsible for potentially unlimited liability for damages, especially consequential damages. Article 2 permits sellers to limit their liability for consequential damages, although **2–719(3)** states that disclaiming consequential damages with respect to personal injury in consumer goods is prima facie unconscionable. Limiting consequential damages may have a similar effect to a disclaimer because it limits the impact of the warranty by limiting the damages a seller may have to pay in the event of a breach.

1. WARRANTY DISCLAIMERS (2–316)

A disclaimer includes modification and exclusion of warranties. Other than the implied warranty of title, the disclaimer rules for warranties are found in **2–316**. It is first important to note that according to **2–316**, a seller may not both give an express warranty and then try to disclaim that same warranty. But, **2–316** does allow for the disclaimer of implied warranties in several different ways. After learning how to properly disclaim implied warranties under the UCC, we will review other state and federal statutes that may prohibit certain disclaimers involving consumer goods.

Although a seller may not disclaim an express warranty, **2–316(1)**, the seller may disclaim implied warranties if the seller follows the rules provided by **2–316**. That section states several alternative ways to disclaim implied warranties. To disclaim only the implied warranty of merchantability, using **2–316(2)**, the seller must use the word "merchantability" and, if the disclaimer is in writing, it must be conspicuous. **1–201(b)(10)** defines conspicuous as being written or presented in a way that a reasonable person ought to have noticed it. For example, the disclaimer may use contrasting font, type, color, or contain a heading in capital letters that is larger than the other language surrounding it. On the other hand, if the seller wants to disclaim just the implied warranty of fitness using **2–316(2)**, this subsection does not require a seller to use specific language. Instead, a rather general disclaimer will work to disclaim a fitness warranty. Read **2–316(2)** for suggested language.

Other permitted methods for disclaiming *all* implied warranties are found in **2–316(3)**. Sellers regularly use **(3)(a)** to disclaim all implied warranties because it merely requires language "which in common understanding calls the buyer's attention to the exclusion of warranties." It suggests phrases like "as is" or "with all faults" as acceptable language to disclaim all implied warranties. If you have ever visited a car dealership that sells used cars, you probably have noticed cars being sold **"AS IS"** because that is a common, easy method for sellers to use when disclaiming warranties. Notice that **2–316(3)** does not require that the language be conspicuous; however, most commentators and courts agree that the disclaimer language must be conspicuous and the drafters simply failed to carry over that requirement from **(2)**. The requirement of conspicuousness may also be gleaned from the words "calls the buyer's attention to" found in **(3)**.

Does that mean that sellers will always be protected as long as they use the words from the statute? The answer is no. This is because **2–316(3)(a)** begins by saying "unless the circumstances indicate otherwise." Circumstances may exist that lead a court to conclude that the parties really did not intend a disclaimer, even if it appears that the seller disclaimed in accordance with **2–316**. Remember that before the UCC, buyers had to be cautious when entering transactions because the old adage of "caveat emptor" (buyer beware) applied. The enactment of the UCC shifted this risk to sellers who sell goods of the kind in most circumstances. Disclaimers shift that risk back to buyers, so courts want to be certain that parties intended to disclaim a warranty. If the circumstances surrounding the transaction suggest otherwise, a purported disclaimer may be ineffective.

There also is a limited exclusion or modification of a warranty when a buyer examines goods fully or refuses to examine them even though the seller has demanded that the buyer examine the goods to look for defects. Those situations require a two-part process. First, the seller must make a demand to put a buyer on notice that she needs to examine the goods. The second step requires a determination of how far the disclaimer will extend.

If the buyer refuses the seller's demands to examine the goods, an exclusion applies only to defects which an examination ought to have revealed—not all defects. Lastly, course of performance, course of dealing, or trade usage may exist that excludes or modifies an implied warranty.

2. WARRANTY DISCLAIMERS FOR LEASES

Because Article 2A was drafted after Article 2 in the 1990s, it used Article 2 as a guide for much of the statute. Nevertheless, some differences exist between the two Articles, but many of them are in the remedy sections. **2A–214**, the section on warranty disclaimers, tracks **2–316** fairly closely with three exceptions. First, to disclaim the implied warranty of merchantability in leases using **(2)**, in addition to using the word merchantability and being conspicuous, it must also be in writing. Article 2 does not contain a writing requirement. Second, the example used in **2A–214(2)** for disclaiming the implied warranty of fitness is much more specific than that used in **2–316**. Article 2A suggests disclaiming the implied warranty of fitness by stating that "there is no warranty that the goods will be fit for a particular purpose." This is much more specific than the language suggested in **2–316**. Finally, Article 2A adds a subsection on excluding or modifying a warranty against interference or infringement.

3. ANTI-DISCLAIMER STATUTES

Now that you understand how sellers may disclaim implied warranties, it is important to recognize how other statutes may interact with those disclaimers when the transaction involves consumer goods. You should always check for other law in your jurisdiction that may modify or exclude **2–316**. One law that every state and the District of Columbia have passed is what is commonly known as a "Lemon Law." It pertains to goods, usually cars, that come with a warranty and are unable to be repaired after a reasonable number of attempts. Lemon Laws vary by jurisdiction. For example, many Lemon Laws only cover new automobiles but others, such as the Song-Beverly Act from California, may include motorcycles, boats, and other types of vehicles.[1] These statutes modify warranties by limiting the number of attempts, usually to about four, sellers may have to repair a vehicle under a warranty before they will have to accept the vehicle's return for a refund of all or part of the purchase price.

In addition to Lemon Laws, a number of states have modified **2–316** and enacted a non-uniform section that protects consumers from certain disclaimers. Once again, the only way to determine this is to check your state's laws and to check them often because they are subject to change.

---

[1] C.R.S.A. § 42–10–101 (Colorado only covers motor vehicles that are not able to carry more than 10 people); FLA. STAT. ANN. § 681.102 (Florida limits its lemon law to on-road, new vehicles); 10 M.R.S.A. § 1161 (Maine includes all motor vehicles except those used for commercial purposes); N.Y. GEN. BUS. LAW., ch. 20, art. 11–A § 198–a (New York includes both new and used vehicles under its lemon law warranty provisions); Cal. Civ. Code § 1793.22 (California Lemon Law).

For example, Mississippi had a far-reaching consumer protection section of Article 2 that was entirely new, but repealed in 2014. Some states' statutes expressly prohibit disclaimers of implied warranties with respect to consumer goods.[2] Other states, such as New Hampshire, permit disclaimers of implied warranties but require a very particular way to do it for transactions involving consumer goods.

Here is an example from the New Hampshire UCC:

(4) . . . in any case in which goods are purchased primarily for personal, family or household use and not for commercial or business use (a consumer sale), disclaimers of the warranty of merchantability or fitness for a particular purpose shall not be effective to limit the liability of merchant sellers, unless the seller provides the buyer with a conspicuous writing which must be signed by the buyer and which clearly informs the buyer, prior to or at the time of the sale, in simple and concise language of each of the following:

(a) The goods are being sold on an "as is" or "with all faults" basis;

(b) The entire risk as to quality and performance of the goods is with the buyer; and

(c) If the goods prove defective after purchase, the buyer, not the manufacturer, distributor or retailer, shall assume the entire cost of all necessary servicing or repair.[3]

4. MAGNUSON-MOSS WARRANTY ACT

In addition to non-uniform versions of **2–316**, the Magnuson-Moss Warranty Act, **15 U.S.C. §§ 2301–2312**, prohibits disclaimers of implied warranties in certain situations. Because this Act is federal law it overrides state law, so it is important to know how it changes the UCC. First, as mentioned in Chapter 1, it only covers consumers and consumer goods. However, it defines consumers quite broadly to include buyers of any consumer products, people who have had consumer products transferred to them while they are under warranty, and anyone else who is entitled to enforce a warranty under the terms of the warranty or state law. *See* **2301(3)**. Remember that Magnuson-Moss defines consumer goods more broadly than the UCC because it includes property *normally* used for personal, family or household purposes. *See* **2301(1)**. Compare that to the UCC's definition that defines a consumer as someone who "enters into a transaction primarily for personal, family, or household use." *See*

<hr>

[2] CONN. GEN. STAT. ANN. § 42A–2–316(5); KAN. STAT. ANN. § 50–639(a); ME. REV. STAT. ANN. TIT. 11 § 2–316(5); MD. CODE ANN. COMM. LAW § 2–316.1; MASS. GEN. LAWS ANN. CH. 106, § 2–316A; MISS. CODE ANN. § 75–2–315.1(1); VT. STAT. ANN. TIT. 9A § 2–316(5).

[3] N.H. REV. STAT. § 382–A:2–316.

1–201(b)(11). So, Magnuson-Moss considers the ordinary use of the product, while the UCC looks at the buyer's particular use of the product.

Magnuson-Moss prohibits a seller from disclaiming any implied warranties in a consumer transaction if the seller has provided a written warranty or sold the consumer a service contract. *See* **2308**. That means that a seller who uses "As Is" to disclaim implied warranties will find it ineffective if that seller also includes a written warranty for a consumer product. In addition to being ineffective, it is a violation of Magnuson Moss, so a consumer may have a cause of action pursuant to **2310**. Further, if a warrantor gives a Full Warranty, that warranty may not even limit the duration of an implied warranty because the federal minimum standards for warranties will apply. *See* **2304**. Magnuson-Moss requires sellers that give written warranties to label them as either "full" or "limited." *See* **2303(a)**. If you want to explore the full requirements of the Magnuson-Moss Warranty Act, you should take a class on consumer law.

5. PRIVITY

As you recall from your first semester contracts class, historically the only people permitted to sue for breach of contract were parties to the contract. If a warrantor breached a warranty, the only one who could sue for that breach was the party in privity with the seller, unless a statute or some other law indicated otherwise. Article 2 eliminates the privity barrier in certain cases through **2–318**. **2–318** provides three different alternatives for states to choose from, so unfortunately this section is non-uniform in every state, not to mention some states enacted privity statutes different from any of **2–318**'s alternatives.

There are two different types of privity issues—horizontal and vertical privity. **2–318** specifically addresses horizontal privity issues. Horizontal privity issues arise when a party who is a stranger to the contract wants to sue a buyer's direct warrantor of a good for an injury. **2–318** allows certain third party beneficiaries to sue for breach of express or implied warranties even though they are not in direct privity with the warrantor. In other words, they did not buy or contract with the warrantor. For example, a passenger or bystander may be able to sue for a breach of warranty on a defective car, although neither one was a party to the contract between the car dealer and the buyer, if she is one of the beneficiaries covered under **2–318**. You can see from the following diagram that both the passenger and the bystander would have horizontal privity issues if they wanted to sue the car dealership for breach of warranty due to an injury from a defective car, unless **2–318** removes that privity bar.

Horizontal Privity

Because **2–318** contains three different alternatives, the results for third parties will vary depending upon jurisdiction. Additionally, as previously mentioned, some jurisdictions developed their own version of **2–318**. For example, Florida used Alternative A, but broadened it by adding "an employee, servant or agent of his or her buyer" to the expanded set of beneficiaries. Fla. Stat. Ann. § 672.318. The chart below illustrates the differences between the three alternatives.

Alternative A	Alternative B	Alternative C
Natural Person	Natural Person	Person
Family or household member, or household guest		
Reasonably expected to use, consume, or be affected by	Reasonably expected to use, consume, or be affected by	Reasonably expected to use, consume, or be affected by
Who is personally injured	Who is personally injured	Who is injured
May not limit or exclude	May not limit or exclude	May limit or exclude economic injury but not personal injury

A review of the text of **2–318** and the above chart reveals the differences between the alternatives. The first difference is that Alternative A and B require a natural person, while Alternative C just requires a person. The UCC's definition of a person includes many entities other than individual human beings such as corporations, governments or other legal or commercial entities. *See* **1–201(b)(27)**. Therefore, Alternative A and B require a human being, but Alternative C includes all the entities listed in **1–201(b)(27)**. Second, Alternative A narrows the group of beneficiaries permitted to sue for breach of warranty to only those individuals who are in either the family, household, or a household guest of the buyer. Alternatives B and C have no such requirement. In fairness to the warrantor, all three alternatives require that there be a reasonable expectation of use, consumption, or that the defective product would affect the individual. The third difference is that Alternative C allows any person with any type of injury to sue, including injuries that are solely economic, but jurisdictions using Alternative C also permit warrantors to limit or exclude their liability for economic losses to third parties. The other two alternatives require personal injury, but a warrantor does not have the usual freedom of contract and may not limit or exclude the consequences of **2–318**.

Vertical privity deals with parties up the distributive chain. For example, consider a person who buys a car from a local car dealer. The local car dealership gets the car from the manufacturer and the manufacturer might get one of the parts, such as the starter, from a different manufacturer, and that business purchased the wire for the starters from yet another supplier. That is an example of a distributive chain, which can be very long. If the car buyer wants to sue for a defective starter in her car she would have a vertical privity problem because she is not in privity with any party except the car dealership. **2–318** does not directly deal with this type of privity.

Vertical Privity

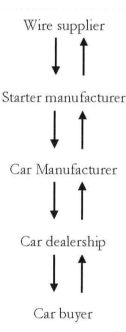

If the car buyer has a defective starter in her car and wants to sue the starter manufacturer and perhaps the wire supplier, the manufacturer and supplier will assert a privity defense. Because the buyer has no contractual relationship with the starter manufacturer or the wire supplier, she will need to find a way around the manufacturer and supplier's defense of privity. The black letter law of **2–318** will not help her because it focuses on horizontal privity. However, some courts have used Comment 3 to broaden the confines of vertical privity to the privity defense. When determining whether a lack of vertical privity will be an issue you must turn to the common law of your jurisdiction to find an answer. For example, many states have removed the vertical privity bar in lawsuits involving personal injury.

6.   MAGNUSON-MOSS AND PRIVITY

Although this book does not attempt to cover the Magnuson-Moss Warranty Act in depth, it is worth reiterating how the Act significantly changes rules in the UCC. As mentioned under the disclaimer section, **2308** restricts the use of disclaimers or modifications of implied warranties to consumers if the supplier gives a written warranty on a consumer product or enters into a service contract within 90 days of the sale of a consumer product. And, through its definition of consumer, the Act expands the number of beneficiaries who may be permitted to sue for breach of warranty or a violation of Magnuson-Moss even though they lack privity with the supplier. For purpose of the Act, **2301(3)** defines a consumer as:

> A buyer (other than for purposes of resale) of any consumer product, any person to whom such product is transferred during the duration of an implied or written warranty (or service contract) applicable to the product, and any other person who is entitled by the terms of such warranty (or service contract) or under applicable State law to enforce against the warrantor (or service contractor) the obligations of the warranty (or service contract).

The second part of the definition, where it uses the term transfer, arguably expands the privity exceptions for consumers because it is broader than the exceptions in **2–318**. Magnuson Moss does not define the term "transfer" but, using that term, some courts have found that Magnuson Moss applies to leases as well as sales. Additionally, Magnuson Moss does not contain a personal injury requirement like **2–318** does.

7.   NOTICE

One final important defense for sellers to consider in a breach of warranty case is the notice requirement in **2–607(3)**. This requirement applies to all breaches, not just a breach of warranty. Further, it is an absolute defense and has an almost draconian effect because a failure to notify leaves the buyer with no remedy under the UCC. This means the buyer essentially loses her day in court for lack of notice. But, in defense of this requirement, it does not require that a buyer notify the seller with great particularity. Comment 4 states that the notice "need merely be sufficient to let the seller know that the transaction is still troublesome and must be watched." The comment states that the notice under 2–607 does not require the same sort of particularity that 2–605 requires when a buyer rejects goods. It is sufficient for the buyer to let the seller know that she claims a breach occurred. A further review of the Comments shows that the UCC treats the notice requirement for buyers differently for 2–607(3) purposes depending on whether the issue involves a consumer or a commercial buyer. Commercial buyers are held to a higher standard.

The buyer must give notice "within a reasonable time after he discovers or should have discovered any breach." The requirement does not apply until a tender has been accepted and then the time begins to run. One issue that often arises relates to *who* must be notified. 2–607(3) specifically states that the buyer must notify the *seller*, but does that mean just the direct seller, or all the sellers in the distributive chain? For example, what happens when a buyer is suing a car dealer and the manufacturer of the car. Is the manufacturer entitled to the same notice as the car dealer? Courts are split on this issue.

Although the discussion of whether the UCC applied to the transaction was omitted from the next case, see if you can imagine the arguments for and against applying the UCC to dental veneers—a question that was posed in a problem in Chapter 1. Also, pay attention to the dentist's use of a clause to disclaim consequential damages because that issue will be discussed later in this chapter.

GOLDEN V. DEN-MAT CORPORATION

47 Kan. App.2d 450 (Kan. Ct. App. 2012)

ATCHESON, J.

Plaintiff Brenda Golden purchased dental veneers—porcelain overlays meant to improve the appearance of teeth—that Defendant Den-Mat manufactured and marketed and Defendant Dr. Carissa M. Gill, a dentist, put in place. Golden contends the veneers became discolored and stained despite representations from Den-Mat and Dr. Gill that they would retain their appearance. So she sued them in Sedgwick County District Court on the grounds the veneers breached implied warranties applicable to goods sold under Article 2—Sales of the Uniform Commercial Code and the transaction entailed deceptive acts and practices and improper limitations of those warranties in violation of the Kansas Consumer Protection Act. The district court granted summary judgment to Den-Mat and Dr. Gill. Golden has timely appealed. We reverse and remand the case for trial, except for one claim under the KCPA on which summary judgment was properly entered.

* * *

Because of the breadth of the issues, this opinion delves into the law governing express and implied warranties under the UCC, deceptive and unconscionable acts and practices under the KCPA, and the interplay of those two statutory schemes as they apply to contracts for the sale of goods to consumers. The unusual nature of the goods involved—dental veneers— has required an especially searching inquiry regarding the UCC. That search turned up no other directly analogous cases. Nonetheless, settled principles developed under the UCC and the KCPA undercut summary judgment based on the substantive grounds the district court actually cited and on the substantive grounds the defendants suggest as legal backstops.

We conclude that factual disputes remain as to: (1) the application of the UCC to the transaction; (2) the scope and breach of express warranties regarding the veneers; (3) the scope and breach of implied UCC warranties of merchantability and fitness of the veneers for a particular purpose; (4) whether Den-Mat or Dr. Gill engaged in deceptive acts or practices in violation of the KCPA; and (5) whether Den-Mat or Dr. Gill improperly attempted to limit those implied UCC warranties in violation of the KCPA. We conclude the district court properly granted summary judgment on Golden's claim that any attempt to limit the UCC warranties amounted to an unconscionable act or practice under K.S.A. 50–627 in violation of the KCPA. That's only because such an attempt specifically violates K.S.A. 50– 639 and is outside the scope of K.S.A. 50–627.

FACTUAL AND PROCEDURAL HISTORY

Because the district court entered summary judgment against Plaintiff Golden, we review the facts in the light most favorable to her. So our narrative presents the events that way. Before turning to that recitation, we note that Defendants Den-Mat Corporation, Cerinate Corporation, and Den-Mat Holdings, LLC appear to be united in interest and are represented by the same counsel. Neither the facts, as we understand them, nor the legal issues on appeal require we distinguish among those defendants. We refer to them collectively as Den-Mat.

In late 2004, Golden wanted to replace the veneers on her teeth with new ones that would give her smile what she described as a "super white" appearance. Veneers are synthetic panels cemented to the front of a person's teeth, thereby covering discoloration or other imperfections in the natural dentition. Golden saw a magazine advertisement for Cerinate veneers, a proprietary product Den-Mat manufactures. In response to her telephone call to the number in the advertisement, Den-Mat sent Golden a brochure describing the Cerinate veneers as "thin porcelain shields . . . bonded to the front of" the teeth "to create dramatic changes in your smile." The brochure touted "long-term clinical research" showing the Cerinate veneers would last up to 16 years "with no discoloration" and "100% retention." The brochure also explained that the porcelain veneers "are stronger and more durable" than comparable products made from plastic.

According to the brochure, "[s]ometimes plastic composites stain and discolor with age, whereas, Cerinate Veneers maintain their beautiful luster and vitality." The brochure referred several times to the durability of the veneers and promoted the "strong, patented adhesive" used to attach them. The brochure, however, contained no unequivocal statement that the veneers would not come loose or crack.

Golden decided to get the Cerinate veneers and contacted Den-Mat for a dentist in the Wichita area. Den-Mat supplied Golden with Dr. Gill's name and contact information as the nearest professional authorized to apply Cerinate veneers. Dr. Gill worked in Wellington, some 35 miles south of Golden's home.

Golden first met with Dr. Gill on November 8, 2004, and they discussed Golden's desire for "really white" teeth. Golden wanted the whitest veneers Den-Mat produced. Golden showed Dr. Gill the Den-Mat brochure and specifically asked about the durability of the veneers and the potential for discoloration. (Dr. Gill contends she first saw the brochure in April 2007, when Golden complained about the veneers. But the conflict is of no moment on summary judgment because the evidence must be taken favorably to Golden as the party opposing the motions.) Apparently without referring specifically to the Cerinate veneers, Dr. Gill assured Golden that porcelain would not discolor. Dr. Gill recalled telling Golden that the whitest veneers might not be the best choice cosmetically because they could look artificial rather than natural. But Golden was adamant she wanted the whitest shade.

Dr. Gill removed the old veneers, took impressions of Golden's teeth, and ordered the new veneers from Den-Mat. On January 10, 2005, Dr. Gill attached the Cerinate veneers to Golden's upper teeth. At the end of that visit, Dr. Gill gave Golden a written warranty for the veneers. The document is entitled "Five Year Limited Warranty" and states the Cerinate porcelain is "warranted against defects in workmanship and materials for a period of five (5) years from delivery date." The warranty covers the "repair or replacement" of the veneers but expressly excludes the costs for "removal or reinsertion," any cash refund, and consequential damages such as lost wages or pain and suffering. The warranty card states in small print that it "is in lieu of all other warranties, whether expressed or implied." The warranty card was filled in with Golden's name and address. Dr. Gill signed the card and a certification that the veneers had been applied using Den-Mat's bonding cement and appropriate preparation techniques.

Golden later testified in her deposition that she felt the veneers seemed darker or less white as soon as they had been affixed to her teeth. Nonetheless, Golden returned to Dr. Gill 3 weeks later and had the remaining veneers applied to her lower teeth. By then, one of the upper veneers had come loose and another appeared to have a crack in it. Dr. Gill ordered replacement veneers and later applied them; she did not charge Golden for that work.

Golden paid $9,875.25 for the Cerinate veneers. The payment was made to Dr. Gill.

Another veneer came off about 6 months later. Dr. Gill reapplied the veneer, again at no cost to Golden. In late March 2007, another veneer came off. Dr. Gill ordered a replacement veneer from Den-Mat. The replacement veneer was considerably whiter than the veneers Golden already had. On April 23, 2007, Dr. Gill spoke with a Den-Mat representative who said it was possible that Golden's veneers had become stained or had darkened over time. Dr. Gill recounted the conversation to Golden the same day.

Later on April 23, 2007, Golden wrote a letter to Dr. Gill expressing her dissatisfaction with the veneers and her belief they had developed "a gray cast" in the 15 months since they were placed on her teeth. Golden asked for Dr. Gill's help in obtaining a new set of veneers from Den-Mat at no cost. Dr. Gill's staff noted the letter in her office chart a week later. Den-Mat declined to replace Golden's veneers.

In the first part of 2008, Golden went to her regular dentist to have the Cerinate veneers removed from her upper teeth and replaced with a similar product from another manufacturer. The replacements cost about $4,500. In the summary judgment materials, Golden submitted a close-up photograph of her teeth after the upper veneers had been replaced. In the photograph, the lower teeth, with the Cerinate veneers, are noticeably duller than the replacement veneers and seem to have what could be stains.

On January 9, 2008, Golden filed a petition against the Den-Mat entities and Dr. Gill alleging breach of express warranties regarding the veneers and breach of implied warranties of merchantability and fitness for a particular purpose. She also alleged violations of the KCPA for a deceptive act or practice based on statements regarding the characteristics of the veneers and an unconscionable act or practice based on an attempt to limit the implied warranties in violation of K.S.A. 50–639. Golden alleged the veneers had become stained and discolored and some of them came off or cracked. Den-Mat and Dr. Gill duly filed separate answers denying liability. The parties conducted significant discovery. In the final pretrial order, Golden sought to recover the cost of the Cerinate veneers; the cost of the replacement veneers she got in 2008; and $5,000 for lost time, inconvenience, and pain and suffering. Den-Mat and Dr. Gill filed separate motions for summary judgment with supporting memorandums and exhibits. Golden responded. The district court requested and received additional briefing on issues related to sales under the UCC.

The district court granted summary judgment to the defendants on all of Golden's claims. In a short letter ruling issued on August 17, 2009, without citing supporting statutes or caselaw, the district court found that warranty claims against Den-Mat were torts filed beyond the 2-year statute of limitations. The district court held that the 3-year statute of limitations on the KCPA claims against Den-Mart expired in September 2007. As to Dr. Gill, the district court found the claims to be for professional negligence and, thus, governed by a 2-year statute of limitations that expired before Golden filed suit. The district court ruled that if the claims were brought under the UCC, Golden failed to give timely notice as required under the UCC. The district court found the KCPA inapplicable to Dr. Gill because the transaction was one for professional services rather than goods. And the district court found that the warranty card Dr. Gill gave to Golden did not limit implied warranties of merchantability or fitness for a particular use and did not otherwise violate the KCPA.

Golden has timely appealed. In their briefing to this court, the parties address an array of issues. . . .

* * *

STATUTES OF LIMITATION AND UCC NOTICE

The defendants asserted and the district court relied on multiple statute of limitations arguments to defeat Golden's claims . . . and her claims against Dr. Gill under the KCPA as common-law torts and granted summary judgment because, so treated, they were filed outside the governing limitations period. The district court also ruled that the KCPA claims against Den-Mat were filed after the 3-year statute of limitations had run. Both Dr. Gill and Den-Mat additionally argue that Golden failed to give timely notice under the UCC that the veneers failed to perform as warranted and, therefore, those claims should be barred. See K.S.A. 84–2–607(3)(a) [**UCC 2–607(3)(a)**]. While not strictly a statute of limitations, the requirement for timely notice that goods sold fail to conform to the contract creates a condition precedent for bringing suit under Article 2 of the UCC and, thus, would be applicable here. The district court erred in granting summary judgment on the grounds that Golden's suit was filed after the governing statutes of limitation had expired or that the notice of breach was untimely for UCC purposes.

* * *

In short, the record evidence fails to support a finding as a matter of law for Dr. Gill that the transaction with Golden was one in which acquisition and use of services predominated over the purchase of goods so that the UCC would not apply. Summary judgment could not be granted to Dr. Gill on the UCC claims on that basis or on any KCPA claims dependent upon an exclusion or dilution of otherwise applicable UCC warranties.

Express Warranty

Dr. Gill contends that even if the UCC applies in this case, she made no express warranty to Golden about the veneers and could not breach any such warranty. The Kansas courts treat the creation and breach of warranties in transactions for goods as questions of fact. [Citations omitted].

Under K.S.A. 84–2–313(1)(a) [**UCC 2–313(1)(a)**], an express warranty entails "any affirmation of fact or promise" a seller makes to a buyer related to the goods that "becomes part of the basis of the bargain." The seller need not label the representations as guarantees, warranties, or the like or even intend to create such an affirmation. K.S.A. 84–2–313(2) [**UCC 2–313(2)**]. A seller's oral representation may constitute an express warranty. And statements in advertising brochures or other promotional materials may create express warranties. To be warranties, the statements must be of a factual nature about the characteristics or utility of the goods. Mere opinions or general, though unquantifiable, expressions of quality or superiority cannot form the basis of an express warranty. A seller's representations that goods are "first rate" or "the finest around" are examples of sales talk or puffing that would not create an express warranty. See *Malul v. Capital Cabinets, Inc.,* 191 Misc.2d 399, 402–03, 740 N.Y.S.2d 828 (2002) (statement that kitchen cabinets were built to "last a lifetime" amounted to puffing, not express warranty). An express warranty once created generally cannot then be limited because, by definition, it has become part of the agreed-upon contract or bargain. The limited written warranty Dr. Gill gave Golden on January 10, 2005, after applying the upper veneers, cannot negate any express warranty created through the earlier affirmations about the veneers. When Golden received the written warranty, the sale contract had already been finalized and at least partly performed, so the terms of the written warranty would not modify the contractual agreement.

The summary judgment record contains sufficient evidence, albeit disputed in material particulars, that Dr. Gill made an express warranty to Golden. Golden testified that she showed Den-Mat's brochure to Dr. Gill and discussed at least some of the contents with her. According to Golden, Dr. Gill assured her that porcelain, the substance used in the veneers, would not discolor. Those discussions took place before the sale was finalized. Dr. Gill's statement, if made, was sufficiently factual that a jury could find it to be a warranty. And a jury could conclude Dr. Gill essentially endorsed or affirmed the representations in the Den-Mat brochure. The brochure's statements about the durability and immutable appearance of the Cerinate veneers could be construed as an express warranty, especially because they were tied to the clinical studies supposedly corroborating the affirmations. A jury, therefore, could reasonably find that Dr. Gill did make representations rising to the level of an express warranty. The summary judgment record also suggests a jury could find otherwise. But that means a jury ought to be making the call.

* * *

Golden's evidence has Dr. Gill reviewing the brochure from Den-Mat before finalizing the sale of the veneers and telling Golden that porcelain dental appliances won't stain or discolor. That course of conduct is comparable to the communication between Black and Don Schmid Motors regarding the warranty. In that case, the warranty terms were briefly noted in writing. But the notation was silent about who would honor the warranty. The absence of a writing in this case goes to the weight of the evidence, something the jury considers, rather than the legal sufficiency of the evidence in its uncontradicted state as the court must view it on summary judgment.

Dr. Gill also submits Golden has presented no "objective evidence" the Cerinate veneers discolored or stained. But nothing requires so-called objective evidence to establish a submissible breach of warranty claim. Golden says the veneers became stained and dull. That's enough to get to the jury. Testimony need not come from a disinterested witness to demonstrate breach. Again, what the jurors may make of Golden's testimony is for them to decide—not for the court to conjecture as a matter of law. Golden, of course, may call witnesses who will corroborate deterioration of the veneers' appearance.

Dr. Gill argues a claim for breach of the express warranty does not lie at least as to chipping and cracking of the veneers because she replaced them. But that misses the point of the express warranty claim. Golden contends Den-Mat and Dr. Gill represented to her that the veneers would not chip or crack. But they did. If the affirmation created an express warranty, the failure of the veneers to perform to the described level constituted a breach. Dr. Gill's efforts to repair or replace the veneers go to the harm the breach caused and the scope of remedy that might be appropriate for Golden now.

Implied Warranties

Dr. Gill contends that the evidence taken favorably to Golden fails to establish either a breach of an implied warranty of merchantability under K.S.A. 84–2–314 [**UCC 2–314**] or a breach of an implied warranty of fitness for a particular purpose under K.S.A. 84–2–315 [**UCC 2–315**]. In turn, the district court would have been correct to enter summary judgment on those grounds, according to Dr. Gill. As we have noted, the scope and breach of those implied UCC warranties typically present questions for the jury.

An implied warranty of merchantability essentially requires that goods sold by a merchant satisfy basic standards of quality or acceptability. See K.S.A. 84–2–314 [**UCC 2–314**], Official UCC Comment 2. As outlined in the pretrial order, Golden specifically claims the veneers fell short of the implied warranty requirement they be "fit for the ordinary purpose for which such goods are used." K.S.A. 84–2–314(2)(c) [**UCC 2–314(2)(c)**]. Based on that warranty, a buyer may reasonably expect an item to be something more than "worthless," though not "the finest of all possible goods of that kind." *Black,* 232 Kan. at 467, 657 P.2d 517. As in *Black,* the purchaser of a used car from a dealer reasonably may expect the vehicle to "provide dependable transportation." 232 Kan. at 467, 657 P.2d 517; see *Dale v. King Lincoln-Mercury, Inc.,* 234 Kan. 840, 843, 676 P.2d 744 (1984) (Consistent with an implied warranty of merchantability, the buyer of a used, low-mileage sedan represented to be in excellent condition may expect the vehicle to "contain a motor and transmission which will give . . . more than a few days' service."). As one court recently stated, a UCC warranty of merchantability " 'does not impose a general requirement that goods precisely fulfill the expectation of the buyer,' " but " 'it provides for a minimum level of quality.' " *Green v. Green Mountain Coffee Roasters, Inc.,* 279 F.R.D. 275, ___ (D.N.J.2011) (unpublished opinion).

The seller's obligation under an implied warranty of merchantability "depends upon the circumstances of the transaction." Courts consider the "reasonable expectations of the ordinary user or purchaser," something based on general "consumer expectations" regarding the goods rather than the subjective beliefs of the particular buyer. In an often cited case, the New York Court of Appeals stated the fitness of goods for ordinary purposes under the implied UCC warranty depends upon "the expectations for the performance of the product when used in the customary, usual and reasonably foreseeable manners." *Denny v. Ford Motor Co.,* 87 N.Y.2d 248, 258–59, 639 N.Y.S.2d 250, 662 N.E.2d 730 (1995).

To establish a breach, the buyer must show the ordinary purpose for goods of the type involved in the transaction and the lack of fitness of the goods actually purchased for that purpose. If the goods fall short, they are considered "defective" under the UCC. See *Miller v. Lee Apparel Co.,* 19 Kan.App.2d 1015, 1031, 881 P.2d 576 (1994) (coveralls that caught fire not defective or unfit for ordinary purposes as work clothing under K.S.A. 84–2–314 [**UCC 2–314**] because buyer had no reasonable expectation they would be flame resistant). Dr. Gill contends the veneers, as a matter of law, were not defective in a way that would breach an implied warranty of merchantability.

But a warranty of merchantability entails some expectation of durability, depending on the circumstances of the transaction and the goods involved. Goods satisfy the warranty of merchantability under **UCC 2–314** when they do "what they were supposed to do for as long as they were supposed to do it." *Prohaska v. Sofamor, S.N.C.,* 138 F.Supp.2d 422, 449 (W.D.N.Y.2001). Thus, a buyer of a handblown glass vase could not reasonably expect it to survive a fall to a tile floor. But the buyer of the car in *Dale* had a reasonable expectation it would run for some time without the engine, transmission, or other principal mechanical systems quitting.

Dr. Gill reads too much into the summary judgment record in suggesting the absence of evidence to support a claim for breach of an implied warranty of merchantability. Veneers are uncommon goods, so there is little in the way of tightly analogous case authority on this issue. Veneers do not particularly resemble used cars or computer software. But the broad principles set out in those and other UCC warranty cases can be adapted to this case. And the more refined application of those principles to the specific facts of this case moves from the realm of legal determination appropriate for summary judgment to factfinding reserved for jury trial.

Given the nature of veneers as permanent dental appliances intended to improve the cosmetic appearance of the user's teeth, a jury could rationally conclude a buyer would reasonably expect the veneers to remain in place and hold their appearance for some period of time after the sale. That is, like a late model used car, veneers ought to have some degree of durability when used as intended. Nobody has suggested Golden somehow misused the Cerinate veneers or subjected them to unusual conditions.

* * *

Other summary judgment evidence supports the breach of an implied warranty of merchantability, suggesting the Cerinate veneers performed below what might be reasonably expected of veneers generally. If credited by the jury, Golden's testimony that Dr. Gill told her porcelain dental products would not discolor or stain reflects some measure of what would be reasonably expected. In other words, if used as intended, porcelain dental appliances ought to retain their general color or appearance. As a practitioner in the field, Dr. Gill reasonably could be viewed as knowledgeable about standard characteristics of those sorts of goods.

* * *

Dr. Gill also argues the veneers were not covered by and, in any event, conformed to any implied warranty of fitness for a particular purpose under K.S.A. 84–2–315 [**UCC 2–315**]. When a seller "has reason to know [of] any particular purpose for which the goods are required" and should understand that the buyer "is relying on the seller's skill or judgment to select or furnish suitable goods," the transaction includes "an implied warranty that the goods shall be fit for such purpose." K.S.A. 84–2–315 [**UCC 2–315**]. Unlike an implied warranty of merchantability, an implied warranty of fitness for a particular purpose depends upon communication between the buyer and seller regarding a specific transaction. A warranty for particular purpose is narrower, based on a tailored use of the specific goods known to the seller rather than on an ordinary characteristic or suitability common to goods of that general type. For example, an implied warranty of fitness for a particular use arises if the buyer of shoes informs the seller he or she intends to go mountain climbing and elicits the seller's help in selecting appropriate footwear.

As we have noted, whether the parties engaged in communication or otherwise created an implied warranty of fitness for a particular purpose in a given transaction typically presents a jury question. The buyer "need not bring home" or emphasize to the seller the particular purpose intended for the goods or the reliance on the seller's skill in choosing among goods to meet that purpose, so long as the seller reasonably should understand the buyer's special use and reliance. The buyer, however, must actually rely on the seller's input.

A jury could conclude that Golden relied on Dr. Gill to keep her from purchasing goods that would fail to meet her expressed desire for exceptionally white teeth, a particular purpose or use. See *Lohmann & Rauscher, Inc. v. YKK (U.S.A.) Inc.,* 477 F.Supp.2d 1147, 1155 (2007) (jury question whether commercial buyer relied on commercial seller's expertise in selecting goods suitable for a particular purpose when it requested welded straps for use in orthopedic braces). While Golden had identified the Cerinate veneers as the product she believed would best fit her needs, she had not already contracted to purchase them when she met with Dr. Gill. According to Golden, they discussed her desire for very white teeth. Dr. Gill recalled suggesting Golden might prefer a more natural shade for the veneers, since the whitest ones might look artificial. Golden, nonetheless, asked Dr. Gill to order the brightest veneers Den-Mat made.

The evidence would support a jury determination that Golden had a particular purpose in mind beyond simply some cosmetic improvement in the appearance of her teeth. She wanted strikingly white teeth, even if some people, apparently including Dr. Gill, might find them unnatural and unflattering. On its face, that looks to be a particular purpose in contrast to a generic characteristic of veneers. Dr. Gill certainly knew of that purpose and knew of Golden's plan to buy Cerinate veneers. In turn, Golden's request of Dr. Gill for some assurance that the veneers would satisfy that purpose and Dr. Gill's purported response that porcelain dental appliances do not discolor or stain could be construed as creating an implied warranty of fitness for a particular purpose. Golden made clear a specific need she wanted the veneers to satisfy and sought affirmation from Dr. Gill the Cerinate veneers would work. The communication may not have been pointed, detailed, or extended. But, as the *Circle Land & Cattle Corp.* case recognizes, the circumstances giving rise to the warranty may be fairly casual. The jury should be permitted to make the call on whether there was an implied warranty of fitness for a particular purpose under K.S.A. 84–2–315 [**UCC 2–315**] and whether the veneers breached that warranty.

Breaches of implied warranties of merchantability and of fitness for a particular purpose are not mutually exclusive. That is, depending on the facts, a seller may be liable for breaching both in a single transaction, although a buyer may not recover duplicative damages. For example, a pair of shoes sold to a person requesting footwear for mountain climbing may have a claim for a breach of warranty for a particular purpose if they fall apart halfway up Denali. If the sole on one of them starts flapping while the person walks through KCI airport to get on a flight to Alaska, the shoes likely breach an implied warranty of merchantability for footwear generally and necessarily breach the more specific and more demanding warranty for the particular purpose of mountain climbing. Here, the claims for breach are more closely connected. The asserted warranty of merchantability related to durability, including resistance to chipping, retention in place, and constancy of color and appearance. The warranty of fitness for a particular purpose appears to depend on constancy of color and appearance alone. That overlap, however, does not impose a legal bar to either claim. The jury, properly instructed, ought to determine the existence and scope of the warranties and any concomitant breach.

[The court then discussed application of the Kansas Consumer Protection Act and Kansas Products Liability Act. That discussion is omitted.]

CONCLUSION

The judgment for Den-Mat and Dr. Gill is reversed, except as to Golden's claim based on an unconscionable act or practice violating K.S.A. 50–627(b)(7), and remanded for further proceedings, including trial. Golden may proceed with her claims for breach of express warranty, for breach of implied warranty of merchantability under K.S.A. 84–2–314 [**UCC 2–314**], for breach of implied warranty of fitness for a particular purpose under K.S.A. 84–2–315 [**UCC 2–315**], for deceptive acts and practices under K.S.A. 50–626, and for improper limitation of implied warranties under K.S.A. 50–639.

Affirmed in part, reversed in part, and remanded with directions.

———————

In the next case we revisit the issue of notice. There is a split in the courts whether **2–607(3)** requires notice only to sellers or also includes manufacturers. A literal reading of the statute seems to indicate only sellers need notice but some courts do not read the statute literally. This case illustrates the differences between jurisdictions on the issue of notice to manufacturers. How a jurisdiction decides this issue will make a difference on whether a plaintiff may go forward with a lawsuit if the plaintiff never notified the manufacturer of problems with the good. Pay attention to what happens when the court determines a plaintiff failed to notify a defendant pursuant to **2–607(3)**. Also, note what actions satisfy the notice requirement in **2–607(3)**.

IN RE MYFORD TOUCH CONSUMER LITIGATION

46 F. Supp.3d 936 (N.D. Cal. 2014)

[24 plaintiffs sued Ford for Warranty related to defective "infotainment" system contained in Ford's automobiles. The Infotaiment system in an integrated communication, navigation, and entertainment system that costs approximately $1,000 to add on to a vehicle as an extra option. The plaintiffs leased or purchased vehicles in fifteen different states, so the court needed to apply the laws of each plaintiffs state. The allegations included fraud and breach of warranty and in the breach of warranty claims Ford raised the issue of lack of notice under **2–607(3)**. What follows is a portion of the lengthy opinion where the court analyzed Ford's claim of lack of notice.]

* * *

4. *Notice*

Ford also contends there is a notice requirement for a claim of express warranty based on **UCC 2–607(3)(a)**. **UCC 2–607(3)(a)** provides that, "[w]here a tender has been accepted, ... the buyer must within a reasonable time after he discovers or should have discovered any breach notify the seller of breach or be barred from any remedy." **UCC 2–607(3)(a).** Ford asserts that, here, eleven Plaintiffs (namely, Ms. Battle, Mr. D'Aguanno, Mr. Sheerin, Dr. Oremland, Mr. Mitchell, Mr. Zuchowski, Mr. Avedisian, Mr. Rodriguez, Mr. Ervin, Mr. Connell, and Mr. Miller-Jones) failed to allege that they satisfied this notice requirement. There is no dispute among the parties that there is a notice requirement for each of the states at issue under the relevant statute.

As the parties agreed at the hearing, the notice issue must be evaluated on a state-by-state basis. The Court first addresses the express warranty claims of Ms. Battle, Mr. Sheerin, and Mr. Zuchowski. Although the Court has already dismissed these Plaintiffs' express warranty claims on the ground of failure to present the car for repair, the dismissal was without prejudice. Here, a failure to comply with the notice requirement is a basis for dismissal with prejudice.

a.   *Ms. Battle (Alabama)*

The Court agrees with Ford that Ms. Battle's express warranty claim should be dismissed for failure to comply with the notice requirement.

First, contrary to what Plaintiffs argue, the notice required here was notice to Ford, the manufacturer of Ms. Battle's car, and not just notice to the direct seller of Ms. Battle's car. Admittedly, **UCC 2–607(a)(3)** on its face refers to notice to the seller. Nevertheless, some states, including Alabama, require notice to the manufacturer where the manufacturer (and not the seller) is the one being sued. *See Hobbs v. Gen. Motors Corp.,* 134 F.Supp.2d 1277, 1285(M.D.Ala.2001) (stating that "remote manufacturers should be afforded the same protections as sellers, either by way of notice provided directly to them, or through notice to them by the direct seller from the buyer").

Second, although Plaintiffs contend that Ms. Battle provided the requisite notice to Ford when Plaintiffs filed the instant lawsuit, that argument lacks merit. Under Alabama law, the filing of a complaint does not constitute notice. *See id.* (stating that notice must "precede the filing of the complaint," at least in a case involving economic harm rather than personal injury); *see also Jewell v. Seaboard Indus.,* 667 So.2d 653, 661 (Ala.1995) (concluding that plaintiff did not give sufficient notice of breach because, before he filed his complaint, he made no attempt to notify defendant that he had experienced problems).

Third, Plaintiffs suggest that the purpose underlying the notice requirement has been satisfied because Ford already knew that many of its customers were having problems with MFT. *See* Opp'n at 37–38 (arguing that "Ford's contention that it lacked the requisite knowledge under **U.C.C. 2–607** is disingenuous in light of the overwhelming allegations in the FAC concerning consumer complaints, the NHTSA database, news articles and direct notice *of this particular problem* Ford received from Plaintiffs and similarly situated consumers"). But similar arguments have been rejected by courts applying Alabama law. For example, in *Smith v. Apple,* No. 08-AR-1498-S, 2009 WL 3958096 (N.D.Ala. Nov. 4, 2009), a district court stated: "[A] general awareness on Apple's part of alleged defects in its iPhone does not extinguish the purpose of the notice requirement, nor does it substitute for that requirement under Alabama law." *Id.* at *1; *see also In re Ford Motor Co. E-350 Van Prods. Liab. Litig.,* No. 03-4558(HAA), 2008 WL 4126264, at *6, 9 (D.N.J. Sept. 2, 2008) (dismissing Alabama warranty claim for failure to comply with notice requirement even though there were allegations that Ford was " 'fully aware of the alleged defect from the earliest stages of the E350's development, [and] was further warned by the NTSB and NHTSA' ").

Accordingly, the Court dismisses Ms. Battle's express warranty claim. The dismissal is with prejudice as Plaintiffs have failed to show that they could make an amendment that would overcome dismissal on this basis.

b.   *Mr. Sheerin (Colorado)*

The Court also concludes that dismissal of Mr. Sheerin's express warranty claim is proper.

Unlike Alabama law, Colorado law does not require notice to the manufacturer. *See Cooley,* 813 P.2d at 741–42 (stating that notice to the immediate seller is required, not to anyone beyond the immediate seller, including the manufacturer). Nevertheless, that does not obviate the requirement that notice still must be given to the seller, and here no notice was given to the seller because, as noted above, Mr. Sheerin did not even bring his car in for a repair.

As above, the Court dismisses the express warranty claim with prejudice—*i.e.,* because Plaintiffs have failed to show that they could make an amendment that would overcome dismissal on this basis.

c.   *Mr. Zuchowski (Ohio)*

For Mr. Zuchowski, the express warranty claim is not subject to dismissal based on the notice requirement.

Ohio law appears to require notice to a manufacturer. *See, e.g., Radford v. Daimler Chrysler Corp.,* 168 F.Supp.2d 751, 754 (N.D.Ohio 2001) (in case where plaintiff sued car manufacturer for damages to her car when it spontaneously caught fire, dismissing Ohio warranty claim based on failure to provide notice).

But, under Ohio law, the filing of a complaint can serve as notice of breach. *See Chemtrol,* 537 N.E.2d at 638 (stating that "we believe in a proper case the filing of a civil complaint could serve as notice of breach" although concluding that "this is not such a case, as Lexington's suit was filed a full two years after the damages were sustained"); *cf. Lincoln Elec. Co. v. Technitrol, Inc.,* 718 F.Supp.2d 876, 883 (N.D.Ohio 2010) (stating that "[t]he circumstances in this case are similar to the circumstances described in *Chemtrol* that would preclude the complaint from constituting sufficient notice: defendant had no prior knowledge of the defects, and the complaint was filed a long period of time after plaintiff's damages were sustained"). Ford argues to the contrary, citing *St. Clair v. Kroger Co.,* 581 F.Supp.2d 896 (N.D.Ohio 2008), where the court stated: "The policy reasons for pre-litigation notice are not satisfied by the filing of a complaint." *Id.* at 903. However, *St. Clair* failed to take into account the Ohio Supreme Court's clear statement in *Chemtrol* that, "in a proper case[,] the filing of a civil complaint could serve as notice of breach." *Chemtrol,* 537 N.E.2d at 638. The district court's decision in *St. Clair* is therefore not persuasive.

Furthermore, *Chemtrol* is not inconsistent with the function of notice. While some courts have observed that the purpose of the notice requirement is to give *pre-litigation* notice of a breach, *see Schmidt v. Ford Motor Co.,* 972 F.Supp.2d 712, 718–19 (E.D.Pa.2013) (stating that the purpose " 'is to allow the seller an opportunity to resolve the dispute regarding an alleged breach before the buyer initiates a lawsuit' "), other courts have framed the purpose underlying the notice requirement more broadly, stating, *e.g.,* that the notice requirement is "designed to allow the defendant seller an opportunity for repairing the defective item, reducing damages, avoiding defective products in the future, negotiating settlements, and protecting against stale claims." *Kerr v. Hunter Div.,* 32 Va. Cir. 497, 507 (1981). While often pre-suit notice best serves those purposes, notice by complaint may serve that function as well. *See Kerr,* 32

Va. at 507 (noting, *e.g.,* that "[n]egotiating settlement does not of course contemplate only pre-suit negotiations").

* * *

d.   *Mr. D'Aguanno (Arizona)*

The Court rejects Ford's contention that, as a matter of law, Mr. D'Aguanno failed to satisfy the notice requirement.

Admittedly, there is case law indicating that, under Arizona law, notice of a breach must be conveyed to the manufacturer of a product. *See, e.g., Hearn v. R.J. Reynolds Tobacco Co.,* 279 F.Supp.2d 1096, 1115–16 (D.Ariz.2003) (in case where plaintiffs sued tobacco manufacturers, dismissing Arizona warranty claims for failure to provide notice within a reasonable time). However, case law also indicates that, under Arizona law, notice can be given through the filing of a complaint. *See id.* (stating that "filing a complaint upon an opposing party (as is the case here) may constitute reasonably timely notice" because " 'notice of the claim of breach need take no special form' and 'where no particular mode of notice is required by the statute[,] what constitutes giving of notice is liberally construed' "); *see also Tasion Comm. Inc. v. Ubiquiti Networks, Inc.,* No. C-13-1803 EMC, 2014 WL 1048710, at *9 (N.D.Cal. Mar. 14, 2014) (stating that "Arizona courts have expressly held that the Complaint itself may constitute notice"); *Yee v. Nat. Gypsum Co.,* 2010 WL 2572976, at *3 (stating that "[t]he notice 'need take no special form,' and the complaint itself may provide adequate notice").

To the extent Ford argues that no timely notice was given, that is question of fact for the jury to decide.

* * *

D. REMEDY LIMITATIONS

One last way for a seller to avoid some liability for breach of warranty is by limiting the remedy for a breach. Sellers accomplish this by providing an exclusive remedy such as only permitting a buyer to obtain a repair or replacement of defective goods. **2–715** allows a buyer to claim consequential damages, although sellers are not afforded the same remedy. While many sellers will be happy to replace a defective good, they are wary of liability for consequential damages. For example, if you own a cell phone and the cell phone burns up, it is likely the seller will gladly replace your phone. However, if you are not home when the cell phone catches fire and the entire home is destroyed, the seller may be much less inclined to readily pay for the consequential damages to your home because the economic liability is potentially enormous. This is why many sellers will disclaim consequential damages in their sales contracts. However, they are not free to avoid all consequential damages. **2–719(3)** states that a limitation on consequential damages for personal injury claims is prima facie unconscionable in cases involving consumer goods.

2–719(1)(a) specifically permits exclusive remedies and remedy limitations such as "limiting the buyer's remedies to return of the goods and repayment of the price or to repair and replacement of non-conforming goods or parts." These exclusive remedies are subject to **2–719**, which places some limits on what a seller may avoid. Consider **2–719(2)**, "Where circumstances cause an exclusive or limited remedy to fail of its essential purpose, remedy may be had as provided in this Act." If an exclusive remedy fails, the Article 2 default rules will fill in the gaps of the contract.

Although the UCC allows parties great freedom of contract in many matters, it recognizes that the essence of any sales contract requires that there be at least minimum adequate remedies available for a breach. Consider a situation where a buyer purchases a new car for $25,000 that comes with a 3-year written warranty and has an exclusive remedy clause that limits the seller's remedy to repair or replace defective parts. After six months, the buyer is driving the car on the interstate when a defective bolt breaks, the engine drops out of the car, the car is totaled, and the buyer is seriously injured. To comply with the exclusive remedy the seller only needs to replace the defective bolt and nothing more. However, the remedy of just repairing the bolt in this scenario would cause the exclusive remedy to fail of its essential purpose and therefore the buyer would be availed of all of the UCC remedies.

Some courts indicate that failure of an exclusive remedy must be a complete failure of purpose and if it was a conscious allocation of risk it does not always mean that a limited remedy will fail of its essential purpose. In *Southern Financial Group v. McFarland State Bank*, 763 F.3d 735, 740–42(7th Cir. 2014), the Seventh Circuit dealt with this issue with regard to the sale of a loan portfolio. Although it was not certain Article 2 applied, it assumed it did for the purpose of the discussion. The court stated:

> The breach at issue in this case was McFarland's inaccurate representation that none of the collateral purportedly securing the loan had been released. In fact, three pieces of collateral property already had been released at the time of sale. This was a non-monetary breach of the contract that entitled SFG to one of the contractual remedies, at McFarland's election. But by the time the case reached the judgment stage, SFG had received through approved sales of collateral more money "in respect of the loans" than it paid to purchase the entire portfolio. Thus, applying the contractually agreed formula, the Repurchase Price was less than zero. Therefore, if the contractual remedies limitation is

enforceable, SFG is not entitled to any recovery for McFarland's breach.

We see no reason to reject the parties' allocation of risk, even if this means that SFG will be uncompensated for McFarland's breach. Wisconsin courts enforce agreements in which parties allocate risk in advance. SFG is a sophisticated, repeat player in the distressed-assets business. It could have negotiated a different contract had it wanted to shift more risk to McFarland. In that case, however, McFarland might have demanded more than 29 cents on the dollar for the portfolio. *Cf. Wis. Power & Light Co. v. Westinghouse Elec. Corp.,* 830 F.2d 1405, 1412 (7th Cir.1987) (Wisconsin law) ("Wisconsin Power cannot accept the favorable purchase price and then disclaim the conditions underlying that price.").

Nor can we write the remedies limitation out of the contract for failure of essential purpose. See Wis. Stat. § 402.719(2) (codification of **U.C.C. § 2–719(2)**). First, the argument that the remedy fails of its essential purpose assumes that Wisconsin interprets U.C.C. Article 2, which governs the sale of goods, to apply to the purchase of a loan portfolio. Perhaps that is so. See Wis. Stat. § 402.102; *S & C Bank v. Wis. Cmty. Bank,* No. 2006AP2142, 309 Wis.2d 233, 747 N.W.2d 527, 2008 WL 302379, at *8 (Wis.Ct.App. Feb. 5, 2008) (unpublished) (citing Wisconsin U.C.C. Article 2 in discussion of warranties regarding sale of loan portfolio); see also *Dittman v. Nagel,* 43 Wis.2d 155, 168 N.W.2d 190, 193 (1969) (applying "legal principles which have developed regarding express warranties as they apply to the sale of goods" to an express warranty regarding a sale of realty). We need not resolve the point, because the remedies limitation here does not fail of its essential purpose even if U.C.C. Article 2 applies.

In Wisconsin, "where [a] limited remedy fails of its essential purpose, the limitation will be disregarded and ordinary U.C.C. remedies will be available," including consequential damages. *Murray,* 265 N.W.2d at 520. A contractual remedy fails of its essential purpose "when the remedy is ineffectual or when the seller fails to live up to the remedy's provisions, either of which deprives the buyer of the benefit of the bargain." *Waukesha Foundry,* 91 F.3d at 1010. Although parties may limit damages remedies by contract, they must provide "at least a fair quantum of remedy for breach of obligations." *Phillips Petrol. Co. v. Bucyrus-Erie Co.,* 131 Wis.2d 21, 388 N.W.2d 584, 592 (1986) (citing **U.C.C. § 2–719, cmt. 1**); see also *Murray,* 265 N.W.2d at 520 (limitations on remedies fail "where they would effectively deprive a party of reasonable protection against breach"). An unconscionable restriction, or one that operates to deprive a party of the substantial value of the bargain, fails of its essential purpose. **U.C.C. § 2–719, cmt. 1**.

SFG suggests that the agreed remedy fails of its essential purpose because it provides no relief to SFG in this case. But the fact that a limited remedy provides no relief in one set of circumstances does not mean the remedy fails of its essential purpose. Indeed, the whole point of limiting remedies is to make some remedies unavailable. See *Wis. Power,* 830 F.2d at 1413 ("[P]laintiffs cannot seriously contend that the contract failed of its essential purpose because they were denied a fair quantum of remedy' when the remedy provided for in the contract was a product of their own making.") (quotation omitted). An agreed remedy does not fail of its essential purpose because it results in the party that bears the risk suffering the risk. Rather, it fails only where a party is unfairly deprived of the substantial value of its bargain. (It is important to note that even the U.C.C. does not assume that *all* anticipated value of the bargain must be preserved; instead, it calls only for "minimum adequate remedies" that address the bargain as a whole. See **U.C.C. § 2–719 cmt. 1**.)

The application of the failure-of-essential-purpose rule in its usual sphere of sales of goods is illustrative. Many contracts for the sale of goods limit the buyer's remedies for breach of warranty to repair or replacement. See *Beal v. Gen. Motors Corp.,* 354 F.Supp. 423, 426 (D.Del.1973) (from seller's perspective, the purpose is "to give the seller an opportunity to make the goods conforming while limiting the risks to which he is subject by excluding direct and consequential damages that might otherwise arise"); *Murray,* 265 N.W.2d at 520 ("The purpose of an exclusive remedy of repair or replacement, from the buyer's standpoint, is to give him goods which conform to the contract . . . substantially free of defects within a reasonable time after a defect is discovered.") (citing *Beal*). "The repair-and-replace remedy fails of its essential purpose when [the] seller is unable or unwilling to repair or replace in a reasonable time." Douglas Laycock, Modern American Remedies 72 (2010). Where the seller fails to honor the repair-or-replace remedy, the buyer loses the benefit of its bargain for the goods.

In this case, by contrast, the only reason that the contract provides SFG no remedy is that SFG already received substantial benefit from its bargain, even if not the full benefit it expected (because it was short three properties). Part of the overall bargain, however, was the clause limiting its remedies. The agreement allowed McFarland to pay back the purchase price less SFG's profits in exchange for return of the loan portfolio. The limited remedy, in other words, was rescission (or McFarland could pay a lesser amount in damages if it preferred). Nothing forced SFG to approve sales of the collateral properties before McFarland repurchased the portfolio. SFG could have held onto the properties, litigated McFarland's liability for the breach and, using the definition of Repurchase Price in the contract, collected money in connection with the rescission. Instead, SFG decided to sell the collateral and collect the profit. By its conduct, SFG showed that it did not want the transaction rescinded. The contractual remedy did not "effectively deprive [SFG] of reasonable protection against breach," see *Murray,* 265 N.W.2d at 520, nor was it "incapable of curing" the breach, *Waukesha Foundry,* 91 F.3d at 1010. Instead, SFG preferred to preserve the imperfect transaction rather than accept the limited remedy for which it negotiated.

Sellers have a dilemma when they want to avoid all liability for consequential damages because their choices for doing this are limited. The choices often are between disclaiming any liability for warranties, disclaiming consequential damages, or trying to limit damages in a way that limits some of the liability for defective products. It may seem that the only way to give a client security is to simply disclaim all implied warranties and be careful not to give any express warranties. In that situation, if a buyer suffers personal injury from a defective good, you may think the seller could avoid liability. Logic would suggest that if there is no warranty, there is no breach, and there should be no damages without a breach. However, a number of courts have used **2–719(3)**, which makes disclaimers of consequential damages prima facie unconscionable in consumer transactions, to eliminate disclaimers of implied warranties when the result of the disclaimer is to limit consequential damages for personal injury in consumer contracts. For example, in *Knipp v. Weinbaum,* 351 So.2d 1081, 1084 (Fla. Dist. Ct. App. 1977) a motorcycle buyer sued a cycle shop where he purchased a defective used motorcycle for personal injuries. The buyer was seriously injured when a rear axle gave way and the buyer lost control while driving on a major highway several hours after purchasing the cycle. The motorcycle was sold "As Is." That type of disclaimer usually excludes all implied warranties, so there should be no liability for a breach of warranty. In that case, the court said:

> The plaintiff in this case alleged that his injuries resulted from a defect in the goods sold. To foreclose consideration of his claim by permitting an "as is" disclaimer to operate as an automatic absolution from responsibility through the mechanism of summary judgment would belie the policy behind Section 672.2–719(3) **[2–719(3)]**, which states that "limitation of consequential

damages for injury to the person in the case of consumer goods is prima facie unconscionable.

PROBLEMS

1.   Independent Grocer and Freshness Bakery have a contract that requires the baker to deliver 20 dozen fresh rolls on Mondays between 6:00 a.m. and 8:00 a.m. every week for 6 months. The contract includes all the necessary terms except when payment is due. See 1–201(3), 1–303, and 2–310.

   a.   Independent and Freshness have been doing business together for the past year and during that time Freshness has made over 40 deliveries. Each time there was a delivery Independent waited 2 weeks before paying seller and Freshness never complained. Freshness Bakery needs cash and would like to be paid at the time of delivery. They call you at your law office and ask whether they can require the grocer to pay for the rolls when delivered. What do you tell them?

   b.   What if the parties had not dealt with each other in the past; however, during the first two months of the contract, the grocer did not pay until 2 weeks after each delivery with no complaints from Freshness. Would your answer change?

   c.   What if both parties are members of the same baker trade and in the trade parties are always allowed 14 days before payment is due. Freshness wants to be paid as soon as the goods are delivered. Does Independent have to pay?

   d.   What if you represented the Independent Grocer and the grocer wanted to have 2 weeks before payment is due. Could you write a contract that ensures that?

   e.   What if the contract says that Independent Grocer has 2 weeks before payment is due and the parties have had the same term in six previous contracts for 2 years, although the grocer always paid upon delivery in previous contracts. Could the grocer use the previous contracts to say the parties have a course of dealing that overrides the default term?

2.   Consider the following situations and for each situation create arguments for and against the creation of an express warranty and state which argument is the most persuasive. See 2–313.

   a.   Duncan visits a used car business in search of a car that will allow him to travel back and forth to work using less gas than his old clunker car uses. The saleswoman, Allie, shows him 2 specific cars and says "both of these cars get great gas mileage." Duncan buys car #1 but within a month he quickly realizes that the car gets less than 20 miles per gallon. Duncan wants to sue the car dealership for a breach of express warranty.

b.   Same facts as (a) except this time Allie says car #1 gets 35–40 miles per gallon. Duncan buys car #1 but within a month he quickly determines that the car gets less than 20 miles per gallon. Duncan wants to sue the car dealership for a breach of express warranty.

c.   What if Duncan did not mention the fact that he wanted a car that got great gas mileage? Instead, he drives car #1, likes it, and buys it. About 3 weeks after he purchased the car he saw an advertisement that said car #1 gets 35–40 miles per gallon, but Duncan knows his car (same as the one advertised) only gets 20 miles per gallon. Duncan wants to sue the car dealership for a breach of express warranty.

d.   Would your arguments for question (c) be different if Duncan had seen the advertisement before he bought the car?

e.   Ginger Holl needed to buy insulation for her vehicle repair shop. She received a brochure from Abe's Paint Shop that described fire retardant characteristics of an insulation product. Shortly after purchasing the insulation and installing it in her shop, the insulation caught on fire through no negligence of Ginger or her employees. Ginger wants to sue for breach of an express warranty and collect damages caused by the fire.

3.   The Greater Diamond City (GDC) transit system has run the transit system in a large metropolitan area for 25 years. The transit system includes subways, trains, buses, and street trolley cars. GDC wanted to upgrade some of its subway cars, so it purchased new cars for the system. When it purchased the new cars, it sold the old trolley cars for scrap. Randy Gold received an invitation to bid on 8 trolley cars no longer being used by the GDC transit system in their subway. After winning the highest bid, he signed a contract with the seller that described the items as "8-scrap P.C.C. Cars complete 'As is' Where is. And without recourse against the seller." The contract further provided that "[a] property listed herein is offered for sale 'as is' and 'where is' and without recourse against the GDC. The GDC makes no guaranty, warranty, or representation, express or implied, as to the quantity, kind, character, quality, weight, size or description of any of the property. . . ." The purchaser was to be "solely responsible for all injuries to persons or damage to property occurring on account of, or in connection with" dismantling the cars and removing them from GDC premises.

One of the 8 cars purchased had been in a fire where 45 fire fighters, a number of passengers, and some GDC employees were treated for possible exposure to PVC fumes, a known toxin. At least one of the damaged cars was covered in drippings of melted plastic that contained the PVC. After buying the cars Randy employed his brother, Joe, to help him dismantle the 8 trolley cars that he purchased including the cars covered in plastic. After scraping off as much plastic as possible, Joe used an acetylene torch to cut through the plastic that could not be scraped away. Joe worked on the car Monday through Friday in very hot weather.

The following week Joe's voice became progressively hoarse, he experienced shortness of breath, and a sore throat. Shortly thereafter he died from acute respiratory failure. The week after Joe's death Randy learned from a GDC employee that there had been something wrong with at least one of the cars and that it had PVC near it or in it.

The executor of Joe's estate wants to sue GDC for injuries caused by a breach of the implied warranty of merchantability due to the defective trolley cars. Answer the following questions:

   a.   Is there an implied warranty of merchantability in the contract between GDC and Randy? Consider whether such warranty exists and the consequence of the disclaimer. See 2–104, 2–314, and 2–316.

   b.   Assume that an implied warranty of merchantability exists, will Joe's case likely be successful when the estate sues the GDC in an Alternative A jurisdiction? In an Alternative B jurisdiction? See 2–318.

   c.   Would it have made a difference if the contract between Randy and the GDC contained an exclusive remedy clause that also limited any remedies for any type of defect to the "repair or replacement of defective parts?" See 2–719.

   4.   Ginger Jones decided to celebrate her 50th birthday by traveling from Pennsylvania (where she lives) to California on a motorcycle. She sold her old motorcycle and bought a new 2017 BMW motorcycle for her trip from "The Bike Shop," a New Jersey dealer that sells new and used motorcycles. She paid $30,000 for the new motorcycle. The sale came with no disclaimers.

A week later Ginger loaned the motorcycle to her twenty-two year old son, Harley (just visiting from his home in California), so he could ride to the beach for the weekend.

Shortly after leaving Ginger's Philadelphia driveway and approaching a "T" intersection, the brakes failed and Harley ran directly into a parked Mercedes Benz sports car doing considerable damage to himself, the motorcycle, and the Mercedes. He felt terrible because he thought that he had wrecked his mother's birthday since her motorcycle could no longer be driven for her big birthday trip and celebration.

Assume that New Jersey is a 2–318, Alternative B jurisdiction and Pennsylvania has enacted 2–318, Alternative A.

   a.   What cause of action should Harley use in a lawsuit? See 2–314.

   b.   Assuming Harley can get jurisdiction in either New Jersey or Pennsylvania, that each State would apply its own law to the dispute, and that all other things would be equal, does it matter for 2–318 purposes whether he sues in one state or the other?

   c.   Does your answer to (b) change if Harley is Ginger's second cousin?

d. Harley also wants to sue BMW. All other things being equal, will he be better off suing in Pennsylvania or New Jersey? Would your answer change if New Jersey had enacted Alternative C?

e. Assume that before Harley even thought about the possibility of suing anyone, Harley worried about his mother's potential responsibility for the damages (he is a wealthy Hollywood executive and does not lack funds) and he didn't want to ruin her birthday, so he decided to pay for the damages himself. A year later, after a few bad investments, Harley decides that he and his mother should sue the Bike shop and BMW due to the defective brakes. Assuming they sue in a state where they can avoid any privity issues, that they can prove the bike was defective and caused the damages, will either or both of those defendants have a good defense to the lawsuit for either or both plaintiffs? Omit any arguments about lack of privity. See 2–607.

5. Marla Maples is the executive director of the National Rescued Greyhound Organization. This job requires that she drive to different parts of the country to pick up rescued greyhounds, transport them to new homes, and meet with local rescue groups. Marla decided to buy a motor home so she could take her two large greyhounds, Athena and Jazz, with her as she traveled around the country. After a month long search, Marla could not find a suitable motor home. She needed a specially built motor home that could accommodate greyhounds. This required a longer home, specially built "doggie doors," and a high fence that could be detached while traveling and reattached when parked. Marla heard about Mars Mobile Vacation Home Builders from a friend. Mars is the only company that produces custom-made motor homes built to a buyer's specifications. They advertise that they will make "your vacation pure pleasure" and that they are "the best vacation homes available for the money."

Marla met with Sam Spade, a salesman for Mars and explained her needs for the motor home. When he told her the motor home would cost $80,000, Marla remarked that the price seemed quite high. Sam explained that the motor home was expensive because it had to be built to the owner's specifications. He also pointed out that $80,000 was not that expensive when you considered the fact that these homes lasted well over 20 years and retained about half their value after 10 years. Further, he pointed out that he was making the motor home so it could accommodate the large dogs with the special doggie doors and detachable fence and that added to the cost.

The 2 page contract contained the following terms, in addition to others that are not relevant:

(1) Buyer will make a $5,000 down payment due upon signing the contract;

(2) Marla's monthly payments will be $850.00 per month for ten years.

(3) There is a Three-Year Limited Warranty on defective parts and Mars will repair or replace parts found to be defective.

Marla took possession of the motor home on August 1 and, on August 15, she and her two greyhounds headed out to Philadelphia. Marla had several scheduled stops along the way. At her first overnight stop in St. Louis on August 16, she discovered that the doggie door did not work properly. It only opened part way and that was not far enough for Jazz & Athena to get through the door. Consequently, Marla had to take them out the front door on a leash so they could get to the yard. Most experts would conclude that this was a design flaw—the doors were not designed to accommodate large dogs. Marla was pleased with the movable fence that came with the motor home because it set up very easily. Unfortunately, when it was time to leave St. Louis, she discovered that the fence did not come down easily. In fact, it was so difficult that she could not do it by herself.

The next stop was Indianapolis on August 17. After attending a meeting, Marla went back to her motor home and started preparing dinner. She discovered a problem with the water pipes. Only a small trickle of water came out of the faucet. At this point, Marla was so disgusted with the entire matter that she located a van rental agency and rented a van to use on the rest of her trip. She made arrangements to have the motor home returned to the seller.

Answer the following questions: See 2–313, 2–314, 2–315, and 2–316.

a.   What warranties exist for this transaction? Include any warranties that the buyer might try to argue exist, even if you are unsure, and consider the arguments on both sides.

b.   For each warranty, state whether it was breached and how.

c.   Would your answer to question (a) change if the contract contained a clause (d) that stated that "this contract comes with no other warranty than what is stated in 'c' of the contract and that means no implied warranties whatsoever"?

6.   Same facts as Problem 5 except Marla mailed the keys, along with her name, address, and a note where the home could be picked up to Mars and left the motor home at the mobile home parking lot in Indianapolis. Seven weeks later, when Marla received a default notice for not making her monthly lease payment, she called Sam and said, "Your motor home was junk, nothing worked right on it and I had to leave it in Indianapolis. You can pick it up there." She then hung up.

After receiving the default notice from Mars, Marla visits an attorney to see what counter measures she can take because Mars was threatening to sue her for the deficiency. See 2–607(3), (5).

a. If Marla sues Mars for breach of warranty, assuming that Marla can prove the existence of both implied warranties and that they have been breached, does Mars have a defense to the lawsuit?

b. Same question as (a.) except Marla wants to sue the manufacturer.

7. Sarah Segal just graduated from college and decided to buy her first car. She visited Luke's Car Palace along with her mother and uncle with the intention of buying a car. A sales person showed Sarah and her family a used 2-year-old Ford SUV. As Sarah looked at the car, the sales person said that "this car is perfect for you; you couldn't buy a better car." Additionally, the sales person said that the car came with a 90-day guarantee "in case anything went wrong." After taking the car for a test drive, Sarah purchased her first car and drove it home.

Unfortunately, Sarah's excitement about her first car quickly turned to exasperation. After a couple of days, she started to have problems with the speedometer cable, three days later she noticed a noise in the rear of the car, and within a couple of weeks she began to see black smoke coming from the exhaust pipe. A few days after the smoke began, the car began stalling regularly, she discovered that the door locks were defective and needed to be replaced, and the dashboard shook when she drove the car. She called Luke's Car Palace and complained to the service manager every time a new problem arose. Each time Sarah called, the service manager had her bring the car in for repair but after 6 or 7 repairs the car continued to have problems. See 2–313, 2–314, 2–315, and 2–316.

Answer the following questions:

a. Did the seller create any express warranties? If so, how were they breached?

b. Can Luke's Car Palace defend against a claim of express warranty by using the fact that Ms. Segal brought her family to the dealership when she bought the car?

c. Are there any implied warranties with this sale?

d. Would your answer to the previous question change if the sales contract contained a clause that said, "This car is sold with NO WARRANTIES: If there are problems with this car YOU, the buyer, are solely responsible for any defects, problems, or complaints about the car?" Would your answer change if this statement was buried in the back of the sales contract in fine print?

8. Assume that Sarah buys a car, it comes with an implied warranty of merchantability, and a month after buying the car Sarah is injured when the brakes failed and she crashed into a tree and an embankment, injuring herself and severely damaging the car. She comes to your law office for help and you notice when you read the sales contract that it contains the following clause: "Buyer agrees to the following exclusive remedy: seller will repair or replace any defective parts, if they fail within the first year of purchase."

a.   Sarah wants to sue Luke's for her injuries that were caused when the brakes failed and she crashed her car. What are her chances of success? See 2–719.

b.   Assume the same facts as the previous question except there is no exclusive remedy clause and Sarah also hit Abraham Podgor, a bystander, when she crashed her car. Will Abraham be able to sue Luke's for his damages? What are his chances of success? See 2–318.

9.   Assume that Sarah buys a car, it comes with an implied warranty of merchantability, and a month after buying the car Sarah is injured when the brakes failed and she crashed into a tree and an embankment, injuring herself and severely damaging the car. This time, however, the car has been fixed and Sarah waited for 1 year before she decided to sue Luke's for her injuries and damages to the car. Does Luke's have a defense? See 2–607.

a.   Would your answer change if Sarah also hit Tara, a bystander, and it is Tara who wants to sue 1 year later?

10.   Whitney Smith visited the Hoosier Motor Dealership and met with Allie Adams to discuss purchasing a used car. After several test drives and an afternoon of negotiation, Whitney finally settled on a 3-year-old Jeep. The purchase price was $18,000 and Hoosier provided Whitney with a 1 year written limited warranty that included the engine of the car and the tires. She also purchased a 1 year service contract. After 3 months, Whitney began to have constant and serious problems with the brakes and the navigation system. Eventually, she was so disgusted with the dealership that she visits your law office and asks for your help dealing with the car dealership. You read the contract and fear that the warranty will not include the problems she is having with the car. You also notice on the bottom of the first page a large disclaimer in capital letters and bolded that says **"THIS CAR IS SOLD AS IS. THERE ARE NO OTHER WARRANTIES SUCH AS THE IMPLIED WARRANTY OF MERCHANTABILITY OR FITNESS WARRANTIES THAT COME WITH THIS CAR. IF IT IS NOT COVERED IN OUR WRITTEN WARRANTY IT IS NOT COVERED."** You determine that the only legal recourse would be a breach of the implied warranty of merchantability, if it applies. Will you have a good argument for Whitney? See 2–314, 2–316 and Magnuson-Moss 2–308, 2–310.

a.   If Whitney also wanted to sue under Magnuson-Moss, what is her cause of action?

b.   Can Whitney sue under both Magnuson-Moss and the UCC? What advantages would exist for Whitney if she sues using both laws?

11.   Karen Smith recently retired from the police force and bought a farm. Her next door neighbor, Neil Strong, bred racehorses for a living. Karen and Neil became friends and Neil started teaching Karen about the breeding business for racehorses. Eventually, Karen decided to buy a racehorse for breeding purposes but, when she told Neil about the horse she wanted, he advised her against making the purchase. Instead, he offered her a 50% interest in one of his horses named Fast Eddie. Neil said that Fast Eddie had

won numerous races and would be a good horse for breeding purposes. Karen bought the 50% interest in Fast Eddie. Several months later Karen discovered that fast Eddie was lame. Karen wants to sue Neil for breach of warranty. What warranties exist with this sale and have any of them been breached? See 2–314 and 2–315.

CHAPTER 3

DETERMINING THE TERMS AND ENFORCEABILITY OF A CONTRACT

■ ■ ■

After reading the last chapter you should now understand the importance of some of the most significant default terms in Article Two, especially the warranty and disclaimer terms. Obviously, the warranty terms are most important to buyers because buyers want to be able to return goods that are defective, do not function the way they were expected to work, or have other unexpected problems or nonconformities. Additionally, if defective goods cause damage to other property, injury to people, or economic loss, buyers want some recourse against the seller of those goods. Often, that recourse is provided through consequential damages.

On the other hand, sellers do not want to constantly worry about liability for goods sold, so they may be inclined to include disclaimers of warranties in their contracts or limit their damages. Even though sellers may be concerned about unlimited liability, many will stand behind their products and repair or replace a defective good. In fact, some sellers willingly go beyond their warranties and repair or replace products, even though the warranty for the product has expired. Since sellers may find that warranting their products helps to increase sales, they must determine how to balance the need to limit liability with their desire to stand behind their products. The tension between the buyer's desire for liability for defective goods and the seller's desire to limit their liability often results in a situation referred to as "the battle of the forms." This is when each party puts boilerplate terms into their contracts that benefit themselves, but not necessarily the other party. To figure out whether various terms are included or excluded from the contract, courts often look to **2–207**.

A. CONTRACT FORMATION

Before turning to **2–207**, the section that will tell us how to determine what terms to include in a contract when there is a battle of the forms, we need to consider contract formation in general under the UCC and how it differs from the common law and the CISG. Recall from your contracts class that determining whether a contract has been formed usually involves an analysis of assent, offer, acceptance, and/or consideration.

1. DIFFERENCES BETWEEN COMMON LAW & THE UCC

Under the common law rules if offer or acceptance is a problem the questions often center around how definite and specific terms are or the mirror image rule. The mirror image rule requires that a party accept the offeror's terms and any additions or variances to those terms usually prevent contract formation. For example, if Juan offered to sell Stella 5 commercial grills for a total of $3,500 and Stella said she would buy the 5 grills for $3,500 but she also wanted Juan to extend his usual warranty by 6 months, there would not be a contract under common law rules because of the mirror image rule. This is so because Stella added a warranty extension, so her acceptance was not on the terms of the offer and therefore not a mirror image of the offer. Instead, Stella's purported acceptance became a counter offer that Juan could either accept or reject. This is what commentators refer to as the "last shot" rule because the party with the last form that contains a different term usually controls the terms of the deal under the common law.

The UCC rejected both the "last shot" and mirror image rules because they do not coincide with the realities of the market place. Article 2 recognizes that parties rarely will include all of the necessary terms in a contract because it is not easy to think of every detail or potential problem that might occur in all contracts. Additionally, it is not economically feasible or efficient to negotiate every term in a contract. Consequently, many buyers and sellers depend on boilerplate forms when ordering goods or acknowledging orders. A final point to note about contract formation is the fact that **2–209**, the section on modification, allows parties to modify their contracts without consideration.

When the Article 2 drafters considered contract formation they used only four sections to cover contract formation and how to deal with different or additional terms. These sections are **2–204** through **2–207**. Read **2–204** and **2–206** to understand how the UCC determines whether a contract exists. You should note that **2–204** requires no formal offer or acceptance and only requires an intent to contract. Evidence of an agreement may be shown through written documentation or conduct, so leaving terms open will not defeat a contract. Basically, as long as there is a way to calculate a remedy and evidence of an intent to contract by the parties, the UCC will find a contract.

2–206 specifically rejects the mirror image rule and states that an offer may be accepted in any manner using any reasonable medium. When a buyer submits an order to a seller, it may be accepted either by promptly shipping the goods or a promise of prompt shipment. Even shipping nonconforming goods will be considered acceptance unless the seller notifies the buyer that the nonconforming shipment is only intended to be an accommodation.

Additionally, there is a special rule for merchants in **2–205** which permits a merchant to make a firm and irrevocable offer in writing without any consideration that may stay open for up to three months. This rule applies to all merchants as defined in **2–104**, not just the special merchants that deal in goods of the kind. This differs from the common law in that it does not require consideration to make an irrevocable offer effective.

Although contract formation is fairly simple under Article 2, determining what terms the contract actually includes is not quite as easy. To understand what terms the UCC will include in a contract where there are one or more written documents, you need to carefully read **2–207**. While reading **2–207(1)**, pay particular attention to the words before and after the comma. They are the "magic words" that will prevent a communication from becoming an acceptance if no assent to additional or different terms is forthcoming. The first part of the sentence, before the comma, makes it clear that the UCC rejects the mirror image rule by allowing a communication to be an acceptance even though it includes different or additional terms. The only way that communication will not be an acceptance (assuming the parties intend a contract) is if the communication includes a clause requiring that the other party expressly agree to any additional or different terms before the acceptance can occur. In other words, the language after the comma in **(1)** prevents a communication, that would normally be an acceptance, from being an acceptance by a party by including the "magic words" of "acceptance is expressly made conditional on assent to the additional or different terms."

2. APPLICATION OF 2–207

Once a purported acceptance includes the language after the comma from **2–207(1)** the only ways to find a contract are for the other party to either expressly assent to the different or additional terms, or through conduct that shows a contract exists. For example, if a buyer sends a purchase order, the seller responds with an acknowledgment that includes the language that "acceptance is expressly made conditional on assent to the additional or different terms," and nothing else occurs there is no contract on the writings. However, if the seller proceeds to ship the goods requested by the buyer, the buyer pays for them, and uses them there is a contract by conduct. This is because performance on both sides shows an intent to contract.

If there is a contract by conduct, the terms of the contract will be determined by using **2–207(3)**, often referred to as the "knockout rule." This means that only the terms that agree in both of the writings become part of the contract, everything else gets knocked out of the contract, and Article 2 fills the gaps with the default rules. There is a split in jurisdictions as to whether the "supplementary terms" referred to in **(3)** include trade usage, course of performance, and course of dealing. Some courts hold that the phrase "supplementary terms incorporated under any other provision of the Act" includes trade usage, course of performance, and course of dealing, while others see it only as referring to the default rules.

Consider the following situation: Terry is a mechanic who owns a garage for repairing sports cars and she specializes in classic Corvettes. She orders an air conditioner and other parts for a 1960 corvette from "Old Cars Supply Shop." Old Cars responds with an acknowledgement that says it will mail the parts within a week, included a warranty disclaimer, and says acceptance is expressly made conditional on assent to the additional or different terms contained in this acknowledgement. If nothing else occurs, there is no contract and failure to send the parts is not a breach because the acknowledgement was not an acceptance. If, instead, Old Cars sends the parts and Terry pays for and uses them, there is a contract created by their conduct. If a problem occurs later with the parts and Terry wants to sue for breach of warranty, does the disclaimer affect her ability to do that? The answer is no. Because the acknowledgment included the specific language after the comma in **(1)** there is no contract on the writings. However, since the parties acted like there was a contract by delivering, paying for, and using the goods, there is a contract by conduct and **(3)** will reveal the terms of the contract. All different and additional terms in both communications are knocked out pursuant to **2–207(3)** and only the terms that agree become part of the contract. The disclaimer is additional so it gets knocked out. Once the disclaimer is knocked out, the default rules fill any gaps and the implied warranty of merchantability becomes part of the contract between Terry and Old Cars Supply Shop because Old Cars is a merchant who sells goods of the kind.

Moving away from **(3)**, if the writing or writings do not contain the language after the comma in **(1)**, then a court will use **(2)** to determine the terms of the contract. The first question to ask when applying **(2)** is whether both parties are merchants. This definition of merchant includes any professional in business as long as the merchant is acting in her mercantile capacity. *See* **2–104**, Comment 2. If both parties are not merchants, then any additional and/or different terms will be mere proposals and will not become part of the contract without assent by both parties. If the parties are both merchants **2–207(2)** allows *additional* terms to become part of the contract unless **(a)**, **(b)**, or **(c)** of that section exist.

After reading **2–207** carefully, you will notice that **(2)** only refers to additional terms while **(1)** mentions different or additional terms. Does that mean that **(2)** does not include different terms? Courts interpret this omission in several different ways. To understand the first interpretation, read Comment 6 to **2–207**. Some courts have used Comment 6 to create a "knockout" rule because that Comment says "[w]here clauses on confirming forms sent by both parties conflict each party must be assumed to object to a clause of the other conflicting with one on the confirmation sent by himself." Using Comment 6 a court may find that the drafters of Article 2 intended to include "different terms" in **(2)** and then knock out the different terms because both parties are objecting to each other's conflicting terms. This is consistent with **2–207(2)(c)** that says notice of objection to a term will keep it out of a contract. This is commonly referred to as the judicially created knock-out rule. For example, Luke Electrical Supply sends a purchase order to Allie Electric and includes in the order a clause stating that the sale includes an implied warranty of merchantability for any goods provided by Allie Electric. If Allie's confirmation of the order contains an effective disclaimer of all warranties, different terms exist. A court that follows the judicially created knock out rule would knock out both terms using **2–207(2)(c)** and the default rules would fill the gap. Of course, that means that the implied warranty of merchantability attaches to the goods sold, as long as Allie Electric sells electrical goods on a regular basis.

The second possible interpretation of the drafters' omission of "different" assumes that the drafters intended to include different terms in **(2)** but inadvertently left it out. After finding that different terms are involved in **(2)**, a court will then apply **(a)**, **(b)** or **(c)** to determine what to do with the different term. Lastly, a court could interpret the omission of the word "different" to mean that the drafters intentionally left out the word because they did not believe a different term should become part of an agreement through boilerplate language. You should always research the cases in your jurisdiction to see how courts use **2–207(2)** when different terms appear.

Even though attorneys and courts often refer to **2–207** as "the battle of the forms" section, this is really a misnomer because **2–207** may apply in situations where only one form exists. The most common instance is when a party sends a written confirmation after an oral agreement has been reached between the parties. If the written confirmation contains an additional term, courts will apply **2–207(2)** to determine whether the term should be added to the previously concluded oral agreement, unless the confirmation contains the language after the comma in **2–207(1)**. Notice that the "magic" language in **2–207(1)** will not have the same effect in a situation involving a concluded oral agreement. That is because the magic language does not have the power to undo the agreement.

What should a court do if a confirmation of an oral agreement also includes a different term? If there has been a previously concluded oral agreement, it does not make sense to use the judicially created knock-out rule because that would allow one party to unilaterally change a negotiated term in an oral agreement. It makes more sense to consider it as a proposal to modify the oral agreement. If the parties agreed on a term it is a negotiated term, and **2–207** should not apply to that term.

The examples we have considered so far involve a form or forms being exchanged between the parties that include boilerplate terms that will be particularly beneficial to each party. Sellers are more apt to use forms that disclaim warranties or limit remedies and buyers usually want all the warranties and remedies available to them. But as a general point, if there is a question between a boilerplate term and a negotiated term, a negotiated term will control. Courts only use **2–207** when parties cannot agree on what to do with the boilerplate terms.

At this point you may find it useful to try to make a flow chart of **2–207** that allows you to see when to apply the various subsections. Then break down each subsection that might apply into a series of questions. For example, your flow chart might start with this question: More than one form, written memo accepting on different or additional terms, or written confirmation of oral agreement with different or additional terms? If the answer is no, the chart will point to **2–204** through **2–206**. If the answer is yes, then break down **2–207(1)**. Is the writing timely? If the answer is no, then there is no contract and the writing will be a counteroffer. If the answer is yes, proceed to parse the section.

As you read the following case pay particular attention to the consequence of using the "magic words" in **2–207(1)**. The court calls those words "the proviso." What risks did SFEG run by including that language in their acknowledgment? How do you think the result would have been different if the acknowledgment had omitted those words?

SFEG CORP. V. BLENDTEC, INC.

2017 WL 395041 (M. D. Tenn. Jan. 30, 2017)

TRAUGER, A.

IV. THE TERMS & CONDITIONS MOTION

A.   Relevant Facts

Between December 29, 2011 and March 3, 2015, Blendtec sent SFEG approximately 32 separate Purchase Orders ("POs") for component parts used in production runs of Blendtec's blenders, as well as non-production run samples, pilot lots, and return orders, although the precise number is disputed. The Purchase Orders for production runs were for component parts that Blendtec planned to install or did install in its blenders that were for sale.

Blendtec's POs included the PO number, a description of the items being ordered, the quantity being ordered, the per unit and total price, and payment terms. After receiving a PO from Blendtec, SFEG's practice was to email Blendtec an Order Acknowledgement confirming the terms of the PO. Among other things, SFEG's Order Acknowledgments referenced Blendtec's PO number and included a description of the items being ordered, the quantity ordered, the per unit and total price, and payment terms. SFEG usually, but not always, sent an Order Acknowledgement upon receipt of a PO from Blendtec.

In addition to the Order Acknowledgement, SFEG sometimes, but not always, sent its Terms and Conditions of Sale ("Terms & Conditions") to Blendtec in response to its POs. Among other things, the Terms & Conditions include language specifying that SFEG's acceptance of any purchase order was "expressly subject" to Blendtec's assent to the conditions set forth in the Terms & Conditions:

> 1. Acceptance: The Seller's acceptance of any order is expressly subject to Buyer's assent to each and all of the terms and conditions set forth below. Any additional or different terms and conditions submitted by Buyer shall be deemed objected to by Seller and shall be of no effect nor in any circumstances binding upon Seller unless accepted by Seller in writing. If Buyer objects to any of the terms and conditions said objections must be specifically brought [sic] the attention of Seller by Buyer by a written instrument separate from any purchase order or other printed form of Buyer. Said objections shall be deemed proposals for different terms and conditions and may be accepted only by a writing executed by an authorized representative of Seller at its offices in Fairview, TN, U.S.A.

In addition, the Terms & Conditions provide for payment of a late fee ("finance charge") by Buyer for any payments not made within 30 days of the invoice date; an express warranty that the equipment manufactured by SFEG would be free from defects in material, workmanship and title as of the date of shipment; a disclaimer of all other implied or statutory warranties; and a disclaimer of liability for damages.

Blendtec's POs are silent on the terms found at paragraphs 1, 5, 10, 11, and 22 of SFEG's Terms & Conditions. Blendtec apparently possessed a document that incorporated its own terms and conditions, but Blendtec never provided SFEG a copy of its terms and conditions.

It is undisputed that Blendtec never expressly objected or assented to SFEG's Terms & Conditions. It accepted shipment of product from SFEG and continued to place orders with it, after having repeatedly received copies of the Terms & Conditions along with SFEG's shipments.

B. Discussion

In its Terms & Conditions Motion, Blendtec asserts that it is entitled to summary judgment on SFEG's Affirmative Defenses 11 and 12 on the basis that SFEG's Terms & Conditions are not, as a matter of law, part of the parties' contract. SFEG opposes that motion and asserts that, at a minimum, there are disputed issues of fact as to whether Blendtec's "continued silence in the face of receiving [SFEG's] Terms and Conditions constitutes assent" to them.

SFEG also seeks summary judgment in its favor, in part, on the basis that all of the Purchase Orders are governed by SFEG's Terms & Conditions, which bar Blendtec's affirmative defenses and Counterclaim. In the alternative, SFEG argues that, "even under the UCC default rules, Blendtec's defense and counterclaim fail as a matter of law." In its Reply in support of its own motion, SFEG changes tack, insisting that its "argument is *not* that silence or inaction constitutes acceptance," but that "Blendtec's repeated ordering, in the face of [SFEG's] terms and conditions, and without validly sending [SFEG] any competing terms and conditions, is a course of dealing that constitutes acceptance to [SFEG's] terms and conditions."

1.   *Section 2–207 of the Uniform Commercial Code*

This matter concerns the terms of a sales contract between merchants. Consequently, Article 2 of the Uniform Commercial Code ("UCC"), and specifically § **2–207** of the UCC, applies to the dispute. As implemented in Tennessee, that section states:

(1)   A definite and seasonable expression of acceptance or a written confirmation which is sent within a reasonable time operates as an acceptance even though it states terms additional to or different from those offered or agreed upon, unless acceptance is expressly made conditional on assent to the additional or different terms.

(2)   The additional terms are to be construed as proposals for addition to the contract. Between merchants such terms become part of the contract unless:

   (a)   the offer expressly limits acceptance to the terms of the offer;

   (b)   they materially alter it; or

   (c)   notification of objection to them has already been given or is given within a reasonable time after notice of them is received.

(3)   Conduct by both parties which recognizes the existence of a contract is sufficient to establish a contract for sale although the writings of the parties do not otherwise establish a contract. In such case the terms of the particular contract consist of those terms on which the writings of the parties agree, together with any supplementary terms incorporated under any other provisions of chapters 1–9 of this title.

Tenn. Code Ann. § 47–2–207 ("Section **2–207**").

This provision of the UCC "recognizes that in current commercial transactions, the terms of the offer and those of the acceptance will seldom be identical." *Dorton v. Collins & Aikman Corp.*, 453 F.2d 1161, 1166 (6th

Cir. 1972). Under the resulting "battle of the forms, each party typically has a printed form drafted by his attorney and containing as many terms as could be envisioned to favor that party in his sales transactions." *Id.* In the usual scenario, the parties never discuss or agree to the new terms, but the seller ships the goods and buyer accepts them as if there were a contract. Section **2–207** defines what terms govern when a dispute arises between the seller and buyer and the dueling forms suddenly become relevant.

Under the common law, changed or additional terms in an order acknowledgment would be construed as a counteroffer accepted by the original offeror when he proceeded to perform under the contract without objecting to the changed or additional terms. Section **2–207(1)** of the UCC effected a significant change to the common law. Under the UCC, "[a] definite and seasonable expression of acceptance or a written confirmation . . . operates as an acceptance," rather than a counteroffer, even if it proposes terms that are additional to or different from those in the offer. However, Section **2–207(1)** is subject to a "proviso": if a definite and seasonable expression of acceptance expressly conditions acceptance on the offeror's assent to additional or different terms contained therein, the parties' differing forms do not result in a contract unless the offeror expressly assents to the additional terms.

If the proviso is *not* implicated and a contract is formed under § **2–207(1)**, the additional terms are treated as "proposals for addition to the contract" under § **2–207(2)**. If, on the other hand, no contract is recognized under § **2–207(1)**, typically because the offeree's acceptance is expressly conditioned on the offeror's assent to the additional or different terms and the offeror did not expressly assent, "the entire transaction aborts at this point." *Dorton*, 453 F.2d at 1166. That is, the parties' writings do not form a contract. If the parties' *conduct* nonetheless recognizes the existence of a contract, § **2–207(3)** comes into play; that subsection provides for the determination of the terms of that contract. "In such case the terms of the particular contract consist of those terms on which the writings of the parties agree, together with any supplementary terms incorporated under any other provisions" of the UCC. § **2–207(3)**.

2.   *Application of § 2–207(1) to the Facts*

In this case, each of Blendtec's Purchase Orders functioned as an offer. SFEG typically responded to such offers with an Order Acknowledgement, sometimes sent with its Terms & Conditions. Because the Terms & Conditions contain additional terms that are not in the Purchase Orders, the case presents a typical battle of the forms.

The Terms & Conditions include language that essentially mirrors that of the § **2–207(1)** proviso: "The Seller's acceptance of any order is expressly subject to Buyer's assent to each and all of the terms and conditions set forth below." *See Dorton*, 453 F.2d at 1168 (to fall within the

"Subsection **2–207(1)** proviso," "an acceptance must be expressly conditional on the offeror's *assent* to [the offeree's additional or different] terms"). SFEG's Terms & Conditions, which are indisputably additional and different terms from those in Blendtec's Purchase Orders, therefore only became part of the parties' contract if Blendtec assented to them. Blendtec insists that it did not assent; SFEG claims that it did.

Undoubtedly anticipating that Blendtec would never expressly assent to the limitations of warranties and liability contained in its Terms & Conditions, SFEG drafted the Terms & Conditions to indicate that silence on the part of Blendtec signaled assent: "If Buyer objects to any of the terms and conditions said objections must be specifically brought [sic] the attention of Seller by Buyer by a written instrument separate from any purchase order or other printed form of Buyer." SFEG argues that Blendtec's repeated acceptance of shipments, despite receiving SFEG's Terms & Conditions at least seven times, gives rise to a jury question as to whether Blendtec assented. Blendtec insists that mere silence and acceptance of the goods shipped by SFEG could never signal assent.

SFEG relies for its position on *Ralph Shrader, Inc. v. Diamond International Corp.*, 833 F.2d 1210, 1215 (6th Cir. 1987), and *Aqua-Chem, Inc. v. D&H Machine Service, Inc.*, No. E2015-01818-COA-R3-CV, 2016 WL 6078566 (Tenn. Ct. App. Oct. 17, 2016). In *Aqua-Chem*, the parties disputed the terms of a contract for services; the UCC did not apply and is not referenced in the opinion. Even if the UCC had applied, § **2–207** would not have been implicated, because there was no battle of forms. Instead, the only written manifestation of the parties' agreement was Aqua-Chem's purchase orders incorporating its terms and conditions. *Aqua-Chem* therefore has no relevance here.

In *Ralph Shrader*, the seller's acceptance fell within the § **2–207(1)** proviso, giving rise to the question of whether the buyer had assented to the additional terms in the acceptance. There, as here, the seller relied on language in the acceptance requiring the buyer to "advise. . .immediately" if it did not agree to the additional terms. The Sixth Circuit held that "failure to so advise obviously does not require a conclusion of assent." *Id.* at 1215 (citing UCC § **2–207(3)**). The court further held that mere acceptance of and payment for goods did not constitute acceptance as a matter of law, but nonetheless remanded the case on the basis that the question of acceptance was a jury question under Michigan law. *See id.* at 1215 (noting that, under Michigan's application of § **2–207(1)**, "[t]he determination of what has or has not been agreed upon will, of course, continue to be made by the trier of fact, but, in making that determination, the fact finder is no longer bound by the last manifestation" (quoting *Am. Parts Co., Inc. v. Am. Arb. Ass'n*, 154 N.W.2d 5, 16 (Mich. Ct. App. 1967)). Michigan law does not apply in this case.

Moreover, where there are competing forms and the § **2–207(1)** proviso is implicated, nearly every court to consider the issue—including the Sixth Circuit—has found that silence and performance without express objection to the additional terms in the acceptance are not sufficient to signal assent to the additional terms. *See, e.g., McJunkin Corp. v. Mechanicals, Inc.*, 888 F.2d 481, 488 (6th Cir. 1989) (where the buyer issued several purchase orders to the seller over the course of five months, and each shipment from the seller in response was accompanied by an order acknowledgment setting forth the seller's additional terms, finding that the § **2–207(1)** proviso applied but that the plaintiff "never explicitly accepted the terms of [seller's] acknowledgment" and that "silence in the face of [the seller's] acknowledgment" did not constitute assent); *Diamond Fruit Growers, Inc. v. Krack Corp.*, 794 F.2d 1440, 1445 (9th Cir. 1986) (holding that the public policy reflected in the enactment of the UCC required "a specific and unequivocal expression of assent on the part of the offeror when the offeree conditions its acceptance on assent to additional or different terms"); *C. Itoh & Co. (Am.) Inc. v. Jordan Int'l Co.*, 552 F.2d 1228, 1235 (7th Cir. 1977) (noting that the buyer must "expressly assent[ ] to the challenged . . . term" under § **2–207(1)**).

In its Reply in support of its own motion for summary judgment, SFEG attempts to avoid the result dictated by the cases referenced above by clarifying that it is *not* arguing "that silence or inaction constitutes acceptance." Rather, SFEG's "argument is that Blendtec's repeated ordering, in the face of [SFEG]'s terms and conditions, and without validly sending [SFEG] any competing terms and conditions, is a course of dealing that constitutes acceptance to [SFEG]'s terms and conditions." (*Id.* (citing *Dresser Indus., Inc. v. Gradall Co.*, 965 F.2d 1442, 1449 (7th Cir. 1992)).)

SFEG apparently conflates the issue of assent with that of ascertaining the terms of the parties' agreement once it has been determined that the § **2–207(1)** proviso applies and there was no express assent to the additional terms. In *Dresser*, upon which SFEG relies, the Seventh Circuit presumed without discussion that the § **2–207(1)** proviso applied and that the offeror had not expressly assented to the offeree's supplemental or different terms. The court therefore proceeded to determine what the terms of the parties' contract were under § **2–207(3)**. *See Dresser*, 965 F.2d at 1451 ("We simply hold that, under Wisconsin law, all of the U.C.C.'s provisions should be used in discerning the terms of a contract under § **2–207(3)**, including those provisions that allow us to examine the parties' performance.").

Here, the court is still on the question of Blendtec's assent to SFEG's Terms & Conditions. Based on *McJunkin* and the other cases cited above, the court finds as a matter of law applied to the undisputed facts that Blendtec's failure to object and continued performance did not constitute assent. Under *Dorton*, "when no contract is recognized under Subsection 2–

207(1) . . . because the offeree's acceptance is expressly conditioned on the offeror's assent to the additional or different terms—the entire transaction aborts at this point." 453 F.2d at 1166. Accordingly, no contract was created by the exchange of forms. However, because there is no dispute that the parties' conduct establishes the existence of a contract, the court must resort to § **2–207(3)** to ascertain its terms.

3. *Application of § 2–207(3)*

SFEG essentially argues that, if the parties failed to create a contract under § **2–207(1)**, the parties' conduct after the exchange of the forms was nonetheless sufficient under § **2–207(3)** to establish a contract that included the supplementary limitations on warranties and liability contained in SFEG's Terms & Conditions.

As set forth above, § **2–207(3)** states that, in a situation where the parties' conduct establishes the existence of a contract even though the writings themselves do not, "the terms of the particular contract consist of those terms on which the writings of the parties agree, together with any supplementary terms incorporated under any other provisions of chapters 1–9 of this title." SFEG argues that the reference to "supplementary terms incorporated under any other provisions of chapters 1–9 of this title" encompasses those terms arrived at through the parties' course of performance and course of dealing.

SFEG argues that the UCC defines the term "agreement" as "the bargain of the parties in fact, as found in their language or inferred from other circumstances, including course of performance, course of dealing, or usage of trade as provided in § 47–1–303 [**UCC 1–303**]." Tenn. Code Ann. § 47–1–201(b)(3) [**UCC 1–201(b)(3)**]. It further insists that Blendtec received SFEG's Terms & Conditions "21 times and repeatedly kept ordering goods. This is not mere silence or inaction. Rather, Blendtec's repeated re-ordering constitutes acceptance, creating a course of performance for Northland's terms."

The fact that Blendtec repeatedly accepted SFEG's performance has no bearing on whether Blendtec assented to SFEG's Terms & Conditions. The court has already determined that silence or inaction, even over the course of repeated transactions, does not constitute "assent" for purposes of § **2–207(1)**. The actual issues presented by SFEG's argument are (1) whether the parties' course of dealing is encompassed within the supplementary terms of the UCC that may be considered in determining the terms of a contract formed under § **2–207(3)**; and (2) if so, whether the course of dealing gives rise to a question of fact as to whether the parties adopted SFEG's warranty disclaimer and limitation of liability in its Terms & Conditions.

In *Dresser*, the Seventh Circuit recognized that courts and commentators had differed on the issue of whether parties' course of performance could be considered under § **2–207(3)**. *See Dresser*, 965 F.2d at 1451 (citing *C. Itoh & Co. v. Jordan Int'l Co.*, 552 F.2d 1228, 1237 (7th Cir.1977) ("[W]e find that the 'supplementary terms' contemplated by Section are limited to those supplied by the standardized "gap-filler" provisions of Article Two."); *Daitom, Inc. v. Pennwalt Corp.*, 741 F.2d 1569, 1579 (10th Cir. 1984) (interpreting § **2–207(3)**'s reference to "supplementary terms" as encompassing terms arrived at through the parties' course of performance, course of dealing, or usage of trade, as well as the UCC's stock gap-fillers); 2 W. Hawkland, Uniform Commercial Code Series, § 2–207:04, at 109–10 (1990) (discussing warranties, opining that the parties' course of conduct should be considered in cases involving § **2–207(3)**); 1 White & Summers, Uniform Commercial Code, § 1–3, at 45 (3d ed. 1988) (recommending that "supplementary terms" be limited to those expressly provided for in the UCC's gap-fillers)). The *Dresser* court ultimately held, however, that Wisconsin's version of the UCC, which is very similar to Tennessee's, permitted courts to consider the parties' course of performance, course of dealing, and usage of trade, as well as the UCC's gap-fillers, in determining the terms of the parties' agreement under § **2–207(3)**:

> We believe that Wisconsin's version of § **2–207(3)** is most amenable to the approach taken by Professor Hawkland and the Tenth Circuit in *Daitom*. That section directs us to fill out a "battle of the forms" contract with "supplementary terms incorporated *under any other provisions of chs. 401 to 409.*" Wis. Stat. § 402.207(3) (emphasis added). Thus, a court is not limited to the standardized gap-fillers of Article 2, but may utilize any terms arising under the entire U.C.C. The statute's reference to "any other provisions," therefore, necessarily encompasses those sections relating to course of performance (§ 402.208) and course of dealing and usage of trade (§ 401.205). This is the most natural reading of the statute. There is no reason to suppose that the legislature would have used the word "any" if it really meant only the usual gap-fillers. This is not to say that the gap-fillers are unimportant; in cases where the parties' performance gives no indication of their understanding of a particular term, the gap-fillers will supply it. We simply hold that, under Wisconsin law, all of the U.C.C.'s provisions should be used in discerning the terms of a contract under § **2–207(3)**, including those provisions that allow us to examine the parties' performance.

Dresser, 965 F.2d at 1451.

The *Dresser* court's analysis remains, to this court's knowledge, the only comprehensive discussion of the topic. Based on the similarity between Tennessee's and Wisconsin's versions of the UCC, this court believes that Tennessee courts and the Sixth Circuit, if directly confronted with the question, would reach the same conclusion—that all of the UCC's provisions should be used to determine the terms of a contract under § 2–207(3), including those provisions that allow consideration of the parties' course of dealing.

The parties' course of dealing in this case, however, does not permit a conclusion that they have adopted SFEG's Terms & Conditions or that there is even a disputed question of fact in that regard. The term "course of dealing" is defined in the UCC as "a sequence of conduct concerning previous transactions between the parties to a particular transaction that is fairly to be regarded as establishing a common basis of understanding for interpreting their expressions and other conduct." Tenn. Code Ann. § 47–1–303(b) [**UCC 1–303(b)**]. Because the record does not reflect that either party ever invoked any warranties prior to bringing this lawsuit, there is no course of dealing between them with regard to that specific conduct. *Accord Step-Saver Data Sys., Inc. v. Wyse Tech.*, 939 F.2d 91, 104 (3d Cir. 1991) ("Ordinarily, a 'course of dealing' or 'course of performance' analysis focuses on the actions of the parties with respect to a particular issue.").

SFEG does not argue otherwise. Rather, the only course of dealing to which it points is Blendtec's continued performance after repeatedly receiving SFEG's Terms & Conditions. Regardless of how many times Blendtec received SFEG's Terms & Conditions, the court, again, has already concluded that Blendtec's silence and continued performance did not manifest assent to those Terms & Conditions for purposes of § 2–207(1). It would be illogical to conclude that silence and continued performance, standing alone, may nonetheless constitute a course of dealing under § 2–207(3), thus bringing in through the back door the same terms rejected at the front door.

In *Dresser*, the Seventh Circuit indeed held that the district court properly permitted the jury to consider the parties' course of dealing and affirmed the verdict in favor of the plaintiff-seller based on the application of its warranties. There, however, the parties' course of dealing included "some activity relating to the terms in question." *Dresser*, 965 F.2d at 1451. The evidence showed that the buyer was actually aware of the contents of the seller's warranty and, in fact, had passed the warranty along to its own customers, who had repairs done in accordance with the warranty's terms. In addition, there was evidence that "the custom in the industry was for the manufacturer of a finished product (here, [the buyer]) to adopt the warranties of the companies who sold them parts (here, [the seller])." *Id.* at 1451 n.2.

The case is therefore distinguishable on the facts from the case at bar, where there is no evidence of activity relating to the terms in question. Those cases more directly on point have consistently declined to find contract terms rejected under § 2–207(1) to be adopted by a course of dealing under **§ 2–207(3)**, where the only course of dealing is silence in the face of repeated delivery of the opposing form. *See, e.g., PCS Nitrogen Fertilizer, L.P. v. Christy Refractories, L.L.C.*, 225 F.3d 974, 982 (8th Cir. 2000) ("Moreover, the fact that Christy repeatedly sent its customer acknowledgment form to PCS does not establish a course of dealing; the multiple forms merely demonstrated Christy's desire to include de the arbitration clause as a term of the contract."); *Step-Saver Data Sys.*, 939 F.2d at 104 ("Because this is the parties' first serious dispute, the parties have not previously taken any action with respect to the matters addressed by the warranty disclaimer and limitation of liability terms of the box-top license. Nevertheless, TSL seeks to extend the course of dealing analysis to this case where the only action has been the repeated sending of a particular form by TSL.").

In sum, the court finds that the parties' course of dealing may be considered in determining the terms of their agreement under **§ 2–207(3)**, but in this case there is no evidence in the record that would permit the finder of fact to conclude that SFEG's Terms & Conditions were adopted by the parties' course of dealing.

C.   Conclusion—Terms & Conditions Motion

The court will grant Blendtec's Motion for Partial Summary Judgment on the question of whether Blendtec's counterclaims are barred by SFEG's Terms & Conditions, as the Terms & Conditions are not part of the parties' agreement. The court will deny SFEG's Motion for Summary Judgment to the extent that it seeks judgment in its favor as a matter of law on Blendtec's counterclaims.

* * *

B. CISG

The CISG rules regarding battle of the forms fall somewhere between the common law and UCC. It is important to understand the differences because the CISG also may impact many contracts governed by the UCC, even if the parties do not realize it.

Read CISG **Article 19**. At first glance, **(1)** seems to adopt the common law mirror image rule because it states that a reply to an offer will be a rejection if it contains differing or additional terms, but you must read the entire rule. A further reading of the next two subsections reveals a softening of the mirror image rule. **(2)** allows different or additional terms in a purported acceptance, that does not materially alter the offer, to be an acceptance. However, **(3)** gives examples of the types of terms that will materially alter an offer and therefore preclude acceptance. Those examples cover many of the terms that are typically added into an acknowledgment or confirmation which, under the CISG, turn a purported acceptance into a counter offer. That is a different outcome than the UCC because **2–207(2)** does not automatically exclude those terms. Similar to the UCC, if the offeror objects to any changes in an acceptance, it precludes the reply from being an acceptance. Unlike the UCC, the CISG says that an oral objection will suffice.

C. PAROL EVIDENCE RULE

2–207 tells us how to handle the boilerplate terms in written communications between the parties. After determining what terms are in the written contract, the next inquiry considers whether any oral or written promises or clauses that occurred before or at the time of the written contract became part of the agreement. This requires a review of the parol evidence rule found in **2–202**. Although **2–202** is called the "parol evidence rule," it is not limited to oral communications. The rule regulates what terms or promises, either oral or written, made before or at the time of the contract will become part of the agreement. It does not deal with any communications that occurred after the contract happened. Post-contract communications are covered by **2–209**, the section on modifications to the contract.

Many people confuse the parol evidence rule with the statute of frauds—don't be one of them! The parol evidence rule only applies to written agreements and the statute of frauds applies to oral contracts. If the agreement is not in writing, the parol evidence rule will not apply. If the parties have a written agreement and one or both of the parties wants to add a term that happened before the contract to that written agreement, the parol evidence rule may apply to determine whether the term will become part of the contract.

After determining that a party wants to add a term to a written contract, there are only 3 steps to consider when analyzing the parol evidence rule—integration, complete or partial integration, and whether the proposed term supplements or contradicts the written agreement. Before analyzing those three steps, it is important to consider what type of evidence is being added to the written agreement. If the evidence is trade usage, course of dealing, or course of performance (*see* **1–303**), the UCC's parol evidence rule eliminates the second step that determines whether an integrated agreement is complete or partial.

1. INTEGRATION

When analyzing if a written agreement is integrated, the first question to examine is whether the writing was intended to be the final agreement between the parties. This refers only to the terms in the agreement and whether the parties intended those terms to be final. That does not mean that the writing contains every single part of the agreement. The question is simply about whether the terms in the written agreement are final. For example, a contract may contain the type and price of goods that are supposed to be delivered under the agreement, as well as any warranties or disclaimers. As long as those terms were intended by both parties to be the final terms on price, type of good, and warranties, then the document is integrated. If the written document contains only the understanding of one party, it is not an integrated document.

2. COMPLETE OR PARTIAL INTEGRATION

After finding an integrated document, the next inquiry requires an analysis of whether the document is a complete and exclusive statement of the terms in the agreement. This entails reviewing the proposed term, comparing it to the written document, and asking whether or not the term would have certainly been included in that document. *See* **2–202**, Comment 3. There is a presumption under the UCC that written contracts are only partially integrated because it is common for parties not to include every necessary item for a contract in one document. Nonetheless, courts do find written contracts that are completely integrated.

To determine whether an agreement is completely or partially integrated you should ask whether the parties would have *certainly* included the proposed term. If they would have certainly included it, the document is a completely integrated agreement and the term may not be added to the contract. Parties may incorporate a merger clause to try to make the agreement a complete and exclusive one. A merger clause states that all promises and agreements are merged into the written document and that there are no other oral or written promises that are not contained in the agreement. These clauses are not conclusive under the UCC.

For example, a business sold a small jet to the president of a corporation who also was a very experienced pilot. The written contract did not contain a warranty about jet speed, however, the pilot claims the seller agreed to such a warranty. The president testifies that the most important thing to him when buying this jet was that the jet could hit a certain speed and that he paid a premium price for the jet because of its ability to reach a high jet speed. After receiving the jet and piloting it on several occasions, he noticed that it did not obtain the speed he wanted, so he now wants to sue for breach of contract. He reviews the written contract and realizes there is no clause guaranteeing that the jet will obtain a high speed. He asks your advice on his chances of success in a breach of contract. When you review the contract you notice that, in addition to not containing any terms about guaranteed jet speed, there are several warranties included, a disclaimer of the implied warranty of fitness for a particular purpose, and a merger clause. As you ponder your chance of adding the term into the contract, you ask, is this the sort of term that the parties certainly would have included in the written agreement? If yes, then the jet speed warranty cannot be added because the agreement is completely integrated and the pilot does not have a good case for a breach of contract based on a guaranteed jet speed. This agreement likely is completely integrated since it contains specific warranties (although not the one the buyer claimed he wanted), a disclaimer of the fitness warranty, a merger clause, and the pilot said the most important factor to him was this jet speed velocity. Because of those facts this is the type of term that the pilot certainly would have included in the contract.

The second step in determining whether an agreement is completely or partially integrated is not necessary if a party wants to add trade usage, course of dealing, or course of performance as evidence. *See* **2–202(a)**. The UCC drafters believed there are often agreements outside of the written contracts. Trade usage, course of dealing, and course of performance seem to be more reliable than other types of evidence, so those additional terms will be added as long as they do not contradict the written document.

3.   CONTRADICTS OR SUPPLEMENTS

If an agreement is only partially integrated or if a party wants to add terms based on trade usage, course of performance, or course of dealing, the final step requires a determination of whether the additional term contradicts the written document or merely supplements it. If it does not contradict, it becomes a part of the agreement.

When analyzing a parol evidence issue be careful not to confuse it with interpretation of a term because the rules that apply to extrinsic evidence differ for interpretation and the Parol Evidence Rule. Extrinsic evidence may be admitted to explain an ambiguous term in a contract, even if the agreement is completely integrated. That is because interpretation does not add to an agreement it simply explains any terms that are already in the contract.

The following chart should help you see the main steps in the parol evidence rule.

Parol Evidence Rule UCC 2–202

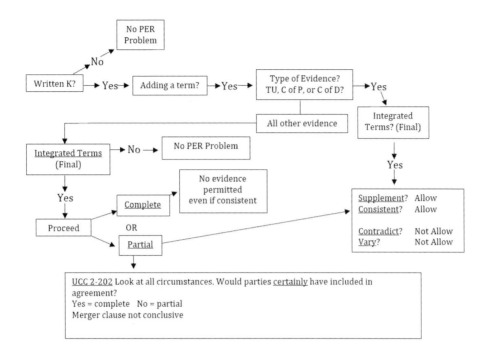

UCC 2-202 Look at all circumstances. Would parties certainly have included in agreement?
Yes = complete   No = partial
Merger clause not conclusive

PAROL EVIDENCE RULE AND CISG

Another area of stark difference between the UCC and the CISG is the Parol Evidence Rule. The CISG contains no parol evidence rule designed to keep some terms from being added to a contract. Instead, **Article 8(3)** is generally interpreted as requiring a court to consider parol evidence in all circumstances. Further, the CISG has no limitation on contradictory parol evidence.

As you read the next case, notice what term Druckzentrum wants added to the contract. Why did the court determine the contract was completely integrated? What facts were important?

DRUCKZENTRUM HARRY JUNG GMBH & CO. v. MOTOROLA MOBILITY, LLC

774 F.3d 410 (7th. Cir. 2014)

SYKES.

A German printing company sued Motorola Mobility LLC, the cell-phone manufacturer, alleging that it breached a supply contract for printing services. In early 2008 Motorola agreed to make a good-faith effort to purchase 2% of its cell-phone user-manual needs from Druckzentrum Harry Jung GmbH & Co., a printer based in northern Germany. Halfway through the two-year contract period, Motorola's cell-phone sales contracted sharply. In response to the downturn, Motorola decided to consolidate its cell-phone manufacturing and distribution operations in China and buy all related print products there. Motorola notified Druckzentrum of the shift, and the two companies continued to do business together for a few more months during the transition.

The loss of Motorola's business did Druckzentrum in; the printer entered bankruptcy in Germany and brought this suit against Motorola alleging breach of contract and fraud in the inducement of the contract. Among other things, Druckzentrum claimed that the contract gave it an exclusive right to all of Motorola's user-manual printing business for cell phones sold in Europe, the Middle East, and Asia during the two-year contract period. The district judge rejected this claim on the pleadings and later entered summary judgment for Motorola on the rest of the case, finding no evidence to support either a claim of breach of contract or fraud.

We affirm. The parties' written contract contains no promise of an exclusive right to all of Motorola's printing business in Europe, the Middle East, and Asia. And because the contract is fully integrated, Druckzentrum cannot use parol evidence of prior understandings to upset the bargain the parties put in writing. Moreover, although Motorola promised to make a good-faith effort to purchase 2% of its cell-phone user-manual printing needs from Druckzentrum for a two-year period, the contract listed several reasons Motorola might justifiably miss the target. These included business downturns of the sort Motorola experienced, and there is no evidence that it acted in bad faith by moving its printing and distribution activities away from Europe. Finally, the evidence is insufficient to create a jury issue on the claim that Motorola fraudulently induced Druckzentrum to enter into the contract or continue performing under it.

I.   Background

Druckzentrum is a printer based in Flensburg, Germany. Motorola is based in Illinois but maintains operations globally. In 1995 Motorola began using Druckzentrum to print user manuals for its cell-phone products marketed in Europe, the Middle East, and Asia—a marketing area apparently known in the trade as the "EMEA" region. During this time period, Motorola manufactured its phones in China and shipped them to a distribution facility in Flensburg, where they were packaged with user manuals printed by Druckzentrum and distributed for sale throughout the EMEA region.

In 2007 Motorola embarked on a program to improve the way it purchased products from vendors. At workshops conducted in fall 2007, Motorola educated vendors on the new process by which they could bid for contracts. Vendors first had to sign a "Corporate Supply Agreement" with a stated effective date of October 1, 2007. Druckzentrum was among the vendors invited to participate. After signing the agreement, Druckzentrum representatives attended a workshop in Illinois.

The materials distributed during the workshop made it clear that vendors would bid for a particular product "segment"—e.g., printed materials, cardboard boxes, plastic packaging, and so forth. It was less clear whether vendors were bidding for a particular *region* as well. Although the bidding materials contain many references to regions and vendors were supposed to state a bid in reference to a particular region, it is not clear whether Motorola would actually award work on a regional basis.

During the bidding process, Motorola shared its sales forecasts with vendors. Bidders needed to know what sales volume they could expect in order to set prices and ensure that they had capacity to meet demand. Motorola told Druckzentrum that it expected to sell 37 million mobile phones in the EMEA region in 2008 and made other rosy projections.

After bidding for the print segment in the EMEA region, Druckzentrum was given an "Initial Award" consisting of a "base share" of 2% and a "swing share" of 8%, meaning that Motorola made a "commitment" to buy 2% of print products from Druckzentrum and could, at its option, buy another 8% of print products from the company. The percentages were stated on the basis of global spending; thus, 2% of print means 2% of global print purchases, not 2% of EMEA print purchases. But there was no "commitment" in an absolute sense; rather, Motorola promised only to make a good-faith effort to hit the target and identified various commercial factors that might lead it to miss. All of this was embodied in a Notice of Initial Award, which the parties refer to as the "NIA" but we will simplify and just call "the contract."

Motorola sent a signed copy of the contract to Druckzentrum on January 23, 2008, although the previously executed Corporate Supply Agreement, which was incorporated by reference, stated an effective date of October 1, 2007. Another quirk is that the parties did not finalize prices until *after* Motorola awarded Druckzentrum the contract. As a result, Motorola purchased nothing from Druckzentrum for the first few months of the contract. As the parties negotiated over prices during the winter and early spring of 2008, Motorola regularly sent updated sales forecasts to Druckzentrum. The updated forecasts showed revised downward sales projections, but they were in a different format than the earlier forecasts; Druckzentrum's fraud claim centers on the change in formatting.

After finalizing pricing, Druckzentrum countersigned the contract in April 2008, and Motorola started placing orders. By its terms, the contract was good through September 30, 2009, "unless terminated earlier." Among various other grounds for early termination, Motorola could terminate the contract "for convenience" on 90 days' written notice.

Throughout calendar year 2008, Motorola's cell-phone sales in the EMEA region dropped precipitously, and by November of that year, Motorola decided to shutter its German operations in favor of a "direct ship" model. Under the new model, everything would happen in China, including the printing of user manuals. Motorola orally notified Druckzentrum of this decision by phone on November 4, 2008. On November 18 Motorola's purchasing agent in Germany notified Druckzentrum by email that all business would conclude by the end of the first quarter of 2009. Motorola and Druckzentrum continued to do business during this transition period. When orders ceased, Druckzentrum sent a notice of cancellation dated April 24, 2009. On July 1, 2009, Motorola faxed a formal letter terminating the contract.

Sometime after losing Motorola's printing business, Druckzentrum entered bankruptcy in German courts. Druckzentrum then sued Motorola in federal court in the Northern District of Illinois alleging claims for breach of contract and fraud. First, Druckzentrum alleged that it had a two-year exclusive right to all of Motorola's print business for cell-phone products destined for the EMEA market, and by moving the work to a Chinese vendor, Motorola breached the contract. Another theory of breach centered on Motorola's failure to meet the 2% purchasing target. On the fraud claim, Druckzentrum alleged that Motorola fraudulently misrepresented its sales prospects during the bidding process, inducing Druckzentrum to bid at lower prices and continue performing to its detriment.

The district court dismissed the exclusivity claim on the pleadings, holding that the contract did not give Druckzentrum an exclusive right to Motorola's printing business in the EMEA region. Following extensive discovery, Motorola moved for summary judgment on the remaining claims, and the court granted the motion. The judge explained that the contract required that Motorola make a good-faith effort to hit the purchasing target but also provided that changes in commercial circumstances would excuse a miss. Because there was no evidence of bad faith—Motorola had moved its operations to China in response to plummeting sales—the judge concluded that there was no breach. The judge also held that Motorola gave proper notice of termination by emailing Druckzentrum on November 18, 2008, saying that business would cease and the Flensburg facility would close by the end of the first quarter 2009.

Finally, Druckzentrum's fraud claim rested on an argument that the sales forecasts Motorola provided during the bidding process were misleading. The judge rejected this claim as well, holding that there was no evidence that Motorola "knowingly misled [Druckzentrum] about its sales forecasts in an attempt to induce [it] to reduce pricing or otherwise enter into an agreement." After resolving a few other disputes not relevant here, the judge entered final judgment for Motorola, and Druckzentrum appealed.

II. Discussion

A. Breach of Contract

Druckzentrum argues that it had an exclusive right to all of Motorola's user-manual printing business for cell phones marketed in the EMEA region during the two-year contract period. If that's true, then Motorola broke its exclusivity promise by moving its printing business to a Chinese vendor halfway through the contract period.

Druckzentrum admits, as it must, that the written contract does not contain an *express* exclusivity promise. Rather, Druckzentrum contends that Motorola made the promise during the bidding process. This argument requires resort to parol evidence, which is foreclosed by the contract's integration clause. The contract contains an "Entire Agreement" provision clearly stating that "[t]his Agreement is the entire understanding between the parties concerning this Initial Award and supersedes all earlier discussions, agreements and representations regarding this Initial Award."

The Uniform Commercial Code, as adopted in Illinois, provides as follows:

> **§ 2–202** Final written expression: parol or extrinsic evidence.
>
> Terms with respect to which the confirmatory memoranda of the parties agree or which are otherwise set forth in a writing *intended by the parties as a final expression of their agreement* with respect to such terms as are included therein *may not be contradicted by evidence of any prior agreement or of a contemporaneous oral agreement but may be explained or supplemented*
>
> > (a) by course of performance, course of dealing, or usage of trade . . . ; and
> >
> > (b) *by evidence of consistent additional terms unless the court finds the writing to have been intended also as a complete and exclusive statement of the terms of the agreement.*

810 ILL. COMP. STAT. **5/2–202** (emphases added).

Druckzentrum tries to fit the facts of this case into subsection **(b)**, which permits the importation of consistent terms from prior agreements but *only* if the contract is not fully integrated. *Id.* § **5/2–202(b)**; *see also id.* Cmt. 1. Motorola counters that the contract is in fact fully integrated and cannot be supplemented by parol evidence of prior agreements. In the words of the Illinois statute, the contract was "intended . . . as a complete and *exclusive* statement of the terms of the agreement." *Id.* § **5/2–202(b)** (emphasis added).

The contract language supports Motorola's position. The integration clause plainly states that "[t]his Agreement is the *entire* understanding between the parties . . . and supersedes *all* earlier discussions, agreements and representations. . . ." (Emphases added.) In an effort to overcome this unambiguous text, Druckzentrum argues that because the contract incorporates extrinsic materials by reference, it cannot reasonably be understood to be an exclusive statement of the parties' agreement despite the presence of an apparently conclusive integration clause. This argument backfires. When a contract expressly incorporates specific extrinsic materials by reference, the proper inference is that other, unmentioned extrinsic agreements are *not* part of the contract.

Moreover, the rule in Illinois is that "[i]f the additional terms are such that if agreed upon, they would certainly have been included in the document in the view of the court, then evidence of their alleged making must be kept from the trier of fact." 810 ILL. COMP. STAT. 5/2–202 cmt. 3 (explaining when a contract is fully integrated). Druckzentrum's claim of exclusivity in the EMEA region suggests that it considers this to be one of the key benefits of the deal. If the parties truly contemplated that Motorola was making such a critical promise, they certainly would have included it in the written contract.

Finally, Druckzentrum argues that the contract award is ambiguous and the presence of ambiguity means that the contract cannot be fully integrated. Even if the factual premise of this argument is correct, the legal conclusion does not follow. The existence of contractual ambiguity may allow consideration of extrinsic evidence to clarify those portions of the contract that are unclear. But it does *not* warrant a conclusion that the contract is not fully integrated such that evidence of prior agreements can be used to import entirely new terms.

And indeed the factual premise is not correct. Druckzentrum's argument about contractual ambiguity hinges on an implausible interpretation of the structure of the initial award. By its terms, the contract awarded Druckzentrum "2% of Base Share for the Print Segment with up to an additional 8% Swing Spend." Druckzentrum points out that 2% + 8% = 10%, and notes that 10% *just happens* to be the percentage of Motorola's worldwide print spending attributable to the EMEA region. Druckzentrum suggests that by stating the award in this way, Motorola promised exclusivity in the EMEA region, and parol evidence would confirm that interpretation.

It's true that the award is stated in technical terms. But it is not unclear. Motorola did not promise Druckzentrum 10% of its worldwide print spend; it promised 2% of its worldwide print spend with another 8% constituting a "swing spend" that it could award at its discretion. Because the contract is fully integrated and unambiguous (or at least unambiguous on this point), Druckzentrum cannot use parol evidence to prove up an enforceable promise of exclusivity in the EMEA region.

* * *

AFFIRMED.

D. STATUTE OF FRAUDS

So far this chapter has focused on finding what terms are included in a written agreement. But what happens if a party wants to enforce a contract and there is no written agreement? The statute of frauds, in **2–201**, requires some form of writing that indicates a contract for sale has been made in contracts for the price of $500 or more. The purpose behind the statute of frauds is to discourage bogus claims and prevent an innocent party from having to pay to litigate a case where there is no evidence of a contract. Additionally, as stated by the court in *MEMC Electronic Materials, Inc. v. BP Solar International*, 196 Md. App. 318, 340 (Md. Spec. App. 2010):

> Furthermore, the purpose of the Statute is to avoid fraud—not to prevent enforcement of legitimate transactions. Consequently, in regard to that purpose, we have stated that the Statute is intended to prevent
>
> > successful fraud [through] inducing the enforcement of contracts that were never in fact made. It is not to prevent the performance or enforcement of oral contracts that have in fact been made; it is not to create a loophole of escape for dishonest repudiators. Therefore, we should always be satisfied with "some note or memorandum" that is adequate, when considered with the admitted facts, the surrounding circumstances, and all explanatory and corroborative and rebutting evidence, to convince the court that there is no serious possibility of consummating a fraud by enforcement.

Even though a party claiming breach of contract defeats a statute of frauds defense, that plaintiff still must prove the existence of the contract. Think of the statute of frauds as a gate to get in to the courthouse. Getting past the statute of frauds only lifts the gate and allows the plaintiff into the courthouse to prove her case. Also, just because a contract is oral does not mean that it is always susceptible to the statute of frauds. If the parties admit there is a contract, there is no basis for a statute of frauds defense.

Consider this example: the parties have an oral contract to buy and sell cotton material to be made into clothing apparel and the material is shipped, paid for, and used to make clothing. After the clothing has been sold, the buyer claims it is defective because customers are complaining that the material fades after several washings and the buyer wants to sue the seller for breach of contract. Will the statute of frauds be an appropriate defense since this transaction is based on an oral contract? No, it is not a good defense because there clearly is a contract.

If, however, there is an oral contract and the statute of frauds is an appropriate defense there may still be a way for a plaintiff to work around the defense. **2–201** lists five ways to avoid having a case dismissed even though a contract is not written. That section states that one term that is essential is quantity. A quantity must be expressed (even if it is the wrong quantity) or there needs to be a way for a court to fairly determine a quantity to enforce when a partial payment has been made. Read Comment 1 to **2–201**.

Read **2–201**. If a party that wants to enforce a contract has something in writing from the person raising the defense, **(1)** may allow her to defeat a statute of frauds defense. Under **(1)** the writing needs to be sufficient to show that a contract for sale has been made, that the person raising the defense signed the writing, and it must contain a quantity of goods that are the subject of the contract. Review Comment 1 and you will see that this writing does not have to contain all of the material terms of the agreement, there only needs to be a basis for the court to believe that the claim is not a fiction. After getting past the statute of frauds through **(1)**, the plaintiff still has to prove the existence of a contract. Additionally, the contract will be limited to the quantity stated in the writing, even if it is incorrect.

Another way to defeat a statute of frauds defense is found in **(2)**; however, it only can be used when the agreement is between merchants as defined by **2–104**. This refers to the broad definition of merchants, including people who are merchants by virtue of their professional status. To use this subsection, the party trying to enforce the contract must have sent a written confirmation of the oral agreement to the person raising the defense. The written confirmation needs to have been sent within a reasonable time, and the party receiving it cannot have sent a written objection within 10 days. The content of this writing has the same requirements as **(1)**. That means it must be signed by the party wanting to enforce the contract, show that a contract for sale occurred, and contain quantity.

For example, Joe Hill, who owns the local farmer supply company, and Holly Sharp, who owns Sunrise Fruit Orchards, orally agree that Holly can buy a used plow truck and spreader for $120,000 to use at her upcoming harvest. If Joe refuses to sell the truck to Holly and she sues Joe to enforce their agreement, she will have a problem if Joe raises the statute of frauds and she has no written documentation from either one of them. If, however, Joe sent her a follow up invoice stating he sold the truck to Holly, signed that invoice, and indicated it was for 1 truck, that invoice would allow Holly to get around a statute of frauds defense using **2–201(1)**, even if it does not mention the price. If, instead, Holly sent a memo to Joe confirming their agreement that she would buy 1 truck for $120,000, signed the memo, and Joe did not assert a written objection within 10 days, Holly could use her memo to defeat a statute of frauds defense using the merchants' exception in **2–201(2)**.

Finally, there are three other exceptions to the statute of frauds in **(3)** that will allow a party to enforce an oral agreement. They include an exception for specially manufactured goods, one where the party raising the statute of frauds defense admits that a contract for sale exists, and when part performance has occurred on either side.

The following case illustrates the merchants' exception. Pay particular attention to the two written communications that Wal-Mart uses to try to satisfy **2–201(2)**.

GENERAL TRADING INTERNATIONAL, INC. V. WAL-MART STORES, INC.

320 F.3d 831 (8th Cir. 2003)

BOWMAN.

General Trading International, Inc. (GTI), sued Wal-Mart Stores, Inc., for breach of contract, action for goods sold, and action on account in a dispute arising out of Wal-Mart's alleged failure to pay for large numbers of decorative "vine reindeer" sold to Wal-Mart for resale to the public during the 1999 Christmas season. Wal-Mart counterclaimed for breach of contract and for fraud. According to Wal-Mart, most of the reindeer, manufactured in Haiti, were "scary-looking" and unsuitable for sale as Christmas merchandise. Wal-Mart claims that GTI orally agreed to absorb $200,000 of the purchase price because of Wal-Mart's dissatisfaction with the quality of the product. GTI, denying the existence of the alleged oral agreement, filed a motion for partial summary judgment, seeking an award of $200,000 of the unpaid balance, by arguing that the alleged oral agreement was unenforceable and violated the statute of frauds. The District Court granted partial summary judgment in favor of GTI and submitted the remaining claims to a jury, which returned a verdict in GTI's favor. Subsequently, the District Court denied Wal-Mart's motion for judgment as a matter of law or for a new trial and GTI's request for attorney fees. Wal-Mart appeals the grant of partial summary judgment and the denial of its motion for a new trial. GTI cross appeals the denial of attorney fees. We affirm.

I. *Background*

Although the factual history of this dispute is set forth in detail in the partial summary-judgment opinion of the District Court, we will summarize some of the major events, especially as they relate to Wal-Mart's claims on appeal. In February 1999, Beth Gitlin, a seasonal buyer for Wal-Mart, began negotiating with Patrick Francis, the president of GTI (a company that sells seasonal craft items to large retailers) for the purchase of 250,000 vine reindeer for resale to Wal-Mart customers during the 1999 Christmas season. In March 1999, GTI executed Wal-Mart's standard vendor agreement. The vendor agreement provided that any changes in the agreement must be in writing and executed by both parties. Wal-Mart issued separate purchase orders, covering price and quantity terms, to GTI for the purchase of the reindeer.

In mid-August 1999, Wal-Mart noticed serious defects with the reindeer when the first shipments began arriving at its stores and warehouses. Gitlin estimated that, at that time, at least seventy percent of the reindeer were of poor quality. A Wal-Mart employee described the reindeer as "[m]oldy, broken grapevines, shapes that no more resembled a deer than they did a rabbit . . . scary-looking." During the next few weeks, Gitlin communicated with Francis about quality problems with the product. On September 13, 1999, Wal-Mart directed GTI to cancel all further shipments of the reindeer.

On September 23, 1999, Gitlin met with Francis and Jeff Kuhn, a GTI representative, to discuss the slow sales and quality problems. During that meeting, Wal-Mart agreed to accept delivery of any reindeer GTI had already manufactured (approximately 25,000), but at a lower price than the prior purchase orders. In addition, Gitlin requested that GTI agree to Wal-Mart's withholding of $400,000 owed to GTI for potential claims for defective merchandise. Finally, according to Wal-Mart, GTI orally agreed, at some point before September 30, to reduce the total amount due from Wal-Mart by $200,000 because of Wal-Mart's price markdown of the reindeer at its stores in view of their poor quality. On September 30, 1999, Gitlin sent Francis and Kuhn an e-mail stating that sales of the reindeer were "too low" and that Wal-Mart would take a price markdown on the product within the next two weeks. E-mail from Gitlin to Francis and Kuhn (Sept. 30, 1999). In that e-mail, Gitlin also stated that she was "also concerned about the defective percentage and claims at the end of the season. You say they normally run less than 10%. I'm going to be conservative and estimate 20%. I'm going to change the reserve on the account to $600,000 and will release the rest of the payments." Gitlin did not receive a response to this e-mail from Francis or Kuhn.

On November 12, 1999, Kuhn sent Gitlin an e-mail stating GTI's frustration in obtaining payment from Wal-Mart on past-due invoices for the reindeer. In that e-mail, Kuhn noted that Gitlin said Wal-Mart was "going to hold $400,000 against future defective claims." E-Mail from Kuhn to Gitlin (Nov. 12, 1999). Gitlin replied three days later asking Kuhn to call her to discuss the matter. Gitlin and Kuhn spoke on November 19, 1999, and Gitlin sent Kuhn an e-mail that same day in which she stated, "As we both agree, we have $600,000 on hold now. $200,000 was to go to

Markdowns and $400,000 was to cover claims. If you are willing to do this, then I will be able to consider reducing the amount on hold from $600,000 to $500,000." Counsel for GTI sent Gitlin a facsimile letter that day demanding payment of the entire balance owed to GTI. Kuhn replied to Gitlin on November 22 and stated that "GTI would accept Wal-Mart withholding the amount of $400,000.00 for present and future charge backs." Kuhn sent Gitlin another e-mail on November 24 and stated that "[t]he principals [sic] of GTI's position is unwavering and non-negotiable. We want a check for $521,429 next week and on 1/15–2/1/2000 the $400,000 reserve will be revisited and adjusted accordingly." Thereafter, during the next several weeks, Gitlin and Kuhn continued to exchange e-mails, which can be characterized primarily as GTI continuing to demand immediate payment of outstanding invoices, or some settlement thereof, and Wal-Mart reiterating its position that GTI agreed to Wal-Mart's retention of funds for defective merchandise claims and $200,000 for price markdowns. GTI never acknowledged the $200,000 for price markdowns in any of its correspondence with Wal-Mart.

In December 2000, GTI sued Wal-Mart for breach of contract, action for goods sold, and action on account, alleging that GTI had shipped Wal-Mart 176,217 vine reindeer at an agreed price of $1,839,777.96, of which Wal-Mart had only paid $1,444,093.79. Wal-Mart counterclaimed for fraud and breach of contract. On October 1, 2001, GTI filed a motion for partial summary judgment, seeking an award of $200,000 of the unpaid balance, by arguing that the vendor agreement precluded any oral modifications and that the statute of frauds barred the alleged oral agreement to deduct $200,000 for price markdowns. The District Court granted GTI's motion on January 15, 2002, concluding that both the terms of the vendor agreement and the provisions of the statute of frauds barred the oral agreement to reduce $200,000 from the amount owed to GTI. The jury heard the remaining claims the next month and returned a verdict in favor of GTI on its breach of contract claim, awarding GTI $63,280, and in favor of GTI on Wal-Mart's counterclaim for breach of contract. Subsequently, the District Court denied Wal-Mart's motion for judgment as a matter of law or new trial and GTI's request for an award of attorney fees. On appeal, Wal-Mart contends the District Court erred in granting partial summary judgment to GTI on the $200,000 claim and abused its discretion in denying Wal-Mart's motion for a new trial on the ground that the erroneous grant of partial summary judgment prejudiced Wal-Mart in the trial of the remainder of the case. GTI cross appeals, arguing the denial of its request for attorney fees was an abuse of discretion.

II. *Discussion*

* * *

A. *Wal-Mart's Appeal*

Wal-Mart first argues the District Court erred when it granted partial summary judgment in favor of GTI by holding that the oral agreement to reduce $200,000 from the amount owed to GTI for price markdowns was barred by the statute of frauds. Subject to certain limited exceptions, the statute-of-frauds provision of the Arkansas version of the Uniform Commercial Code (U.C.C.) renders unenforceable any unwritten contract for the sale of goods with a value of more than $500 "unless there is some writing sufficient to indicate that a contract for sale has been made between the parties and signed by the party against whom enforcement is sought." Ark.Code Ann. § 4–2–201(1) [**UCC 2–201(1)**]. Both parties agree the case is governed by the so-called "merchants' exception" to the statute of frauds. Under the merchants' exception, a confirmatory writing setting forth the terms of the agreement is sufficient if the recipient of the writing knows its contents and fails to object in writing within ten days. *See* § 4–2–201(2) [**UCC 2–201(2)**]. Here, Wal-Mart claims GTI did not object within ten days of Wal-Mart's sending GTI a confirmatory writing of the oral agreement for the $200,000 allowance. Specifically, Wal-Mart argues Gitlin's September 30 e-mail as well as her other e-mails to Kuhn and Francis are confirmatory memoranda to which GTI did not object in writing.

The question of whether a writing constitutes a confirmation of an oral agreement sufficient to satisfy the statute of frauds is a question of law for the court. In this case, the District Court concluded that as a matter of law none of Wal-Mart's e-mails were sufficient. We agree.

We turn first to Gitlin's September 30 e-mail to Francis and Kuhn. In that e-mail, Gitlin stated that she was "going to change the reserve on the account to $600,000." According to Wal-Mart, this e-mail clearly indicates that Wal-Mart believed the original contract had been changed. Moreover, Wal-Mart argues that "although the breakdown of the $600,000 into a $400,000 reserve allowance for defective merchandise claims and a $200,000 for a markdown allowance is not explicit, it is strongly implied by the text of the e-mail." GTI does not dispute that it never responded to this e-mail. Instead, GTI argues that Gitlin's September 30 e-mail is not a confirmatory writing under § 4–2–201(1) [**UCC 2–201(1)**].

While the merchants' exception does not require a confirmatory writing to be signed by the party to be charged, *see* § 4–2–201(2) [**UCC 2–201(2)**], the writing still must satisfy the dictates of § 2–201(1) [**UCC 2–201(1)**]. Under the U.C.C., "[a]ll that is required [for a writing to indicate a contract for sale has been made under § **2–201(1)**] is that the writing afford a basis for believing that the offered oral evidence rests on a real transaction." U.C.C. § 2–201 cmt. 1. Most courts that have interpreted the "sufficient to indicate" requirement "have required that the writing indicate the consummation of a contract, not mere negotiations." *Howard Constr. Co.,* 669 S.W.2d at 227. Thus, writings that contain language evincing a tentative agreement or writings that lack language indicating a binding or complete agreement have been found insufficient.

Based upon our review of Gitlin's September 30 e-mail, we agree with GTI that this e-mail fails sufficiently to indicate the formation or existence of any agreement between the parties through inference or otherwise. This e-mail is simply devoid of any language concerning an agreement on the issue of $200,000 for markdowns. While the e-mail references a $600,000 reserve, it does not state what, if any, portion of that amount was agreed to be set aside for markdowns. At most, the e-mail shows Wal-Mart's unilateral effort at taking a markdown on the reindeer and changing the reserve, e.g., "I will be taking a MD on this either next week or the following . . . I'm going to change the reserve on the account to $600,000." Gitlin's Sept. 30 e-mail. In summary, the language in the e-mail does not constitute a sufficient writing for purposes of the statute of frauds because it does not evince any agreement between the parties on price markdowns.

Wal-Mart next argues that even if the September 30 e-mail is not a sufficient writing, Gitlin's subsequent e-mails to Kuhn and Francis constitute confirmatory memoranda. In particular, Wal-Mart points to Gitlin's e-mail to Kuhn on November 19 in which she stated, "As we both agree, we have $600,000 on hold now. $200,000 was to go to Markdowns and $400,000 was to cover claims. If you are willing to do this, then I will be able to consider reducing the amount on hold from $600,000 to $500,000." GTI does not directly refute that this or subsequent e-mails from Gitlin could constitute confirmatory memorandums. Instead, GTI argues that it filed timely objections to these writings. Specifically, Kuhn replied on November 22 and 24 and offered to sign a letter authorizing Wal-Mart to retain $400,000 for defective merchandise claims, but he also demanded immediate payment on all outstanding invoices, noting that GTI's position was not negotiable.

Section 4–2–201(2) [UCC 2–201(2)] does not prescribe any particular form for an objection to a confirmatory writing. Nonetheless, both parties agree that courts require an unequivocal objection to a confirmatory writing alleging an oral agreement. *See, e.g., M.K. Metals, Inc.,* 645 F.2d at 592 (holding response to a purchase order was not an adequate objection under § 2–201(2) because it did not challenge the price term in the purchase order, but rather stated that "there was someone who was willing to pay more than the amount stated in the purchase order") Here, Wal-Mart argues that GTI did not unequivocally object to its confirmatory writing because GTI failed specifically to object to the $200,000 for price markdowns in its November 22 and 24 e-mail responses to Gitlin's e-mails.

In analyzing these e-mails, the District Court concluded that GTI's "reply e-mails including different terms and containing demands for payment of the amount due on the invoices, less a reserve, constitute objections under § 2–201(2)." Though GTI failed to mention the $200,000 in its responses, it is clear when viewing the responses as a whole that GTI never agreed to Gitlin's assertion that they had reached an agreement on markdowns. Instead, GTI's responses, with a demand for full payment, less a reserve for defective merchandise claims, can only be characterized as unequivocal objections to any agreement on markdowns.

On the facts of this case, the merchants' exception to the statute of frauds has not been satisfied. Accordingly, we find the District Court did not err in granting partial summary judgment in favor of GTI on its claim for $200,000 of the unpaid balance of the reindeers' purchase price.

* * *

III. *Conclusion*

For the reasons stated, we affirm the orders of the District Court granting partial summary judgment in favor of GTI and denying GTI's request for attorney fees.

---

1. STATUTE OF FRAUDS AND THE CISG

The CISG does not contain a statute of frauds provision and in fact CISG **Article 11** affirmatively states that a contract of sale does not need any evidence of a writing, nor is there any requirement as to form. The CISG allows a contract to be proved by any means. Because the CISG was a compromise between common law and code countries, the drafters agreed to add Article 96 that allows a country whose laws require a writing for sales to opt out of **Article 11** and enforce their law. The United States did not do this, so contracts governed by the CISG arising in the United States have no statute of frauds requirement.

E. TITLE

One last Article 2 default rule to understand before moving on to performance in the next chapter is title. The two main issues to focus on are warranty of title and how title is transferred.

1. WARRANTY OF TITLE

Unlike the warranties covered in the last chapter, the warranty of title, found in **2–312**, is not a quality warranty. This warranty exists in every contract for sale unless disclaimed and it cannot be disclaimed by using the disclaimers in **2–316**. Under **2–312**, a seller warrants that goods sold have good title and that the seller has the power to transfer that title unless the buyer is aware that there is a problem. Additionally, a seller warrants that the goods being sold come free of any security interests or other encumbrances. A disclaimer of the warranty of title requires specific language or special circumstances as stated in **2–312(2)**.

2. PASSING TITLE

In a normal sale of goods with no problems, good title passes from a seller to a buyer. The seller has the right to convey title to the buyer and the buyer becomes the owner of the goods with good title. The opposite of this scenario happens when the seller passes void title to the buyer. Void title occurs simply when no title passes between the parties. It is the very absence of title. For example, if a thief breaks into a garage and steals a car, that thief has void title. If the thief tried to sell the vehicle, the buyer also would receive void title. The more difficult issue is voidable title because a person with voidable title has the power to pass both good and voidable title to another party depending on the circumstances of the transaction. A person receives voidable title when she obtains a good by deceit. The difference between void and voidable title is that in voidable title the possessor of the good intentionally transfers it, whereas with void title the person with the good does not voluntarily deliver the good.

2–401 covers at what point in time title passes. **2–401** follows the contractual approach in providing that title cannot pass prior to the identification of the goods to the contract. **2–401(1)** specifies that "title to goods passes from the seller to the buyer in any manner and on any conditions explicitly agreed on by the parties."

Although when title passes usually does not cause a problem, issues generally arise with regard to whether and what type of title passes. **2–403** addresses those issues. The issue of whether title passes centers on two concepts—voidable title and entrustment. Both of those concepts create a safe harbor for the person acquiring the good because they may allow good title to pass from a party who does not hold good title as long and that person had voidable title. **2–403(1)** covers voidable title and **(2)** and **(3)** involve entrustment.

As just mentioned, **2–403** uses a term called voidable title. Although Article 2 does not define voidable title, it explains how a party obtains voidable title. A person may acquire voidable title to a good if she receives the good from a party by using some means of trickery. The trickery often involves a criminal matter such as passing counterfeit money in exchange for the good or writing a bad check. The most important factor needed to create voidable title is intent. The person transferring the good must intend to transfer it to the other party, even if that transfer was caused by deception. **2–403** makes it clear that a party who holds voidable title has the power to pass good title to a good faith purchaser for value. If the transfer is to a good faith purchaser for value that good faith purchaser acquires good title, even though the other party only had voidable title.

First, **2–403(1)** requires a purchase. Read the definition for purchase in **1–201(b)(29)**. It is very broad. A purchase requires that the party transferring the good do so voluntarily and with the intention of creating an interest in property. This may include a sale, a lease, or even a gift. When a purchase occurs the party transferring the property usually transfers whatever title she possesses. That means in a purchase transaction, usually a party with good title transfers good title, voidable title transfers voidable title, and void title transfers void title. That changes when the person transferring the goods holds voidable title and transfers it to a good faith purchaser for value. When that occurs the good faith purchaser for value receives good title, even though the party who transferred title only had voidable title.

Why is there an exception for a good faith purchaser for value? The best answer is that the party who initially had good title could have stopped the deception in the beginning if she had been more careful and avoided handing over the goods. Also, the original owner intended to transfer title to the person who received the goods, even though it may have involved deception or trickery. For example, she could have made sure there were sufficient funds before taking a check or been more careful before taking counterfeit money. Since that was not done, the party who acquires the goods by deception holds voidable title and is able to transfer good title to a good faith purchaser for value. The subsequent purchaser does not have the same opportunity to detect the problem. If there are indications of a potential problem with title, the good faith requirement may not be satisfied. Remember you cannot use **2–403(1)** unless there is a purchase. If there is no purchase the only other safe harbor is entrustment, covered in **2–403(2)** and **(3)**.

The second way to obtain good title from a party who does not hold good title is when there is an entrustment. Entrustment occurs when a person voluntarily delivers or allows goods she possesses to be delivered to another party. If the goods are entrusted to a merchant who deals in goods of that kind, then the entrusted merchant has the power to transfer good title (or whatever title is held by the entruster) to a buyer in the ordinary course of business. Read **1–201(b)(9)** for the definition of a buyer in the ordinary course of business. This type of buyer is more narrowly defined than a good faith purchaser for value and it requires two things. First, the buyer must have no knowledge that by buying the goods she is violating the rights of another person and second, the goods must be bought in the usual manner that goods would normally be purchased from that business.

To illustrate, when Josephine leaves her computer with the local computer store for repairs it is an entrustment because she is allowing the computer store to possess her computer. When Mark buys it from the salesperson at the store during normal working hours he is a buyer in the ordinary course of business. Mark will obtain good title to Josephine's computer through entrustment and therefore, Josephine's only recourse is to sue the computer store, not Mark. If, however, Mark buys the computer off the back of a truck in the parking lot of the computer store after hours, Mark would not acquire good title because he is not a buyer in the ordinary course of business.

The court in *Kozar v. Christies, Inc.*, 109 A.D.3d 967, 968 (N.Y. 2013), held that title did not pass to a buyer who purchased a painting outside of the ordinary course of business.

> Contrary to the appellants' contention, the evidence at trial did not establish that they were good faith purchasers of the subject painting under **UCC 2–403(2)**. UCC **2–403(2)** provides: "Any entrusting of possession of goods to a merchant who deals in goods of that kind gives him power to transfer all rights of the entruster to a buyer in ordinary course of business." This "'entruster provision' of the [UCC] is designed to enhance the reliability of commercial sales by merchants (who deal with the kind of goods sold on a regular basis) while shifting the risk of loss through fraudulent transfer to the owner of the goods, who can select the merchant to whom he entrusts his property. *It protects only those who purchase from the merchant to whom the property was entrusted* in the ordinary course of the merchant's business" (*Porter v. Wertz*, 53 N.Y.2d 696, 698, 439 N.Y.S.2d 105, 421 N.E.2d 500 [emphasis added]). Here, the evidence presented at trial supports the conclusion that the appellants did not purchase the subject painting from the "merchant to whom the property was entrusted" (*id.* at 698, 439 N.Y.S.2d 105, 421 N.E.2d 500). Accordingly, we decline to disturb the Supreme Court's determination.

The following chart breaks down the two major concepts for transferring title contained in **2–403**. The purchase transaction is found in **2–403(1)** and entrustment is in **2–403(2), (3)**. GF/P/V means good faith purchaser for value. Each one of those elements are necessary to transfer good title from a person who hold voidable title. **1–201(b)(19)** contains the definition of a buyer in the ordinary course of business—BOCB.

Title Transfer Under 2-403

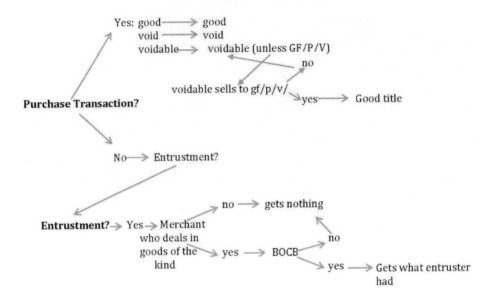

See if you can follow the next case using the **2-403** chart. In this case the plaintiff tries to argue he obtained good title either through a transaction of purchase or an entrustment, the only two ways that he can acquire good title using **2-403**.

MELLEN, INC. v. BILTMORE LOAN AND JEWELRY-SCOTTSDALE, LLC

2017 WL 1133031 (D. Ariz. 2017)

RAYES, D. L.

This case was brought to determine ownership of a four-carat blue diamond worth nearly $2 million. Plaintiff Mellen, Inc. bought the diamond in 2013. Two years later, Defendant Biltmore Loan and Jewelry obtained the diamond through a pawn transaction and subsequent purchase.

On March 8, 2016, Mellen filed a complaint against Biltmore asserting claims for declaratory judgment, replevin, and conversion. Biltmore has alleged slander and tortious interference counterclaims. In June 2016, the Court issued a preliminary injunction enjoining the sale or transfer of the diamond pending resolution of this case. The diamond presently is stored by Biltmore in a safe deposit box at a local bank.

Before the Court are cross motions for summary judgment. The motions are fully briefed. The Court heard oral argument on March 22, 2017. For reasons that follow, Mellen's motion is granted in part and Biltmore's motion is denied.

* * *

BACKGROUND

For purposes of the summary judgment motions, the following facts are not genuinely disputed. Mellen is a wholesale diamond dealer specializing in colored and other high-quality diamonds. In June 2013, Mellen acquired the diamond at issue—a flawless, four-carat blue heart-shaped stone—by purchasing it from another diamond dealer in California.

On January 23, 2015, Mellen and a diamond dealer from Florida, Scott Meyrowitz, entered into a memorandum agreement concerning a potential future sale of the diamond. Pursuant to its terms, the diamond was given to Meyrowitz "on memo," which is a customary practice in the diamond trade. The memo provides, in pertinent part:

> The merchandise described below, is delivered to you on *memorandum* . . . [and] only for examination and inspection by prospective purchasers, upon the express condition that all such merchandise shall remain the property of [Mellen], and shall be returned on demand, in full in its original form. . . . You acquire no right or authority to sell, pledge, hypothecate or otherwise dispose of the merchandise, or any part thereof, by memorandum or otherwise. . . . A sale of all or any portion of the merchandise shall occur only if and when we agree and you shall have received from us a separate invoice. . . . (This is NOT an INVOICE or BILL of Sale).

Meyrowitz received the diamond on January 26, 2015.

About two months earlier, Meyrowitz had reached out to the owner of Biltmore, David Goldstein, regarding a potential $1 million loan with the diamond as collateral. Meyrowitz thereafter introduced Goldstein to Joe Gutekunst, who purported to own the diamond and expressed interest in pawning it for $1 million. Goldstein and Gutekunst spoke about the pawn transaction the same day Meyrowitz entered into the memo with Mellen.

The transaction between Goldstein and Gutekunst was completed on March 2, 2015, the terms of which are set forth in a pawn ticket signed by Gutekunst. Biltmore wired the $1 million to Gutekunst the next day, and he immediately transferred $955,000 to Meyrowitz. Biltmore bought the diamond outright from Gutekunst on November 18, 2015, for a sale price of $1.3 million. This suit followed several months later to determine lawful ownership of the diamond.

DISCUSSION

It is undisputed that Mellen owned the diamond when it was given to Meyrowitz on memo. Mellen argues that neither Meyrowitz nor Gutekunst acquired any ownership rights in the diamond, and Biltmore cannot show that it obtained good title to the diamond as a good faith purchaser for

value or through an entrustment or consignment under the Uniform
Commercial Code (U.C.C.). Mellen further argues that Biltmore's
counterclaims for slander and tortious interference fail as a matter of law
because Mellen is the true owner of the diamond.

Biltmore initially asserted that the dispute is governed by Article 2 of
the U.C.C., which covers transactions in goods by merchants. Biltmore
argued that it had good title to the diamond under both the "good faith
purchaser rule" provided in U.C.C. § **2–403(1)** and the "entrustment rule"
set forth in § **2–403(2)**. Biltmore now takes the position that Article 9 of
the U.C.C., which covers secured transactions, governs the dispute.
Biltmore argues that Mellen's delivery of the diamond to Meyrowitz
constitutes a consignment under § **9–201** and Biltmore therefore has good
title to the diamond as a purchaser for value of goods from a consignee
under § **9–319**. Despite taking the position that Article 9 controls, Biltmore
does not waive any prior arguments made under Article 2. The Court
therefore will address the arguments made under each article.

I. Biltmore Did Not Obtain Good Title to the Diamond Under U.C.C. § 2–403(1)

Relying on the good faith purchaser rule, Biltmore argues that it has
good title to the diamond because Meyrowitz obtained voidable title
through a "transaction of purchase" under U.C.C. § **2–403(1)**. That section
provides, in pertinent part:

> A person with voidable title has power to transfer good title to a
> good faith purchaser for value. When goods have been delivered
> under a transaction of purchase the purchaser has such power
> even though . . . the delivery was procured through fraud[.]

U.C.C. § **2–403(1)(d)**. Mellen argues, correctly, that § **2–403(1)** does
not apply because neither Meyrowitz nor Gutekunst obtained the diamond
under a transaction of purchase.

A transaction of purchase is limited to those situations in which a
person delivers goods "intending for the subsequent seller to be the owner
of the goods." *Touch of Class Leasing v. Mercedes-Benz Credit*, 591 A.2d
661, 667 (N.J. Super. Ct. App. Div. 1991). "Applying that definition to the
case at bar, no 'transaction of purchase' occurred because it is clear from
the record that [Mellen] never intended for [Meyrowitz] to become the
owner of the [d]iamond." Rather, Mellen gave it to Meyrowitz "on memo,"
and the express terms of the agreement preclude the finding that
Meyrowitz was to have an ownership interest in the diamond.

The diamond was given to Meyrowitz "only for examination and
inspection by prospective purchasers, upon the express condition that all
such merchandise shall remain the property of [Mellen]." Meyrowitz
"acquire[d] no right or authority to sell, pledge, hypothecate or otherwise
dispose of the [diamond], or any part thereof, by memorandum or

otherwise[.]" A sale of the diamond could occur "only if and when [Mellen] agree[d] and [Meyrowitz] shall have received from [Mellen] a separate invoice." The diamond was to be returned to Mellen "on demand, in full in its original form." The memo concludes by making clear that it "is NOT an INVOICE or BILL of Sale[.]"

In short, the memo could not be more explicit that the transaction between Mellen and Meyrowitz was not one of "purchase." Stated differently, in delivering the diamond to Meyrowitz on memo, Mellen never intended for him to become the owner of the diamond. Thus, even if Biltmore was a good faith purchaser for value, any title Meyrowitz might have had in the diamond was void, not voidable, and good title could not pass to Biltmore under § 2–403(1).

The Fifth Circuit made this clear in *American Standard Credit, Inc. v. National Cement Co.*, 643 F.2d 248 (5th Cir. 1981). The court explained that a "transaction of purchase" occurs where the deliverer of the goods intended, however misguidedly, that the subsequent seller would become the owner of the goods. Thus, "the con artist who fraudulently induces a manufacturer to deliver goods to him by means of a forged check has voidable title because he obtained delivery through a transaction of purchase[.]" *Id.* Under § 2–403(1), "the defects in the con artist's voidable title would be cured by a sale to a good faith purchaser for value, and the good faith purchaser would obtain clear title[.]"

Where the con artist, however, "merely converts the goods to his own use after having obtained possession of them in some manner other than through a transaction of purchase, he does not even have voidable title; *instead, he has void title, and cannot pass good title even to a good faith purchaser for value.*" *Id.* (emphasis added). This is because a "purchaser of goods acquires [only the] title which his transferor had or had power to transfer [.]" U.C.C. § 2–403(1).

Here, there is no genuine dispute that Meyrowitz obtained possession of the diamond via "some manner other than through a transaction of purchase." *Am. Standard*, 643 F.2d at 268. The record shows that in giving the diamond to Meyrowitz on memo, Mellen never intended for Meyrowitz (or Gutekunst) to become the owner of the diamond, and Mellen reserved unilateral authority to determine whether a future sale of the diamond would occur. This is clear on the face of the memo, and courts interpreting similar language have found that it precludes a "transaction of purchase" in the wholesale diamond market.

      * * *

Because Meyrowitz did not obtain the diamond through a "transaction of purchase," he had only void title to the stone and could not pass good title to Biltmore even if it was a good faith purchaser for value. Thus,

Biltmore's "attempt to shoehorn [its] case within the confines of section 2–403(1) fails."

II. Biltmore Did Not Obtain Good Title to the Diamond Under U.C.C. § 2–403(2)

Section **2–403(2)** of the U.C.C. is known as the "entrustment rule." The section provides that "[a]ny entrusting of possession of goods to a merchant who deals in goods of that kind gives him power to transfer all rights of the entruster to a buyer in the ordinary course of business." U.C.C. § **2–403(2)**. The entrustment rule "is designed to enhance the reliability of commercial sales by merchants (who deal with the kind of goods sold on a regular basis) while shifting the risk of loss through fraudulent transfer to the owner of the goods, who can select the merchant to whom he entrusts his property." *Porter v. Wertz*, 421 N.E.2d 500, 500–01 (N.Y. Ct. App. 1981). In order for the buyer to have good title under § **2–403(2)**, three conditions must be met: (1) the goods must be entrusted to a merchant, (2) the merchant must deal in goods of that kind, and (3) the buyer must purchase the goods from the merchant in the ordinary course of business. U.C.C. § **2–403(2)**.

For example, if the owner of a new car takes it back to the dealership for service and the dealer puts it on the car lot and sells it to an unsuspecting buyer, the entrustment rule would give good title to the buyer. The original owner, of course, would have various claims for damages against the dealership, but the owner would bear the risk of loss by entrusting possession of the car to the dealership. The innocent buyer, by contrast, would not suffer the loss given his reasonable expectation that the dealership had clear title to the car and the right to sell it because the dealership regularly "deals in goods of that kind[.]" U.C.C. § **2–403(2)**.

The result would be different, however, if the buyer bought the car from the salesman at a vacant parking lot not knowing he was employed by the dealership. It is "well settled that § **2–403(2)** protects 'only persons who buy in the ordinary course out of inventory'" from a merchant who deals in goods of that kind.

A. The Diamond Was Not Entrusted to Gutekunst and He Is Not a Merchant

Mellen argues that Biltmore's claim to good title under the entrustment rule fails because Mellen never entrusted the diamond to Gutekunst, he is not a diamond merchant, and Biltmore did not buy the diamond in the ordinary course of business. Biltmore does not dispute that Mellen never entrusted the diamond to Gutekunst, or that he is not a diamond merchant (Biltmore was told that Gutekunst was in the vitamin supplement business but he in fact sells allergy drops). Rather, Biltmore contends that these facts are irrelevant because Meyrowitz was the one who sold the diamond to Biltmore through a purported agency relationship with Gutekunst. Biltmore asserts that Meyrowitz's alleged transfer of the diamond to Biltmore through his agent Gutekunst is protected by the entrustment rule. The Court disagrees.

The plain language of the rule provides that entrusting goods "to a merchant who deals in goods of that kind gives *him* the power to transfer" the goods to a buyer. U.C.C. § **2–403(2)** (emphasis added). The entrustment rule "is meant to safeguard unsuspecting buyers who purchase goods *from merchants* in good faith." *Great Am. Ins. Co. v. Nextday Network Hardware Corp.*, 73 F. Supp. 3d 636, 640 (D. Md. 2014) (emphasis added). The sale of goods from the merchant himself is an essential underpinning of the entrustment rule. This is because the rule's purpose is to "facilitate the free flow of goods based on a buyer's reasonable expectation that a merchant in possession of goods it ordinarily sells has title to them." *Lakes Gas Co. v. Clark Oil Trading Co.*, 875 F. Supp. 2d 1289, 1305 (D. Kan. 2012). This purpose would be defeated if, as Biltmore contends, the entrustment rule were to protect the purchase of a rare $2 million diamond from an apparent vitamin salesman.

The narrow definition of a "merchant that deals in goods of that kind" supports this conclusion. Unlike the general definition of "merchant" in § **2–104**, which includes the merchant's own skill or knowledge that might not be apparent to a buyer, the concern of § **2–403(2)** is with a narrower class of merchants based on appearances. "An individual buying a product from an apparent dealer in such goods expects to get good title." *Id.* (citation omitted). Thus, one "expects to get good title when buying a shiny new car from a General Motors dealer, [but] one buying goods from a mere warehouseman trying to recover storage costs knows that the seller is dealing with somebody else's goods." *Id.* The entrustment rule would not apply even if, unbeknownst to the buyer, the car in fact belonged to the dealership and was sold by the warehouseman at its request.

In short, § **2–403(2)** "enables a merchant to transfer rights to an entrusted good only if the person is a 'merchant' who 'deals in goods of that kind,' in this case diamonds or other high-end jewelry." *Zaretsky*, 820 F.3d at 520. Biltmore's purchase of the diamond from Gutekunst is not protected by § **2–403(2)**. Biltmore should have known that a four-carat fancy blue diamond worth nearly $2 million did not belong to a purported vitamin salesman. Stated differently, Biltmore had no reasonable expectation that it was buying the stone from a diamond merchant. It therefore finds no safe harbor in the entrustment rule.

Biltmore contends that reliance on the part of the buyer has no place in the entrustment rule, but the rule is specifically "designed to enhance the *reliability* of commercial sales by merchants who deal with the kind of goods sold on a regular basis[.]") For this very reason, the rule protects "*only those who purchase from the merchant to whom the property was entrusted*[.]" (Citation omitted.)

Biltmore asserted at oral argument that it would have been easy for Biltmore to believe it was buying the diamond from Meyrowitz because he was involved in the transaction, had dealings with the Gemological Institute of America (GIA), and the pawn ticket states that Gutekunst was either the owner of the diamond or authorized to act on the owner's behalf. But the undisputed evidence shows that Biltmore did not *actually* believe it was buying the diamond from Meyrowitz, to whom the stone was entrusted, nor did Biltmore buy the diamond from someone it *knew* to be an agent of Meyrowitz. Goldstein testified that he believed Meyrowitz was brokering the sale of the diamond for Gutekunst, not the other way around. Meyrowitz told Goldstein that Gutekunst wanted to sell the diamond to get money to expand his vitamin business. Goldstein made clear that the initial pawn transaction was with Gutekunst, not Meyrowitz, and Goldstein wired the $1 million loan directly to Gutekunst's bank account. Goldstein further testified that he later purchased the diamond outright from Gutekunst for $1.3 million, and again the money was sent directly his way.

This testimony is consistent with express terms of the pawn ticket. The customer listed on the ticket is "Joe Gutekunst." In pledging the diamond as security for the loan, Gutekunst indicated that he "was the owner of the pledged goods free and clear of all security interest liens." The pawn ticket was signed by Gutekunst himself, not Meyrowitz. The pawn ticket, combined with Goldstein's own testimony, undisputedly shows that Biltmore believed it was buying the diamond from a vitamin salesman, not from a diamond merchant. Courts have long held "the ultimate purchaser can demonstrate reliance and invoke [the protection of § **2–403(2)**] only if he believed he was buying from a dealer. The proof here is wholly lacking in [this] respect." *Atlas Auto Rental Corp. v. Weisberg*, 281 N.Y.S.2d 400, 404 (N.Y. Civ. Ct. 1967).

Biltmore contends that it does not matter that it was misled into believing Gutekunst owned the diamond because in reality Gutekunst was Meyrowitz's agent and Biltmore therefore purchased the diamond from Meyrowitz. Although it may be true that the entrustment rule protects a buyer who reasonably knows he is dealing with the lawful agent or employee of a merchant of goods (such as a salesman at a car dealership), the evidence in this case—even when construed in Biltmore's favor—does not support a finding that Biltmore knew it was purchasing the diamond from Meyrowitz through his agent.

Rather, the undisputed evidence shows that Biltmore did not know about the purported agency relationship, nor did it otherwise believe that it was buying the diamond from Meyrowitz. As explained above, the entrustment rule is meant to protect a buyer where there is a "reasonable expectation" that he is buying from a merchant who actually trades in the goods bought. This is what promotes the "reliability of commercial sales by

[such] merchants." *Porter*, 421 N.E.2d at 500. The fact that Biltmore did not believe, reasonably or otherwise, that Gutekunst was acting as Meyrowitz's agent, precludes a finding that Biltmore bought the diamond from a "merchant who deals in goods of that kind" under § **2–403(2)**.

Biltmore's reliance on *Canterra* and *Standard Leasing* is misplaced. In each of those cases, goods were transferred to sham corporations which reasonably appeared to be merchants in the types of goods sold in the ordinary course of business. Neither case addressed the law of agency or applied the entrustment rule where the seller did not appear to be a merchant of the goods sold.

* * *

B. Biltmore Did Not Buy the Diamond in the Ordinary Course of Business

The entrustment rule set forth in § **2–403(2)** is limited to sales to a "buyer in the ordinary course of business." A sale is not in the ordinary course of business unless it is from a person "*in the business of selling goods of that kind.*" U.C.C. § **1–201(9)** (emphasis added). As explained above, Gutekunst is not in the business of selling diamonds.

But even if Biltmore had purchased the diamond believing Gutekunst was Meyrowitz's agent, the entrustment rule still would not apply. A buyer in the ordinary course of business "does not include a person that acquires goods . . . as security for or in total or partial satisfaction of a money debt." *Id.* Biltmore contends that it did not acquire the diamond in this manner, but the record shows otherwise.

Biltmore acquired the diamond as security for the $1 million loan it extended to Gutekunst as part of the pawn transaction on March 2, 2015. The pawn ticket's security interest provision makes this abundantly clear:

> SECURITY INTEREST: To secure my payment of this Loan and Security Agreement, I [Joe Gutekunst] hereby grant Lender [Biltmore] a security interest in the pledged goods described herein. . . . I promise to pay to the Lender, on or before the Maturity Date, the Amount Financed, plus all accrued interest and fees set forth in this Loan and Security Agreement.

When Biltmore later purchased the diamond outright for $1.3 million, it paid an additional $250,000 and forgave the $1 million loan ($50,000 was withheld as interest on the loan). Because a buyer in the ordinary course of business does not include someone who acquires goods "as security for or partial satisfaction of a money debt," Biltmore does qualify for protection under § **2–403(2)**.

Biltmore claims that it actually purchased the diamond when Gutekunst pawned it on March 2, 2015, because the U.C.C. deems a "pledge" to be a purchase and pawn transactions are considered purchases under Arizona law. But the pawn ticket undisputedly includes a provision creating a security interest in the diamond. Although Gutekunst had no obligation to fully redeem the pledged diamond, he promised to make payments on the loan or risk forfeiting the diamond to Biltmore after the loan's 90-day maturity date unless the redemption period was extended, as occurred here. Gutekunst made multiple $40,000 interest payments to "keep the loan/pawn open." Moreover, Goldstein—an experienced diamond trader and pawnbroker—has himself testified that the pawn transaction was not converted to a purchase until he forgave the $1 million loan on November 18, 2015. Similarly, Biltmore affirmatively alleges in its third-party complaint that Gutekunst conspired to "initially pawn the diamond" and then later to "convert the pawn to an outright sales transaction."

Despite Biltmore's contention that it purchased the diamond on March 2, 2015, the undisputed evidence shows that the diamond was pledged as security for the $1 million loan and Biltmore later forgave the loan when it bought the diamond outright. These facts preclude a finding that Biltmore bought the diamond in the ordinary course of business under § **2–403(2)**.

In summary, none of the conditions of the entrustment rule can be met given that the diamond was not entrusted to Gutekunst, he is not a diamond merchant, and the diamond was not bought in the ordinary course of business. U.C.C. § **2–403(2)**.

* * *

PROBLEMS

1.   Consider the following facts:

Athena Corporation manufactures and sells swimming gear to retail sporting goods stores in the southeastern United States. Some of their more popular items are their high-tech Aztec swimming suits for competitive swimming. On July 1, Athena sent fliers to all of the retail buyers it usually did business with to advertise the following special:

> For every order of 20 Aztec suits you place, we will give you 2 sets of Light-N-Easy swim fins, free of charge. If your customers try them, they will love them! Order now because the special is only good until the end of the month.

The order form had various blanks to fill in for quantity, date of delivery, etc. It was silent as to the mode of dispute resolution. Abraham Adams, the buyer for the Gunnar Sporting Goods Shop, ordered the Aztec swimming suits to use in an upcoming promotion that he intended to have in several months. He completed the form sent to him by Athena and ordered 50 Aztec swimming suits with a stated delivery date of Aug. 1. See 2–204, 2–206, 2–207, and CISG Article 19.

a.   If the next action that occurs is Athena sending Gunner 45 Aztec swimming suits that are delivered on Aug. 1, is there a contract between the parties?

b.   What if, instead of sending 45 swimsuits on Aug. 1, the next action that occurs is Athena sending Gunner 50 Aztec swimming suits that are delivered on Nov. 1. Is there a contract between the parties?

c.   What if instead of sending swimsuits, Athena sends 50 kickboards, is there a contract between the parties?

2.   Same facts as problem 1 except instead of sending the swimsuits, Athena sends an acknowledgment form and that form contains a term that requires the parties to submit any disputes to arbitration.

a.   Is there a contract?

b.   If a contract exists, will disputes have to go to arbitration?

c.   Would there be a contract if the court applied the common law instead of UCC Article 2?

d.   Would there be a contract if the CISG applied to this transaction?

3.   Using the facts from problem 1, assume again that Athena sent an acknowledgment form after receiving the order and that form contained a term that required the parties to submit any disputes to arbitration. The acknowledgement form sent by Athena also had a term that said: "Our acceptance is expressly made conditional on your accepting any additional or different terms" and expressly disclaimed consequential damages. See 2–207.

a.   After receiving the acknowledgement but before goods are shipped, is there a contract? If so, what are the terms?

b.   What if Gunnar received the acknowledgement, Athena sent the swimsuits, Gunnar paid for them, Abraham began to sell them in his sporting goods store, and a dispute arises over the quality of the goods? Is there a contract? If so, what are the terms?

4.   Assume that Gunnar and Athena agreed over the telephone to all the necessary terms of the contract for the swimsuits that are stated in problem 1 including quantity, price, etc. and that the seller, Athena, would not be responsible for consequential damages. After concluding the telephone call, Gunnar sent a letter to Athena restating the terms of the deal with the quantity, price, etc., stating that all disputes would go to arbitration, seller was liable for consequential damages, and that Athena's acceptance is expressly made conditional on acceptance to these terms.

Athena then sends the swimsuits to Gunnar and, after accepting and paying for the goods, a dispute arises over the quality of the swimsuits. Assume that Gunnar can prove that the swimsuits are defective and that is not an issue. See 2–207.

a.   Should a dispute over the quality of the goods be settled in court or will it be handled in arbitration?

b.   Will the seller be responsible for consequential damages?

5.   Consider the following facts:

On June 1, Sabrina West met Randy Gold at a crystal trade show. Randy showed her a variety of crystal goods he recently crafted that looked very similar to Waterford, a famous brand of crystal originally manufactured in Ireland, but were considerably less expensive. Sabrina invited Randy to dinner to explore the possibility of buying his crystal for her shop, Crystal Ball. Sabrina said that the Crystal Ball would carry his line of "Merlin Table Lamps" and all the vases he could produce during the year, if he agreed to a one-year contract, but at a rate that Randy considered very low. Randy was hesitant because of the low price but he also knew this was a big break for his new company. Sabrina thought it was fair because during the first six months she would put a lot of time and energy into marketing his goods. She assured Randy that after six months, they would renegotiate for a higher price. Sabrina pulled a contract out of her briefcase and told Randy that it was a standard contract that everyone in the industry signed. Randy was new to the industry and he thought having his goods in Sabrina's store was a great opportunity for him. Since he would only have to accept the low price for 6 months, Randy decided to sign the contract. See 1–303, 2–202, and CISG Article 8(3).

a.   Six months has passed and Randy comes to your office for advice. He tells you that he just met with Sabrina and she refuses to renegotiate the price she is paying Randy for his crystal. You review the contract and see that there is no merger clause and the contract only contains the basic terms about price, the output contract, delivery terms, and proposed dates for shipment. What are Randy's chances of adding the promise to renegotiate the price?

b.   Would your answer to (a.) change if there was a merger clause in the contract?

c.   How would your answer to (a.) change if Sabrina's store was in Toronto, Canada and Randy's shop was in Minneapolis, Minnesota?

d.   Does your answer to (a.) change if the promise to renegotiate was made after Randy and Sabrina signed the contract?

e.   Randy also tells you that he found out from friends that due to the price of cut crystal it is common to allow a termination clause after 6 months. He wants to know what his chances are of terminating the contact if he cannot get Sabrina to renegotiate the price. The contract does not contain a termination clause.

6.   Shawn Builder was very proud of the custom-made motorcycles that he built in his workshop. They are highly sought after by motorcycle enthusiasts and a few have been purchased for over $100,000. Shawn found a Boss audio system that he wanted to have added to his latest custom built motorcycle that he called the Raven, so he took the Raven into Moe's Motorcycle Sales and Repair shop. Moe's told Shawn that they had to do some measurements, make a few adjustments on the bike, and then special order a

system to fit the Raven, so he left it at the shop to give them time to do everything they needed. Shawn arranged to pick up the Raven in 4 weeks.

Several weeks after leaving the motorcycle in the shop Shawn saw a woman riding the Raven on the highway. He followed her and when she stopped at a restaurant he got out of his car and went to talk to her. When he confronted her, he found out that her name was Hunter Hawkins and she told him that she had purchased it from a man named Jack Harley for $50,000 through a classified ad. He took her name and address and drove to the motorcycle shop to demand some answers.

Here is what he found out from Moe who had been trying to track down the motorcycle ever since he found out they sold it: A sales man at Moe's accidentally sold it to a customer named Will Saturn for $45,000. Will Saturn sold it the next day to Lucy Steed for $50,000 but it turned out that Lucy had paid for the Raven with a check that bounced. Lucy then gave it as a birthday gift to her boyfriend Marley Smith but after a fight with Lucy, Marley sold it to Hunter Hawkins who now has the Raven. See 1–201(b)(9), (20), (30), 1–204, and 2–403.

Trace the title to the Raven in this problem by answering the following questions

  a.   What type of title did Shawn have when he took the Raven to Moe's?

  b.   What type of title did Moe's possess when they sold it?

  c.   What type of title did Will Saturn get from Moe's?

  d.   What type of title did Lucy Steed possess when she bought the Raven from Will?

  e.   What type of title did Marley Smith get from Lucy?

  f.   What type of title does Hunter Hawkins have?

  g.   Does Shawn have any recourse against anyone in this mess and what are the chances that Shawn will be able to get the Raven returned to him from Hunter?

  7.   Trace the title in the following transactions: See 1–201(b)(9) and 2–403.

  a.   Ginger takes her car to Miley's used and new cars for repairs. After repairs, the mechanic accidentally drives it to the used car lot. Stella, a saleswoman at Miley's, sells it to Athena. Ginger returns to retrieve her car and discovers what has happened. Can Ginger recover her car from Athena?

  b.   Ginger takes her car to Miley's used and new cars for repairs. After repairs, Miley gives it to Tom to satisfy a debt of $10,000 that Miley's owes him for parts. Can Ginger recover her car from Tom?

  c.   Ginger loans car to a friend, Hans, for a week because he needs transportation to and from work and she has 2 cars. The car is parked in front of Hans's house when Hans's father, Abe, sells it to Sarah.

Ginger discovers what happens and wants to recover her car from Sarah—can she?

d. Ginger takes her car to Miley's used and new cars for repairs. After repairs, the mechanic accidentally drives it to the used car lot. Stella, a saleswoman at Miley's, takes it out as a loaner and sells it to her neighbor because she needs some cash. Can Ginger recover her car from the neighbor?

e. Ginger takes her cool purple car (with dark lavender stripes) to Miley's used and new cars for repairs. Athena, a classmate, gives her a ride home and Ginger tells her she will find another ride to pick up the car tomorrow after her car is repaired. After repairs, the mechanic accidentally drives it to the used car lot.

Athena goes back to Miley's by herself to look for a car, sees it on the lot, has always admired it, and finds a saleswoman to show it to her. The saleswoman shows it to Athena and then sells it to her. Ginger returns to retrieve her car and discovers what has happened. Can Ginger recover her car from Athena?

8. On Oct. 1, Julie Mast, the owner of Mast Industries, met with Trevor Tank, president of Super Clothing stores, to discuss the sale of certain textiles that Mast was closing out. That afternoon the two of them spent about an hour negotiating all of the details of an oral agreement except price. The following day Julie and Trevor met again to talk about price and, after another hour of negotiation, they agreed on a price of $230,000 with each bundle of textiles costing $46,000 (5 total). Julie told Trevor that they would receive the invoices in the next day or two and the textiles would be delivered shortly. When Trevor did not receive the invoices he called Julie. She told him not to worry and that the invoices were on their way. When no invoices had arrived by Oct. 9, Trevor faxed 5 purchase orders on Super Clothing's letterhead to Mast's office. The handwritten fax stated that the purchase orders were being faxed in accordance with the agreement between Mast and Super Clothing reached on Oct. 1 and 2. The purchase orders contained detailed quantity, description, price, and payment terms but Trevor did not sign them. Mast never objected or acknowledged the purchase orders.

Several weeks later Trevor called Julie to find out when his order will arrive and she said, "We don't have any written agreement so we have no deal." See 2–201, 1–201(b)(37), and CISG Article 11.

a. When Trevor sues to enforce his agreement with Mast, Julie raises a statute of frauds defense. Will Trevor be able to enforce the agreement?

b. Would your answer to (a.) change if the CISG governs this agreement?

c. What if Julie receives the purchase order and immediately calls Trevor and says, "That is not the price we agreed to—you can just forget it?"

    d.   Would your answer to (c.) change if Julie puts the above statement in writing?

    e.   Same facts as the problem above, except that Trevor does not send a purchase order but instead sends a check for $92,000 that says down payment on textile deal. If Julie raises a statute of frauds defense will Trevor be able to enforce the agreement and, if yes, for how many bundles?

    9.   On March 1, Nick Archer, a law student, visited Planet Chevrolet to look at their fleet of used Chevy Silverados. He spoke with the owner, Buzz Star, about purchasing a Silverado that was several years old. After a test drive and about an hour of negotiations, he agreed to buy a 3-year-old Silverado for $20,000. Before his credit could be checked and any documents signed, a bad storm hit the area and knocked all of the power out. When the power had not come back on within an hour, Nick left and Buzz said that he would be back in touch. Nick could not get off of work to go back to Planet Chevrolet for several days and he could not reach Buzz by phone, so he decided to send him a letter. The letter said that he now had the cash for the 3-year-old Silverado truck that he agreed to buy and he would like to pick up the truck within 10 days. When he never heard back from Buzz, he drove to the dealership. When he arrived Buzz said that he had sold the truck to someone else for $23,000. See 2–201 and CISG Article 11.

    a.   If Trevor sues to enforce the agreement and the dealer raises the statute of frauds defense, what are Trevor's chance of success?

    b.   If this contract is enforced under the CISG, would your answer to (a.) change?

CHAPTER 4

PERFORMANCE AND RISK OF LOSS

■ ■ ■

Now that you understand many of the important default terms in Article 2, how the UCC handles contract formation, the use of boiler plate terms in a contract, when contracts have to be in writing, and how to add terms to a written contract, it is time to turn to performance of the contract. Performance issues arise when a seller sends nonconforming goods, a buyer does not pay, a party repudiates a contract or some other breach occurs. Performance of a contract is intertwined with issues regarding risk of loss, such as which party has the risk of loss if goods are lost, damaged, or destroyed. Because performance and risk of loss issues are often connected they will be combined in this chapter.

Before turning to performance, you should understand the concept of good faith that permeates contract performance. The law implies good faith into a contract, so parties will be held to a minimum standard of good behavior with their contracting partners. Although a breach of good faith may not be actionable by itself, it may help convince a court that other breaches are particularly egregious. Additionally, the non-merchant definition of good faith in Article 1 is not entirely uniform among the states.

A. REQUIREMENT OF GOOD FAITH

Read **1–201(b)(20)**, **1–302**, **1–304**, and **2–103(1)(b)**. Remember that the UCC is a series of default rules, so the parties may choose to contract around them by adding clauses in the contract that cover the same subjects as the default rules, except they use different terms. However, in the UCC there are some default rules that parties may not negotiate out of or contract around. Good faith is one of those default rules that contracts always contain. It is a concept that you undoubtedly remember from your studies in contracts. In contracts the common law implies a good faith requirement and the UCC follows the same trend. **1–304** states that every contract imposes an obligation of good faith and **1–302** makes it clear that this obligation may not be disclaimed by agreement.

So, how does the UCC define good faith? Until Article 1 was amended in 2006 the definition of good faith depended on whether a party was a merchant or a non-merchant. For a merchant, the definition has remained the same and includes both a subjective component (honesty in fact) and an objective component (observance of reasonable commercial standards). The non-merchant definition used to contain only the subjective component. However, when Article 1 was amended in 2006, an objective component was added to the non-merchant definition of good faith. A number of states chose not to amend the non-merchant section in their statutes, so it remains as one of those non-uniform sections that varies depending on jurisdiction. For your studies, you should rely on the amended version of the good faith definition found in the UCC. But, this serves as a good example of why you should always check your state's version of the UCC!

B. PERFORMANCE IN NON-INSTALLMENT CONTRACTS

Performance issues in a contract usually stem from a breach by one of the parties. **2–301, 2–507** and **2–511** state the basic obligations of a buyer and seller. **2–507** requires the seller to deliver goods before the buyer must accept and pay for them. **2–511** makes payment a condition of the seller's duty to deliver goods. These duties may be breached in a variety of ways depending on the terms of the contract.

The UCC treats breach differently than the common law. Remember from your study of the common law in contracts that there has to be a material breach before a party can cancel a contract, a minor breach is not sufficient. And even with a material breach the breaching party usually has a right to cure before the injured party may try to avoid the contract. Article 2 does not use the terms material or minor breach, although several rules on breach talk about a breach that "substantially impairs the value" of a contract and that concept is similar to material breach. Some courts use cases analyzing material breach when they are discussing whether a breach substantially impairs the value of an installment or when considering revocation.

Article 2 rules regarding performance examine when a buyer may avoid a deal by returning defective or nonconforming goods to the seller. You should note as an aside that at some point it is too late for a buyer to do that and she has to keep the goods. While a buyer can still sue for breach in that situation, her remedies will be more limited if she has to retain the goods. Whether a buyer can return nonconforming goods depends on whether the transaction is a single delivery contact, such as a car purchase, or if it is an installment contract. Installment contracts are covered later; but before turning to installment contracts, this chapter will consider how the UCC deals with breaches and delivery of nonconforming goods in a single delivery contract.

1. REJECTION AND ACCEPTANCE

The first step in recognizing how the UCC handles breaches and nonconforming goods is to understand the concepts of rejection, acceptance, revocation, and cure. Unlike common law, Article 2 permits a buyer to reject goods if they are not a perfect tender. Even a minor breach allows a buyer to reject goods, although the UCC softens the harshness of that rule by allowing cure in many situations. Read **2–601** and **2–602**. If a seller delivers defective goods and the buyer wants to reject them, she needs to notify the seller within a reasonable amount of time. A failure to reject in a reasonable amount of time likely will be construed as acceptance under the UCC whereas a rejection within a reasonable time is effective under **2–602**, even if it is unwarranted. It is important to note the difference between an effective rejection that is rightful and a wrongful but effective rejection. A buyer may *effectively* reject goods as long as she complies with **2–602**—even if that rejection is *wrongful* because the goods are not defective. On the other hand, a buyer may rightfully and effectively reject goods if they are defective or nonconforming. If a rejection is wrongful but effective the seller still will have recourse to sue, although the remedies may be limited due to the rejection. This will be important in the next chapter when we consider the remedy of specific performance for a seller.

When a buyer rightfully rejects goods she should state ascertainable defects with some particularity instead of just a general rejection because **2–605** requires a buyer to tell the seller why she is rejecting the goods, with some exceptions. A failure to state the defects with particularity could result in a buyer losing the ability to rely on that defect later when trying to justify rejection and prove breach. Additionally, rejection usually causes the goods to go back to the seller. Until the buyer actually returns them, the buyer has a duty to take reasonable care of the goods until the seller may retrieve them.

If the buyer does not effectively reject the goods under **2–602**, you should consider whether an acceptance has occurred. Read **2–606** regarding the rules on acceptance. That section lists four different ways that a buyer may accept goods. Subsection **(a)** describes the first way to accept goods which envisions an affirmative act whereby the buyer tells the seller she is accepting the goods even if they are nonconforming. Comment 3 of **2–606** states that payment is not conclusive, although it may be a factor to consider when ascertaining whether an acceptance has occurred under subsection **(a)**.

Subsection **(b)** creates an acceptance by a buyer's failure to act, which is how most acceptances occur. It states that after a reasonable amount of time, if a buyer has not rejected the goods, an acceptance occurs. However, this subsection must be read together with **2–513**, the section that gives the buyer a right to inspect the goods before payment or acceptance. Comment 2 to **2–513** makes it clear that the buyer does not have to inspect the goods immediately, but just within a reasonable amount of time. What amounts to a reasonable amount of time depends on many factors, including the type of goods and the different circumstances of each case. However, if a buyer waits an unreasonably long time before inspecting the goods, it may affect her ability to reject the goods if she later finds a defect. That is because, as discussed previously, **2–602** requires the buyer to notify the seller within a reasonable amount of time if she wants to reject. Although the buyer initially must pay for any inspection costs, if the goods are defective the buyer may be able to recoup the amount paid for inspection. *See* **2–513(2)**.

The last two ways to accept goods are found in **2–606(1)(c)**. Read subsection **(c)** and Comment 4 to see if you can determine the two different possibilities for acceptance. You should see that the first part of subsection **(c)** (the words before the semicolon) results in an automatic acceptance once a buyer "does any act inconsistent with the seller's ownership." You cannot decide whether an act is inconsistent with the seller's ownership without considering the buyer's right to inspect under **2–513**. The buyer's right to inspect will likely entail some action inconsistent with the seller's ownership. For example, if you order a new computer you may need to use it to see if software is installed, see if the keys are working, and perform other acts to ensure the computer functions properly. If you continue to use the computer, at some point you will cross the line of inspection rights into acts inconsistent with the seller's ownership. A common act inconsistent with the seller's ownership is one that alters the goods. For example, you order a chair but, because it did not come in the color you wanted, you paint it lavender as soon as it arrives. This is inconsistent with the seller's ownership rights. Under the first part of **2–606(1)(c)** you will have accepted the goods.

Now read the rest of the sentence in **(c)** after the semicolon that starts with "but if such act is wrongful. . ." Read Comment 4 to **2–606** and **2–602(2)(a)**. Notice the difference between the first and second part of **2–606(c)**. In the first part of **2–606(c)** the acceptance is automatic and in the second part of **(c)** the acceptance is not automatic. Instead, acceptance has to be ratified by the seller. So, what is the difference between the two types of acceptance? When you read **2–602(2)(a)** you should have noticed that once a buyer rejects goods, "any exercise of ownership . . . is wrongful as against the seller." As such, you should recognize that the second part of **2–606(1)(c)** seems to refer to post rejection acts, while the first part of **(c)**, probably occurs before rejection.

This can be confusing, so consider two similar situations that illustrate the difference between the pre and post semicolon language in **(c)**. Compare the situation where the buyer immediately paints the chair to a situation where a buyer promptly calls the seller upon arrival of the goods and tells the seller she does not want the goods any longer, so she is rejecting them. Once that rejection occurs, those goods are the property of the seller and any act by the buyer of ownership is wrongful against the seller per **2–602(2)(a)**. That means the buyer may not simply change her mind and paint the chair lavender. If she does, it is wrongful against the seller and it will only be an acceptance as long as the seller ratifies it. Whereas painting the chair before or without rejection automatically creates acceptance. However, the buyer should be careful because acceptance post rejection may not be without consequences. For example, if the buyer rejected because the goods were defective but then decided it would be less expensive to repair the goods and use them because the price of the goods had escalated, the buyer may owe the seller damages. Damages may occur if the seller already had made plans to resell them or if there was a change in the price.

2. REVOCATION

Once a buyer accepts goods she loses the ability to reject them. *See* **2–607(2)**. However, a buyer still has another opportunity to rightfully return defective goods to the seller through revocation of acceptance. Read **2–608**. The type of defect required for a revocation is more substantial than for rejection. Before a buyer may revoke, the defect must "substantially impair [the value of the good] to the buyer." The standard required for revocation contains both a subjective and an objective element. Whether a nonconformity impairs the value of the good to the buyer is judged from a subjective standpoint; however, the issue of whether the impairment is substantial is judged objectively using the reasonable person standard. Compare that to the perfect tender rule in **2–601**, where any breach allows a buyer to reject the goods.

After determining that the defect is substantial enough to move forward with revocation, the next step is to see if the buyer knew of the defect when the goods were accepted. If she did, **2–608(1)(a)** applies and if not **(1)(b)** applies. **(1)(a)** states that if the buyer knew about the defect and still accepted the goods, the acceptance must have been on the reasonable assumption that the seller would cure the defect. If the buyer was not aware of the defect when she accepted the goods because the defect was difficult to discover or the seller had made assurances about the good, then the buyer may revoke her acceptance under **(1)(b)**.

2–608 contains several other limitations on the buyer's right to revoke acceptance. The buyer needs to revoke acceptance within a reasonable time after she discovers or should have discovered the nonconformity and that revocation must happen before there is a substantial change in the goods not caused by the original defects. For example, if a car buyer notices problems with a steering mechanism and decides to drive the car back to the seller for analysis and repairs and on the way has a wreck, the cause of that wreck may impact the buyer's ability to revoke acceptance of the car. If the steering mechanism's defect caused the steering wheel to fail, then the substantial change caused by the accident may not affect the buyer's ability to revoke acceptance. However, if the buyer swerved to avoid hitting something in the road, the substantial change in the car will impact the buyer's ability to revoke her acceptance. Once a buyer revokes acceptance, the buyer has the same responsibilities as if she had rejected the goods. *See* **2–608(3)**.

Like with rejection, the buyer must hold the goods with reasonable care. However, a buyer who has paid part of the price, the entire price, or paid other expenses to care for the goods has a security interest in the goods as provided by **2–711(3)**. The advantage for a buyer of rejecting or revoking nonconforming goods is that it allows the buyer to return the goods to the seller and pursue whatever remedies may be available such as suing for cover (**2–712**) or for contract/market damages (**2–713**). A buyer who is unable to reject or revoke must retain the goods and pay for them. Although she still can sue the seller for damages for breach of warranty (**2–714**) or other contract breaches that may have occurred, the remedies are much more limited. These remedies will be covered in the next chapter.

C. PERFORMANCE IN INSTALLMENT CONTRACTS

Now that you understand the rules for how a buyer may reject or revoke nonconforming goods in a single delivery contract, we will consider the rules for installment contracts. Read **2–612**. An installment contract is one that requires or authorizes delivery in separate lots that are accepted separately, even if the agreement states that each delivery is a separate contract.

The standard for rejection in an installment contract is similar to the standard for revocation because it requires that the defect substantially impair the value of the installment before a buyer may reject that particular installment. Plus, this section adds the requirement that the seller needs to be given the opportunity to cure before a buyer can reject the installment. If the nonconformity substantially impairs the value and cannot be cured the buyer may reject that installment.

Even though a buyer rejects an installment, the seller still has the right to perform the remainder of the contract (the remaining installments) unless the buyer can show that the substantial impairment of the installment that cannot be cured also impairs the value of the entire contract as a whole. If that is the case, the buyer may cancel the entire contract. For example, imagine a computer store orders five computers to be delivered every month for four months. After the seller delivers the first installment of five computers the buyer notices that the keys on all of the computer boards are not working properly. When the buyer alerts the seller to the problem, the seller cannot cure because all of its keyboards are promised to other customers. The buyer had a contract to sell those computers to the government; but, due to the defective keyboards, the government cancels. In that situation, the buyer should argue that not only was the installment's value substantially impaired but the failure to cure in a timely fashion caused the government to cancel its contract and therefore the buyer can no longer use those specific computers. In that instance, the buyer should be able to argue that the seller breached the entire installment contract.

As you read the excerpts from the following case, ask yourself why neither party filed their claims under the CISG. Should they have done so? More important, ask whether the attorneys' lack of knowledge about the UCC hurt their clients. The judge cited their "total disregard" of the relevant portions of the UCC.

EXPORT DEVELOPMENT CANADA V. T. KEEFE AND SON, LLC

2016 WL 8488125 (Conn. Nov. 9, 2016)

WILSON, J.

* * *

IV

FINDINGS OF FACT

The court finds the following facts to have been proven by a fair preponderance of the evidence.

The plaintiff is a Federal Crown Corporation of the Government of Canada organized and doing business in Canada. The defendant is a limited liability company organized and existing under the laws of the state of Connecticut, with an office in Guilford, Connecticut. The defendant is an ironworks company which is in the business of the installation of steelwork, that involves anything in the ironworkers trade.

Metal Perreault is a Canadian corporation that has been in business since 1987 as a structural and miscellaneous steel fabricator. The defendant, who is an ironworks subcontractor, secured a contract with a general contractor, Perini Building Company (Perini), to supply and erect certain metal components at a garage structure being constructed by Perini at the Foxwoods Casino in Ledyard, Connecticut. In connection with the contract, the defendant sought bids from suppliers of structural and miscellaneous metals for the metal components to be supplied and erected at the project, including a bid from Metal Perreault. At the request of the defendant, Metal Perreault submitted its written bid quotation to the defendant on or about September 15, 2006, and the defendant accepted Metal Perreault's bid quotation in a written purchase order on or about October 12, 2006. Jason Keefe, owner and member of the defendant, was the project manager on the construction project.

Metal Perreault's quotation provided a detailed breakdown by category of metal goods to be supplied with prices allocated to each category. Each category of metal goods is referred to in the quotation as a "breakdown" and numbered 1 through 10 and 15. The total agreed-upon price for all breakdowns in the quotation was $377,000. The quotation provided that the metal goods would be made in conformity with the original architect's drawings for the project, which are referenced in the quotation by drawing numbers and dates, but are not attached to the quotation. The architect's drawings referred to in the quotation were drawings showing the intended construction of the concrete garage structure that did not reflect the actual measurements of the "as built" structure after it was erected. In order for Metal Perreault to fabricate the required metal goods, it had to know the actual dimensions of the "as built" concrete structure erected by others. According to Simon Harnois, vice president and project manager for Metal Perreault, concrete structures frequently vary from the original design drawings because of normal variations that occur in concrete construction. The actual as-built measurements are determined by taking "field measurements" at the project site. The quotation provided that it was the defendant's responsibility to take field measurements of the as-built structure and to provide those measurements to Metal Perreault, which Metal Perreault relied upon and used to fabricate the steel goods. The quotation also provided that Metal Perreault was responsible for preparing shop drawings. Shop drawings showed the details of the metal goods to be fabricated. Shop drawings had to be approved by Perini before Metal Perreault could begin fabrication. Shop drawing approvals were significantly delayed by Perini, thereby delaying Metal Perreault's ability to begin fabrication.

Neither the quotation submitted by Metal Perreault nor the defendant's written purchase order contain a delivery date or time, or a date or time for performance. The quotation order states that "delivery dates to be confirmed at time of order." The defendant's written purchase order accepting Metal Perreault's quotation, states: "Delivery date: To be determined."

At issue in this case is breakdown # 1 as listed in Metal Perreault's quotation, which is described in the quotation to include steel guardrails and hand rails for six concrete staircases in the garage structure, numbered 1 through 6. The guardrails and handrails for all six staircases were manufactured and delivered by Metal Perreault in eight separate deliveries between February 18, 2007, and May 24, 2007, as reflected in the itemized packing slips that were signed by the representative of the defendant, acknowledging receipt.

The only evidence of an agreed delivery date is a fax communication from Metal Perreault to the defendant dated February 14, 2007, confirming a voicemail left on Jason Keefe's cell phone regarding the February delivery, which states that: "Our carrier cannot leave today because of the snowstorm. We have to postpone the delivery [to] next Monday February

19th . . . at the site." Keefe did not check his voicemail. Keefe did not check the fax machine because he went directly to the job site and not to his office on the morning the delivery was expected, which was on or about February 15, 2007. Consequently, he did not receive notice that the scheduled delivery could not be made on February 15, 2007 and, therefore, he did not cancel the rental of a crane for which he claimed the defendant incurred expenses, nor did he instruct his employees to not come to the job site on February 15, 2007. The first shipment was delivered three days later on February 18, 2007, and included guardrails for stairs number 1 and 4. The defendant signed the packing slip dated February 18, 2007, indicating that the shipment was received. In fact, the defendant stipulated during trial that all product shipped by the plaintiff for which the plaintiff claims the defendant owes $189,500, was in fact received by the defendant.

After the first delivery of the goods, the defendant notified Metal Perreault that there was a problem with the metal parts fabricated for stair number 4. Metal Perreault received a photograph of stair number 4 from the defendant on or about the end of February 2007, depicting the problem. In response to the notification from the defendant, Metal Perreault initially looked at the shop drawings to determine if the drawings were done correctly. Metal Perreault determined that there were no problems with the drawings. Thinking that there might be a mis-fabrication, which Harnois testified is unusual, Metal Perreault refabricated a portion of the metal parts for stair number 4 as per the same drawing. They then shipped the refabricated metal parts for stair number 4 to the project site. The refabricated metal parts for stair number 4 however, again did not fit. As a result, Metal Perreault was notified again by the defendant that there was still a problem with the refabricated metal parts for stair number 4. T. Keefe did not notify Metal Perreault at this time that it was rejecting the goods.

In response, sometime in March 2007, Metal Perreault sent someone to the project site to look at the problem and to perform a field survey so they could conduct their own field measurements, although the taking of field measurements under the contract was the responsibility of the defendant. In addition, Metal Perreault looked at the rise and the run of the stairs and the location of the treads. They then put the results of the field survey into their detailing software. They then realized that there were some differences between what they surveyed and from what they built the original guardrails. Based on these field measurements, Metal Perreault refabricated the guardrails for stair number 4 which was then shipped to the defendant on or about April 6, 2007, which the defendant received on April 10, 2007.

After the delivery of the refabricated metal parts for stair number 4, there was still a problem, however, the defendant did not notify Metal Perreault that there was still a problem, nor did the defendant notify Metal

Perreault that it was rejecting the goods. Notwithstanding this continuing problem with the parts for stair number 4, the defendant field modified and installed some of the refabricated metal parts. The defendant at this point did not notify Metal Perreault that the goods were still not usable or that it was rejecting the goods, but rather accepted the parts and modified some of them for its use in constructing stair number 4, and discarded, or as Jason Keefe testified, "scrapped" the remaining parts.

Metal Perreault was also notified that there were problems in a portion of the metal parts shipped for stair number 1. Harnois could not recall when Metal Perreault was notified of the problems with the metal parts for stair number 1. Metal Perreault refabricated the metal parts for stair number 1 and redelivered them on or about May 14, 2007, and on or about May 25, 2007. Metal Perreault did not receive further notice regarding stair number 1 after redelivering the refabricated metal parts. Again, the defendant did not notify Metal Perreault that it was rejecting the goods.

Metal Perreault did not receive any notice about any defects in any materials it supplied for stairs 2, 3, 5 or 6 under breakdown # 1. Moreover, there is no credible evidence that the defendant rejected the metal parts for stairs 1, 2, 3, 4, 5, or 6 under breakdown # 1. The evidence demonstrates, as this court will discuss, that the defendant did not effectively reject the metal materials supplied to it by Metal Perreault, but instead accepted the materials.

According to Jason Keefe, the defendant was able to complete its installation of the metal goods supplied by Metal Perreault by making field modifications. Keefe's testimony in this regard is consistent with the letter he wrote to the general contractor, Perini in which Keefe sets forth the reasons for the stop work order between the defendant and Metal Perreault. The letter states in relevant part: "1. Predominant issue is poor craftsmanship of fabricated handrail materials for Parking Garage. Some sections of the handrail [materials] were fabricated three times and all three times failed to meet standards required for installation. Due to time constraints of the Parking Garage opening, T. Keefe and Son, LLC was forced to field modify well above and beyond normal circumstances. Due to this field modification on all stairs, T. Keefe and Son, LLC incurred large losses in time and money due to extra re-work. This required additional manpower and crane costs to dismantle the incorrect handrails and scrap the materials that were provided by Metal Perrault. If time was not an issue, T. Keefe and Son, LLC would have sent the incorrectly fabricated materials back for a third time and would have had Metal Perrault re-fabricate all materials . . ."

According to Jason Keefe, due to its contractual obligations to the general contractor to establish two means of ingress and egress to those using the parking garage for the construction at Mashantucket, the defendant faced liquidated damages of $5,000 per day for each day that the defendant went beyond its delivery deadline to the general contractor. Consequently, faced with no other alternative, the defendant was required to use the goods and therefore hired workers to cut apart the goods and field modify the goods. The defendant cancelled the contract with Metal Perreault and contracted with Logan Steel to fabricate the same metal goods so that it could complete its obligations under its contract with the general contractor. Although the defendant characterizes the goods as having been "rejected," the defendant failed to plead and prove, as this court will later discuss, that it rightfully rejected the goods by giving Metal Perreault proper notice in accordance with General Statutes § 42a–2–602 [UCC 2–602]. Instead, as just stated, the defendant accepted the goods and used some of the goods to complete the project to meet its obligations under the contract it had with Perini.

Moreover, as indicated in Jason Keefe's letter to Perini, time also became an issue. However, the timing of delivery of the metal goods became an important issue because of delays in obtaining approvals of shop drawings from Perini. Metal Perreault's bid quotation provides that it is the responsibility of the defendant to obtain approval of shop drawings within 14 days. The bid quotation states: "If shop drawings are under [Metal Perreault's] responsibility, approval time is 14 calendar days and RFI [requests for information] reply is 48 hours." Thus, according to Jason Keefe's letter to Perini, the defendant conceded that if time was not an issue, it would not have terminated the contract, but rather, would have provided Metal Perreault an opportunity to cure any defects.

In early June 2007, after the defendant had used some of the metal goods shipped to it by Metal Perreault and "scrapped" the remaining unused goods, the defendant terminated its contract with Metal Perreault and orally notified Metal Perreault to stop work on the contract. Metal Perreault made its last delivery which completed the fabrication and delivery of metal goods required under breakdown number 1 in the quotation at the end of May 2007.

Metal Perreault also fabricated and delivered structural steel to be used in roof framing, described in the quotation as "breakdown # 10." There is no evidence that the defendant complained about any of the structural steel included in breakdown # 10, for which the quotation set a line item price of $56,300.00. There is no evidence that the items in breakdown # 10 were defective in any manner or that the defendant rejected or did not use the materials.

Metal Perreault began to prepare drawings for breakdown # 6, # 11 and # 15, but did not complete the fabrication of those items due to the defendant's termination of the contract. Metal Perreault invoiced the defendant for the partial work on those drawings in the respective amounts of $3,400.00, $200.00 and $5,100.00. Prior to the termination of the contract, Metal Perreault invoiced the defendant for the work completed in the total amount of $189,500. The defendant has made no payments to Metal Perreault in connection with the contract. The court may find additional facts as necessary in deciding the merits.

V

DISCUSSION

"Before [the] court address[es] the merits of [the plaintiff's claims and the defendant's defenses, the court] must observe that this case has been presented with virtually total disregard of the relevant provisions of [this state's] statutes, in particular Article 2 of the Uniform Commercial Code, General Statutes § 42a–2–101 *et seq.*" *Bead Chain Mfg. Co. v. Saxton Products, Inc.,* 183 Conn. 266, 270, 439 A.2d 314 (1981). Such is evident in the pleadings of the parties, the presentation of evidence during trial and in the parties' post-trial briefs. The plaintiff's complaint alleges what appears to be a simple debt collection action with no reference whatsoever to the UCC, despite this being a commercial contract for the fabrication of miscellaneous and structural steel parts at a contract price of $377,000 which is well over $500. The plaintiff in its complaint simply alleges that between January 31, 2007, and May 28, 2007, the plaintiff's assignor, Metal Perreault sold and delivered goods to the defendant the value of which was $189,500 which the defendant failed to pay. The plaintiff also alleges that Metal Perreault assigned to the plaintiff a debt originally owed to Metal Perreault by the defendant which sum the defendant has failed, refused and neglected to pay.

Notwithstanding that the contract between Metal Perreault and the defendant was for the sale of goods well in excess of $500, which brings the contract within the scope of the UCC, and that the defendant claims it rejected the goods due to their nonconformity, the plaintiff fails to allege that Metal Perreault complied with all of the required provisions of the UCC in the tender and delivery of the goods, and that the defendant failed to comply with said provisions that are applicable to it as the buyer of the goods, which resulted in a breach of the contract. In addition, given that the UCC provides for various remedies available to the seller and buyer in the event of a breach by either, the plaintiff's complaint is devoid of any allegations of the statutory provisions that would cover remedies available to the assignor, Metal Perreault, under the contract, which as assignee of the contract, would be available to the plaintiff. With the exception of the use of the words "sold and delivered goods to defendant, the value of which was $189,500," and that the defendant failed to pay, the plaintiff makes no reference in its complaint to any of the relevant provisions of the UCC.

The defendant's answer is no better. The sole special defense, after its failed attempts to plead a claim under the UCC, is accord and satisfaction. Both parties, knowing full well that this was a substantial commercial contract with an international company, presented this case as if it were a simple common-law breach of contract claim. Except for the plaintiff's passing references to the UCC in its post-trial brief, by use of terms here and there extracted from various UCC provisions, and its vague citations to certain statutory provisions, and the defendant's passing reference to certain UCC terms in its post-trial brief, such as "rejection of goods," without any substantive legal analysis applied to the facts as adduced at trial, this court is left with resolving a relatively substantial commercial contract dispute that falls squarely within our commercial code, the application of which can be complex. This case is far from a simple debt collection action based on a simple common-law breach of contract.

[Notwithstanding the failure of the parties to properly plead under the UCC, the court will consider this case under the UCC default rules].

* * *

D

Nonconforming Goods

Buyer's Rights on Improper Delivery—§ 42a–2–601
[UCC 2–601]

Buyer's Right of Rejection—§ 42a–2–602
[UCC 2–602]

Seller's Right to Cure—§ 42a–2–508
[UCC 2–508]

General Statutes § 42a–2–508, which corresponds to § **2–508** of the Uniform Commercial Code provides: "(1) Where any tender or delivery by the seller is rejected because nonconforming and the time for performance has not yet expired, the seller may seasonably notify the buyer of his intention to cure and may then within the contract time make a conforming delivery. (2) Where the buyer rejects a nonconforming tender which the seller had reasonable grounds to believe would be acceptable with or without money allowance the seller may if he seasonably notifies the buyer have a further reasonable time to substitute a conforming tender."

When the seller has the right to make a curative tender and the buyer improperly refuses to accept the tender, the buyer is not entitled to damages for breach of contract or breach of warranty with respect to the goods tendered. Citations omitted.

However, '[t]he seller's right to cure, as provided in [§ **2–508**], is in terms limited to the situation where nonconforming goods have been *rejected* by the buyer.' *Bonebrake v. Cox,* 499 F.2d 951, 957 (8th Cir. 1974); (citations omitted). There is no right to cure after goods have been accepted. Citations omitted.

The defendant in its post-trial brief characterizes the metal goods shipped by Metal Perreault as having been rejected by it. The court disagrees. The defendant failed to plead any facts in its answer to establish that it had rightfully rejected the goods and gave Metal Perreault notice of the rejection pursuant to § 42a–2–602 [**2–602**]. Nor did the defendant prove that it had rightfully rejected the goods.

"The elements for a common law breach of contract action are the formation of an agreement, performance by one party, breach of the agreement by the other party and damages.' (Internal quotation marks omitted.) *Rosato v. Mascardo,* 82 Conn.App. 396, 411, 844 A.2d 893 (2004). Breach of contract actions involving the sale of goods, however, are governed by Article II of the UCC and require the parties to plead and prove additional facts. Under the UCC, [if the goods or the tender of delivery fail in any respect to conform to the contract], the buyer may '(a) reject the whole; or (b) accept the whole; or (c) accept the commercial unit or units and reject the rest.' General Statutes § 42a–2–601 [**2–601**]. Yet, '[r]ejection of goods must be within a reasonable time after the delivery or tender' and 'is ineffective unless the buyer seasonably notifies the seller.' General Statutes § 42a–2–602(1) [**2–602(2)(b)**]. Additionally, 'if the buyer has before rejection taken physical possession of goods in which he does not have a security interest . . . he is under a duty after rejection to hold them with reasonable care at the seller's disposition for a time sufficient to permit the seller to remove them.' General Statutes § 42a–2–602(2)(b) [**2–604**]. Additionally, 'if the seller gives no instructions within a reasonable time after notification of rejection, the buyer may store the rejected goods for the seller's account or re-ship them to him.' General Statutes § 42a–2–604."

T. Keefe's counterclaim in which it attempted to plead that it rejected the goods because the goods were nonconforming, was stricken by the court and T. Keefe did not replead or attempt to amend its answer prior to trial. Furthermore, the evidence does not support a finding that T. Keefe rightfully rejected the goods since it failed to seasonably notify Metal Perreault that it was rejecting the goods because it accepted the goods by field modifying and using the goods and discarding the remainder of the goods that it did not use. There is no evidence that T. Keefe had a security interest in the metal goods. Thus, since T. Keefe had physically taken possession of the metal goods, in addition to notifying Metal Perreault of rejection, it was "under a duty to hold the goods with reasonable care at Metal Perreault's disposition for a time to permit Metal Perreault to remove the goods." General Statutes § 42a–2–602(b) [**2–602(2)(b)**]. Instead, T. Keefe accepted the goods, used some of the goods and scrapped the remainder of the goods it did not use.

With respect to the procedural requirements for rejection of nonconforming goods, White, Summers and Hillman state: "[The] Code imposes two procedural requirements for rejections. Under **2–602** [which is the same as § 42a–2–602], a rejection must be 'within a reasonable time' after delivery or tender of the goods, and it is 'ineffective unless the buyer seasonably notifies the seller . . .' Although the Code does not require written notice, buyers who have depended on non-written notice, or on equivocal notice, have not fared well in the courts. [White Summers and Hillman] counsel that notice be written, unequivocal, and sufficiently detailed." 1 J. White et al., *supra* 9:11, 791, 792.

* * *

Here, not only did T. Keefe fail to plead the requisite facts to demonstrate that it rejected the goods, it also failed to prove that it rejected the goods in accordance with § 42a–2–601(1) [**2–601(1)**]. The evidence elicited at trial demonstrates that although T. Keefe complained of defects contained in the metal parts for stairs 1 and 4, it never notified Metal Perreault either in writing or orally that it was rejecting the goods. Although T. Keefe allowed Metal Perreault to refabricate the metal parts for stairs 1 and 4, it failed to effectively reject the parts. T. Keefe used some of the metal parts and discarded the remainder. Likewise, with respect to stairs 2, 3, 5 and 6, and the structural steel for breakdown number 10, T. Keefe neither complained about the metal parts nor rejected them.

The evidence demonstrates that T. Keefe accepted the goods, and thus, once T. Keefe accepted the goods, it did not effectively reject them. Therefore, once T. Keefe accepted the goods, there was no right to cure. Moreover, "[a]lthough rejection is not comprehensively defined in the Uniform Commercial Code; *Ramirez v. Autosport*, 88 N.J. 277, 288, 440 A.2d 1345 (1982); it is inconsistent with acceptance. See *Dunleavy v. Paris Ceramics, U.S.A., Inc., supra*, 47 Conn.Sup. 572. Here, the evidence clearly demonstrates that T. Keefe failed to rightfully reject the goods, and therefore it accepted them.

E

Acceptance of Goods—§ 42a–2–606 [**UCC 2–606**] and § 42a–2–607 [**UCC 2–607**]

"Acceptance of goods occurs when the buyer (a) after a reasonable opportunity to inspect the goods signifies to the seller that the goods are conforming or that he will take or retain them in spite of their nonconformity; or (b) fails to make an effective rejection as provided by subsection (1) of section 42a–2–602, but such acceptance does not occur until the buyer has had a reasonable opportunity to inspect them; or (c) does any act inconsistent with the seller's ownership; but if such act is wrongful as against the seller it is an acceptance only if ratified by him." General Statutes § 42a–2–606. "Acceptance of goods by the buyer precludes rejection of the goods accepted . . ." General Statutes § 42a–2–607(2) [**2–607(2)**].

Here, T. Keefe accepted the goods. T. Keefe notified Metal Perreault of the problems it had with the metal parts for stairs 1 and 4, and allowed

Metal Perreault to refabricate the parts. T. Keefe, however, never effectively rejected the goods by providing Metal Perreault with notice of rejection. With respect to the metal parts for stairs 2, 3, 5, and 6, and the structural steel for the roof framing, T. Keefe neither complained to Metal Perreault about problems it was experiencing with these parts, nor notified Metal Perreault that it was rejecting the parts. In early June 2007, after T. Keefe had accepted the goods and used them, did it notify Metal Perreault that it was canceling the contract.

T. Keefe accepted the goods, did not notify Metal Perreault that it was rejecting them, and used some of the goods to fit the stairs. Although use of tendered goods for a short time is not necessarily acceptance; here, the totality of circumstances clearly evidences acceptance. See *Quiet Automatic Burner Corp. v. Wetstone,* 143 Conn. 276, 279, 121 A.2d 635 (1956) (buyer's conduct, after delivery of goods, in ordering carrier to deliver goods to third party was inconsistent with seller's ownership and justified finding of acceptance to buyer); *Urbansky v. Kutinsky,* 86 Conn. 22, 27, 84 A. 317 (1912). T. Keefe's failure to notify Metal Perreault that it was rejecting the goods, as well as its use of the goods was inconsistent with Metal Perreault's ownership, and is evidence of acceptance. Accordingly, this court finds that T. Keefe accepted the goods.

F

Revocation of Acceptance—§ 42a–2–608 [UCC 2–608]

This court must again point out that the defendant did not plead revocation in its answer. As previously noted, the court (Woods, J.) struck the defendant's counterclaim which attempted to allege various claims under the UCC. The defendant failed to replead, and further, did not seek an amendment of its answer prior to trial. "Under the code, a buyer's revocation of acceptance is a distinct cause of action, not to be confused with rescission by mutual consent; . . . nor is it an alternative remedy for breach of warranty . . ." *Conte v. Dwan Lincoln-Mercury, Inc.,* 172 Conn. 112, 119, 374 A.2d 14 (1976). Here, the defendant failed to plead a cause of action for revocation of acceptance under § 42a–2–608. However, even if the defendant had pled a cause of action under § 42a–2–608, the claim would fail since there is no evidence that T. Keefe revoked its acceptance of the goods.

[The Court's reprinting of **2–608** omitted.] "Whether goods are substantially impaired by nonconformity and whether revocation of acceptance is given within a reasonable time are questions of fact subject to the [trier of fact's] determination . . ." (Citations omitted.) *Conte v. Dwan Lincoln-Mercury, Inc. supra,* 172 Conn. 121.

(i)

Substantial Impairment—§ 42a–2–608(1) [**UCC 2–608(1)**]

The court must first determine substantial impairment as a factual matter. "The test for substantial impairment is both subjective and objective: it focuses first, on the needs and circumstances of the particular buyer seeking to revoke, and then considers whether, from an objective standpoint, the value of the goods to the buyer has in fact been impaired." *Web Press Services, Corp. v. New London Motors, Inc.,* 203 Conn. 342, 346–47, 525 A.2d 57 (1987). "Each case must be examined on its own merits to determine what is a 'substantial impairment of value' to the particular buyer." *Conte v. Dwan Lincoln-Mercury, Inc., supra,* 172 Conn. 121. "The subjective component of the test takes into consideration the particular buyer's needs and expectations. The objective element focuses on the actual defects, which must not be trivial or insubstantial." *Kesner v. Lancaster,* 180 W.Va. 607, 612, 378 S.E.2d 649 (1989).

First, with respect to the metal parts for stairs 2, 3, 5 and 6, and the structural parts for the roof framing in breakdown number 10, there is simply not enough evidence from which the court can conclude that there was any nonconformity in the goods that substantially impaired the value of the entire shipment of goods to T. Keefe. There is no evidence to show that, after these parts were delivered, T. Keefe notified Metal Perreault of any defects or problems. The evidence demonstrates that after the parts were delivered, T. Keefe accepted the parts and used them. T. Keefe failed to demonstrate that there was any nonconformity in the metal goods for stairs 2, 3, 5, and 6 or in the structural metal for the roof framing in breakdown number 10, upon which it could base a revocation of acceptance of those goods. Furthermore, T. Keefe did not return the goods to Metal Perreault, but rather accepted the goods and used them which is inconsistent with Metal Perreault's ownership, and which undermines any claim that the value of the goods to T. Keefe was substantially impaired.

With respect to the metal parts for stairs 1 and 4, when the parts were initially delivered, T. Keefe notified Metal Perreault of problems with the parts. Metal Perreault refabricated the parts and redelivered the refabricated parts to T. Keefe. T. Keefe accepted the refabricated parts, used them and did not notify Metal Perreault of any further problems. The court cannot conclude from this evidence that the metal parts for stairs 1 and 4 substantially impaired the value of the goods shipped to T. Keefe because after Metal Perreault refabricated the parts, T. Keefe accepted the goods, used them, did not return them, and did not notify Metal Perreault of any further problems.

T. Keefe did not substantiate any measurable losses it sustained as a result of any nonconformity. Although T. Keefe submitted a spread sheet containing expenses it claims it incurred as a result of the claimed defective metal parts, as this court will discuss in its discussion of damages, T. Keefe did not present any evidence of payment of the outstanding amounts. Additionally, T. Keefe's invoices submitted as proof of expenses it claims it incurred for replacing defective steel were overstated by $104,185.79 which puts into doubt the credibility of all of the losses it claims it incurred as a result of the claimed defective parts. Thus, the court cannot conclude on the evidence before it, that there was any nonconformity that substantially impaired the value of the metal parts for stairs 1, 2, 3, 4, 5 and 6 and the structural steel for the roof framing for breakdown number 10 to T. Keefe.

Even if T. Keefe had proven that there was a nonconformity that substantially impaired the value of the goods to it, there is no evidence that the goods were accepted on the reasonable assumption that Metal Perreault would cure the nonconformity and that the nonconformity was not seasonably cured. With respect to the metal parts for stairs 2, 3, 5, and 6 and the structural metal for the roof framing, the only evidence before this court is that T. Keefe accepted the goods and failed to notify Metal Perreault of any problems with those parts.

With respect to stairs 1 and 4, Metal Perreault refabricated the parts, after which T. Keefe accepted and used the parts and did not notify Metal Perreault of any further problems. Thus, there is no evidence that after Metal Perreault refabricated the metal parts for stairs 1 and 4, that T. Keefe accepted the refabricated parts under the reasonable assumption that Metal Perreault would further cure. In addition, T. Keefe was aware of the problems it was having with the metal parts for stairs 1 and 4, and there is no evidence that its acceptance of those metal parts after it discovered the problems, was induced by any assurances made by Metal Perreault to further cure and that Metal Perreault failed to do so. General Statutes § 42a–2–608(1)(b). Indeed, the evidence demonstrates that T. Keefe accepted the goods and used them because it was under a time constraint to complete its obligations under the contract it had with Perini. In its letter to Perini explaining the reasons for the stop work order with Metal Perreault, T. Keefe concedes that it did not notify Metal Perreault of further problems. The letter states: "[s]ome sections of the handrail were fabricated three times and all three times fail to meet standards required for installation . . . If time was not an issue, T. Keefe and Son, LLC would have sent the incorrectly fabricated materials back for a third time and would have had Metal Perreault refabricate all materials." Clearly T. Keefe did not accept the nonconforming goods under the reasonable assumption that Metal Perreault would further cure, or based upon any assurances made by Metal Perreault that it would further cure. T. Keefe accepted and used the goods without notifying Metal Perreault of further problems because "time was an issue." *Id.*

(ii)

Notice—§ 42a–2–608(2) [UCC 2–608(2)]

Even if T. Keefe had pled or proven "substantial impairment," it still failed to give Metal Perreault any notice of revocation of acceptance of the goods. "Not only must there be a substantial impairment of value to the buyer, but the revocation must take place 'within a reasonable time after the buyer discovers or should have discovered' the defect. 'What is a reasonable time for taking any action [under the code] depends on the nature, purpose and circumstances of such action.' [§]42a–1–204(2)." *Conte v. Dwan Lincoln-Mercury, Inc., supra*, 172 Conn. 122.

Section 42a–2–608(2) provides that a buyer's revocation of acceptance "is not effective until the buyer notifies the seller of it." "Comment 5 to this subsection states '5. The content of the notice under subsection (2) is to be determined in this case as in others by consideration of good faith, prevention of surprise, and reasonable adjustment.' At § 8–4, page 572 of Volume 1, Uniform Commercial Code, 5th ed. White and Summers cite cases to the effect that: 'One line of cases between merchants holds that the essential content of the notice of revocation must set forth "the nonconformity in the goods materially impairing their value to the buyer." The notice must inform the seller that the buyer *does not wish to keep the goods*. If the buyer equivocates in word or in deed, his purported revocation may be invalid. While the buyer's notice of revocation needs to be unequivocal, it need not be formal.' See *HCI Chemicals, Inc. v. Henkel,* 966 F.2d 1018, 1023 (C.A.5, 1992); *Agarian Grain Co., Inc. v. Meeker,* 526 N.E.2d 1189, 1191 (2nd App.) (actual knowledge by seller buyer is dissatisfied with goods does not unequivocally equate with revocation even where buyer stops payment). Another case cited in White and Summers says '. . . notice of breach of revocation of acceptance. While the latter need not be in any particular form, *it must inform the seller that the buyer does not wish to keep the goods.' Allis-Chalmers Corp. v. Sygitowicz,* 18 Wash.App. 658, 571 P.2d 224, 226 (Ct. of App. Wash., 1977)." (Citations omitted.)

It is clear that as early as February 2007, T. Keefe upon receiving the goods for stairs 1 and 4, and after reasonable inspection, discovered a problem and notified Metal Perreault. T. Keefe was aware of the problems, allowed Metal Perreault to refabricate the parts, however, even after its dissatisfaction with Metal Perreault's refabrication, T. Keefe still accepted the goods, used some of them and "scrapped" the remainder. After accepting the refabricated parts, T. Keefe never notified Metal Perreault that it was revoking its acceptance of the parts. With respect to stairs 2, 3, 5, 6 and breakdown number 10, there is no credible evidence of any complaints T. Keefe made to Metal Perreault about these parts. T. Keefe, therefore, accepted the parts and did not, after acceptance, notify Metal Perreault of any problems with the goods relating to stairs 2, 3, 5, 6 and breakdown number 10 or that it was revoking its acceptance of the goods. T. Keefe failed to notify Metal Perreault that it wished to return the goods and revoke its acceptance.

Moreover, neither does T. Keefe's June 2007 cancellation of the contract constitute reasonable notice of revocation of its acceptance of the goods. T. Keefe was well aware of the problems with the metal parts for stairs 1 and 4 in February 2007, three months prior to its cancellation, yet it neither effectively rejected the parts nor notified Metal Perreault, after the refabrication of stairs 1 and 4, that it was rejecting the goods. T. Keefe used the goods and discarded the rest. Because T. Keefe had knowledge of the problems with the steel parts as early as February 2007, its notice of cancellation to Metal Perreault in June 2007 was not seasonable and thus, it failed to revoke its acceptance of the goods.

Finally, T. Keefe's right to revoke acceptance of the goods expired when it modified and then discarded the goods. "[T]he buyer's right to revoke acceptance *automatically* expires under [§ 42a–]2–608(2) [**2–608(2)**] if the goods undergo a substantial change in condition 'which is not caused by their own defects.' According to Comment 6, a buyer should not be allowed to revoke acceptance of goods that have 'materially deteriorated in the buyer's hands except when the deterioration is attributable to original 'defects' in the goods. Examples of such 'deterioration' not attributable to original defects are buyer's cutting of a fabric, *buyer's use of the goods after modifying them,* buyer's cutting of goods into narrow strips in accord with specifications of sub-purchaser, and buyer's knitting defective yarn." (Emphasis added) 1 J. White et al., *supra,* § 9:18, pp. 816–17 (2012). Here, the evidence shows that the goods had materially deteriorated in T. Keefe's hands since they field modified the parts by cutting them to fit, and they discarded the goods that they did not use.

T. Keefe failed to notify Metal Perreault that it wished to return the goods and that it was revoking its acceptance. Accordingly, even if T. Keefe had properly pled a cause of action for revocation of acceptance pursuant to General Statutes § 42a–2–608 [**2–608**], it failed to prove that it revoked acceptance of goods it claimed were nonconforming.

* * *

_____

D. SELLER'S RIGHT TO CURE

The last issue that may arise is cure and the impact of **2–508** on a buyer's ability to return goods to the seller after either a rejection or revocation. Additionally, **2–612** gives the seller a right to cure a nonconforming installment, so cure impacts rejection in all contracts governed by Article 2. First, read **2–508** and see if you can find a reference to revocation. Both subsections **(1)** and **(2)** refer to a buyer's rejection. The first subsection applies when a seller delivers nonconforming goods before time for performance is due. In that situation, the seller may remedy a defective tender and cure by delivering conforming goods by the date of performance.

Subsection **(2)** is a little more problematic because it only allows a seller to cure a rejected nonconforming tender "which the seller had reasonable grounds to believe would be acceptable." Also, the right to cure needs to be read in conjunction with **2–605**, the section that requires the buyer to state objections with particularity when she rejects a good. As noted earlier, a failure to list defects or nonconformities with particularity may cause the buyer to lose the right to rely on an unstated defect later. Compliance with **2–605** puts the seller on notice of what defects need to be cured. After the seller learns of the defects, the seller only has the right to cure the nonconformity if she had reasonable grounds to believe the goods were acceptable in the first place.

Sellers may prove that they believed the goods would be acceptable by showing that they had a reasonable quality assurance process in place and were not in the business of selling defective goods. Another way a seller may show reasonable grounds is when the seller knew about the nonconformity but still believed the goods would be acceptable. For example, Alex orders a new pair of contact lenses from Contacts International (CI) for $200. CI only has lenses that sell for $250 available, so a representative sends Alex the better quality lens but only charges $200. It would be reasonable to think that a customer would be happy to receive a better product for a lesser price. If, however, Alex is unable to wear those lenses due to an anomaly with her right eye, she may reject them as nonconforming. When that happens, CI should be able to cure under **2–508(2)** because it believed that the better lens would work just as well for the buyer.

Let us revisit the revocation question posed earlier: does a buyer who properly revokes a nonconforming tender have to accept a cure tendered by the seller? You should have noticed that **2–508** contains no reference to revocation. Consequently, some courts have held that a revoked seller does not have the same right to cure as a rejected seller. Yet, a few other courts have held that a revoked seller may cure a nonconforming tender even though **2–508** does not specifically refer to revocation. You should always check to determine how the courts in your jurisdiction handle this issue.

1. SHAKEN FAITH DOCTRINE

One last issue may arise when a seller wants to cure a nonconforming tender and a buyer does not want to allow the seller to do so. Even if the seller is able to cure, there may be situations when she will not be allowed to cure due to the buyer's shaken faith in the seller's ability to provide safe and/or conforming goods. This may have to do with the buyer's concern relating to the safety of the goods or it may be that the seller has already tried to fix the defects numerous times and the buyer eventually lost confidence in the seller's ability to cure.

In *Hemmert Agricultural Aviation Inc. v. Mid-Continent Aircraft Corp.*, 663 F.Supp. 1546, 1552 (Kan. 1987) the court addressed the issue of "shaken faith," in terms of cure and when analyzing whether a substantial impairment existed that justified a revocation.

> In considering the subjective element [in **2–608**], the courts have employed a term, "shaken faith." In determining whether value was substantially impaired, the courts have weighed the cost of repairs, the inconvenience resulting from the nonconformities, and the entire impact the defects had on the buyer's confidence in the goods purchased. Lost confidence has been adopted by a number of courts and labelled as the "shaken faith" doctrine. Where the buyer's confidence in the dependability of the machine is shaken because of the defects and possibly because of seller's ineffective attempts to cure, revocation appears justified.

> Kansas appellate courts have not specifically addressed whether a buyer's lost confidence is a relevant factor for determining substantial impairment. In summarizing the recurring defects with the pickup in *Johnson v. General Motors Corp.*, 233 Kan. at 1045, 688 P.2d 139, the Kansas Supreme Court concluded: "(r)epairs were attempted under GMC's warranty agreement but the Johnsons had lost confidence in the truck." While only dicta, this is an indication that Kansas courts would recognize this doctrine to be an appropriate factor within the subjective element of substantial impairment and a necessary companion in concept to the seller's right to cure. This court considers the buyer's lost confidence in a product to be a relevant consideration in determining a substantial impairment in value.

In the next case, *Rester v. Morrow*, the court considered a situation where a car buyer had brought his car back to the seller on numerous occasions to fix many problems with the car. The Supreme Court of Mississippi analyzed whether the buyer had grounds for revocation of acceptance and, if so, whether the seller had a right to cure. In *Rester* the court was not troubled by the lack of revocation terminology in **2–508**.

RESTER V. MORROW
491 So.2d 204 (Miss. 1986)

ROBERTSON.

* * *

Norman L. Rester purchased a 1981 Renault on April 13, 1981, and encountered repeated difficulties through and including September 15, 1981, at which time he abandoned the vehicle back to its seller. The ultimate issue is whether the automobile failed to conform to the seller's contractual and legal obligations incident to the sale and whether such nonconformity substantially impaired the value of the automobile to Rester. Miss.Code Ann. § 75–2–608(1) [**2–608(1)**] (1972). The resolution of such a question of ultimate fact may be taken from the jury only in conformity with our familiar rule emanating from *Paymaster Oil Mill Co. v. Mitchell,* 319 So.2d 652, 657 (Miss.1975) and progeny. Because the evidence on the substantial impairment issue is quite disputed, the trial judge committed error when he sustained the seller's motion for directed verdict.

Without question, Rester had accepted the automobile, not necessarily on April 13, 1981, but when he failed to make an effective rejection after having had a reasonable opportunity to inspect it. Rester's acceptance was reasonably induced by the difficulty of discovery of defects before acceptance and by the seller's assurances.

Rester then attempted to revoke his acceptance. This revocation occurred when he returned the automobile to the seller on September 15, 1981. The ultimate question, as indicated above, becomes whether on the facts of this case he was entitled to revoke. The outcome determinative question on this appeal is, in the present state of the record, to what decision making authority—the trial judge or the jury—has our law committed the making of the factual determinations whether the Renault "non-conformed" and whether that non-conformity substantially impaired its value to Rester.

IV.

There are two fundamental errors in the trial judge's approach to this case, the first having to do with the UCC conception of substantial impairment and the second, as indicated, having to do with when that issue may be taken from the jury. First, the trial judge seems to have considered that the only bases for rejection are the specific complaints of Rester the day he returned the automobile to his seller. On that occasion Rester pointed out a soiled carpet, an unrepaired fuse panel and an unreplaced piece of chrome. Unquestionably, these are minor defects.

Rester's entitlement to revocation, however, turns upon whether, under the totality of the circumstances—temporally and structurally—the automobile failed to be what the seller was by private and public law obligated to provide Rester and whether that aggregate nonconformity substantially impaired the value of the automobile to Rester. Put another way—and having in mind the testimony in this case, the seller has a right to attempt cure. *Cf.* Miss. Code Ann. § 75–2–508 [**2–508**] (1972). But our law does not allow a seller to postpone revocation in perpetuity by fixing everything that goes wrong with the automobile. There comes a time when enough is enough—when an automobile purchaser, after having to take his car into the shop for repairs an inordinate number of times and experiencing all of the attendant inconvenience, is entitled to say, "That's all," and revoke, notwithstanding the seller's repeated good faith efforts to fix the car. (Citations omitted.)

The Florida case of *Orange Motors of Coral Gables v. Dade County Dairies,* 258 So.2d 319 (Fla.App.1972) made the point this way:

> The buyer of an automobile is not bound to permit the seller to tinker with the article, indefinitely in the hope it may ultimately be made to comply with the warranty. . . [citations omitted] At some point in time, if major problems continue to plague the automobile, it must become obvious to all people that a particular vehicle simply cannot be repaired or parts replaced so that the same is made free of defect.

258 So.2d at 321.

In this setting it is appropriate to reiterate the aggregate of problems Rester encountered with the automobile:

(1)   the presence of the odor of gas fumes;

(2)   the problems with the air conditioner which at times bordered on the bizarre;

(3)   the stalling problem;

(4)   the problems with the battery;

(5)   the problems with the oil indicator gauge;

(6)   the problems with the fuse panel;

(7)   the problems with the ratchet adjustment on the passenger seat;

(8)   the problem of the soiled carpet due to water leaking on it;

(9)   the missing piece of chrome.

These problems required repeated servicing.

The trial judge—and the seller on this appeal—concentrate only upon the straw said to have broken the camel's back. In our view, the whole camel—including its performance over the five month period Rester's use of the Renault—is relevant to the question of whether Rester had the right to revoke.

For a majority of people the purchase of a new car is a major investment, rationalized in part by the peace of mind that flows from its dependability and safety. Once the purchaser's faith is shaken, the vehicle loses not only its real value in his eyes, but becomes an instrument whose integrity is substantially impaired and whose operation is fraught with apprehension. The attempted cure in the present case was ineffective.

Our law tells a buyer such as Rester that he may revoke only if there is substantial impairment of the value of the car "to him." Substantial impairment is determined by reference to the particular needs of the buyer, even though the seller may have no advance knowledge of those needs and even though those needs may change after acceptance of the automobile.

While the statute imports a subjective standard of nonconformity and impairment, we regard that it nevertheless contains an important objective component. The "to him" language in the statute requires that courts proceed by reference to the unique circumstances of the buyer. Once those circumstances have been determined, we proceed to an objective determination of whether the nonconformity would substantially impair the value of the automobile to a reasonable person in the circumstances of the buyer.

Rester's circumstances are set forth adequately above. They involve considerable regular travel. Those circumstances suggest an unequivocal need for a properly functioning automobile. When one pays for a car what Rester paid for the Renault, he is entitled to frills as well as essentials that are relatively trouble free.

* * *

E. RISK OF LOSS

Before performance begins or even while a party is performing a contract, some loss or damage to the goods may occur, so it is necessary to determine who is responsible when a loss occurs. Typically, sellers will either ship goods via carrier or the buyer will pick up the goods from the seller or seller's representative. The rules on who is responsible for any loss are different for each of those situations.

First, if the loss is caused by the neglect or an intentional act of the buyer or seller, that party will be responsible. Otherwise, Article 2 contains default terms to determine who is responsible for the loss, although this usually means the responsible party will have to pursue the carrier or their insurance company. Before you can determine which party bears the risk of loss, make sure you ask whether either party is in breach of the contract because breach changes the rules.

If there is no breach, **2–509** contains the rules for determining which party will carry the risk of loss. If there is a breach, then **2–510** will govern risk of loss issues. If the loss happens while the goods are in transit, a buyer may need to review the shipper's records to determine whether the seller breached the contract. For example, if the seller was supposed to ship 12 black refrigerators but the documents show there were only 10 or that 10 were silver and two were black, the buyer can determine that the seller is breached and then turn to **2–510** to see where the risk of loss lies. Additionally, the risk of loss rules intertwine with performance because they often require a determination of whether there has been a rejection, acceptance, or revocation.

When a contract requires shipment by a carrier there are typically three parties involved in the transaction that include the buyer, seller, and carrier. You have undoubtedly seen many semi-trucks driving back and forth using the interstate system and other highways to deliver goods across America. Some companies such as Wal-Mart are large enough that they have their own dedicated carriers that deliver and pick up goods. Other buyers and sellers hire carrier companies to deliver goods for them. When parties hire carriers to deliver goods they will typically choose a shipment term to specify who is responsible for certain payments and risks while the goods are in transit. If the parties fail to include a shipment term or designate a place for delivery in the agreement, the default rules provide that the place of delivery is the seller's place of business. *See* **2–308**. As such, before we can discuss loss, it is necessary to understand the meaning of several shipment terms frequently used.

1. SHIPMENT TERMS

You should be familiar with two common shipment terms that use the abbreviation "F.O.B." F.O.B. literally means free on board. F.O.B. will usually be accompanied by a named place, such as F.O.B. seller's warehouse or F.O.B. buyer's warehouse. These terms will help you understand who must pay for the shipment, the place of tender for the goods, and who has the risk of loss if the goods are lost, damaged, or destroyed during performance of a contract. Read **2–319(1)**. This section distinguishes between a shipment contract and a destination contract. A seller's duty in a shipment contract generally occurs when the seller delivers the goods to the carrier and completes that part of performance at the seller's place of business or city. Alternatively, a destination contract requires a seller to deliver the goods at a place designated by the buyer. For example, if a contract provides for shipment of the goods F.O.B. Seller's warehouse, Seattle, Washington this is a shipment contract. If, instead, the term is F.O.B. Buyer's warehouse, Dallas, Texas the shipment is a destination contract.

A shipment contract must comply with **2–504**. It requires a seller to deliver conforming goods to the carrier and pay any expense to transport the goods to the carrier. Additionally, it requires the seller to make a reasonable contract for shipping taking into account the nature of the goods, to tender any documents required for the buyer to take possession of the goods, and to promptly notify the buyer of shipment. Despite these requirements, a failure to notify the buyer of the shipment or to make a proper contract is not a proper ground for rightful rejection by the buyer unless the buyer is damaged due to a loss or material delay. If the contract does not specify whether it is a shipment or destination contract, the default rules designate it as a shipment contract. *See* **2–308**.

Instead of a shipment contract, the parties may agree on a destination contract. A destination contract requires goods to be delivered to a particular destination. The destination may be the buyer's place of business or it may be a different location chosen by a buyer. This type of contract carries more risk and expense for a seller because it requires the seller to be responsible for paying for the shipment, including any insurance, and the seller is responsible for any potential loss to the goods until they are delivered to the required destination.

2. RISK OF LOSS WHEN THERE IS NO BREACH

Without a breach, **2–509** controls who is responsible for any loss or damage to the goods. The first subsection, **(1)**, only applies when the contract calls for delivery by carrier. If there is no carrier involved, you need to check to see if a bailee is being used, **(2)**, and, if not, then who has to deal with the loss will depend on whether the seller is a merchant, **(3)**. Of course, the parties are free to change these rules in their contract if they wish and **2–509(4)** expressly gives the parties that control.

If the contract calls for shipment by carrier, then the first step is to see whether the goods were being shipped using a shipment contract (F.O.B. seller's place) or a destination contract (F.O.B. buyer's place or buyer's chosen destination). Remember if the contract omits the delivery term, the default rule in **2–308** is for a shipment contract. In a shipment contract the risk of loss shifts to the buyer when the goods are "duly delivered to the carrier." *See* **2–509(1)(a)**. Comment 2 states that the term "Duly Delivered" requires the seller to comply with **2–504**, the section titled "Shipment by Seller." As long as the seller delivers the goods to the carrier, makes a reasonable contract for their shipment, delivers or tenders the necessary documents, and promptly notifies the buyer, the risk will move to the buyer and any loss or damage after that is borne by the buyer. If, however, it is a destination contract, the risk of loss will not pass to the buyer until the seller tenders the goods at the designated destination for the buyer to take delivery. In that case, the seller will be responsible for paying to ship the goods, obtaining insurance, and any loss or damage that occurs while in transit.

If there is no shipment by a carrier or a bailee holding the goods, then the next issue is whether the seller is a merchant (**2–104**). If the seller is a merchant, **2–509(3)** requires that the buyer receive the goods before risk of loss will pass. If there is no merchant involved, then the risk of loss will not pass until the seller tenders the goods to the buyer. Consider the definitions of receipt and tender. **2–103(1)(c)** defines receipt as taking actual physical possession of the goods whereas **2–503** provides that tender requires the seller to "put and hold conforming goods at the buyer's disposition" and to give the buyer any notice the buyer needs. Make sure not to confuse the two definitions. The contract should specify the time, place, and manner of the tender. If the contract does not cover this, then it will be a reasonable time, place, and manner. Of course, as mentioned previously, the parties may change these rules by contract if they wish.

3.   RISK OF LOSS WHEN THERE IS A BREACH

If the seller or buyer breaches the contract, **2–510** changes the risk of loss rules. Subsections **(1)** and **(2)** apply to situations where the seller breached and **(3)** applies in the event of a buyer's breach. After determining there is a breach by the seller, the next step is to consider the buyer's response. This requires an understanding of when and how a buyer may reject goods, when an acceptance occurs, and whether there has been a rightful revocation. After a seller's breach there needs to be a determination of whether the buyer has a right of rejection under **2–601** or, with regard to an installment contract, **2–612**; if the breach has been cured under **2–508**; or if the goods have been accepted under **2–606**. If there has been no cure or acceptance and the breach gives the buyer the power to reject, the risk of loss stays with the seller. If an acceptance occurred, then you need to determine whether the buyer rightfully revoked acceptance (**2–608**).

The rules change if the buyer accepts the goods but then rightfully revokes that acceptance. *See* **2–608**. In that case, the risk of loss depends on the buyer's insurance coverage. This tends to keep the risk of loss with the party in possession of the goods because that party is most likely to carry insurance on the goods. After a buyer rightfully revokes acceptance the buyer's insurance usually picks up the loss, except that the seller is responsible for any deficiency in the buyer's insurance coverage for the lost or damaged goods.

When a buyer breaches after the goods have been identified to the contract, but before risk of loss has passed to the buyer, the seller usually still has possession of the goods. Consequently, subsection **(3)** states that the risk of loss shifts to the buyer only to the extent of any deficiency in the seller's insurance and only for a commercially reasonable time.

As you read the following case, note the importance of the FOB term and how the defendant, Gibbs International, attempts to interpret the term through course of performance, course of dealing, and trade usage. Also, pay attention to the other cases described in detail in the following opinion. They should help your understanding of how to use FOB terms and their importance when determining risk of loss.

SOUTHERN RECYCLING, LLC v. GIBBS INTERNATIONAL, INC.

2016 WL 1258402 (D.S.C. Mar. 31 2016)

Opinion and Order

HENDRICKS, B. H.

This matter is before the Court on Plaintiffs' motion for partial summary judgment and Plaintiffs' motion to exclude Defendant's additional evidence. For the reasons set forth in this Order, Plaintiffs' motion to exclude is denied and Plaintiffs' motion for partial summary judgment is granted.

BACKGROUND

This diversity action stems from an alleged breach of contract. On November 6, 2012, Plaintiff Southern Recycling, LLC ("Plaintiff Southern" or "Southern") contracted with Defendant Gibbs International, Inc. ("Defendant" or "Gibbs") to purchase 500,000 pounds of scrap copper wire. The purchase contract contained a delivery term stating:

> F.O.B., loaded in bulk into Buyer's 20′ sea container at Port of Manila, Philippines. Shipments and delivery to be completed no later than November 30, 2012. Seller [sic] buyer and seller will mutually agree upon dates, location, and loading times for containers. Buyer will have a representative at each loading and will sign each trucker's bill of ladings [sic], along with Sellers [sic] representative.

The payment term of the purchase contract stated:

> Payment to be made via wire transfer to Seller's designated banking account the following business day upon Buyer's inspection and acceptance of goods, and Seller's delivery as described above. Incremental payments will be made on each shipment.

Gibbs purchased the scrap copper wire it sold to Southern Recycling from a third party, Regent Phoenix Imports and Exports ("Regent Phoenix"). A total of thirteen (13) shipping containers, generally two (2) per day, were sent to an inland warehouse in Sucat, Philippines in order to load the copper wire. The containers were trucked from the warehouse in Sucat to the Port of Manila, transported by ocean carrier to Long Beach, California, and then transported to their final destination in Dallas, Texas. Plaintiffs allege that when the containers were opened in Dallas, they contained debris, e.g. cement blocks and slag, not copper wire. Although this allegation was denied for lack of sufficient knowledge in Gibbs' answer, later deposition testimony from Gibbs' witness appears not to contest that the copper wire was substituted for debris at some point during the shipping process. Plaintiff CNA Insurance Company Limited ("Plaintiff CNA") is Plaintiff Southern's marine cargo insurer, and performed an investigation into the loss of the scrap copper wire.

* * *

DISCUSSION

I.   Motion for Partial Summary Judgment

Plaintiffs seek partial summary judgment on a discreet legal issue in this case. Specifically, Plaintiffs request that the Court find as a matter of law that, pursuant to the terms of the purchase agreement, Gibbs was obligated to deliver the copper wire in containers to the Port of Manila, Philippines and, if Gibbs failed to satisfy this obligation, Gibbs bore the risk of loss. As set forth fully below, the Court agrees with Plaintiffs' position and grants summary judgment on this narrow legal issue.

* * *

A.   The F.O.B. Term and Its Meaning under the Commercial Code

Turning to the purchase contract at issue here, the "Delivery" term plainly states: "F.O.B., loaded in bulk into Buyer's 20′ sea container *at Port of Manila, Philippines.*" Section 36–2–319 [**UCC 2–319**] of the South Carolina Commercial Code, entitled "F.O.B. and F.A.S. terms," states in relevant part:

(1)   Unless otherwise agreed the term F.O.B. (which means "free on board") at a named place, even though used only in connection with the stated price, is a *delivery term* under which

(a)   when the term is F.O.B. the *place of shipment*, the seller must *at that place* ship the goods in the manner provided in this chapter (Section 36–2–504) and *bear the expense and risk of putting them into the possession of the carrier.* . . .

S.C. Code § 36–2–319 [**UCC 2–319**] (emphasis added). The Official Comment section of the statute describes the general purpose of the F.O.B. provisions in the Commercial Code, stating: "This section is intended to negate the uncommercial line of decision which treats an 'F.O.B.' term as 'merely a price term.' " Moreover, the associated South Carolina Reporter's Comments state, "In addition to being a price term, the parties also use the term to indicate the point at which title passes and delivery takes place," and with respect to § 36–2–319(1)(a) [**UCC 2–319(1)(a)**], "In addition to the allocation of payment of freight charges, the risk of loss during handling and shipment passes to the buyer at the F.O.B. point."

Against this backdrop of what the Court considers to be clear, unambiguous contractual language and fairly straightforward statutory application, Defendant makes numerous arguments regarding why, in its view, Plaintiffs have failed to establish, as a matter of law, that Gibbs bore the risk of loss prior to the Port of Manila. Defendant hangs the majority of its argument on a caveat built into § 36–2–319(1) [**UCC 2–319(1)**], which states: "*Unless otherwise agreed* the term F.O.B. . . . at a named place. . .is a delivery term. . . ." Citing *Williston on Contracts*, Gibbs argues that the statutory meaning of the term F.O.B. is subject to (1) any contrary agreement of the parties, (2) the parties' course of performance and course of dealing, and/or (3) usage of trade.

Defendant first cites two cases to support its general argument that the F.O.B. term should glean its meaning from sources other than the statute; however, neither case effectively supports Defendant's position. In *Black Prince Distillery, Inc. v. Home Liquors*, 148 N.J. Super. 286 (N.J. Sup. 1977), a liquor distiller (seller) brought an action against a liquor retailer (buyer) to recover the cost of liquor ordered by the retailer but hijacked during delivery. The retailer had been purchasing whisky from the distiller for about twenty-five years. The retailer prepared the shipping documents which did not designate a destination for the goods. The retailer's telephone purchase order was confirmed by a writing executed by the retailer and directed to the distiller, entitled 'Request for Release,' and setting forth the quantity and type of goods being purchased. The writing contained no instructions as to where the goods were to be delivered. The trucking cost was either totally or partially paid by the distiller. Subsequently, the goods were allegedly hijacked while in the possession of the carrier en route to a destination designated by the retailer. In evaluating who bore the risk of loss, the trial judge used a letter written after the alleged hijacking to infer that the parties' arrangement had always been such that the distiller was required to make delivery to the retailer's locations, and thus must bear the loss resulting from the theft. The appellate court reversed, finding that the trial judge disregarded the course of dealings between the parties that had existed for many years, and holding that title passed when the distiller turned the goods over to the carrier, from which point the risk of loss was born by the retailer.

The *Black Prince* case is wholly different from the instant case for any number of reasons, not the least of which are: (1) the parties in *Black Prince* had no written agreement indicating a point of delivery, (2) there was no

F.O.B. term applicable to the transaction at issue, and (3) the parties in *Black Prince* had a twenty-five year course of dealings from which the court could discern their intentions. Here, the purchase contract contained an unambiguous F.O.B. term specifying the point of delivery, and the parties had no dealings prior to the transaction in question. The Court need say no more, *Black Prince* does not support Gibbs' arguments.

In re Julien Co., 128 B.R. 987 (Bankr. W.D. Tenn. 1991), *aff'd*, 44 F.3d 426 (6th Cir. 1995), involved an adversary proceeding brought to determine entitlement to proceeds from the sale of cotton, which had been delivered to the debtor (buyer) but not paid for. The debtor (buyer), a cotton merchant, contracted to purchase cotton from a broker (seller). The bankrupt merchant failed to pay for 360 bales of cotton, and the cotton broker made a claim in the merchant's bankruptcy case to recover payments it was forced to make to its suppliers, which were cotton producers. The contract provided that the cotton would be transported "F.O.B. trucks at Oakland Gin Company, Oakland Alabama," the seller's gin.

The *In re Julien* court applied the "unless otherwise agreed" language from the Uniform Commercial Code ("UCC") in finding that the parties varied the meaning of the F.O.B. term supplied by the UCC. There, the court found that the parties' true agreement was that "F.O.B. trucks at Oakland Gin" was to mean simply that the buyer would pay for the cost of shipment rather than that "delivery" or performance by the seller was completed by the loading of the trucks. Importantly, the *In re Julien* court made this conclusion based on the parties' testimony and an *additional term* in the contract, styled "PLACE OF PERFORMANCE," which essentially provided that performance included the seller invoicing the cotton at a provisional price and drawing a draft on the buyer's bank with an accompanying bill of lading at the time the cotton was loaded. Thus, the court held that "neither the seller's performance nor delivery was completed at the time the trucks were loaded. Rather, the seller's performance was completed upon delivery to The Julien Warehouse."

In the instant case, the purchase contract contains no additional term that expressly varies the meaning of the F.O.B. term, and the Court finds that none of the existing terms manifest the parties' intent to transfer the risk of loss prior to delivery or alter the statutory meaning of F.O.B. as a delivery term. The precise facts of *In re Julien*, seem to cut against, not in favor of, Defendant's argument, since the *In re Julien* court held that the seller's performance was not completed at loading, even though the F.O.B. term itemized seller's gin as the relevant location. Moreover, the features of the purchase contract in this case are meaningfully distinguishable from *In re Julien*, where the court held that the "PLACE OF PERFORMANCE" term was, in substance, the delivery term, and the "F.O.B. trucks at Oakland Gin" term merely indicated that the buyer was to pay for shipping.

Here, the delivery term is clearly delineated, and performance of Gibbs' obligation under the contract was contingent upon the purchased copper being delivered *to the Port of Manila*. As will be discussed more thoroughly *infra*, the fact that the delivery term provided that, "Buyer will have a representative at each loading and will sign each trucker's bill of ladings [sic], along with Sellers [sic] representative," does not, in the Court's view, alter the statutory meaning of the F.O.B. term.

B.   The Agreement of the Parties and the Parties' Intent

First, Defendant argues that the meaning of "F.O.B. Port" in the purchase agreement should be varied from its statutory meaning because the agreement between the parties and their contractual intent establish that the risk of loss was meant to pass from Gibbs to Southern at the inland warehouse in Sucat. In support of this assertion, Defendant states that the "agreement between the parties" means that the purchaser (Southern) must: "(1) inspect and accept the cargo at the inland warehouse in Sucat; (2) inspect and accept the loading of the containers at the inland warehouse in Sucat; (3) seal the containers at the inland warehouse in Sucat; [and] (4) re-inspect after traveling from Sucat to the inland warehouse in Manila." In reviewing the purchase contract, the Court is unable to find all of these purported elements of the parties' agreement. Rather, the delivery term requires that Southern have a representative at the loading to sign off on each bill of lading *along with Gibbs' representative*, and the payment term indicates that payment will be made the following business day upon Southern's "inspection and acceptance" of the goods, *"and Seller's delivery as described above."* It seems abundantly clear to the Court that, under the explicit terms of the contract, "delivery" was not achieved until Gibbs' put the goods into the hands of the carrier at the Port of Manila.

The Court finds that, contrary to Defendant's assertions, nothing in the "inspection and acceptance" phrase of the payment term indicates that the parties expressly intended to transfer the risk of loss to Southern at the inland warehouse. Furthermore, to focus on that phrase narrowly is to ignore the remainder of the payment term which makes payment contingent upon Gibbs' fulfillment of its delivery obligations "as described above." This language makes it abundantly clear that the F.O.B. Port delivery described in the foregoing delivery term was a distinct contractual obligation, independent from the buyer's inspection and acceptance, an obligation uniquely born by Gibbs. By relying on the "inspection and acceptance" phrase and ignoring the phrase immediately following thereafter, Defendant's argument fails to interpret the purchase contract as a whole. But holistic interpretation of the contract is the Court's duty. *See McGill v. Moore*, 672 S.E.2d 571, 574 (S.C. 2009) ("A contract is read as a whole document so that one may not create an ambiguity by pointing out a single sentence or clause.") The language of the purchase contract alone simply does not show an express intent by the parties to vary the statutory meaning of the F.O.B. Port delivery term.

One provision within the delivery term that both parties appear to have overlooked in their arguments reads, "*Shipments and delivery* to be completed no later than November 30, 2012." Thus, "shipments" of the copper are conceived as distinct from its eventual "delivery" to the F.O.B. location. The only rational construal of the word, "shipments," is that it denotes the transport from the location where the copper was to be loaded (inland warehouse) to the location where it was to be delivered (Port of Manila). This common sense reading of the delivery term is at odds with Gibbs' assertion that its obligations, and associated risk of loss, were satisfied at the time the containers were loaded, and it is undisputed that Gibbs paid for the transport from the inland warehouse to the Port.

Defendant highlights that Southern's inspection agent, Mr. Joel Dignos, (1) was present at the inland warehouse when all of the copper was loaded, (2) saw the copper in person, (3) verified that all of the copper was present on the chart he inspected, (4) determined the copper he saw was in acceptable condition, and (5) watched the loading, sealed the containers himself, and took photographs. But these facts do not advance Defendant any closer to nullifying an explicit, unambiguous term within the purchase contract that dictated delivery was achieved when the seller put the copper into the hands of the carrier at the Port of Manila. Rather, Mr. Dignos' actions are indicative that Southern upheld its end of the bargain during the loading phase. It is natural that these steps were taken by Southern's agent during the time period when and at the place where it made most sense to observe the quality, quantity, and condition of the copper—loading at the inland warehouse. It does not follow that merely because Southern, through its agent, availed itself of this opportunity to inspect the copper it was buying, that risk of loss passed to Southern at that point. This is a non sequitur.

Defendant further asserts, "If [Southern] truly was not accepting the risk of loss at the inland warehouse in Sucat, all it need say was: '[Southern] does not accept the risk of loss at the inland warehouse in Sucat,'" and asks the rhetorical question, "If that was truly [Southern's] intent, why not include those fourteen words?" But this argument sets up a straw man. In the Court's view, Southern communicated the precise concept that it did not accept the risk of loss prior to the Port when it negotiated the inclusion of the F.O.B. Port term within the purchase contract. Pointing to the absence of hypothetical language does not call into question the force and application of the existing contractual language.

Gibbs advances the deposition testimony of its 30(b)(6) witness, Mr. Greg Boozer, as support for the notion that Gibbs' contractual intent was that risk of loss would pass at the inland warehouse. Mr. Boozer testified:

Q: At what point under the purchase contract, Gibbs Exhibit 22, does Gibbs believe the risk of loss for the copper wire passed from Gibbs to Southern Recycling?

. . .

A: When the goods were loaded on the container and accepted by Southern Recycling.

However, as already explained, the construction of clear and unambiguous contractual language is a question of a law for the Court. Mr. Gibbs' testimony, while certainly serving of his company's interests, amounts to little more than a *post hoc* legal conclusion about the meaning of the contract. The same goes for the deposition testimony of Mr. Blair Biggerstaff, a former employee of Gibbs, who signed the purchase contract on Gibbs' behalf. Defendant quotes Mr. Biggerstaff's testimony at length, but fails to introduce information that would call the Court's conclusions on this *matter of law* into question.

C. Course of Performance and Course of Dealing

Second, Defendant argues that independent of the terms of the purchase contract, the parties' course of performance and course of dealing establish that the risk of loss passed to Southern at the inland warehouse in Sucat. By "course of performance" and "course of dealing," Defendant refers to the undisputed facts that an agent of Southern inspected and accepted the cargo at the inland warehouse, observed the loading of the cargo, sealed the containers himself, monitored the transportation to the port by keeping track of departure and arrival times, and re-inspected the containers just outside the Port. These circumstances, asserts Defendant, show the passing of the risk of loss at the inland warehouse.

Put simply, Defendant has not established that the parties' course of performance modified the statutory meaning of the F.O.B. term because there is no course of performance at issue in this case. Section 36–1–303(a) **[UCC 1–303(a)]** of the South Carolina Commercial Code states:

(a) A "course of performance" is a sequence of conduct between the parties to a particular transaction that exists if:

(1) the agreement of the parties with respect to the transaction involves repeated occasions for performance by a party; and

(2) the other party, with knowledge of the nature of the performance and opportunity for objection to it, accepts the performance or acquiesces in it without objection.

There is no "course of performance" here because there is no "sequence of conduct" that involves "repeated occasions for performance." The purchase agreement at issue involves a single transaction between Southern and Gibbs, and it is undisputed that this transaction was the first and last time these companies had commercial dealings. Thus, Defendant has not presented evidence of a "course of performance" for the Court to consider. Moreover, many of the actions by Southern's inspection agent that Gibbs relies upon as evidence that the parties modified the F.O.B. term through their "course of performance" were simply contractual obligations, laid out in the delivery and payment terms, that Southern needed to fulfill to keep its part of the bargain (e.g. inspecting the copper at the inland warehouse, observing the loading and accepting the goods, signing the bills of lading). The Court need say no more, there is no evidence that the parties modified the F.O.B. term through a course of performance.

Similarly, Defendant has not established that the parties' course of dealing modified the statutory meaning of the F.O.B. term because there is no course of dealing between the parties. Section 36–1–303(b) [**UCC 1–303(b)**] of the South Carolina Commercial Code states: "A 'course of dealing' is a sequence of conduct concerning previous transactions between the parties to a particular transaction that is fairly to be regarded as establishing a common basis of understanding for interpreting their expressions and other conduct." Defendant has not presented any evidence regarding previous transactions between the parties, and, again, cannot do so because the transaction at issue is the only commercial dealing the parties ever had. Given this undisputed fact, there is no "course of dealing" for the Court to consider.

D. Usage of Trade

Third, Defendant argues that the usage of trade establishes that the risk of loss passed to Southern at the inland warehouse in Sucat. In its response brief, Gibbs asserts, "The 'usage of trade' by inspecting and approving the cargo, the loading and sealing the containers itself with its own seals and the subsequent monitoring of the transportation of the cargo along with the re-inspection just outside the Port establish that the risk of loss passed to [Southern]." Defendant's assertions on this point are little more than a rehash of arguments already made with respect to the intent of the parties, course of performance, and course of dealing, and are likewise insufficient to establish a usage of trade.

By way of an affidavit styled as "Expert Designation Report of Norwood ('Woody') Ezzell" submitted five months after its response in opposition to Plaintiff's motion for partial summary judgment, Defendant sought to remedy the dearth of evidence regarding usage of trade in its original submission. The substance of Mr. Ezzell's affidavit is contained on one page and states in relevant part that he is the owner of a freight forwarding business, he has been in that business since 1992, and "The usage of trade in the industry is that the risk of loss passes upon inspection and acceptance of the cargo, loading and sealing of the containers. That is particularly true when theft is known in the area." Mr. Ezzell does not offer any support for this proposition other than his employment, and his own "experience and expertise."

Prior to offering this opinion about the "usage of trade in the industry," Mr. Ezzel indicates that he has reviewed the purchase contract between Gibbs and Southern as well as some of the pleadings in the case. He states: "Based on my experience and expertise in the area of shipping and transporting cargo internationally, it is my interpretation that the risk of loss passed to the purchaser when they first inspected and accepted the cargo." Mr. Ezzel then opines that based on the fact that Southern's agent inspected and accepted the cargo, observed the loading of the containers, and sealed the containers himself, "the purchaser accepted the risk of loss by engaging in these activities in an inland warehouse in the Philippines." Mr. Ezzell's opinions, and the particular facts on which he bases those opinions, are unmistakably linked, both in their basis and in their resultant conclusions, to Gibbs' arguments that the F.O.B. term's statutory meaning has been modified by the parties' "course of performance," "course of dealing," and/or usage of trade. Notably, Mr. Ezzell's affidavit says nothing about F.O.B. terms, or how the purported usage of trade interacts with such F.O.B. terms when they are present in a purchase contract such as this one.

The Court finds that Mr. Ezzell's affidavit, though tendered as evidence of a usage of trade to bolster Defendant's position that the statutory meaning of the F.O.B. term was modified, is insufficient to preclude the entrance of summary judgment on the risk of loss issue. Section 36–1–303 [**UCC 1–303(c)**] of the South Carolina Commercial Code states:

> (c) A "usage of trade" is any practice or method of dealing having such regularity of observance in a place, vocation, or trade as to justify an expectation that it will be observed with respect to the transaction in question. The existence and scope of such a usage must be proved as facts. If it is established that such a usage is embodied in a trade code or similar record, the interpretation of the record is a question of law.

To begin with, Mr. Ezzell's proffer about *when* the risk of loss passes from seller to buyer in the international shipping industry is a legal conclusion couched in thinly veiled factual terms as a "usage of trade." Nevertheless, assuming *arguendo* that usage of trade were a question of fact relevant to construction of the instant purchase contract, it is questionable whether Mr. Ezzell's affidavit construes "usage of trade" in a manner narrow enough to be helpful to a trier of fact on the putative question of whether risk of loss transferred prior to the Port of Manila. He opines with sweeping scope, "The usage of trade *in the industry* is that the risk of loss passes upon inspection and acceptance of the cargo, loading and sealing of the containers."

In general, extrinsic evidence may not be considered to ascertain the meaning of an unambiguous contractual term. "If the contract's language is clear and unambiguous, the language alone, understood in its plain, ordinary, and popular sense, determines the contract's force and effect." *Beaufort Cty. Sch. Dist. v. United Nat. Ins. Co.*, 709 S.E.2d 85, 90 (S.C. Ct. App. 2011). "A contract is ambiguous only when it may fairly and reasonably be understood in more ways than one." *Padgett v. S.C. Ins. Reserve Fund*, 531 S.E.2d 305, 307 (S.C. Ct. App. 2000). "It is a question of law for the court whether the language of a contract is ambiguous. Once the court decides the language is ambiguous, evidence may be admitted to show the intent of the parties. The determination of the parties' intent is then a question of fact." *S.C. Dep't of Nat. Res. v. Town of McClellanville*, 550 S.E.2d 299, 302–03 (S.C. 2001) (internal citations omitted); *see also Wallace v. Day*, 700 S.E.2d 446, 449 (S.C. Ct. App. 2010).

However, as Defendant correctly argues, in cases under the UCC, a finding of ambiguity in the contractual language is not required before extrinsic evidence concerning the meaning of the contract, including usage of trade, may be considered. Nevertheless, usage of trade does not simply trump unambiguous contractual terms, for "[t]here can be no doubt that the [UCC] restates the well-established rule that evidence of usage of trade and course of dealing should be excluded whenever it cannot be reasonably construed as consistent with the terms of the contract." Still, evidence of usage of trade to explain or supplement terms should not be excluded simply because a contract appears to be complete. Rather, "the test of admissibility is not whether the contract appears on its face to be complete in every detail, but whether the proffered evidence of course of dealing and trade usage reasonably can be construed as consistent with the express terms of the agreement."

Applied to the instant case, the Court finds that the usage of trade proffered by Mr. Ezzell, to the extent it constitutes more than a bare legal conclusion, cannot be reasonably construed as consistent with the express terms of the purchase agreement, and is therefore not admissible to preclude the entry of summary judgment. Specifically, Mr. Ezzell's proffer of the usage of trade regarding transfer of the risk of loss cannot be reasonably reconciled with the delivery term, "F.O.B., loaded in bulk into Buyer's 20′ sea container at Port of Manila, Philippines," because it flatly contradicts that term on the central issue, namely, *when* the risk of loss passes. Thus, to the extent the affidavit raises an issue of material fact regarding usage of trade, the issue is not *genuine* because it would not permit a reasonable jury to return a verdict for Defendant based on the proffered evidence. The remaining opinions in Mr. Ezzell's affidavit unquestionably constitute legal conclusions, not facts or permissible expert opinions, and are insufficient to withstand summary judgment on the risk of loss issue.

E. Questions of Fact

Fourth, Defendant argues that at a minimum, the intentions of the parties, course of dealing, and/or usage of trade as to the timing of the passing of the risk of loss involve issues of fact to be resolved at trial. Citing *Wallace v. Day*, 700 S.E.2d 446, 449 (S.C. Ct. App. 2010) for the rule that when a contract is ambiguous the parties' intent becomes a question of fact, Defendant asserts that this rule has been applied to deny summary judgment in the context of determining the time at which risk of loss passed. Here, Defendant relies on a ruling from the District Court of Appeal of Florida, *Ladex Corp. v. Transportes Aeros Nacionales, S.A.*, 476 So.2d 763 (Fla. App. 1985). In *Ladex*, the court was unable, due to an undeveloped record, to determine as a matter of law who had title to the goods at the time of loss. The *Ladex* court found that factual issues remained as to the type of contract that existed between the parties, reversed the trial court's grant of summary judgment, and remanded for further proceedings accordingly.

No such problem exists in the instant case. The record is amply clear about the type of contract at issue, as well as the various facts and circumstances that might conceivably operate to alter the statutory meaning of the F.O.B. term. Additionally, Gibbs' 30(b)(6) witness acknowledged his belief that title did not pass until the copper was delivered to the Port. Put simply, Gibbs has not produced evidence of any genuine issue of material fact on the risk of loss issue, and the Court finds that summary judgment is appropriate.

 * * *

PROBLEMS

1. Consider the following facts:

Armani ordered a new desk from Gibson Office Supply for his office. When he received it he noticed that there was a water stain on the back left leg. Although it was not visible once the desk was placed in his office, he was not happy with the water stain. See 2–508, 2–513, 2–601, 2–602, 2–605, and 2–612.

 a. Does Armani have a valid basis for rejecting the desk? If so, what steps should he take to reject?

 b. If Armani rejects the desk, what rights does Gibson have to keep the deal going?

 c. Would it matter if Armani's contract were for 12 desks with scheduled deliveries of 4 desks at the 1st of the month for the first 3 months of the year?

2.   Consider the following situations and determine whether the buyer has accepted the goods. See 2–513, 2–601, 2–602, 2–606, and 2–607.

a.   Computer Store ordered 25 boxes of paper from Pulp Manufacturing. When Pulp delivered the paper on February 2, the manager from Computer Store had the delivery person place the boxes in the front of the warehouse. The manager carefully counted to be sure that there were 25 boxes. After verifying the number of boxes, the manager of Computer Store paid for the paper in full. A week later the manager pulled several reams of paper from the boxes and discovered that Pulp sent the wrong weight of paper. When the manager sees this, she calls Pulp and attempts to reject the delivery but Pulp claims she accepted the paper on February 2 and it is too late to reject.

b.   Roger Dodger ordered a new motorcycle and CC Bike Shop delivered it to his house as he requested so it would be waiting for him when he got home from work. After arriving home, he decided the motorcycle needed to look a little more "racy," so he painted a racing stripe on the right side before he took it out for a spin. He then took it out for a test drive. About 5 minutes into his test drive, Roger noticed that the motorcycle kept pulling to the right and that there was a 3-inch scratch across the speedometer. He immediately stopped the drive, called CC Bike Shop, and told them they needed to pick up the defective bike. The bike shop refused saying he had accepted the motorcycle.

c.   Same facts as (b), except that when Roger got home he did not paint a racing stripe and he immediately noticed the 3-inch scratch across the speedometer. He then took the motorcycle for a 10-minute test drive to CC Bike Shop. When he arrived, Roger told the sales person that he did not want the motorcycle because it had a big scratch across the speedometer. The bike shop refused to take the motorcycle back.

d.   Sally Construction Company ordered 4000 PSI strength concrete from Bulldog Concrete Company to use when building a retaining wall at Charlie Smith's home. After the seller delivered the concrete to the Smith's house as the contract required, Sally poured the concrete into the mixer and built the first half of the wall. After allowing it to dry, Sally had the concrete tested to be sure it was the strength ordered because she could not test it until it was mixed. As soon as Sally tested the wall, she discovered that the concrete was 3000 PSI weight and not the 4000 weight she had ordered. She does not want to pay for the concrete, so she calls the seller and tells them she is rejecting the delivery. Bulldog claims it is too late because she already accepted the concrete.

e.   Dobie Lumber Yards delivered a truckload of wood to Miller Home Builders. Right after the delivery Miller notices that Dobie delivered oak instead of walnut, so the manager called Dobie immediately and rejected the wood delivery. The next day Miller discovers that the homeowner actually would prefer that the office be built with oak wood, so Miller has the workers take the oak to the customer's home and begin building the home office. When Dobie Lumber Yards arrives the next day to pick up the oak planks, Miller said they decided to keep the wood and had already begun to use it. Dobie Lumber Yards had already sold it to another customer. Has Miller accepted the wood? If so, does the seller have any recourse against Miller?

f.   Arrow Smith goes to the local Jeep dealer and purchases a new Jeep Cherokee. After signing all of the documents and making the initial payment, Arrow drives it to her family's home in another town about 30 miles away. After a nice visit with her family, Arrow drives the new Jeep back to her home. On the way back, the check engine light came on 5 times and the Jeep stalled at 3 or 4 different red lights. Arrow called the dealer the next day and said she was bringing the Jeep back because of the defects. Has Arrow accepted the Jeep?

g.   Same facts as (f) except that dealer repaired the Jeep. Two days after the repair, Arrow is driving the Jeep to work when the check engine light comes on and within a minute the engine caught fire. A fire truck came to the scene and put out the fire. Arrow was not injured. She had the Jeep towed back to the dealer and insisted they keep it and refund her the money she paid. The dealer refused, saying they can fix the Jeep. Does Arrow have a right to get her money refunded or will dealer be able to repair the Jeep? See 2–508.

3.   Assume that there was no acceptance and the buyer rejected delivery in all the scenarios described in Problem 2 except g. Will the seller be permitted to cure the defects? See 2–508.

4.   Now assume that there was acceptance in each situation described in Problem 2. Will the buyer be able to revoke that acceptance? See 2–607(2), 2–608, and 2–612.

a.   If the buyer is able to revoke acceptance, will the seller be permitted to cure the defective or nonconforming goods? See 2–508.

5.   Consider the following facts:

Ginger Dawg recently won a national singing competition and she thought that meant she was destined to be the next big singing star who would soon be making millions of dollars and playing in front of millions of adoring fans. She determined to use part of her prize money to buy a new Yamaha top of the line acoustic guitar. After an extensive search, Ginger found just what she wanted advertised online by the Music as Art store located in Nashville, Tennessee for $5,000. She called the store and talked to the owner, Young Neil. After about an hour on the phone, Young assured Ginger the guitar was top of the line and would be a great one for her to work with on her first album.

Young e-mailed the contract to Ginger with the following pertinent terms, among others: Ginger agrees to pay $5,000 with 50% down and 50% due within 30 days after delivery. Young promises to deliver the guitar to Ginger's home no later than March 15. Poodle Carrier Lines will ship it and it will be FOB Nashville. The delivery between Nashville and Ginger's home costs $350.

Ginger signed the contract, provided her credit information, and sent it back to Young. On March 8, Young delivered the guitar to the carrier but forgot to give notice to Ginger. Ginger received it on March 12.

As soon as Ginger took it out of the box to play it, she was not sure she liked the way it felt in her hands. She decided to wait a while to see if she would like it a little better. On March 15, Ginger's grandmother bought her a brand new Fender guitar as a surprise to celebrate her win at the competition. After playing the Fender guitar for two weeks, Ginger decided it was definitely the guitar for her. She was trying to decide what she wanted to do with the Yamaha guitar when she dropped a guitar pick in the hole of the guitar. While trying to carefully retrieve the pick, she noticed a large imperfection on the inside of the guitar for the first time. It did not affect the music but it certainly detracted from the beauty of the instrument. It was an imperfection about the size of a silver dollar.

Ginger called Young that afternoon and told him that she was returning the guitar immediately due to the imperfection. When he asked to see the imperfection she took a picture of it and texted it to him. He told her it was just a normal indentation in the wood and that it was too late for him to accept a return even if it was defective, which he asserted it was not. As luck would have it, Ginger was flying to Nashville at the end of the week, so she took it with her, dropped it off at the Music as Art store, and refused to take it back even when Young insisted she could not return it. She stopped payment on her check, said he needed to fix the imperfection in the wood, and told him it was his problem now. She left the guitar at the store and went on to her way.

    a.   Ginger comes to you for advice because Young has just sued her for the price of the guitar using 2–709(1)(a) because he contends the goods were accepted. She wants to know whether Young will win the case or if she has a valid defense. Advise her as to whether you think the guitar was accepted. See 2–319, 2–504, 2–513, 2–601, 2–602, 2–606, and 2–709(1)(a).

    b.   Assume that Ginger did not receive the Yamaha guitar because the carrier's truck was hit by lightning. Who is responsible for the risk of loss? See 2–319, 2–504, 2–509, and 2–510.

    c.   Would your answer to (b) change if the contract's delivery term was F.O.B. Ginger's residence?

    6.   Consider the following facts:

JJ Enterprises manufactures children's wooden toys in Farmington, Minnesota. They recently negotiated a contract whereby JJ agreed to sell 100 toy trucks to Morgan's Toy Store in Indianapolis on or before June 1. Morgan's insisted that the contract include the delivery term FOB Indianapolis. JJ made arrangements with Happy Delivery to ship the toys from Farmington to Indianapolis. Happy picked the shipment up, but while it was in transit thieves broke into the truck and stole everything in the truck including the toys intended for Morgan's Toy Store. See 2–319, 2–504, 2–509, 2–510, and 2–601.

    a.   Between JJ and Morgan's, who is responsible for the loss of the toys?

    b.   Would it make a difference in your answer to the previous question if JJ contracted with FBN Delivery Company, a company well-known as a "fly by night" company that JJ had refused to use in the past because of FBN's reputation for losing or damaging goods while in transit?

    c.   Would your answer to (a.) change if the contract between JJ and Morgan's contained a delivery term that said FOB Seller's place, Farmington Minnesota?

    d.   Would your answer to (a.) change if the shipment contained 95 toy trucks?

    e.   Would your answer to (a.) change if, while the goods were in transit, the buyer called JJ Enterprises and repudiated the contract?

7.   Patti Paulson agreed to purchase a MacBook Pro from the Nelson Computer Store but the seller needed to load some new software on the computer before it would be ready for Patti. After they agreed to the terms of the sale, Patti signed the contract agreeing to pay Nelson within 30 days of picking up the computer. She told the sales person that she would stop by the store on Friday to pick it up. She did not make it to the store on Friday and the computer was stolen early Tuesday morning. See 2–103, 2–104, 2–503, 2–509, and 2–510.

    a.   Who is responsible for the loss?

    b.   Assume the same facts as 7 except that the contract said that Patti promised to bring the cash to Nelson within 2 days. After 4 days had passed, Patti had not brought the cash and the computer was stolen from Nelson's store. Nelson's insurance did not cover $1500 of the loss.

    c.   Would your answer to (b.) change if Nelson's store had no insurance on their computers?

    d.   Would your analysis in (a.) change if Patti Paulson made the purchase as general manager of her law firm?

8.   Bill Ward, a university student, agreed to buy a computer for $1,000 from another student, Matt Boon. Bill signed a short contract that described the computer and said he would pay for it when he picked it up. On the way out of class, Bill said he would stop by within the week to pick it up. Unfortunately, before he could pick it up, Matt's home was burglarized and the computer was stolen. See 2–503, 2–509, and 2–510.

    a.   Who is responsible for the stolen goods?

b.   Would your answer to the above question change if Bill had not picked up the computer and it was stolen from Matt's home about 3 weeks after Bill signed the contract?

CHAPTER 5

REMEDIES

■ ■ ■

This final chapter in our coverage of Article 2 covers remedies available under Article 2. Understanding remedies is critically important because it will not help clients if you win their case, but do not know how to turn that win into financial relief. Additionally, from a defense perspective, you need to know how to lessen the financial impact of losing a case. You can do this for your clients by learning how to use and apply the remedy sections to your advantage.

This chapter is divided into seller's remedies and buyer's remedies because Article 2 has a different set of remedies for buyers and sellers. Seller's remedies are less complex than buyer's because the most significant breach by the buyer is usually a failure to pay for goods delivered or wrongfully rejecting or revoking acceptance of the goods. A breach by a seller, however, has the potential to cause more complicated damages for the buyer due to the fact that a breach by a seller may involve defective goods, as well as delivery problems. Defective goods have the capability to cause personal injury, property damage, and various other kinds of damage which the buyer will want to be compensated for. These types of extra damages are called consequential damages. Additionally, parties may spend money after a breach caring for or transporting goods. These types of damages are called incidental.

At first glance remedies may seem fairly easy because they can be reduced to formulas. But, deciding what numbers actually go into the formulas often is more difficult than it seems. This chapter will cover seller's remedies, buyer's remedies, a few of the major differences with the remedies for leases, and then consider two defenses called impractability and unconscionability. The material you learned in the previous chapter is very important and understanding that chapter will help you better comprehend remedies. For example, if you do not understand delivery terms, rejection, acceptance, and revocation you will have difficulty determining how to work through the various formulas to arrive at a proper remedy.

In a survey course, there is not enough time to go deeply into all of the possible remedy sections; that will be left to a more comprehensive course on the UCC or remedies. In this chapter we will consider remedies for a seller of resale damages (**2–706**), contract-market damages (**2–708(1)**), lost volume seller (**2–708(2)**), and an action for price (**2–709**). This chapter also deals with buyer's remedies of cover damages (**2–712**), contract-market damages (**2–713**), damages for accepted goods (**2–714**), and the buyer's right to specific performance (**2–716**).

It is very important to keep **1–305** in mind when considering which remedy to pursue because courts often use that section to justify veering away from a strict interpretation of a damages section. **1–305** directs the court that the remedies "must be liberally administered to the end that the aggrieved party may be put in as good a position as if the other party had fully performed[.]" So in essence, the UCC strives to give injured parties their expectation damages.

Next, this chapter will examine a few important differences between remedies in leases and sales, although we will not study the specific formulas contained in Article 2A. Lastly, we will consider the defense of excuse (**2–615**), and then look at how a court may refuse to enforce parts of a contract or the entire contract if it finds the contract or any clause in the contract to be unconscionable (**2–302**).

A. SELLER'S REMEDIES

An index of all of the remedies available to sellers can be found in **2–703**. The UCC drafters rejected the common law doctrine of election of remedy. That doctrine required an injured party to elect a remedy and, once that election was made, a plaintiff could not pursue alternate and perhaps inconsistent remedies. Under the UCC, remedies are cumulative and the facts of any particular case will determine whether a plaintiff is barred from any particular remedy. *See* **2–703**, Comment 1. For example, after a wrongful repudiation by the buyer, a seller may do all of the following: refuse to deliver goods, cancel the contract, and pursue a suit for damages. If the seller is still in the process of manufacturing the goods when a repudiation occurs, **2–704** permits the seller to choose between stopping production *or* completing the goods, as long as she uses commercially reasonable judgment. If the seller believes she will be unable to sell the goods once they are completed, the seller may quit manufacturing the goods and sell what remains for salvage value; however, under different facts, where a market for the manufactured goods exists, it may make more sense to complete the goods and resell them.

All of the remedy sections permit a seller to include incidental damages when suing for a breach of contract. **2–710** defines seller's incidental damages. These are usually costs that the seller has to spend after the breach to either stop delivery or care for the goods. One important difference between the seller's and buyer's remedies relates to the ability to sue for consequential damages. **1–305** states that a party may not sue for consequential damages unless specifically allowed in the UCC. None of the seller's remedies permit a seller to sue for consequential damages. The only section on consequential damages is **2–715**, which covers the buyer's incidental and consequential damages. Although this chapter does not cover damages under the CISG, an important difference between the CISG and the UCC is that the CISG has no prohibition against a seller receiving consequential damages.

Why does the UCC only authorize consequential damages for a buyer? Buyers are more likely to have consequential damages than sellers because there are many more variations of damages caused by defective goods than there are from simply failing to pay the price. Although some scholars argue that a seller, in a proper case, should be able to sue for consequential damages most courts interpret **1–305** as not allowing a seller to win consequential damages. In *Stamtec, Inc. v. Anson Stamping Co., LLC*, 346 F. 3d 651, 658–660 (6th Cir. 2003), the seller argued it should be able to recover interest from the lost use of money and interest paid to third parties as a result of the buyer's breach. The court stated:

> Nor did the district court err when it concluded that Stamtec could not recover either the interest charges paid to Chin Fong or interest based on its lost use of money because these costs are consequential damages, which are not available to an aggrieved seller. Like the district court, we find the reasoning in *Firwood* persuasive. The *Firwood* court considered whether an aggrieved seller could collect the cost of its lost use of money (interest) as an element of its incidental damages. The *Firwood* court began by noting that the Uniform Commercial Code entitles sellers to collect incidental, but not consequential damages. Focusing on the issue of how Michigan had defined incidental damages, the court found that Michigan courts had not permitted an aggrieved seller to collect interest payments on a loan secured to maintain a business after a buyer's breach on the ground that such interest payments fell within the definition of consequential damages. Because the Michigan courts had not addressed the specific issue of incidental damages arising from the lost use of money, the *Firwood* court considered the competing positions taken by the Seventh and Second Circuits. In doing so, the *Firwood* court looked to the general structure of the Uniform Commercial Code for guidance. The *Firwood* court "agree[d] with the Seventh Circuit's view that sellers are not entitled to [lost use of money] as an element of the damage award" because "a foregone profit from exploiting a valuable opportunity that the breach of contract denied to the victim of the breach fits more comfortably under the heading of consequential damages than of incidental damages." *Id.* at 171 (quoting *Afram Export Corp. v. Metallurgiki Halyps, S.A.*, 772 F.2d 1358 (7th Cir.1985)). The *Firwood* court "decline[d] to follow the Second Circuit's embrace of an expansive definition of incidental damages because [that] Court appeared to conflate the definition of consequential damages with that of incidental

damages" when it determined that recovery depended on whether the interest payments were foreseeable, an element of the test for consequential damages. *Id.* at 170 n. 2. Thus, it was the considered opinion of the *Firwood* court that the general structure of the Uniform Commercial Code precluded the award of interest, whether claimed as charges arising from a bank loan or the buyer's lost use of money, as incidental damages because such costs fell outside the immediate buyer-seller transaction.

We believe that the *Firwood* court was correct in its analysis of recoverability of interest costs as an element of incidental damages. We do not see a meaningful distinction between costs incurred due to the lost use of money and interest paid on a commercial loan. Each involves a financial transaction that falls outside the immediate scope of the buyer-seller transaction at issue: the first involves a bank transaction necessary to maintain an entity's financial viability and the second involves a transaction with an unspecified party that would produce uncertain results. Thus, we conclude that the Tennessee Uniform Commercial Code, which adopted the relevant Uniform Commercial Code provisions without modification, does not permit a seller's claim for damages based on either lost use of money or interest paid to a third party (which is analogous to interest paid on a commercial loan) because these costs represent consequential damages. Given that a seller is not entitled to consequential damages, and the Commercial Code portion of the Tennessee law precludes the award of consequential damages except as specifically provided by statute, TENN.CODE ANN. § 47–1–106(1) **[UCC 1–106(1)]**, Stamtec cannot recover the interest-charge payments made to Chin Fong nor the cost of its lost use of money as an element of incidental damages under § 47–2–710 **[UCC 2–710]**.

* * *

(The court proceeded to permit Stamtec to recover prejudgment interest pursuant to the Tennessee Code.)

1. RESALE DAMAGES (2–706)

This section allows a seller to enter into a substitute transaction with another buyer and resell the goods after the original buyer has breached. If the difference between the resale price and the breached contract price is a loss, the seller may recover the difference along with any incidental damages under **2–710**. As stated by **2–710**, incidental damages are recoverable, however the seller should not be put in a better position than she would have been had the buyer not breached. This means that any expenses saved as a result of the breach must be subtracted from the final damages award. The formula for **2–706** damages is contract price **(KP)** – resale price **(RP)** + incidental damages **(ID)** – expenses saved **(ES)**.

When a seller pursues damages under **2–706**, the resale must be made in good faith and in a commercially reasonable manner. Additionally, the seller must give the buyer reasonable notice of the intent to resale the goods. Failure to notify the buyer, act in good faith, or act properly under this section will keep the seller from collecting damages under **2–706**. See Comment 2. In *Fuji Photo Film USA v. Zalmen Reiss & Associates*, 31 Misc. 3d 1240(A), *2–3 (N.Y. 2011), the plaintiff resold merchandise that had been returned by the buyer at a very discounted price and sued for **2–706** damages. The discounted price was significantly lower than the market price and the market price was essentially the same as the contract price. Additionally, the seller failed to notify Zalmen of its intent to resale the goods. The court found both the resale and lack of notice to be a problem as you can see in the following excerpt:

> However, the mandate of UCC § **2–706(3)**, that notice be provided to a buyer which has wrongfully revoked acceptance prior to effecting a private sale of goods so returned, is unequivocal when seeking to recover damages pursuant to UCC § **2–703(d)**. Recovery of the difference between the contract price and the amount recovered upon resale is unavailable to the seller upon failure to comply. [Citations omitted].

> The only alternative is to seek recovery pursuant to UCC § **2–708** for "the difference between the market price at the time and place for tender and the unpaid contract price". UCC § **2–708(1)**; *B & R Textile,* 1979 WL 30097. The burden, however, is upon the seller under that section to establish the applicable market price so as to demonstrate that the unnoticed private sale resulted in a fair price reflective of the actual value. *See Acuri,* 91 Misc.2d at 835–836; *Karen v. Cane,* 152 Misc.2d 639, 643 [CCCNY, Queens Co, 1991]. Here, the evidence adduced by plaintiff established that the market value of the cards when returned to it in 2009 remained at $19.49 per unit, exactly the contract price. The merchandise at issue was not custom-made or in any manner unique. Fuji sold a product that it maintained in its inventory and marketed from a catalog. Plaintiff's witness testified that the returned items were not damaged and were "A Stock". Presumably, they could have been returned to inventory and sold at Fuji's market price of $19.49, without a loss.

> Having failed to give notice to defendant pursuant to UCC § **2–706(3)** so as to afford it the opportunity to participate in the private sale or perhaps determine to pay plaintiff's invoice so as to avoid the greater loss to be sustained under the terms of plaintiff's proposed private sale, plaintiff had the burden to prove

that its resale to a third party represented a transaction made in good faith and in a commercially reasonable manner (see UCC § 2–706). This plaintiff failed to do. Plaintiff's evidence actually established that the resale of the returned merchandise, significantly below market value, to a single vendor selected by plaintiff, was not conducted in a commercially reasonable manner. Plaintiff has not, therefore, sustained its burden and its complaint must be dismissed.

2. CONTRACT-MARKET DAMAGES (2–708)

Although an action for price or resale damages usually will get a seller closest to her expectation measure of damages, the contract-market differential is an option if the seller has not resold the goods, does not qualify for resale damages, or cannot bring an action for price. 2–708(1) allows a seller to collect the difference between the market price, at the time and place for tender, and the contract price. Additionally, like in 2–706, the seller may add in any damages that qualify as incidental damages but will need to subtract expenses saved. The formula is market price **(MP)** – contract price **(KP)** + incidentals **(ID)** – expenses saved **(ES)**.

When determining damages for this section, the delivery terms are critical because those terms will affect the time and place for tender. Review 2–503 for the requirements of tender of delivery and 2–319 for the meaning of FOB terms. For example, if a contract calls for the sale of lumber between a seller in Seattle and a buyer in New Orleans the delivery term will let the parties identify where and when tender will occur. If the term is FOB Seattle, then the seller tenders the goods in Seattle and 2–708 will use the market price in Seattle; however, if it says FOB New Orleans then the tender cannot occur until the goods reach New Orleans and the New Orleans market price will be used when calculating damages. The FOB term also relates to expenses saved. If there is a destination contract, as in FOB New Orleans, and the buyer repudiates before the goods are shipped, the seller will save the expense of shipping the goods to New Orleans and those saved expenses will be subtracted from the final award.

One issue relating to 2–708(1) and 2–706 is whether the seller may choose the remedy she wants, regardless of whether she has resold the goods. This issue may come up when the market price is lower than the resale price. If these two sections are read in conjunction with 1–305, it appears that a seller should only receive her expectation damages and not a windfall. On the other hand, 2–703 Comment 1 clarifies that the UCC rejected the doctrine of election of remedy. Some scholars have suggested that a seller who has resold may not collect 2–708(1) damages, yet other courts have allowed sellers to pursue damages under 2–708(1)—even when it results in a windfall—reasoning that the seller is the injured party, so she should be able to choose her remedy. Courts are split on how to resolve this issue, as you will see when you read the next case written by the Oregon Supreme Court.

PEACE RIVER SEED CO-OPERATIVE, LTD. V. PROCEEDS MARKETING, INC.

355 Or. 44 (Or. 2014)

BALLMER, C. J.

In this breach of contract case, we examine the availability of different remedies under the Uniform Commercial Code (UCC) for an aggrieved seller of goods after a buyer breaches a contract to purchase those goods. Specifically, we consider the relationship between ORS 72.7080(1) [**UCC 2–708(1)**], which measures a seller's damages as the difference between the unpaid contract price and the *market* price at the time and place for tender, and ORS 72.7060 [**UCC 2–706**], which measures a seller's damages as the difference between the contract price and the *resale* price. We examine those provisions to determine whether an aggrieved seller who has resold goods can recover a greater amount of damages using the market price measure of damages than the seller would recover using the resale price measure of damages.

Plaintiff, a seller seeking damages from a buyer that breached contracts to purchase goods, argued at trial that it was entitled to recover its market price damages. The trial court determined that plaintiff was entitled to the lesser of its market price damages or its resale price damages, and the court ultimately awarded plaintiff its resale price damages. The Court of Appeals reversed and remanded, because the court determined that plaintiff could recover its market price damages, even though it had resold some of the goods at issue. *Peace River Seed Co-Op. v. Proceeds Marketing,* 253 Or. App. 704, 717, 293 P.3d 1058 (2012). The Court of Appeals also reversed the trial court's decision not to award plaintiff its attorney fees under the parties' contracts, and remanded for the trial court to determine whether the parties intended the ambiguous contract term "charges for collection" to include attorney fees. *Id.* at 724–25, 293 P.3d 1058. For the reasons that follow, we agree that plaintiff was entitled to recover its market price damages, even if those damages exceeded plaintiff's resale price damages. We conclude, however, that plaintiff is not entitled to recover its attorney fees under the parties' contracts.

FACTS AND PROCEEDINGS BELOW

The facts material to our discussion are mostly undisputed. Peace River Seed Co-Operative ("plaintiff") is a Canadian company that buys grass seed from and sells grass seed for grass seed producers. Proceeds Marketing ("defendant") is an Oregon corporation that purchases grass seed from various sources to resell to end users. A broker prepared and the parties agreed to multiple contracts for defendant to purchase from plaintiff the total production of grass seed from a certain number of acres for a fixed price over a period of two years. The contracts incorporated the NORAMSEED Rules for the Trade of Seeds for Planting, which have been adopted by the American and Canadian Seed Trade Associations to govern the trade of seed. The NORAMSEED Rules provide that the UCC applies to transactions within the United States, and both parties have litigated this case under the UCC.

Under the contracts, defendant was to provide shipping and delivery instructions to plaintiff. During the contract period, however, the price of grass seed fell dramatically. Although defendant initially provided shipping instructions and plaintiff shipped conforming seed, defendant eventually refused to provide shipping instructions for delivery of additional seed under the contracts. After multiple requests for shipping instructions, and defendant's continued refusal to provide them, plaintiff cancelled the contracts. Over the next three years, plaintiff was able to sell at least some of the seed that defendant had agreed to purchase to other buyers.

The parties submitted their contract dispute to arbitration. Following an arbitrator's award in plaintiff's favor, plaintiff sought to enforce the award in court, and the trial court entered judgment over defendant's objection. Defendant appealed, and the Court of Appeals remanded for trial after concluding that the arbitration was not binding. In the subsequent bench trial, the court concluded that defendant had breached the contracts and that plaintiff had been entitled to cancel the contracts and seek damages. When the trial court awarded plaintiff its damages, the court noted that the parties had entered into fixed price contracts, "regardless of the market price at the time of harvest and shipment," and the court explained that "[e]ach party takes certain risks and hopes for certain benefits in this type of a contract." Nonetheless, the court concluded that plaintiff had an "obligation to mitigate damages" and was "not entitled to recover damages in an amount greater than actually incurred." Accordingly, the trial court awarded plaintiff the lesser of two measures of damages: the difference between the unpaid contract price and the market price (the measure under ORS 72.7080(1)) [UCC 2–708(1)] or the difference between the contract price and the resale price (the measure under ORS 72.7060 [UCC 2–706]). The trial court directed plaintiff to submit calculations of each measure of damages.

Both parties sought reconsideration. At a hearing on those motions, the trial court stated that it would not be "absolutely one-hundred percent convinced" about the appropriate measure of damages until it could see how each party calculated market price damages and resale price damages. The trial court acknowledged that plaintiff previously had submitted its calculation of market price damages and had proven those damages, but the court also directed the parties to calculate damages to account for any seed that had been resold. Subsequently, defendant submitted its analysis of damages based on the prices that plaintiff had received when it resold. Plaintiff criticized defendant's analysis and stuck by its calculation of market price damages, without submitting an analysis of damages based on resale prices.

Each party's calculation of damages for one of the breached contracts, contract 1874, illustrates the implications of using the market price or the resale price to calculate damages. The evidence at trial showed that the contract price for contract 1874 was $0.72 per pound. Plaintiff sought damages of $3,736.00 for that contract, apparently based on a market price of $0.64 per pound, resulting in a contract price minus market price differential of $0.08 per pound for 46,700 pounds of seed not accepted by defendant. Defendant argued, however, that plaintiff had resold at least some of that seed for $0.75 per pound, $0.03 per pound above the contract price and $0.11 per pound above plaintiff's market price calculation. Thus, according to defendant, plaintiff did not have any damages for that resold seed because plaintiff had resold for more than the contract price. If plaintiff recovered $0.08 per pound in market price damages, in addition to the $0.75 per pound that plaintiff allegedly had received on the resale, plaintiff ultimately would recover $0.83 per pound, which was $0.11 more than the contract price.

For that same contract, however, where the contract price was $0.72 per pound, defendant noted that some of the seed had been resold for $0.60 per pound. That meant that the resale price damages would be $0.12 per pound. That is, for at least some of the resold seed from contract 1874, plaintiff's resale price damages of $0.12 per pound would exceed plaintiff's claimed market price damages of $0.08 per pound. In sum, the parties' calculations of damages for contract 1874 showed that, with regard to some seed, the market price damage calculation would lead to a larger award, but that, with regard to other seed, the resale price damage calculation would lead to a larger award. On the whole, however, defendant calculated that plaintiff would receive a smaller amount of damages using the resale price measure of damages than plaintiff calculated that it would receive using the market price measure of damages.

The trial court awarded plaintiff damages using the resale price measure of damages as calculated by defendant. The trial court reasoned that plaintiff had not calculated damages as ordered by the court. The court stated that "even if Plaintiff [was] correct that Defendant's calculations [were] somehow flawed or incorrect, no alternative calculation ha[d] been offered." Thus, the trial court concluded that it was "left with no option but to accept Defendant's calculation."

The trial court also denied plaintiff's request for attorney fees. The court concluded that plaintiff had not adequately alleged its request for attorney fees, and, on the merits, rejected plaintiff's argument that it was entitled to recover attorney fees under a provision of the NORAMSEED Rules, which the parties had incorporated into their contracts. Those rules allowed a seller to recover "charges for collection of payment" if the buyer did not pay in full and immediately when due. Rather than construing the phrase "charges for collection of payment," however, the trial court stated that the term "fees" in the NORMASEED Rules was ambiguous, and the court purported to construe the term against plaintiff as the drafter of the contracts that had incorporated those rules.

Plaintiff appealed. As relevant on review, plaintiff argued that the trial court erred in not awarding plaintiff its market price damages under ORS 72.7080(1) [**UCC 2–708(1)**] or its attorney fees under the NORAMSEED Rules. *Peace River,* 253 Rapp. at 711, 722–23, 293 P.3d 1058.

The Court of Appeals reversed and remanded. On the first issue, the court noted that, at least on its face, the UCC allows a seller to recover damages as calculated under either ORS 72.7060 [**UCC 2–706**] (contract price less resale price) or ORS 72.7080(1) [**UCC 2–708(1)**] (contract price less market price). After reviewing the relevant statutory provisions, the court went on to conclude that, "[i]n the absence of a restriction within the UCC that precludes an aggrieved seller from seeking its remedy pursuant to ORS 72.7080 [**UCC 2–708**] if the seller has resold, we would decline to impose such a restriction." In support of that conclusion, the court explained that, once the buyer breaches, the buyer loses any right to control the goods or to "insist upon a different measure of damages." Moreover, the court noted, market price damages require the buyer to fulfill only the bargain to which it agreed. Although the court acknowledged that the UCC policy is that remedies should put an aggrieved party "in as good a position as if the other party had fully performed," ORS 71.3050(1) [**UCC 1–305(1)**], the court concluded that the intent of the UCC is to allow an aggrieved seller to recover market price damages, even if the seller has resold the goods. The court remanded the case for a proper calculation of plaintiff's market price damages.

On the issue of attorney fees, the Court of Appeals determined that the trial court had erred in its contract interpretation analysis by both interpreting the wrong contract term and failing to follow the contract interpretation framework in *Yeoman v. Parrott,* 325 Or. 358, 361, 363–64, 937 P.2d 1019 (1997). Applying the *Yeoman* analysis, the Court of Appeals first determined that the relevant contract term, "charges for collection," was ambiguous. The court went on to note that the trial court had failed to determine the intent of the parties as necessary under the second step of *Yogman.* Because the court concluded that there was some evidence in the record of the parties' intent regarding that contract term, the court remanded to the trial court to consider the parties' intent in the first instance.

Defendant sought review and now urges this court to reverse the Court of Appeals and affirm the trial court on both issues.

AN AGGRIEVED SELLER'S REMEDIES UNDER THE UCC

The UCC provides a variety of remedies to an aggrieved seller. *See* ORS 72.7030 [**UCC 2–703**] (providing an index of a seller's remedies). As noted, the issue in this case is whether an aggrieved seller who has resold goods can recover the difference between the unpaid contract price and the market price under ORS 72.7080(1) [**UCC 2–708(1)**], even when market price damages would exceed resale price damages under ORS 72.7060 [**UCC 2–706**].

Commentators and courts have taken two different approaches to this issue. Relying on the text and context of the sellers' remedies provisions, some commentators have argued that the drafters of the UCC intended for sellers to be able to recover either market price damages or resale price damages, even if the seller resold the goods for more than the market price. (Citations omitted.) On the other hand, Professors White and Summers, whose view has been adopted by a number of courts, have argued that the UCC's general policy is that damages should put a seller only in "as good a position as if the other party had fully performed," ORS 71.3050(1) [**UCC 1–305(1)**], meaning a seller who has resold should not be allowed to recover more in market price damages than it could recover in resale price damages. We agree with those commentators who have observed that the drafters did not clearly resolve this issue. (Citations omitted.) Nonetheless, we conclude that the text, context, and legislative history of the sellers' remedies provisions support a seller's right to recover either market price damages or resale price damages, even if market price damages lead to a larger recovery.

We analyze the relevant statutory provisions using the framework described in *State v. Gaines,* 346 Or. 160, 171–72, 206 P.3d 1042 (2009). We begin by examining the statute's text and context to determine the legislature's intent regarding a seller's remedies under the UCC. Because the relevant statutes are part of the UCC, we also consider the official UCC comments as an indication of the legislature's intent. In addition, "the legislative intent to make the UCC a uniform code makes relevant the decisions of other courts that have examined these questions and the discussions of the questions by scholars in the field, especially those scholars who participated in drafting the UCC." We also examine legislative history. The Oregon legislature enacted the UCC in 1961 "with little debate or discussion of the legislative intent," but the UCC was proposed so that Oregon could "obtain the same advantages that other states had gained from the adoption of a uniform and comprehensive set of commercial statutes." Given "the legislative intent to make the UCC a uniform code," *id.*, we consider prior drafts of the UCC, as drafted by the National Conference of Commissioners on Uniform State Laws (NCCUSL), as part of the legislative history.

Before examining the statutory scheme, however, we briefly review the law as it existed prior to the enactment of the UCC in Oregon. At common law, an aggrieved seller

> "ha[d] the election of three remedies: (1) To hold the property for the purchaser, and to recover of him the entire purchase money; (2) to sell it, after notice to the purchaser, as his agent for that purpose, and recover the difference between the contract price and that realized on the sale; (3) to retain it as his own, and recover the difference between the contract and market prices at the time and place of delivery[.]"

Krebs Hop Co. v. Livesley, 59 Or. 574, 588, 118 P. 165 (1911). *Krebs Hop Co.* suggests that, before Oregon adopted the UCC, an aggrieved seller had to elect between remedies, and if the seller resold the goods, it had elected its remedy and could recover only resale price damages, but not market price damages. Although the UCC retained some aspect of each of the remedies available at common law, as explained below, it specifically rejected the doctrine of election of remedies. *See* Legislative Comment 1 to ORS 72.7030 [**UCC 2–703**]. (Citation omitted.)

* * *

The UCC comments to the statute describing a seller's remedies confirm that interpretation. Although the comments acknowledge that, in a particular case, the pursuit of one remedy may prevent a seller from obtaining certain damages, the comments also state that the UCC chapter on sales "reject[s] any doctrine of election of remedy as a fundamental policy and thus the remedies are essentially cumulative in nature and include all of the available remedies for breach." Legislative Comment 1 to ORS 72.7030 [**UCC 2–703**] at 101. In contrast, the comments to the statute describing a buyer's market price remedy explain that that remedy "is completely alternative to 'cover' under ORS 72.7120 [**UCC 2–712**] and applies *only when and to the extent that the buyer has not covered.*" Legislative Comment 5 to ORS 72.7130 [**UCC 2–713**] at 110 (emphasis added). Thus, while the comments to the statute describing a seller's remedies expressly reject the doctrine of election of remedies, the comments to the statute describing a buyer's market price remedy appear to adopt that doctrine. Those comments further indicate that a seller who resells goods after a buyer's breach would not be considered to have "elected" the resale remedy and thus would not be precluded from seeking a larger damage recovery using the market price measure of damages.

The text of ORS 72.7060 [**UCC 2–706**], which sets forth the seller's resale remedy, similarly suggests that a seller who resells goods is not necessarily precluded from using the market price measure of damages, even if it leads to a larger recovery. ORS 72.7060(1) [**UCC 2–706(1)**] states that "the seller *may* resell the goods concerned or the undelivered balance thereof," which suggests that an aggrieved seller is not required to resell. (Emphasis added.) Similarly, the text of ORS 72.7060 [**UCC 2–706**] indicates that a seller who resells is not required to seek damages using the resale remedy. *See* ORS 72.7060(1) [**UCC 2–706(1)**] ("Where the resale is made in good faith and in a commercially reasonable manner the seller *may* recover the difference between the resale price and the contract price * * *." (Emphasis added.)). In fact, the unqualified text of ORS 72.7080(1) [**UCC 2–708(1)**] seems to suggest that market price is in fact the default measure of damages. *See* ORS 72.7080(1) [**UCC 2–708(1)**]. Thus, the text of the remedy provisions does not limit a seller who resells to its resale price damages.

As defendant notes, however, one of the comments to ORS 72.7060 [**UCC 2–706**] does indicate that the drafters intended ORS 72.7060 [**UCC 2–706**] to be a seller's primary remedy, and did not intend to allow a seller to recover more under the market price remedy. Comment 2 to ORS 72.7060 [**UCC 2–706**] explains that "[f]ailure to act properly under ORS 72.7060 [**UCC 2–706**] *deprives* the seller of the measure of damages there provided and *relegates* him to that provided in ORS 72.7080 [**UCC 2–708**] [market price damages]." Legislative Comment 2 to ORS 72.7060 [**UCC 2–706**] at 104 (emphasis added). That language suggests that the comment drafters viewed market price damages as less favorable, but it does not indicate *why* they viewed them that way. The pejorative language used in the comments does not necessarily lead to the conclusion that a seller who resells cannot use the market price remedy or must use the resale price remedy if it would yield the same or a smaller amount of damages than the market price remedy. That language instead could indicate that market price damages are considered less favorable because market price is often hard to prove, as many commentators have noted. As a result, that comment language is not dispositive, particularly in light of the text of the remedy provisions.

Turning to legislative history, prior drafts of the UCC provide additional insight into the drafters' intent to allow a seller to recover its market price damages, even if the seller has resold. In particular, in an earlier draft of the section describing the resale price remedy, section **2– 706**, one of the comments stated that that section provided

> " 'the *exclusive* measure of the seller's damages where the resale has been made in accordance with the requirements of this section. Evidence of market or current prices at any particular time or place is relevant *only* on the question of whether the seller acted with commercially reasonable care and judgment in making the resale.' "

See Gabriel, 23 Wake Forest L Rev at 436 (quoting UCC § **2–706** cmt. 3 (May 1949 Draft) (emphasis added)). Under that version of the UCC, a seller who had met the resale requirements would be required to use the resale price measure of damages. That comment later was revised, however, and when Oregon adopted the UCC, the comment included language that also had been in the 1949 draft comment, but the mandatory language had been removed, leaving only the permissive wording: "If the seller complies with the prescribed standard of duty in making the resale, he *may* recover from the buyer the damages provided for in subsection (1)." Legislative Comment 3 to ORS 72.7060 [**UCC 2–706**] at 104 (emphasis added). That shift, from resale as the exclusive remedy to resale as a permissible remedy, indicates that the drafters intended for a seller to be able to choose to recover market price damages, even after reselling under ORS 72.7060 [**UCC 2–706**].

Defendant argues, however, that even if a seller who resells can recover market price damages under ORS 72.7080(1) [**UCC 2–708(1)**], those damages cannot exceed the seller's resale price damages. Defendant primarily relies on the general policy statement set forth in ORS 71.3050 [**UCC 1–305**] to support its argument. ORS 71.3050(1) [**UCC 1–305(1)**] provides,

> "The remedies provided by the Uniform Commercial Code must be liberally administered to the end that the aggrieved party may be put *in as good a position as if the other party had fully performed* but consequential damages, special damages or penal damages may not be had except as specifically provided in the Uniform Commercial Code or by other rule of law."

(Emphasis added.) Defendant reasons that the reference in ORS 71.3050(1) [**UCC 1–305(1)**] to putting an aggrieved party "in as good a position as if the other party had fully performed" acts as a limit on the damages that a party can receive. Commentators and courts likewise have relied on that provision in concluding that a seller's market price damages should be limited to the actual loss suffered, by taking into account any goods that have been resold. (Citation omitted.)

The text of ORS 71.3050(1) [**UCC 1–305(1)**] indicates that the drafters of the UCC intended a seller's remedies to be compensatory. *See* Legislative Comment 1. The text of that section, however, also provides that the remedies in the UCC are to be "liberally administered." ORS 71.3050(1) [**UCC 1–305(1)**]; *see also* Legislative Comment 4. Nonetheless, we agree with defendant that the general policy of compensation provided in ORS 71.3050(1) [**UCC 1–305(1)**] must be taken into account.

We do not agree, however, that that policy necessarily limits an aggrieved seller who has resold to its resale price damages. Defendant argues that if it had fully performed, plaintiff could expect to recover only the contract price, and that limiting plaintiff to the difference between the contract price and the resale price therefore gives it the benefit of its bargain. As Professor Gabriel notes, however, limiting a seller to its resale price damages does not account fully for either party's expectations upon entering into the contract. He explains that a seller expects to be able to recover the difference between the contract price and the market price because it is the "logical and expected measure of damages," and because the ability to recover market price damages "is the natural assumption the seller makes in return for the risk inherent in the contract that the sale may not turn out to be economically beneficial to the seller. That the seller then resells the goods in no way diminishes this expectancy regarding the first contract." *Gabriel,* 23 Wake Forest L Rev at 449, 453. From the buyer's perspective, he argues that "the [buyer] has specific obligations and will suffer the consequences of the failure to perform these obligations because this is the [buyer's] expectation." *Id.* at 450. In other words, contrary to defendant's argument, an aggrieved seller expects to be able to recover market price damages under the contract, and a breaching buyer expects to have to fulfill its obligation to the seller—even if a seller resells and recovers market price damages, "the buyer's obligation is no more than the right the buyer originally conferred upon the seller." *Id.* at 449.

Moreover, limiting an aggrieved seller to its resale price damages ignores the risk for which the parties bargained. When parties bargain for fixed price contracts, each party assumes the risk of market price fluctuations. The parties are willing to take that risk because of the benefits that they might receive: if the market price decreases, the seller benefits, and if the market price increases, the buyer benefits. In a fixed price contract, therefore, market price damages represent the risk for which both parties bargained. For those reasons, we conclude that a seller can recover market price damages, even if the seller resells some of the goods at above the market price at the time and place for tender.

Defendant argues, however, that that conclusion does not account for an aggrieved party's duty to mitigate, which is consistent with the UCC's policy of minimizing damages. We do not understand the duty to mitigate to be a limit on a seller's market price damages because, as noted, the text demonstrates and commentators agree that a seller is not required to resell goods after a buyer's breach. If the duty to mitigate does not require the aggrieved seller to resell its goods, we do not think that the duty to mitigate can require the seller to use the resale price measure of damages. The comments to the resale remedy provision also acknowledge that the seller who resells does so for its own benefit, and not for the benefit of the breaching party as mitigation. *See* Legislative Comment 2 to ORS 72.7060 [**UCC 2–706**] at 104 (noting that the seller resells "in his own behalf, for his own benefit and for the purpose of fixing his damages"); *cf.* ORS 72.7060(6) [**UCC 2–706(6)**] ("The seller is not accountable to the buyer for any profit made on any resale."). Therefore, the principle of mitigation does not appear to limit an aggrieved seller's recovery to resale price damages under ORS 72.7060 [**UCC 2–706**]; the seller may instead seek market price damages under ORS 72.7080(1) [**UCC 2–708(1)**].

In sum, when viewed in light of the bargained-for market risks and the UCC's rejection of the doctrine of election of remedies, the text, context, and legislative history of the sellers' remedy provisions demonstrate that an aggrieved seller can seek damages under either ORS 72.7080(1) [**UCC 2–708(1)**] or ORS 72.7060 [**UCC 2–706**]. That means that an aggrieved seller can seek damages under ORS 72.7080(1) [**UCC 2–706(1)**] even if the seller has resold the goods and market price damages exceed resale price damages.

* * *

CONCLUSION

The decision of the Court of Appeals is affirmed in part and reversed in part. The judgment of the circuit court is affirmed in part and reversed in part, and the 11 case is remanded to the circuit court.

---

3. LOST VOLUME SELLER (2–708(2))

There are certain situations where sellers resell goods from a breached contract but neither **2–706** nor **2–708(1)** will allow the seller to recover their true expectation damages. A typical lost volume situation occurs when a seller shows that she would have made two sales but for the breach and so does not want the second sale to be considered a resale when calculating damages under **2–706**. The two sales refer to the expected sale from the breached contract and the second sale the seller actually made. In that situation, the seller's resale of the good should not be considered a resale under **2–706** because the seller deserves the profits she would have made from both sales. Similarly, in a situation like the one described above, **2–708(1)** will suffer from the same problem because it only attempts to determine the profit on the basis of a hypothetical resale at the time performance was due, using the market price at the time and place for tender. It does not consider the fact that the seller should be allowed to keep the profit on the second sale in addition to recouping the profit from the buyer on the breached contract.

To illustrate, imagine Jim's Computer Store regularly sells computers to its customers. Jim's contracts with Keith Rich to sell him a laptop computer for $1800, but Keith breaches the contract and refuses to buy the computer. If Keith had not breached, the computer store would have earned a profit of $200 from that sale (including overhead as permitted in **2–708(2)**). Jim sells several more identical computers to other customers for $1800. What happens if a court considers one of those sales as a resale of the breached contract and uses **2–706** to calculate seller's damages? You should see that the difference between the contract price and the resale price equals zero, so the only damages the computer store might be able to recover are any incidental damages that it can prove. In that case, the computer store earns the profit on the second sale but no profit on the first sale. However, if the computer store can show that the store would have made both sales, then the seller should be able to collect the profit it lost from the breached sale with Keith as well as the profit on the second sale. That means that the second sale will be disregarded when calculating damages and the seller will be awarded the lost profit on the breached contract.

In the computer store example, you should see that **2–706** damages would not award the seller its expectation damages. If the seller used **2–708(1)** it still would not recoup Jim's expectation damages even if we assume there is a market price a little lower than the contract price that Keith had agreed to pay. In that scenario, Jim would only get the difference between the lower market price and the contract price but would not get his full lost profit. This is a typical example of a lost volume seller.

The seventh circuit dealt with this issue in 1987 in the case of *R.E. Davis Chemical Corp. v. Diasonics, Inc.*, 826 F.2d 678, 683–685 (7th Cir. 1987). The court permitted the seller of a MRI machine to collect under **2–708(2)** as a lost volume seller. However, the court added a requirement that the seller show it would have been profitable to make both sales. It also addressed the problematic language in **2–708(2)** that says to account for "allowance for costs reasonably incurred and due credit for payments or proceeds of resale." Obviously, in the example above, if the resale of the computer is credited then Jim's Computer Store will be in the same situation as collecting under **2–706** and will not get its expectation damages. Here is what the *Diasonics* court said:

> We agree with Diasonics' position that, under some circumstances, the measure of damages provided under **2–708(1)** will not put a reselling seller in as good a position as it would have been in had the buyer performed because the breach resulted in the seller losing sales volume. However, we disagree with the definition of "lost volume seller" adopted by other courts. Courts awarding lost profits to a lost volume seller have focused on whether the seller had the capacity to supply the breached units in addition to what it actually sold. In reality, however, the relevant questions include, not only whether the seller could have produced the breached units in addition to its actual volume, but also whether it would have been profitable for the seller to produce both units. Goetz & Scott, *Measuring Sellers' Damages: The Lost-Profits Puzzle,* 31 Stan.L.Rev. 323, 332–33, 346–47 (1979). As one commentator has noted,

under the economic law of diminishing returns or increasing marginal costs [,] . . . as a seller's volume increases, then a point will inevitably be reached where the cost of selling each additional item diminishes the incremental return to the seller and eventually makes it entirely unprofitable to conclude the next sale.

Shanker, *supra* p. 7 n. 6, at 705. Thus, under some conditions, awarding a lost volume seller its presumed lost profit will result in overcompensating the seller, and **2–708(2)** would not take effect because the damage formula provided in **2–708(1)** does place the seller in as good a position as if the buyer had performed. Therefore, on remand, Diasonics must establish, not only that it had the capacity to produce the breached unit in addition to the unit resold, but also that it would have been profitable for it to have produced and sold both. Diasonics carries the burden of establishing these facts because the burden of proof is generally on the party claiming injury to establish the amount of its damages; especially in a case such as this, the plaintiff has easiest access to the relevant data. (Citations omitted.)

One final problem with awarding a lost volume seller its lost profits was raised by the district court. This problem stems from the formulation of the measure of damages provided under **2–708(2)** which is "the profit (including reasonable overhead) which the seller would have made from full performance by the buyer, together with any incidental damages provided in this Article (Section **2–710**), due allowance for costs reasonably incurred and due credit for payments or *proceeds of resale*." Ill.Rev.Stat. ch. 26, para. **2–708(2)** (1985) (emphasis added). The literal language of **2–708(2)** requires that the proceeds from resale be credited against the amount of damages awarded which, in most cases, would result in the seller recovering nominal damages. In those cases in which the lost volume seller was awarded its lost profit as damages, the courts have circumvented this problem by concluding that this language only applies to proceeds realized from the resale of uncompleted goods for scrap. (Citations omitted.) Although neither the text of **2–708(2)** nor the official comments limit its application to resale of goods for scrap, there is evidence that the drafters of **2–708** seemed to have had this more limited application in mind when they proposed amending **2–708** to include the phrase "due credit for payments or proceeds of resale." We conclude that the Illinois Supreme Court would adopt this more restrictive interpretation of this phrase rendering it inapplicable to this case.

We therefore reverse the grant of summary judgment in favor of Davis and remand with instructions that the district court calculate Diasonics' damages under **2–708(2)** if Diasonics can establish, not only that it had the capacity to make the sale to Davis as well as the sale to the resale buyer, but also that it would have been profitable for it to make both sales. Of course, Diasonics, in addition, must show that it probably would have made the second sale absent the breach.

─────────────

In summary, for a seller to qualify as a lost volume seller she needs to show that the seller has more inventory than buyers and that there is a reasonable likelihood that the seller would have made both sales—the one from the breached contract and the second sale. If a seller can prove those two factors exist, then the seller can show that the measure of damages in **2–708(1)** is "inadequate to put the seller in as good a position as performance would have done." Keep in mind, the seventh circuit added a requirement that both sales had to be profitable.

If a seller qualifies as a lost volume seller, the next step is to determine the lost volume seller's damages. The formula is deceptively simple. It is: contract price, minus direct costs, plus incidentals (**KP – DC + ID**).

Recall, you need to determine what profit the seller lost on the breached contract and **2–708(2)** permits a seller to include reasonable overhead as part of the profit. The biggest problem arises when trying to determine what the direct costs are. The courts have broken costs down into two categories. Those categories are fixed costs and variable costs. Fixed costs do not qualify as direct costs and variable costs do. Fixed costs include overhead; they are the type of costs that are not usually affected by a breach. Conversely, variable costs are those costs that a seller can stop once the buyer breaches. Thus, any variable costs will be subtracted from the contract price under the category of direct costs in the formula above. A buyer wants to maximize the amount of direct costs to lower overall damages, while a seller will want to minimize the amount of direct costs.

Do not get led astray by the term net profit. The term net profit usually considers all revenues and subtracts all expenses from those revenues. In other words, the expenses subtracted to determine net profit include those fixed expenses referred to as part of overhead. **2–708(2)** tells us not to subtract those types of expenses as direct costs; therefore, a seller's net profit is not relevant when determining **2–708(2)** damages.

Fixed expenses may include administrative costs such as permanent employees who keep working after a breach occurs, mortgage or rental payments for a building, bookkeepers, etc. Direct costs do not include those types of expenses. However, direct costs will include expenses that can be stopped because of the breach, such as the cost of the material to make a product, or subcontractors that no longer need to be hired. Incidental damages may include storage costs, upkeep charges, or restocking fees.

Consider the following example: Jamal Smith builds and sells greenhouses for consumers for use in their back yards. Myra Hall agreed to purchase one for $7500, but changed her mind and breached the contract. By the time that Myra breached the contract, Jamal had already delivered half of the glass windows to her house. Assume that Jamal can show he is a lost volume seller and the second sale is also for $7500. If the cost of materials is $6,000, those costs would go into the formula as direct costs, so they will be subtracted from the overall award. If Jamal has to pay $200 to have the glass windows removed from Myra's yard and returned to his shop, the damage formula would include those payments as incidental costs. A breach of one contract would not cause Jamal to lay off any employees or shut down any part of the business, so none of those expenses would be included in direct costs. In this simple scenario, the formula would be $7500 (KP) – $6000 (DC) = $1500 + $200 (ID) = $1700 total lost profit. What if you could show that Jamal was actually operating at a negative net profit because he was a new business and the startup costs were high? You should see that does not matter and is not considered anywhere in the formula. Jamal still lost a profit. The lost profit for **2–708(2)** purposes would remain $1700 regardless of net profits.

There are 2 other types of sellers that may try to recover using **2–708(2)**. The first one is often called a "jobber" and is not just a seller. A jobber is the middle person who is in the business of finding both buyers and sellers and then putting the contract together for the parties. For example, Matilda Enterprises knows that Joe Hill Electronics needs a supplier of cell phones and she knows that Louis Pratt is in the business of supplying cell phones. Matilda brokers a deal whereby Joe Hill agrees to buy 50 cell phones every other month for a year and Louis Pratt agrees to provide them. Matilda makes her money by finding a supplier who will supply the desired goods at a reasonable cost, then she may tack on a fee for her services to the final contract, and she finds a buyer who agrees to pay one price that includes her fee plus the supplier's costs. If Joe Hill or Louis Pratt breach the contract Matilda will lose the profit she expected to make from putting the two clients together. That profit is the difference between what the buyer agreed to pay and the seller's price for providing the cell phones. She may try to recover her lost profit using **2–708(2)**.

The other type of seller that may try to recover using **2–708(2)** is the seller who, after learning the buyer breached the contract, chooses to stop performance in the middle of manufacturing to mitigate her costs as permitted by **2–704**. The formula for this type of seller is quite complicated, but this book does not cover it.

4. ACTION FOR PRICE (2–709)

The UCC allows a seller to obtain specific performance in three situations enumerated in **2–709**. First, when a buyer has accepted goods, the seller may bring an action for price. This situation requires an understanding of the UCC sections related to performance—specifically **2–606** on acceptance, **2–601**, and **2–602** relating to rejection, and **2–608** on revocation. Pay particular attention to the default rule in **2–606(1)(b)** because it does not require a buyer to take any action, so many acceptances take place here. After a reasonable time to inspect has expired, an acceptance automatically occurs. If a buyer effectively rejects goods, it will prevent an acceptance under **2–606(1)(b)**, even if it is a wrongful rejection. This is not true of a wrongful revocation. If a buyer attempts to wrongfully revoke goods, it will not avoid an acceptance, so a seller may still win an action for price. *See* Comment 5 to **2–709**.

What happens if Marla agrees to purchase a new furniture set from Deek's Furniture Store and when it arrives she decides she does not want to buy the set, so she immediately calls the seller and rejects the furniture? As soon as Marla calls with the rejection, she has effectively rejected the goods by notifying the seller within a reasonable time as required by **2–602**. It is a wrongful rejection because there are no defects in the furniture but it is still effective. Once there has been an effective rejection, there cannot be an acceptance without the buyer taking some type of affirmative step that would qualify as an acceptance under **2–606(1)(c)**. Consequently, in the situation just described, Deek's will not be successful if it tries to pursue an action for price because there was no acceptance. Deek's will need to use one of the alternative remedies if he wants to sue for damages.

A wrongful revocation has a different result from a wrongful but effective rejection in an action for price. What happens in the example above if Marla accepts the furniture but after several weeks decides she does not like the color and attempts to revoke her acceptance? Will it affect the seller's ability to pursue an action for price? This time it should not because the UCC does not allow a buyer to wrongfully but effectively revoke. So, a wrongful revocation is not a revocation, the buyer would still have the goods, and they are still accepted goods. In that scenario, Deek's should be able to win an action for price because the goods were not defective, time to effectively reject has expired, and there was no basis for a rightful revocation.

A second possible scenario that will allow an action for price is where the seller sends conforming goods and they are lost or damaged along the way. This requires an understanding of the sections on risk of loss (**2–509** and **2–510**), tender and shipment (**2–503** and **2–504**), and delivery terms (**2–319**). If the risk of loss has passed to the buyer and the goods are lost or damaged within a commercially reasonable time after the risk has passed, the seller can sue for price. For example, Sam's Orange Groves in Miami,

Florida agrees to sell 2 pallets of oranges (about 2,600 pounds) to a buyer in Indianapolis, Indiana, FOB seller's warehouse, Miami. If the carrier has an accident en route to Indianapolis, the seller could sue the buyer for price and should be successful. Because this is a shipment contract, the risk of loss passed to the buyer when the oranges were loaded on the trucks at the seller's warehouse. Alternatively, if the delivery term had been FOB Indianapolis, the seller could not sue for price because the risk of loss has not transferred to the buyer.

The third possibility for an action for price occurs when a seller has either made reasonable efforts to resell the goods and cannot find a buyer willing to pay or the seller can show that, under the circumstances, she will not be able to resell the goods at a reasonable price. Two issues that may arise when a seller sues for price using this subsection are whether: (1) the seller made a reasonable effort to resell the goods and (2) whether the price a buyer was willing to pay was reasonable.

Also, this subsection requires that the seller identify the goods to the contract before reselling them. **2–501** provides the rules on identification. Often it may be as simple as putting aside goods for the buyer, shipping the goods, marking the goods, or any other way that the seller designates certain goods are intended for a particular buyer. If the contract is for fungible goods contained in a bulk, such as grain in a grain elevator, that is sufficient to identify them to the contract. *See* **2–105(4)**. For example, if a seller, Country Grains, sells 25,000 bushels of wheat that are contained in a grain elevator holding 100,000 bushels of grain, the fact that all of the wheat is comingled will not matter for identification purposes. The wheat is sufficiently identified to the contract.

If a seller successfully sues a buyer for price, the seller usually holds the goods until payment is received. Once the buyer pays the judgment, the seller will release the goods to the buyer.

B. BUYER'S REMEDIES

Before considering the specific damages available to the buyer, it is important to note that the buyer has several self-help remedies that may be used before resorting to litigation. These remedies include rejection or revocation for non-conforming goods. After that, the buyer's possible remedies look quite similar to the seller's. They include damages when a buyer finds a substitute transaction under **2–712**, contract-market differential under **2–713**, damages for accepted goods using **2–714**, and specific performance under **2–716**. For an index of these remedies see **2–711**. In addition to actual and incidental damages, a buyer often sustains other losses caused by the breach that are called consequential damages. Remember that a seller does not have a right to sue for consequential damages under the UCC.

When deciding which remedy section to use for damages for an aggrieved buyer, the first issue to consider is whether the buyer has accepted the goods. If a buyer has accepted goods and time for rejection or revoking that acceptance has passed there is only one relevant remedy section to use and that is **2–714**, the section for breach with regard to accepted goods. Obviously, if the buyer has accepted the goods, she cannot cover or sue for market price because she has the goods in her possession. And specific performance is not appropriate because the seller no longer has the goods.

1. COVER (2–712)

Like a seller, a buyer may decide to look for a substitute transaction after a seller breaches. **2–712** is a corollary to the seller's remedy section on resale. It is called cover. Cover occurs when a buyer searches on the open market for the same or similar goods as she had contracted for in the breached contract. Cover often permits the buyer to avoid other negative consequences of the seller's breach because it allows her to proceed with her business. **2–712** requires that when the buyer makes a substitute purchase it must be: (1) in good faith, (2) without unreasonable delay, and (3) a reasonable purchase. The UCC does not require a buyer to seek a substitute transaction and she is free to pursue market damages in lieu of cover. However, if the buyer is also suing for consequential damages, **2–715** mandates the buyer try to mitigate those damages by pursuing cover or otherwise.

There are various issues a seller may raise in an attempt to defeat the buyer's claim for cover. The first relates to timeliness. **2–712**'s comments make it clear that a buyer is allowed to take the necessary time to consider the options available before deciding the best way to cover. The facts of each case may impact the length of time a buyer has to look for a substitute transaction. For example, if market prices are rapidly rising, the seller may have less time to pursue cover than if market prices are falling. Therefore, reasonableness in this instance depends on the situation of each buyer.

The other issues that sellers often litigate concern whether the buyer's substitute purchase was reasonable or made in good faith. Note the goods do not have to be identical and in some cases replacement goods may even be better goods. **2–712**, Comment 1 states the issue as whether the substitute goods are "commercially usable as reasonable substitutes under the circumstances of the particular case." It does not always have to be the cheapest or most effective substitute, as long as it was reasonable at the time the buyer covered. For example, if a seller promises to deliver 12 Carrier brand central air conditioning units to a construction company, but repudiates the contract before delivery, the buyer may search for 12 comparable units. If the buyer is only able to locate 12 comparable Trane brand units at a slightly higher price, those units should qualify as cover.

The buyer will then ask the seller for the difference between the cover price and the contract price. The formula under **2–712** is cost to cover, minus contract price, minus expenses saved, plus incidental and consequential damages. **(CC) – (KP) – (ES) + (ID) + (CD)**. Additionally, if the buyer has paid any of the contract price to the seller the buyer is entitled to have that returned.

2. CONTRACT-MARKET DIFFERENTIAL (2–713)

This section is the corollary to the contract-market differential section for the seller (**2–708(1)**). The appropriate formula is market price, minus contract price, minus expenses saved, plus incidental and consequential damages. **(MP) – (KP) – (ES) + (ID) + (CD)**. As with cover, the seller has to return any money paid by the buyer toward the contract price. These damages are a little less straightforward than the seller's market damages because of the way **2–713** determines market price.

2–713 says to use the market price "at the time when the buyer learned of the breach" and the place to set the market price will depend upon the location of the goods. The market price is set at the place for tender unless the goods have been shipped to the buyer. If they have been shipped and the buyer has rejected or revoked acceptance, the market price will be set at the place of arrival.

Complications can arise because of when **2–713** sets the market price at the time the buyer *learns of the breach*. First, when does breach occur? Technically it cannot happen until the time performance is due. Market price is not a problem if the breach occurs on that date. But, what happens if there is an anticipatory repudiation? For example, if time for performance is set for December 1, but the seller calls the buyer and repudiates the contract on November 1, when does the buyer learn of the breach? A literal reading requires setting the market price on December 1 because an actual breach cannot occur until time before performance is due. However, if the market price is rising, then waiting until the date of performance can produce a windfall for the buyer. On the other hand, if the market price on the date of repudiation is used, that allows the breaching party to set the date and does not give a buyer an opportunity to search for a substitute transaction. Additionally, **2–610** permits an aggrieved party to wait a commercially reasonable time for the repudiating party to change her mind and perform. In trying to balance these two interests, the courts have not been consistent in their rulings on when to set the market price when the breach involves an anticipatory repudiation. The court in the following case had to wrestle with this issue and it decided on a compromise between the earliest and the latest dates.

COSDEN OIL & CHEMICAL COMPANY V. KARL O. HELM AKTIENGESELLSCHAFT

736 F.2d 1064 (5th Cir. 1984)

REAVLEY.

* * *

II. TIME FOR MEASURING BUYER'S DAMAGES

Both parties find fault with the time at which the district court measured Helm's damages for Cosden's anticipatory repudiation of orders 05, 06, and 07. Cosden argues that damages should be measured when Helm learned of the repudiation. Helm contends that market price as of the last day for delivery—or the time of performance—should be used to compute its damages under the contract-market differential. We reject both views, and hold that the district court correctly measured damages at a commercially reasonable point after Cosden informed Helm that it was cancelling the three orders.

Article 2 of the Code has generally been hailed as a success for its comprehensiveness, its deference to mercantile reality, and its clarity. Nevertheless, certain aspects of the Code's overall scheme have proved troublesome in application. The interplay among sections **2.610**, **2.711**, **2.712**, **2.713**, and **2.723**, Tex.Bus. & Com.Code Ann. (Vernon 1968), represents one of those areas, and has been described as "an impossible legal thicket." J. White & R. Summers, *Uniform Commercial Code* § 6–7 at 242 (2d ed. 1980). The aggrieved buyer seeking damages for seller's anticipatory repudiation presents the most difficult interpretive problem. Section 2.713 describes the buyer's damages remedy:

Buyer's Damages for Non-Delivery or Repudiation

(a) Subject to the provisions of this chapter with respect to proof of market price (Section **2.723**), the measure of damages for non-delivery or repudiation by the seller is the difference between the market price *at the time when the buyer learned of the breach* and the contract price together with any incidental and consequential damages provided in this chapter (Section **2.715**), but less expenses saved in consequence of the seller's breach. (emphasis added).

Courts and commentators have identified three possible interpretations of the phrase "learned of the breach." If seller anticipatorily repudiates, buyer learns of the breach:

(1) When he learns of the repudiation;

(2) When he learns of the repudiation plus a commercially reasonable time; or

(3) When performance is due under the contract.

[Citations omitted].

We would not be free to decide the question if there were a Texas case on point, bound as we are by *Erie* to follow state law in diversity cases. We find, however, that no Texas case has addressed the Code question of buyer's damages in an anticipatory repudiation context. Texas, alone in this circuit, does not allow us to certify questions of state law for resolution by its courts.

Fredonia Broadcasting Corp. v. RCA Corp., 481 F.2d 781 (5th Cir.1973) (*Fredonia I*), contains dicta on this question. The court merely quoted the language of the section and noted that the time for measuring market price—when buyer learns of the breach—was the only difference from pre-Code Texas law. *Id.* at 800. *See* Anderson, *Learning of Breaches under Section 2–713 of the Code,* 40 Tex.B.J. 317, 320 (1977). We have found no Texas case quoting or citing *Fredonia I* for its dicta on damages under section 2.713. Although *Fredonia I* correctly stated the statutory language, it simply did not address or recognize the interpretive problems peculiar to seller's anticipatory repudiation.

Since *Fredonia I,* four Texas courts have applied section **2.713** to measure buyer's damages at the time he learned of the breach. (Citations omitted.) In all of these cases the aggrieved buyer learned of the breach at or after the time of performance.

Two recent Texas cases indicate that appropriate measure for buyer's damages in the anticipatory repudiation context has not been definitively decided. In *Aquamarine Associates v. Burton Shipyard,* 645 S.W.2d 477 (Tex.App.—Beaumont 1982), *aff'd,* 659 S.W.2d 820 (Tex.1983), seller anticipatorily repudiated its obligation to construct and deliver ships. After seller learned of the repudiation, it covered by contracting with another party to complete the vessels. Since buyer covered under section **2.712**, the jury's answer to the section **2.713** damages issue was properly disregarded. Referring to comment 5 of section **2.713**, however, the Texas Court of Civil Appeals cited two cases that measured buyer's damages for anticipatory repudiation at different times. *Id.* at 479 & n. 8. *Cargill, Inc. v. Stafford,* 553 F.2d 1222 (10th Cir.1977), held that buyer's damages for anticipatory repudiation should be measured at a commercially reasonable time after he learned of the repudiation if he should have covered, and at the time of performance if buyer had a valid reason for failure or refusal to cover. In *Ralston Purina Co. v. McFarland,* 550 F.2d 967 (4th Cir.1977), the court measured buyer's damages at the market price prevailing on the day seller anticipatorily repudiated. The two citations in *Aquamarine* reveal uncertainty concerning the applicable time for measuring damages.

Hargrove v. Powell, 648 S.W.2d 372 (Tex.App.-San Antonio 1983, no writ), also indicates that the interpretation of section **2.713** in an anticipatory repudiation case has not been settled in Texas. In referring to the hypothetical case of seller's repudiation, the *Hargrove* court cited

Cargill and Professor Anderson's article, which presents the argument that "time when the buyer learned of the breach" means the time for performance or later.

We do not doubt, and Texas law is clear, that market price at the time buyer learns of the breach is the appropriate measure of section **2.713** damages in cases where buyer learns of the breach at or after the time for performance. This will be the common case, for which section **2.713** was designed. In the relatively rare case where seller anticipatorily repudiates and buyer does not cover, the specific provision for anticipatory repudiation cases, section **2.610**, authorizes the aggrieved party to await performance for a commercially reasonable time before resorting to his remedies of cover or damages.

In the anticipatory repudiation context, the buyer's specific right to wait for a commercially reasonable time before choosing his remedy must be read together with the general damages provision of section **2.713** to extend the time for measurement beyond when buyer learns of the breach. Comment 1 to section **2.610** states that if an aggrieved party "awaits performance beyond a commercially reasonable time he cannot recover resulting damages which he should have avoided." This suggests that an aggrieved buyer can recover damages where the market rises during the commercially reasonable time he awaits performance. To interpret **2.713**'s "learned of the breach" language to mean the time at which seller first communicates his anticipatory repudiation would undercut the time that **2.610** gives the aggrieved buyer to await performance.

The buyer's option to wait a commercially reasonable time also interacts with section **2.611**, which allows the seller an opportunity to retract his repudiation. Thus, an aggrieved buyer "learns of the breach" a commercially reasonable time after he learns of the seller's anticipatory repudiation. The weight of scholarly commentary supports this interpretation. (Citations omitted.)

Typically, our question will arise where parties to an executory contract are in the midst of a rising market. To the extent that market decisions are influenced by a damages rule, measuring market price at the time of seller's repudiation gives seller the ability to fix buyer's damages and may induce seller to repudiate, rather than abide by the contract. By contrast, measuring buyer's damages at the time of performance will tend to dissuade the buyer from covering, in hopes that market price will continue upward until performance time.

Allowing the aggrieved buyer a commercially reasonable time, however, provides him with an opportunity to investigate his cover possibilities in a rising market without fear that, if he is unsuccessful in obtaining cover, he will be relegated to a market-contract damage remedy measured at the time of repudiation. The Code supports this view. While cover is the preferred remedy, the Code clearly provides the option to seek damages. *See* § **2.712(c)** & comment 3. If "[t]he buyer is always free to choose between cover and damages for non-delivery," and if **2.712** "is not intended to limit the time necessary for [buyer] to look around and decide as to how he may best effect cover," it would be anomalous, if the buyer chooses to seek damages, to fix his damages at a time before he investigated cover possibilities and before he elected his remedy. Moreover, comment 1 to section **2.713** states, "The general baseline adopted in this section uses as a yardstick the market in which the buyer would have obtained cover had he sought that relief." *See* § **2.610** comment 1. When a buyer chooses not to cover, but to seek damages, the market is measured at the time he could have covered—a reasonable time after repudiation. *See* §§ **2.711** & **2.713**.

Persuasive arguments exist for interpreting "learned of the breach" to mean "time of performance," consistent with the pre-Code rule. If this was the intention of the Code's drafters, however, phrases in section 2.610 and **2.712** lose their meaning. If buyer is entitled to market-contract damages measured at the time of performance, it is difficult to explain why the anticipatory repudiation section limits him to a commercially reasonable time to await performance. *See* § **2.610** comment 1. Similarly, in a rising market, no reason would exist for requiring the buyer to act "without unreasonable delay" when he seeks to cover following an anticipatory repudiation. *See* § **2.712(a)**.

The interplay among the relevant Code sections does not permit, in this context, an interpretation that harmonizes all and leaves no loose ends. We therefore acknowledge that our interpretation fails to explain the language of section **2.723(a)** insofar as it relates to aggrieved buyers. We note, however, that the section has limited applicability—cases that come to trial before the time of performance will be rare. Moreover, the comment to section **2.723** states that the "section is not intended to exclude the use of any other reasonable method of determining market price or of measuring damages. . . ." In light of the Code's persistent theme of commercial reasonableness, the prominence of cover as a remedy, and the time given an aggrieved buyer to await performance and to investigate cover before selecting his remedy, we agree with the district court that "learned of the breach" incorporates section **2.610**'s commercially reasonable time.

* * *

3. BREACH OF ACCEPTED GOODS (2–714)

When the buyer has accepted goods and has lost the right to reject or revoke acceptance, **2–714** is the only section available to the buyer for damages. In addition to suing for any general damages, the buyer may sue for damages caused by a breach of warranty. The formula for those damages is the difference between the value of the nonconforming goods, (VNCG) and the value they would have had if the goods had conformed and there had not been a breach of warranty (VCG). Additionally, any incidental or consequential damages will be added to the amount of damages. The formula is **(VCG) – (VNCG) + (ID) + (CD)**.

The difference in value between conforming and nonconforming goods often is the cost to repair or replace the defective goods. However, if the buyer has owned the goods for a significant period of time this may complicate the matter because the goods will have depreciated and/or the buyer may have used the goods. The court may take this into account when determining damages. For example, if Duncan buys a new car and, after 1 year, the engine starts to have major problems, may Duncan sue for repair costs that essentially will give him a new engine that will now last much longer than the original one? Because this would give the buyer an unintended windfall, most courts will take into account the extra benefit a buyer will receive and deduct that from the total recovery. If repair or replacement are not an option, the parties may need to use an expert witness to help determine the value of the goods at the time they were accepted.

Another potential issue with **2–714** damages is whether to value the nonconforming goods using a subjective or an objective measure. Most courts use an objective measure, although some courts have been convinced to use the subjective value of the goods. In *Irmscher Suppliers, Inc. v. Schuler*, 909 N.E.2d 1040, 1050 (Ind. App. 2009), home owners complained of problems with screen windows they had purchased for almost $13,000 and sued for breach of the implied warranty of merchantability. Although not all of the windows were defective, the trial court awarded the home owners the value to replace all of the windows because they were bought as a single system. Additionally, the trial court allowed the buyers to recover more than the original contract price. The appellate court upheld the first part of that ruling but reversed the second.

> We have found several appropriate measures to value direct damages under Indiana Code § 26–1–2–714 [**UCC 2–714**]. The primary focus of all these measures is whether the award of damages is reasonable. Namely, we have approved in the past the following methods: (1) the cost of repair (but seldom have we allowed repair costs to exceed the initial value of the goods); (2) the fair market value of the goods as warranted minus the salvage value; (3) the fair market value of the goods as warranted at the time of acceptance less the fair market value of the goods as accepted; and (4) the replacement costs less the value of the plaintiff's use of the good up to the time of trial.

> * * *

We now turn to the case at hand. First, Pella and Irmscher challenge the portion of the replacement cost related to the twelve fixed casement windows. As for the cost to replace the twelve fixed casement windows, the Schulers introduced evidence that the twelve fixed casement windows and the twenty hinged casement windows with Rolscreens were purchased together as a functional and aesthetic system in consultation with both their contractor and an Irmscher sales representative. As such, the trial court could reasonably conclude that the defendants knew that the Schulers would need to replace all thirty-two windows if the Rolscreens were defective so that the windows on the plaintiffs' house would match and function together. We cannot say that the trial court abused its discretion in granting the Schulers damages for the cost of replacing the twelve fixed casement windows with double-hung windows.

Second, Pella and Irmscher challenge the amount of damages in excess of the original purchase price of the thirty-two windows. We agree with Pella and Irmscher that awarding the Schulers direct damages greater than the costs of the initial windows is not reasonable. Because the Schulers are replacing all the windows in their home with more expensive double-hung windows, the cost of replacement is not an appropriate measure of damages in this case, as the plaintiffs would receive something worth more than the original bargain. This damage award put the Schulers in a better position than had Pella and Irmscher fully performed. We conclude that, in this case, the damages for replacement of the windows cannot exceed the initial value of the windows. Rather, a more reasonable method to determine damages is the difference between the fair market value of the goods as warranted and the salvage value. Since the trial court ordered that Irmscher and Pella are entitled to possession of the windows in question, they in essence received the salvage value of the windows. As such, we determine that the reasonable amount of direct damages related to the replacement costs of the windows in this case is the fair market value of the goods as warranted, which is $12,986.13, and accordingly order these damages reduced to that amount.

———————

The difference between the value of conforming and non-conforming goods occasionally overlaps with consequential damages. This can be particularly problematic when the seller has disclaimed consequential damages. This issue occurred in the case of *T.Co Metals, LLC v. Dempsey Pipe & Supply, Inc.*, 592 F.3d 329, 339–341 (2d Cir. 2010). Although the seller shipped defective pipes the buyer was able to repair the pipe and use it in its business. Repairing the pipes affected the profit the plaintiff made on the contract when it resold the repaired pipe. The seller argued that the buyer's lost profit on the second contract was consequential damages that had been properly excluded from the breached contract. The buyer, however, argued that the amount it lost on the second contract was simply a reflection of the damages on the breached contract that were the same as the cost to repair the pipe. If the damages claimed by the buyer are the cost of repairing the pipe on the first contract, then they should be recoverable. However, if those damages were a result of a lost profit on the second contract, they were consequential damages and not properly recoverable because the seller had included a valid disclaimer of consequential damages. After finding that the arbitrator correctly awarded the buyer diminution-in-value damages pursuant to **2–714(2)**, the court considered the seller's argument against that award.

> In arguing to the contrary, T.Co errs by making the unwarranted assumption that the breach-of-warranty damages that the arbitrator calculated pursuant to N.Y. U.C.C. § 2–714(2) inescapably amount to an award of "lost profits," which in turn constitute consequential damages. There is a difference between the loss of the inherent economic value of the contractual performance as warranted, which N.Y. U.C.C. § 2–714(2) addresses, and the loss of profits that the buyer anticipated garnering from transactions that were to follow the contractual performance. The fact that the N.Y. U.C.C. addresses consequential damages in a separate section from diminution-in-value damages supports the inference that these two measures of damages are not necessarily equivalent. *See* N.Y. U.C.C. §§ 2–714(2), 2–715(2); *see also id.* § 2–714(3) (noting that, in addition to breach-of-warranty damages under § 2–714(2), "[i]n a proper case any incidental and consequential damages under the next section may *also* be recovered" (emphasis added)). New York case law similarly demonstrates that a buyer may recover the diminution in the value of the contractual goods as warranted even where there is a contractual exclusion of consequential damages. Our case law has also recognized in an analogous context that a contractual exclusion of consequential damages "does not foreclose liability for lost profits to the extent those profits merely reflect the value of the goods at destination." *Jessica Howard Ltd. v. Norfolk S. Ry. Co.,* 316 F.3d 165, 169 (2d Cir.2003).
>
> T.Co's attempts to undermine the weight of this authority are unpersuasive. Moreover, the sources T.Co cites in favor of equating Dempsey's damages under § 2–714(2) to consequential damages fall short of demonstrating that this result is conclusively established by New York law. For example, T.Co cites a Uniform Commercial Code treatise by James J. White and

Robert S. Summers for the proposition that § 2–714(2) damages are not appropriate where the contract excludes consequential damages. But the White and Summers treatise is more equivocal than T.Co acknowledges. It notes that "reasonable persons often differ whether an item of damage is 'consequential' or not," 1 James J. White & Robert S. Summers, UNIFORM COMMERCIAL CODE § 10–2 (5th ed.2006), *available at* 1 WS-UCC § 10–2 (Westlaw), and it specifically recognizes that "[i]n many cases, the consequential damages that appear to be recoverable under 2–715(2) may overlap with the direct 'difference-in-value' damages recoverable under 2–714(2)," *id.* The legal distinction between diminution-in-value damages and consequential damages, therefore, resembles the kind of "ambiguous law" that eludes analysis under the manifest disregard doctrine.

When assessing damages in the present case, the arbitrator properly looked not only to Dempsey's plans for the pipe, but also assessed a cross section of invoices from other companies that dealt in the pipe in order to determine the pipe's fair market value at the time and place of acceptance. In doing so, the arbitrator was engaged in determining "the value differential component of the buyer's total loss," not the subjective lost profits and lost business opportunities of Dempsey. This process of calculating damages constituted a reasonable interpretation of the legal distinction between the diminution-in-value damages that were available to Dempsey under the N.Y. U.C.C. and the consequential damages that were excluded by the parties' contracts. Accordingly, we perceive no manifest disregard of the law under any understanding of the current status of that doctrine. Whatever the scope of the manifest disregard doctrine may be in the wake of *Hall Street,* therefore, the arbitrator's decision to award diminution-in-value damages does not qualify. We therefore affirm the district court's denial of T.Co's motion to vacate the award of diminution-in-value damages to Dempsey.

4. SPECIFIC PERFORMANCE AND REPLEVIN (2–716)

Usually a buyer will pursue damages by using one of the vehicles previously mentioned in this chapter including cover, the contract-market differential, or breach of contract for accepted goods and breach of warranty. When one of those remedies does not properly compensate the buyer, she may sue for specific performance using 2–716. This section of the code is not as specific as the seller's right to sue for specific performance in 2–709. Instead of listing particular situations where specific performance is appropriate, 2–716 states that a court may award specific performance "where the goods are unique or in other proper circumstances." This sounds very similar to the common law approach that only allows specific performance when the subject matter is so unique that a damage award would not be appropriate. However, **2–716**, Comment 1, clarifies that the UCC is trying to be more expansive than the common law when it comes to awarding specific performance. The comments make clear that the drafters intended to allow specific performance in a larger number of situations than the common law. Comment 1 states that "this Article seeks to further a more liberal attitude than some courts have shown in connection with the specific performance of contracts of sale." And Comment 2 adds that when a court is using the uniqueness test for specific performance, it should consider the "total situation which characterizes the contract." Unlike common law, **2–716** does not require that the remedy at law be inadequate before a court can award specific performance. The code envisioned the court considering the realities of the market place and the commercial world when determining whether goods are unique enough to require specific performance.

Additionally, **2–716** adds two other situations where a buyer may sue for specific performance, similar to the situations specified in **2–709**. This section gives the buyer a right to replevin the goods in certain situations including where the buyer has made reasonable efforts to obtain cover, but the market is such that she cannot procure cover. Second is when the goods were shipped under reservation and the buyer has satisfied or tendered any security interest on the goods.

5.   INCIDENTAL AND CONSEQUENTIAL DAMAGES (2–710 AND 2–715)

The UCC allows buyers and sellers to collect incidental damages as long as they are reasonable expenses caused by the breach. The seller's incidental damages under **2–710** include charges related to caring for goods, returning goods, or extra costs incurred when reselling goods. The buyer's incidental damages are similar to sellers. **2–715(1)** permits buyers to collect charges related to caring for rejected goods or effecting cover. These charges can be quite high. One case allowed incidental damages over a million dollars for a charge of storing nuclear material.

Consequential damages, however, are treated differently. UCC remedies only permit buyers to recover consequential damages. These damages compensate a buyer for losses, other than direct damages, caused by the breach. **2–715** divides them into two categories. The important distinction between **2–715(2)(a)** and **(b)** relates to foreseeability and mitigation. A buyer may collect damages to property or a person proximately caused by a breach of warranty under **2–715(2)(b)** without having to prove they were foreseeable to a seller or that they could have been prevented. **(2)(a)**, however, is more narrow because it limits the recoverable losses for the buyer to those that the seller had reason to know about and "could not reasonably be prevented by cover or otherwise."

Sellers are typically wary of consequential damages because they can cause much larger losses. For example, if a laptop battery burns up and destroys a laptop a seller may not worry about being responsible for those damages because the seller only has to replace the laptop computer. However, if the burning laptop causes a fire that destroys a home, it will be much costlier for a seller to fully compensate the buyer. Consequential damages also may include lost profits and losses caused by an interruption of buyer's business. So, sellers worry more about these damages and, as a result, may try to limit their exposure to consequential damages. Although the UCC allows a seller to limit or exclude consequential damages, that right is not boundless. **2–719** prohibits a limitation of consequential damages where the result is unconscionable. Further, **2–719(3)** states that a "limitation of consequential damages for injury to the person in the case of consumer goods is prima face unconscionable." So, a seller does not have the same ability to limit damages in consumer cases where personal injury could arise. Remember that **1–201(b)(11)** defines consumer as "an individual who enters into a transaction primarily for personal, family, or household purposes."

The following case considers a variety of consequential damages for the buyer in addition to the cost to cover. Notice the consequential damages that the court did not allow and the court's reasoning for that denial.

ELDESOUKY V. AZIZ

2015 WL 1573319 (S.D.N.Y. Apr. 8, 2015)

COTT, J. L.

By Opinion and Order dated December 19, 2014, the Court granted summary judgment against Hatem Abdel Aziz on Plaintiffs' breach of contract claim. The Court now considers the damages to which Plaintiffs are entitled by virtue of obtaining summary judgment against Aziz. For the reasons that follow, the Court directs that judgment be entered against Aziz in the amount of $1,237,301.36, plus prejudgment interest, as well as $8,310.13 in attorneys' fees.

I.   *BACKGROUND*

* * *

A.   Factual Background

On January 13, 2011, plaintiffs Tasneem Company ("Tasneem") and Al-Yasmin Company ("Al-Yasmin"), through their principals Eldesouky and Abbas Elsayed Abbas ("Abbas"), respectively, entered into a contract with defendant General Trade Corporation, Inc. ("General Trade") to purchase 2,000 metric tons of flaxseed at $420 per metric ton. Eldesouky agreed to pay 10% of the total cost, Abbas 75%, and Aziz 15%. After confirming that the flaxseed met the contracted-for quality specifications, Plaintiffs paid Aziz $721,590 in installments over the next several months.

Sometime thereafter, Plaintiffs learned that Aziz had contracted, through Pyramid, with a Canadian company named Richardson International Limited ("Richardson") to purchase 4,000 metric tons of flaxseed at $660 per metric ton. They further learned that Aziz had paid Richardson using $443,750 of Plaintiffs' money. Plaintiffs therefore contacted Richardson, and Richardson agreed to credit the money it had received from Aziz towards Plaintiffs' own purchase, but only if they agreed to acquire 4,000 metric tons of flaxseed at the same price Pyramid had agreed to pay. Plaintiffs agreed to these terms, and Aziz was to transfer $278,360 to Richardson as the remainder of the money Plaintiffs had paid him. Ultimately, Aziz did not deliver this money either to Richardson or to Plaintiffs nor did Plaintiffs receive the flaxseed they contracted to purchase from General Trade.

Plaintiffs began receiving shipments of flaxseed from Richardson in August 2011. Richardson's first shipment was 989.062 metric tons of flaxseed. Richardson credited a pro rata portion of the money received from Aziz towards Plaintiffs' purchase. Plaintiffs resold this flaxseed at a loss due to its poor quality. Because Plaintiffs allegedly had a difficult time finding buyers for further shipments, Richardson then sold 750 metric tons of flaxseed on Plaintiffs' behalf, crediting a pro rata portion of Aziz's payment towards the flaxseed, which again resulted in a loss to Plaintiffs. Richardson sent a third and final shipment of 242.193 metric tons of flaxseed to Plaintiffs in approximately September 2012; however, it was seized by Egyptian authorities due to the low quality of grain. In total, Plaintiffs received 1981.255 of the 4,000 metric tons contracted for from Richardson. During this period, Richardson also charged Plaintiffs storage fees for the flaxseed.

B. Procedural History

On November 26, 2013, Plaintiffs moved for summary judgment against Aziz and default judgment against General Trade and Pyramid. Neither Aziz nor the corporate defendants submitted any responsive papers, and the Court granted summary judgment against Aziz with respect to Plaintiffs' breach of contract claim in an amount to be determined upon further submissions by the parties. The Court then held a conference to discuss conducting an inquest on damages on January 22, 2015, but Aziz did not appear. The Court now has before it Plaintiffs' submissions on damages and a separate application for attorneys' fees in connection with their motion for discovery-related sanctions. Aziz has not submitted any opposition papers.

II. *DISCUSSION*

* * *

B. Damage Calculations under the Uniform Commercial Code

The UCC provides that its remedies "must be liberally administered" with the goal of placing the non-breaching party "in as good a position as if the other party had fully performed." N.Y. U.C.C. Law § **1–305(a)**.

Section **2–711(1)** of the UCC provides an aggrieved buyer with a number of options where, as here, a seller fails to deliver goods: the buyer may "(a) 'cover' and have damages under [§ **2–712**] as to all the goods affected whether or not they have been identified to the contract; or (b) recover damages for non-delivery as provided in [§ **2–713**]." Both sections **2–712** and **2–713** also provide that a buyer may recover any incidental and consequential damages "less expenses saved in consequence of the seller's breach."

The UCC defines incidental damages to include, among other things, "any commercially reasonable charges, expenses or commissions in connection with effecting cover and any other reasonable expense incident to the delay or other breach." *Id.* § **2–715(1)**. Consequential damages, on the other hand, are those "resulting from the seller's breach" and may include "any loss resulting from general or particular requirements and needs [of the buyer] of which the seller at the time of contracting had reason to know and which could not reasonably be prevented by cover or otherwise." *Id.* § **2–715(2)(a)**; *see also Kenford Co. v. County of Erie,* 73 N.Y.2d 312, 321 (1989) (Consequential damages "are restricted to those damages which were reasonably foreseen or contemplated by the parties during their negotiations or at the time the contract was executed."). Where a contract is silent as to consequential damages, "the court must take a 'common sense' approach, and determine what the parties intended by considering 'the nature, purpose and particular circumstances of the contract known by the parties . . . as well as what liability the defendant fairly may be supposed to have assumed consciously.'" *Schonfeld v. Hillard,* 218 F.3d 164, 172 (2d Cir.2000) (quoting *Kenford,* 73 N.Y.2d at 319).

1. General Damages

Here, upon learning of Aziz's breach, Plaintiffs attempted to "cover" by purchasing flaxseed from Richardson. Under the UCC, a "buyer may 'cover' by making in good faith and without unreasonable delay any reasonable purchase of or contract to purchase goods in substitution for those due from the seller." N.Y. U.C.C. Law § **2–712(1)**. Although Richardson's flaxseed price was higher than General Trade's, and Richardson required Plaintiffs to purchase twice as much flaxseed, there is nothing to suggest that Plaintiffs' decision to purchase cover from Richardson was not in good faith or otherwise unreasonable. (Citations omitted.) Upon learning of Aziz's breach, Plaintiffs promptly contacted Richardson and contracted with it for flaxseed because if they had not, Richardson would have kept the money that Aziz had already transferred. Therefore, Plaintiffs are entitled to "recover from the seller as damages the difference between the cost of cover and the contract price . . . less expenses saved in consequence of the seller's breach." N.Y. U.C.C. Law § **2–712(2)**.

The difference in price between the Richardson and the General Trade contracts is calculated as follows: Plaintiffs agreed to pay General Trade $420 per metric ton exclusive of shipping fees, which, because they agreed to pay only 85% of the total costs, is effectively $357 per metric ton. Richardson required Plaintiffs to pay $660 per metric ton exclusive of shipping costs. Plaintiffs therefore paid $303 more per metric ton to purchase 2,000 metric tons of flaxseed from Richardson than they would have paid Aziz/General Trade absent the breach, and are therefore entitled to **$606,000** as a result ($303 per metric ton multiplied by 2,000 metric tons).

Additionally, after transferring $443,750 of Plaintiffs' money to Richardson, Aziz still retained $277,840 of the money Plaintiffs had paid under the General Trade contract ($721,590 minus $443,750). Aziz has not returned this sum to Plaintiffs or provided an equivalent amount of flaxseed. Therefore, Plaintiffs are entitled to receive **$277,840** in addition to their cover damages, for total general damages of **$883,840** ($606,000 plus $277,840).

2. Incidental Damages

Plaintiffs seek as incidental damages the storage fees they incurred in connection with the Richardson flaxseed purchase. The Court finds that storage fees are both commercially reasonable and related to the breach. Richardson charged Plaintiffs $41,239.51 for storage from November 30, 2011 to April 30, 2012 ($0.12 per metric ton of flaxseed per day) as well as $221.85 in connection with the September 2012 flaxseed shipment. Together, this equals **$41,461.36** in storage fees ($41,239.51 plus $221.85).

3. Consequential Damages

Plaintiffs seek consequential damages for: (1) their lost profits, (2) costs associated with the lower quality of flaxseed received from Richardson, and (3) the cost of purchasing an additional 2,000 metric tons of flaxseed from Richardson. The Court will address each of these categories of consequential damages in turn. For the reasons that follow, Plaintiffs are entitled to $312,000 in lost profits. However, Plaintiffs have not demonstrated that they are entitled to any damages related to additional flaxseed purchased from Richardson or that Aziz is responsible for the losses they suffered as a result of the poor quality of Richardson's flaxseed.

a. Lost Profits

First, Plaintiffs seek lost profits, which they calculate by reference to the Egyptian market price for flaxseed "[a]t the time that the flaxseed from Aziz was to be delivered." Where, as here, a contract for the purchase of goods contemplates that the buyer will resell those goods, lost profits are found to constitute consequential damages that the seller should have reasonably foreseen at the time of contracting. (Citations omitted.) Plaintiffs contend that the market price for flaxseed in Egypt was $816 per metric ton at the time they had intended to resell it. Because the difference in price between the Richardson and General Trade contracts was already accounted for as part of cover damages, the Court will calculate lost profits using the $660 per metric ton price from Richardson, as Plaintiffs suggest. Accordingly, Plaintiffs' lost profits on 2,000 metric tons of flaxseed are $156 per metric ton ($816 minus $660), or **$312,000** in total ($156 per metric ton multiplied by 2,000 metric tons).

b. Poor Quality of Flaxseed from Richardson

Second, Plaintiffs seek damages to compensate them for the lower quality (and consequently, lower value) of the flaxseed they received from Richardson. The Court finds that such damages are not appropriate based on the record presented here. The Court agrees with Plaintiffs that, in a resale contract such as the one at issue here, it is reasonably foreseeable that if the buyer does not receive goods meeting the quality specifications in the contract, losses would result. Here, Plaintiffs' contract with General Trade specified the quality of flaxseed to be sold and included a provision that, if upon testing, the flaxseed did not meet these requirements, Plaintiffs would be entitled to receive their contractual down payment back. Therefore Aziz can be deemed to have understood at the time of contracting that flaxseed quality was one of Plaintiffs' "particular requirements and needs." N.Y. U.C.C. Law § **2–715(2)(a)**.

Nevertheless, Aziz's breach was not the proximate cause of Plaintiffs' losses in this regard; rather, Richardson's failure to deliver flaxseed of a higher quality represents a break in the causal chain. Therefore, regardless of whether such a category of damages may have been foreseeable, Aziz is not liable for losses due to the poor quality of flaxseed Richardson provided to Plaintiffs.

c. Additional Flaxseed Purchased from Richardson

Finally, Plaintiffs seek recompense for having to purchase an additional 2,000 metric tons of flaxseed from Richardson. While it may have been foreseeable that, upon a breach, Plaintiffs' source of cover flaxseed might require them to purchase extra grain, Plaintiffs have not shown that they did, in fact, purchase this additional flaxseed. The record reflects that Plaintiffs agreed to purchase 4,000 metric tons of flaxseed from Richardson, but that they have paid for only 1981.255 metric tons to date, the last shipment of which was more than two years ago. At the Court's January 22, 2015 conference, Plaintiffs' counsel represented that, after receiving flaxseed from Richardson of such poor quality, plaintiffs "basically said they weren't going to take anymore shipments," and instead initiated arbitration. Despite representations to the contrary, Plaintiffs have not provided the Court with any information on the result of this arbitration or argued its impact on any damage calculation. The record thus does not support any damages in this category.

4.   Prejudgment Interest

Plaintiffs also seek prejudgment interest, which they characterize as "incidental damages." "The law of the state which was applicable in determining liability in the first instance, is applicable in determining whether an award of prejudgment interest is appropriate." *Vitol S.A., Inc. v. Koch Petroleum Grp., LP,* No. 01-CV-2184 (GBD), 2005 WL 2105592, at *12 (S.D.N.Y. Aug. 31, 2005) (citing *In re Gaston & Snow,* 243 F.3d 599, 609 (2d Cir.2001)). Here, the Court has applied New York law, and in New York, prejudgment interest *"shall* be recovered upon a sum awarded because of a breach of performance of a contract," at a rate of nine percent per year. N.Y. C.P.L.R. § 5001(a) (emphasis added), § 5004.

New York law further provides that interest "shall be computed from the earliest ascertainable date the cause of action existed, except that interest upon damages incurred thereafter shall be computed from the date incurred." N.Y. C.P.L.R. § 5001(b). "[I]n breach of contract actions, 'the earliest ascertainable date' referenced in C.P.L.R. § 5001(b) for the purposes of computing prejudgment interest 'arises when the alleged breach occurred.'"'Citibank, *N.A. v. Barclays Bank, PLC,* 28 F.Supp.3d 174, 185 (S.D.N.Y.2013) (quoting *McNally Wellman Co. v. New York,* 63 F.3d 1188, 1200 (2d Cir.1995)). Here, the Court finds that the date on which Aziz entered into a contract with Richardson (April 26, 2011) is the date of the breach, and correspondingly, the date upon which interest begins to accrue with respect to Plaintiffs' general damages and lost profits. Plaintiffs' incidental damages, however, accrued at a later date; specifically the dates on which Richardson charged them for flaxseed storage (May 1 and July 25, 2012), and interest on these amounts shall be calculated accordingly.

＊ ＊ ＊

6.   ARTICLE 2A REMEDIES

Similar to the Article 2 division of buyer's and seller's remedies, Article 2A divides remedies into remedies for the lessor and lessee. **2A–523** is the index of lessor remedies. Two major differences between lessor and seller remedies are found in **2A–523(1)**. **(1)(c)** gives the lessor the ability to repossess the leased good and **(1)(f)** mentions lessor's right to pursue any other remedies allowed by the contract. **2A–527** is comparable to the seller's remedy of resale except that the substitute lease transaction has to be substantially similar to the breached lease. One last difference from sales can be found in **2A–523** that allows the lessor to collect compensation for any loss to the residual interest. The main remedies for a lessee are analogous to a buyer's remedies and an index of those remedies can be found in **2A–508**.

C. DEFENSES

Two last arguments that may be used as defenses by a party in breach and consequently may impact an aggrieved party's ability to obtain damages are impracticability and unconscionability. The section on impracticability (**2–615**) excuses a breaching seller from paying damages when certain unanticipated situations arise. Unconscionability is not a vehicle for excusing a breach. Instead, **2–302** allows a court to refuse to enforce all or any part of a contract that it finds unconscionable. Although attorneys tend to think of using it more often with a consumer case, it applies to all contracts including commercial ones.

1. EXCUSE (2–615)

This section applies to delays in performance as well as non-performance. Impracticability is often broken down into four questions: (1) is performance impracticable, (2) was this impracticability caused by an unforeseen contingency, (3) was the non-occurrence of the contingency a basic assumption of the contract, and (4) was the risk of the contingency allocated to either party? The answers to the first 3 questions need to be in the affirmative and the answer to the last question needs to be in the negative for the party claiming impracticability to be successful.

Although sellers have tried to use increased cost as an excuse for breach, those arguments have not been very successful. **2–615**, Comment 4 states that "increased cost alone does not excuse performance unless the rise in cost is due to some unforeseen contingency which alters the essential nature of the performance." Also, a rise or fall in the market is not going to be a successful reason for claiming impracticability.

If the situation causes a failure of part of the performance instead of the entire performance, the seller needs to determine how to allocate production and deliveries in a fair and reasonable manner. Additionally, the seller needs to seasonably notify the buyer of the problem and whether performance will be delayed or will not be forthcoming.

2–615 only refers to sellers and the doctrine is more appropriate for sellers than buyers because usually the only performance required of a buyer is to pay for goods. Some courts have indicated that buyers can use **2–615** in proper circumstances. If a buyer has any issues using **2–615**, she may want to use the more appropriate doctrine of frustration of purpose. That common law doctrine should apply to UCC cases because **1–103** directs that the principles of law and equity supplement the UCC, unless displaced by the code.

One other section, **2–613**, allows a seller to be excused from performance when goods identified to the contract "suffer casualty" while risk of loss is still with the seller. This section refers to goods specific to a contract and not fungible goods. For example, if a seller has a contract to sell the Batmobile from the Batman movie and it is destroyed, **2–613** may offer the seller an excuse. If the loss is only partial, **(b)** allows a buyer to inspect the goods and decide whether to accept the goods, taking into account the damages.

2. UNCONSCIONABILITY (2–302)

The courts originally developed the doctrine of unconscionability to police against grossly unfair contracts. When the doctrine was first codified in the UCC, there were some skeptics who were not sure it belonged in a commercial code. Yet, it remains a powerful policing tool for a grossly one-sided bargain. When a party claims a contract, or any part of it, is unconscionable the court will take evidence from both sides before deciding the result of the claim. **2–302** gives the court considerable leeway to fashion a fair remedy. It may refuse to enforce the entire contract, refuse to enforce the offending clause, or "limit the application of any unconscionable clause as to avoid any unconscionable result."

Most courts require a party claiming unconscionability to show both substantive and procedural unconscionability before a court will find a contract or any part of it to be unconscionable. Substantive unconscionability refers to the actual terms of the contract and procedural unconscionability is about the process or how the parties agreed to the contract. Additionally, unconscionability is judged at the time the contract is made. Where a contract is so unfair and one-sided that it "shocks the conscience" a court may find it to be unconscionable.

PROBLEMS

1. At the end of the Sockeye salmon season, Sam's fishery of Seattle, finds that it has a considerable amount of processed salmon fillets. On August 1 it contracts to sell a large number of the fillets to Super Fishes in Dallas, Texas for a price of $2.00 per pound, FOB Dallas. Delivery is due by rail on or before August 21 and payment is due within 30 days of the buyer receiving the goods. On August 4, before the shipment has been delivered to the railroad, Super Fishes contacts Sam's and repudiates the contract. Additional facts that you may or may not need to answer this question are: (these prices are per pound so your answer should state the damages as a price per pound):

Market prices of filets in Dallas on August 1	$2.04
Market prices of filets in Seattle on August 1	$1.54
Market prices of filets in Dallas on August 4	$1.92
Market prices of filets in Seattle on August 4	$1.40
Market prices of filets in Dallas on August 21	$1.14
Market prices of filets in Seattle on August 21	$1.00
Cost of shipping from Seattle to Dallas	$ .05
Cost to store the filets per day in Dallas	$ .03
Cost to store the filets per day in Seattle	$ .04

See 2–319 and 2–708.

a.   If Sam's sues Super Fishes and asks for damages under 2–708(1), what amount should it receive?

b.   Would it make a difference if the price had been agreed to as **$1.98 FOB Seattle**?

c.   Assume that the price was **$2.00 FOB Dallas** and that Super Fishes did not repudiate. Instead it rejected the shipment for no valid reason when it arrived in Dallas on August 20. What damages would Sam's be able to get?

2.   Professor Ginger Binger, a professor at a nationally known college of music, recently won a singing contest and decided to use her winnings to buy a new state of the art Roland V piano for $7,000 from Saul Goldstein's piano store. The day it arrived she asked the delivery service to place it in her music studio. The next day she heard about a different piano for sale that was less expensive and decided to buy it instead. She called Saul's and told them to pick up the piano because she did not want it. See 2–601, 2–602, 2–606, 2–608, 2–708, and 2–709.

a.   If Saul's sues Ginger Binger in an action for price what are the chances he will be successful?

b.   Would your answer to (a.) change if Ginger waited for a month before calling Saul's and then Saul's sues for price?

3.   Sarah Seller owns a store in the Tampa Bay area that sells pet food and toys and also has a small grooming business as a sideline. Sarah wanted to get into the business of handling show dogs and she thought the best way to do that was to concentrate on the grooming side of her business, so she decided to sell the entire inventory in her store and get completely out of the retail business. She had an extensive collection of high-end organic gourmet food and chew toys and a rare line of raw frozen dog food items that had to be stored in a special airtight freezer that Sarah rented for $50 per week. On February 1, after extensively examining Sarah's inventory, Hans Buyer, also in Tampa, contracted to buy the entire inventory for $150,000. Hans agreed to pick up the inventory on April 1. For reasons that are not particularly relevant to this

inquiry, Hans Buyer repudiated the contract on March 1. Sarah located a substitute buyer in Miami on March 7 and contracted to sell the inventory for $130,000 with delivery on March 15, FOB Miami. She did not give Hans Buyer notice of the resale and resold the inventory on March 15.

On March 13, a major scandal broke out in the organic gourmet pet food and toy industry having to do with chemicals being found in the organic food and dangerous pesticides found in the toys. Many pets throughout the United States became very ill as a result of eating the tainted food and playing with the tainted toys. This created such an uproar among pet owners that it caused many customers to boycott the sale of organic pet food and toys. Because of these events, the value of Sarah's entire inventory drastically declined. On March 15, the inventory that Sarah planned to sell to Hans Buyer was worth $90,000 and on April 1 it was worth $75,000. Sarah had to pay a freight service $500 to deliver the inventory to Miami. See 1–305, 2–703 Comment 1, 2–706, and 2–708.

   a. Sarah retains you to handle her breach of contract against Hans Buyer. What is the appropriate measure of damages for a court to award and why? Consider all possibilities from both buyer's and seller's perspectives.

   4. Matthew Electronics, a high volume seller of custom computers hardware, made a contract to sell a top-of-the-line personal computer to Bowser for a "package price" of $5,000, delivery to be made on December 10. On December 5, Bowser repudiated saying he had been ill and missed a lot of work so he was unable to buy the computer right now. It was a relatively slow holiday season so the computer sat on Matthew's shelf until Dec. 20 when he notified Bowser that he was selling his computer at a discount. Matthew put this computer and all the other computers in the store on sale for 20% off. This reduced the computer that had been set aside for Bowser to $4000 and Matilda bought it for that price. The market price for comparable computers was $5,000.

Matthew bought the computer components for a total of $1500. He hired "independent contractors" who charged him $500 per computer to assemble and test components. The share of Matthew's business overhead apportioned to the computer was $100. See 2–706 and 2–708.

   a. What would Matthew need to show to be able to recover as a lost volume seller?

   b. Assume Matthew's is a lost volume seller. What would its damages be?

   c. Assume Matthew's is not a lost volume seller. What would its damages be?

   d. Would your answer to (c.) change if Matthew's did not give Bowser notice of the resale?

   5. Josie Hills owns a manufacturing business in Kansas City, Missouri that specializes in making high-end light fixtures for very expensive homes.

Josie regularly supplies Unicorn Housing with a variety of light fixtures. She intended to use the bronze from Jeff's metals to fulfill her contractual obligations with Unicorn Housing. Josie had a contract with Unicorn Housing to sell them 100 dozen bronze light fixtures at $200 per fixture. That contract contained a liquidated damages clause that required Josies to pay $1,000 per day for each day of delay in supplying the light fixtures. She also contracted with Jeff's Metals of Milwaukee, Wisconsin to supply her business with 4,000 pounds of bronze at $1.00 per pound, FOB Josie's business, Kansas City. Josie did regular business with Jeff's metals and they usually supplied about 80% of the bronze metal that she needed in her manufacturing business. Jeff Smith, the owner of Jeff's Metals, had visited Josie's business and was aware that Josie resold her light fixtures to a variety of businesses in the construction industry. About three weeks before Jeff's was scheduled to deliver the 4,000 pounds of bronze, Jeff called Josie and told her that his buyers had made a number of errors and they would not be able to deliver the 4,000 pounds of bronze as promised.

Josie immediately began a search for 4,000 pounds of bronze she needed to manufacture the light fixtures for Unicorn Housing. Josie's contract with Unicorn Housing had a liquidated damages clause that reduced Josie's final payment by a significant amount for each day of delay. Due to a growing shortage in bronze metal, the price of bronze had been slowly escalating for several months and Josie had some trouble locating enough bronze to meet her contractual needs. She found 2 other suppliers. Several days after Jeff's repudiated Josie located Orca Metals and they agreed to sell Josie 3000 pounds of similar quality bronze at $1.25 per pound but it would take several weeks to deliver. The bronze from Orca would not be enough to allow her to meet her contractual obligations because she could not make the required number of light fixtures for Unicorn Housing and it would cause a delay of 3 weeks. Pelican Quality Metals of Chicago said they could supply the full amount needed, 5,000 pounds, three days later than originally scheduled for Jeff's delivery, but the cost would be $1.50 per pound and the quality of the bronze would be slightly better than the bronze that Jeff's Metals was supposed to supply. Josie agrees to buy 5,000 pounds of the slightly better bronze from Pelican FOB Chicago. The cost of shipping the metal from Milwaukee to Kansas City is $1,500 and the cost of shipping the metal from Chicago to Kansas City is $1,200. Additionally, Josies delivery to Unicorn Housing will be delayed by 3 days. See 2–712 and 2–715.

    a.   Is Josie entitled to sue for cover damages?

    b.   Assume that she will be able to sue for cover and determine her damages.

    c.   Assume that Josie's was not able to cover due to a supply shortage in the bronze market. The price of bronze metal was $1.30 per pound on the day of repudiation, $1.40 per pound 10 days after the repudiation, and $1.60 per pound 20 days after repudiation on the day performance was due. What would Josie's contract-market damages be?

6. Lane Yar contracted to buy a new Cessna jet for $325,000 for her family textile business. She took delivery on September 1 and immediately took it on several business trips. She began to have problems the third week after she purchased the plane and she immediately called Cessna and demanded they repair the problem. Although they attempted to fix the problems on several different occasions they were never able to get the jet to reach its full potential. After a month of attempted repairs Lane finally had an independent mechanic examine the jet and he advised her that the cost of repair would be $50,000. Additionally, Lane lost 2 jobs because the jet was in the shop and each one would have produced a profit on $35,000. See 2–714.

    a.   If Lane wants to keep the jet, what damages should she sue for?

7. Enviro Wood Co. contracted with Red Forest Co. to purchase cross ties. Both companies were in the business of treating cross ties for industrial and commercial use. Enviro had a forward contract with Shannon railroad to resell the cross ties it would be receiving from the contract with Red. The cost of ties had risen considerably during the pendency of the contract and, as a result, Red notified Enviro that it would be unable to perform under the contract. Enviro tried on numerous occasions to get Red to perform under the contract, but it refused to do so because of the increased cost. Enviro obtained price quotations from several other suppliers but the cost was so high that Enviro realized it could produce the cross ties in its own business for less money than it could purchase them from other sources. Instead of spending more money to cover from other suppliers, Enviro produced the cross ties internally and resold them to Shannon railroad.

Additionally, Enviro claimed $40,000 in lost profits from using its own facilities to produce cross ties to replace the ones that Red refused to provide. It argued that it covered by internally manufacturing the cross ties, although it could have been producing cross ties and selling them to new or different customers instead of producing cross ties to substitute for the ones that Red failed to provide. See 2–712 and 2–715.

    a.   When Enviro sues for damages will it be entitled to cover and will it be able to recover the $40,000 in lost profits?

8. In a completely separate matter, Enviro Wood, located in Kansas City contracted to buy 1000 gallons of micronized copper, a non-toxic preservative used to treat softwoods, for $60,000 from Clean Chemical Co. located in San Diego. The contract was FOB San Diego with a delivery date of October 1. Clean chemical called Enviro on September 22 and repudiated the contract. The market price of micronized copper on September 22 was $65,000 in San Diego and $63,000 in Kansas City. The cost to ship the chemical from San Diego to Kansas City is $2,000. See 2–308, 2–319, and 2–713.

    a.   If Enviro does not cover, what are its damages?

    b.   How would your answer to (a.) change if the contract was FOB Kansas City?

c. How would your answer to (a.) change if the contract did not contain a delivery term?

d. How would your answer to (a.) change if the chemical was delivered to Enviro in Kansas City? Upon arrival Enviro's accepted the chemicals but after testing found that the product was defective and properly revoked its acceptance?

9. Joe Jones was an automobile enthusiast with a penchant for corvettes. He was particularly thrilled when the manufacturer announced it would produce a limited number of special edition Corvettes to commemorate the selection of the Corvette as the Pace Car for the Indianapolis 500. Joe visited Smith's Chevrolet and spoke to Chris Engle, a salesman at the dealership, about the possibility of ordering one of the special edition corvettes. After about an hour of discussion, they reached an agreement that allowed Mr. Jones to purchase the car if Smith Chevrolet could secure one from the manufacturer with the specific options that Joe wanted included. Only 6,000 cars were going to be manufactured and a dealer was entitled to only order one. The price was $130,000 with the options Joe requested. Four months later, Joe called Chris and asked him when the car would arrive. Chris said they expected to receive it within a month. Chris asked if they could keep the car at the dealership for promotional purposes for several weeks and Joe agreed. On May 1, Chris called Joe and told him that the car had arrived; but, he also informed Joe that, due to the publicity and demand for these cars, the value had been greatly inflated and Joe could not buy it for $130,000. Instead, the dealer was taking bids and he already had received bids for over $150,000 from people all over the US, including Hawaii. Chris informed Joe that he could bid on the car. Joe refused and filed suit for specific performance. The dealer argued that the corvette is not unique because it is not an heirloom or one of a kind. See 2–716.

a. Should Joe be awarded specific performance?

10. Fresh Air Manufacturing manufactures and sells incinerators. Carmen Parker owned a 40-acre recreational camp that accumulated considerable garbage, so Carmen decided to see if there was a way to dispose of the trash economically and in a way that would cause much less pollution than his current method. He contacted Fresh Air and, after telling them what he wanted, the manager of Fresh Air invited him to visit their plant and inspect the equipment they sold and operated. Carmen was very impressed with what he saw, so after being assured that the units would meet the camp's specific needs, he contracted to buy 2 incinerators for $30,000. The contract contained written warranties and did not disclaim any implied warranties.

Carmen had two concrete slabs installed as advised by Fresh Air. Several days later, a representative from Fresh Air visited him and told him that he needed to sign some new papers. He told Carmen that the previous papers had a problem and the ones he had now were essentially the same except they had a new manager's signature. The representative said they needed to be signed so Fresh Air could be paid and they could deliver the incinerators to the camp.

Carmen quickly read over the papers and signed them so he could have the incinerators installed. They were delivered the next day.

Unfortunately, the incinerators never worked properly. Every time Carmen complained to Fresh Air they tried to fix the problem, but were never successful. Carmen made four payments but after he determined that the incinerators were useless and would not work he stopped making payments. After refusing to make any more payments, Fresh Air sued the Parker Camp for all of the money due on the contract.

Carmen comes to your office for advice. You look at his contract and notice that it contains what appears to be a valid disclaimer of all implied warranties and no other written warranties. When you show that to Carmen he is shocked. He said the original contract did not have a disclaimer and he was assured that Fresh Air would stand behind their work. You realize that without any written warranties, the only good argument Carmen has is to argue that Fresh Air breached the implied warranty of merchantability and maybe the fitness warranty, but you keep rereading the disclaimers and they seem to track 2–316 word for word.

Carmen wants you to help him win this lawsuit and he also wants to recoup the money he has already paid Fresh Air. See 2–314 and 2–302.

a. What arguments can you make for Carmen to defend against the breach of contract suit filed by Fresh Air? What arguments will Fresh Air make?

b. Will Carmen be able to sue Fresh Air for breach of an implied warranty?

c. What options does the court have to fashion a remedy in this case?

CHAPTER 6

INTRODUCTION TO PAYMENT SYSTEMS AND NEGOTIABILITY

■ ■ ■

The following five chapters are concerned with Payment Systems. This area of law is governed by UCC Articles 3 and 4 together with other state and federal law. Because of the risk and inconvenience associated with carrying large sums of currency, commerce is often transacted using non-cash forms of payment. The two means of payment that Articles 3 and 4 cover are drafts, which include checks, and promissory notes. Article 3 provides the basic rules governing notes and drafts, while Article 4 covers the bank-collection process and is, therefore, primarily concerned with checks.

This chapter discusses the characteristics of drafts and notes, showing examples of each. The concept of negotiability is also introduced in this chapter. This concept is important because whether an instrument is negotiable or nonnegotiable affects its marketability and value. This chapter explains the relationship between a negotiable instrument and the underlying transaction (such as a sale of goods or services) that prompted its issuance. This chapter also presents the seven requirements for negotiability and the concept of negotiable instruments as "couriers without luggage" that each holder can evaluate at face value without engaging in time-consuming research. As this chapter will show, negotiable instruments must be signed writings with certain indicia of ready transferability, containing unconditional language promising or ordering only the payment of a fixed sum of money at a time certain, without imposing additional obligations.

Chapter 7 builds upon Chapter 6, introducing three types of parties who may have rights in a negotiable instrument: assignees, holders, and holders in due course. Holders in due course have superior rights of enforcement, as compared with the other two, that enable them to take instruments free from certain defenses that might otherwise limit their rights, thus protecting the marketplace and their own expectations. Chapter 7 also shows how parties' indorsement (or failure to indorse) affects their rights and obligations vis-à-vis one another and with regard to the instrument. Note that the word "indorsement," in this context, is spelled with an "i" rather than the more familiar spelling with an "e."

Chapters 6 and 7 are concerned with Article 3. Chapter 8 covers the bank-collection processes in Article 4. Chapter 8 also explores the relationship between a bank and its customers, describing the rights and responsibilities of both regarding the payment of items and allocation of losses.

Chapter 9 presents the various ways parties can sue and be sued under theories of contract liability, tort liability, and breach of warranty found in Articles 3 and 4. Chapter 9 discusses which theory of liability is most appropriate, and which party is most likely to bear the loss, under a variety of potential litigation scenarios.

Chapter 10 introduces several kinds of payments that fall outside Articles 3 and 4, including wholesale funds transfers and letters of credit, as used in what are called "documentary sales" transactions. These forms of payment involve Articles 4A and 5, respectively. Chapter 10 also covers payments with credit and debit cards. Credit and debit cards are included because they are so central to daily life, even though they fall outside the UCC and are governed by federal law. Chapter 10 concludes with non-bank financial services and several forms of payment governed primarily by contract law, including mobile payments and virtual currency such as Bitcoin.

A. INTRODUCTION TO PAYMENT SYSTEMS LAW

Most readers probably use electronic payments as a primary, or even exclusive, means of payment. Electronic payment systems are governed by laws originally written with traditional paper instruments—paper checks and promissory notes—in mind. Thus, to understand the law of electronic payment systems, it is important to become familiar with the paper-based systems on which the law was built and to understand when these paper-based systems are still used.

Article 3, entitled "Negotiable Instruments," and Article 4, entitled, "Bank Deposits and Collections," were part of the original UCC published in 1952. Both were based on the Negotiable Instruments Law (NIL), which the Uniform Law Commission (ULC) promulgated in 1896. The NIL was the ULC's first successful uniform act, and each of the states adopted it. Articles 3 and 4 were revised in 1990 and 1991, respectively, and amended in 2002.

B. AN INTRODUCTION TO NOTES AND DRAFTS

3–102(a) indicates that Article 3 applies to negotiable instruments. Notes and drafts are the two types of instruments with which Article 3 is concerned. A note is an unconditional written promise by one party to pay money to another, and is normally an instrument of credit to be repaid at a designated future date rather than a "demand" item payable immediately at issuance. Notes are two-party paper, the two parties being (1) the promisor, or maker, and (2) the promisee, or payee. In a loan transaction, the borrower is normally the maker of the promissory note, and the lender is the payee. **3–104(e)** provides the definition of "note," and **3–103(a)(12)** defines "promise."

The following is a graphic representation of a simple promissory note:

> ### PROMISSORY NOTE
>
> For value received, I do hereby promise to pay to Payee or order, one hundred fifty thousand and no/100 dollars ($150,000.00) The terms and conditions of such note are as follows: . . .
>
> */signed/ Maker*

Drafts, by contrast, are three-party paper, the three parties being (1) the drawer, who orders payment to be made, (2) the drawee, which is the party that receives the order and, if it accepts the order, makes payment accordingly, and (3) the payee, to whom the draft is payable. "Draft" and "order" are defined in **3–104(e)** and **3–103(a)(8)**, respectively. "Drawer" and "drawee" are defined in **3–103(a)(4)** and **(5)**, respectively. A draft is generally used as an instrument of convenience and is thus usually payable on demand, although "time drafts" payable at a future date do exist. The most common kind of draft is a check. Checks are, by definition, payable on demand, as **3–104(f)** indicates. In the case of a check, the bank customer is the drawer, and the bank on which the check is drawn is the drawee.

The following is a simplified graphic representation of a check:

> *Drawer's Name*
> *123 Main Street*
> *Detroit, MI 76543*   *Date of Check* _____
>
> Pay to the
> Order of   *Payee* _____   *$ amount* _____
>
> *Amount of check and no/100* ------------------------- _____
>
> *Drawee National Bank*
>   */signed/ Drawer*
> MEMO _____

On the "memo" line might appear a notation such as "April rent," designating the purpose for the check. Such information is not required, however, and the memo line is frequently left blank.

What is pictured above is a traditional paper check. Electronic payments, such as those made on-line via credit card or debit card, in addition to on-line bank payments or mobile payments, are increasingly replacing the paper check as a payment mechanism. Even so, some individuals and businesses still prefer paper checks. As you will learn in these materials, paper checks present better protections against fraud or unauthorized use than some of their electronic counterparts.

In most cases, even when an individual writes a paper check, the check will be converted to an electronic image for processing. This conversion facilitates rapid check-processing and eliminates some historical sources of check fraud—such as the "check kiting" featured in the popular movie "Catch Me If You Can."

C. THE CONCEPT OF NEGOTIABILITY

3–104, which will be the primary focus of Section F of this chapter, provides an overview of the features that make a payment instrument negotiable. Before we get there, it is useful to explore the concept of negotiability in more general terms. Negotiability is a characteristic of Article 3 instruments and certain other commercial documents such as negotiable warehouse receipts and bills of lading. These other commercial documents are briefly discussed in Chapter 10.

Negotiability is probably the hardest concept in this chapter for most students to master, for one, simple reason: The word is familiar, but has a completely different meaning in the context of payment systems. "Negotiable," as that term is used in Articles 3 and 4, means "easily transferable." Thus, a "negotiable instrument" is one that a person or entity who was not the original payee can purchase with confidence and without having to do much more than verifying the authenticity of the instrument and the identity of the presenter. To understand this concept, imagine that you have been given a check as a birthday gift. You are the payee of this check, because it is payable to you. You present the check to your bank for cash or for deposit, and it either gives you cash or credits your account for the amount of the check. In this sense, the bank "purchases" the check. Although the teller probably will verify your identity (at least if you request cash) and will examine the instrument for any obvious irregularities, he or she probably will not question you about how and why you were given the check. The reason for this is simple: the check is a negotiable instrument. Therefore, the bank's right to enforce the check does not depend on knowing the story behind the check.

Purchasers of negotiable instruments—such as the bank in our example—rely on the information found on the face of such instruments to disclose defects or risks that affect their value. In addition, as Chapter 7 shows, only negotiable instruments can be transferred in such a way that a transferee can be a "holder in due course," a denomination that carries superior rights of enforcement under some circumstances.

To understand Article 3's concept of negotiability, it may be useful to begin with a contrasting Article 2 example involving a theft of goods. The graphic below shows a theft of goods from their true owner, who then seeks to reclaim the goods from a bona-fide (good faith) purchaser for value ("BFP") who bought the goods from the thief.

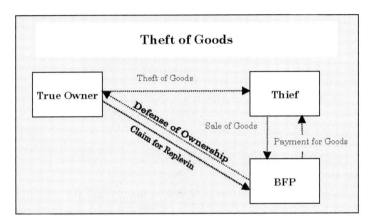

It is impossible for a purchaser of stolen goods, even a "good faith purchaser for value" within the definition of **2–403(1)** such as the BFP in this graphic, to obtain good title. Instead, because the thief had no title to those goods, the thief had no rights to convey. Thus, if the owner and the BFP were to assert competing claims to the goods, the owner would prevail unless either the thief or the BFP had acquired title to the goods via the property law doctrine of adverse possession.

The opposite result can be reached in some cases under Article 3, if what is stolen is a negotiable instrument rather than goods. First, consider the possibility of a stolen check. As the discussion below shows, several conditions must be satisfied before the bona-fide purchaser of a stolen check (who is called a "holder in due course") may keep the check, but it is possible.

These are the conditions that must be met: (1) The check must be a "negotiable instrument" within the meaning of **3–104**, (2) The check must be transferred in such a way as to constitute a "negotiation" as defined in **3–201** instead of a mere assignment of rights, (3) The possessor of the instrument must qualify as a "holder in due course," as defined in **3–302**, and (4) There must not be any "real defenses" against enforcement of the instrument, as outlined in **3–305**. "Personal defenses," as presented in the same code section, are less serious and do not prevent a holder in due course from enforcing the instrument. If each condition is met, then the holder in due course may be entitled to enforce the stolen check, unlike the BFP described above. This chapter explains how a note or draft can qualify as a negotiable instrument. The concepts of negotiation, holders in due course, and real and personal defenses are introduced in Chapter 7. For now, understand that a holder in due course is much like a BFP.

This graphic shows what happens when a check is stolen:

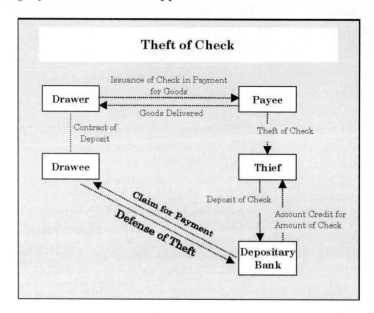

This illustration shows a theft of a check from the payee. The thief deposited the check in his or her bank account. Because a depositary bank is often a holder in due course, it may be able to enforce the check despite the theft. As Chapter 7 will explain, a depositary bank that qualifies as a holder in due course can enforce this check because theft is a "personal defense."

When a note is stolen instead of a check, some labels change, but the outcome is similar:

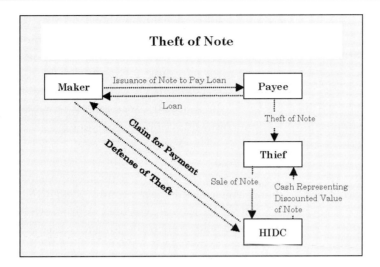

As with the check, the note was stolen from the payee. The thief then sold the note to a holder in due course, who paid for the note. The payment would almost certainly be less than the face value of the note. Because notes are instruments of credit, this discount would take into consideration the time value of money and the risk that the maker would fail to pay the note when it came due. As between the maker of the stolen note and the holder in due course, the holder in due course would prevail.

Favors v. Yaffe, 605 S.W.2d 342 (Tex. Civ. App. 1980), illustrates the superior rights of a holder in due course. In 1971, a salesman selling land in Arizona approached Mr. and Mrs. Favors in New Orleans. The salesman represented that the land purchase was backed by a six-month money-back guarantee. There were some limitations attached to the guarantee. Buyers could get their money back only if, "upon their on-site inspection of the property in Arizona, they wished to back out." After this disclosure, Mr. and Mrs. Favors purchased the property sight-unseen. They made payment via a promissory note payable to the land-sale company.

About six months later, Mr. and Mrs. Favors traveled to Arizona to exercise the refund option. When they arrived in Arizona, a company representative offered to extend the guarantee for another year, during which time the company would try to sell the Favors' land to another person, and would split any profit with Mr. and Mrs. Favors. Mr. and Mrs. Favors agreed and continued to make payments on the property for some time. Later, they made a second attempt to exercise their refund option.

Unbeknownst to Mr. and Mrs. Favors, twelve days after they purchased the property, the land-sales company sold the note to a third party. The third party knew nothing about the guarantee, which did not appear on the face of the note but was instead contained in a separate document. The third party testified that it would not have purchased the note had it known that Mr. and Mrs. Favors had been promised a money-back guarantee. The third party refused to honor the guarantee and sought to enforce the note, and Mr. and Mrs. Favors resisted the claim for payment on the ground that they had been defrauded by being denied the promised guarantee.

Because the court found the third party was a holder in due course, and because Mr. and Mrs. Favors' defense of fraudulent inducement is a personal defense that does not bind a holder in due course, the third party was entitled to enforce the note. Mr. and Mrs. Favors had recourse only against the land-sale company that actually defrauded them. Unfortunately, wrongdoers are frequently unavailable for suit or judgment-proof. As between Mr. and Mrs. Favors and the third-party who purchased the note, Mr. and Mrs. Favors were in the better position to avoid this loss by insisting that the guarantee appear on the face of the note. Thus, Mr. and Mrs. Favors were required to pay the note even though they did not get the promised guarantee.

D. SPECIALIZED INSTRUMENTS

Sometimes, an ordinary check or promissory note is ill-suited to the parties' needs for one of a variety of reasons, so a specialized instrument is employed instead. Consider a transaction involving a sale of goods. Out of concern that a buyer's personal check may be dishonored for insufficient funds, a seller might insist that the buyer provide a cashier's check (3–104(g)), teller's check (3–104(h)), or certified check (3–409(d)). If a buyer lacks a personal checking account, he or she might pay with a money order (3–104(f)) purchased with cash, especially if he or she is planning to send payment through the mail. Article 3 defines and governs each of these instruments.

1. CASHIER'S CHECKS

A cashier's check (3–104(g)), sometimes called a "bank check," "treasurer's check," or "official check," is often used in real estate closings or to purchase big-ticket items such as vehicles. From a payee's point of view, such a check is more reliable than a personal check because the bank's own funds are involved, such that the check cannot be dishonored due to insufficient funds.

Here is how a cashier's check might work in the case of a car sale: The buyer of the car would obtain the final sale price from the seller and would then go to a bank to obtain a cashier's check. This buyer, who would normally be a customer of that bank such that there is some banking history between the parties, would either give the bank cash in the amount of the sales price or ask the bank to withdraw the funds from one of his or her accounts with the bank. The bank customer is called a "remitter" (3–103(a)(15)) because he or she has remitted payment for the cashier's check. Having received funds from the remitter, the issuing bank would deposit those funds and then draw the cashier's check on its own funds. Thus, the remitter is not a party to the cashier's check. Instead, the bank issues the cashier's check against its own funds.

In *Warren Finance, Inc. v. Barnett Bank*, 552 So.2d 194, 195–96 (Fla. 1989), the Supreme Court of Florida described the effect of a cashier's check, as follows:

> The purpose of a cashier's check is to act as a cash substitute in dealings between parties. . . . A cashier's check, unlike an ordinary check, stands as on its own foundation as an independent, unconditional, and primary obligation of the bank. . . . People accept a cashier's check as a substitute for cash because the bank stands behind the check, rather than an individual. . . . Because the bank. . . is personally liable, the holder of a cashier's check knows that upon presentment the issuing bank will honor its obligation. . . . When used in the place of a personal check, . . . the parties' expectation is that the cashier's check will remove all doubt as to whether the instrument will be returned to the holder unpaid due to insufficient funds in the account, a stop payment order, or insolvency.

The following image represents a cashier's check. Because the remitter is not a party to the check, his or her name appears on the check only for informational purposes. Thus, on this check, the remitter might be Luke Smith and the memo line might read, "for Mustang convertible."

2. TELLER'S CHECKS

To avoid drawing on its own funds, a bank may issue a teller's check instead of a cashier's check. A teller's check is like a cashier's check in that it is drawn at the request of a remitter, after the bank receives funds from the remitter. However, a teller's check is not drawn on the bank's own funds like a cashier's check, but on another bank's funds or, occasionally, a nonbank drawee's funds. A teller's check requires a pre-existing deposit or credit relationship between the drawer bank and the bank on which the funds are drawn. The remitter of a teller's check remits payment to the drawer bank. Like a cashier's check, a teller's check is considered substantially more reliable than an ordinary, uncertified personal check.

The following image represents a teller's check. Note that the names of both the drawer bank and the drawee bank appear as parties to the instrument. As before, the remitter's name appears only for informational purposes. Once again, our remitter might be Luke Smith and the memo line might read, "for Mustang convertible."

Drawer National Bank Teller's Check   No. 1234567

                                                  Date of Check
_____

Pay to the
Order of   **Payee** _____ $ amount ___

Amount of check and no/100 ----------------------

Drawn On
Drawee National Bank

Remitter: _____

MEMO _____   */signed/ Drawer's Agent* ___

---

3. MONEY ORDERS

A money order, which can be thought of as a prepaid check, may be used to pay for goods or services when the purchaser does not have access to, or does not wish to use, a personal checking account. In fact, money orders are defined in **3–104(f)** as a form of check. The purchaser pays for the money order up front, and then the issuer (which may be a bank, a post office, or even a convenience store) draws the money order on its own funds. Although this description may sound like a cashier's check or teller's check, there is an important distinction to keep in mind: Some money orders are subject to a customer's stop-payment order just as an ordinary check is. Such a money order is less reliable than a cashier's check or teller's check, neither of which is subject to a stop-payment order. In *Trump Plaza Associates v. Haas*, 692 A.2d 86, 88, 90 (N.J. Super. Ct. App. Div. 1997), the court describes money orders as follows:

> A personal money order has been described as an instrument "for the convenience of anyone who does not have an ordinary checking account and needs a safe, inexpensive and readily accepted means of transferring funds." . . . There is a public perception that personal money orders are the equivalent of cash or have the credit of the issuing bank behind them. . . . However, this perception is at odds with legal reality. . . . [M]erchants who will not accept personal checks are happy to accept money orders. To their misfortune, this confidence is misplaced. . . . [I]n purchasing

a money order, an individual deposits a sum with a bank and essentially receives one blank check.

The following image represents a money order. The serial number, date, amount of the money order, and issuing office will be filled in when the money order is purchased. The name and address of the purchaser and payee, along with the memo line, might be filled in either at or after purchase.

4. CERTIFIED CHECKS

Certified checks are ordinary checks that have had an extra step completed prior to issuance. An ordinary check is issued to a payee, perhaps transferred to one or more additional holders, and ultimately presented to the drawee bank for payment. At the time of presentment, the drawee bank determines whether the check is properly payable and decides whether to pay the check. This decision is called acceptance. A certified check (**3–409(d)**) is different in that the acceptance decision is made prior to issuance. In the case of a certified check, the drawer normally presents the check to his or her bank for acceptance prior to delivering the check to the payee. Before accepting the unissued check, the bank representative should ensure that sufficient funds exist to pay the check, and should consider placing a hold on those funds. A stamp or other notation on the front of the check shows that the drawee bank has accepted it. Because the bank has already committed to pay the check, a certified check functions like a cashier's check; it cannot be dishonored due to insufficient funds, and it is not subject to a stop-payment order.

The following image represents a certified check. The "Accepted" stamp is its most prominent feature:

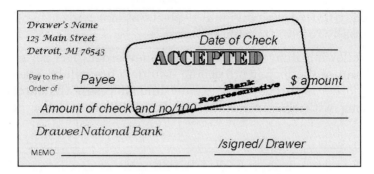

5. "PAYABLE THROUGH" DRAFTS

Comment 4 to **3–104** makes reference to insurance claim settlement drafts. Although laypeople refer to these drafts as checks, they are actually not checks within the Article 3 definition because they are "payable through" the bank on which they are drawn, rather than being drawn on the bank itself. *Harper v. K & W Trucking Co.*, 725 P.2d 1066, 1068 (Alaska 1986), explains how a "payable through" draft is unique:

> A "payable through" draft is similar to an ordinary check, but it is different in that a check is drawn on a bank, whereas a "payable through" draft is actually drawn on the [drawer] itself. . . . The upshot is that the bank named on the draft has no authority to make payment, but must present the draft to the [drawer] for payment. The "payable through" draft is used for a variety of reasons. . . . It provides the drawer with greater control over payment than ordinary checks.

Continuing with the example of the insurance settlement, imagine that an insurance company sends a "payable through" draft, along with a proposed settlement agreement, to a policyholder who has an active insurance claim. If the policyholder deposits the draft, the bank on which the draft is drawn will contact the insurance company before making payment. This is important because the insurance company would want to make sure the policyholder agreed to the settlement terms for the claim before paying the instrument. By using a "payable through" draft, the company avoids the risk that the policyholder will keep the funds but refuse to settle. The following graphic represents a "payable through" instrument that might have been sent to a policyholder named Ann Insured along with settlement-and-release documents.

```
Citizens Insurance Co.
123 Main Street
Detroit, MI 76543                September 8, 1977

        Pay to the
        Order of    Ann Insured                    $4,450.00

     Four thousand four hundred fifty and no/100 -------------------
  Payable through  First National Bank of Howell

           Claim 1234 Stolen Car          Mr. Herbert Citizen
  MEMO
           8/15/77. Policy No. 6789     President, Citizens Insurance
```

When Ann Insured deposits this draft, First National Bank will contact Citizens Insurance to ask whether the draft should be paid. Before responding, Citizens will review its files to see whether it has received a signed release from Ms. Insured.

To review several of the key points from the prior discussion, the following case discusses the importance of negotiability and the unique role of cashier's checks. This case also previews security interests, which you will learn about starting in Chapter 11.

PRESTIGE IMPORTS, INC. v. SOUTH WEYMOUTH SAVINGS BANK

916 N.E.2d 1015, 71 UCC Rep. Serv. 2d 191 (Mass. Ct. App., 2009)

McHUGH, J.

Prestige Imports, Inc. (Prestige), had a banking relationship with South Shore Bank (SSB). Using Prestige's funds, Wajahat Malick, Prestige's comptroller, fraudulently procured treasurer's checks from SSB and used them to pay personal loans he had obtained from South Weymouth Savings Bank (South Weymouth). After the fraud was discovered and related litigation began, Prestige and Helmut and Renate Schmidt (collectively, Prestige) impleaded South Weymouth and asserted claims for mishandling the SSB checks. Ultimately, a judge of the Superior Court granted South Weymouth's motion for summary judgment and dismissed the Prestige claims. Prestige appeals, and we affirm.

Background. Viewing the record in the requisite fashion, . . . it appears that Prestige, a Weymouth automobile dealership, financed its purchase of new vehicles with "floor plan" financing from SSB. Under the plan, SSB provided Prestige with a revolving line of credit, advancing funds to pay for, and taking a security interest in, each vehicle the dealership acquired. Prestige paid monthly interest until the vehicle was sold and then paid SSB the balance due.

In 1987, Prestige hired Malick as its comptroller. Malick's duties included depositing checks at SSB pursuant to a depositary agreement that was part of the financing plan. On nine occasions between February and October of 1990, however, Malick exchanged Prestige checks intended as payment on SSB loans for SSB treasurer's checks made payable to South Weymouth, which had no banking relationship with Prestige. All the Prestige checks Malick used in the scheme were made payable to SSB, and Prestige owner Helmut Schmidt had properly cosigned all of them. A "remitter" line on the face of each SSB treasurer's check stated that the check had been "purchased by" Prestige. The nine checks totaled $432,895.

Malick presented the nine checks to South Weymouth with instructions to deposit them into his personal account, where the proceeds were used, at least in part, to repay loans he had obtained from South Weymouth. The instructions were part of a fraudulent scheme through which Malick, during a two-year spree lasting from 1988 to 1990, embezzled over $1.5 million from Prestige.

For Prestige, Malick's fraud was financially ruinous. Various lawsuits ensued, one of which was this action, in which Prestige alleged that South Weymouth was negligent in accepting the SSB treasurer's checks and in failing to investigate Malick's transactions.

* * *

On appeal, Prestige claims that there is a genuine issue of material fact whether South Weymouth was a holder in due course and whether it negligently allowed Malick to deposit the treasurer's checks into his own account.

* * *

South Weymouth has filed affidavits and deposition testimony of the requisite type. In response, Prestige urges that genuine issues of material fact regarding South Weymouth's notice arise from the remitter statement on the face of each check indicating that it had been "purchased by" Prestige and from South Weymouth's general knowledge of Malick's suspicious behavior, including the size and number of the checks Malick was presenting. We are unpersuaded.

* * *

The "purchased by" notation on the front of each SSB check was notice to South Weymouth, and to everyone else who handled the check, that Prestige was the check's "remitter." The 1998 version of the Code defines the "remitter" as "a person who purchases an instrument from its issuer if the instrument is payable to an identified person other than the purchaser." G.L. c. 106, § 3–103(11) (1998) [UCC **3–103(a)(15)**].

* * *

A remitter's purchase of a treasurer's or cashier's check is typically designed to facilitate the purchase and sale of commercial goods. See, e.g., Official Comment 2 to Uniform Commercial Code § **3–201**, 2 U.L.A. 102–

103 (revised art. 3). However, even if the bank delivers the check to the purchasing remitter, the remitter is not a party to the instrument and he or she has neither a right to enforce it, . . . nor a right to order the issuing bank to dishonor it for reasons arising out of the underlying commercial transaction. . . .

Notwithstanding the remitter's limited rights to and on a treasurer's check, Prestige asserts that the appearance of Prestige's name on the remitter line put South Weymouth on notice of Prestige's claims to the checks or, at least, imposed on South Weymouth an obligation to inquire of Prestige before following Malick's instructions regarding disposition of the proceeds.

* * *

Prestige relies on *In re Nordic Village, Inc.*, 915 F.2d 1049 (6th Cir. 1990), for the proposition that the appearance of Prestige's name on the remitter line was alone sufficient to put a holder such as South Weymouth on notice of Prestige's claims when Malick, the possessor of the check, instructed South Weymouth (the transferee) to use the check and its proceeds for purposes other than those that appeared to be consistent with Prestige's interests.

Nordic Village is a case in which a Nordic Village officer used Nordic Village funds to purchase a cashier's check payable to the Internal Revenue Service (IRS). The officer then delivered the check to the IRS with instructions to apply it to the outstanding tax liabilities of a separate corporate venture with which he was involved. *Id.* at 1050–1051. Nordic Village subsequently entered bankruptcy proceedings, and the bankruptcy trustee sought to recover the funds from the IRS under provisions of the Bankruptcy Code allowing recovery unless the IRS took the check "for value, in good faith and without knowledge of the voidable nature of the transfer." *Id.* at 1055. The court held that the trustee could recover, reasoning that

> the IRS gave value for the check by crediting it against [the officer's] outstanding tax liability. However, because of the words 'REMITTER: SWISS HAUS, INC.,' it cannot be said that the IRS acted without knowledge of the voidability of the transfer. It is not an ordinary business practice for corporate entities to pay one another's taxes. This notation is sufficient to place a reasonable person on notice that the transfer was illegitimate, and by extension, that it was voidable.

Id. at 1056.

Nordic Village was decided under the Bankruptcy Code, not under the Uniform Commercial Code. To the extent we are asked to apply its reasoning to the record before us, we decline to do so, for to expand the court's rationale to include any use of a treasurer's check that does not appear to be in the remitter's interests would destroy the check's commercial utility. "It is an assurance of negotiability tantamount to a cash transfer which a cashier's check represents. If we are to begin requiring parties to investigate, despite this representation of negotiability, we are subverting the purpose for which the cashier's check was proffered." *Wohlrabe v. Pownell*, 307 N.W.2d 478, 485 (Minn. 1981).

Concerns about preserving the assurance of negotiability lie at the heart of decisions that have declined to find notice of a remitter's claim from the mere appearance of the remitter's name in the remitter line. Thus, in another bankruptcy case, the court said that "[r]emitter notations on a cashier's check are 'information to the maker and not conditional or notice of the payee.' . . . [F]illing in of the remitter line on a cashier's check is akin to filling in of the memo line on a personal check; helpful, but not required, and of no legal effect." *In re Spears Carpet Mills, Inc.*, 86 B.R. 985, 993 (W.D.Ark. 1987). . . .

　　　* * *

Even if its name on the remitter line did not provide notice of its claim to the checks, Prestige argues, its name at least imposed on South Weymouth an obligation to inquire of Prestige as to the proper disposition of the funds. Here Prestige analogizes its position as a remitter to that of the drawer in other check fraud cases and premises its claim on the proposition that[,]

> [w]here a check is drawn to the order of a bank to which the drawer is not indebted, the bank is authorized to pay the proceeds only to persons specified by the drawer; it takes the risk in treating such a check as payable to bearer and is placed on inquiry as to the authority of the drawer's agent to receive payment.

Govoni & Sons Constr. Co. v. Mechanics Bank, 51 Mass.App.Ct. 35, 40, 742 N.E.2d 1094 (2001), quoting from *Bank of S. Md. v. Robertson's Crab House*, 39 Md.App. 707, 715, 389 A.2d 388 (Ct.Spec.App. 1978).

　　　* * *

In the present context, at least, the difference between the drawer and the remitter is fundamental, for, at bottom, a check is the drawer's order to pay money in a specified fashion from the drawer's account. . . . The drawer is a party to the instrument, has certain rights in the instrument, and knows how it intends the funds to flow. A remitter is in an entirely different position. As we noted earlier, the check is not drawn on the remitter's account; the remitter is not a party to the check, cannot enforce it, cannot order the drawee to dishonor it for reasons arising out of the underlying transaction, and is not in a position to direct disposition of the funds.

　　　* * *

This case illustrates the very limited role of the remitter in a cashier's check transaction, which is one characteristic that distinguishes a cashier's check from an ordinary, uncertified check. Another such characteristic is explained in the following section.

E. MERGER AND CONDITIONAL PAYMENT

Two related concepts—merger and conditional payment—describe the relationship between a negotiable instrument and the transaction motivating its issuance. Both concepts are captured in **3–310**, although neither phrase appears in the statute.

"Merger" describes how the obligation giving rise to the issuance of the instrument (such as a loan or the purchase of goods or services) is fused to the instrument such that payment of the instrument satisfies the underlying obligation. Thus, a negotiable instrument and the transaction motivating its issuance are merged, together representing a single right to payment. Because the negotiable instrument symbolizes the entire obligation, possession of the instrument is exceedingly important.

Disputes can arise when the obligor pays someone not in possession of the instrument, and another person later produces the instrument and demands to be paid, as well. In *Lambert v. Barker*, 232 Va. 21, 348 S.E.2d 214 (1986), the court addressed such a situation. Barbara and William Barker purchased real estate from Robert Davis, executing a promissory note to Davis in payment for the property. The Barkers then sold the property to David Beloff, who sold the property to Charles and Ann Harwood, each of whom, in turn, expressly agreed to pay the note to Davis. Some time later, Davis transferred his right to receive payment on the note to Katherine Lambert, to secure a loan that Lambert's company made to him. When the Harwoods sold the property to Bryce and Nancy Bugg, Davis appeared at the closing with an affidavit in which he falsely represented that he had lost the note. He was paid out of the closing proceeds. Lambert subsequently sued both the Harwoods and the Barkers to recover payment, presumably because Davis was either judgment-proof or unavailable for suit. The defendants claimed their obligations had already been satisfied through payment to Davis. The court held in favor of Lambert, noting that "[p]ayment or satisfaction discharges the liability of a party only if made to the holder of the instrument. . . . [T]he payor may protect himself by demanding production of the instrument and refusing payment to any party not in possession unless in an action on the obligation the owner proves his ownership."

As a practical matter, the Harwoods should have required Davis to obtain a surety bond or otherwise provide security against the possibility that someone else—in this case, Lambert—would later produce the note and demand payment.

The term "conditional payment" reflects the reality that anyone who accepts a promissory note or an ordinary, uncertified check as payment for a loan or a sale of goods or services assumes the risk that the note or check will be dishonored—that is, that it will remain unpaid after payment is demanded. A cashier's check, teller's check, or certified personal check, by contrast, is considered unconditional payment because such instruments cannot be dishonored due to insufficient funds and are not subject to stop-payment orders. In recognition of this fact, **3–310** provides that payment via certified check, teller's check, or cashier's check discharges the underlying obligation as soon as the payee takes the instrument, while other forms of payment merely suspend the obligation until the item is presented for payment. At the time of presentment, a conditional item will either be paid—thus discharging the underlying obligation—or dishonored—thus reviving the underlying obligation as a separate cause of action.

Harper v. K & W Trucking Co., 725 P.2d 1066, 1068 (Alaska 1986), explains the effect of **3–310**, as it relates to an ordinary, uncertified check:

> The statute strikes a balance between two possible approaches. Under one approach, the mere acceptance of the instrument would discharge the obligation. Under a second approach, acceptance of the instrument would have no effect, and the underlying obligation would remain in force until cash actually changed hands. The statute effectuates a compromise between these two approaches by suspending the obligation, but only until it is satisfied.

One odd result of the second approach would have been that the payee could accept a check in payment for a delivery of goods, then separately sue the drawer of the check demanding payment for those same goods, without first seeking to enforce the check.

As an application of the prior discussion of merger and conditional payment, the following case explains how payment with an ordinary personal check affects the obligation for which the check was given.

WHITE V. HARTFORD LIFE INSURANCE CO.

2008 WL 4104487, 66 UCC Rep. Serv. 2d 796 (W.D. Ky. 2008)

HEYBURN, II, C.J.

Plaintiff William G. White ('Plaintiff') filed this lawsuit against Defendants Hartford Life Insurance Company and Pacific Insurance Company, Limited (jointly referred to as 'Defendant') seeking to recover annuity payments which he alleges Hartford wrongfully and/or negligently paid to another party over a forged endorsement or by direct deposit to an account without White's authorization.

Now that discovery is complete, White has moved for summary judgment on his claim. Defendant objects primarily on the grounds of existing disputed material facts. Hartford opposes the motion on expected grounds and argues that White's claim is barred by the statute of limitations and under the equitable doctrines of waiver, laches, and failure to mitigate damages. However, Hartford has not formally moved for judgment as a matter of law on any of these grounds. For the reasons described below, the Court denies White's motion. In doing so the Court discusses but does not rule on the statute of limitations issues.

I.

An extensive statement of the facts in a light most favorable to Hartford follows.

On October 7, 1980, White who was employed in Hawaii as a crane operator, suffered back, arm, leg, and neck injuries. He subsequently filed a worker's compensation claim in Hawaii which was settled under the terms of a Compromise and Settlement Agreement and Release ('Agreement') dated March 4, 1987. The Agreement provided payments as follows:

> The total amount of $800.00 will be paid to the Claimant each month in a single lump sum, with payments to begin within 30 days of formal approval of this Agreement by the Department of Labor and Industrial Relations, and with said payments *to continue at monthly intervals for the remainder of Claimant's life,* with payments guaranteed to continue for a period of ten years from the date of the first annuity payment to be made to the Claimant or to whomever of Claimant's heir, beneficiaries, representatives, successors, or assigns that Claimant may so designate to receive the same. . . .

Pl.'s Depo. Exh. 1 pp. 4–5.

White began receiving monthly checks for $800 from Hartford once the Agreement was approved. In April or May of 1994, White moved to Louisville, Kentucky to live with his brother, John White and a woman named Thelma Simpson ('Simpson') on Lotus Avenue. He continued to receive the monthly annuity checks in Louisville. After Bill arrived in Louisville he began working with his brother doing long-haul trucking which required him to be on the road for weeks at a time. White opened a checking account in Louisville and deposited $15,000 in it. He gave signature rights on that account to Simpson so that she could get him money while he was on the road, but White says that when he returned from a trucking trip the account had been entirely depleted. He says that Simpson had explained to him that she had used it to pay a tax bill.

White says that while he was on the road, he arranged for Simpson to call him as mail came in and read him the address. If he thought it was important, he would instruct her to open it and see what it was and relay that to him over the phone. White says that while he was traveling out of town with his brother around March 1995, he received a phone call from Simpson informing him that he had received a letter at the residence he shared with his brother and Simpson from Hartford stating that his annuity payments were ending. White says he 'pretty much took [Simpson's] word for it' that the annuity payments were ending and he did not attempt to contact Hartford to inquire further. In fact, Hartford continued to mail annuity checks to White at the Lotus Avenue address he had provided to Hartford when he first moved there.

Around July 1995, White, his brother, and Simpson temporarily moved to an apartment on Halsley Court. Though it is unclear how Hartford learned that White's address had changed, in the months of July–October 1995, Hartford mailed White's annuity checks to Halsley Court. At some point after October 1995, White, his brother, and Simpson moved back to Lotus Avenue and Hartford resumed sending the annuity checks to White at Lotus Avenue. So although Hartford mailed the monthly annuity checks to White at the addresses where he was residing, he maintains that from March 1995 onward he never received them. He believes that after Simpson had told him the checks were ending she 'was apparently intercepting the checks and cashing them herself.' Mot. for Summ. J. 5. Though some of the checks dated after March 1995 bear the signature 'William White,' White says that those signatures are forgeries.

In 1996, White stopped living with his brother and Simpson and moved in with his future wife, Roxy White. Later in the year, White's brother and Simpson moved to a house on Wurtele Avenue. In August 1996, Hartford received handwritten correspondence stating, 'I William White gave Thelma Simpson power of attorney for me. She is my beneficiary. If you need anything call her.' In response to that correspondence, a Hartford employee named Angie Lee mailed a letter stating, in part, 'Prior to updating our records we will need Power of Attorney paperwork from the courts appointing Thelma Simons (sic) as such. . . .' Hartford subsequently received a letter dated August 21, 1996, stating, 'Angie/ Would you please change William White address from 1033 Lotus Ave to 1502 Wurtele Ave Louisville Ky 40208/ Thank you/ William White.' Hartford began sending the annuity checks to White at Wurtele Avenue in December 1996, though White never lived at Wurtele Avenue. On March 21, 1997 Hartford received an Electronic Funds Transfer request purportedly signed by William White instructing it to directly deposit White's annuity payments into Thelma Simpson's checking account. A voided check from Simpson's account was attached to the request. Thereafter, Hartford began [to] electronically transfer[ ] the annuity payments directly to Simpson's account and mailed paper confirmation notices addressed to White at Wurtele Ave.

Some time after April 1997, Simpson moved with White's brother to Utah Avenue. In 1999 White and his wife moved to Loretto, Kentucky. By at latest January 2000, Hartford's mailed EFT confirmation notices were being returned with an attached notice indicating that the forwarding order had expired. On March 7 and June 1, 2000, Hartford wrote to White at the Utah Avenue address (where White had never resided) requesting an address correction in the form of a notarized letter. Hartford continued to transfer the funds to Simpson's checking account and mail the EFT confirmation notices to Wurtele Avenue through at least the end of 2004.

According to White, some time in early 2005, he received an EFT confirmation notice at his home in Loretto confirming the monthly deposit of $800 into Simpson's account. Precisely what series of events prompted Hartford to send the confirmation to White at his home in Loretto is not clear. After White received a second such notice the next month, he reports that he and his wife checked with their bank to investigate whether any funds from Hartford had been deposited into their account. No deposit from Hartford was recorded. In April 2005, White sent a letter to Hartford stating that he had not received his annuity payments since 1994. The next month White filled out a criminal complaint intake form with the Jefferson County attorney against Simpson. Since June 2005, Hartford has been electronically transferring White's monthly annuity payments directly to White's checking account.

White's brother's and Simpson's deposition testimony is evidence that White and Simpson shared a romantic relationship. White has also been previously convicted for insurance fraud, having been caught in a scheme to register and insure cars and then report them as stolen.

White filed suit on May 25, 2006, seeking $98,400.00 from Hartford, a figure which represents the sum of the monthly annuity payments from March 1995 through and including May 2005. He also seeks interest at a rate of 8% from the date each monthly payment was due.

In his motion for summary judgment, White argues that Hartford failed to discharge its contractual obligations for each month that Simpson allegedly forged White's endorsement on the checks for payment that Hartford mailed (from March 1995 through March 1997) and for each month that Hartford made annuity payments via EFT to the account allegedly established by Simpson without White's knowledge (from April 1997 through May 2005). Hartford responds that a reasonable jury could decide that an agency relationship existed between White and Simpson or that White ratified Simpson's actions in directing that the checks be sent to her address and later electronically transferred to her checking account. . . .

III.

The Court now considers the framework for addressing the statute of limitations issues. In so doing, the Court begins by discussing White's cause of action, and the time and place this cause of action accrued. White asserts that 'fundamentally, the issue in this case is whether or not Hartford has performed its obligation to White under the Agreement and is thus discharged of its obligation.' Mot. for Summ. J. 11. Framing the issue as a matter of pure contract law neglects consideration of the legal effect of the issuance of a negotiable instrument, like a check, on an underlying obligation, which is addressed by Article 3 of the Uniform Commercial Code ('UCC'), governing commercial paper and which has been adopted by Kentucky. Ky.Rev.Stat. Ann. §§ 355.3–101 *et seq.*

When a party takes a check for an underlying obligation, that check does not discharge the underlying obligation, but rather suspends the obligation until the check is paid 'to a person entitled to enforce' it. Ky.Rev.Stat. Ann. §§ 335.3–310(2)(a) [UCC **3–310(b)**]; 355.3–602(1)(b) [UCC **3–602(a)**]. In addition to suspending the underlying obligation, a party's decision to issue a negotiable instrument also triggers separate contractual liability on the check itself.

In some cases a party's underlying obligation and the obligation on the negotiable instrument become divided. This occurs, for example, when a check given for the obligation is stolen from the payee, the payee's signature is forged, and the forger then obtains payment. In such a situation, per Ky.Rev.Stat. Ann. § 355.3–310(2)(d) [UCC **3–310(b)(4)**]:

> If the obligee is the person entitled to enforce the instrument but no longer has possession of it because it was lost, stolen, or destroyed, the obligation may not be enforced to the extent of the amount payable on the instrument, and to that extent the obligee's rights against the obligor are limited to enforcement of the instrument.

The Official Comment to this section of Article 3 explains that if the payor bank pays a person not entitled to enforce the instrument, the suspension of the underlying obligation continues, because the check has not been paid within the meaning of § **3–602(a)**. § **3–310 cmt. 3–4**. Under these circumstances, the payee could sue the depositary or payor bank in conversion under Section **3–420**, or the drawer under Section **3–309**. Kentucky has adopted the 2000 Amendment to Section **3–309**.

However, as the Official Comment explains, 'the payee cannot merely ignore the instrument and sue the drawer on the underlying contract. This would impose on the drawer the risk that the check when stolen was indorsed in blank or to the bearer.' § **3–310 cmt. 4**. In other words, if the payor bank pays the forger, 'the suspension on the underlying obligation for which the check was given continues because the check has not been paid.' Henry J. Bailey & Richard B. Hagedorn, Brady on Bank Checks: The Law of Bank Checks, ¶ 30.1, (A.S. Pratt & Sons updated 2007)(accessed electronically).

Thus, White's ability to enforce the underlying obligation turns largely on whether the annuity checks could properly be considered 'delivered' to him. 'Delivery' in the context of UCC means 'voluntary transfer of possession.' Ky.Rev.Stat. Ann. § 355.1–110(14). [Note: Citation should probably be to Ky.Rev.Stat.Ann § 355.1–201(*o*), [UCC **1–201(b)(15)**] definition of 'Delivery.' Editor.] If the checks were 'delivered,' regardless of what happened afterward, § **3–310** governs the effect of the check on the underlying obligation. By contrast however, if the checks were never delivered, White retains his right to enforce the underlying obligation.

A.

Until July 1995, Hartford mailed the annuity checks to the address White had provided and where he actually resided. As the Official Comment to § **3–420**, 'the payee received delivery when the check comes into the payee's possession, as for example when it is put into the payee's mailbox.' § **3–420 cmt. 1**. Here, the Court concludes that for at least so long as Hartford mailed his annuity checks to the address that White had provided to Hartford, and where he was actually living, those checks were 'delivered' within the meaning of Article 3. The 'delivery' analysis is complicated for the time period when, according to White, someone other than White was notifying Hartford of his changes of address. It appears that from July 1995 until the point at which White moved out in early 1996, Hartford mailed the check to the address where he lived despite White's professed lack of knowledge of such delivery. At the very least, White had constructive possession of mail delivered to him at the address where he lived. Accordingly, for this period of time White's claim against Hartford arises pursuant to § **3–309** of Article 3, and not as a claim to enforce the underlying obligation under contract law. *See* Ky.Rev.Stat. Ann. § 355–3.310 [UCC **3–310**].

By contrast, when Hartford began mailing checks to addresses where White had never lived (apparently in December 1996, with delivery to the Wurtele address), whether 'delivery' occurred, which could operate to suspend Hartford's obligation on the underlying obligation, depends on the disputed agency relationship between White and Simpson and the level of knowledge White had about his annuity checks. Thus White would retain his rights to enforce Hartford's underlying obligation after December 1996, . . . unless Hartford is successful in proving an agency relationship or actual knowledge on White's behalf. *See* § 355.**4A–406** (describing the effect of an electronic funds transfer on an underlying obligation).

In sum, the facts presently before the Court suggest that Hartford suspended its underlying obligation when it sent checks to the address where White lived, and for the time period that this occurred White is entitled to enforce the check under Article 3. From December 1996 onward, Hartford's delivery of annuity checks to addresses where White did not reside would not seem to effect 'delivery' under the UCC. On this view, the underlying obligation would not even be suspended let alone discharged, and White would retain full common law contractual rights to enforce it.

* * *

[The court then went on to consider the statute-of-limitations implications of its holding with respect to delivery. Because White's cause of action for the pre-1996 payments arose under **3–309**, the statute of limitations for these checks, as provided in **3–118**, was just 3 years. This is because his claim arose under a conversion theory, which is further explained in Chapter 9. For the post-1996 payments, his cause of action arose under the common law of contracts, and Kentucky prescribes a 6-year limitations period for such cases. His claim for the pre-1996 checks was time-barred, but his claim for the post-1996 checks was not.]

This case allocates the responsibility between Hartford and White differently at various points during Simpson's fraudulent scheme. This allocation reflects which party was, at the time, in the better position to identify the fraud and avoid the loss.

F. REQUIREMENTS FOR NEGOTIABILITY

The prior discussion introduced the concept of negotiability and how negotiable instruments are related to the obligations that motivate their issuance. We now turn to the formal requirements of negotiability, found in **3–104**. Comment 1 provides an introduction to the seven requirements for negotiability discussed throughout the rest of the chapter. The test for whether an item is a negotiable instrument is formal rather than functional; that is, the form of the instrument, rather than its function or the parties' intent, dictates whether the instrument is negotiable. **3–104** provides the exclusive mechanism by which an item is deemed negotiable; a non-negotiable instrument cannot be made negotiable by custom or agreement of the parties.

1. THE "WRITING" REQUIREMENT

A negotiable instrument must be a writing. "Writing" is defined in **1–201(b)(43)**, and the requirement of a writing is part of the definitions of "order" (in the case of a draft such as a check) and "promise" (in the case of a note) found in **3–103(a)(8)** and **(12)**, respectively.

The writing requirement is normally satisfied by reduction of the instrument to paper form. The following graphics represent typical paper-based negotiable instruments that would satisfy the "writing" requirement.

```
Drawer's Name
123 Main Street                    Date of Check
Detroit, MI 76543                  _____

Pay to the
Order of    Payee                                 $ amount
           _____

Amount of check and no/100 ------------------------

Drawee National Bank
                                   /signed/ Drawer
MEMO _____         _____
```

```
               PROMISSORY NOTE

    For value received, I do hereby promise to pay to
    Payee or order, one hundred fifty thousand and
    no/100 dollars ($150,000.00).  The terms and
    conditions of such note are as follows: . . .


    /signed/ Maker
```

The key to understanding the "writing" requirement is to differentiate the word "writing" from the word "record." Whereas **1–201(b)(43)** defines a writing as an "intentional reduction to tangible form," a record is defined in **1–201(b)(31)** as "information that is inscribed on a tangible medium *or that is stored in an electronic or other medium and is retrievable in perceivable form.*" (Emphasis added). The term "record" is broader than "writing." An Article 3 "writing," unlike a "record," which is a term used elsewhere in the UCC, must take tangible form.

2. THE "SIGNATURE" REQUIREMENT

A negotiable instrument must be signed, but the signature requirement is fairly flexible. For example, the signature requirement may be satisfied by initials, the letter "X," a machine-generated facsimile signature, or even an assumed name. When an illiterate person marks an "X" to sign a document, parol evidence would be used to determine whose signature the "X" was, since many persons use the same mark.

In addition to the nontraditional forms a signature might take, a party might sign an instrument through a representative. Signatures by representatives are discussed in Chapter 7; other aspects of the signature requirement are explored in this section. In the graphics below, Drawer and Maker have satisfied the signature requirement.

The "signature" requirement is part of the definition of "order" (in the case of a draft such as a check) and "promise" (in the case of a note) found in **3–103(a)(8)** and **(12)**, respectively. **1–201(b)(37)** defines "signed." **3–401(b)** requires that the signature be made with "present intention to authenticate [the] writing," and allows a party to sign with an assumed name. Note, however, that using an assumed name might constitute fraud or forgery under other law.

3. "MAGIC WORDS" OF NEGOTIABILITY

Some negotiable instruments must contain words indicating the issuer's intention that the instrument be negotiable. The so-called "magic words" of negotiability, which are "to bearer" or "to order," are required for any promissory note and also for any draft that is not a check. The "magic words" requirement is found in **3–104(a)(1)**, the exemption for checks is found in **3–104(c)**, and the difference between items payable "to bearer" and "to order" is explained in **3–109**.

The language "pay to the order of [name of payee]" denotes negotiability by indicating that the named payee may enforce the instrument personally or may transfer the item to another party, who should also be permitted to enforce the item. The language "pay to bearer" indicates that whoever is in possession of the item—even if not named in the item—should be permitted to enforce it. The former language creates what is called "order paper," while the latter denotes "bearer paper." The difference between order paper and bearer paper becomes significant in the next chapter.

The following are examples of bearer paper:

A promissory note that reads, "Pay to [payee's name] or bearer." **3–109(a)(1)**.

A check that reads, "Pay to the order of bearer." **3–109(a)(1)**.

A promissory note that reads, "Pay to the order of _____," where the blank has not been filled in. **3–109(a)(2)**. Once the blank is filled in with an identified payee, the item becomes order paper.

A check that reads, "Pay to Merry Christmas." **3–109(a)(3)**.

A check that reads, "Pay to the order of cash." **3–109(a)(3)**.

In *Horvath v. Bank of N.Y., N.A.*, 641 F.3d 617, 621 (4th Cir. 2011), the court clarified the effect of bearer paper: "Negotiable instruments . . . that are [bearer paper] may be freely transferred. And once transferred, the old adage about possession being nine-tenths of the law is, if anything, an understatement. Whoever possesses an instrument [that is bearer paper] has full power to enforce it."

Although checks are exempt from the "magic words" requirement because they are generally assumed to be negotiable, most checks nevertheless contain such words, as in the image below:

The following image represents a note that satisfies the "magic words" requirement:

> ## PROMISSORY NOTE
>
> For value received, I do hereby promise to **pay to Payee or order**, one hundred fifty thousand and no/100 dollars ($150,000.00). The terms and conditions of such note are as follows: . . .
>
>
> */signed/ Maker*

According to **3–104** Comment 3, although the words, "Not Negotiable" or similar language would be effective to render a promissory note or a non-check draft non-negotiable even if it would otherwise be negotiable, such language would not keep a check from being negotiable. This result makes sense because checks do not need the "magic words" to qualify as negotiable, in the first place.

4. THE "UNCONDITIONAL" REQUIREMENT

For an instrument to be negotiable, payment must not depend on the occurrence of some event; instead, the obligation to pay must be unconditional. The "unconditional" requirement is found in **3–104(a)** and further explained in **3–106**. The purpose of the "unconditional" requirement is to ensure that holders are not saddled with the burden of conducting research to determine whether a condition stated in the item has been satisfied. This is consistent with the fact that a negotiable instrument should be a "courier without luggage." Only express conditions render an item non-negotiable; **3–106** Comment 1 provides an example of an express condition: "I promise to pay $100,000 to the order of John Doe if he conveys title to Blackacre to me."

Although the "unconditional" requirement is intended to ensure that holders are not required to research their rights and responsibilities, **3–106** provides that an instrument can make reference to another record "for a statement of rights with respect to collateral, prepayment, or acceleration" without becoming non-negotiable. One potential policy reason for this distinction is that such clauses provide the holder with more rights, rather than fewer, and the holder can elect not to track down and review the other record without losing the face value the instrument represents.

An acceleration clause protects a creditor because it allows the creditor to make the entire balance due at once. The creditor hopes it will be able to exercise acceleration rights when the debtor's finances first start to fail, before all of his or her assets are exhausted. Acceleration is subject to the Article 1 "good faith" requirement found in **1–309**, which incorporates by reference the definition of good faith in **1–304**. *State National Bank of El Paso v. Farah Manufacturing Co., Inc.*, 678 S.W.2d 661, 785 (Tex. App. 1984), explains how acceleration clauses are to be used, given the good-faith limitation:

> Even where an insecurity clause is drafted in the broadest possible terms, the primary question is whether the creditor's attempt to accelerate stemmed from a reasonable, good-faith belief that its security was about to become impaired. Acceleration clauses are not to be used offensively such as for the commercial advantage of the creditor. They do not permit acceleration when the facts make its use unjust or oppressive.

Consider the following graphics, noting that the bolded language in the first item is an impermissible condition, while the bolded language in the second is acceptable as a mere "reference to another record" as contemplated in **3–106(a)**.

The precise language the parties choose can affect whether an item is impermissibly conditional and thus non-negotiable. In *First Federal*

Savings & Loan Association v. Gump & Ayers Real Estate, Inc., 771 P.2d 1096, 1096 (Utah Ct. App. 1989), the court considered a promissory note with the following language:

> This Note is secured by that certain Purchase and Security Agreement dated June __, 1984. Reference is made to the Purchase and Security Agreement for additional rights of the holder thereof.

In finding the note negotiable, the court held that the quoted language was a "mere reference" to another document that did not affect its negotiability.

By contrast, in *Guniganti v. Kalvakuntla*, 346 S.W.3d 242, 249–50 (Tex. Ct. App. 2011), the court held that the following language in a promissory note rendered the note impermissibly conditional and thus non-negotiable:

> NOT ALL of the principal amount of this Note has been advanced on the date hereof. Additional advances will be made *in accordance with the terms and conditions of the Loan Agreement, reference to same being here made for all purposes.* Interest shall accrue only on funds from date of advancement. A default under said Loan Agreement will constitute a default hereunder.

Because the italicized language was more than a "mere reference" to the Loan Agreement, and instead "burdened the Note with the conditions of the Loan Agreement," the note was conditional and thus non-negotiable.

The following chart summarizes the rules found in **3–106**:

Conditional	Unconditional
"I promise to pay $100,000 to the order of John Doe if he conveys Blackacre to me." **3–106(a)(i)** and Comment 1	"In consideration of John Doe's promise to convey Blackacre to me, I promise to pay $100,000 to the order of John Doe." **3–106** Comment 1
"This note is subject to a loan and security agreement dated April 1, 1990, between the payee and maker of this note." **3–106(a)(ii)** and Comment 1	"This note is secured by a security interest in collateral described in a security agreement dated April 1, 1990, between the payee and maker of this note. Rights and obligations with respect to the collateral are [stated in] [governed by] the security agreement." **3–106(b)** and Comment 1

"Rights and obligations of the parties with respect to this note are stated in an agreement dated April 1, 1990 between the payee and maker of this note." **3–106(a)(iii)** and Comment 1	"This note is issued as per a loan and security agreement dated April 1, 1990 between the payee and maker of this note." **3–106(a)**
"This note incorporates by reference the agreement dated April 1, 1990 between the payee and maker of this note." **3–106(a)**	"Payment of this note is limited to resort to the ABCD Fund." **3–106(b)(ii)**

5. THE "NO ADDITIONAL PROMISE" REQUIREMENT

Students often confuse the "unconditional" requirement with the "no additional promise" requirement. The "unconditional" requirement fails when the maker of a note or drawer of a draft agrees to pay only if certain conditions are met. The "no additional promise" requirement fails when the maker of a note or drawer of a draft promises to pay money and to take on some additional obligation, as well.

As with the "unconditional" requirement, certain additional promises are expressly permitted. Under **3–104(a)(3)**, a "promise or order may contain (i) an undertaking or power to give, maintain, or protect collateral to secure payment, (ii) an authorization or power to the holder to confess judgment or realize on or dispose of collateral, or (iii) a waiver of the benefit of any law intended for the advantage or protection of an obligor."

Looking at the images below, **3–104(a)(3)** expressly permits the language appearing on the memo line in the first example, while the second example includes an impermissible additional promise.

> **PROMISSORY NOTE**
>
> For value received, I do hereby promise to pay to Payee or order, one hundred fifty thousand and no/100 dollars ($150,000.00). **I also agree to convey real estate to Payee with a market value of at least $25,000.** The terms and conditions of such note are as follows: . . .
>
> /signed/ Maker

There has been significant controversy in recent years as to whether notes secured by mortgages should be considered negotiable instruments. In his Memorandum to the Uniform Law Commission dated February 11, 2013, in his capacity as co-reporter for the Residential Real Estate Mortgage Foreclosure Process and Protections Act, Professor Jim Smith stated as follows:

> [Q]ualification of a secured note as a negotiable instrument usually turns on one issue: whether the note says too much about the maker's obligations with respect to the mortgaged property, so that it exceeds the bounds of the [no additional promise requirement]. Although one might conceivably interpret Section **3–104** to allow a note directly to incorporate a full range of standard mortgage covenants into the note, without destroying negotiability, conventional wisdom is that the drafter must avoid doing too much.

Overton v. Tyler, 3 Pa. 346 (1846), a pre-UCC case, is the origin of the phrase "courier without luggage," which is the famous description of the requirement that a negotiable instrument be capable of being fully understood, and fully appraised, without reference to other sources. The facts of the case are omitted because the holding of *Overton* is no longer good law, but the following language remains useful in understanding the "no additional promise" requirement:

> [A] negotiable bill or note is a courier without luggage. It is a requisite that it be framed in the fewest possible words, and those importing the most certain and precise contract; and though this requisite be a minor one, it is entitled to weight in determining a question of intention. To be within the statute, it must be free from contingencies or conditions that would embarrass it in its course; for a memorandum to control it, though endorsed on it, would be incorporated with it and destroy it. But a memorandum which is merely directory or collateral, will not affect it. . . .

In concluding that the note in question was not negotiable, the court returned to the language of intent from the paragraph above: "[T]hese parties could not have intended to impress a commercial character on the note, dragging after it, as it would, a train of special provisions which would materially impede its circulation."

Linking Professor Smith's analysis with *Overton v. Tyler*, language that "do[es] too much" creates "a train of special provisions" that makes an instrument non-negotiable.

6. THE "FIXED AMOUNT OF MONEY" REQUIREMENT

A draft or note must show on its face how much the drawer of the draft is ordering to be paid, or the maker of the note is promising to pay. The "fixed amount of money" requirement ensures that the holder of a draft or a note will be able to make an educated decision as to how much to offer, in terms of goods, services, or money, in exchange for the instrument. The "fixed amount of money" requirement is found in **3–104(a)**, and "money" is defined in **1–201(b)(24)**. **3–104(a)** indicates that the "fixed amount of money" may include interest, although the rate may be subject to other law, such as state usury law. **3–112** explains that interest may be presented as a fixed or variable interest rate. Although early cases did not permit variable interest rates, courts now allow any rate that provides "commercial certainty." *Amberboy v. Societe de Banque Privee*, 831 S.W.2d 793, 794, 796 (Tex. 1992), explains the reasoning behind this change:

> [T]he drafters of the UCC expressly contemplated that the courts would advance the basic purpose of the Code by construing the UCC's provisions "in the light of unforeseen and new circumstances and practices." [Citing **1–103**, Comment 1.]
>
> * * *
>
> Section **3–106** lists several instances in which reference to sources outside the instrument are necessary to determine the sum payable under the instrument.
>
> Section **3–106** does not explicitly mention variable rate notes ("VRNs") because, when the UCC was developed in the 1950s and adopted in the 1960s, VRNs were virtually unknown.
>
> * * *
>
> A VRN which contains provision for interest to be paid at a variable rate that is readily ascertainable by reference to a bank's published prime rate is compatible with the Code's objective of "commercial certainty." The Code does not require "mathematical certainty" but only "commercial certainty."

The distinction between "commercial" and "mathematical" certainty can be articulated as follows: VRNs with specific interest-rate references such as "interest payable at three percent above the prime rate established by the Chase Manhattan Bank of New York City" are permissible, but vague language failing to indicate how interest will be calculated, such as "interest payable at the current rate" is not.

Both of the items below satisfy the "sum certain" requirement.

Other disputes over the "fixed amount of money" requirement arise when an instrument includes numeric and textual descriptions of the sum to be paid that contradict one another. As **3–114** indicates, handwritten terms prevail over typewritten terms, which prevail over printed terms. The drafters assumed that these rankings reflect parties' expectations as to which terms best capture the parties' intentions. In addition, expressions of amount in words prevail over numbers. The assumption is that typographical errors in words are less common than in numbers.

7. THE "PAYABLE ON DEMAND OR AT A DEFINITE TIME" REQUIREMENT

For an instrument to be negotiable, it must either be payable on demand or payable at a definite time. If the instrument is not payable on demand, then the time when it will come due must be ascertainable when the instrument is issued. For example, an instrument payable at the maker or drawer's death would fail because no one would know, at the time when the instrument was issued, when the maker or drawer would die. The requirement that an instrument be payable on demand or at a definite time (sometimes called the "time certain" requirement) is found in **3–104(a)(2)** and further explained in **3–108**. The "time certain" requirement is important for at least two reasons. First, when an instrument is payable at a definite time in the future (as with an instrument of credit such as a promissory note), it is necessary to know its due date so that the instrument can be discounted to present value. Second, as Chapter 7 discusses, for a holder to be a holder in due course, the holder must not have notice that the instrument is overdue or has been dishonored. This requires that he or she know the instrument's due date.

In the graphics below, the check is "payable on demand" (**3–108(a)(ii)**), while the promissory note is "payable at a definite time" (**3–108(b)**).

```
Drawer's Name
123 Main Street
Detroit, MI 76543                    December 13, 2001

Pay to the   Payee                                    $ amount
Order of   _____

Amount of check and no/100  -------------------------

Drawee National Bank
                              /signed/ Drawer
MEMO _____
```

```
              PROMISSORY NOTE

For value received, forty-five days after sight, I do
hereby promise to pay to Payee or order, one
hundred fifty thousand and no/100 dollars
($150,000.00). The terms and conditions of such note
are as follows: . . .

/signed/ Maker
```

The following chart summarizes the rules found in **3–108**:

Payable on Demand	Payable at a Definite Time
A promissory note with no due date listed. **3–108(a)(ii)**	A promissory note, payable on "Leap Day 2008." **3–108(b)**
A draft "payable at the will of the holder." **3–108(a)(i)**	A promissory note "payable on April 21, 2018, or on demand." This item is actually payable at a definite time, subject to acceleration. **3–108(c)**
A promissory note "payable at sight." **3–108(a)(i)**	A promissory note "payable on April 21, 2018, or at such later date as the holder may determine. This item is payable at a definite time, subject to extension at the holder's election. If the language were "payable on April 21, 2018, or at such later date as the maker may determine," the item would be non-negotiable. **3–108(b)**
A check, regardless of whether it is dated. **3–104(f)** Post-dated checks are specifically addressed in Chapter 8.	A promissory note, payable on January 16, 2016. **3–108(b)**

Chapter Conclusion: In leaving this chapter behind, you should be comfortable with the basic concept of negotiability, the basic attributes of a promissory note and check, the specialized items presented here, and the seven elements of negotiability. One way to test your comfort level with these materials is to answer the following problems:

PROBLEMS

1.   Tommy Lee McCubbins obtained two loans from Bullitt Federal Savings and Loan Association, one in the amount of $16,000, and one in the amount of $1,600. Both loans were secured by a mortgage on his home, had the same term, and were paid via a combined monthly payment. About a year before the last payment was to be due, Mr. McCubbins visited the bank and requested the payoff amount. He was told that the payoff amount was $20.41. He paid this amount shortly thereafter and received both notes in the mail stamped "Paid in Full," along with a letter from the bank's loan administrator regarding his "recently paid loan." A Deed of Release of the Mortgage signed

by the bank's senior vice president was recorded in the county records. About two years later, the bank sued Mr. McCubbins for $6,657, which it claimed was the balance still owed. The bank supplied an affidavit that only the smaller loan had actually been paid off.

a. What (if any) significance should be given to the fact that Mr. McCubbins received both notes in the mail stamped "Paid in Full"? Also look at 3–601. You have not yet been introduced to this Code section, but it builds upon the concepts presented in Part E. Had both of Mr. McCubbins' loans been discharged? Why or why not?

b. Taking the prior question a step further and introducing another new. Code section, do the bank's actions in this case qualify as an "intentional and voluntary act" within the meaning of 3–604(a)? Why or why not?

2. Read 3–104(f) through (h) and 3–409(d) and consider the following facts:

Charles Dermenjian entered into a five-year lease agreement with Asian American Bank & Trust Company, whereby the bank leased certain property from Dermenjian. The lease included an option to purchase the property for $400,000. To exercise the option, the bank was required to give written notice not less than six months prior to the expiration of the lease term, accompanied by a certified check payable to Dermenjian in the amount of $25,000. About a year and a half before the lease was to expire, the bank sent Dermenjian a letter indicating its intention to exercise the purchase option. The letter accompanied a check for $25,000 issued by the bank and drawn on the bank's own funds. The word "certified" did not appear on the check. Dermenjian rejected the check, as well as the bank's offer to supply a new check bearing the word "certified."

a. Is the check a cashier's check?

b. Is the check a certified check?

Assume that Dermenjian's concern, in requiring a certified check, was making sure the payment instrument was "the next best thing to cash."

c. Does the check satisfy that concern?

d. Would a money order or teller's check satisfy that concern in the same way?

Assume that Dermenjian did not want to include a purchase option in the contract in the first place, and does not want to sell the property.

e. Can he reject this check?

3. Consider the following proposed statutory language:

Unless another form of payment is agreed to by the policyholder or beneficiary, an insurance company doing business in this state may not pay a judgment or settlement of a claim in this state for a loss incurred in this state with an instrument other than a negotiable bank check payable on demand and bearing even date with the date of writing or by electronic funds transfer.

Assume that you were advising your state legislature when it was considering this law.

a. As a practical matter, what kinds of instruments would such a statute prohibit?

b. What is the reasoning behind this statute, and what are its risks and benefits?

4. Think back to the *White* case and consider the following facts:

Bob Lawson was an employee of the State of Kentucky for 26 years prior to retirement. He was a member of the Kentucky Employees Retirement Systems (KERS). After meeting with a KERS counselor on August 2, 2004, prior to his retirement, he selected the "Life with 15 Years Certain" payment option. At the time, Lawson believed incorrectly that his wife would receive benefits for 15 years after his death, regardless of when he died. In actuality, his wife would receive no benefit if he lived more than 15 years after his retirement. The KERS form included the following language: "I realize that, after my first retirement allowance payment has been issued by the state treasurer, I *cannot change* to another payment option or change my beneficiary." The KERS form also indicated that Lawson would receive his first monthly payment on or around September 27, 2004.

On September 16, 2004, realizing he had misunderstood the benefit he selected, Lawson called the KERS office to request a change in his payment option. He was told that the State Treasurer had produced the initial check and that this meant the "first retirement allowance payment [had] been issued" such that the benefit option could not be changed.

a. Had Lawson's first retirement allowance payment been "issued" within the meaning of 3–105(a)? Was it "delivered" within the meaning of 1–201(b)(15)?

b. What, if any, significance should be given to the fact that Lawson was told he would receive his first monthly payment on or around September 27, 2004, and he contacted KERS on September 16?

5. Lester Construction performed construction work in Kentucky for Dayton Home Construction and Renovation, LLC. As payment, Dayton issued six checks payable to Lester for a total amount of $38,500. Dayton delivered the checks to Chris Ruchala, falsely believing that Ruchala was the authorized agent of Lester. In fact, Ruchala had no affiliation with Lester whatsoever. Ruchala indorsed the checks and presented them to the bank on which the checks were drawn, which cashed them. Lester has now sued the bank, alleging conversion of the checks.

a.   Were the checks ever delivered to Lester within the meaning of 1–201(b)(15)?

The statute of limitations for the payment obligation between Lester and Dayton will be the ordinary Kentucky limitations period for breach of contract. The statute of limitations for Lester's conversion claim against the bank will be 3–118(g).

b.   Find the relevant Kentucky statute for breach of contract. Which cause of action—contract or conversion—has the more favorable limitations period?

6.   Matthew Livingston, a student at the University of Oklahoma, executed and delivered to the University a promissory note which was to repay a student loan administered by the University. The note was for $10,000 plus 5% interest per annum. The note provided that interest was due on July 1 of every year in which principal payments were not made, and that principal was to be paid in "equal monthly installments" starting "three months after the maker ceased to carry a normal full-time academic workload."

a.   Is this instrument payable at a definite time?

b.   Does this instrument provide a sum certain?

c.   According to 3–112, when does interest begin to accrue?

7.   M.S. Horne executed a $100,000 promissory note "to the order of R.C. Clark." On the note appeared the following language:

This note may not be transferred, pledged, or otherwise assigned without the written consent of M.S. Horne.

a.   Is this note negotiable? 3–104(d) and Comment 3 may help you to answer this question.

b.   Look at 3–117, which is a Code section you haven't seen before. After reading this Code section, would your answer to the first question change if Horne had separately delivered a letter to Clark authorizing transfer of the note?

8.   On June 5, 1984, Air Terminal Gifts, Inc. executed a note for $125,000 to First Federal Savings & Loan Association. The note stated as follows: "This Note is secured by that certain Purchase and Security Agreement dated June 5, 1984. Reference is made to the Purchase and Security Agreement for additional rights of the holder thereof." The Purchase and Security Agreement described the collateral given for the note and gave First Federal Savings & Loan Association a security interest in the collateral, which it could foreclose upon in the event of Air Travel Gifts' default on the note.

a.   Does the note contain an impermissible additional promise?

b.   Is it impermissibly conditional?

9.   John and Evelyn Leavings signed a retail installment sales contract containing the following language:

> We agree to pay Solar Marketing $8,495 for a home improvement solar heating system at 16.5% interest per annum, payable in 120 installments of $146.82 each beginning 60 days from the date the Completion Certificate is signed, which is estimated to be December 15, 1984. Solar Marketing will retain a security interest in the tank, pipes, and valves of the solar water heating system and a mechanic's and materialman's lien will be placed on our residence. Any holder of this consumer credit contract is subject to all claims and defenses which the debtor could assert against the seller of goods or services obtained pursuant hereto or with the proceeds hereof.

The reverse side of the retail installment contract contained additional terms and conditions.

  a. Does this retail installment sales contract qualify as a negotiable instrument?

  b. If so, is it a promissory note or a draft?

  c. If not, what element or elements of negotiability are missing?

  d. What effect, if any, should the last sentence of the excerpt from the contract have on negotiability? In answering this question, look at 3–106(d).

10. Consider the following typed document, to which the parties refer as a note:

> Receipt is hereby acknowledged of U.S. $318,778 as full and final payment by Sami and/or Jacqueline Tamman to be invested by Samy and Isaac Schinazi. Samy and Isaac are fully responsible for the funds. At any end of month this amount can be reimbursed on request to the owner.

By way of background, Sami and Jacqueline Tamman are a married couple, Isaac Shinazi is Sami Tamman's cousin, and Samy Shinazi is Isaac's father. Isaac and Samy Shinazi signed this document and dated it May 8, 1998. In the summer of 2000, the Tammans made a demand for the return of their money, but were told that their money had been lost. Nevertheless, the Shinazis' bank account reflected a balance at that time of almost $1.4 million.

  a. Is this instrument payable on demand within the meaning of 3–108(a)?

  b. Does the instrument include a promise to pay within the meaning of 3–104(a)?

      Assume that Sami and Jacqueline can provide credible testimony that they were verbally promised interest in the amount of ½% per month.

  c. If the document is a negotiable promissory note, is this interest enforceable as part of the note? In answering this question, look at 3–117.

11. Is a "Federal Reserve Note" such as a dollar bill a promissory note within the meaning of Article 3? If not, which element or elements of negotiability fail?

12. Consider the following language:

> A promissory note is defined to be a written engagement by one person to pay absolutely and unconditionally to another person therein named, or to the bearer, a certain sum of money at a specified time or on demand.

     a.   Is this an accurate and complete description of the standards for negotiability under the Uniform Commercial Code?

     b.   What is the Article 3 name for a person who engages to pay another person a certain sum of money?

     c.   What is the Article 3 name for a person to whom such a payment promise is made?

13. Lawyers sometimes encounter cases in which one party to a note or draft claims the item should be deemed non-negotiable because it was issued gratuitously—in other words, without consideration. Chapter 7 shows that this fact is relevant in determining whether a holder is a holder in due course.

     a.   Based upon what you have learned in this chapter, is this fact also relevant to the issue of whether the item is a negotiable instrument?

14. As the text mentioned, instruments with variable interest rates are now recognized as satisfying the "sum certain" requirement. However, if the parties executed a promissory note during a time when variable interest rates were understood to defeat negotiability, a court will not apply a statute changing this rule retroactively.

     a.   Why not?

CHAPTER 7

NEGOTIATION, HOLDERS IN DUE COURSE, AND REAL AND PERSONAL DEFENSES

■ ■ ■

The prior chapter introduced the following analysis: If (1) a financial instrument qualifies as a "negotiable instrument" within the meaning of 3–104, (2) it is transferred in a way that qualifies as a "negotiation" as defined in 3–201 rather than a simple assignment, and (3) the person seeking to enforce the instrument qualifies as a "holder in due course," as defined in 3–302, then the holder in due course has the right to enforce the instrument notwithstanding the existence of certain defenses called "personal defenses" that may otherwise bar enforcement. In the prior chapter, you were introduced to the general concept of negotiability, as well as the seven elements an instrument must satisfy to be a negotiable instrument. Thus, you have already explored the first step of the analysis above. The materials that follow explain the second and third steps. Thus, the next task is to understand when a transfer is a "negotiation."

A. NEGOTIATION AND WHAT IT MEANS TO BE A HOLDER

In the context of Article 3, a "negotiation" is "a transfer of possession . . . of an instrument by a person other than the issuer, to a person who thereby becomes its holder." This language comes from 3–201. Thus, to understand when a transfer qualifies as a negotiation, it is important to understand when the transferee qualifies as a holder. A negotiation may be either voluntary or involuntary; thus, under certain circumstances, a theft can constitute a negotiation and a thief can be a holder. 3–201 Comment 1 explains how this can occur.

1–201(b)(21)(A) defines a "holder" as "the person in possession of a negotiable instrument that is payable either to bearer or to an identified person that is the person in possession." Thus, as a preliminary matter, a holder must possess the instrument. A holder can be the initial payee to whom the instrument was issued (3–105(a)) or a later transferee to whom the instrument was negotiated, as per 3–201.

Consider the following graphic. The movement of the check runs clockwise—that is, the check is issued by Drawer to Payee, which then transfers it to Transferee 1, followed by Transferee 2, which then presents the check to Drawee for payment. The double-sided arrows indicate that each exchange is supported by consideration. Assuming the check was not a gift, Payee gives Drawer goods or services in return for the check. Transferee 1, which might be a check-cashing company, gives Payee cash for the check. Transferee 2, which might be a bank, gives the check-cashing company account credit for the check. And finally, Drawee gives Transferee 2 account credit for the check. The line appearing between Drawer and Drawee represents the contractual relationship between those parties, which is explored in Chapter 8.

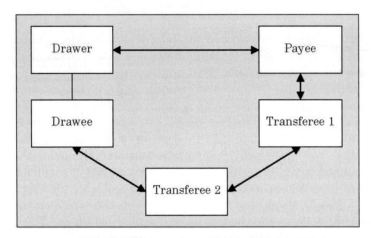

Payee, Transferee 1, and Transferee 2 would all be holders of the instrument during their time of possession so long as the instrument is payable to them, or to bearer, when they come into possession of it. Drawer is not a holder of this instrument, because the instrument is an obligation of Drawer, not an asset. Drawee is also not a holder, because Drawee pays the instrument rather than being paid for the instrument.

In studying these materials, note that ownership of an instrument and the right to enforce the instrument are not the same thing. Property law determines who owns an instrument, while Article 3 covers rights of enforcement. Thus, it is possible to own an instrument without having the right to enforce it. It is also possible to have the right to enforce an instrument without owning it.

Although a person must possess an instrument to be considered a holder, Article 3 recognizes the possibility of constructive possession. In *Bronco Printer Service & Supplies, Inc. v. Byte Laserecharge, Inc.*, No. 2-04-105-CV, 2005 WL 451475 (Tex. Ct. App. Feb. 24, 2005), the court held that "[c]onstructive possession exists when a person does not actually possess land or chattel [such as a note] but has the intent and capability to maintain control and dominion over it." The facts of that case were as follows: The owners of Byte Laserecharge, Inc., Mike and Jan McNicholas, agreed to sell all of the assets of Byte to Bronco Printer Service & Supplies. Inc. At closing, Richard Carbaugh, as President of Bronco, signed a note for

$47,000 payable to Byte. Danny Murphy, a third party, notarized the note and made a copy, which he provided to the McNicholases. Murphy returned the original to Carbaugh, who held the original up until the time of trial. The court found that, although neither Byte nor the McNicholases ever had actual possession of the note, they obtained constructive possession when Carbaugh surrendered the note to Murphy after signing it. The court thus held that Byte was the holder of the note. Importantly, possession of a copy, without this additional evidence, would not suffice, and thus the court's willingness to recognize constructive possession was significant.

Being a holder requires not only possession of an instrument, but also that the instrument be either payable to the person in possession, or payable to bearer. If the holder meets additional qualifications set forth later in this chapter, the holder may be a holder in due course. Holders in due course may enforce instruments notwithstanding the existence of certain "personal" defenses such as theft or certain kinds of fraud or duress.

A transfer that does not qualify as a negotiation is called an "assignment." The distinction between negotiation and assignment is important because, although a holder in due course sometimes has greater rights in an instrument than his or her transferor, an assignee can never have greater rights than his or her assignor. Because an assignee is not a holder, an assignee can never be a holder in due course, even if the assignee is a bona-fide purchaser for value. This rule was applied in *Holly Hill Acres, Ltd. v. Charter Bank of Gainesville*, 314 So. 2d 209 (1975). In that case, the court held that a bank purchasing a non-negotiable mortgage note would be bound by the borrower's personal defense of fraudulent inducement to the contract, to the same extent as the original payee would have been. This result is compelled because the purchaser of a non-negotiable instrument is an assignee of the instrument.

Proving "holder" status is the most common means of proving that one is a "person entitled to enforce" an instrument, as that term is used in **3–301**. The court's opinion in *In re Wells*, 407 B.R. 873, 879 (Bankr. N.D. Ohio 2009), explains how this works. This excerpt also introduces the concept of indorsement, which will be explored in the next section:

> A promissory note is usually a negotiable instrument, which provides the person entitled to enforce the note the right to payment of the obligation it represents. A person is entitled to enforce a note when that person falls into one of three categories. One such category is when the person is a holder of the note. Generally, a person is a holder of the note by having physical possession of the note, which has either been [i]ndorsed to that person or [i]ndorsed in blank. A note may be [i]ndorsed by an allonge, which is a paper "affixed to the instrument," which then becomes part of the instrument.

Once a note is [i]ndorsed, its negotiation is complete upon transfer of possession. The transfer of possession requires physical delivery of the note "for the purpose of giving the person receiving delivery the right to enforce the instrument. . . ."

The *Wells* court alludes to three ways of being a "person entitled to enforce" an instrument, but discusses only the first and most common one, which is being a holder of the instrument. The second option is being a nonholder in possession of an instrument. This concept is explained in *In re Wilhelm*, 407 B.R. 392 (Bankr. D. Idaho 2009). Once again, note the importance of indorsement:

> A "nonholder in possession of the instrument who has the rights of a holder," [**3–301(ii)**], includes persons who acquire physical possession of an unindorsed note. . . . As the statutory comments [to **3–203**] explain, however, such nonholders must "prove the transaction" by which they acquired the note:
>
>> If the transferee is not a holder because the transferor did not indorse, the transferee is nevertheless a person entitled to enforce the instrument under Section **3–301** if the transferor was a holder at the time of transfer. Although the transferee is not a holder, under subsection (b) the transferee obtained the rights of the transferor as holder. Because the transferee's rights are derivative of the transferor's rights, those rights must be proved. Because the transferee is not a holder, there is no presumption under Section **3–308** that the transferee, by producing the instrument, is entitled to payment. The instrument, by its terms, is not payable to the transferee and the transferee must account for possession of the unindorsed instrument by proving the transaction through which the transferee acquired it. [**3–203** Comment 2.]

However, if a person "proves the transaction" by which he or she acquired the note, but fails to show possession, he or she cannot enforce the note. *See generally* 11 Am.Jur.2d Bills and Notes § 210 (2009) (discussing differences between a "holder" and an "owner"). Again, the statutory comments explain:

> [A] person who has an ownership right in an instrument might not be a person entitled to enforce the instrument. For example, suppose X is the owner and holder of an instrument payable to X. X sells the instrument to Y but is unable to deliver immediate possession to Y. Instead, X signs a document conveying all of X's right, title and interest in the instrument to Y. Although the document may be effective to give Y a claim of ownership of the instrument, Y is not a person entitled to enforce the instrument until Y obtains possession of the instrument. No transfer of the instrument

occurs under Section **3–203(a)** until it is delivered to Y. [**3–203** Comment 1.]

The third means of enforcing an instrument under **3–301** is to be "a person not in possession of the instrument who is entitled to enforce the instrument pursuant to **3–309** or **3–418(d)**." **3–309** deals with lost or stolen instruments, while **3–418(d)** deals with instruments paid by mistake. As the court held in *In re Harborhouse*, No. 10-23078-HJB, 2014 WL 184743 (Bankr. D. Ma. Jan. 15, 2014), "A person seeking to enforce a lost note must meet two tests: it must have been both in possession of the note when it was lost and entitled to enforce the note when it was lost." The "lost note" scenario frequently arises with notes issued in connection with mortgages. In *Secretary v. Leonhardt*, 29 N.E.3d 1 (Ohio Ct. App. 2015), the court permitted the assignee of a mortgage note to enforce a note it had lost, because the assignee was able to prove by a preponderance of the evidence that it had been in possession of the note when it was lost, and that the note, when lost, was indorsed in blank and thus payable to bearer.

A mortgage transaction involves two documents—the mortgage and the note. In some transactions, a deed of trust is used in lieu of a mortgage. For purposes of this discussion, mortgages and deeds of trust can be treated similarly. The traditional view is that the "mortgage follows the note," meaning that the owner of the note has standing to foreclose under the mortgage. Thus, as the court found in *In re Knigge*, 479 B.R. 500 (Bankr. App. 8th Cir. 2012), a bank in possession of a note indorsed in blank and secured by a deed of trust had the standing to enforce both the note and the deed of trust that secured it. Under the Restatement (Third) of the Law of Property: Mortgages, transfer of either the note or the mortgage transfers ownership of both. *In re Veal*, 450 B.R. 897, 915–16 (Bankr. App. 9th Cir. 2011) illustrates the traditional approach: "[U]nder the common law, . . . the transfer of a mortgage without the transfer of the obligation it secures renders the mortgage ineffective and unenforceable in the hands of the transferee." Thus, under the traditional approach, the mortgage is "incident or accessory to the debt" while the note is "essential."

In understanding how mortgage notes are enforced, it is helpful to be aware of the role of the Mortgage Electronic Registration System ("MERS"). In *Ellington v. Federal Home Loan Mortgage Corp.*, 13 F.Supp.3d 723, 725 (W.D. Ky. 2014), the court described the role of MERS as follows:

> Under the MERS system, "when a home is purchased, the lender obtains from the borrower a promissory note and a mortgage instrument naming MERS as the mortgagee (as nominee for the lender and its successors and assigns)." In the mortgage, "the borrower assigns his right, title, and interest in the property to MERS, and the mortgage instrument is then recorded in the local land records with MERS as the named mortgagee. When the

promissory note is sold (and possibly re-sold) in the secondary mortgage market, the MERS database tracks that transfer. As long as the parties involved in the sale of promissory note are MERS members, MERS remains the mortgagee of record (thereby avoiding recording and other transfer fees that are otherwise associated with the sale) and continues to act as an agent for the new owner of the promissory note.

* * *

[T]he MERS system aids in the ability to determine the lienholder and advances the aim of the legislative attempt to ensure the timely release of liens. Once a loan held by a MERS member is registered in the MERS database, MERS serves as the nominal mortgagee for the lender and any successors and assigns. When the security instrument is recorded, the local land records list MERS as the mortgagee. Thus, when members transfer an interest in a promissory note to another MERS member, MERS privately tracks the assignment within its system, but remains mortgagee of record. Thus, the borrower knows who to go to get it released.

Note that this excerpt uses the term "assigns," which is closely related to the term "assignee," and serves to denote a person to whom property is transferred by conveyance, by intestacy, or through a will.

Now that you know a little bit about what it means to be a holder, the next step is to explore the role of indorsement.

B. INDORSEMENT ← *UNLOCK + ASSUME RESPONSIBILITY FOR*

The prior section quoted language from **1–201(b)(21)(A)** indicating that a holder is "the person in possession of a negotiable instrument that is payable either to bearer or to an identified person that is the person in possession." When an instrument is issued to the payee, the payee is the first holder. If the payee would like to negotiate the instrument to another party, the payee must make the instrument payable either to bearer (if it is not already bearer paper) or to the person to whom the payee intends to transfer the instrument (which makes the instrument "order paper" payable to that person). This is done via indorsement.

The way an item is indorsed determines whether it has been negotiated, such that the transferee is a holder and might be a holder in due course. First, assume that a check has been made payable to "Pamela Payee." This check is "order paper" because it is payable "to the order of" (according to the directions of) Pamela Payee. If Pamela Payee applies a "blank indorsement" **(3–205(b))** consisting solely of her signature, she changes this "order paper" into "bearer paper." Since the check is now bearer paper, any person who possesses the check will be a holder. If, following her blank indorsement, Pamela Payee applies an indorsement reading, "pay to the order of Helen Holder," this "special indorsement" (3–205(a)) changes what was previously "order paper" payable to Pamela Payee into "order paper" payable to Helen Holder.

The following graphic represents this series of events:

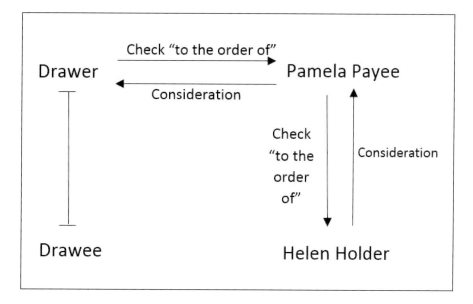

Thus, a single instrument can be both bearer paper and order paper at different points in the negotiation process.

A specially indorsed item cannot be negotiated without the signature of the named party or his or her agent, while an item indorsed in blank can be negotiated by mere transfer of possession. A payee who wishes to cash a check made payable to him or her might use a blank indorsement, but should be careful to apply the indorsement only when ready to hand the check directly to the person who will cash the check. Otherwise, if the payee indorses the item, leaves it somewhere, and another person finds it, the finder will be a "person entitled to enforce" the instrument.

A special indorsement designates a specific party as the new payee. The designated person must indorse the item to negotiate it. Thus, a special indorsement "locks" the instrument until the identified person indorses. Here is an example in which a special indorsement might be useful: A child purchases goods with his or her own money, and the parent completes and submits documentation for a rebate. If the rebate is made via a check payable to the parent, the parent might apply a special indorsement: "Pay to the order of [Child's Name], [Parent's Name]." This indorsement changes the check from order paper payable to the parent into order paper payable to the child.

Another form of indorsement is the "anomalous indorsement," defined in 3–205(d). An anomalous indorsement is for the purpose of suretyship; a party making such an indorsement is not a holder and does not enter into the chain of title for the item. Instead, a party making this kind of indorsement is simply promising to pay the item if it is dishonored. There is a presumption that "every party whose signature appears on the instrument has become a party for value," so an anomalous indorsement runs against this presumption. *Brault v. Grayton*, No. CV054003196, 2006 WL 1738257 (Conn. Super. Ct. June 5, 2006).

The final kind of indorsement is a "restrictive indorsement," defined in 3–206. A restrictive indorsement allows a holder to control the funds an instrument represents. The most common restrictive indorsement is "for deposit only." An individual doing business with an out-of-state bank might use this kind of indorsement if she wishes to mail a deposit consisting of several large checks made payable to her. Applying the indorsement "for deposit only" along with her account number puts later would-be holders on notice of her desire to have the checks deposited in a certain account. This example also shows why remote deposit capture, a form of banking technology that allows items to be deposited via electronic image rather than being physically presented, has become so popular—and is much more convenient than sending a check through the mail for deposit.

Although it is common for a negotiable instrument to be indorsed on the back of the instrument, sometimes it is unclear whether a signature is an indorsement because it appears in an unusual place or takes an unusual form. The signer's intent determines whether a signature is an indorsement. Even so, 3–204(a) provides that a signature is an indorsement, regardless of the signer's actual intent, unless the evidence clearly shows the signature was not for the purpose of indorsement. Comment 1 provides the example of a check presented for cashing by the payee's employee, after the payee properly indorsed it. If the bank requires the employee to initial the back of the check to show that the employee received cash, it would not be reasonable to assume that the initials were intended to function as an indorsement. Instead, the initials clearly function as a receipt in this context.

The prior discussion assumes the payee's identity is clear. Sometimes, however, there are questions about the payee's identity—and thus questions about who has the authority to indorse. To handle such cases, 3–110 provides a series of rules, some of which are highlighted in the chart below.

Rule	Policy Explanation
An instrument is payable to two persons alternatively, rather than jointly, when the language of the instrument is ambiguous.	It makes sense not to require both parties to sign when the maker or drawer has not specifically required both signatures.
The intent of the maker or drawer controls to whom an instrument is payable, even if the name on the instrument is not the true name of the payee.	The fact that the maker or drawer has made an error in writing the payee's name should not keep the intended payee from enforcing the item.
When an instrument is made payable to an account number represented as being associated with an identified person, the instrument is payable to the identified person rather than the holder of the account, if the account is not held by the identified person.	It is easier to make an error writing a number than a name.
If an instrument is made payable to an office or to a person described as holding an office, the instrument is payable to the named person, the incumbent, or the successor of the incumbent.	The assumption is that the funds were intended to go to the office or officeholder rather than to a specific individual.

It is possible for a draft or note to be negotiated many times, to many holders, before being presented to the maker or drawee for payment. The last indorsement controls what is required for the instrument to be negotiated again. If the last indorsement creates bearer paper, then negotiation to a new holder requires only transfer of possession. If the last indorsement creates order paper, then further negotiation requires not only transfer of possession, but also indorsement by the named person.

Sometimes, holders of order paper neglect or forget to indorse before transferring possession of the instrument to someone else. In such a case, the transferee of the unindorsed item has a specifically enforceable right, pursuant to **3–203(c)**, to require the transferor to supply an unqualified indorsement of the item, so long as the transferee gave value for the instrument as defined in **3–303**. Until the indorsement is given, however, the transferee cannot be a holder. **4–205** provides an additional option for depositary banks: they are holders of instruments their customers neglected to indorse before delivering them to the bank for collection, so long as the customers were holders at the time of delivery.

1. SIGNATURES BY AGENTS

One who signs an instrument—whether as a drawer of a check, maker of a note, or indorser of a check or note—must pay the instrument under certain circumstances. As you will learn in Chapter 9, the maker of a note must pay the note when it matures and is presented for payment, and the drawer of a check or indorser of a check or note must pay the instrument if it is dishonored by the drawee or maker. Thus, signing an instrument is legally significant. Sometimes, as in the case of a business entity, an instrument is signed by an agent. When a purported agent signs an instrument on behalf of some principal, two issues are raised: (1) whether the principal is bound by the agent's signature, and (2) whether the agent is personally liable on the instrument. These are independent questions. **3–402(b)** governs the agent's liability. This subsection establishes a "gold standard" by which agent signatures can be measured to see whether the agent can escape personal liability. This "gold standard" is satisfied when the form of the agent's signature (1) names the principal and (2) indicates he or she is signing the item in a representative capacity. "John Doe, as President for ABC Company" is one example of a signature that would satisfy this "gold standard" and allow agent John Doe to avoid personal liability. If the standard is not met, then the agent may be personally liable for the instrument if it is dishonored, just as if the instrument were a personal obligation of the agent. Even when the "gold standard" is not met, as **3–402(b)(2)** indicates, unless the item is held by a holder in due course, parol evidence may be used to show that the original parties did not intend the agent to be personally liable. In addition, **3–402(c)** provides an exception for checks signed by agents. So long as the agent has express, implied, or apparent authority to sign a check drawn on the principal's account, the agent will not face personal liability even if its signature does not meet the "gold standard." As Comment 3 indicates, the assumption is that no person who accepts an entity check will be misled into thinking the agent who signed it intended to be personally liable.

3–402(a) governs the liability of a principal when an agent signs on the principal's behalf. A principal is liable (even if its name does not appear on the instrument) if the putative agent has express, implied, or apparent authority to sign for the principal. If the alleged agent lacks authority of any kind, then **3–403(a)** applies and only the unauthorized signer will be liable.

The following chart summarizes the basic attributes of express, implied, and apparent authority:

Type of Authority	Example
Express authority. This is authority that is given specifically to an agent. This authority often appears as part of a contract, job description, or hiring letter.	A bank president's job description may indicate that he or she is charged with directing and administering the bank's financial performance, credit quality, business development, operations, regulatory compliance, and risk management. If so, all of these are within the president's express authority.
Implied authority. This is authority that has never specifically been given to the agent, but can be considered reasonably necessary to carry out his or her express authority.	The bank president with the above job description would have the implied authority to draft policies and hire people to help him or her carry out the items enumerated above.
Apparent authority. This is authority that the agent does not actually have, but which others may reasonably believe he or she has, given the position the principal has assigned to the agent.	Even if the bank president has been told that only the chief financial officer may sign contracts on behalf of the bank, third parties may reasonably assume the bank president has the authority to do so as well, if bank presidents usually have such authority. This would be an example of apparent authority.

Security Pacific National Bank v. Chess, 58 Cal. App. 3d 555, 561 (1976) illustrates how **3–402** can be applied. This case involved a series of notes payable to Petroleum Equipment Leasing Company of Tulsa, Oklahoma (PELCO). PELCO properly indorsed the notes and transferred them to Equipment Leasing Company of California (ELC). Once in ELC's possession, some of the notes were indorsed "Richard L. Burns" or "Richard L. Burns, Pres.," and it was not clear whether these indorsements were valid. In finding that Burns' signature would bind ELC, the court held as follows:

> Burns was at the time the president of ELC, and there is no question of his authority, or any reason to doubt his intention thereby to effect a transfer of the notes to [a third party now seeking to enforce them]. His handwriting therefore constitutes the signature of the corporation, under the principle that a party

may adopt any form or symbol as its signature for a particular transaction.

Under **3–402**, Burns may also be personally liable on the notes because his signature did not meet the "gold standard" and thus did not make it clear that he signed only as an agent. It would have been better to sign, "Richard L. Burns, as President for ELC."

The outcome in the *Security Pacific National Bank* case would have been different if it involved a check rather than a note. This is because **3–402(c)** contains an exception for checks signed by agents. *Pollin v. Mindy Manufacturing Co.*, 236 A.2d 542 (Pa. Super. 1967), illustrates the exception. Benjamin and Arthur Pollin owned the Girard Check Exchange, where employees of Mindy Manufacturing Company brought payroll checks drawn on Continental Bank and Trust to be cashed. The Pollins cashed the checks and then indorsed and deposited them into Girard Check Exchange's account with Provident National Bank of Philadelphia. After going through the collection process described in Chapter 8, the checks were presented to Continental, which refused to pay because insufficient funds remained in Mindy Manufacturing's account after the bank had exercised its right of set-off to satisfy a pre-existing debt. The Pollins contacted Mindy Manufacturing, which refused to reimburse Girard Check Exchange for the bad checks. The Pollins then sought to recover from Robert F. Apfelbaum, president of Mindy Manufacturing, on a theory of personal liability. The checks were pre-printed with the name of the company, and Apfelbaum signed the checks with only his signature, providing no indication that he was signing as an agent.

In finding Mr. Apfelbaum not personally liable, the court noted that the checks clearly showed on their face that they were drawn on a payroll account over which Apfelbaum had no control as an individual. The court found that (1) the check, when completed, was clearly that of an entity and not of any individual, (2) the company could not be liable on any check unless an authorized individual had signed it, and (3) because companies act only through individuals, it is natural (and necessary) that an individual sign a company check. Because Apfelbaum was authorized to sign checks for Mindy Manufacturing, the court held that he was not personally liable for the payroll checks in issue.

C. REAL AND PERSONAL DEFENSES

A holder in due course escapes any "personal defenses" the drawer of a draft or maker of a note might raise, but is bound by any "real defenses." Other transferees are bound by both real and personal defenses. Real defenses generally involve problems with mutual assent that are sufficiently serious to make the obligation void, while personal defenses generally involve less severe circumstances that make the obligation voidable. The exception is minority incapacity, also known as infancy. As

3–305 Comment 1 provides, **3–305(a)(1)(i)** "allows assertion of the defense of infancy against a holder in due course, even though the effect of the defense is to render the instrument voidable but not void. The policy is one of protection of the infant even at the expense of occasional loss to an innocent purchaser."

When an obligation is void, no person may enforce it. An example would be a contract to purchase a car signed by a person who has been adjudicated mentally incompetent. Neither the seller of the car nor the buyer may enforce this contract. Now assume that the mentally incapacitated person signed a promissory note as part of this transaction. Mental incapacity is a real defense to the enforcement of a negotiable instrument, and thus not even a holder in due course could enforce the instrument against the incapacitated person.

When an obligation is voidable, the party with the legal entitlement to raise the defense has the option to enforce the obligation or avoid it. An example would be a contract to purchase a car that involved fraud as to some term of the contract. For example, the seller of the car might have lied to the buyer, claiming the seller owned the car outright when, in fact, there was a lien on the car. The buyer might be able to avoid this contract due to fraudulent inducement, but she might also choose to enforce the contract anyway, because she might still want the car. Now assume that the transaction included a promissory note from the buyer to the seller. Fraudulent inducement is a personal defense to the enforcement of a negotiable instrument, and thus a holder in due course could enforce the note despite the fact that the buyer could raise the fraud against the seller. As **3–305(a)** indicates, state common law determines when obligations are void or voidable, but the following table provides a general overview:

Real Defenses	Personal Defenses
Fraud in the Factum	Fraudulent Inducement
Illegality	Failure of Consideration
Discharge in Bankruptcy	Discharge by Payment
Physical Duress	Economic Duress
Infancy & Mental Incapacity	Theft

Although most of the personal and real defenses are fairly self-explanatory, *Bankers Trust Co. v. Litton Systems, Inc.*, 599 F.2d 488 (C.A.N.Y. 1979), demonstrates a layer of complexity in the law of illegality that can be a trap for the unwary. Litton Systems, Inc., needed photocopiers for the branch offices of its telephone business. Royal

Typewriter Company was a subsidiary of Litton, and a Royal salesperson recommended that Litton obtain copiers from Regent Leasing Corporation. As it turned out, this salesperson was receiving kickbacks from Regent. Regent purchased the equipment from Royal and leased it to Litton.

To finance the purchase of the machines, Regent borrowed money from Bankers Trust Company and assigned the Litton leases as security. Litton later defaulted on the leases. In defending against the lender's suit for collection, Litton claimed the kickbacks rendered Litton's obligations void and therefore served as a defense, even as against a holder in due course such as Bankers Trust.

The court noted, as a preliminary matter, that there is nothing illegal about leasing copiers, and thus whether the real defense of illegality applies requires a more nuanced analysis. Only the bribery contract between the Royal salesperson and Regent was illegal. Because there was a direct connection between the bribery contract and the leasing contract, Regent would not be permitted to enforce the leases.

The more difficult question was whether Bankers Trust would be subject to the same defense. Thus, the question was whether the bribery rendered the obligation between Litton and Regent void or simply voidable. Making an analogy to the personal defense of fraud in the inducement, the court concluded that Bankers Trust as the lender should be able to enforce the contract despite the salesperson's illegal conduct, thus rendering the contract voidable rather than void and the real defense of illegality inapplicable.

The lesson from this case is that, when a negotiable instrument has been issued in a matter involving bribery, the instrument is treated as illegal (and the contract supporting the instrument is void) only if there is a direct connection between the instrument and the bribery. In this particular case, no such direct connection existed, and thus the obligation was voidable rather than void and the instrument was subject to the personal defense of fraudulent inducement rather than the real defense of illegality. This is why Regent could not enforce the leases, but Bankers Trust could enforce its interest in the leases.

A second important case in understanding the illegality defense is *Kedzie and 103rd Currency Exchange, Inc. v. Hodge*, 619 N.E.2d 732 (Ill. 1993). As that case shows, for illegality to prevent enforcement of an instrument, there must be a clear connection in existing law between the illegal conduct and the enforceability of the instrument.

In that case, Fred Fentress agreed to install a flood-control system at the Chicago home of Eric and Beulah Hodge for $900. In partial payment, Mrs. Hodge wrote a $500 check payable to "Fred Fentress—A-OK Plumbing," drawn on the Hodges' joint account at Citicorp. Fentress never performed the promised work for the Hodges, so Eric Hodge called Fentress to tell him the contract was cancelled. The same day, Hodge placed a stop-payment order with Citicorp. Stop-payment orders are briefly explored below in *Lynwood Sand & Gravel, Inc. v. Bank of Everett* and further explained in Chapter 8. For now, understand that a stop-payment order is a direction the drawer of a check gives to the bank on which the check is drawn, directing the bank to dishonor the check. Stop-payment orders are normally used when the drawer is disappointed with the goods or services for which the check was issued.

Fentress took the check to the Kedzie and 103rd Currency Exchange, a check-cashing company, indorsed it as sole owner of A-OK Plumbing, and received cash in return. Currency Exchange presented the check to Citicorp, which returned the check unpaid due to the stop-payment order. Currency Exchange sued Mrs. Hodge for the value of the check. As you will learn in Chapter 8, Currency Exchange could not sue Citicorp because the drawee of an unaccepted check has no obligation to anyone but its own customer, the drawer.

In the ensuing litigation, Mrs. Hodge admitted that Currency Exchange was a holder in due course, but claimed the check was void under a theory of illegality. Illinois required that all plumbing be performed by licensed plumbers, and made noncompliance a misdemeanor. Currency Exchange admitted that Fentress was not a licensed plumber, but argued that it should be able to enforce the check anyway.

In holding for Currency Exchange, the court distinguished between an illegal transaction and the enforceability of an instrument issued in connection with the transaction: "Unless the instrument arising from a contract or transaction is itself made void by statute, the illegality defense under Section 3–305 is not available to bar the claim of a holder in due course." The court noted, by way of comparison, that usury is illegal, but usurious instruments are not usually void. Instead, courts typically grant relief targeted at the usury alone—such as reducing the interest to be paid.

Consider the following language from the dissent, which claimed Currency Exchange did not prove it was a holder in due course and probably was not one:

> It can hardly be doubted that any currency exchange would question whether it would be able to collect on an uncertified personal check. Further, the check in this case was made payable to "Fred Fentress—A-OK Plumbing. . . ." Any currency exchange presented with such a check and indorsement would have to question whether the named individual was indeed the sole owner of the named business and entitled to the proceeds of the check.

> Also, this personal check was made payable to the order of a business. It is reasonable to assume that a businessperson would have a business bank account where the check could be negotiated

without a fee. Why would such a person choose to pay a fee to a currency exchange?

Some commentators have argued that check-cashing companies such as Currency Exchange should not be considered holders in due course. In addition, perhaps Mr. and Mrs. Hodge could have prevented their loss by waiting until the services were finished before paying, or (as you will learn in Chapter 10) paying by credit card.

Turning from illegality to duress, duress, as **3–305** Comment 1 indicates, "is a matter of degree." Thus, "[a]n instrument signed at the point of a gun is void, even in the hands of a holder in due course. One signed under threat to prosecute the son of the maker for theft [, however,] may be merely voidable, so that the defense is cut off."

Fraud, like duress, is sometimes a real defense and sometimes a personal defense. Fraud in the factum, which Comment 1 describes as "real" or "essential" fraud, is a real defense, while fraudulent inducement is a personal defense. Comment 1 provides the following illustration of fraud in the factum: "[A] maker . . . is tricked into signing a note in the belief that it is merely a receipt or some other document." In such a case, the fraud relates to the essential nature of the transaction, or even perhaps the fact that a transaction is being proposed at all. By contrast, the personal defense of fraudulent inducement can be raised when a party is deceived as to some aspect of the transaction (such as the quality of the goods or the interest rate being charged) but is aware of the essential nature of the transaction.

D. PROVING HOLDER-IN-DUE-COURSE STATUS

For the distinction between real and personal defenses to affect a holder's rights, the holder must be a holder in due course. **3–302(a)** identifies six elements that must be satisfied for a holder to be a holder in due course:

(1) The holder must take the item for value;

(2) The holder must not have notice that the item is overdue or has been dishonored;

(3) The item must bear no indicia of suspicious irregularity or incompleteness;

(4) The holder must not have notice that the item contains an unauthorized signature or has been altered;

(5) The holder must act in good faith; and

(6) The holder must have no notice of any claim to the instrument, defense to the enforcement of the instrument, or claim in recoupment.

As is the modern trend, this section will deal with elements (3), (4), (5), and (6) together. Whether a holder is a holder in due course is determined when the holder acquires the item. As the court held in *Lynnwood Sand and Gravel, Inc. v. Bank of Everett*, 630 P.2d 489 (Wash. App. 1981), "[s]ubsequent notice of infirmities in the instrument has no effect upon the rights of a holder in due course, absent a showing of bad faith."

1.   WHEN A HOLDER GIVES VALUE

3–303 explains when a holder gives value for the purpose of qualifying as a holder in due course. It is obvious that a holder gives value when it receives a note in exchange for a loan, or a check in exchange for goods. In fact, there will be a presumption that the payee gave value for the instrument unless the maker or drawer proves otherwise. In *Oupac, Inc. v. Sam*, 89 So.3d 402 (La. Ct. App. 2012), the court made it clear that the maker of a note bears the burden of proving that the note was issued without consideration, rather than requiring the holder to prove the existence of consideration. More complex situations arise when performance has been promised in return for an instrument, but not yet given. Although an executory promise is "consideration" under contract law, only a completed promise constitutes "value" for purposes of Article 3.

Other issues arise in the "value" context when a holder agrees to buy an item at a discount but does not pay the full sum promised. As **3–302(d)** indicates, the drafters have indicated that the following "percentage" test should be followed in such a case:

$$\text{Amount for which H is HIDC} = (\text{amount paid} / \text{amount promised}) \times \text{item's face value}$$

Assume a holder promised to pay \$800 for a note with a face value of \$1,000, but paid only \$400. Under the percentage test, the equation is 400/800 × 1000, or \$500. Thus, the holder ("H") is a holder in due course ("HIDC") for only \$500 of the instrument, not the full \$1,000. The holder's rights to the other \$500 are subject to both real and personal defenses.

Although paying a discounted sum for an instrument constitutes giving value within the meaning of **3–303**, if the discount is too high, the holder is deemed to have notice of a problem with the item's enforceability. Such a transaction would pass the "value" element of holder-in-due-course status but fail "good faith and without notice."

Other questions regarding value arise when items are deposited in bank accounts. A depositary bank is an agent of the depositor and does not itself become the owner of the item. Determining when a bank gives value after crediting a check to the depositor's account requires an understanding of how funds are credited to—and spent from—accounts. **4–210(b)** supports the following description of deposited funds: Like cartons of milk in a grocery store, the newest deposit is "loaded from the back of the shelf," pushing older deposits forward to be spent first.

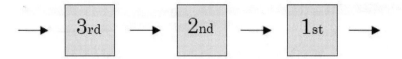

The last funds to be deposited in the account will be the last to be spent, and the bank gives value for the funds in the order in which they were deposited.

The following case further explores the "value" requirement in the context of provisional credit given by a bank, and also explains what happens when a holder receives notice of a problem with an instrument only after taking possession of it. The case also discusses the right of stop payment, further explored in Chapter 8, and shows that a stop payment order does not necessarily defeat the rights of a holder in due course.

LYNNWOOD SAND & GRAVEL, INC. V. BANK OF EVERETT
29 Wash.App. 686, 33 UCC Rep.Serv. 1703 (Wash Ct. App. 1981)

JAMES, J.

Plaintiff Lynnwood Sand and Gravel, Inc. (Lynnwood) appeals entry of summary judgment in favor of defendant Bank of Everett (Everett) in a suit to recover the amount of a check drawn by Lynnwood and paid by Everett over a stop payment order. We affirm.

On December 23, 1977, Lynnwood issued its check No. 1555 in the amount of $30,000 drawn on Everett and payable to Western Cedar Products (Western). Western deposited the check in its checking account at Peoples National Bank (Peoples) the same day. Also on December 23, Peoples gave provisional credit for the check, reducing an existing overdraft of $32,328.71 in Western's account by the full amount of the check.

Lynnwood contends it issued a stop payment order to Everett on December 27, with respect to check No. 1555. For purposes of the summary judgment motion, it was assumed that a valid stop payment order was given. On December 28, Everett returned the check to Peoples with the notation, "non-collected funds, refer to maker." On January 5, 1978, Peoples resubmitted the check to Everett, and Everett paid the check.

If Peoples was a holder in due course of the check, Everett is subrogated to its rights. RCW 62A.4–407 provides:

If a payor bank has paid an item over the stop payment order of the drawer or maker . . . , to prevent unjust enrichment and only to the extent necessary to prevent loss to the bank by reason of its payment of the item, the payor bank shall be subrogated to the rights

> (a) of any holder in due course on the item against the drawer or maker; . . .

Because Lynnwood presented no defense valid against a holder in due course, Lynnwood cannot recover against Everett if Peoples was a holder in due course. A holder in due course is defined by RCW 62A.**3–302**, which states:

> (1) A holder in due course is a holder who takes the instrument
>
> > (a) for value; and
> >
> > (b) in good faith; and
> >
> > (c) without notice that it is overdue or has been dishonored or of any defense against or claim to it on the part of any person.

That Peoples acted in good faith and was without notice of dishonor or of claims or defenses regarding the check when provisional credit was given is not disputed. Lynnwood does, however, contend that Peoples did not take the instrument for value. RCW 62A.**3–303** provides:

> A holder takes the instrument for value
>
> > (a) to the extent that the agreed consideration has been performed or that he acquires a security interest in or a lien on the instrument otherwise than by legal process; or
> >
> > (b) when he takes the instrument in payment of or as security for an antecedent claim against any person whether or not the claim is due; . . .

RCW 62A.4–209 [UCC **4–211**] provides:

> For purposes of determining its status as a holder in due course, the bank has given value to the extent that it has a security interest in an item provided that the bank otherwise complies with the requirements of RCW 62A.**3–302** on what constitutes a holder in due course.

RCW 62A.4–208 [UCC **4–210**] provides:

> (1) A bank has a security interest in an item and any accompanying documents or the proceeds of either
>
> > (a) in case of an item deposited in an account to the extent to which credit given for the item has been withdrawn or applied;

(b)   in case of an item for which it has given credit available for withdrawal as of right, to the extent of the credit given whether or not the credit is drawn upon and whether or not there is a right of charge-back; or

(c)   if it makes an advance on or against the item.

Lynnwood contends that Peoples neither allowed a withdrawal nor applied credit given for the item by merely granting a provisional credit to its depositor, and thus did not take for value. Everett responds that value was given because the credit was applied to reduce an existing overdraft in the depositor's account. The issue, then, is whether a bank takes an item for value for purposes of becoming a holder in due course by giving provisional credit for the item which is applied against an existing overdraft in the depositor's account. We conclude that a bank does give value and becomes a holder in due course under these circumstances.

It is well established that the mere granting of provisional credit, without more, does not constitute a taking for value. *Marine Midland Bank-New York v. Graybar Electric Co.*, 41 N.Y.2d 703, 363 N.E.2d 1139, 395 N.Y.S.2d 403 (1977). . . .

But it is also well established that a depository bank gives value when it allows its depositor to make withdrawals against uncollected checks for which the bank has given credit. . . .

A bank makes a loan to its customer by allowing an account overdraft. *State v. Larson*, 119 Wash. 259, 205 P. 373 (1922). This creates an "antecedent claim" within the meaning of RCW 62A–.3–303(b) [UCC **3–303(a)(3)**]. By applying credit given for a check to reduce an existing overdraft in the depositor's account, a bank gives value for the check, even if the credit is provisional. . . . Peoples became a holder in due course no later than when it granted provisional credit for the check and applied that credit to reduce an existing overdraft in Western's account.

Lynnwood relies primarily upon *Marine Midland Bank v. Graybar Electric Co., supra.* The case is distinguishable. There, the depositor of a check had both a checking account and an independent loan from the bank. The bank applied credit for a subsequently dishonored check against the depositor's loan obligation. The court reasoned that because the depositor's loan and checking account were not interconnected, the bank did not take the check in satisfaction of an antecedent claim but merely took unilateral action to protect its security. Here, Peoples granted provisional credit against an overdraft in Western's checking account for a check deposited in Western's account.

Citing RCW 62A.4–202(1)(b) [UCC **4–202(a)(2)**], Lynnwood finally contends that Peoples, if a holder in due course, lost that status by breaching its duty of ordinary care through failing to reverse the provisional credit upon receipt of the notice of dishonor and by failing to return the item. We do not agree.

Subsequent notice of infirmities in the instrument has no effect upon the rights of a holder in due course, absent a showing of bad faith. . . . There is no contention that Peoples acted in bad faith. Moreover, RCW 62A.4–202(1)(b) [UCC **4–202(a)(2)**] is designed for the protection of the bank's customer. When returning an item, the collecting bank (here Peoples) acts as agent for the owner of the item, RCW 62A.**4–201**, who is the depositor (here Western). . . . See generally Comments, RCW 62A.**4–201**. The statute does not provide that failure to use ordinary care deprives the bank of holder in due course status as to a check on which a third party is obligated.

The judgment is affirmed.

DURHAM-DIVELBISS and WILLIAMS, JJ., concur.

———————

As this case demonstrates, a holder in due course does not lose its status by later receiving information (such as the non-collectability of the instrument) that, had the information been known when the holder took possession of the instrument, would have disqualified the holder from holder-in-due-course status. This case also illustrates the majority position that a bank gives value for purposes of holder-in-due-course status when it credits a deposit against a customer's existing overdraft.

2. DETERMINING WHETHER THE ITEM IS OVERDUE

If the face of an item shows that it is already overdue, a subsequent holder will have reason to doubt that it will be paid and thus cannot be a holder in due course. A check that was dishonored due to insufficient funds or bears a date more than 90 days old is overdue (**3–304(a)(1)** and **(2)**). **3–304(b)(1)** applies to installment notes: A note is overdue when any installment is owed and unpaid, until the default is cured. For a single-payment note, **3–304(b)(2)** applies, and the note becomes overdue the day after it matures if it is not paid. Under **3–304(c)**, a default as to interest only will not cause the item to be overdue if the principal is current.

Applying these rules, if the face of a note indicates a maturity date of October of one year and the note is bought in November of the following year, the buyer is on notice that the note is overdue and cannot be a holder in due course. Likewise, in *Dorchester Financial Securities v. Banco BRJ, S.A.,* No. 02 Civ. 7504(KMW)(KNF), 2009 WL 5033954 (S.D.N.Y. Dec. 23, 2009), the court rejected a party's claim that it was the holder in due course of two forged cashier's checks. Notably, the checks showed on their face that they were more than eight years old when the party sought to assert holder-in-due-course rights.

3. DETERMINING THE HOLDER'S GOOD OR BAD FAITH AND LACK OR PRESENCE OF NOTICE

Because a holder in due course is similar to a bona-fide purchaser for value, a holder cannot be a holder in due course unless it took the item in good faith and without notice of any irregularity or defense to enforcement. *Branch Banking & Trust Co. v. Gill*, 237 S.E.2d 21, 32 (1977), describes the relationship between good faith and notice of irregularity or defenses in a way that shows why these elements are often covered together. In that case, which involved the issuance of negotiable warehouse receipts as part of a grain elevator's fraudulent scheme, the court held as follows in considering whether the bank that accepted the receipts had acted in good faith and without notice of any issue with the transaction, so as to be a holder in due course:

> Good faith ... and notice, although not synonymous, are inherently intertwined. Therefore, the relation between the two cannot be ignored. "The same facts which call a party's 'good faith' into question may also give him 'notice of a defense.'"

The following cases illustrate the kind of conduct that does—and does not—violate the "good faith and without notice of any irregularity or defense" requirement.

NEW RANDOLPH HALSTED CURRENCY EXCHANGE, INC. V. REGENT TITLE INSURANCE AGENCY, LLC

405 Ill.App.3d 923, 73 UCC Rep.Serv.2d 341 (Ill Ct. App. 2010)

NEVILLE, J.

New Randolph Halsted Currency Exchange (New Randolph) cashed a check drawn on a bank account of Regent Title Insurance Agency (Regent). Regent stopped payment on the check. New Randolph sued Regent for payment, claiming that New Randolph qualified as a holder in due course of the check. Following a bench trial, the trial court held that New Randolph was not a holder in due course because the check-cashing transaction raised several warning signals that should have alerted New Randolph to the possibility of fraud. The court entered judgment in favor of Regent.

* * *

On New Randolph's appeal, we find that New Randolph took commercially reasonable precautions before cashing the check, and therefore it qualifies as a holder in due course, and we reverse the trial court. . . .

BACKGROUND

Regent served as a settlement agent for closing real estate transactions. Regent cut checks to distribute funds to all the parties to such transactions.

On December 23, 2005, New Randolph cashed a check from Regent, made out to Charae Pearson, for $1,945.99. Four days later, New Randolph cashed another check for Pearson, again from Regent, this time for $2,500. On January 11, 2006, Pearson brought to New Randolph Regent's check number 22221, for $29,588.31. Unlike the prior checks, which spelled Pearson's name correctly, this check showed the payee as "CHAREA PAERSON." The check indicated that Pearson received it as a "LOAN PAYOFF." Pearson presented the check to Patrice Keys, manager of New Randolph. Pearson showed Keys her state identification card, which had been issued on December 30, 2005. Pearson told Keys that Regent issued the check to her to pay her a commission she earned from the sale of property.

Police arrested Pearson on January 23, 2006, charging her with check fraud. Two days later, police arrested Tatiana Auson, an employee of Regent, on the same charge. Regent had hired Auson to work as a funder, meaning that Regent authorized Auson to cut checks for the parties to real estate transactions. According to Regent's investigator, Auson cancelled checks intended for parties to real estate transactions, then issued new checks to different payees for the amounts of the original checks. Pearson admitted that Auson gave her the three checks New Randolph cashed for Pearson. Pearson kept about $5,000 of the proceeds from the checks, and she gave the remainder to Auson. All three checks appeared to bear the signature of Karen Hendricks, who had authority to sign checks on behalf of Regent.

Regent told its bank to stop payment on the check. New Randolph sued Regent for payment of the check, claiming that its status as a holder in due course entitled it to payment, despite the evidence that Auson and Pearson conspired to defraud Regent. . . .

* * *

At the trial, Keys testified that she looked up Pearson in PLS's database and found that she had recently cashed two other checks from Regent for lesser amounts. Keys called Regent, using a phone number she found in PLS's database. The person who answered the call for Regent confirmed that Regent issued the check to Pearson for the dollar amount shown, as payment of a commission. According to the person who answered the call for Regent, Pearson earned the commission from her work as an employee of Regent.

Arizaga, who worked as director of operations for PLS, testified that she approved about three checks each week for amounts exceeding the amount of Regent's check number 22221. She spoke with Keys about the check, and then she looked up the phone number for Regent at Regent's Web site. Arizaga testified that she called the number and asked to speak with someone about verifying a check. The woman with whom she spoke confirmed that Regent issued the check to Pearson in the amount shown. Arizaga then contacted [drawee] American Chartered Bank, which confirmed that the check came from a valid account with sufficient funds to cover the check, and Regent had not stopped payment on the check.

On cross-examination, Arizaga admitted that according to PLS's manual, the misspelling of Pearson's name could signal fraud. Pearson's recent identification card should also raise suspicion. Arizaga did not remember whether she noticed that the check indicated its purpose as "LOAN PAYOFF," instead of listing the payment as a commission.

Regent introduced PLS's manual into evidence. The manual emphasizes that PLS earns its fees by cashing checks, so the employee should "[s]pend * * * time proving that the check can be cashed and not looking for excuses not to cash it." (Emphasis omitted.) The manual identifies several signs that a check might not be valid, including several of the factors present in this case. According to the manual, the employee should "verify that the check is good" by "phoning the maker." (Emphasis omitted.)

William Andrews, the president of Regent's commercial division, testified that Pearson never worked for Regent, and no woman working at Regent would have fielded a call about who worked at Regent. Andrews admitted that the check appears to bear Hendricks's authorized signature. Andrews did not know whether Hendricks actually signed the fraudulently issued check.

The trial court summarized its findings of fact. It found that Arizaga and Keys called Regent to verify the check. When they called, they failed to ask about the discrepancy between the purpose shown on the check and the purpose Pearson stated. According to the court, that discrepancy "was enough to cause the currency exchange to pause and think twice about cashing the check. And then when * * * they decided to go ahead with negotiating the check * * * they did it at their own risk." The court added:

> "[I]t's not a question of anybody being dishonest or anything of that nature.
>
> * * *
>
> So I'm not talking about any kind of dishonesty or illegality. I'm just simply saying perhaps a mistake was made."

The trial court entered an order on December 18, 2008, finding in favor of Regent on New Randolph's complaint.

* * *

ANALYSIS

Holder in Due Course

The trial court entered judgment for Regent following a trial. We defer to the trial court's findings of fact, reversing only if the court committed clear error, but we review rulings of law de novo. . . .

The trial court awarded the judgment based on its finding of fact that New Randolph did not qualify as a holder in due course of the check. . . . The Uniform Commercial Code defines a holder in due course as:

the holder of an instrument if:

> (1) the instrument when issued or negotiated to the holder does not bear such apparent evidence of forgery or alteration or is not otherwise so irregular or incomplete as to call into question its authenticity, and

> (2) the holder took the instrument (i) for value, (ii) in good faith, (iii) without notice that the instrument is overdue or has been dishonored or that there is an uncured default with respect to payment of another instrument issued as part of the same series, (iv) without notice that the instrument contains an unauthorized signature or has been altered, (v) without notice of any claim to the instrument * * *, and (vi) without notice that any party has a defense or claim in recoupment * * *." 810 ILCS 5/3–302 (West 2006).

The trial court found that New Randolph did not qualify as a holder in due course because the check at issue was "so irregular * * * as to call into question its authenticity." However, grounds for suspicion about a check will not always prevent one from taking the check as a holder in due course. . . . Where all of the evidence available to the holder shows that it lacked notice of a defense, it becomes a holder in due course. . . . " 'To defeat the rights of one dealing with negotiable securities it is not enough to show that he took them under circumstances which ought to excite the suspicion of a prudent man and cause him to make inquiry, but that he had actual knowledge of an infirmity or defect, or of such facts that his failure to make further inquiry would indicate a deliberate desire on his part to evade knowledge because of a belief or fear that investigation would disclose a vice in the transaction.' " *Valley Bank & Trust Co. v. American Utilities, Inc.*, 415 F.Supp. 298, 301–02 (E.D.Pa.1976), quoting *First National Bank of Blairstown v. Goldberg*, 340 Pa. 337, 340, 17 A.2d 377, 378–79 (1941). . . .

A federal case involved a similar issue. In *McCook County National Bank v. Compton*, 558 F.2d 871 (8th Cir. 1977), McCook cashed a check despite several irregularities, including a discrepancy in the amount of the check. McCook contacted Northwestern, the bank on which the payor drew the check, and Northwestern confirmed the correct amount and assured

McCook the check was " 'okay to cash.' " *McCook*, 558 F.2d at 873. The trial court held that McCook did not qualify as a holder in due course. The *McCook* court said:

> "McCook bank was presented with a check that had an obvious $10,000 discrepancy on its face. As any prudent bank would, McCook contacted the Northwestern bank to ascertain the correct amount and whether adequate funds existed to cover the check. Assured by the bank and indirectly by Compton, who issued the check, that the check was 'okay', McCook proceeded to cash the check and issue money orders. There were no remaining irregularities in the instrument itself. Since this court has found no actual notice and insufficient constructive notice from the reporting service, and no other notice at the time the check was cashed, we can find no bad faith or dishonesty on the part of McCook bank in cashing the check.
>
> In sum, while a better judgment concerning the negotiability of the check might have been made we cannot find the requisite notice or bad faith that would deprive McCook bank of its status as holder in due course." *McCook*, 558 F.2d at 877.

* * *

Here, New Randolph had some grounds for suspecting that the check could be invalid. Regent misspelled Pearson's name, the purpose stated on the check did not match the purpose Pearson described, the check greatly exceeded the amount of prior checks made out to Pearson, and Pearson had only recently renewed her state identification card. However, when it cashed the check, New Randolph also knew that Regent had issued two other checks to Pearson, and those checks had cleared. Most significantly, Arizaga and Keys called Regent and Regent directly confirmed that it issued the check to Pearson for the stated amount.

We agree with the trial court's finding that irregularities involving the check called its authenticity into question. But New Randolph investigated those irregularities in a commercially reasonable manner by calling Regent to verify the check. In this case, unlike *McCook*, the holder did not rely on an indirect verification from the payor. New Randolph contacted Regent directly, as well as American Chartered Bank. New Randolph might have acted more cautiously and asked more questions of the person who spoke to them when they called Regent. But that person's verification of the check made the decision to cash the check commercially reasonable. We find that the trial court committed clear error when it found that New Randolph was not a holder in due course of check number 22221. Therefore, we reverse the judgment entered in favor of Regent and remand for entry of judgment in favor of New Randolph for payment of the check.

* * *

The prior case examined whether certain characteristics of an instrument create notice of an irregularity in a way that defeats holder-in-due-course status. The case that follows analyzes whether a high discount paid on a promissory note provides evidence that the purchaser either suspected or must have known of some problem with the instrument or defense to its enforcement and thus cannot be a holder in due course.

NORTHWESTERN NATIONAL INSURANCE CO. v. MAGGIO
976 F.2d 320, 18 U.C.C. Rep. Serv. 2d 808 (7th Cir. 1992)

POSNER, J.

This diversity suit on a promissory note was brought by Northwestern National Insurance Company against the note's maker, Anthony Maggio. The district court, holding that Northwestern was a holder in due course and had therefore taken the note free of any defenses Maggio might have had to a suit by the promisee, gave judgment for Northwestern on the latter's motion for summary judgment.

In 1981, Maggio had purchased a limited partnership in a new venture created by a former astronaut to develop an optoelectronic scanner designed to provide perimeter security for sprawling properties such as airfields, oil fields, and pipelines. As consideration for his partnership interest, Maggio gave the partnership a noninterest-bearing note for $55,000, maturing October 31, 1990. The partnership negotiated the note to a venture-capital company that in turn negotiated it to Goldman Sachs, which in 1988 negotiated it to Northwestern, along with other notes of the limited partners, at a 50-percent discount. When the note matured on October 31, 1990, Northwestern demanded payment from Maggio of the full face amount. He refused.

Maggio claims that he was induced to purchase the limited partnership by fraud. If so, he has of course a claim against the partnership itself and perhaps the general partner and others, but he has no claim against Northwestern if the latter is a holder in due course. It is not if it did not take the note "in good faith" . . . .

＊ ＊ ＊

The . . . substantial issue is whether the 50-percent discount at which Northwestern bought the note should have made Northwestern inquire into the possible existence of defenses. Maggio does not argue that the discount itself established bad faith—only that it was a sufficiently suspicious circumstance to make Northwestern guilty of ostrich conduct, or more precisely to raise a jury issue and thus forestall summary judgment. Bad faith is a conscious state, but it includes the deliberate avoidance of inquiry by one who fears what inquiry would bring to light.

Northwestern reminds us that a noninterest-bearing note at fixed maturity must sell at a discount. No one will pay $1,000 today for the right to receive $1,000 in two years, and Northwestern bought Maggio's note from Goldman Sachs two years before it was to mature. But a 50-percent discount on a note bought two years before maturity implies an interest rate of about 40 percent a year, and Maggio asks us to infer that no one would compensate the buyer of a note at such a rate unless the promisor had defenses. . . . But this overlooks an obvious reason for the discount besides compensation for the time value of Northwestern's money—the risk that Maggio, even if he had no defenses to a suit for collection brought by the original promisee, would raise some anyway, as he has done, or wouldn't have the assets to pay the note when it matured. A bird in the hand is said to be worth two in the bush. Goldman Sachs got the bird in the hand; Northwestern got the two birds in the bush.

The fact that a note is sold at a discount is thus not in itself a suspicious circumstance that triggers a duty of inquiry by the buyer.

———————

Judge Posner's opinion raises the question of what evidence would have been sufficient to defeat Northwestern's holder-in-due-course status. To support his claim that Northwestern should not be a holder in due course because it paid too little for the note, and thus presumably knew there was a reason to be concerned about its enforcement, Maggio should perhaps have introduced evidence about his own credit-worthiness, as well as standard discount rates in the industry.

This case also discusses the time value of money. Computing present values is a key component of determining whether the amount a party pays for a note is reasonable. The formula is as follows:

$$PV = \frac{FV}{(1+r)^n}$$

FV is the future value (often also the face value) of the item, *r* is the interest rate compounded annually, expressed as a decimal, and *n* is the number of years until the item reaches maturity. Applying this formula, the present value of the $68,000 promissory note in *Northwestern National Ins. Co. v. Maggio*, assuming a six-percent annual interest rate and a four-year term, is $68,000/([1.06]^4), or $53,862.

The financial health of the maker or drawer, in addition to the face value of the instrument, may affect what a holder would be willing to pay. Such information can also affect whether the holder is a holder in due course. A number of cases address how much negative information a holder may have about the transaction, or a party's financial condition, before it will be unable to qualify as a holder in due course. In *Citizens National*

Bank of Englewood v. Fort Lee Savings & Loan Association, 213 A.2d 315, 318 (N.J. Super. 1965), the court addressed whether allowing a customer to draw on uncollected funds when its account was either very low or overdrawn would keep the bank that permitted the withdrawal from being a holder in due course. In that case, the remitter of a cashier's check alleged that the payee, Mr. Winter, procured issuance of the check by fraud. In finding the bank had not acted in bad faith in allowing the payee to withdraw the uncollected proceeds of the check, the court held as follows:

> Winter's account was low in funds. However, this fact, or the fact that Winter's account was overdrawn, currently or in the past, if true, would not constitute notice to the collecting bank of an infirmity in the underlying transaction or instrument and is not evidence of bad faith chargeable to the bank at the time it allowed withdrawal against the deposited check.

> Moreover, a depositary bank may properly charge an account by honoring a check drawn by a depositor even though it creates an overdraft. It would be anomalous for a bank to lose its status as a holder in due course merely because it has notice that the account of its depositor is overdrawn.

The remitter in the *Citizens Bank* case claimed that the depositary bank knew this was the account of a "troubled customer." The depositary bank prevailed because its knowledge that the depositor's account was overdrawn cannot be equated with having knowledge that the checks the customer deposited were procured through fraud.

Likewise, merely requesting verification of a check's validity will not prevent a party from being a holder in due course if the party had no actual knowledge of any bad faith or notice of any claims against the instrument, defenses to enforcement, or other irregularities. In *I&B Check Cashing Corp. v. Jensen*, 927 N.Y.S.2d 816 (City of NY. 2011), the court found that a check cashing company was a holder in due course of two checks, each written for more than $5,000, which were ultimately dishonored and returned. The defendant who presented the checks was a plumber who asked I&B's employee to "check the checks," which he had received in return for plumbing services he provided, because he did not know the person who had given him the checks.

The issue of notice of irregularity introduced in the *New Randolph* case has additional layers of complexity when a fiduciary relationship is involved. In *Smith v. Olympic Bank*, 693 P.2d 92 (Wash. 1985), the court addressed a dispute arising from a guardian's misuse and personal appropriation of funds intended for the support of a minor. The child's father, Charles Alcombrack, had wrongfully deposited in his personal account a check made payable to "Charles Alcombrack, Guardian of the Estate of Chad Stephen Alcombrack, a Minor." The child's representative sued the bank that accepted the deposit. Because the check clearly indicated on its face that it was to be paid in a guardianship capacity and thus should have been deposited in a guardianship account, and because the child's attorney had communicated with the bank regarding the requirements for setting up such an account, the court concluded the bank acted in bad faith by accepting the check.

When an item is facially incomplete, as when it is irregular in some way, a holder has notice of potential enforcement problems that may prevent the holder from being a holder in due course. In *Winter & Hirsch, Inc. v. Passarelli*, 259 N.E.2d 312 (Ill. App. 1970), Mr. and Mrs. Passarelli borrowed money through Equitable Mortgage, a brokerage firm that arranged for them to borrow money from Winter & Hirsch, Inc. at a usurious interest rate. Mr. and Mrs. Passarelli executed a note to Equitable. Equitable sold the note for $11,000 to Winter & Hirsch. The Passarellis defaulted, and Winter & Hirsch sued them to enforce the note. The Passarellis counterclaimed, seeking to recover a penalty under state law based on usury.

The usurious interest rate did not appear on the face of the note, which simply recited a total amount (including interest) of $16,260 as being given for "value received." Because Winter & Hirsch gave Equitable the money before the note was executed, the court found Winter & Hirsch knew or should have known the note's terms. Even if Winter & Hirsch had not paid Equitable until it saw the note, the court found Winter & Hirsch knew a usurious interest rate was being charged, because otherwise it would make no sense that Equitable was willing to sell a note with a face value of $16,260 for only $11,000. Under such facts, the court found Winter & Hirsch had a duty to ask more questions. One lesson of this case is that, even though the Code interposes no general duty to inquire into the transaction underlying the issuance of a note, a holder may not choose to remain ignorant when the item raises suspicions.

4. THE FTC HOLDER IN DUE COURSE RULE

3–106(d) and **3–302(g)** indicate that the UCC's rules on holder-in-due-course status are subject to other law limiting the ability of a party to qualify as a holder in due course. The most important such rule is found in **16 CFR Part 433**, known as the Federal Trade Commission Holder in Due Course Rule. Under this rule, consumers receive special protections when they execute negotiable promissory notes for certain consumer credit sales. In the typical transaction, a consumer executes a promissory note payable to a dealer for goods and gives a security interest in the goods to the dealer. The dealer normally does not finance the transaction itself, but instead negotiates the note to a third-party financing company. The third party would like to enforce the debt free of any personal defenses the consumer could raise against the dealer. To do so, the third party must be a holder in due course.

A policy decision has been made that, in the commercial setting, it is appropriate for a holder in due course to escape the personal defenses of a purchaser or lessee. In the consumer context, however, the decision was that consumers should have an opportunity to assert personal defenses against any holder in an action for payment on a negotiable credit instrument. This result is accomplished by way of a required notice, found in **16 CFR 433.2**, which warns any holder of a promissory note issued as part of a consumer-credit contract that it cannot be a holder in due course, but will instead be subject to any defenses the consumer could have raised against the original payee.

In *Courtesy Financial Services, Inc. v. Hughes*, 424 So. 2d 1172, 1175 (La. App. 1st Cir. 1982), the court addressed what happens when the required FTC legend does not appear on the note:

> An FTC regulation requires that notice be given that the holder of a consumer credit contract is subject to all claims and defenses which the debtor could assert against the seller. However, it is the inclusion of the required language that prevents a subsequent holder from becoming a holder in due course.

If the required language is omitted, a holder can be a holder in due course, but the payee may be subject to a civil penalty of $10,000 as a matter of federal law. States can add additional penalties if they wish. The fine is levied upon the payee, not the holder, since it is normally the payee who drafts (and thus controls) the terms of the note.

5. PAYEES AS HOLDERS IN DUE COURSE

As **3–302** Comment 4 indicates, it is possible, albeit not common, for a payee of a negotiable instrument to be a holder in due course. Examples of this phenomenon typically involve an isolated payee dealing with the maker or drawer through an intermediary. Whatever the specific facts, the payee must lack notice of any irregularity with the transaction or the instrument and otherwise qualify as a holder in due course.

First, consider Comment 4, Case #4, which could be titled, "The Case of the Sneaky Secretary." An employer gave a blank, signed check to the corporate secretary to type in the name of A Corporation, to which the employer owed money. Instead, the secretary typed in the name of B Corporation, to which the secretary owed money personally, and delivered the check to B Corporation. B Corporation, as the payee, could be a holder in due course if it had no reason to know of the secretary's deceit. Note the "information wall" between the drawer and payee in the following graphic. Also note the single-sided arrow between Employer and B Corporation, indicating that Employer received no consideration from B Corporation for the check (although Secretary did, in the form of the reduction or elimination of Secretary's personal debt to B Corporation):

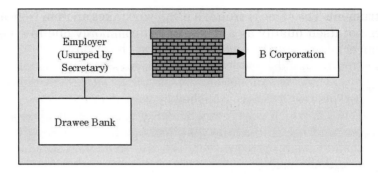

Another example in Comment 4 is Case # 3, which could be called, "The Case of the Sneaky Corporate Officer." The corporation drew a check payable to Bank. A corporate officer was given the check to deliver to Bank in payment of the debt the corporation owed Bank. The corporate officer also had a personal account at Bank. Instead of giving Bank the check to pay the corporate debt, the officer deposited the check in his personal account. If Bank had no reason to know of the fiduciary capacity in which the officer was given the check, Bank could be a holder in due course. Once again, note the "information wall" between Corporation and Payee Bank and the lack of consideration for the check flowing to Corporation from Payee Bank.

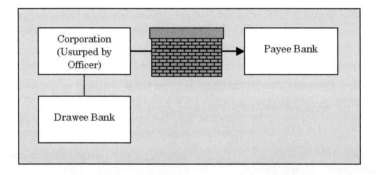

6. THE SHELTER DOCTRINE

Sometimes, a transferee fails to be a holder because an indorsement is missing, or a holder fails to qualify as a holder in due course because it received the instrument as a gift and therefore did not give value for the instrument. In such cases, the "shelter doctrine" can be helpful. Pursuant to **3–203(b)**, a transferee of an instrument will acquire all rights of the transferor unless the transferee engaged in fraud or illegality, or the transferee was a prior holder with knowledge of a defense or claim against the instrument. The shelter doctrine makes it possible for a party who does not qualify as a holder in due course to assert the rights of a holder in due course if it took the instrument from a party who was a holder in due course, so long as it was not personally involved in wrongdoing affecting the instrument. The same is true of a party who takes an item from a holder but does not itself qualify as a holder (most commonly due to a failure of indorsement).

Note the specific language used here: **3–203(b)** does not state that the transferee of a holder in due course will be a holder in due course, but that the transferee will have the rights of a holder in due course. The important distinction is found in Comment 2 to **3–203**: "Because the transferee's rights are derivative of the transferor's rights, those rights must be proved." This is a burden that would not be required of the transferee if it actually qualified as a holder or holder in due course. The doctrine makes it possible for a party who does not qualify as a holder to prove its entitlement to payment, a status that cannot be presumed since the transferee is not a holder.

Chapter Conclusion: After this chapter, you should be familiar with the differences between negotiation and assignment, real and personal defenses, and between holders in due course and other holders and assignees. You should be able to recognize the various forms of indorsement and the issues involved when instruments are signed by agents. You should know how to prove each element of holder-in-due-course status and should be able to recognize payees as holders in due course, consumer credit contracts, and transferees claiming rights through their transferors.

PROBLEMS

1.   Victor Ukpe obtained a $224,000 mortgage loan from Countrywide Home Loans (CHL) in July 2005 to buy a house. During this time, Ukpe was employed as a taxi driver. He informed the mortgage broker, who worked for Morgan Funding Corporation, that he could not afford to make a mortgage payment exceeding $1,000 per month, and the broker assured him that his payment would not exceed this amount. During the closing, Ukpe learned for the first time that his monthly payment would be $1,488.67. When he raised this as a concern, the broker assured him that he could refinance in "a few months" and decrease the payment to $1,000. Ukpe proceeded with the closing, signing a note "payable to the order of the lender." Mortgage Electric Recording System (MERS) initially held the note as a nominee for CHL. A few months later, the mortgage was securitized, such that Ukpe's mortgage was pooled and transferred to Bank of New York (BNY) as a trustee, which held the mortgages for the benefit of investors. The note was indorsed in blank and transferred to BNY as part of this transaction. CHL continued to service the loans and would, from time to time, remit to BNY all sums paid on the mortgages, minus a service fee. Ukpe tried, without success, to refinance on several occasions. In August 2007, he stopped making payments and defaulted on the note; in March of 2008, BNY filed a foreclosure complaint.

    a.   Is BNY a holder of the note within the meaning of 3–201? Is it a holder in due course within the meaning of 3–302?

b.   Review 3–305. What defense, if any, could Mr. Ukpe raise against the mortgage broker? CHL? BNY?

c.   Does the FTC Holder-in-Due-Course rule apply? Why or why not?

2.   Mark Peoples was the sole member of a company called Pyramid Title, LLC. He signed a check drawn on an account identified in the upper-left corner of the check as follows:

Pyramid Title LLC
Escrow Account
PH 504-484-0900
4332 Canal Street
New Orleans, LA 70119

Immediately above his signature in the bottom right corner of the check appeared the words "authorized signature." Mr. Peoples signed his name, with no additional identifying information. Read 3–402 and consider the following questions:

a.   Is Pyramid Title LLC liable for the amount of the check?

b.   Is Mark Peoples personally liable for the amount of the check?

c.   To what extent should parol evidence be admitted to demonstrate that the payee knew Mr. Peoples did not intend to have personal liability for the check?

d.   How, if at all, would your answer to the prior question change if the instrument in question were a note instead of a check?

3.   Several partners in a law firm executed a note to a bank in return for the bank's loan to the firm. Later, the law firm declared bankruptcy, the partners defaulted on the note, and the FDIC sought to collect from the partners as successor in interest to the bank, which had become insolvent. The partners responded by claiming they signed the note only because they were told that their wages and standing in the firm would suffer if they refused.

a.   Read 3–305. If the partners proved their claim, could the FDIC, a holder in due course, enforce the note anyway? Why or why not?

4.   Jim and Marie Estepp consolidated their debt via a loan from United Bank and Trust Company. United Bank was unwilling to loan money to them unless they obtained the signature of a third party who owned property locally. Mr. Estepp approached Marvin O. Schaeffer, who worked under Estepp as a groundskeeper at the Tantallon Country Club and owned real estate in the area. Schaeffer had known Estepp for eight years at the time and later testified, "I thought he was a wonderful guy," adding that Estepp had assisted him in making funeral arrangements when his wife died. Upon Estepp's request, Schaeffer signed the Estepps' note to United Bank as a surety.

Consider the following exchange between Schaeffer, who completed third grade, had a limited ability to read, and suffered loss of vision earlier in his life due to a bottle explosion, and the attorney for United Bank, which sought to recover from Schaeffer after the Estepps defaulted.

Q: Well, Mr. Schaeffer, will you please tell us why you do not feel apparently that you should pay this debt?

A: Because Jim Estepp, when he told me to sign that paper it wasn't for paying a debt.

Q: Well now, you are saying Jim Estepp. You are not saying United Bank and Trust Company; is that correct?

A: No. Jim told me that when I filled the application out to sign and I signed it. He said it was a character witness.

Q: Are you stating nobody explained to you that this was a note?

A: No, sir.

a.   Based on 3–305, who should prevail? (United Bank is a holder in due course).

b.   What facts are most important in your analysis?

5.   Weston Wade Sleater was the sole member and manager of Atlas Capital, LLC. Enlightened Management, LLC loaned a total of $4,000,000 to Atlas. In return for the loans, two notes were executed for a total amount of about $4.5 million. The body of each note identifies Mr. Sleater numerous times as the note's maker. The signature block of each note contains only Sleater's signature, although the caption below each signature reads, "Weston Wade Sleater & Atlas Marketing Group, LLC." Each note also includes a personal guarantee clause, which Sleater signed in his individual capacity. Other than the caption below each signature, neither note mentions Atlas.

a.   Is Atlas Capital liable for the notes?

b.   Is Sleater personally liable for the notes?

c.   What effect, if any, should the personal guarantees have on Sleater's personal liability for the notes?

d.   Should parol evidence be admissible for the purpose of showing that the parties' intent was that Sleater not be personally liable for the notes?

6.   Consider these statements, each taken from a court's holding:

Check cashing businesses are a major source of traditional banking services for low-income and working poor consumers.

The concept of "fair dealing" includes not being an easy, safe harbor for the dishonest.

Check cashing companies are the pariahs of holder-in-due-course law.

The need for speed in a business transaction is usually less acute than for someone cashing a paycheck or welfare check to pay for life's necessities.

a.   Would you support a law that check cashing companies are presumptively not holders in due course? Why or why not? What are the counter-arguments?

b.   Would your opinion change based on the fee that a check cashing company earns by cashing a check? For example, some check cashing companies charge a fee of between 3% and 5% for cashing a check, such that cashing a check for $18,000 would generate a fee of as much as $900. Is this too much?

c.   What steps should a check cashing company take before cashing a check, to preserve its holder-in-due-course status? For example, should a check cashing company obtain a fingerprint from any customer who is not a prior customer, or establish a "membership" requirement to encourage repeat business?

7.   Liccardi Ford, Inc. issued a post-dated check to one of its employees, Charles Stallone, Jr. JCNB Check Cashing, Inc., a New Jersey check cashing company, cashed the check for Stallone before its issue date and deposited the check into its own bank account. The drawee refused to pay the check because it was postdated.

a.   Does the fact that JCNB cashed the check prior to its issue date prevent it from being a holder in due course? Why or why not? Consult 3–302, 3–113 and 4–401 as needed in preparing your answer.

b.   If JCNB sold the Liccardi check, along with seven others, to attorney Robert J. Triffin for the purpose of collection after the checks were dishonored, could Triffin be a holder in due course? Based on 3–304 and 3–302, why or why not?

c.   The New Jersey Legislature, as part of the Check Cashers Regulatory Act of 1993, prohibited check cashing companies from cashing postdated checks. Would this affect JCNB's ability to be a holder in due course?

8.   Mr. Wajahat Malick worked as the comptroller for Prestige Imports, Inc., which had a banking relationship with South Shore Bank. Malick fraudulently drew on Prestige's funds and had South Shore issue cashier's checks made payable to South Weymouth Savings Bank, where Malick banked. South Weymouth had no relationship with Prestige. Prestige owner Helmut Schmidt cosigned each check, as company policy required. The remitter line on each cashier's check indicated that the check had been "purchased by Prestige." South Weymouth permitted Malick to deposit the checks into his personal account, and then to transfer funds to pay his personal debts with South Weymouth.

a.   Which entity was in the best position to discover Malick's fraud?

b.   Was South Weymouth a holder in due course of the checks? Why or why not?

c.   Did the presence of the Prestige name on the remitter line compel South Weymouth to contact Prestige before accepting the checks for deposit?

d.   What would be the benefits and risks of a rule requiring a depositary bank to look into any situation in which a cashier's check was presented to be deposited or cashed in a way that does not appear to be in the remitter's interest?

9.   Is the following a correct and complete statement of the shelter doctrine found in 3–203(b)? If not, why not?

> [A] note that is un[i]ndorsed can still be transferred to a third party. Although that third party technically is not a holder of the note, the third party nevertheless acquires the right to enforce the note so long as that was the intent of the transferor.

10.   Sonic Engineering, Inc. obtained a judgment for about $218,000 against Konover Construction Company South. Having no success in collecting the judgment, Sonic requested state marshal Timothy Poeti to serve a writ of execution on the office of People's Bank where Konover had funds. He requested that the bank issue a bank check representing the amount of the judgment plus interest and other costs. Norma Junnack, the People's Bank employee with whom the marshal spoke, told him she would not know until the next day whether she could comply with his request. After he told her he could not return the next day due to other commitments, she agreed to go ahead and issue the check "on the condition that he hold on to the check until she could confirm if there were any difficulty with the bank's complying with the execution." This was at 1:30 p.m. Assume that the check was issued with a blank payee line. Two and a half hours later, at about 4 pm, Junnack phoned Poeti to inform him that he must return the check. He returned the call the following morning, and Junnack informed him that a stop payment order had been placed on the check. Even so, Poeti attempted to deposit the check into his personal account, but it was returned unpaid.

a.   Was Poeti a holder of the check? Was Sonic?

b.   Was Poeti a holder in due course of the check? Was Sonic?

11.   American International Group issued a check payable to Jermielem Merriwether in connection with a personal injury matter. Merriwether took the check to A-1 Check Cashing Emporium, which cashed the check for him but failed to obtain his signature. John Carter, the A-1 employee who cashed the check, simply wrote Merriwether's name on the back of the check about half an hour after he left the store, and A-1 deposited the check. Carter called Merriwether and left a message asking him to return to the store to indorse the check, but received no response. Before the drawee paid the check, Merriwether signed an affidavit falsely attesting that the check had been stolen, and the check was returned to A-1 unpaid.

Consider 1–201(b)(21), 3–203(c), and 4–205 in preparing the answers to these questions:

a.   Was Merriwether a holder of the check when he presented it to A-1?

b.   Is A-1 a holder of the check? Is it a holder in due course?

c. Would your answer change if A-1 were a bank?

12. Patricia Ann Woodberry executed a note in the amount of about $68,000 to South Star Financing. Although there was room on the note for an indorsement, South Star indorsed the note on an allonge stapled to the note. The allonge included, in addition to the indorsement, Woodberry's name, her address, the original loan amount and date, the original lender's name, the interest rate, and the loan number.

Consider 3–204(a) and 3–205 in answering the following questions:

a. Is the indorsement on the allonge effective?

b. Would your answer change if the allonge were paper-clipped to the note?

c. Now assume that the allonge read, "Pay to the order of without recourse." Is this an effective indorsement? If so, what kind of indorsement is it, and to whom is the instrument now payable?

13. Jack Wilkins purchased a trunk at an estate sale in 1974 as part of a bulk purchase of goods for $250 total. Inside the trunk, which he opened immediately, were 390 bearer bonds with the denomination of $1,000 each. Fort Smith, Subiaco and Rock Island Railroad had issued the bonds in 1919 as thirty-year bonds expiring in August 1949. They were then renewed and extended in July 1954 with a new due date of 1984. Mercantile Trust Company bank was the original trustee of the bonds. Due to time constraints, Wilkins did not research the notes or seek to enforce them until 2004. When he sought to enforce the bonds, the successor in interest to Mercantile Trust Company informed him that, because the trust money securing the bonds had been embezzled, the bonds would not be honored. He was further advised that he should consider the bonds only collector's items due to the bankruptcy of the railroad that had issued the bonds.

a. Is Wilkins a holder of the bonds? Is he a holder in due course? Think of two reasons to substantiate your answer.

b. Can any defense can be raised against enforcement of the bonds? Is this a real or personal defense?

14. Freestyle Sports Marketing, Inc. employed Cassandra Demery as a bookkeeper for several years before she was terminated for embezzling over $200,000 in company funds and other misbehavior. Demery agreed to repay Freestyle and, in return, Freestyle agreed not to notify the authorities so long as she made repayment. Demery then went to work for Metro Fixtures Contractors, Inc., which her parents owned, also as a bookkeeper. After lying to Freestyle's president, Clinton Georg, telling him that her parents had loaned her the money to repay Freestyle, Demery wrote a check payable to Freestyle, drawn on Metro's account, in the amount of $189,000. Assume that Demery, who issued the check without her parents' permission and knowledge, delivered the check to Georg on behalf of Freestyle.

a. Is Georg a holder of the check? Is Freestyle?

b.   Is Georg a holder in due course? Is Freestyle?

c.   Is Metro liable for the amount of the check?

d.   Is Demery personally liable for the amount of the check?

e.   Would your answer to the two prior questions change if writing checks were not part of Demery's job description—and not part of a typical bookkeeper's job?

CHAPTER 8

THE COLLECTION PROCESS

■ ■ ■

A. INTRODUCING THE COLLECTION PROCESS

Articles 3 and 4 are closely related, but serve distinct purposes. Whereas Article 3 provides the general rules for all negotiable instruments, including notes as well as drafts, Article 4 deals with those items (mostly checks) that are collected through the banking system. As one would expect, since the UCC is domestic, state law, Article 4 deals only with checks collected through United States banks. Although checks are the primary focus of this chapter, 4–102 Comment 1 explains that banks may also collect bonds and certain investment securities.

The word "item," defined in 4–104(a)(9), is a catch-all term for instruments paid or collected through one or more banks. Article 4 provides the rules for how banks handle items for the purpose of collection and payment. As 4–103(a) and Comment 2 indicate, parties can contract around the provisions of Article 4, subject to the "good faith and ordinary care" limitations found in 4–103(a).

Article 4 also introduces some new vocabulary. The *depositary bank* is the first bank to take the item for collection. The *payor bank* (also called the drawee) is the bank on which the item was drawn; in the case of an ordinary personal or business check, the payor bank is the bank where the drawer maintains an account. *Intermediary banks* participate in the collection process, but are neither drawee/payor nor depositary banks. Instead, as the name would suggest, they serve as intermediaries between depositary banks and drawee/payor banks. Federal Reserve Banks are a common example. *Collecting banks* are all banks that participate in the collection process other than the drawee/payor bank. Thus, the depositary bank and any intermediary bank are collecting banks. The *presenting bank* is the bank that presents an item to the drawee/payor bank for payment. This can be either the depositary bank or an intermediary bank. Thus, a bank can have more than one label. These labels are all found in 4–105.

When a depositary bank receives a check drawn on another bank, it may (1) present that check to the other bank directly, (2) deliver the check to the other bank via a local clearinghouse exchange or correspondent bank, or (3) utilize the check-collection services of the Federal Reserve. The illustration below shows a collection through the Federal Reserve System. In this illustration, the Federal Reserve Bank is a collecting, intermediary, and presenting bank. It serves as an intermediary between the payee's bank in New York and the drawer's bank in Florida. As in the prior chapter, note the double arrows showing that each transaction is supported by consideration, as well as the line between the drawer and drawee representing the parties' contractual relationship. You will learn more about each of these concepts in this chapter.

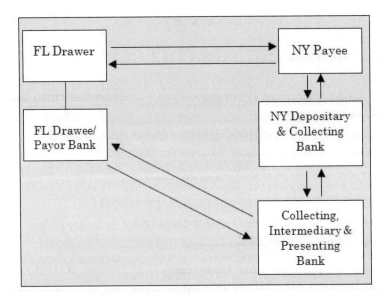

The Florida drawer issued this check to the New York payee in return for goods or services. It was deposited at a New York depositary bank in return for provisional credit. The New York bank transferred the check to an intermediary bank (the Federal Reserve) in return for provisional credit once again. Finally, the check was presented to the Florida bank on which it was drawn, in return for provisional credit. Assuming everything went well and the check was honored, the Florida bank would make final payment on the check and all provisional credits would become final.

The collecting banks' task is to get the item processed in a timely manner, in accordance with Article 4's deadlines, so that the drawee/payor bank can determine whether the item will be paid. As part of this process, the accounts of all parties in the collection process are credited and debited along the way.

Sometimes an item is dishonored due to insufficient funds, a stop payment order, or some other reason. In addition, sometimes an item is altered or forged. The rules presented in Article 4, coupled with certain rules in Article 3 that we will explore in this chapter and the next one, establish who bears the loss in each situation.

Article 4 does not, however, address every dispute that can arise in the collection of an item. For example, as **4–101** Comment 3 states, Article 4 "does not regulate the terms of the bank-customer agreement." Instead, the contract of deposit between the bank and its customer provides the primary rules for their relationship. Another body of authority, as indicated in **4–103(b)** and Comment 3, consists of Federal Reserve regulations, operating circulars, and clearing-house rules. These rules, which address many of the logistics of check collection, are capable of preempting Article 4.

1. ELECTRONIC PRESENTMENT

4–101, Comment 2 refers to some ways in which the technology of check processing has changed since Article 4 was drafted in 1950. Most checks are now processed as electronic images, even if they were originally issued in paper form. The Federal Reserve Bank has described the process as follows:

> The process of converting a paper check to an electronic item creates a collection of data records for each item that includes:
>
> - The MICR line data of the check;
> - Front image;
> - Rear image; and
> - Electronic Indorsements

MICR is Magnetic Ink Character Recognition, a technology the American Bankers Association developed in the late 1950s and early 1960s. In *First National Bank of Boston v. Fidelity Bank, National Association*, 724 F.Supp. 1168, 1168–69 (E.D. Pa. 1989), the court described the MICR line data and its use, as follows:

> The form of each bank check is preprinted with magnetic characters, along the bottom of the check, toward the left-hand side. These characters [include the "routing and transit" numbers that] designate the bank upon which the check is drawn, and the account number of the [drawer]. When a check is presented to another bank (the "depositary bank"), that bank adds additional magnetic encoding, at the lower right-hand side of the check, specifying the amount of the check. From that point on, the check works its way through the bank-clearing system to the bank on which the check is drawn and is charged against the [drawer's] account—all without further human intervention. Thus, the role of the encoder at the depositary bank is crucial, since all subsequent steps in the processing of the check for payment depend upon the accuracy of the encoded information; ordinarily, no other human being actually examines the check from that point on. The development of this method of processing checks, it is generally agreed, has enabled the banking system to meet the needs of our ever-expanding economy.

In the image above, the number between the two colons is the routing and transit number designating the bank on which the check is drawn. The longer number beginning with the four zeroes is the drawer's bank account number. The shortest number, which corresponds with the number in the upper right corner of the check, is the check number. All of these numbers are pre-printed in magnetic characters on the blank checks when the drawer first receives them. Note that, when the check is first issued to Paula Payee, there is a blank area at the lower right corner of the check. This is the area where the depositary bank will encode the check amount.

The following image shows the check as encoded with the correct amount, $100.00.

Sometimes, the amount of an item is encoded incorrectly. As 4-209 Comment 2 indicates, either an over-encoding or an under-encoding can cause the drawee/payor bank to suffer a loss, either by paying out more than the face value of the item, as in the case of an over-encoded amount, or honoring an item that would have been dishonored if correctly encoded, as in the case of an under-encoded amount.

The following image shows the check under-encoded as if it were drawn for $10.00:

If the drawer's account has $90 on deposit when the under-encoded check is presented for payment, the check will clear due to the under-encoding, even if it would have been dishonored due to insufficient funds if correctly encoded. Because the drawee/payor bank, having accepted the under-encoded check, is now liable for the full $100 face amount of the check, this could result in a loss for the drawee/payor bank if it cannot recover the additional $10 from the drawer. 4–209 allows the drawee/payor bank to shift the loss to the depositary bank, which made the error.

The following image shows the check over-encoded as if it were drawn for $1,000.00:

If the drawer's account has $1,500 on deposit when the check is presented for payment, the check will clear, but the drawee/payor bank will be required to refund $900 to the drawer since the check was written for $100. Again, 4–209 allows the drawee/payor bank to shift the loss to the bank that made the error. The mechanics of this loss-shifting provision are discussed in the next chapter.

Sometimes, drawers try to take advantage of under-encoding. In *Georgia Railroad Bank & Trust Co. v. First National Bank & Trust Co of Augusta*, 229 S.E.2d 482 (Ga. 1976), the court considered the under-encoding and processing of a $25,000 check for $2,500. When the depositor discovered the error, his bank credited his account for the additional $22,500, then sought to recover from the drawee/payor bank. When the drawee/payor bank contacted the drawer, he "told the [bank] not to 'bother' his account," refusing to pay the additional sum although his account contained sufficient funds and even though he had written the check. The court found the drawer liable for the full sum of the check as drawn, notwithstanding the error in encoding.

Encoding technology has created opportunities for new kinds of fraud. In *United States Fidelity and Guaranty Co. v. Federal Reserve Bank*, 620 F. Supp. 361 (S.D.N.Y. 1985), the court considered the proper allocation of loss among banks who were victims of a check-fraud scheme that utilized MICR technology. Readers who have seen the movie "Catch Me If You Can" will recognize the scheme. The fraudfeasor had created and deposited a series of worthless checks drawn on a non-existent account. By manipulating the routing and transit numbers to be read by a MICR-processing machine, the wrongdoer ensured that the check would be routed to several different banks before the fraud was discovered. In the meantime, the fraudfeasor withdrew the funds and disappeared. *Northpark National Bank v. Bankers Trust Co.*, 572 F. Supp. 524, 526 (S.D.N.Y. 1983), provides insight into how such a scheme might operate. The "hold" referenced in the excerpt below is discussed in Section 3 of this chapter.

> [I]t is clear how a fraud of this type is accomplished. Its object is to cause a worthless check deposited for collection to take a sufficiently long detour in its progress to the drawee bank, to insure that the notice of non-payment will not arrive at the depositary bank until after the expiration of the hold which it placed on the availability of the proceeds from transit items. Having received no such notice before the expiration of the hold, the depositary bank supposes the items to have been paid and allows its proceeds to be withdrawn. By the time notice arrives the malefactor has, of course, absconded with the spoils. The crucial detour is caused by imprinting the fraudulent check with the wrong MICR routing number—i.e., one that does not correspond to the bank designated on the face of the check as the drawee bank, but to a different bank, preferably one that is distant from the institution designated as the drawee bank on the face of the check. The fraudulent check in our case bore the MICR routing

number of Bankers Trust Co. in New York and identified the "Bank of Detroit"—a fictitious institution—as the drawee bank.

As the *United States Fidelity and Guaranty Co.* court held, "because only the depositary bank possesses [the] ability to examine both the depositor and the check, it is appropriate to place upon it the initial burden of care." Thus, the depositary bank is "the first line of defense against MICR fraud, and the most efficient point at which to take precautions against it." Therefore, in a case involving MICR fraud, the depositary bank, rather than a later collecting bank, most commonly bears the loss.

2. THE FEDERAL RESERVE SYSTEM

The Federal Reserve is the central bank for the United States. President Woodrow Wilson established the Federal Reserve in 1913, and it has primary responsibility for the country's monetary policy. There are twelve regional Federal Reserve Banks in major cities around the country. The following information from the Federal Reserve Bank of New York website describes the role of the Federal Reserve in check processing:

> Regardless of whether checks are processed as paper or electronic items, financial institutions have several alternative ways to receive payment for, or clear, checks deposited with them.
>
> . . . [I]nterbank checks . . . are checks that are deposited at and drawn on different depository institutions. . . . "[O]n-us" checks . . . are deposited at and drawn on the same depository institution.
>
> To clear on-us checks, the institution makes the appropriate entries on its books, by debiting the payor's account and crediting the depositor's account. To collect the remaining interbank checks, a financial institution may:
>
> - present the paper checks or transmit images of the checks directly to the paying bank,
>
> - forward the paper checks or images of the checks to a correspondent for collection,
>
> - exchange checks, in paper or electronic form, with a group of banks participating in a clearinghouse arrangement, or
>
> - forward the paper checks or images of the checks to a Federal Reserve Bank for collection.

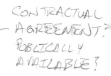

Generally, smaller deposit-taking financial institutions either deposit checks for clearing with a Federal Reserve Bank or with a correspondent. A correspondent may be a larger commercial bank, . . . or a corporate credit union. Larger institutions may deposit exclusively with a Federal Reserve Bank or use a combination of methods to clear checks. All depository institutions, either directly or in conjunction with a correspondent, may deposit checks with a Federal Reserve Bank. Check deposits are received as either bundles of paper checks called "cash letters" or, more commonly, computer files of imaged checks called "image cash letters." The Federal Reserve Banks charge depositors a fee for check-clearing services.

When cash letters or image cash letters are deposited with Federal Reserve Banks, they credit the Federal Reserve account of the depositing institution or its correspondent. The Reserve Banks debit the Federal Reserve account of the paying institution or its correspondent when the checks drawn on the paying institution are presented to that institution for payment. . . . The paying institution then charges the accounts of the customers who wrote the checks in accordance with its account agreement.

Thus, the Federal Reserve functions as the bankers' bank, facilitating forward collection and charge-backs in a way that allows items to be processed very quickly.

3. REGULATION CC AND DEPOSIT HOLDS

While an item is being collected, a depositary bank may wish to hold the funds, to guard against the possibility of losing money if the check representing the funds is ultimately dishonored by the drawee/payor bank. The Expedited Funds Availability Act (EFAA), which is federal law, governs how long a bank may hold funds before making them available for withdrawal. **12 U.S.C. §§ 4002, 4003, and 4004** include pertinent provisions of the EFAA, which was implemented by Regulation CC, including **12 CFR 229.10, 229.12, and 229.13.** The EFAA provides a schedule with which depository banks are required to comply in making funds available to depositors. The schedule differentiates among different kinds of items based on the expected risk involved in collecting the funds in question. When funds are held, the EFAA also requires that a certain amount of money be made available the next banking day for immediate needs.

These rules often require depositary banks to release uncollected funds to their customers. The following information, presented on-line by the Federal Reserve Board, summarizes the relevant deadlines:

_____

Disclosing Your Availability Policy

Regulation CC requires that financial institutions provide customers who have a transaction account with disclosures stating when their funds will be available for withdrawal. . . .

* * *

Posting Your Policy Where Employees Accept Deposits

Your institution must post, in each location where employees accept consumer deposits, a notice of your availability policy pertaining to consumer accounts. The notice must specifically state the availability periods for the various types of deposits that may be made to consumer accounts. The notice need not be posted at each teller window, but it must be posted in a place where consumers seeking to make deposits are likely to see it before making their deposits. For example, the notice might be posted at the point where the line forms for teller service in the lobby. The notice is not required at drive-through teller windows or at night depository locations, but it is required at all automated teller machines.

Printing Your Availability Notice on Deposit Slips

Regulation CC requires that financial institutions include a notice of funds availability on the front of all preprinted deposit slips. The notice need state only that deposits may not be available for immediate withdrawal. The notice is required only on deposit slips that are preprinted with the customer's name and account number and furnished by your institution in response to a customer's order. It need not appear on deposit slips that are not preprinted—such as counter deposit slips—or on special deposit slips used to secure next-day availability for state and local government, cashier's, certified, or teller's checks. In addition, your institution is not responsible for ensuring that the notice appears on deposit slips that the customer does not obtain from or through [your institution].

Determining Funds Availability

Regulation CC states when deposits of various types must be made available to your customers, measured in business days following the banking day on which the deposit is made. Business days are defined as Mondays through Fridays except federal holidays. A banking day is any business day (up to the bank's cut-off hour) when your institution is open for substantially all of its banking activities. All references to the number of days to funds availability in this guide indicate maximum time limits for making funds available; your institution may provide earlier availability of funds if it chooses and may extend the time when funds are available up to periods set by Regulation CC on a case-by-case basis.

The following types of deposits must be made available on the first business day following the banking day of deposit ("next-day availability"):

1. **Cash** deposited in person to one of your employees.

2. **Electronic payments** received by your institution for deposit in an account. An electronic payment (a wire transfer or an ACH credit) is considered received (deposited) when your institution has received both payment in collected funds

and information on the account and the amount to be credited. (Under other rules, funds for most electronic deposits are made available on the day of deposit.)

3. **U.S. Treasury checks** deposited in person to one of your employees or at an ATM owned by your institution (a "proprietary" ATM) and into an account held by a payee of the check.

4. **U.S. Postal Service money orders** deposited in person to one of your employees and into an account held by a payee of the check.

5. **Federal Reserve Bank and Federal Home Loan Bank checks** deposited in person to one of your employees and into an account held by a payee of the check.

6. **State or local government checks** deposited in person to one of your employees and into an account held by a payee of the check, if your institution is in the same state as the payor of the check. . . .

7. **Cashier's, certified, or teller's checks** deposited in person to one of your employees and into an account held by a payee of the check. . . .

8. **Checks drawn on an account held by your institution** ("on-us checks") deposited in person to one of your employees or at on-premises ATMs or night depositories.

9. **The Expedited Funds Availability Act** requires up to the first $200 of a non-"next-day" check(s) to be made available the next day. [handwritten: $225]

[handwritten margin note: AMOUNT UPDATE SCHEDULE?]

Exceptions: When deposits of types 1, 4, 5, 6, and 7 are not made in person (for example, when they are made at one of your ATMs), the funds must be made available by the second business day. Deposits, cash or check, made at an ATM that you do not own (a "nonproprietary" ATM) must be made available by the fifth business day.

For checks of types not discussed above, funds generally must be made available in accordance with a schedule specified in Regulation CC. That schedule differentiates between "local" or "nonlocal" checks. Since there is now only one Reserve Bank check-processing region, however, there are no longer any "nonlocal" checks for purposes of Regulation CC.

Funds from local checks must be made available by the second business day following the day of deposit.

There are minor exceptions involving, for example, certain checks deposited outside the continental United States and cash withdrawals of the proceeds of certain checks.

* * *

This does not apply to deposits at nonproprietary ATMs or to deposits subject to certain exception holds. . . .

Delaying Funds Availability

For certain types of deposits, Regulation CC permits financial institutions to delay, for a "reasonable period of time," the availability of funds. A "reasonable" time period is generally defined as one additional business day (making a total of two business days) for on-us checks, and five additional business days (total of seven) for local checks; your institution may impose longer exception holds, but you may have the burden of proving that they are "reasonable."

If you decide to hold funds beyond the period specified in your institution's general availability policy, you must give the customer a notice at the time of the deposit explaining why the funds are being held and when they will be available. If the deposit is not made in person to an employee of your institution or if you decide to extend the time when deposited funds will be made available after the deposit has been made, you must mail or deliver the notice to the customer not later than the first business day after the banking day on which the deposit is made.

Deposits of cash and electronic payments are not eligible for exception holds. The six types of deposits that are eligible are

- **Large deposits** (greater than $5,000)—Any amount exceeding $5,000 may be held. Your institution must make the first $5,000 of the deposit available for withdrawal according to your availability policy and the remainder within the "reasonable" time frames discussed above.

- **Redeposited checks**—May be held unless the check was returned because an endorsement was missing or because the check was postdated. In such a case, if the deficiency has been corrected, the check may not be held as a redeposited check.

- Deposits to accounts that are **repeatedly overdrawn**—An account may be considered repeatedly overdrawn and items may be held if

  1. On six or more banking days during the previous six months the account had a negative balance, or would have had a negative balance had checks and charges been paid, or

  2. On two or more banking days during the previous six months the account balance was negative in the amount of $5,000 or more, or would have been had checks and charges been paid.

- **Reasonable cause to doubt the collectibility** of a check—Doubtful collectibility may exist for postdated checks, checks dated more than six months earlier, and checks that the paying institution has said it will not honor. The general criterion for doubting collectibility is "the existence of facts that would cause a well-grounded belief in the mind of a reasonable person" that the check is uncollectible. The reason for your belief that the check is uncollectible must be included in your notice to the customer.

- Checks deposited during **emergency conditions** that are beyond the control of your institution—Such checks may be held until conditions permit you to provide availability of the funds. Examples of emergency conditions are natural disasters, communications malfunctions, and other situations that prevent your institution from processing checks as it normally does.

- Deposits into accounts of **new customers** (open for less than 30 days)—Next-day availability applies only to cash, electronic payments, and the first $5,000 of any other next-day items; the remaining amount from next-day items must be available by the ninth business day. You may choose any availability schedule for deposits of other checks into the accounts of these new customers.

Building on this information, ordinary, uncertified business and personal checks are often subject to standard two-day Regulation CC holds. A bank may also place an "exception" hold of up to five additional banking days on items it believes present a higher level of risk. By contrast, the "next day" items described in the first section are unlikely to be dishonored in most cases. Notably, EFAA never requires a bank to hold funds, and banks routinely release funds for immediate use even though they could have been held, for customers who have a well-established banking history and sufficient funds on deposit to cover the check in question if it is dishonored.

4. THE MIDNIGHT RULE AND MIDNIGHT DEADLINE

Each bank in the collection process, from the depositary bank to the drawee/payor bank, must adhere to a strict schedule in moving the check forward. Once the check reaches the drawee/payor bank, that bank decides whether to honor the check by making final payment, or dishonor the check, returning it unpaid.

Just as, by the end of 2013, the Federal Reserve was receiving more than 99.9% of checks presented for forward collection as electronic images, almost the same percentage of checks are returned in electronic form in the event of dishonor.

You have previously learned how holders indorse paper checks before transferring them to another party. The following information from Federal Reserve Bank Services, a service of the Federal Reserve Bank, explains how banks indorse checks for forward collection once they have been converted to electronic images:

> When processed as paper, [a] financial institution's indorsements appear as printed ink characters on the back of a check. In an electronic check processing environment, the paper is converted to an image and processed electronically. Indorsements are represented electronically in Addenda records as opposed to being physically printed on the back of the check.
>
> * * *
>
> Each subsequent financial institution that processes an electronic item adds its indorsement electronically to the data records for that item.

The deadlines for timely processing items are captured in two main rules—the midnight rule and the midnight deadline. As similar as the two names sound, these are actually separate and independent Article 4 requirements.

4–104(a)(10) defines the "midnight deadline" with which every bank in the Article 4 collection process must comply in moving an item forward or returning it unpaid. This deadline requires that a bank act upon the item no later than midnight on the next banking day following the banking day of receipt. Assume that a bank provides notice pursuant to 4–108 that its banking day ends at 2 p.m., as many banks do. If the bank receives a check at 3 p.m. on a Monday, its midnight deadline will expire on Wednesday at midnight, since the banking day of receipt will be Tuesday, not Monday.

The policy behind the midnight deadline has been explained as follows:

> The midnight deadline was designed to contribute to the goal of having checks act, as closely as feasible, like cash. It deters banks from simply holding a check and using a drawer's money as long as possible, . . . by imposing liability for a delay in processing regardless of whether the check was "properly payable or not[.]". . . . *Triffin v. Mellon PSFS*, 855 A.2d 2, 6 (N.J. Super. A.D. 2004).

4–302 provides that, in addition to the "midnight deadline" each bank must meet, the drawee/payor bank is required to meet a separate deadline commonly called the "midnight rule." The "midnight rule" requires drawee/payor banks to make provisional settlement by midnight on the banking day of receipt. The bank then has until the midnight deadline to dishonor the item by revoking the provisional settlement. This process is described in **4–301** and Comments 1 and 3 as "deferred posting." Failure to meet either deadline will cause the drawee/payor bank to become accountable for the item.

Although the UCC imposes liability on a drawee/payor bank that meets the midnight deadline after missing the midnight rule, one court has challenged this approach:

> The importance of the midnight deadline in promoting certainty in banking relationships is obvious. . . . The importance of the midnight rule, however, is less obvious. If that time limit is not met but the item is settled for by the midnight deadline, the damages would be [only] one day's interest.
>
> * * *
>
> "Where a timely return has been made, there is a serious question whether the accountability proposed by the first midnight rule should be imposed at all."

Hanna v. First National Bank of Rochester, 207 A.D.2d 181 (N.Y. App. Div. 1994) (quoting the Hawkland, Leary & Alderman treatise). This court would favor liability only when the midnight deadline is violated.

The clock begins to run for purposes of the midnight rule and midnight deadline when the bank receives the checks. In *Heartland State Bank v. American Bank & Trust*, 791 N.W.2d 638 (S.D. 2010), the depositary bank unsuccessfully argued that the drawee/payor bank received the checks in question when they were delivered to the postal service, rather than when the bank received them, in an effort to argue that the midnight deadline expired earlier than if it began to run at actual delivery.

5. ACCEPTANCE AND FINAL PAYMENT

The midnight rule and midnight deadline also control when acceptance and final payment occur. These terms are defined in **3–409(a)** and **4–215(a)** respectively, and are two closely related processes that take place at the drawee/payor bank. Acceptance is the drawee/payor bank's agreement to pay an item, and final payment is the point at which the amount provisionally credited during the collection process becomes final. As **4–215(a)(3)** indicates, a drawee/payor bank may revoke a provisional settlement made in compliance with the midnight rule, so long as it does so before the midnight deadline expires. If it takes no action, its provisional settlement becomes final. Final payment also occurs when a bank pays an item in cash. Once a drawee/payor bank has accepted an item, it is obligated to make final payment on that item.

In considering the process by which checks are presented for final payment, take a look at the following image from *J. Walter Thompson USA, Inc. v. First BankAmericano*, 518 F.3d 128 (2d Cir. 2008), which shows how the check-collection process works:

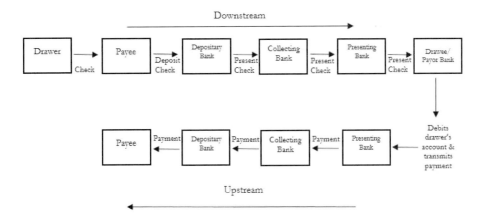

Making final payment is the unique role of the drawee/payor bank, which is why the drawee/payor bank appears as the midpoint in the chart above. There are several cases involving e-mail scams and counterfeit cashier's checks in which a depositor has sued a depositary bank, alleging that the depositor relied to its detriment on statements of tellers and other representatives of the depositary bank that the check had "cleared." These cases are almost always resolved in favor of the bank rather than the depositor because they reflect a misunderstanding of how final payment works. No other bank can make final payment or obligate the drawee/payor bank to do so. This makes sense because the drawee/payor bank is in the best position to know whether there are funds available in the drawer's account to pay the check. Thus, only the drawee/payor bank decides whether to honor and pay the check, or to dishonor and return it.

Once the drawee/payor bank has accepted an item and made final payment, it generally cannot reverse its decision. As **3–418** and Comment 4 indicate, a bank may revoke acceptance only in exceptional circumstances, such as when the payee knows it received payment in error. *Morgan Guaranty Trust Co. of New York v. American Savings and Loan Association*, 804 F.2d 1487, 1496 (9th Cir. 1986), illustrates such a situation. That case involved a dispute between a drawee/payor bank and a payee that received payment on two bearer notes after it learned the maker had filed for bankruptcy. After the bank realized its error, it sought to recover the funds from the payee, which refused. In requiring the payee to restore the funds, the court held as follows:

> The payee who receives payment aware that he is not entitled to it does not have the same expectation of finality as an innocent

REQUIRES KNOWLEDGE

payee, and the payor bank in this circumstance does not have superior knowledge. A party who accepts payment on an instrument knowing that the payor was entitled to dishonor it justifiably receives less favorable treatment by a court of equity than a payee ignorant of any problem.

6. NOTICE OF DISHONOR

Dishonor is the opposite of acceptance. When an item is dishonored, indorsers are entitled to notice of dishonor before they can be required to pay a dishonored instrument, but drawers of checks are not. You will learn about an indorser or drawer's obligation to pay a dishonored instrument in Chapter 9. Notice of dishonor is explained in **3-503**. (The "drawers" referenced in **3-503(a)** who are entitled to notice of dishonor are drawers of non-check drafts such as trade acceptance drafts, which are beyond the scope of these materials.) The midnight deadline as set forth in **3-503(c)** provides banks' timeline for giving notice of dishonor. Returning the item to the indorser provides sufficient notice of dishonor; nothing additional is required. Likewise, when actual notice of dishonor is received, returning the item is not necessary. In *NBT Bank, National Association v. First National Community Bank*, 393 F.3d 404 (3d Cir. 2004), the court rejected a depositary bank's argument that the drawee/payor bank should be liable for failing to give timely notice of dishonor, notwithstanding the fact that the depositary bank received actual notice of the drawee/payor bank's decision prior to the expiration of the midnight deadline, where the insufficient funds check itself had been improperly encoded with the routing and transit number for another bank such that there was a delay in returning the check to the depositary bank.

7. CHARGE-BACK

4-214 describes a bank's right to charge back the amount of a dishonored check against its customer's account. This right is commonly invoked when a depositary bank has either chosen—or been required under the EFAA—to allow the depositor to access uncollected funds. Charge-back is thus a reversal of the provisional credit a collecting bank gives for an item.

The following case illustrates the interplay between a depositary bank's right of charge-back and the midnight deadline.

SMALLMAN V. HOME FEDERAL SAVINGS BANK OF TENNESSEE

786 S.W.2d 954 (Tenn. Ct. App. 1989)

GODDARD, J.

Home Federal Savings Bank was sued by David Smallman and his wife Tommie after Home Federal charged back funds from the Smallmans' checking account because a check in the amount of $703.87 deposited in their account was returned unpaid. After the charge-back 14 outstanding checks written by the Smallmans on their account were returned because of insufficient funds. The jury awarded the Smallmans $703.87, the amount of the check, and $30,000 in other damages. Both sides have appealed.

Home Federal insists on appeal that the Trial Court erred in failing to direct a verdict as to the amount of the check and the other damages claimed to have been suffered by the Smallmans, in admitting evidence of Home Federal's net worth and in charging the jury that it might award damages for embarrassment and humiliation. The Smallmans insist that the Court erred in directing a verdict for Home Federal as to their punitive damage claim.

The facts are essentially undisputed. The Smallmans made a sale of some business inventory to Linda Petruzello, a sister-in-law of a friend of the Smallmans, for $703.87. Ms. Petruzello tendered a check dated April 18, 1985, drawn on AmSouth Bank in Alabama in that amount to the Smallmans which they deposited in their checking account at Home Federal on April 22. Home Federal then submitted the check for processing and collection. This process involved the check first going to First American National Bank, then to First Tennessee Bank, then to the Federal Reserve Bank of Atlanta, then to AmSouth Bank which refused to pay the check because Ms. Petruzello's account contained insufficient funds. At some point in the return process to Home Federal the check was lost in the mail.

On July 30, slightly more than three months after it was deposited, Home Federal received a photocopy of the check and notice that the check was being returned for non-payment. It received no explanation for the delay. Believing that the check had not been processed in a timely fashion, Gary Underwood, an officer of Home Federal, embarked on a course of conduct designed to collect the check because he thought that it was just a problem among the banks that were involved in the collection process. The Smallmans were not notified of any potential problem with the check when Home Federal received the notice.

On August 30, more than four months after the check was deposited, Home Federal received a second notice that the check would not be paid and that a time delay had not occurred relative to collection but that the check had been lost in the return process to Home Federal. The dishonor notice to the Smallmans was prepared on September 5, and received on September 12 or 13 in an envelope dated September 10.

On Sunday, September 8, the Smallmans tried to withdraw cash from an automatic teller machine but the machine showed a zero balance despite a recent deposit of $900. The Smallmans testified that they had no knowledge of dishonor of the Petruzello check until September 9 when Mr. Smallman contacted Mr. Underwood at Home Federal to inquire about the zero balance on the ATM machine. It was then that Mr. Underwood informed the Smallmans that the Petruzello check had not cleared and $703.87 had been taken out of their account. The charge-back occurred on September 5.

Because of the charge-back, the Smallmans had 14 checks returned unpaid, all but two of which were written prior to the conversation on September 9 between Mr. Underwood and the Smallmans which is the point in time that the Smallmans received actual notice that the check had been returned unpaid and that their account had been charged back. The Smallmans had employed counsel on or before the date they received the written notice and notified Home Federal, in accordance with their counsel's advice, that they would be making no further deposits in their account. The account, consequently, was closed on September 20.

The Smallmans offered no proof to show that the check could have been collected had they received timely notice of dishonor.

At trial, Home Federal's motion for a directed verdict was denied. The evidence adduced included evidence of the bank's net worth which was admitted over Home Federal's objections. A verdict was rendered in favor of the Smallmans as hereinbefore stated.

We now turn to the first issue raised by Home Federal questioning whether a directed verdict should have been granted in its favor at the close of all the proof. In support of its position, Home Federal asserts that: (1) there was no evidence to show that it was negligent in handling the check; (2) even if there was proof sufficient to establish negligence, it could charge-back on the unpaid item anyway; (3) the Plaintiffs failed to establish damages within the purview of [4–103(e)]:

> The measure of damages for failure to exercise ordinary care in handling an item is the amount of the item reduced by an amount which could not have been realized by the use of ordinary care, and where there is bad faith it includes other damages, if any, suffered by the party as a proximate consequence.

[4–202] imposes a duty of ordinary care on a collecting bank in notifying its customer of non-payment or dishonor. Also of importance here is [4–214(a)] which permits a bank to charge-back the amount of any credit extended to a customer's account "if by its midnight deadline or within a longer reasonable time after it learns the facts it returns the item or sends notification of the facts." The midnight deadline is "midnight on its next banking day following the banking day on which it receives the relevant item or notice or from which the time for taking action commences to run, whichever is later." [**4–104(a)(10)**].

August 30, when the copy of the check was returned a second time, was a Friday, and due to the Labor Day Holiday on September 2, the midnight deadline was Tuesday, September 3. On that date, which was the next banking day, Mr. Underwood attempted to contact AmSouth, the Bank upon which the check was drawn, to determine if the check would clear. Upon learning that it would not he decided that a charge-back was in order. The charge-back was effected on September 5.

As to Home Federal's first point under the first issue, the jury could reasonably find Home Federal was negligent in failing to notify the Smallmans of the dishonored check prior to the midnight deadline.

Apropos of [**4–214**] relative to charge-back, the authors of Anderson's Uniform Commercial Code (Volume 3, Page 261) make the following observation:

> In order to exercise the right of charging back a credit provisionally given to its customer, the collecting bank must act before its midnight deadline. If the bank does not learn of the facts justifying such action within time to act before that deadline, it may act after the deadline has passed if it does so within a reasonable time after it learns of the facts justifying such action against its customer.

Notwithstanding the foregoing, Home Federal argues that the measure of damages is found in [**4–103(e)**], hereinbefore set out.

It argues that in view of the fact the Smallmans adduced no proof to show that they suffered damages because of the negligence of Home Federal they are not entitled to recover.

If the suit were predicated upon negligence other than failure to meet the midnight deadline, we would be inclined to agree. However, the real question is whether Home Federal was entitled to charge-back notwithstanding its failure to meet the midnight deadline and its failure to show it learned any facts justifying an extension thereof.

It seems clear that Home Federal's right to charge back depends on whether the statute establishes a condition precedent or whether it defines the duty of care relative to the right of charge-back, which also would require a showing of damages by reason of the breach of the duty.

* * *

Our reading of the statute persuades us that . . . under the plain language of the statute the Bank is not entitled to charge-back a returned check unless it meets the requirements as to the midnight deadline.

* * *

It is appropriate to discuss together Home Federal's insistence as to the other damages and the Smallmans' insistence as to their right to have the question of punitive damage determined by the jury.

The Smallmans' right to additional damages beyond the amount of the check is governed by [4–103(e)], hereinbefore set out.

* * *

Counsel for the Smallmans' principal assertion that they are entitled to damages for bad faith as well as punitive damages is based upon their contention that Home Federal laid in wait, so to speak, to pounce on their meager checking account after watching it for a number of days until they had made a deposit sufficient to satisfy the returned check. The fallacy of this argument is that from the date it was learned on September 3 that the check would not clear after it had been returned the second time, until it was charged back, there were sufficient funds in the account to satisfy the check.

Additionally, there are the following undisputed facts which belie any contention that Home Federal was guilty of bad faith:

1.   An officer of Home Federal offered to hold the Smallmans' checks a few days to enable them to cover them with a deposit.

2.   Home Federal waived all "not sufficient funds" charges against the Smallmans' account and credited their account accordingly.

3.   An official of Home Federal offered to contact individuals or firms where the Smallmans' checks had been returned and explain to the recipients the circumstances surrounding their return.

We accordingly conclude the Trial Court was correct in directing a verdict as to punitive damages and that he likewise should have directed one as to damages predicated upon bad faith.

––––––––––

The court of appeals held that the Smallmans were entitled to recover the amount of the check ($703.87) because the charge-back was outside the midnight-deadline period and thus unauthorized. The court reversed the lower court holding insofar as the $30,000 in "other damages" for bad faith was concerned, however, as it found that the lower court should have directed a verdict as to that portion of the Smallmans' claim.

In addition to the right of charge-back, a bank may also set off against a customer's account other monies owed to the bank. For example, if a customer holds both a mortgage account and a checking account at the same bank and defaults on the mortgage, the bank may satisfy the mortgage obligation out of funds in the checking account. This is a common-law right recognized in most bank-customer agreements. **4–303** acknowledges this right and describes certain limitations for its application.

8. RESPONSIBILITIES OF COLLECTING BANKS

A few final observations about the relationship between depositary banks and their customers are needed. **4–201(a)** provides that a collecting bank (which includes a depositary bank) acts as an agent of the owner of an item presented for collection. Thus, the customer remains the owner of the check while it is being collected. **4–202** describes the duty of ordinary care that collecting banks are required to exercise with respect to both the time and manner of processing checks.

The language of **4–210** describes a collecting bank as having a security interest in items being collected. As **4–211** indicates, this security interest makes it possible to satisfy the "value" requirement so that otherwise qualified collecting banks can be holders in due course. **4–210** Comment 3 describes the security interest as "self-liquidating" because, when a collecting bank receives final payment, the interest ends.

B. DRAWEE/PAYOR BANKS AND THEIR CUSTOMERS

We turn now from the relationship between depositary banks and their customers who deposit checks to the relationship between drawee/payor banks and their customers who draw checks.

1. THE "PROPERLY PAYABLE" RULE

A drawee/payor bank may debit a drawer's account for any item that is properly payable, as defined in **4–401(a)**. An item is properly payable when the drawer has authorized the payment and the payment does not violate any agreement between the bank and the drawer. For example, if there is an agreement in place for a joint account providing that no check will be paid unless both accountholders have signed it, a check bearing only one signature would not be properly payable. An item is properly payable even if it creates an overdraft, although the bank has the prerogative not to pay such an item. In addition, a bank may accept postdated checks as properly payable prior to the date of the check, unless a customer provides notice as described in **4–401(c)**.

When a drawee/payor bank pays an item into overdraft, it will demand that funds be deposited to cover the overdraft and typically also charge the drawer a substantial fee, often $35 or more per item. Should the bank not be able to recover from the drawer, it will not normally be able to reclaim the funds from the holder receiving payment. The assumption is that the bank could have dishonored the check and avoided the loss.

Despite the well-accepted rule that a drawee/payor bank may pay items into overdraft if it wishes, in several cases drawers have alleged that their bank engaged in practices that caused them to incur more overdrafts—and thus more overdraft fees—than expected. The most common complaint is that banks do not post checks in the order in which they are presented for payment. Assume that an account has $1000 on deposit, and checks for $100, $200, $100, $150, $200, $50, $200, and $800 are presented in that order on a given day. If the checks were paid in the order presented, then only the $800 check would bounce. Instead, however, the bank might engage in what is called "high-low posting," in which higher-value checks are honored first. In this example, if "high-low posting" were used, only the $800 check and one $200 check would clear; six checks would be dishonored rather than one. As this example shows, "high-low posting" typically results in more checks being dishonored; the higher-value checks exhaust the account balance quickly, thus resulting in lower-value (and generally more numerous) checks being dishonored. The Office of the Comptroller of the Currency has generally approved this practice, based on its interpretation of the National Bank Act and its implementing regulations.

The case of *Hassler v. Sovereign Bank*, 374 Fed. Appx. 341 (3d Cir. 2010) presents a typical "high-low posting" scenario and a court's typical response. In that case, at the beginning of the day in question, Hassler had an available balance of $112.35. He made a payment of $39.58 from his account in the morning and then withdrew $140.00 in the afternoon. If the payments had posted to his account in the order in which they occurred, only the second transaction would have resulted in an overdraft. Because the transactions were posted in reverse chronological order instead, his account was charged with two overdrafts. In affirming the lower court's dismissal of Hassler's complaint, the court cited language from the Account Agreement between the customer and the bank providing in relevant part that "We reserve the right to pay the withdrawals you make from your Account regardless of the method of withdrawal in any order we determine." The court further held that the bank's apparent motive— "simply seeking profit"—was not the kind of "bad motive" that would support a breach of the bank's duty of good faith and fair dealing.

Another court, however, allowed a case to proceed past dismissal where the plaintiffs claimed that the bank "routinely enforce[d] a policy whereby charges incurred [were] posted to customers' accounts in order of largest to smallest amounts, even where larger charges [were] received *days after* smaller charges." (Emphasis added). *White v. Wachovia Bank*, 563 F. Supp. 2d 1358 (N.D. Ga. 2008). The differing outcomes make sense, as the conduct alleged in *White* is egregious.

The "properly payable" rule becomes relevant when a drawee/payor bank chooses to pay an item, and its customer—the drawer—disputes its decision to do so. A drawee/payor bank is normally liable to the drawer for paying any item that is not properly payable. Altered items or items bearing a forged drawer's signature or forged indorsement are not properly payable within the meaning of **4–401**, and thus a drawee/payor bank would normally be liable for paying any such item. However, banks sometimes implement policies pursuant to **4–103(a)** to change this default rule. For example, in *Cincinnati Insurance Co. v. Wachovia Bank, Nat. Ass'n*, 72 UCC Rep.Serv.2d 744 (D. Minn. 2010), the bank required its commercial customers to either implement a fraud-detection program called "Positive Pay" or assume liability for any losses due to fraud caused by the customer's failure to do so:

> Positive Pay is a software program that enables a customer to transmit to its bank pertinent information about every check that the customer issues. For example, when a customer who uses Positive Pay issues check number 7394 to "Acme, Inc." in the amount of $15,286.25, the customer's bank is promptly *informed* that the customer has issued check number 7394 to "Acme, Inc." in the amount of $15,286.25. When a bearer then presents check number 7394 for payment, the bank's computer can compare the information on the check to the information that was transmitted by the customer. If the information does not match—if, for example, the name of the payee on check number 7394 is "Jane Smith" instead of "Acme, Inc.," the bank can contact the customer before clearing the check.

The court held that requiring Positive Pay was "unquestionably reasonable." Thus, because the customer had not implemented the software program as required, the bank was not liable for paying an altered item that was not properly payable.

Along the same lines, a bank and drawer can agree that the bank will honor—and charge the drawer's account for—"all checks bearing a facsimile signature resembling the specimen on file even if it is created by a forgery or the stamp is affixed by an unauthorized person." The court examined such an arrangement in *Lor-Mar/Toto, Inc. v. 1st Constitution Bank*, 871 A.2d 110 (N.J. Super. 2005). In such a case, assuming the parties used "clear and unambiguous language defining the scope of the bank's obligation, identifying the customer's responsibility, and expressly shifting the risk of loss to the customer," a check with a forged or unauthorized signature will be properly payable.

Applying **4–401**, and absent an agreement like the one described in the *Lor-Mar* case, an accountholder is not normally responsible for a check if his or her signature is forged, unless he or she violates the bank-statement rule described later in this chapter by failing to notice and advise the drawee/payor bank of any such forgery. Having said this, if the situation falls within the scope of **3–404**, **3–405**, or **3–406**, the bank may be able to shift the loss to the accountholder. **3–404**, which includes the "impostor rule" and "fictitious payee rule," applies when an impostor induces a drawer to issue a check to him or her by impersonating a legitimate payee, or when an instrument is made payable to a fictitious payee as part of a fraudulent scheme. **3–405**, the "faithless employee rule," covers situations in which an employee entrusted with responsibility for checks forges the indorsement of either the employer as payee of a check, or the legitimate payee of a check the employer issued. **3–406** addresses other situations in which a party's negligence contributes to a forged signature or an alteration of an instrument.

3–404 uses the term "impostor" to describe one who "induces the issuer of an instrument to issue the instrument to the impostor, or to a person acting in concert with the impostor, by impersonating the payee of the instrument or a person authorized to act for the payee." *Covington v. Penn Square National Bank*, 545 P.2d 824, 826 (Okla. Civ. App. 1975), illustrates how the rule works.

In November 1972, James F. Beaird, Jr. contacted Mr. A.M. Covington, offering to sell him an oil lease and claiming to work for Western Geophysical Company of Houston, Texas. He showed Covington maps of test holes and logs indicating oil sand had been discovered in each test area. Covington contacted Western Geophysical Company and, upon asking whether "James Beaird" was an employee, was told that "James Baird" was in charge of the data processing department. When Covington tried to clarify the spelling of Beaird's name, Beaird responded "that his name was spelled with an 'I.' "

On November 16, Covington purchased a cashier's check from Boulder Bank in the amount of $6,400, made payable to "James Baird." On November 17, James Beaird cashed the check at Penn Square National Bank, where he had banked for five years. He informed the teller that his name had been misspelled and, at the teller's request, indorsed the check twice, once using each spelling.

On November 18 and 19, Covington began to investigate Beaird more carefully, having become suspicious. He found that Beaird was not the "James Baird" whom Western Geophysical employed and that there had been no exploration on the land he had agreed to lease. On November 20, he asked Boulder to stop payment on the cashier's check, and the bank agreed to do so in return for Covington's agreement to indemnify the bank for any losses it suffered by doing so. When Penn Square presented the check for payment, Boulder initially returned the item stamped "payment stopped," but relented and paid the check when Penn Square demanded that it do so.

Covington sought to recover from Boulder and Penn Square, claiming Boulder was liable for its failure to stop payment and Penn Square was liable because it indorsed the check "with all prior indorsements guaranteed." In rejecting both claims, the court held as follows:

> Statutory language and case law unmistakably place the burden of loss from a forged instrument on the party who deals with the forger.
>
> * * *
>
> The policy underlying this rule is that the person who is taken in by an impost[o]r or a dishonest employee should bear the burden of loss rather than a collecting bank. This is so despite the fact that the transaction with the collecting bank is based on a forgery.

Covington trusted someone who turned out to be a thief, but then sought to pass his loss to one of the two banks involved. He lost on both claims, which makes sense because he was in the best position to avoid the loss. He also had no legal right to stop payment on the cashier's check pursuant to **4–403** Comment 4, which is why Boulder was required to pay the check when Penn Square insisted that it do so.

If a check is altered (as, for example, with a raised amount), **4–401(d)(1)** allows a bank to pay the item according to its original terms. In addition, **4–401(d)(2)** indicates that the bank generally may pay a holder for an item that was incomplete at issuance (as with a blank amount), according to its terms as completed.

2. WRONGFUL DISHONOR

The flip side of the properly payable rule is the wrongful dishonor doctrine, which imposes liability on a drawee/payor bank for failing to pay an item that is properly payable. Exceptions exist for items that are drawn on insufficient funds or stale; both are properly payable but can be dishonored at the bank's election. **4–402** establishes that drawee/payor banks are liable for actual damages caused by wrongful dishonor. This cause of action is available only to a drawer or someone subrogated to the rights of the drawer. Thus, even if a drawee/payor bank has verbally promised a payee that a check will be paid and then declines to do so, the payee has no cause of action against the drawee/payor. The payee may, however, have a claim against the drawer based on the underlying contract. In *W.B. Farms v. Fremont National Bank & Trust Co.*, 756 F.2d 663 (8th Cir. 1985), the court explained this outcome as follows:

> Checks are not instant assignments of the drawer's funds to the payee. In fact, drawers have no money in banks. Only bankers have money in banks. Drawers have choses of action against banks. A bank's failure to pay a check, therefore, may be a breach

of its contract of deposit with the drawer, but it is neither a breach of contract nor a tort actionable at the instance of the payee.

The term "chose of action" refers to a right to sue. Again, only the drawer has this right. Actual damages, which may include consequential damages, are normally awarded for wrongful dishonor, but punitive damages may be awarded in exceptional circumstances such as those presented in *Northshore Bank v. Palmer*, 525 S.W.2d 718 (Tex. 1975).

In *Northshore Bank*, an unknown fraudfeasor obtained some of Marvel Fikes' blank checks and made one of them payable to James T. Palmer in the amount of $275. The wrongdoer took the check to Northshore Bank, where Palmer had an account, and had the bank cash the check. The teller did not verify the identity of the person presenting the check, and thus did not discover that the wrongdoer had assumed Palmer's identity. Several days later, the drawee/payor bank returned the check to Northshore, having noted Fikes' forged signature. Northshore charged the returned check against the account of Palmer, who had no knowledge of the forgery and asserted his innocence. The bank also closed Palmer's account and recalled several valid checks Palmer had written to various payees, on which it had already made final payment, stamping them "paid in error" or "account closed." The bank charged Palmer an "insufficient funds" fee for each recalled check and placed the matter with a collection agency when he refused to pay.

When Palmer went to the bank to clear up the matter, a bank employee had an armed guard escort him from the premises. Palmer reported the forgery to the police, personally contacted Fikes and his bank, and telephoned the payee of each recalled check. The bank never repaid the funds taken from Palmer's account. The court upheld the jury award of $3,500 in punitive damages along with $2,000 actual damages.

3. STALE CHECKS

4–404 allows the drawee/payor bank to decide whether to pay stale checks, so long as it acts in good faith. Thus, a decision to dishonor a stale check would not be a wrongful dishonor, even though the bank could have paid the check. An item is considered stale if it is dated more than six months previously.

If a bank refuses to pay a stale item, the holder can recover from the drawer or whoever transferred the check to the holder, by pursuing a cause of action under the contract giving rise to the issuance or transfer of the check. Certified checks, cashier's checks, and teller's checks are excluded from 4–404. The drawee/payor bank accepted these items prior to issuance and thus has no right to dishonor them.

In *IBP, Inc. v. Mercantile Bank of Topeka*, 6 F. Supp. 2d 1258 (D. Kan. 1998), the court considered a bank's payment of a very stale check. On July

15, 1986, IBP, Inc. issued a check to Meyer Land & Cattle Company for approximately $135,000 for the purchase of cattle. The check was drawn on IBP's account with Mercantile Bank of Topeka. Meyer lost the check, and Tim Meyer found it behind a desk drawer in 1995. Although he noticed the check was 9 years old, he assumed correctly that it represented payment for a sale of cattle. He indorsed the check and deposited it in his account at Sylvan State Bank. Sylvan accepted the check for deposit, as Meyer frequently presented checks of similar amount. The check was routed to Mercantile via an automated clearing-house. Mercantile paid the check and debited IBP's account.

IBP sued Mercantile in <u>conversion,</u> claiming it had improperly honored the stale check. IBP claimed Mercantile had an affirmative duty to ascertain for itself whether IBP still owed money to Meyer before it paid this stale check. **4–404** does not, however, support such a duty. The best approach for a drawer of a stale check who wishes to prevent the check from being paid would be to stop payment on the check and renew the stop-payment order for the entire limitations period. The logistics of stop payment are explored in the next section. <u>Because IBP</u> had not placed a <u>valid stop-payment order</u>, Mercantile was not liable for paying the check.

[handwritten margin note: THESE WERE ACTUALLY MEYER'S NOT IBP]

4. STOP-PAYMENT

Building on the prior discussion of the "properly payable" rule, a drawer may wish to stop payment on a check that was issued fraudulently (as, for example, with a forged drawer signature) or has an altered amount. In both circumstances, because the check is not properly payable, the drawer will not be liable on the check even absent the stop-payment order. Even when a check is properly payable, however, a drawer may wish to stop payment on a check if he or she is dissatisfied with the goods or services obtained in return for the check, or in the case of staleness, as mentioned above. **4–403** describes the right to stop payment, and **4–303** indicates when a drawer can exercise the right. Notably, as **4–403** Comment 7 explains, a stop-payment order does not affect a holder in due course's right to enforce an item.

Banks normally require drawers to follow specific instructions—and pay a fee—to stop payment. When a drawer fails to follow the bank's instructions, the bank has no obligation to stop payment.

Courts have addressed the issue of when a stop-payment order, although incorrect in some way, nevertheless provides a bank with sufficient information to act on the order. One such case is *Staff Service Associates, Inc. v. Midlantic National Bank*, 504 A.2d 148, 152 (N.J. Super. 1985). Staff Service Associates, Inc. maintained an account with Midlantic National Bank. On July 2, 1982, a representative of Staff Service, Raymond Nelson, issued a check drawn on the Midlantic account to Lynn Gross for $4,117.12.

On July 7, John Tracy, Staff Service's president, contacted the bank to stop payment on the check. In writing the stop-payment order, Tracy incorrectly wrote the amount of the check as $4,117.72, thus making an error in one digit. At the bottom of the stop-payment form, which Tracy admits he read, was the following statement:

> IMPORTANT: The information on this Stop-payment Order must be correct, including the exact amount of the check to the penny, or the Bank will not be able to stop payment and this Stop-payment Order will be void.

Because of the error, Midlantic's computers were not able to stop payment on the check, and Staff Service brought suit. In finding the bank liable for any damages Staff Service could prove it suffered, the court held as follows:

> Staff Service's representative did not know that Midlantic utilized a computer to effect stop payment of a check. In addition, Midlantic never informed Staff Service that the exact amount of the check is necessary for the computer to pull the check. It chose a computerized system which searches for stopped checks by amount alone. By electing this system, Midlantic assumed the risk that it would not be able to stop payment of a check despite the customer's accurate description of the account number, the payee's name, the number and date of the check, and a *de minimis* error in the check amount. Midlantic should not be permitted to relieve itself of this risk unless it calls attention to its computerized system and the necessity for the exact check amount to meet computer requirements.

> The court is not persuaded by the clause in the stop-payment order which states that Midlantic cannot stop payment unless the information provided by the customer is correct, including the exact amount of the check to the penny. Indeed this clause is inaccurate since, as Midlantic's representative explained in his certification, "if the amount of the check is correct, the check will be stopped, although a discrepancy may exist in the remaining elements of the stop-payment order, unless and until the customer instructs otherwise."

More accurate language would have been something like this: "The exact amount of the check on this Stop-Payment Order must be correct to the penny, or the bank will not be able to stop payment and this Stop-Payment Order will be void."

When a bank pays an item over a valid stop-payment order, it is liable to the drawer, but only if the drawer proves he or she suffered a loss. For example, if a drawer stops payment on a check issued to pay for goods that were entirely satisfactory and the bank pays the check anyway, the bank will not be liable. Had the bank stopped payment, the customer would have received a windfall by not paying for the goods. If, however, the bank had failed to stop payment on a check issued to pay for worthless goods, the drawer would suffer a loss because the drawer should not have to pay for the goods. Thus, there is a distinction between a *valid* stop-payment order and a *rightful* stop-payment order, and the drawee/payor bank will be liable only for losses associated with a stop-payment order that is both valid and rightful.

4–407 provides a drawee/payor bank with subrogation rights in the event of a dispute involving a stop-payment order. Both of the following examples implicate the drawee's right of subrogation:

1)   A drawer might sue the drawee after an item is charged against the drawer's account over a valid stop-payment order. Because the drawee has already paid the item, the payee will have no reason to participate voluntarily in litigation regarding payment of the item. The drawee, wishing to avoid double liability, may assert against the drawer any defenses the payee could have raised. For example, if the payee could have shown stop-payment was unwarranted as a matter of contract law because the drawer received valuable goods or services from the payee for which the disputed item represented payment, the drawee could assert those facts in defending against the drawer's claim, thus proving the drawer suffered no harm from payment of the item. As the graphic below shows, the pre-litigation posture of the parties is that the drawer is disappointed that the check was paid, the payee is satisfied because the check was paid, and the drawee, who is neutral as to the underlying dispute between the drawer and payee, is simply trying to avoid paying twice.

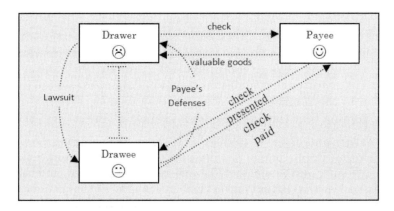

2)   The drawee, having paid a check over a valid stop-payment order, might re-credit the drawer's account immediately to avoid rancor. The drawer would therefore have no reason to participate voluntarily in litigation involving payment of the item. The bank, having already paid twice the value of the item, might then seek to recoup its loss. To do so, the

Formal Valid - Yes
Rightful - Yes

bank might sue the payee, asserting any rights the drawer could have asserted. For example, if the payee engaged in fraud that prompted the issuance of the item, the bank could sue the payee to recover the value of the item and, in so doing, could raise the fraud claim that originally belonged to the drawer. As the graphic below shows, the pre-litigation situation is that the drawee has satisfied both the drawer and payee by paying the value of the instrument twice, thus drawing on its own funds (to its financial detriment), and is trying to recover the double payment.

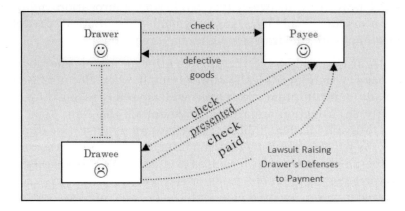

It is not normally possible to stop payment on a cashier's check, certified check, or teller's check, since the drawee/payor bank has already "accepted" the item within the meaning of **4–303(a)(1)**. In fact, **4–403** Comment 4 and **3–411** provide that a bank may be liable if it wrongfully refuses to pay such a check, as in the case when a bank stops payment on a cashier's check either on its own initiative or because its customer asked it to do so. In *State ex rel. Chan Siew Lai v. Powell*, 536 S.W.2d 14, 16 (Mo. 1976), the court considered a remitter's request to enjoin enforcement of a cashier's check he had purchased and delivered to the payee, after he had sought (without success) to stop payment through the bank's ordinary channels. The remitter contended the payee had misrepresented a business transaction to the remitter. The court held as follows, denying injunctive relief and finding that the bank could not refuse to pay:

> The nature and usage of cashier's checks in the commercial world is such that public policy does not favor a rule that would permit stopping payment of them. It is aptly stated in *National Newark & Essex Bank v. Giordano*, 111 N.J. Super. 347, 268 A.2d 327 (1970): "A cashier's check circulates in the commercial world as the equivalent of cash. . . . People accept a cashier's check as a substitute for cash because the bank stands behind it, rather than an individual. In effect, the bank becomes a guarantor of the value of the check and pledges its resources to the payment of the amount represented upon presentation. To allow the bank to stop

payment on such an instrument would be inconsistent with the representation it makes in issuing the check. Such a rule would undermine the public confidence in the bank and its checks and thereby deprive the cashier's check of the essential incident which makes it useful. People would no longer be willing to accept it as a substitute for cash if they could not be sure that there would be no difficulty in converting it into cash."

A bank may, however decline to pay a forged or counterfeit cashier's or teller's check. In *Savesmart, Inc. v. Bowery Savings Bank*, 445 N.Y.S.2d 963 (City Court of NY 1982), the court explained its holding to that effect, as follows:

> [T]he legal effect of delivery of a forged teller's check may be paralleled to the delivery of counterfeit cash. In neither case does the deliveree acquire a claim against the issuer (the bank or the government).

The application of stop-payment principles to money orders, which is more complicated than for other instruments, is explored in *Garden Check Cashing Service, Inc. v. First National City Bank*, 25 A.D.2d 137, 141 (N.Y. App. Div. 1st Dept. 1966). That case demonstrates that the purchaser of a money order can sometimes stop payment. On April 13, 1962, Mr. Higgins purchased a money order from Garden Check Cashing Service, Inc. in the amount of $130.37. He did not fill in the name of the payee. Later that day, Mr. Higgins reported the money order lost and requested stop-payment. The same day, Mr. Walker—a stranger to Mr. Higgins—found and presented the money order to First National City Bank, having filled in his own name as payee. First National paid him the face value of the money order, minus a small fee. Upon presentment of the money order for payment, the item was returned unpaid due to Mr. Higgins' stop-payment order.

> In upholding the stop-payment order, the court held as follows:

> We see small difference between the present transaction and one where a person deposits with the bank a sum of money and receives a quantity of blank checks. The obvious difference [with a money order] is that a single deposit was made and a single blank check received with the amount of the deposit inserted therein.

Notwithstanding the *Garden City Check Cashing* case, many money orders expressly exclude the right of stop payment, by contract.

Other cases address whether the issuer of a money order has the right to stop payment. In *Sequoyah State Bank v. Union National Bank of Little Rock*, 621 S.W.2d 683, 684 (Ark. 1981), the court addressed an issuing bank's attempt to stop payment on a money order upon discovering that the check it accepted in payment for the money order was drawn on insufficient funds. In denying the bank's attempt, the court held as follows:

> The personal money order constituted an obligation of Union [National Bank, the issuer,] from the moment of its sale and issuance. The fact that Union was frustrated in retaining the funds because instead of cash it accepted a check drawn on insufficient funds is no reason to hold otherwise. . . . We note by analogy that the Uniform Commercial Code on Sales . . . provides [in **2–403(1)(b)**] that a purchaser of goods, who takes delivery in exchange for a check which is later dishonored, transfers good title to the goods.

Thus, a remitter of a money order, but not the issuer, may have a right to stop payment on a money order, unless the parties have waived or excluded the right by contract.

5. LEGAL PROCESS

Whereas stop payment on an ordinary business or personal check is the drawer's right, service of legal process terminates a drawee/payor bank's authority to pay items drawn on the drawer's account, without the drawer being involved in the decision at all. The most common form of legal process served on a bank is garnishment. When litigation arises in this context, it is usually because checks have bounced after a bank was served with an order of garnishment that drew most or all of the funds out of an account, or because the accountholder withdrew funds immediately before a garnishment order attached, so that the account was greatly diminished or even emptied of funds to be garnished.

4–303 provides rules that establish the relative priority between garnishment and competing claims (including checks posted to the account and other requests to withdraw funds from the account) As **4–401** Comment 6 states, "the effective time for determining whether [a garnishment order was] received too late to affect the payment of an item and a charge to the customer's account by reason of such payment, is receipt plus a reasonable time for the bank to act on [the garnishment]."

W&D Acquisition, LLC v. First Union National Bank, 817 A.2d 91 (Conn. 2003), addressed the issue of how quickly a drawee/payor bank must comply with a garnishment order, in determining "a reasonable time for the bank to act" within the meaning of **4–303(a)**. In that case, garnishment papers were served on the bank around noon. On that same day, the accountholder entered the bank around 3:30 p.m. and withdrew almost the entire balance of the account, leaving virtually no funds to which the garnishment could attach. The garnishor brought suit, alleging the garnishee bank had sufficient time to secure the funds prior to the withdrawal and seeking to recover the amount of money it contended it should have received pursuant to the garnishment. The court quoted **1–205** for the proposition that a "reasonable time" within the meaning of **4–303** would be a fact-specific inquiry and need not be synonymous with the "midnight deadline" in **4–104(a)(10)**. Because the lower court inappropriately applied the "midnight deadline," the court reversed and remanded.

In such a case, the bank should be prepared to present evidence regarding its communication processes and any industry standards. As **4–303** Comment 6 states, "Usually a relatively short time is required to communicate to the accounting department advice of one of these events, but certainly some time is necessary."

6. DEATH OR INCOMPETENCE OF DRAWER

A drawer's death or adjudicated incompetence will terminate a bank's authority to pay items drawn on that drawer's account, but such termination of authority does not become effective immediately. **4–405** and Comment 2 provide the relevant rules. First, it is not death or adjudicated incompetence that is the trigger point here, but the bank's actual knowledge of death or adjudicated incompetence. In addition, there is a ten-day window after death, in which a bank may continue to pay checks, even if it has knowledge of the death, so long as no person claiming an interest in the account orders otherwise. No similar window exists after a person is adjudicated incompetent.

As the following case shows, items issued near death can raise issues of estate-planning law, especially when the court believes an item was intended as a will substitute. This case also involves a different form of legal process—a temporary restraining order rather than an order of garnishment, and reminds readers of the role of final payment.

DELUCA v. BANCOHIO NATIONAL BANK, INC.
74 Ohio App. 3d 233, 598 N.E.2d 781 (Ohio Ct. App. 1991)

PETREE, J.

This case involves a dispute over a $75,000 check allegedly given to Carolyn DeLuca on Friday, January 27, 1989, by decedent Joseph G. Rotondo. At the time, decedent was a seventy-eight-year-old practicing attorney and Carolyn DeLuca was his secretary.

On Friday, January 27, 1989, decedent, who for years had suffered from emphysema, heart problems, and other ailments, felt very ill. He called Carolyn in the morning to take him to the hospital. They stopped first at his office. Despite his discomfort, he signed several blank payroll checks [drawn on BancOhio National Bank] that were on his desk. Before they left for the hospital, decedent told Carolyn, who usually did the payroll banking, that he had one check for her in his desk.

At the hospital, decedent was treated in the emergency room. Carolyn remained with him, and eventually her daughter Jacqueline arrived as well. Further, decedent's son, Eric P. Rotondo, also visited. Eric is an attorney practicing law in the same office as his father. Earlier that morning, Eric had seen the blank checks on his father's desk and had overheard his father's comment about a check left for Carolyn.

Carolyn was at decedent's side in his hospital room. At one point, she maintained that decedent told her that he wanted to pay her debts and asked her how much she needed. She told him that her debts were $75,000. So, decedent told her that if anything happened to him, she was to take the blank check in his desk and fill it in for that amount. No one else was present to hear this conversation.

Carolyn remained at the hospital until decedent died at 4:46 p.m. . . .

After decedent died, Carolyn returned to decedent's office to pick up some personal items, finish the payroll, and pick up her check. Subsequently, she went home.

Eric remained at the hospital to make funeral arrangements. When he returned to the law office, he noticed that the payroll checks were properly in their envelopes, except that one was missing.

Eventually, Carolyn filled in the blank check as decedent had instructed. She filled in her name as payee, the amount of $75,000, and the date. She then went to the Bexley branch of BancOhio with Jacqueline on Saturday, January 28, 1989. She presented the check to the next available teller, Kathleen R. Miller, who in fact was head teller. Carolyn indicated that she needed the funds deposited in her BancOhio account. After some discussion about the availability of the funds to pay bills, Miller told Carolyn that the funds would be available on the next banking day. Miller then deposited $75,000 into plaintiffs' account.

Thereafter, Eric, who is co-executor of his father's estate, learned about the transaction at BancOhio. He consulted an attorney who filed for an ex parte temporary restraining order [(TRO)] on Monday, January 30, 1989, to stop-payment on the check and the transfer of any funds. After the trial court granted this relief, the TRO was presented to BancOhio on Monday afternoon.

The bank then dishonored the check, removed a provisional credit from plaintiffs' account, recredited decedent's account, and returned the check to Carolyn with a stamp on it and an explanation that the check had been dishonored due to the TRO. Decedent's estate was then able to withdraw the $75,000 for the benefit of the estate.

Plaintiffs filed suit on March 22, 1989, alleging that BancOhio removed $75,000 from their joint bank account without authority to do so and refused to repay the funds. Both parties filed motions for summary judgment, but the trial court overruled them. At trial, at the close of plaintiffs' case, BancOhio orally moved for a directed verdict and the trial court granted it.

In findings of fact and conclusions of law, the court wrote that BancOhio obeyed the TRO and dishonored the check. The court acknowledged that Carolyn ". . . took the check to defendant's Bexley branch to deposit the funds in plaintiffs' savings account. . . ." But the court found that Carolyn did not inform the bank that the maker of the check was dead nor that she had completed the check . . . by naming herself as payee and by inserting the amount of $75,000. The court concluded that the check was ". . . invalid, payment was properly denied, and the account of plaintiffs was properly debited."

In their assignments of error, plaintiffs argue that BancOhio cashed the $75,000 check on Saturday and could not thereafter undo such final payment.

　　　　　* * *

. . . By contrast, BancOhio submitted affidavits and other evidence to establish that Carolyn only deposited the check, which allowed the bank to revoke any provisional credit granted prior to its so-called midnight deadline. . . .

[The portion of the court's opinion addressing whether the check was cashed before deposit, which would have constituted final payment because this was an on-us check, has been omitted. The court held for Carolyn on this point. The portion of the court's opinion addressing the bank's response to the son's TRO has also been omitted.]

BancOhio's last line of defense is based on the theory that . . . Carolyn had no authority to fill in the incomplete check after decedent's death. On this score, we are compelled to agree.

In her deposition, Carolyn squarely admitted that the subject check was intended as a gift to her. As is evident from the deposition, it is at least arguable that decedent attempted to effectuate a gift *causa mortis* of the check in question. However, the law as it stands cannot permit this on these facts.

Lord Chancellor Ashbourne once said that: ". . . , I do not look with particular favor on these death-bed gifts." The same sentiment applies in Ohio.

Although such gifts are enforceable in Ohio, gifts by check pose a special problem. The almost uniform rule at common law was that a donor's own check not paid or accepted prior to death could not establish a gift *inter vivos* or *causa mortis*. The same effect was said to obtain under the Negotiable Instruments Law [that preceded UCC Articles 3 and 4.]

The theoretical underpinning for this rule is that a check is not an assignment of funds and therefore, any intended gift could not be complete because the donor retains the power to stop payment on his order. The Code today also provides that a check is not an assignment of funds.

* * *

On the evidence presented, Carolyn's authority to fill in the check was revoked by decedent's death. . . . For this reason, the court should have directed a verdict for BancOhio.

Because this case involved an on-us check, which is generally subject to "next day" availability, the only hold BancOhio could have placed under Regulation CC would have been an exception hold due to the amount of the check. Specifically, **12 CFR Part 229.13(h)(4)** would allow one additional business day for an on-us check of this size. Although the bank could place a longer hold, the bank would bear the burden of establishing its reasonableness. Thus, the son was wise to seek injunctive relief.

Applying the language of **3–115** and Comments 2 and 3 regarding completion of incomplete items, DeLuca's authority to act on the decedent's behalf with respect to payroll matters, including this particular check, terminated at his death. Since the item was incomplete at issuance and it was completed by a person who lacked the authority to complete it—even though the decedent had directed her to do so—her completion of the check was legally considered an alteration within the meaning of **3–407**.

A bank's knowledge of adjudicated incompetence, like death, terminates a bank's authority to pay items drawn on its customer's account. The case of *Republic National Bank of Miami v. Johnson*, 622 So. 2d 1015 (Fla. 3d Dist. App. 1993), is illustrative. As a result of a third party's exploitation, 76-year-old Maria Johnson depleted her savings before she was adjudicated incompetent. Her legal guardian sued her bank, asserting that red flags such as the rapid withdrawal of large sums from a personal checking account using starter checks and counter checks should have put the bank on notice of a problem. The court held that the UCC relieved the bank of liability because she had not yet been adjudicated incompetent. After this litigation, Florida adopted legislation requiring banks to report suspected financial abuse of elders.

Concerns about elder incapacity present a difficult policy question. On the one hand, a bank's quick intervention may protect the funds of an older person like Mrs. Johnson from being tragically depleted. On the other hand, a bank might find itself accused of ageist behavior if it blocks (or even delays) certain transactions. Consider a person who decides to take a spontaneous, expensive trip. If a 35-year-old customer would not be questioned about making a large withdrawal to finance such a trip, one might reasonably ask why a 90-year-old should not expect the same privilege.

7. THE BANK STATEMENT RULE

In many situations, a careful review of bank statements can reveal fraudulent account activity and halt future fraud. Under the "Bank Statement Rule" found in 4–406, an accountholder must report any items with an unauthorized drawer signature or alteration within a reasonable time after the bank sends a bank statement or makes a statement available. Items with unauthorized signatures or alterations are not properly payable, but an accountholder who does not timely notice and report them loses the right to require the bank to re-credit his or her account. 4–406 does not require banks to provide account statements, but creates incentives for them do so through the loss-shifting features of the statute. Thus, upon receiving a bank statement, an accountholder is well advised to compare it against his or her record of expenditures.

NEGATES
– NEVER AUTH
– ALTERED

– MUST ACT W/IN TIME LISTED IN DEP. AGREEMENT

When a bank sends a statement to the account address of record, the clock begins to run under the Bank Statement Rule even if the accountholder was incapacitated or hospitalized and a caregiver intercepted the statements such that the accountholder never actually saw them. In *Peters v. Riggs National Bank, N.A.*, 942 A.2d 1163 (D.C. Ct. App. 2008), for example, the court affirmed the legal effectiveness of statements mailed to an accountholder during a 153-day period during which she suffered a serious stroke, was hospitalized, then was transferred to an assisted living facility where she remained seriously ill and later died. During that period, the accountholder lacked the capacity to review bank statements and likely never even saw them.

4–406 sets forth a maximum period of one year for accountholders to report suspicious activity, although banks generally impose a significantly shorter limitations period by contract. In *Clemente Bros. Contracting Corp. v. Hafner-Milazzo*, 14 N.Y.3d 277 (NY. Ct. App. 2014), the court upheld a contractual provision shortening the notice period from one year to fourteen days. The court found that the modification was not "manifestly unreasonable" as applied to Clemente Brothers, an entity "with numerous employees and hundreds of thousands of dollars under its control . . . [which had] acknowledged its responsibility to [monitor its accounts once a month, within 14 days of each statement] in a corporate resolution." The court went on to say, "That expectation is all the more reasonable in this age, when customers can monitor their account transactions minute by minute online from around the world."

The court went on, however, to emphasize that its holding would be "limited to the case of a corporate entity that either is financially sophisticated or has the resources to acquire professional guidance." "It could well be unreasonable," the court continued, "for banks to use contracts of adhesion to impose an exacting 14-day limit on unsophisticated customers, small family businesses, or individual consumers, including, for example, the elderly, people suffering from certain disabilities, or others for whom the 14-day rule could be too unforgiving." Explaining this limitation, the court continued, "These customers may lack the time, technology, or other resources to check their account statements within such a limited period each month. They are more susceptible to unforeseen events disrupting their routines or normal business operations. And it may be that banks need less protection on these accounts because the total assets may be less than those of larger companies."

More stringent rules apply when the same wrongdoer engages in repeated misdeeds against the accountholder. In such cases, if the accountholder does not notice and report the first bad act by this wrongdoer within a reasonable time not exceeding thirty days, the accountholder will be liable for any loss from that wrongdoer's additional misdeeds. This "same-wrongdoer rule" is found in **4–406(d)(2)**, and the thirty-day period runs from the time that the bank sends or otherwise makes available the statement showing the first wrongdoing by this person.

The following case illustrates the Bank Statement Rule and the same-wrongdoer rule, showing how the duty of ordinary care found in **3–103(a)(9)** applies to the relationship between a bank and an accountholder. The case also illuminates some pertinent provisions of a typical deposit contract.

SPACEMAKERS OF AMERICA, INC. v. SUNTRUST BANK

271 Ga. App. 335, 55 U.C.C. Rep. Serv. 2d 893 (Ga. Ct. App. 2005)

ELLINGTON, J.

Spacemakers of America, Inc. sued SunTrust Bank after the bank processed approximately 65 checks that had been forged by the company's bookkeeper. The trial court granted the bank's motion for summary judgment on Spacemakers' claims for negligence, conversion, and unauthorized payment of forged items. Spacemakers appeals, claiming the trial court erred when it misapplied the law, granted summary judgment on its tort claims, and found the bank was not negligent as a matter of law. Because summary judgment was properly granted in this case, we affirm.

* * *

. . . Jenny Triplett applied with Spacemakers of America, Inc. for a bookkeeping position in November 1999. Triplett listed no prior employment on her application, and the application did not inquire about her criminal history. Prior to hiring Triplett, employees of Spacemakers did not ask her about her criminal history or conduct a criminal background check. Had it done so, Spacemakers would have learned that Triplett was on probation from a 1997 conviction for thirteen counts of forgery in the first degree, as well as from convictions for theft by taking and theft by deception in March 1999, just eight months before she applied for the Spacemakers job. All of these convictions were the result of Triplett forging the checks of previous employers.

Spacemakers hired Triplett as a bookkeeper on December 1, 1999, delegating to her the sole responsibility for maintaining the company's checkbook, reconciling it with the monthly bank statements, and preparing financial reports. According to Dennis Rose, Spacemakers' president, Triplett also handled the company's accounts payable and regularly presented him with invoices from vendors and payroll records for employees. Rose stated that he spent several hours reviewing the vendor invoices each month before giving Triplett specific directions about which ones should be paid. After Triplett wrote the checks, she gave them to Rose so he could sign them. No other Spacemakers employee . . . looked at the company's checkbook register to ensure that Triplett wrote only authorized checks on the company's account. Further, Rose admitted that no other employee checked the accuracy of Triplett's financial reports and that he simply relied on Triplett's representations regarding how much money was in the bank account at any given time.

On January 3, 2000, just weeks after starting her job at Spacemakers, Triplett forged Rose's signature on a check for $3,000. She made the check payable to her husband's company, "Triple M Entertainment Group," which was not a vendor for Spacemakers. By the end of her first full month of employment, Triplett had forged five more checks totaling $22,320.30, all payable to Triple M. Then, over the next nine months, Triplett forged fifty-nine more checks totaling approximately $475,000. Triplett made all of these checks payable to Triple M. Most of the checks were for amounts between $5,000 and $10,000, and only two of the checks were for an amount over $20,000: a check for $24,500 dated September 1, 2000, and a check for $30,670 dated October 5, 2000. There is no evidence that anyone at Spacemakers other than Triplett reviewed the company's bank statements between January and October 2000 or that Spacemakers ever notified SunTrust that there had been any unauthorized transactions during that period.

On October 13, 2000, a SunTrust loss-prevention employee visually inspected the $30,670 check. She became suspicious of the signature and immediately contacted Rose. The SunTrust employee faxed Rose a copy of the check, which was made payable to "Triple M." Rose knew that Triple M was not one of the company's vendors and that he had not authorized the check. During the phone conversation, a Spacemakers employee reminded Rose that Triplett's husband owned Triple M. Rose's wife immediately called the police, and Triplett was arrested.

On November 9, 2000, Spacemakers sent a letter to SunTrust demanding that the bank credit $523,106.03 to its account for the forged checks. The bank refused, contending that Spacemakers' failure to provide the bank with timely notice of the forgeries barred its claim under the notice provisions of the account agreement between the bank and Spacemakers, as well as under the notice provisions of the Georgia Commercial Code, specifically OCGA § 11–4–406. The bank also contended that Spacemakers' negligence in hiring and failing to supervise Triplett, a convicted felon, barred the company's claim under OCGA §§ 11–3–406 and 11–4–406. Spacemakers subsequently sued the bank for negligence, conversion, and unauthorized payment of forged items.

* * *

Spacemakers claims the trial court erred in applying OCGA § 11–4–406 to the facts of this case.

* * *

[T]his rule imposes upon a bank customer the duty to promptly examine its monthly statements and notify the bank of any unauthorized transaction. If the customer fails to report the first forged item within 30 days, it is precluded from recovering for that transaction *and for any additional items forged by the same wrongdoer....* The underlying justification for this provision is simple: one of the most serious consequences of the failure of a customer to timely examine its statement is that it gives the wrongdoer the opportunity to repeat his misdeeds. Clearly, the customer "is in the best position to discover and report small forgeries before the [same] wrongdoer is emboldened and attempts a larger misdeed."

In this case, . . . [t]here is every reason to believe that, if Spacemakers had simply reviewed its bank statement for January 2000, it would have discovered the forgeries. More importantly, it would have been able to timely notify the bank of its discovery and avoided its subsequent losses of almost $475,000. Clearly, Spacemakers' extensive and unnecessary loss due to forgery is precisely the scenario that the duties created by OCGA § 11–4–406 were designed to prevent. Accordingly, we find that Spacemakers is precluded as a matter of law from asserting claims based upon the forgeries in this case. The trial court did not err in granting summary judgment to the bank.

Spacemakers also contends the trial court erred in finding that there was no evidence that the bank failed to use ordinary care in processing customers' checks. Specifically, Spacemakers claims a jury issue existed as to whether the bank was negligent because it did "absolutely nothing" to verify signatures on commercial checks written for less than $20,000. Further, Spacemakers argues that, if *both* the customer and the bank are negligent, then the loss from the forged checks is allocated between the two parties according to the extent each party's negligence contributed to the loss. See OCGA §§ 11–3–406; 11–4–406(e). Therefore, according to

Spacemakers, the bank should be liable for at least part of the company's losses from the forged checks. . . .

Under OCGA § 11–3–103(a)(7) [UCC **3–103(a)(9)**], . . . [o]rdinary care in this context is comparable to a "professional negligence" standard of care and does not refer to what a "reasonable person" would do under the circumstances.

The bank . . . presented a prima facie showing that it exercised ordinary care in this case. According to the affidavit of Jeffrey Dalrymple, a SunTrust Senior Vice-President, the bank's regional operations center handles between 650,000 and 1,200,000 checks per day, and its fraud-detection software, ASI/16, is "an industry standard and one of the most sophisticated rules-based fraud detection software systems available." This fraud-detection software program reviews every check written for $250 and over and looks for certain suspicious characteristics which may indicate fraud on an account. These characteristics include, but are not limited to, the following: check numbers that are out of sequence; checks that have duplicate, missing, or out-of-range serial numbers; checks for high dollar amounts; checks for an amount greater than average for the account; and checks for an amount which exceeds the largest found in the account's history. If a check meets any of these characteristics, it is "outsorted" and visually inspected by SunTrust employees. Further, commercial checks for $20,000 or greater are automatically reviewed and verified by SunTrust employees. Dalrymple's affidavit also stated that he has personal knowledge of commercial standards in the banking industry in general and in the Atlanta area, as well as SunTrust's policies and procedures regarding the processing of checks. According to Dalrymple,

> SunTrust's standards with respect to thresholds for sight inspection of checks drawn on commercial accounts not only meet, but are in fact more stringent than, the standards for sight inspection of such checks among other banks in the Atlanta, Georgia area and are in observance and in fact exceed reasonable commercial standards.

Finally, Dalrymple's affidavit stated that SunTrust followed its standard procedures when it processed checks drawn on Spacemakers' account.

. . . The only evidence Spacemakers presented to refute SunTrust's showing was an expert witness, who testified that he had never analyzed fraud-detection systems in any national bank in the Atlanta area. He also admitted that he did not know what fraud-detection procedures SunTrust actually performs on commercial checks under $20,000. Even so, the witness deposed that, in his opinion, the bank was negligent because it did not visually inspect the signature on every check it processes, regardless of the check's amount. The expert witness later abandoned that position, however, and admitted that he did not think that reasonable commercial standards for national banks in the Atlanta area required banks to visually inspect every check. The witness had no opinion as to how large a check amount would have to be for the bank to be required to visually inspect it for fraud in order to comply with reasonable commercial standards in the Atlanta area. He also deposed that he was not aware of any provision in the Georgia Commercial Code which requires a bank to visually examine every check it processes. Further, although the expert witness claimed SunTrust was negligent for failing to notify its customers of its fraud detection policies and procedures, he admitted that he did not know what SunTrust told its customers, or what other banks in the area tell their customers, regarding their fraud detection program.

Accordingly, we find the record supports the trial court's conclusion that Spacemakers failed to create a jury issue as to whether the bank exercised ordinary care under the circumstances.

We also find that, even if OCGA § 11–4–406 did not preclude Spacemakers from recovering from the bank, there was a second basis for granting summary judgment on the company's claims. The evidence showed that Spacemakers' commercial account with SunTrust was subject to certain terms, which were documented in a booklet entitled "Rules and Regulations [for] Non-Personal Deposit Accounts." The booklet expressly notified commercial customers that the bank does not verify the signatures on every check paid against their account and instructed customers to promptly examine their monthly statements to verify that only authorized checks have been paid. In fact, a second provision specifically detailed the customer's duty with regard to recognizing account discrepancies and its liability to fulfill this duty:

> You should carefully examine the statement and canceled checks (including the face and back), if included in the statement, when you receive the statement. The Bank will not be liable for any unauthorized signature, alteration, miscoding, or other error on the face of any item in your statement, or for any incorrect amount or other error on the statement itself . . . unless you notify the Bank within thirty (30) calendar days from the date the Bank . . . makes your statement available to you or anyone to whom you request it be sent. . . . Moreover, because you are in the best position to discover an unauthorized signature . . . , you agree that the Bank will not be liable for paying such items if . . . you did not examine the statement and the canceled checks (if included) or you have not reported the unauthorized signatures . . . to us within the time period set forth above.

Most importantly, the booklet contained the following provision: "Bookkeepers. In the event you authorize any third person . . . to retain possession of or prepare items for [your company], you agree to assume full responsibility for any errors or wrongdoing by such third person . . . if the

Bank should pay such items." Therefore, under these express provisions, Spacemakers cannot recover from the bank for the payments on the forged checks.

* * *

Accordingly, summary judgment was appropriate and there was no error.

_____

The policy behind the UCC's allocation of risk and loss for checks that are not properly payable reflects a balancing of several policy considerations. Thus, while customers bear the burden of some kinds of preventable loss (like that shown in the preceding case), banks bear the burden of loss that neither the bank nor the customer could prevent—like a forged indorsement.

Chapter Conclusion: This chapter should have given you a clear picture of each bank's role in the Article 4 collection process, from the depositary bank to the drawee/payor bank. Leaving these materials, you should also understand the allocation of rights and responsibilities between banks and their customers.

PROBLEMS

1.   Bradley Union was the beneficiary of two trusts his father established in 1977 and 1981, respectively. In April of 1998, Union executed a power of attorney to James Johnson, who had been his caretaker and personal ⟶ AGENT assistant since the 1960s, authorizing him to handle Union's banking. In December 2000, Union was adjudicated incompetent, and C. Douglas Maxwell, Jr. became his guardian. Maxwell revoked Johnson's power of attorney and requested Union's financial records from his bank, Branch Banking & Trust Co. At that time, Maxwell discovered that Johnson and members of his family had forged Union's signature on checks and had converted a large sum of money, from before 1997 through December 2000. Throughout this time, the bank had provided statements of Union's account. Maxwell sued the bank.

   a.   Did the bank have the authority to pay items drawn on Union's account through December 2000?

   b.   Were the items Johnson drew on Union's account properly payable?

   c.   Is Branch Banking & Trust Co. protected by the Bank Statement Rule?

2.   Neal and Helen Rogers were in their eighties, and Neal was bedridden. Helen hired Jackie Reese to help care for her husband, run errands, and do chores. Over the course of about a year, Jackie forged checks on four checking accounts that Mr. and Mrs. Rogers maintained with Union Planters Bank, totaling more than $58,000. Some were written to "Helen Rogers," some to "cash," and some to "Jackie Reese." Jackie hid or disposed of the statements

from the bank during this time period. After Neal died, his son Neal, Jr., worked with Helen to straighten out the family finances, and the two discovered the forgeries. The last forged checks were written about a month before the forgeries were discovered.

a.   Does 4–405 apply in this case? Why or why not?

b.   Does the bank-statement rule, coupled with the "same-wrongdoer rule" found in 4–406(d)(2), protect Union Planters Bank from liability to Helen Rogers?

c.   Have the bank statements been "sent" to Mr. and Mrs. Rogers, within the meaning of 4–406(a)? Which Code section answers this question?

d.   Can Neal, Jr. recover for the last forged checks written about a month before the forgeries were discovered?

3.   VR Electric, Inc. banked with Bank of Texas. One day in October 2003, VR's bookkeeper Beverly Pennington placed an unsigned check for $8,276 made out to Viohl Electric on the counter in front of VR President Terry Viohl's office. This was Pennington's usual practice because Viohl was very disorganized, and she feared that he would otherwise lose the check. The counter was next to the front entrance and accessible to anyone who entered VR's office.

Anthony Burlew, who worked for a contractor doing business with VR, took the unsigned check. Burlew forged Viohl's signature on the front of the check and indorsed the check to himself. Burlew then took the check to a used car dealer, to whom he indorsed the check in exchange for a car and cash. The dealer accepted the check and deposited it into his account. Pennington and Viohl noticed the check was missing but did not request a stop payment order because they concluded that the check must have been lost in Viohl's office.

Bank of Texas processed and paid the check. Although the bank did not verify Viohl's signature, the Vice President of Operations for the bank testified that this was consistent with the bank's verbal policy not to review the signature manually for any item less than $100,000. (On another occasion, she indicated that the threshold amount for manual review was $250,000.)

When VR received its October statement, it immediately notified Bank of Texas that Viohl's signature had been forged and asked that its account be credited for the amount of the check.

a.   Does this case fall within 3–404, 3–405, or 3–406? How do you know?

b.   As between VR and Bank of Texas, who should prevail and why? - BoT

4.   Read 3–418 and consider the following facts:

Park Corporation agreed to sell used mining equipment to DAI International Investment Corporation. For its down payment, DAI provided Garland Caribbean Corporation, the agent for the sale, with a check for $75,000. The equipment was not to be delivered until the purchase price was fully paid. Before indorsing the check to Park, a representative of Garland called the drawee to find out whether DAI had sufficient funds in its account to cover the check. After learning that it did not, and without relating this information to Park, Garland transferred the check to Park, which sought to enforce the check. The check cleared by mistake, and Park refused the drawee's demand for repayment.

 a. Is Park entitled to enforce the check notwithstanding the erroneous payment? You may assume that Park is a holder in due course.

 b. Which portion of 3–418 is applicable in this situation?

 c. How, if at all, would your answer change if Park had not yet delivered the mining equipment to DAI, but had merely promised to do so?

 d. Which portion of 4–215 would you cite to explain how and when the drawee bank made final payment on this check?

 5. Review Regulation CC and consider the following facts:

Essex Construction Corporation deposited a check for about $120,000 into its account with Industrial Bank before 2 p.m. on March 31. The check was drawn on East Side Manor Cooperative Association's account with Signet Bank. Industrial provisionally credited Essex's account for the amount of the check, but notified it that only $100 of the deposit would be available until April 6. April 1 and 2 were weekend days, and the bank was closed both of those days.

 a. Has Industrial complied with Regulation CC's rules for ordinary holds?

 b. Could Industrial have placed an exception hold? If so, for how long?

   On April 6, Signet informed Industrial that East Side had stopped payment on the check, and Industrial revoked the provisional credit to Essex's account. On April 7, Industrial mailed a notice to Essex, informing it that the check had been returned and enclosing the checks so Essex could pursue payment of the check if desired. That same day, Essex wrote two checks totaling approximately $40,000 against the East Side check funds, which it expected to be in its account at that time. Essex received notice of dishonor on April 11 and brought suit against Industrial, claiming that "it [was] entitled to recover because Industrial failed either to provide notice of dishonor or to make the funds available by April 6, the date specified in the notice it provided."

 c. What is the legal flaw in Essex's argument? (4–214 may be helpful.)

 d. What was the deadline for Industrial to provide notice of dishonor to Essex?

 e. Applying 3–503 and 4–214(b), when was notice effective?

 6. Livestock dealer Ned Maryott had done business with First National Bank of Eden, South Dakota for almost twenty years and had never incurred an overdraft or made a late loan payment. The bank dishonored three checks drawn on his account despite the fact that sufficient funds were on deposit

because it suspected (incorrectly) that Maryott was involved in a check-fraud scheme.

At the same time, and based on the same suspicions, the bank exercised its right of setoff and appropriated a significant portion of Maryott's account to pay off almost the entire balance of several loans Maryott owed to it. These loans were not overdue at that time.

Based on the bank's actions, two of the payees on the dishonored checks made claims on the bond Maryott was required to maintain as part of his business. Because these claims exceeded the amount of the bond, Maryott forfeited his state license to sell livestock and lost his livelihood.

   a.   Did the bank's actions constitute wrongful dishonor? Why or why not? *- Yes*

   b.   If so, what damages would you expect to see awarded, and what Code section would you cite in support of an award of damages? *- Actual Dam*

   c.   Could punitive damages be available? (See 4–402 Comment 1.) *- No, No Indica of Malicious*

   7.   On Sunday, May 13, 1979, Kenneth and Vicki Isaacs noticed their checkbook was missing. They reported this fact to their bank, Twin City Bank, on Monday, May 14. Two forged checks totaling about $2,000 had been cashed against their account on May 11 and 12. On Monday morning, after the Isaacs notified the bank of the loss, the bank "froze" the account, which contained a balance of about $2,000. Because Mr. Isaacs had been convicted of burglary some years before, the bank was initially concerned that he might be involved in some kind of wrongdoing. By May 30, however, the police had apprehended the forger and notified Twin City that the Isaacs were not involved. The police repeated this information to the bank in mid-June, but the bank continued to keep the account "frozen" for approximately four years, even though the Isaacs' credit with Twin City was "impeccable." During this four-year period, not only was the Isaacs' credit impaired with Twin City, but they were unable to obtain credit elsewhere as well and were forced to borrow from relatives and friends. A check they wrote as "earnest money" for a house they planned to purchase shortly before the account was frozen was dishonored, and the sale fell through. At one point, one spouse filed for divorce; although the petition was dropped, the Isaacs testified that the matter had placed considerable strain upon their marriage. In addition, Twin City repossessed two vehicles because the Isaacs did not have access to the funds in their account to make car payments. One vehicle was repossessed before the parties' five-day grace period had expired.

   a.   What, if any, action on the bank's part constituted wrongful dishonor? *- Freezing Acct.*

   b.   Are punitive damages appropriate? *- Yes*

   8.   Francis A. Dziurak had a savings account with Chase Manhattan Bank containing about $18,000. Mario Staveris convinced him to enter a business relationship in which Dziurak would acquire a one-third interest in a restaurant for about $22,000. Pursuant to the parties' oral contract, Dziurak paid $5,000 down and requested that his bank issue an official check for the balance, payable to the order of Staveris. Mr. Monaco, an officer of the bank, advised Dziurak to have the check made payable to himself rather than

Staveris, and further advised him to seek the advice of an attorney, who would instruct him in how to indorse the check to Staveris. Dziurak assented, and a check for $17,000 was issued in Dziurak's name. His savings account was debited for the amount of the check.

Ignoring Monaco's advice to seek the advice of an attorney, Dziurak wrote on the back of the check, "Francis Dziurak. Pay to order Mario Staveris" and delivered the item to Staveris. Instead of depositing the check in the restaurant account as promised, Staveris appropriated the check for his own use.

 a. What do you think Monaco was trying to accomplish?

In the meantime, before the check had cleared, Dziurak sought the advice of counsel. The attorney advised him to try to get the bank to stop payment on the check. The bank refused, believing it could not do so absent a court order.

 b. Based on 4–403, what do you think of the attorney's advice?

 c. Under 4–303, how long would Dziurak have had to obtain a court order, to keep the bank from paying the check?

Assume Dziurak declined to get a court order, and the check was paid.

 d. If the bank had stopped payment, would Staveris have had a cause of action under 3–411?

 9. In May 1998, Linda Kressler, also known as Madam Linda, the "spiritual advisor" to Benito Dalessio's girlfriend Jennifer Lopez, informed Dalessio that Lopez could not marry her unless he paid Lopez's debts first. On Monday, November 9 of that year, Dalessio went to his bank, Republic National Bank of New York, and asked the bank to certify a personal check for $107,000 made payable to Kressler for the purpose of paying Lopez's debts. The following day, November 10, Dalessio returned to cash a check for $15,000. Noting Dalessio appeared nervous, the teller referred him to the branch manager. In the conversation that ensued, Dalessio informed the branch manager that Lopez and Kressler had visited Dalessio in his home to tell him that Lopez "would only be free to marry him if he paid her the funds requested." The branch manager notified Dalessio's sister, who was the co-owner of the account, and recommended that she have an attorney get a court order to stop payment on the certified check. On November 11, the courts and banks were closed for Veteran's Day. On November 12, Justice Irving S. Aronin signed a temporary restraining order directed to the bank, enjoining payment of the check. The bank received the court order prior to paying the check. It paid the check without responding to the order or appearing in court to contest the order, based on its assumption that it was legally required to pay the check, having certified it.

 a. Could Dalessio's sister simply have stopped payment on this check rather than seeking a court order? Why or why not?

 b. Was the bank correct that it was legally required to pay the check? 4–303 and Comment 1 may assist you in formulating your answer.

c.   Would your answer to the prior question change if Kressler held the check for three years before presenting it for payment? Why or why not?

d.   What is the significance of the fact that the courts and banks were closed for Veteran's Day on November 11?

10.   Courts have routinely held that a drawee/payor bank does not engage in wrongful dishonor when it charges non-accountholder payees a "presentment fee" to cash checks drawn on the bank, and refuses to cash such checks unless the fee is paid. The typical fee is about $10.

a.   Look carefully at 3–501. Is such action actually a dishonor under 3–502? Why or why not?

11.   In 1993, Doris Coyle opened a checking account with Regions Bank. The signature card for the account indicated that only she was authorized to draw on the account. She also established a number of certificates of deposit with Regions Bank. Mrs. Coyle was the sole owner of the CDs.

In late 1997, at age 90, Mrs. Coyle became seriously ill. She was in a coma for about three weeks, and her health was compromised for the rest of her life. At that time, her monthly income from two pensions and Social Security totaled about $1,000.

After Mrs. Coyle became ill, Walter and Laquana Massey insinuated themselves into her affairs and began to exercise influence over her. They were members of her extended family and convinced her of their business expertise. They began writing checks on her Regions Bank account and forging her signature. From the middle of 1999 until Mrs. Coyle died in January 2003, they wrote $257,000 of checks on her account. Not only was this volume of expenditure highly unusual for her account, but the complaint later filed on behalf of Mrs. Coyle's estate asserted that the items being purchased were also unlike anything she would have bought:

These . . . expenditures included large amounts for food even though Mrs. Coyle's diet was primarily made up of liquid supplements. The expenditures also included numerous checks for large individual amounts to Wal-Mart, electronic gaming stores, sporting goods stores, gourmet markets, liquor stores, restaurants, fast food, Harley Davidson motorcycle shops, academic tutoring, acne medication, and lingerie, to name only a few. Further, the Masseys used Coyle's funds to pay their MasterCard and Home Depot charge accounts. In 2002 alone, $16,700.00 was paid from Coyle's . . . account to the Masseys' personal Sears MasterCard charge account. The Masseys also paid their utilities and their son's truck insurance from Coyle's account. Payments were also made from the Regions account to a McRae's/Saks credit card for purchases of jewelry, watches and menswear by and for the benefit of the Masseys. [The Bank] participated with the Masseys and honored those payments from Coyle's account. The vast majority, if not all, of these expenditures were for the Masseys' personal benefit.

The Masseys ultimately overdrew Mrs. Coyle's account. Regions Bank permitted the overdrafts, and charged fees accordingly. The bank continued to pay checks drawn on Mrs. Coyle's account even after it received notice of her death. The bank also permitted the Masseys to cash in several of Mrs. Coyle's CDs, which resulted in penalties for earlier withdrawal, lower yields, and lower interest rates being paid on the CDs. At no time did Regions Bank question the Masseys' authority to take these actions. You may assume that, at all times, statements were mailed to the address of record for Mrs. Coyle.

a. Would 3–404, 3–405, or 3–406 apply here?

b. Were the forged checks and the checks causing overdrafts properly payable? If not, should the bank be responsible for paying them?

c. How, if at all, does 4–405 affect the bank's liability in this case?

12. Ama Afiriyie opened a checking account, savings account, and secured credit card account with Bank of America. In February of 2007, she received a letter from Bank of America telling her that her credit card was being "graduated" to unsecured status. On March 8, 2007, she received a check for $300 from Bank of America drawn upon a Bank of America corporate account with an attached stub indicating that the check represented a refund of her $300 security deposit for the credit card. The letter stated, "Enclosed you will find a check which represents a credit balance refund from *your* Bank of America *account*." (emphasis added). She called the toll-free number on the stub to learn more about the check and whether it was "good." The representative told her that "the check was valid and could be cashed at any [Bank of America] branch."

Later that day, she went to a Bank of America branch in a local supermarket, about 30 minutes before she needed to pick her daughters up from a nearby daycare facility. She was called to a teller's window, and teller swiped her bank card. She handed over the card, along with her identification and the check.

When the teller ran the check through the MICR reading device, a warning came up, advising her to seek additional verification before completing the transaction. Thus, she took the check to the bank manager. When the bank manager pulled up the account on which the check was drawn, she found a large number of small checks for just a few cents each, so she found the $300 amount of this check suspicious even though she stated that nothing on the face of the check itself appeared suspicious. The manager then spoke with the customer, asked her where she had gotten the check, and told her that "Bank of America does not issue checks like this."

Upon hearing Afiriyie's explanation of how she received the check, the manager then called the secured credit card department, which advised her that "the customer never should have received this check" because her account had been open just a few months and there was no record that she had graduated to an unsecured account.

The manager advised Afiriyie that she would not be able to cash—or return—the check that day because she could not verify the check. The manager's story and Afiriyie's story differ, with each accusing the other of becoming loud and angry. The manager then retreated to her office and called the local police department, advising them of a female trying to cash a fraudulent check. She was taken to the police station, placed in a holding cell, handcuffed, photographed, fingerprinted, questioned, and charged. She was released after about two and a half hours, after an officer advised her that "it had all been a mistake."

a. Would Regulation CC have permitted a hold of any kind on this check?

b. Is this wrongful dishonor? If so, would Afiriyie have a cause of action for wrongful dishonor?

c. What kind of legal theory might Afiriyie employ in this case? What kind of damages would you expect to see awarded?

13. Chapter 6 introduced the "payable through" draft. 4–106(a) provides that the bank on which such an item is drawn is considered a "collecting bank" within the meaning of 4–202 rather than a drawee/payor bank.

a. What policy considerations support this designation?

In answering, consult 4–103(e), 4–302, and 4–402(b) to see why this classification makes a difference. Also consider whether the bank is in control of whether it meets the "midnight rule" and "midnight deadline" on a "payable through" draft.

14. F&M law firm received what appeared to be an official Wachovia Bank cashier's check from a new client, in the amount of $225,351. The check was payable to F&M. F&M deposited the check which, it was advised, represented partial payment of a debt that another entity owed to the client, into its account with Wells Fargo Bank. Four days later, the client asked F&M to transfer a portion of the funds by wire transfer to an account in South Korea. Two days later, the client asked that a portion of the funds be sent to an account in Canada. The transfers had a combined value of slightly less than the cashier's check. Before making either transfer, F&M accessed its Wells Fargo account on line and confirmed that the "available funds" balance could cover both transfers.

The afternoon of the second transfer, the Federal Reserve dishonored the check as counterfeit. Wells Fargo phoned F&M, advised them of the situation, reversed the credit to F&M's account, and transferred funds from an F&M money market account to cover the wire transfer. F&M asked the bank to cancel the wire transfers, but it could not do so because the funds had already been withdrawn.

a. Could the depositary bank have placed a Regulation CC hold on these funds? Why or why not? Consult the Regulation CC materials in this chapter, as well as 12 CFR 229.10(c), and 229.13(b) and (h), in answering this question.

b. Can F&M rely upon the "available funds" balance in its account to support an argument that the bank had represented that the funds had been collected and thus were not susceptible to charge-back? Why or why not?

c. What Code section or sections would you cite to support Wells Fargo's actions in notifying F&M, reversing the account credit, and transferring funds from another F&M account to cover the transfers?

CHAPTER 9

LIABILITY UNDER ARTICLES 3 AND 4

■ ■ ■

Negotiable instruments can give rise to contract, tort, or warranty liability, just as each kind of liability can exist under the underlying contract.

A. CONTRACT LIABILITY UNDER ARTICLES 3 AND 4

A negotiable instrument is a contract. Under **3–401**, when a drawer signs a check, a maker signs a note, or an indorser signs either a check or a note, that party takes on contractual responsibility for the instrument. In the case of the maker of a note, this means that he or she promises to pay the note when due. In the case of the drawer of a check or indorser of a note or check, this means that he or she promises to pay the instrument if it is dishonored. Thus, contract liability under Articles 3 and 4 is relevant when a demand for payment of an instrument is made. There are two kinds of contract liability under Articles 3 and 4—primary and secondary liability. Primary liability, by definition, has no condition precedent; secondary liability is subject to some condition precedent. Normally, the conditions precedent for secondary liability include presentment to the party with primary liability, dishonor, and notice of dishonor. Only once the party with primary liability does not pay, does secondary liability come into play.

1. PRIMARY AND SECONDARY LIABILITY

Primary and secondary liability function differently for notes and drafts. Starting with a note, **3–412** establishes the expectation that the maker (referred to in **3–412** as the "issuer") will pay the note when it matures. Thus, the maker has primary liability for the note. All indorsers of that same note have secondary liability under **3–415(a)**. This means that, if the note is presented to the maker and dishonored, any indorser may be called upon to pay the note. In the following chart, the maker takes on primary liability for the note at issuance and the payee assumes secondary liability when it indorses.

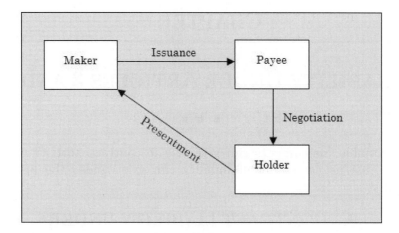

Thus, if the holder presents the note to the maker, who does not or cannot pay, the holder can require the payee to honor the instrument. Paying the instrument on the maker's behalf gives the payee a cause of action against the maker under **3–412**.

In the case of a check, at the time of issuance the drawer has secondary liability, meaning that the drawer will be asked to pay the instrument only if it has been presented to the drawee for payment and dishonored. **3–414(b)** establishes the secondary liability of drawers. Comment 2 provides that "[t]he liability of the drawer of an unaccepted [check] is treated as a primary liability." This somewhat confusing language is meant to capture the practical reality that the drawer of a check is the party who has the greatest moral responsibility for the instrument.

Any indorser of this check also takes on secondary liability, under **3–415(a)**. In the graphic below, this would be the payee, depositary bank, and Federal Reserve bank. Like the drawer, they will not be called upon to pay the instrument unless and until the instrument is presented to the drawee and dishonored. Indorsers' secondary liability is more limited than the drawer's. First, as **3–415(e)** states, the liability of an indorser is discharged thirty days after indorsement, while the drawer is liable under **3–414(b)** for the full limitations period as set forth in **3–118**. Second, as **3–415(c)** provides, an indorser's liability is discharged if **3–503** requires notice of dishonor and it is not given. By contrast, as explained in Chapter 8, drawers of checks are not entitled to notice of dishonor.

Thus, at the time of issuance, the drawer has secondary liability on the check and no other party has any liability at all. Each indorser takes on secondary liability when it indorses the check. This means that, until the check is presented for payment, no party has primary liability on the instrument. If the drawee accepts the item for payment, it takes on primary liability, and the secondary liability of the drawer and all indorsers is discharged. **3–413**, **3–414(c)**, and **3–415(d)** provide these rules.

Conversely, under **3–408**, unless and until the drawee accepts the check, it will have no contract liability for the item. It may, however, face liability to the drawer for wrongful dishonor under **4–402** if it refuses to pay an instrument that is properly payable within the meaning of **4–401**.

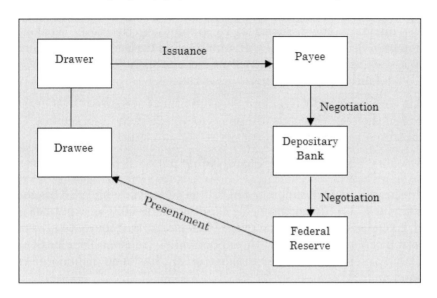

Putting these pieces together in the graphic above, if the check is presented to the drawee and dishonored, the drawee may face liability to the drawer under **4–402** if the instrument was properly payable and wrongfully dishonored, but the drawee will not face liability to the presenting party (in this case, the Federal Reserve) or to any indorser. The Federal Reserve may then call upon the drawer pursuant to **3–414(b)** or the payee or depositary bank as prior indorsers under **3–415(a)** to pay the instrument. If the depositary bank is required to pay the instrument, it may seek to recover from the payee as a prior indorser or from the drawer, using the same code sections identified above. If the payee is required to pay the instrument, it may seek to recover from the drawer under **3–414(b)**. If the drawer is required to pay, it cannot recover from any other party, which makes sense given the language of **3–414** Comment 2 quoted above.

3–415(b) provides that instruments can be indorsed "without recourse." This language, explained below, indicates that the indorser refuses to accept secondary liability for the instrument.

2.   INDORSEMENT WITHOUT RECOURSE

Indorsement without recourse allows an indorser to escape contractual exposure, but will not entirely insulate the indorser from liability. Other remaining potential sources of liability, such as warranty and tort, are discussed later in this chapter. *Hartford Life Insurance Co. v. Title*

Guarantee Co., 520 F.2d 1170, 1174–75 (D.C. 1975), explains how contractual liability can be disclaimed, yet other forms of liability may remain:

> A "without recourse" [i]ndorsement is a qualified [i]ndorsement; it does not eliminate all obligations owed by the transferor of an instrument to his transferee. By [i]ndorsing the note "without recourse," [the payee] still warranted to [its transferee] that it had no knowledge of any fact which would establish the existence of a good defense against the note.

The practical effectiveness of a "without recourse" indorsement depends on the transferee's willingness to accept such indorsement. Often, the transferee will refuse.

3.   DISHONOR AND NOTICE OF DISHONOR

One prerequisite of indorser liability is notice of dishonor. This concept was introduced briefly in the prior chapter. As **3–503(b)** explains, notice may be given by any person and given in any form, whether verbal, written, or electronic. The key is that the notice must "reasonably identif[y] the instrument and indicate[ ] that the instrument has been dishonored or has not been paid or accepted."

Brannons Number Seven, Inc. v. Phelps, 665 P.2d 860, 861–62 (Okla. Civ. App. 1983), explains the connection between indorser liability and notice of dishonor. Robert Phelps worked for Jet Service Company, which issued payroll checks to him totaling about $800. Brannons Number Seven, a grocery store, cashed the checks after Phelps indorsed them. When Brannons presented the checks to the drawee, they were dishonored for lack of funds. Brannons sought to recover from Phelps. In finding that Phelps would not be liable unless he received notice of dishonor, the court held as follows:

> An indorser's liability is contingent and does not become fixed unless and until the holder complies with the requirement of notice of dishonor. This notice is an element of Brannons' cause of action, and Brannons thus has the burden of proving that it gave notice.

Under some circumstances, a failure to give notice may be excused, or an indorser may be deemed to have notice of the dishonor. For example, **3–504(b)** provides that notice of dishonor is excused when the instrument provides that it may be enforced without notice of dishonor. Likewise, if the indorser has already received information that the instrument will not be paid, the indorser will be deemed to have notice of dishonor, such that no further notice will be required. The standard for the kind of information that will suffice is, however, a stringent one. In *Hane v. Exten*, 259 A.2d 290 (Md. 1969), the holder of a note that the maker had dishonored sought to recover from an indorser based on **3–415**. The indorser defended on the ground that it had not received notice of dishonor. The holder claimed its failure to provide notice should be excused because the indorser knew the maker was insolvent and therefore "ha[d] no reason to expect . . . that the instrument [would] be paid." In rejecting this argument, the court held that "[a]n indorser's knowledge of the maker's insolvency, standing alone, will not excuse the giving of notice of dishonor" and does not establish that the indorser "knew or should have known that the note would not be paid."

Because dishonor triggers secondary liability, it is important to understand when an item has been dishonored. Promissory notes payable at a definite time (as opposed to those payable on demand, which are less common) are considered dishonored when they are not paid on the day of presentment, if presentment is required, or the day on which they become payable, whichever is later. These rules are found in **3–502(a)(2)** and **(3)**. Checks that are presented "over the counter" for payment are dishonored, according to **3–502(b)(2)**, if not paid when presented. This makes sense because checks are considered "demand items" that are, as the name would suggest, payable on demand. Checks that are presented through Article 4's check-collection process are considered dishonored if timely return or timely notice of dishonor is given under **4–301** or **4–302**. This rule is found in **3–502(b)(1)**. **3–502** contains other rules applicable to "demand notes" and non-check drafts, as well, but those are beyond the scope of these materials.

4.   DISCHARGE BY PAYMENT

A party will sometimes claim he or she has already paid the debt an instrument represents and thus should not have to pay the instrument. For example, the maker of a note might claim that he or she has already paid off the loan the note represented and thus should not be required to pay the note. This concept, called discharge by payment, is one of the forms of discharge addressed in **3–601**. **3–601** also covers other forms of discharge, such as discharge in bankruptcy. Discharge by payment, unlike discharge in bankruptcy, is ineffective against a holder in due course. This means that a party may have to pay twice if he or she makes payment to a person not entitled to payment, and a holder in due course produces the instrument and demands payment. In *Groover v. Peters*, 202 S.E.2d 413, 414 (Ga. 1973), the court addressed the prospect of double liability, as follows:

> The maker of a negotiable note . . . must determine at the time of payment whether the payee is the holder of the instrument or the authorized agent of the holder in order to protect himself against liability for double payment. If the original grantee has assigned the instrument to another, who is a holder in due course, the

burden rests with the maker to determine same and pay only the holder or his authorized agent. . . .

The long and short of the matter is that the borrower must be as careful in repaying the debt as the lender presumptively was in making the loan.

A party can protect itself against double liability by insisting that someone demanding payment either produce the instrument or, if it cannot do so, be willing to provide a surety bond or other protection in case another claimant later produces the instrument.

5.   TENDER OF PAYMENT

If the maker of a note or drawer of a check has already tendered payment, which was refused, the question becomes whether it should be required to tender payment again. **3–603** describes how tender of payment affects liability. Note that this situation can be considered the opposite of dishonor: rather than the maker of a note or drawer of a check *refusing to pay*, the maker or drawer is *offering to pay*, and the offer is being refused. If tender of payment is made to a person entitled to enforce the instrument and is refused, the liability of any indorser or accommodation party (a concept introduced later in this chapter) will be discharged entirely, and the liability of a drawer or maker will be discharged insofar as any after-accruing interest is concerned.

Thus, for example, if the maker of a $10,000 promissory note bearing a 10% per annum interest rate tenders payment in full to the holder of the note, who refuses payment because he or she wishes for the note to continue to accrue interest, the holder cannot later demand payment of the note from any indorser of the note or any accommodation party. The holder can later demand that the maker of the note pay the principal amount plus any interest that had accrued as of the tender date, but will not be entitled to any after-accruing interest. Whether tender has occurred will be a matter of state common law. In *Davis v. Dillard National Bank*, 50 UCC. Rep. Serv. 2d 877 (M.D. N.C. 2003), the court applied North Carolina law and held that "[m]erely offering to produce payment or showing a readiness to perform is insufficient to establish tender; actual production of payment is necessary."

6.   PRESENTMENT

Because the secondary contract liability of drawers and indorsers does not come into play until the item is presented and dishonored, it is important to understand the rules for presentment set forth in **3–501**. Presentment is a demand for payment or acceptance of an instrument, made by or on behalf of the holder or someone else entitled to enforce the instrument. In the case of a check, presentment is made to a drawee; in the case of a note, presentment is made to the maker. Presentment may include verification of the presenter's identity. For example, the drawee of a check may properly refuse to pay if the presenting party does not provide reasonable identification to prove it is the party entitled to payment. Until presentment is made, and unless presentment is excused under **3–504**, a refusal to pay an instrument is not dishonor.

7. ACCORD AND SATISFACTION

Up to this point, this chapter has addressed the contract liability arising under Articles 3 and 4. However, the negotiable instrument is not only itself a contract, but often also represents payment pursuant to some underlying contract. For example, a check may be issued to pay for repairs made to a car. After the check is written, the drawer may decide the repairs were unsatisfactory and that the payee therefore breached the contract to repair the car, while the payee may dispute this contention.

The accord-and-satisfaction doctrine found in **3–311** provides a common way of settling contract disputes. Under this doctrine, tender and payment of a check presented in full satisfaction of a disputed debt, if handled correctly and in good faith, discharges the debt. Thus, in our example involving the car, the drawer might stop payment on the *first* check representing payment in full for the car repairs, and then issue a *second*, smaller check representing what he or she believes is a fair price to pay for the repairs given that they were not entirely satisfactory. This second check implicates the accord-and-satisfaction doctrine. If the payee cashes or deposits the accord-and-satisfaction check, then the drawer's obligation to pay for the car repairs is discharged, and the dispute has been resolved without any need to involve the court system.

Another common example is an insurance settlement check. The parties may dispute fault and the value of the claim, but if the insurance company tenders a check in final settlement of the matter and the claimant cashes or deposits the check, the claim is discharged. As the court held in *McMahon Food Corp. v. Burger Dairy Co.*, 103 F.3d 1307 (7th Cir. 1996), "[t]he purpose of **3–311** is to encourage informal dispute resolution by full-satisfaction checks. Its drafters intended to codify the common law of accord and satisfaction with some minor variations to reflect modern business conditions."

Solomon v. American National Bank, 612 N.E.2d 3, 4–7 (Ill. App. 1st Dist. 1993), shows that a drawer must act carefully when preparing and tendering a check in satisfaction of a disputed debt, to ensure that cashing or depositing the check will have the desired effect. In that case, a landlord tendered a check to his former tenants for $452.33 bearing the legend, "Security deposit pd. in full." The tenants' original security deposit had been $1,350. The tenants crossed out the legend and cashed the check, then sought to recover the balance of the security deposit as well as certain state statutory damages for the landlord's delay in refunding the full deposit owed. When the landlord defended on the ground that cashing the check had extinguished the tenants' claim, the court held as follows in rejecting this argument:

> To constitute an accord and satisfaction there must be: (1) a *bona-fide* dispute; (2) an unliquidated sum; (3) consideration; (4) a shared and mutual intent to compromise the claim; and (5) execution of the agreement. An accord and satisfaction is contractual in nature; thus, the intent of the parties is of central importance. The debtor must show that the creditor intended to accept the payment of less than what is claimed as full satisfaction; otherwise, the payment operates only as a discharge of the amount paid. To determine the intent of the parties, it is necessary to examine the language of the relevant documents.
>
> The language of the checks the landlord sent to the tenants clearly refers to plaintiffs' security deposits being paid in full. However, this language does not establish that the landlord intended that cashing the checks would extinguish the plaintiffs' claims for [the] landlord's failure to refund the security deposit within the time prescribed by law.

The landlord should have included a letter making it clear that the check was being given in full satisfaction of a disputed debt. Language such as, "This check is being tendered as full accord and satisfaction of your disputed claim for a refund of your security deposit" would suffice. (He might even have added, "Please note that cashing this check will bar any further claim.") Had he included this kind of language, then the tenants' action in crossing out the words "Security deposit pd. in full" would have had no effect, and the landlord would have prevailed. Upon receipt of a clearly marked "full satisfaction" check, a payee can protect its interest in pursuing the entire disputed sum only by refusing the check.

In determining whether a check is tendered in settlement of a bona fide dispute, the court must examine whether the parties in good faith disagreed as to the amount owed—or even whether any amount was owed—at the time when the check was tendered. As the court held in *Hunter-McDonald, Inc. v. Edison Foard, Inc.*, 579 S.E.2d 490 (Ct. App. N.C. 2003), it is not sufficient to show that the parties disagreed as to the amount owed later, when a lawsuit was filed. In addition, although some courts have held otherwise in error (*see Johnston v. First Union National Bank*, 271 Va. 239 (2006)), a party's simple error as to the amount due, even if the error is an honest one, does not suffice to establish the kind of "bona fide dispute" that can be settled via accord and satisfaction.

Parties can contract around the accord-and-satisfaction doctrine. In *Eaton v. Citibank (South Dakota)*, 73 UCC Rep.Serv.2d 107 (M.D. Pa. 2010), the court considered a $110 check that a Citibank cardholder alleged she had submitted as full satisfaction of her account obligation to Citibank.

Setting aside the question of whether the check was tendered in settlement of a bona fide dispute, the court noted that the cardholder agreement included the following language: "We can accept late or partial payment, as well as payments that reflect 'paid in full' . . . without losing any of our rights under the Agreement." Such language, the court held, established dispositively that the check could not be used for accord and satisfaction.

The following case provides an example of a check that was not tendered in satisfaction of a good-faith dispute, and also explains why **3–311** was added to Article 3 in 1993.

ALPINE HAVEN PROPERTY OWNERS ASSOCIATION, INC. V. DEPTULA

830 A.2d 78 (Vt. 2003)

AMESTOY, C.J., DOOLEY, JOHNSON, SKOGLUND, JJ., AND GIBSON III, J.

¶ 1. Defendants Edward Deptula and Bertrand and Joseph Emmett, homeowners in the Alpine Haven development, appeal a summary judgment order to pay three years of overdue fees, plus interest and costs, for road maintenance and other services rendered by plaintiff Alpine Haven Property Owners Association, Inc. (the Association). Defendants argue that the trial court erred by . . . (3) dismissing defendants' accord and satisfaction defense and consumer fraud counterclaim; and (4) improperly granting the Association summary judgment. We affirm in part, reverse in part, and remand.

¶ 2. This case began as a collection action filed by the Association against a small group of homeowners, including defendants on appeal, for fees owed for three annual assessment periods (from November 1, 1996 to October 31, 1999). The dispute, however, goes back much further than that. The Alpine Haven development was founded in the 1960s and, at the time of this dispute, included approximately eighty units, mostly chalets. Pursuant to deed covenants, the original developer, Alpine Haven, Inc., provided defendants with garbage removal and street lighting, and maintained roads within the development, in return for a "reasonable annual fee." The developer later constructed a swimming pool, tennis courts, and other recreational facilities to which individual homeowners could subscribe for a separate fee.

¶ 3. In the late 1970s, fees for deeded services began to increase, leading to more than ten lawsuits between the developer and certain homeowners over the reasonableness of the fees. In one of those actions, Deptula sought a declaratory judgment in Franklin Superior Court that the developer had breached the deed covenants and that the fees assessed by Alpine Haven, Inc. over the previous five years were excessive. In its 1992 decision, the court held that a common scheme existed for the maintenance of street lighting and rights-of-way, and thus Deptula was obligated to contribute rateably to these services, although he was not obligated to pay for optional services such as garbage removal and private driveway plowing. The court found the $1,200 per year charged by the developer to all lot owners was reasonable. However, the court allowed Deptula to subtract the average costs of driveway plowing and garbage removal, since he did not receive those services, and found that the fair and equitable fee for the remaining services was $1,050 per year. For future years, the court required that the percentage increase assessed against Deptula must be equal to the percentage increase for all other lot owners in the community, and warned that Deptula could become liable for litigation expenses if he refused to pay. The litigation continued, however, and in 1996, in one of six small claims actions between Deptula and Alpine Haven, Inc., the Orleans Superior Court ordered Deptula to pay $1,102.50 per year—a five percent increase over the 1992 superior court judgment. This increased amount was also assessed against all other lot owners in the community receiving the same services.

¶ 4. That same year a majority of the community's homeowners formed the Alpine Haven Property Owners Association, Inc., and contracted with the soon-to-retire developer to purchase and assume ownership of the development's common lands, roads, and recreational facilities and to provide all deeded and recreational services. Although membership was initially granted to all homeowners in the development, some homeowners, including defendants, opted out of the Association. As a result, during the period in dispute (November 1, 1996 to October 31, 1999), nonmembers were provided deeded services only—garbage removal, street lighting, and road maintenance and snow removal—while members were provided all deeded services plus access to recreational facilities. Nonmembers were billed a base fee as established by the 1992 and 1996 Deptula judgments, plus an annual increase based on the Consumer Price Index, and, since 1998, a pro rata share of payments on a Federal Emergency Management Agency (FEMA) loan to repair flood-damaged community roads. Members were billed a pro rata share of all expenses remaining after the nonmembers' fee assessment was subtracted from the annual budget.

¶ 5. Since the Association took over on November 1, 1996, defendants have refused to pay the full assessment. In 1997, the Association sued to collect, initiating this case. Defendants counterclaimed and moved for summary judgment, alleging, inter alia, unreasonably high fees, accord and satisfaction, and violation of the Vermont Consumer Fraud Act. . . .

* * *

¶ 18. . . . Deptula asserts accord and satisfaction with respect to one of the three years at issue in this litigation. For that year, he sent a check to the Association treasurer in the amount of $278.59. The check was accompanied by a letter stating that he refused to pay the billed amount because the Association provided "no substantiation" that the billed amount reflected the actual cost of road maintenance for his lot. The Association deposited the check after writing "without prejudice" on it. Under *Frangiosa v. Kapoukranidis*, 160 Vt. 237, 244, 627 A.2d 351, 355 (1993), the reservation of rights language the Association added to the check would have avoided defendant's accord and satisfaction defense. However, the law was changed by the Legislature's addition of § **3–311** to the Uniform Commercial Code. With respect to payments "by use of instrument," the law of accord and satisfaction is now governed by § **3–311**.

¶ 19. Under 9A V.S.A. § **3–311(a)**, accord and satisfaction may apply if the person against whom the claim is asserted acts "in good faith" in tendering the instrument in full satisfaction of the claim and does so with respect to a claim that is "unliquidated or subject to a bona fide dispute." *Id*. § **3–311(a)(i)**, **(ii)**. At least in part, the section is intended to codify the common law of accord and satisfaction. *Id*. § **3–311, cmt. 3**. Our common law has required a bona fide dispute as to the amount owed. See *Adams v. B.P.C., Inc.*, 143 Vt. 308, 309–10, 466 A.2d 1170, 1171 (1983). In *Adams*, this Court quoted *Loizeaux Builders Supply Co. v. Donald B. Ludwig Co.*, 144 N.J.Super. 556, 366 A.2d 721, 726 (Law Div. 1976), as follows: "While it is not necessary that the dispute or controversy should be well-founded, it is necessary that it should be in good faith. Without an honest dispute, an agreement to take a lesser amount in payment of a liquidated claim is without consideration and void." *Id*. at 311, 466 A.2d at 1172. "Good faith" under the UCC means "honesty in fact and the observance of reasonable commercial standards of fair dealing." 9A V.S.A. § 3–103(a)(4). [UCC **3–103(a)(6)**].

¶ 20. We conclude that the trial court had sufficient undisputed facts before it to find that Deptula did not act in good faith in disputing the assessment bill for 1996–97, and that the bill was not subject to a bona fide dispute. Deptula had litigated his arguments that the assessment amounts were excessive and unfair in the 1992 action and lost, and thereafter lost in successive years when the developer was required to sue him to obtain payment of the assessment. By the time that Deptula sent the check for which he claims accord and satisfaction, he no longer was raising a "bona fide dispute" over the amount owed or acting "in good faith." We thus reject his defense of accord and satisfaction.

Thus, had Deptula's check met the requirements of the accord-and-satisfaction doctrine under **3–311**, the "without prejudice" language added by the Association would have had no effect, and any further claim by the Association would have been barred. The same is true of the tenants' crossing out the "full satisfaction" legend in the *Solomon* case discussed earlier in this section.

The following section addresses contract liability of a completely different kind – that of parties who sign an instrument only for the purpose of guaranteeing another party's debt. These are called accommodation parties.

8.   LIABILITY OF ACCOMMODATION PARTIES

3–419 describes the rights and responsibilities of accommodation parties. An accommodation party is sometimes referred to as a secondary obligor. Despite the similarity in vocabulary, a secondary obligor is not the same as a person who has secondary liability. Secondary liability refers to any liability that is subject to a condition precedent and was discussed earlier in this chapter; a secondary obligor under **3–103(a)(17)** is a party to an instrument who, if called upon to pay the instrument, has recourse against another party. The party against whom the secondary obligor has recourse is called the "principal obligor," as defined in **3–103(a)(11)**.

An accommodation party is a party serving as a surety for the principal obligor's indebtedness who thus agrees to pay the debt if the primary obligor fails to do so. In the suretyship context, the principal obligor is called the "accommodated" party and the secondary obligor is called the "accommodation" party. One example of an accommodation transaction is a parent co-signing a promissory note for a child.

As an aside, because you now know that an indorser, if called upon to pay an instrument that has been dishonored, has recourse against the issuer or drawer of that instrument pursuant to **3–412** or **3–414**, as well as recourse against prior indorsers, you now understand that an indorser has secondary liability under **3–415** and can also be considered a secondary obligor under **3–103(a)(17)**. This is true even if the indorser is not an accommodation party. This is further explained in **3–605** Comment 3: "Unless an indorser signs without recourse, the indorser's liability under **3–415(a)** is functionally similar to that of a guarantor of payment." By contrast, the drawer of a check has secondary liability but does not qualify as a secondary obligor under **3–103(a)(17)**. This is because the drawer of a check, if called upon to pay pursuant to **3–414(b)**, has no such right of recourse. This reality is captured in the previously-quoted language of **3–414** Comment 2: "The liability of the drawer of an accepted draft is treated as a primary liability."

The main distinguishing characteristic of an accommodation party is that such party receives no direct benefit from the transaction. The parent who serves as a co-signer for a child on an educational loan is an accommodation party because he or she does not get the direct benefit of the transaction (the education); instead, the child does.

An accommodation relationship requires three contracts:

(1) An underlying contract between the accommodated party and the creditor. This is the central contract motivating the transaction. In our example, this would be the contract between the child and the lender pursuant to which the child receives an educational loan.

(2) The contract of guaranty between the accommodation party and the creditor. This is the contract by which the accommodation party takes on contractual liability to the accommodated party's creditor, to guarantee payment of the accommodated party's debt. In our example, this would be the contract between the parent and the lender pursuant to which the parent guarantees the loan.

(3) The contract for reimbursement between the accommodation party and the accommodated party. This contract allows the accommodation party to recover from the accommodated party if required to pay that party's debt. In our example, this would be a contract between the parent and child. Especially when the accommodated and accommodation parties are family members, this third contract may not have been formalized.

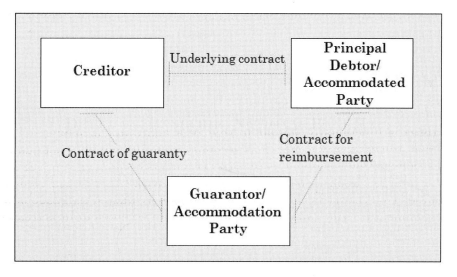

An accommodation relationship is sometimes referred to as a guaranty. The following is a typical guaranty, from *Langeveld v. L.R.Z.H. Corp.*, 376 A.2d 931 (N.J. 1977):

> To induce the said JOHN P. LANGEVELD to accept the above note, the undersigned hereby guaranty performance of all obligations of the obligors under the note and under the mortgage securing the indebtedness described in the note. The said undersigned guarantors agree to be principally liable on the indebtedness jointly and severally, and further agree to their obligation jointly and severally without the necessity of presentment, demand, or notice of dishonor.
>
> The undersigned guarantors agree to pay the tenor of this instrument notwithstanding that [the primary obligor] may effectuate an assignment for the benefit of creditors, be declared a bankrupt, be discharged from bankruptcy, or otherwise be excused, except by payment, of the debt.
>
> /s/ Joseph A. Higgins, Sr.
>
> /s/ Albin H. Rothe
>
> /s/ Louis J. Zoghby

3–419(b) provides that "[a]n accommodation party may sign the instrument as maker, drawer, acceptor, or indorser and, subject to subsection (d), is obliged to pay the instrument in the capacity in which the accommodation party signs." Often, the accommodation party signs as a co-maker (as in the example above involving the parent and child) or an indorser. If an accommodation party signs as a co-maker, the accommodation party takes on primary liability along with the accommodated party. The *Langeveld* guaranty language above requires Higgins, Rothe, and Zoghby to take on primary liability along with whoever the maker of the "above note" was. We see this in the language in which they "agree to be principally liable on the indebtedness." If the accommodation party signs as an indorser, the accommodation party takes on secondary liability. This kind of indorsement is referred to as an anomalous indorsement. This term is defined in **3–205(d)** and was introduced in Chapter 7.

3–419(d) allows an accommodation party to guarantee collection rather than guaranteeing payment, thus taking on somewhat less potential liability.

9. RIGHTS AND DEFENSES OF ACCOMMODATION PARTIES

If an accommodation party pays an item, he or she has the right to be reimbursed by the accommodated party. In addition, he or she has the right under **3–305(d)** to assert many of the accommodated party's rights against the creditor. This right is called subrogation. The accommodation party may not, however, assert the defenses of infancy, insolvency, or lack of legal capacity. This distinction makes sense, as concern about the existence of these particular defenses is frequently the very reason why a creditor insisted upon an accommodation party. In the parent-and-child example above, the educational lender likely would insist that the parent co-sign the loan due to concerns about the child's youth and lack of solvency.

3–605 addresses discharge of secondary obligors, including accommodation parties. A creditor's release of a principal obligor (such as an accommodated party) will generally also release the secondary obligor (such as an accommodation party). Thus, in our example involving the parent and child, if the lender forgives the child's educational debt, then the lender would not (absent the parties' agreement to the contrary) be able to recover from the parent, either. **3–605(b)** addresses how an extension of time to the principal obligor will affect the liability of the secondary obligor, and **3–605(c)** addresses the effect that other modifications to the agreement between the principal obligor and the creditor will have on the secondary obligor. A secondary obligor normally is not discharged by an extension of time because such a change generally benefits the secondary obligor by making it more likely that the primary obligor will be able to pay. When the agreement is modified in other ways, such as by a change in interest rate or other terms, the secondary obligor is more likely to be able to show that the changes would otherwise cause the secondary obligor a loss and thus be discharged to the extent of such loss.

When the secondary obligor has guaranteed an obligation secured by an interest in collateral, **3–605(d)** provides that the secondary obligor will be released from liability when the creditor (or other person entitled to enforce the instrument) impairs the value of the collateral held as security. The release operates to the extent of the impairment. *Langeveld v. L.R.Z.H. Corp.*, 376 A.2d 931, 934 (N.J. 1977), explains the policy behind this rule, using the terms "principal debtor" and "surety" in place of "accommodated party" and "accommodation party":

> The doctrine is an equitable one, designed to protect the surety's right of subrogation. Upon paying the debt, the surety is, as a matter of law, subrogated to all the creditor's rights against the principal debtor and is entitled to all benefits derivable from any security of the principal debtor that may be in the creditor's hands. The rule forbidding impairment of collateral has as its chief aim the protection of these potential benefits made available through subrogation.

3–605 Comment 7 provides an example of impairment of an interest in collateral.

As **3–605** Comment 2 states, "[l]ike the law of suretyship and guaranty, Section **3–605** provides secondary obligors with defenses that are not available to other parties to instruments." Several of these defenses are explained above. Even so, it is common for secondary obligors to waive these defenses by contract. Accommodation parties who waive their suretyship defenses may later regret doing so. In *Agribank, FCB v. Whitlock*, 621 N.E.2d 967, 975–76 (Ill. App. 4th Dist. 1993), the court rejected an argument that a common waiver provision allowing the lender to pursue the accommodation parties even if it released the accommodated party from liability, violated the UCC's good-faith provisions. The accommodation parties claimed the waiver showed bad faith because the lender knew the parties intended that the accommodated party, rather than the accommodation parties, would repay the loan obligation. In upholding the waiver, the court held as follows:

> We do not believe we can construe the duty of good faith imposed by the Code to prevent the lender from inserting a provision in the instrument or accompanying documents, when the use of such a provision has been expressly sanctioned by the Code. Rather, we believe the effect of the good-faith obligation in the context of the advance consent to release the accommodated party, is to place the obligation upon the lender to act in good faith when releasing the accommodated party.

> As a practical matter in most accommodation situations, the accommodation party intends only to lend his credit so the accommodated party may obtain a loan. Both the accommodated party and accommodation maker intend, at the time of the signing of the contract, that the accommodated party will make the payments of the loan. The lender who is aware one individual is an accommodation maker may be cognizant that the accommodation maker merely intends to help the accommodated party obtain a loan, but has no expectation that he (the accommodation maker) will be called upon to satisfy the indebtedness. . . .

> While many accommodation parties may be surprised to learn the consent provisions in the instrument or accompanying documents essentially preclude them from asserting suretyship defenses and render little difference between their liability and the liability of the accommodated party, such consent provisions are sanctioned by the Code and routinely utilized by lenders.

It can be useful to advise a client who has expressed interest in serving as an accommodation party for a child, friend, or business partner to consider guaranteeing collection rather than payment and to also consider not waiving the **3–605** protections.

As **3–116** shows, parties signing in the same capacity, such as the co-makers of a note, are jointly and severally liable with one another, unless the instrument provides otherwise. In the example of a note signed by two co-makers, a holder can recover the full amount of the item from either. Once the holder has recovered from either co-maker, the co-makers' rights against one another depend on whether either is serving as an accommodation party for the other.

Assuming neither party is an accommodation party for the other, **3–116(b)** applies and, unless the parties have agreed otherwise, the co-maker who was required to pay can seek contribution from the other, such that each pays a proportional share. Thus, if the amount of the note was $10,000, the holder could recover the full amount from either co-maker, who could then recover $5,000 from the other.

However, if the co-maker who was required to pay is an accommodation party for the other, as in our example involving the parent and child, then **3–419(f)** applies. In such a case, the accommodation party has a right of reimbursement against the accommodated party. Thus, assuming the child is solvent and available for suit, the parent can recover the full amount of the note from the child. As a practical matter, a parent may simply pay his or her child's debt without seeking reimbursement.

Although the UCC generally allows a creditor to proceed against an accommodation party before pursuing the accommodated party, some jurisdictions that adopted the doctrine of *Pain v. Packard*, 7 Am. Dec. 369 (N.Y. Sup. 1816), allow an accommodation party to insist that the creditor obtain a judgment and return of execution against the accommodated party before the accommodation party's liability will come into play. The *Pain v. Packard* doctrine is described in *Amick v. Baugh*, 402 P.2d 342 (Wash. 1965). Thus, unless the doctrine of *Pain v. Packard* applies, the lender in our example may choose to demand payment from the parent first rather than proceeding against the child.

To be liable as an accommodation party, one must have intended to be a surety. Determining whether a party had the requisite intent can present a challenge. *Transamerica Commercial Finance Corp. v. Naef*, 842 P.2d 539 (Wyo. 1992), addresses this issue. Transamerica Commercial Finance Corporation sought to recover from Linda Naef under a note she signed for her husband's business. The business and the husband had filed for bankruptcy protection, and Transamerica pursued payment from Mrs. Naef under **3–305(d)**, which provides that an accommodation party cannot raise the accommodated party's insolvency to avoid liability. The court rejected Transamerica's claim against Mrs. Naef because the evidence showed she owned no interest in the business and lacked the intent to be a party to the note. In fact, when she was asked to sign the note, she initially refused because she could not guarantee her husband's obligation. The bank officer assured her that her signature was not important. Under these facts, Mrs. Naef was not liable as an accommodation party.

B. WARRANTY LIABILITY UNDER ARTICLES 3 AND 4

1. TRANSFER AND PRESENTMENT WARRANTIES

The second kind of liability under Articles 3 and 4 is warranty liability. Warranty liability is relevant when an instrument is altered, a signature is forged or unauthorized, or other issues with the enforceability of the instrument arise, because these are occurrences that constitute a breach of warranty.

There are three periods in the life of an instrument: Issuance, Transfer, and Presentment. Two of these—transfer and presentment—correspond with warranties. The issuer of an instrument makes no Article 3/Article 4 warranties; instead, any warranties the issuer made under Article 2 or other contract law are part of the underlying contract being paid via the instrument. When the instrument is transferred, each transferor makes a transfer warranty. There are two transfer warranties—one in Article 3 (**3–416**) and one in Article 4 (**4–207**). This section will explore the substance of these warranties, the differences between the Article 3 and Article 4 warranties, and to whom these warranties are owed.

In addition to the transfer warranties, there are two presentment warranties. The Article 3 presentment warranty is found in **3–417** and the Article 4 presentment warranty is found in **4–208**. In the case of a check, the party presenting the check to the drawee/payor bank for payment makes a presentment warranty to the drawee/payor bank, as does every prior transferor that participated in delivering the check to the drawee/payor bank. In the case of a note, the party presenting the note to the maker for payment, along with every prior transferor, makes a limited presentment warranty to the maker. The substance of these warranties is explored below.

Before exploring the substance of the transfer and presentment warranties, it is helpful to determine when the Article 3 warranties will apply and when the Article 4 warranties apply. The key to understanding this concept is remembering that Article 4 covers bank collections, while Article 3 covers all negotiable instruments. Thus, in the chart below, only checks implicate warranties in both Articles 3 and 4; notes and non-check drafts involve only Article 3 because they are not collected through banks. In addition, note that the "full" presentment warranty that will be explored below applies only to checks and non-check drafts; with respect to notes, the only warranty made to the maker is that the warrantor is (or was, at the time he or she transferred the instrument) entitled to enforce the instrument or acting on behalf of someone entitled to enforce the instrument. This limited warranty makes sense, given that the other presentment warranties really are intended to protect the interests of a drawee.

Conversion = civil COA for theft

	Transfer Warranty	Presentment Warranty
Note	Article 3 transfer warranty applies exclusively.	Only the very limited warranty found in 3–417(d) applies. *THAT NOTE END. SIG. IS NOT FORGED*
Check	Article 3 transfer warranty applies before check is introduced into Article 4 check-collection system and becomes an "item" handled for collection; Article 4 transfer warranty applies after that point.	Article 3 presentment warranty applies before check is introduced into Article 4 check-collection system and becomes an "item" handled for collection; Article 4 presentment warranty applies after that point.
Non-check draft	Article 3 transfer warranty applies exclusively.	Article 3 presentment warranty applies exclusively.

2. THE SUBSTANCE OF THE WARRANTIES

The following chart compares the transfer warranties, as found in **3–416** and **4–207**, with the presentment warranties found in **3–417** and **4–208**. These warranties are similar, but not the same. "Instrument" is used in the Article 3 warranties, while "item" is used in Article 4, so both terms are used below.

	Transfer Warranty	Presentment Warranty
Entitlement to Enforce	I am a person entitled to enforce this instrument or item. As 3–416 Comment 2 indicates, this is "in effect a warranty that there are no unauthorized or missing indorsements that prevent the transferor from making the transferee a person entitled to enforce the instrument." This	I am, or was, when I transferred the instrument or item, a person entitled to enforce the instrument or item or authorized to obtain acceptance or payment on behalf of a person entitled to enforce it. As with the transfer warranty, this resembles a warranty of title. This is the only

	warranty resembles a warranty of title.	presentment warranty made with respect to a note.
Signatures	All signatures on the instrument or item (including mine) are authentic and authorized.	To the best of my knowledge, the drawer's signature is authorized.
Alterations	The instrument or item has not been altered.	The instrument or item has not been altered.
Defenses	This instrument or item is not subject to any defenses or claims in recoupment that could be raised against me.	No warranty made.
Solvency	Insofar as I know, the maker of this note or drawer of this draft is not insolvent.	No warranty made.

In the chart above, references to accepted drafts and remotely-created consumer items have been left out for the purpose of simplicity.

Note that the presentment warranty includes no warranty with respect to defenses or solvency. This makes sense because any defenses against enforcement of the instrument would not affect the drawee in the same way that it would affect a transferee, since the drawee is not seeking to enforce the instrument. In addition, the drawee at least arguably has more information about the drawer's solvency than other parties do, so no warranty to the drawee as to the drawer's solvency would be appropriate.

As the chart above shows, with transfer warranties, the fact that signatures are authorized and authentic is generally warranted; with presentment warranties, the warranty is only that "the warrantor has no knowledge that the signature of the drawer . . . is unauthorized." The assumption is that the drawee is generally in a better position than any indorser to know whether the drawer's signature is authorized. Thus, as the court held in *Clean World Engineering, Ltd. v. MidAmerica Bank, FSB*, 793 N.E.2d 110 (Ill. Ct. App. 2003), the UCC follows the 1762 English case of *Price v. Neal*: The drawee assumes the risk that the drawer's signature is unauthorized, unless the party presenting the draft for payment has actual knowledge that the drawer's signature is not authorized.

The next step is to explore in further detail who makes these warranties and to whom the warranties are owed. Let's start with a check issued and negotiated as order paper. The fact that this check remains order paper throughout the negotiation process means that every transferor indorses the check. Under these circumstances, each transferor of order paper owes (1) a transfer warranty to each later transferee (not just his or her immediate transferee), and (2) a presentment warranty to the drawee.

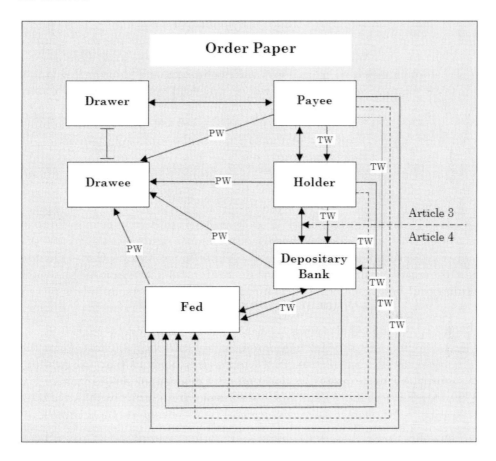

In the example above, Payee owes a transfer warranty to Holder, Depository Bank, and Fed. Holder owes a transfer warranty to Depository Bank and Fed. Depository Bank owes a transfer warranty to Fed. Payee, Holder, Depository Bank, and Fed all owe a presentment warranty to Drawee.

If the check were bearer paper such that each transferor did not indorse the instrument, the results would differ slightly:

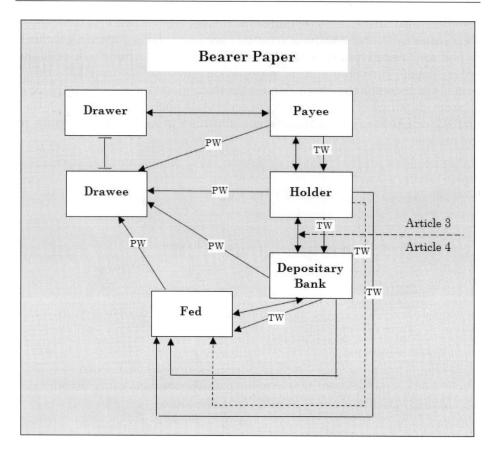

Transferors of bearer paper do not make warranties to later transferees under **3–416**. This makes sense; because they don't indorse, later transferees likely could not find them. Thus, in the chart above, Payee owes a transfer warranty to Holder but not to Depositary Bank or Fed. The presentment warranty is, however, unaffected by the lack of indorsement: Payee, Holder, Depositary Bank, and Fed all owe a presentment warranty to Drawee.

There is one caveat to the distinction between bearer paper and order paper. Under **4–207**, unlike **3–416**, the existence of transfer warranties to later transferees does not depend on whether the transfer was by indorsement. Thus, Holder (as a "customer" of Depositary Bank within the meaning of **4–207(a)**) owes a transfer warranty to both Depositary Bank and Fed, not just Depositary Bank.

3. BREACH OF THE TRANSFER AND PRESENTMENT WARRANTIES

Damages for breach of warranty are based on the loss the breach caused. Such damages may not exceed the amount of the instrument plus any expenses and loss of interest due to the breach. The following discussion provides examples of conduct that does, and does not, constitute a breach of the transfer and presentment warranties.

When a check is payable to two payees, presentment of the check to the drawee for payment after only one payee has indorsed violates the presentment warranty. In *First Atlantic Federal Credit Union v. Perez*, 918 A.2d 666 (N.J. Super. 2007), the court considered a check Allstate Corporation tendered in payment of a claim for the total loss of a vehicle. The check for just over $4,200 was written jointly to Charles Perez, who owned the car, and First Atlantic Federal Credit Union, which had provided financing for the car and still had a lien for the unpaid balance of the loan. United Check Cashing cashed the check for Perez without First Atlantic's indorsement, and the court held that doing so violated the presentment warranty United Check Cashing owed to Bank of America, the bank on which the check was drawn. United Check Cashing breached the portion of the warranty promising that the warrantor is a person entitled to enforce the instrument and thus has "good title" to the instrument. When indorsements are missing, later transferees are not persons entitled to enforce the instrument, and the chain of title to the instrument is broken.

The above example involved a presentment warranty. Next, we will examine how a forged signature can violate a transfer warranty. *Aetna Life and Casualty Co. v. Hampton State Bank*, 497 S.W.2d 80, 83 (Tex. Civ. App. 1973), involved a transfer-warranty claim based on a stolen check bearing a fictitious payee and a forged drawer's signature. The depositary bank credited the check to a customer's account and, after the drawee returned the check unpaid, sought to recover the loss from its own insurance company. (The customer was presumably either unavailable for suit or judgment-proof.) One of the issues before the court was the possibility of warranties owed to and by the depositary bank. The court stated, "It may seem odd to speak of a warranty of title to a forged check, but that is exactly what we have here." The court explained its holding as follows:

> Title to a check does not necessarily mean the right to collect it from the drawer, since the drawer may have a good defense. A person (other than the drawee bank) who has paid value for a forged check has title to the spurious instrument which enables him to recover against his transferor . . . and against prior indorsers. . . . A warranty of title is nothing more than an assurance that no one has better title to the check than the warrantor, and therefore, that no one is in a position to claim title as against the warrantee, as the payee or other owner of a genuine check could do if his indorsement were forged. *Id.* at 84.

The court uses the phrase "warranty of title." The transfer and presentment warranties in **3–416(a)(1)**, **3–417(a)(1)**, **3–417(d)(1)**, **4–**

207(a)(1), and **4–208(a)(1)** can appropriately be compared with the warranty of title in **2–312**.

A counterfeit check, unlike a check with a forged indorsement, actually does not implicate the Article 3/Article 4 warranties. In *Bank of America, N.A. v. Amarillo National Bank*, 156 S.W.3d 108, 109–11 (Tx. Ct. App. 2004), the court considered a check fraudulently copied from an existing check. The original check, drawn on Amarillo National Bank, was in the amount of $522,000, numbered 036830, issued by Western Builders, dated April 15, 1999, and payable to Megadoor, Inc. The copy bore the same check number, was dated April 27, 1999, purported to be drawn on Western Builders' account, had the correct account number at Amarillo National Bank, was in the amount of $500,000, and was payable to Robert L. Surber, who indorsed the check and deposited it into his Bank of America account.

Amarillo National Bank paid the check and was required to re-credit its customer's account for the funds it could not recover from Surber, since the check was not properly payable. Amarillo National Bank sought to recover from Bank of America on a presentment warranty theory. In rejecting this claim, the court held as follows:

> [B]efore [4–208(a)(2)] applies, any alteration must appear to be made on the body of the original instrument, as opposed to appearing simply on a copy of the original. Yet here, the check presented by Surber to BOA was not an actual check issued by Western. No one disputes that. Rather, it was one created by Surber or someone else and made to look like a Western check.
>
> * * *
>
> In short, and akin to the "Mona Lisa," there was but one check issued to Western, numbered 036830, and made payable to Megadoor, Inc., in the amount of $522,000. Neither Surber nor his compatriot (if any) altered it by copying the item and then changing the terms appearing on the face of the copy. He or they simply made another, separate instrument. And, in making a separate check, the individual who created the fake item did not alter the original, as contemplated by [the presentment warranties found in Articles 3 and 4]. . . . Consequently, and as a matter of law, BOA could not have been held liable for breaching warranties that arise when passing an altered check.

Thus, a counterfeit check does not involve the kind of "alteration" that violates the Article 3/Article 4 warranties. It is important to realize, however, that nothing in the court's analysis lessens the culpability of Surber or anyone who assisted him; the court's holding relates only to the liability of Bank of America under a presentment warranty.

To recover for a breach of presentment warranty, a drawee/payor bank must pay or accept the instrument in good faith within the meaning of **3–**

417 and **4–208**. In *Savings Banks Trust Co. v. Federal Reserve Bank of New York*, 577 F. Supp. 964 (S.D.N.Y. 1984), the court held that a drawee is not a "payor in good faith" if it pays an item over a valid stop-payment order or is aware of any defense or claim against it. By contrast, as the court held in *Wachovia Bank, N.A. v. Federal Reserve Bank of Richmond*, 338 F.3d 318 (4th Cir. 2003), a drawee does not act in bad faith merely by failing to review high-value checks manually before paying them. Even if the bank's conduct were negligent, the court held, it was not the kind of "unfair or dishonest" behavior that rises to the level of bad faith.

Now, let's examine how the transfer and presentment warranties can work together in the same fact pattern. Warranty liability is often implicated when a check is stolen from the payee. If the thief forges the payee's indorsement, the check is no longer properly payable, but the drawee may pay the check because it may not be aware of the theft until after the check is paid. In such a case, the matter might proceed according to the following chart. In this chart, note that the only transfer not supported by consideration is Forger's theft of the check from Payee. Here's why: Assuming that Assignee in the chart below is a check-cashing company, if Assignee cashes the check for Forger, none of the consideration from the check flows to Payee. In reading the chart below, "TW" refers to transfer warranty, and "PW" refers to presentment warranty.

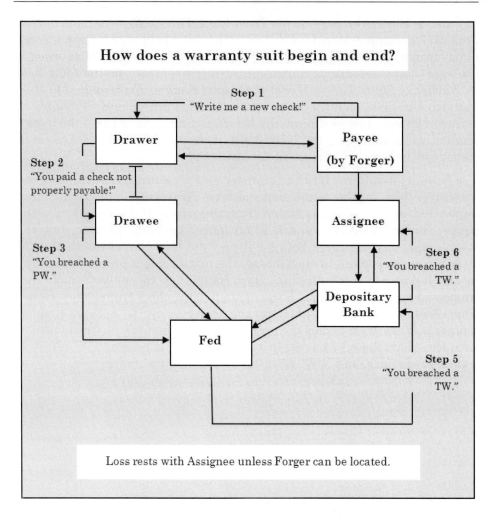

Note that the word "Assignee" is used in this chart in place of "Holder" because no transferee of order paper with a forged indorsement can be a holder.

In a perfect world, Payee would simply locate and sue Forger. More likely, Forger will be unknown (or will have no assets), and Payee will instead reach out to Drawer—the party most accessible to Payee—and demand that a new check be issued. Because Payee has not yet received the funds the check represented, and because Payee gave consideration to Drawer in return for the check, Drawer must honor this request.

After paying Payee, Drawer will demand that Drawee re-credit its account. Because the check was not properly payable due to the forged indorsement, Drawee must honor this request. In this chart, Drawee can use a presentment warranty to pass the loss to Fed, Depositary Bank, or Assignee. The specific portion of the presentment warranty that is breached is found in **3–417(a)(1)** or **4–208(a)(1)**. Fed can use a transfer warranty to pass the loss to Depositary Bank or Assignee, and Depositary Bank can use a transfer warranty to pass the loss to Assignee. The specific portions of the transfer warranty that are breached are found in **3–416(a)(1)** and **(2)** and **4–207(a)(1)** and **(2)**. If Forger could be found, Forger would be liable to Drawee on a presentment warranty and to Assignee, Depositary Bank, and Fed on a transfer warranty.

As this chart suggests, a plaintiff may sue any party with legal responsibility for the instrument, even if that party is not ultimately the most culpable for the loss. The party that is sued may, in turn, use transfer and presentment warranties to move the loss to another party with a closer connection to the breach. The goal is that the loss rest with the wrongdoer (in this case, Forger), or at least with the party that dealt with him or her (in this case, Assignee).

4. ENCODING AND RETENTION WARRANTIES

Article 4 also provides encoding and retention warranties, found in **4–209**. The person or bank that encodes the amount term on a check after it has been issued makes an encoding warranty to every subsequent collecting bank as well as the drawee/payor bank.

Encoding and retention warranties facilitate electronic presentment by allowing later transferees to rely on prior encoding. Otherwise, each bank would have to examine each item individually, which would make electronic presentment impossible. Retention warranties allow access to the original item for a certain period of time should it ever be needed for the purpose of comparing it to the electronic image.

If a bank allows its customer to encode items before delivering them to the bank, both the bank and the customer may be liable under an encoding warranty. Typically, a large institutional customer would have the technology to encode its own instruments. A bank that allows a customer to encode items prior to deposit should require the customer to indemnify the bank for any loss resulting from the misencoding.

As **4–209** Comment 2 indicates, a drawee/payor bank can incur a loss if (1) a check is under-encoded, (2) the drawee pays the encoded amount and thus becomes liable for the full amount of the check (since, according to Comment 2, misencoding does not alter the check), and (3) the drawer's account balance does not cover the full amount of the check but did cover the under-encoded amount.

In such a situation, if the drawee/payor bank receives a notice of adjustment and there are insufficient funds in the drawer's account to pay the check, the bank has two options. Notably, both options place the loss upon the depositary bank, which made the error. First, it can refuse payment. In such a case, if the depositary bank has given provisional credit for the full value of the check and the depositor has withdrawn the funds, the loss will rest upon the depositary bank. Second, the drawee may choose to honor the adjustment notice and recover from the depositary bank under an encoding warranty theory. These facts were explored in *Troy Bank and Trust Co v. Citizens Bank*, 84 UCC Rep.Serv.2d 880 (Ala. 2014).

Along the same lines, if a check is over-encoded, the drawee/payor bank will be able to draw from the drawer's account only the amount of the check as originally written (since, again, misencoding does not alter the check). If the depositary bank has allowed its customer to draw upon the funds as wrongly credited for the larger amount, the loss will rest with the depositary bank.

C. TORT LIABILITY UNDER ARTICLES 3 AND 4

Tort liability is relevant when a party claims to be harmed by another's negligence, or when one party claims another has converted funds rightfully belonging to it. The first tort we will examine is conversion.

3–420 explains how the common-law tort of conversion applies to negotiable instruments. The chart that follows shows which parties may have a cause of action for conversion, and which parties may be sued under a conversion theory.

A typical conversion fact pattern involves a check that a drawer properly issued as order paper, which was stolen from the payee. A wrongdoer forged the payee's indorsement and obtained payment of the check. The check was then presented through the Article 4 collection process and paid, presumably because the drawer was not made aware of the theft and forgery in sufficient time to stop payment on the check. Thus, as a preliminary matter, note that this is substantially the same fact pattern as was presented in the prior section regarding warranty liability. The difference is that, this time, the payee seeks to recover "downstream" from the party that cashed the check for the wrongdoer or from one of the banks that participated in the collection of the check, rather than asking the drawer to re-issue the check. As the chart below shows, Payee (the probable plaintiff) can potentially sue any of these parties, although Fed is the least likely defendant due to its limited liability, as explained below. Payee would also, of course, have a cause of action against Forger, assuming that person could be found and had assets.

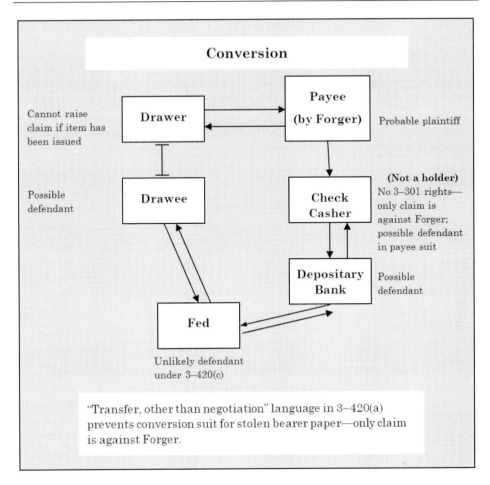

In this example, because the check was stolen from Payee, Payee is the expected plaintiff in a conversion action. Drawer has no conversion claim, because an instrument, once issued, is an obligation of a drawer rather than the drawer's property.

In the chart above, Payee may sue Forger, Check Casher, or any of the banks, as **3–420** Comment 3 indicates. The measure of damages for conversion is normally the amount payable on the instrument, but will in no event exceed the claimant's interest in the instrument. Other than Depositary Bank, those collecting banks that have acted in good faith with regard to the instrument will not be liable for any funds exceeding the amount of the item that is yet to be paid out. This is why Fed is an unlikely defendant in a conversion action, as indicated in the chart above.

If Payee sues Drawee in conversion, Drawee can pass the loss to any earlier bank using a presentment warranty as explained earlier in this chapter. If Fed is sued (either by Payee, in conversion, or Drawee, under a presentment warranty), it can use a transfer warranty as explained earlier in this chapter to pass the loss to Depositary Bank, Check Casher, or

Forger. Depositary Bank will charge the check back against Check Casher's account, and Check Casher will try to recover from Forger.

3–206(c) brings restrictive indorsement and conversion together. The rightful owner of an instrument has a conversion claim against a bank or other party that pays an item for a forger. In addition, when a holder indorses a check or other item with a restrictive indorsement such as "for deposit only," a bank may be liable in conversion if it handles the item in a manner inconsistent with these instructions.

Conversion must be understood in the context of **3–405**'s "faithless employee" rule. As the court held in *Auto-Owners Insurance Co. v. Bank One*, 879 N.E.2d 1086 (Ind. 2008), this rule

> shifts the responsibility for monitoring possibly wayward employees away from a bank and onto the employer. The rationale . . . is that an employer is in a better position to select and supervise its employees than an outside bank. . . . [A]n employer is also better able to put in place measures to prevent fraud among its employees. The effect is that, when an employee wrongfully [i]ndorses a check made payable to the employer, after having been entrusted with the responsibility for handling such checks, the [i]ndorsement is as good as the employer's as far as a taker in good faith is concerned.

Thus, when a faithless employee forges the employer's indorsement on a check, the employer has no conversion claim against parties who dealt with the faithless employee, although it will, of course, have a claim against the employee. Having said this, if a bank failed to exercise ordinary care in paying or taking the check and "that failure substantially contributes" to the employer's loss, the employer can recover to the extent of the bank's negligence.

The following case provides context for the rule that a drawer of a check with a forged indorsement cannot sue the depositary bank for conversion. This case also introduces the tort of negligence in the payment context.

CONDER V. UNION PLANTERS BANK, N.A.
384 F.3d 397 (7th Cir. 2004)

POSNER, J.

This appeal from the dismissal of a diversity suit (governed by Indiana law) for failure to state a claim requires us to consider a bank's liability to victims of a Ponzi scheme for allowing checks made out to the malefactors to be deposited without proper endorsements. According to the complaint, which is our only source of facts, Johann Smith and three other individuals used a number of corporations and other business entities controlled by them, collectively the "Heartland Financial Group," to extract money from the plaintiff and the members of her class on the promise that the money would be invested and yield a high rate of return. Instead of investing the money, Smith and his associates rebated some of it to the earliest investors as the promised high return on their investment (the signature move in a Ponzi scheme, designed both to delay discovery of the fraud and to attract additional investors) and used the rest to support an extravagant lifestyle. Before being shut down by the SEC the scheme had fleeced the investors of some $35 million.

The plaintiff made out numerous checks, one for as much as $150,000, to "Johann M. Smith Escrow Agent." Smith, or someone acting on his behalf, stamped each check

PAY TO THE ORDER OF
UNION PLANTERS BANK
FOR DEPOSIT ONLY
LINCOLN FIDELITY ESCROW ACCOUNT
074014213 0001266190

The number at the bottom is not Smith's, the payee's, bank account number (anyway his account is in another bank), but that of Lincoln Fidelity, one of the Heartland entities; thus the check was not endorsed by the payee. Nevertheless, Union Planters Bank, the defendant, accepted each of the checks for deposit in Lincoln Fidelity's escrow account in the bank. The money was transferred to that account from the plaintiff's bank account when Union Planters Bank presented the plaintiff's check to her bank for payment, and was then checked out from Lincoln Fidelity's account to various of the schemers.

The plaintiff's theories of the bank's liability are two: conversion and negligence, and we begin with the former. Obviously an endorsement signed not by the payee but instead by the person to whom the check is endorsed is ineffective to transfer rights over the check from the payee to the endorsee and thus to the bank in which the endorsee deposits the check. UCC § **3–201(b)**. So Union Planters Bank was not a holder in due course of the money when it arrived and was deposited in the bank, *id.*, § **3–302(a)**; . . . and therefore, the plaintiff argues, the bank stood in the shoes of Lincoln Fidelity (part of Heartland, the Ponzi enterprise, remember) and has the same liability to the plaintiff as Lincoln Fidelity would have. Since she could have sued Lincoln Fidelity for conversion, she can, she argues, sue Union Planters Bank for conversion. Section **3–306** of the Uniform Commercial Code provides that "a person taking an instrument, other than a person having rights of a holder in due course, is subject to a claim of a property or possessory right in the instrument or its proceeds, including a claim to rescind a negotiation and to recover the instrument or its proceeds." The transferee of a negotiable instrument who is not a holder in due course is simply the assignee of a contract and has no greater rights than any other assignee. UCC §§ **3–305(a)**, **3–306**; ... A thief cannot convey a good title, by assignment or otherwise. . . So the Ponzi schemers, by depositing Conder's check in Union Planters Bank, could not convey good title to the bank.

Or so it might seem; but in fact this hallowed principle of property law is no longer applied in cases in which a transfer of money is effected by negotiation of an instrument rather than by physical conveyance, even if as in this case the recipient (the bank) is not a holder in due course. UCC § **3–420(a)**; compare *Douglass v. Wones*, 120 Ill.App.3d 36, 76 Ill.Dec. 114, 458 N.E.2d 514 (1983). The Uniform Commercial Code, as revised in 1990 to wipe out some earlier cases, including one from Indiana, . . . is explicit that a drawer (the plaintiff in this case) cannot sue the depositary bank (the defendant, Union Planters Bank) for conversion. UCC § **3–420(a)(i)** and Comment 1 . . . As the UCC comment explains, the plaintiff has an adequate remedy by way of suit against her own bank, the bank that paid the check even though it wasn't properly endorsed. We haven't been told whether the plaintiff has sued her own bank as well as Lincoln Fidelity's bank. As we'll see, such a suit might fail for want of proof of causation; but a remedy is not inadequate merely because it does not yield the plaintiff a windfall.

The plaintiff's alternative theory is that Union Planters Bank violated a duty of care to her in allowing her improperly endorsed checks to be deposited in Lincoln Fidelity's account. In other words, she is accusing the bank of having negligently failed to prevent the Ponzi schemers from defrauding her. . . .

Even if Indiana imposed such a duty of care, this suit would fail for several reasons, including a lack of a showing of negligence. There was nothing to arouse the suspicions of Union Planters Bank when it was instructed to deposit improperly endorsed checks in Lincoln Fidelity's account. Improper endorsements are common enough, and usually innocent. Depositary banks can be holders in due course of unendorsed checks if the payee is its customer, UCC § **4–205(1)** . . . while the "intended payee" rule, as we shall see, provides a safe harbor for banks that honor unendorsed or improperly endorsed checks.

There is a little more in the way of suspicious circumstances here because remember that the plaintiff's checks were deposited in Lincoln Fidelity's *escrow* account. The plaintiff argues that the checks that the malefactors wrote on the account should have alerted the bank that the money in the account was being used for purposes that would not be legitimate for an escrow agent. Statutes impose various monitoring duties on banks, such as the duty to report large currency transactions, and depositors who are on terrorist watch lists, 31 U.S.C. §§ 5313(a), 5318(*l*), but excuse banks from knowing the terms of its escrow accounts. Ind.Code §§ 30–2–4–5, –6, –7, –9. . . . Tasking banks to read every check to make sure that the payee's identity was consistent with the character of the account would impose an unreasonable burden, and so the failure to perform the task would not be negligence even if banks did have a general duty of care to noncustomers (which, to repeat, they do not).

Our recent decision in *Kaskel v. Northern Trust Co.*, 328 F.3d 358 (7th Cir.2003), provides still another defense to the bank. Mrs. Kaskel had written a check to a company called MLS, which had agreed to invest the money for her. MLS mailed the check, without however endorsing it, to a Dr. Shook, who was to make the actual investment. Shook deposited the check in his personal account, and his bank presented it for payment to the Northern Trust Company, the bank on which Kaskel's check had been drawn. Northern Trust paid despite the absence of an endorsement, with the result that Kaskel's money ended up in Shook's account, from which it subsequently disappeared. Kaskel sued Northern Trust, claiming that it had broken its contract with her, UCC § 4–401(a), because the contract authorized the bank to disburse money in her account only to a payee or endorsee of her checks, and Shook was neither. We held, so far as bears on the present case, that while there was indeed a breach of contract, Mrs. Kaskel was not entitled to more than nominal damages because there was no causal relation between the breach and the loss of her money. For had the bank noticed that the check was not endorsed, and therefore returned it to MLS, MLS would have endorsed it to Shook, Shook would have redeposited the check, this time Northern Trust would have paid, and so Kaskel would still have lost her money. 328 F.3d at 360 . . .

Likewise had Union Planters Bank noticed the improper endorsement, it would have returned the check to Johann Smith, he would have endorsed it to Lincoln Fidelity, the check would have been redeposited with the bank, and the bank would have credited Lincoln Fidelity's account with the amount of the check. So the plaintiff would have lost her money all the same, and is therefore no worse off because of the bank's mistake. She faults the district court for "absolving [the bank] of any accountability for looking the other way and neglecting its duties under the UCC while millions of dollars of stolen funds passed through its hands," but fails to see that the same millions of dollars would have passed through the bank's hands, with a delay of only a few days, had the bank returned the checks either to Smith or to her.

Imposing liability on someone who hasn't actually caused a harm (because the harm would have occurred anyway) creates incentives to take excessive, and therefore socially wasteful, precautions, . . . with the effect of impeding commerce. . . . Hence the "intended payee" rule, recognized in Indiana as elsewhere, . . . and a further obstacle to Conder's claim, unless the rule is considered, as probably it should be, as just a restatement of the general tort requirement of proving a causal relation between the tortious conduct and the plaintiff's injury.

The rule provides that if a bank transfers a check without a proper endorsement but the transfer is to a person whom the drawer of the check wanted (or would if consulted have wanted) to have the money, the bank is not liable for any loss the drawer may have suffered as a result of the transfer, since the transfer would have gone through even if the bank had insisted that the check be properly endorsed. The plaintiff's criticism of the application of the rule to the facts of *Franklin v. Benock*, 722 N.E.2d 874 (Ind.App. 2000), may be well founded, but the rule itself is sound; there is no liability in tort if the victim would have suffered the loss of which he is complaining even if the defendant had not violated its legal duty.

The principle is equally applicable to a suit for fraud or conversion— the plaintiff's other claim, with which we began. She argues that requiring proof of a causal relation between the defendant's conduct and the plaintiff's loss is strictly an aspect of tort law and section **3–306** is a rule of property law. That is doubly wrong: *Kaskel* was a contract case, not a tort case; and all that section **3–306** does is, by lifting the holder in due course defense, to open the way to a tort suit. See UCC § **3–307** Comment 2 . . . It removes a defense, rather than altering the claim, and the claim is governed by the principles of tort law, which require proof of causation. . . .

AFFIRMED.

As this case demonstrates, negligence is another source of potential tort liability.

First National Bank of Commerce v. Anderson Ford-Lincoln-Mercury, Inc., 704 S.W.2d 83 (Tex. App. 5th Dist. 1985), elucidates the practical difference between contract and tort liability, in the context of a negotiable instrument. A vice president of First National Bank of Commerce, presumably acting as the bank's agent, told an employee of Anderson Ford Lincoln Mercury, Inc., "Draft on me for $13,000," which was the price of the new truck that Anderson Ford customer Jerry McKnight wished to purchase. This was a common, informal way of securing financing. Based on the bank's representation, the dealership sold McKnight the truck, gave him a rebate of about $1,600, and prepared a draft on the bank in the amount of $13,000. The dealership then presented the draft to the bank for its signature. The bank refused to sign the written draft when presented, claiming it had changed its mind and did not wish to finance the purchase. The dealership sued, and the court held the bank could not be liable in contract because it never signed the draft, but could be liable in tort for failing to exercise ordinary care toward the dealership. Thus, the triggering facts for contract obligations, on the one hand, and tort liability, on the other, are different. Contract obligations are generally triggered by a party's signature on an instrument, while tort liability is triggered by other facts independent of whether the party has signed the instrument.

In addition to the tort claims recognized in Article 3, parties sometimes attempt to recover under a common-law tort theory. The economic loss rule may, under some circumstances, limit a plaintiff to a contract or warranty cause of action rather than a common-law tort claim. In *Great Lakes Higher Education Corp. v. Austin Bank of Chicago*, 837 F. Supp. 892, 896 (N.D. Ill. 1993), both plaintiffs—Great Lakes Higher Education Corporation and First Wisconsin Bank—raised a common-law negligence claim against Austin Bank. This case arose after Great Lakes issued 224 checks to the order of various payees as proceeds of student loans, and the checks were presented and paid without the indorsement of any named payee. The court held as follows, rejecting this claim:

> Plaintiffs invoke the law of common-law negligence against Austin. . . . When only economic loss is incurred, the plaintiff may only raise contract theories, even if the defendant's alleged conduct constituted a tort as well as a breach of contract."

> . . . Here, First Wisconsin and Great Lakes have other remedies under the UCC which they have alternatively plead in their complaint, thus showing that a common-law action for negligence is unnecessary and may not be alleged here.

The economic loss rule is a way of creating a reasoned distinction between tort law (which compensates parties for injury) and contract law (which focuses on giving parties the benefit of their bargain). Economic losses are better suited to the latter analysis than the former.

D. ARTICLES 3 AND 4 STATUTES OF LIMITATIONS

Now that you are familiar with the various causes of action that are available under Articles 3 and 4, the last step is to become familiar with the relevant limitations periods. **3–118** and **4–111** provide the Article 3 and Article 4 statutes of limitations, respectively. Article 4 supplies a three–year limitations period, while Article 3 is more complex in this respect. Under Article 3, the limitations period for tort and warranty claims is three years after the cause of action accrues. The following chart summarizes when contract actions to enforce the most common items under Article 3 must be commenced:

TYPE OF INSTRUMENT	MUST COMMENCE ACTION TO ENFORCE
Note payable at a definite time	Within 6 years after due date on note or accelerated due date
Unaccepted draft (including an ordinary check that the drawee has dishonored)	Within 10 years of date of draft or 3 years from dishonor, whichever is first
Certified, teller's, and cashier's checks	No time limit to make demand Within 3 years of demand
Other accepted drafts (including an ordinary check that the drawee has accepted but refused to pay)	Within 6 years of date of acceptance

3–118 also contains limitations periods for actions arising from demand notes, drafts payable at a definite time (rather than on demand), traveler's checks, and certificates of deposit, but those are beyond the scope of these materials.

Chapter Conclusion: As you leave this chapter, you should be comfortable with the three major sources of liability under Articles 3 and 4: contract, warranty, and tort, including the special contract rules relating to accommodation parties and accord and satisfaction. You should feel confident that you could dissect a fact pattern and advise a potential client as to each cause of action that it could raise, and each cause of action that it should anticipate being raised against it.

PROBLEMS

1. After reviewing 3–415, is this transfer made with or without recourse?

FOR VALUE RECEIVED, the undersigned TWIN CITY STATE BANK, hereby sells, transfers, sets over, and assigns to the ANDERSON LOAN ASSOCIATION its entire right, title, and interest in and to each and all of the following described bona-fide mortgages executed to or held by the undersigned, all prior mortgages held by the undersigned, all prior mortgages held by the assignor having been fully paid and released, together with all of the promissory notes and any other indebtedness thereby secured which said mortgages are hereinafter described and identified by the names of the mortgagors, the dates of execution, and the amounts of the original loans, the book and page of recordings in Grant County, Indiana, and the exact principal balances due on each at this transfer date as follows: (a list then followed)

We hereby assign the within note to First Savings & Loan Ass'n.

(Date)

Twin City State Bank

/s/ Donald F. Hundley

/s/ Donald F. Hundley, Pres.

    a.   What, if any, difference would it make if the evidence showed that the bank subjectively intended that its indorsement be without recourse?

    2.   Read 3–116, 3–415, and 3–419 and consider the following facts:

Jerry Iguess executed a promissory note to Calcasieu Marine Bank for $7,000. On the reverse side of the note were the signatures of Alvin Daigle, Alvin's wife Marlene, and David Chaisson, along with the word "indorser" under each. The three signatures appeared horizontally across the back of the note, coupled with the following language: "The undersigned hereby jointly and severally guarantee to the bank . . ." Before the note came due, Iguess filed for bankruptcy and received discharge on the note. After the note became past due, the bank demanded payment from the indorsers. Alvin Daigle paid and then sued Iguess and Chaisson.

Consider this language from the court's opinion: "Plaintiff, Alvin Daigle, an indorser and presently the holder of the note, seeks indemnity or, in the alternative, contribution from the defendant, David Chaisson, a co-indorser."

    a.   What status is Alvin Daigle claiming? Read 3–419(c) and Comment 3 carefully. Is the "guarantee" language helpful in establishing this status?

    b.   Why is Alvin Daigle "presently the holder of the note"? The "entitled to enforce" language in 3-419(f) may help you answer this question.

    c.   On what theory could Alvin Daigle sue Chaisson?

    d.   Read 3–415(a) and Comment 5. Should David Chaisson be considered a "subsequent indorser"? Why would this matter?

    e.   On what theory could Daigle sue Iguess?

    f.   Can Alvin Daigle, Marlene Daigle, and David Chaisson use 3-305(d) to escape liability on the note due to Iguess' discharge in bankruptcy? Why or why not?

    3.   Donald F. Boyer executed two notes payable to People's National Bank of Mora in return for two loans. His parents, Donald E. and Dorothy Boyer, indorsed as accommodation parties. In their contract of guaranty with the bank, they consented to any extension of time or renewal of the loans. In accordance with this consent, each loan was renewed several times. In August 1981, the two loans were consolidated. Mr. and Mrs. Boyer never signed the

renewed notes, nor did they sign the consolidated note, even though the bank contacted them three times, asking them to do so. The consolidated note bore a higher rate of interest than the two initial notes did. In addition, the credit-life-insurance policies issued in conjunction with the two original notes were cancelled and new insurance was issued, with the new premiums added to the consolidated balance. In March 1982, the son filed for bankruptcy. The bank sued the parents, who raised the defense of discharge.

  a. Identify all parties with primary and secondary liability, as well as all primary and secondary obligors.

  b. Should the bank prevail in arguing that the renewals and consolidation represent a mere "extension of time" under 3–605 that will not discharge the liability of Mr. and Mrs. Boyer?

  c. Are Mr. and Mrs. Boyer bound by the terms of the original notes as renewed, the new, consolidated note, neither, or both?

  d. If, instead of filing for bankruptcy in March 1982, the son had tendered payment to People's National Bank, which had refused to accept his payment, what would be the effect on his liability? What would be the effect on his parents' liability?

4. Walter Fithian and Richard Jamar formed a business partnership and applied to the People's Bank of Chestertown, Maryland for a loan of $11,000 to buy equipment for their new business. The bank was willing to extend credit only if Walter's wife Connie, Richard's wife Janet, and Walter's parents Bill and Mildred would co-sign the note along with Walter and Richard. When Walter and Richard asked why these additional signatures were required, the bank's Vice President replied, "They will make the bank more secure." Each of the six parties signed the note in the bottom right-hand corner.

After the partnership failed, Walter and Richard defaulted on the note, and the bank demanded payment from Bill and Mildred. After paying, Bill and Mildred demanded payment from Richard.

  a. In what capacity did each party sign?

  b. Who had primary liability on the note?

  c. Who, if anyone, had secondary liability?

  d. Who, if anyone, served as an accommodation party? Who, if anyone, was an accommodated party?

  e. What rights, if any, do each of the following parties have as against the others?

  • Richard v. Connie NONE
  • Janet v. Connie CONTRIB 25%
  • Richard v. Walter CONTRI
  • Janet v. Walter REIMBURSE

f.   Under 3–118, how long do the various parties have to bring suit?

5.   Carlisle Distributing Co. delivered a check for $10,000 to William Paladino, who pledged the check to Wildman Stores, Inc., as security for a loan of $8,000, which he later paid in full. After having the check for seventeen months, Wildman sought to enforce it, and the drawee/payor bank dishonored it. Wildman then sued Carlisle on a theory of secondary liability.

a.   Was the bank required to dishonor the check? Was Carlisle entitled to notice of dishonor?

b.   Is Carlisle still liable on the check? If so, what Code section would you cite to prove its liability, and what is the relevant limitations period?

c.   Assume Paladino indorsed the check before delivering it to Wildman. Is he still liable on the check? If so, what is the relevant limitations period?

6.   An individual in Africa contacted Impact Computers and Electronics, Inc., claiming to be associated with Westgate Fabrics, Inc., a Texas corporation. Impact agreed to sell computers to this individual that were worth about $63,000. After Impact received a check from this individual drawn on an unfamiliar bank, it deposited the check in its account with Bank of America and, once the bank indicated the check had cleared, shipped the computers to Africa. A Bank of America representative ostensibly informed Impact that "nothing could affect the funds" after the check cleared. Bank of America subsequently learned that the check had been altered as to both its amount and the identity of the payee. After notifying Impact, Bank of America debited the amount of the check from its account, which created an overdraft of approximately $22,000.

a.   Based upon these facts, are any warranties owed

•   From Impact to Bank of America?

•   From Bank of America to Impact?

•   From Bank of America to the drawee/payor bank?

•   From Impact to the drawee/payor bank?

b.   Have any warranties been breached?

c.   Where should the loss ultimately rest in this case, and why?

7.   Read 3–402 and consider the following facts:

Theresa Piotrowski defaulted on a note for a 1957 Ford automobile. She refused to pay because she claimed she had neither purchased the car nor signed the note. The bank holding the note then sought to recover the balance due from the Ford dealer, which was the original payee that indorsed and transferred the note to the bank. The bank acknowledged Ms. Piotrowski never signed the note, but claimed an authorized agent, Edward Rogalia, signed on her behalf.

a.   What facts are needed to determine whether Piotrowski and/or Rogalia are liable on the note?

b.   On what theories can the bank sue the car dealer?

c.   Can the dealer escape liability if it indorsed the note "without recourse?"

8.   Interamerican Business Institute owner Diego Aguirre perpetrated a scam involving student-loan proceeds. Great Lakes Higher Education Corporation issued 224 student-loan checks drawn against its account with First Wisconsin Bank and delivered the checks to Interamerican, where the students named as payees on those checks were presumably enrolled. The students' indorsements were forged, and the checks were deposited at Austin Bank of Chicago, where Interamerican banked. First Wisconsin paid the checks. The following excerpts from a Department of Education report describe the scam:

> Investigation showed that most of the students for whom the checks were issued had canceled their enrollment and never attended [Interamerican], or only attended the school for a short time. Aguirre . . . converted the funds for his own use. Aguirre also destroyed the files for these students before he closed the school in 1992, thereby hindering the investigation.

a.   Are any warranties owed to Great Lakes, to Austin Bank, or to First Wisconsin Bank?

b.   Have any warranties been breached?

c.   Can Great Lakes sue Austin Bank under 4–202?

d.   Could First Wisconsin sue Austin Bank in conversion?

9.   Read 3–203(a). Is each a transfer?

a.   Depositing a check with a bank other than the drawee.

b.   Presenting a check to the drawee for cashing.

c.   Presenting a check to a drawee who is also a payee, to make payment on a mortgage held by the drawee.

10.   Read 4–209 Comment 2, and 3–310 and consider the following facts:

Harold France financed the purchase of a tractor with Ford Credit and decided to pay off the note early by writing two checks to Ford Credit for the remaining balance. Due to an encoding error by the creditor's agent, the first check was encoded and debited from his account as $506 rather than the correct amount of $8,506. Due to an error by France's wife, the amount of the second check was written in numbers as $8,000 and in words as "eight dollars." The creditor's agent made a second error, encoding this check for $800. Once again, the drawee/payor bank debited France's account for only the encoded amount. Upon demand for the balance due, Mr. France refused to make further payment, claiming his obligations were eliminated by these repeated errors.

    a.   Will he prevail?

    b.   How does 3–310 apply to this fact pattern?

    c.   Does 4–209 provide a cause of action to Ford Credit?

    d.   Was the second check over-encoded or under-encoded? As a hint, what was the amount of the second check under 3–114?

11.   Jeff Messing was the holder of a check for about $1,000, drawn on the account of Toyson J. Burruss, d/b/a Prestige Auto Detail Center. On August 3, 2000, Messing presented the check for payment at Bank of America, the drawee. The teller confirmed that sufficient funds were in the drawer's account and stamped the check with the date, time, check amount, account number, and teller number. At the same time, the teller placed a hold on Burruss' account for the amount of the check. Upon the teller's request, Messing produced two forms of identification and signed the back of the check. The teller counted out cash equal to the value of the check and inquired as to whether Messing was a customer of Bank of America. Upon learning that he was not, she informed him that, pursuant to bank policy, he would be required to place a thumbprint on the check before it would be cashed. Messing refused and, following a conversation in which the branch manager refused to waive the thumbprint requirement, left the bank with the check. At that time, the teller released the hold on Burruss' account, returned the cash to her drawer, and voided the transaction on her computer terminal. Messing brought suit against Bank of America, claiming conversion and wrongful dishonor. The allegations of conversion are based upon Messing's claim that the bank exercised unauthorized dominion and control over the proceeds of the check to the complete exclusion of Messing after the bank accepted the check and refused to distribute the proceeds, counted out by the teller, to him.

    a.   Had Messing presented the check within the meaning of 3–501? Had the bank accepted the check? Why or why not?

    b.   Does any cause of action in conversion exist under these facts?

    c.   How will the bank respond to the claim of wrongful dishonor?

12.   You received the following letter and enclosed check at your home address. Assume your legal name is Winifred Robins, you have never heard of Tony Davis or James Powell, and you know nothing of the transaction to which the letter makes allusion. Further assume you are experiencing urgent financial need at this time and $2,500 would make an appreciable difference in your fiscal situation. Several friends have urged you to "just deposit the check and see what happens, hoping for the best."

a.   What is the mysterious sender of this letter seeking to accomplish?

Sorry for the delay in getting the check, I will like you to deduct your charges for the item and send the remaining balance to the shipper via Western Union Money Transfer TODAY so that they can schedule a date for the shipment and come for the pickup in your base. Here is the information you are to use for the transfer of the funds via Western Union.

NAME: TONY DAVIS

ADDRESS   50 SCRIVEN STREET
*   HACKNEY*
*   LONDON*
*   E8 4HY*
*   UNITED KINGDOM.*

After the transfer of the funds you are to get back to me with the below information which I am to give to the shipper to get the money today and schedule a time for the pickup.

AMOUNT SENT AFTER WESTERN UNION CHARGES

SENDERS NAME AND ADDRESS

MTCN (MONEY TRANSFER CONTROL NUMBER)

b.   What possible liability (if any) could you face if you deposit the check, and to whom might you be liable?

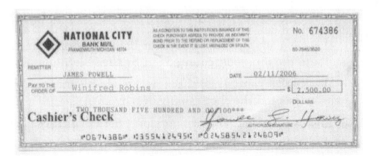

13. Mississippi Bulk Transport, Inc., a trucking transport broker, employed Amy Jaco for about 18 months, during which time she embezzled more than $100,000 from the company by arranging for more than 70 Mississippi Bulk Transport checks to be made payable to a fictitious company and then depositing those checks into her personal checking account with Union Planters Bank, N.A., which was also the bank on which the checks were drawn.

a.   Does Mississippi Bulk Transport have a cause of action against Union Planters Bank under 3–404? In answering this question, you may assume that Jaco is "a person whose intent determines to whom an instrument is payable" within the meaning of 3–404(b).

b.   Why does Mississippi Bulk Transport not have a claim in conversion or under one of the warranties presented in this chapter?

14. Carolyn Hartsock was owed a series of payments pursuant to a structured settlement. She directed Prudential Reinsurance Company, the entity making payment, to remit one such payment in the amount of $60,096 to Singer Asset Finance Company. Singer never received the payment; instead, it was intercepted by Anne McCardy, who altered the check to make it payable to her. McCardy deposited the check in her account with Rich's Employees Credit Union. The drawee/payor bank, CoreStates Bank of Delaware, paid the check, and McCardy withdrew the proceeds and disappeared.

    a.   What cause of action does Hartsock have against Prudential?

    b.   Why does Singer not have a conversion cause of action against CoreStates Bank of Delaware or Rich's Employees Credit Union?

15. Consider the following language from a court's opinion:

> You cross continents and spend years trying to collect a judgment for your client. Late one Friday afternoon, the debtor's lawyer walks into your office and hands you a cashier's check for almost $13 million, covering the entire judgment and all accumulated interest. Do you accept the check or say, "No thank you, I need to make a motion for attorney fees first"? Put another way, is a bird in the hand worth two in the bush?

A company called Gray1 obtained a judgment against SCC Acquisitions. Two years later, SCC tendered a cashier's check, through its attorney, covering the judgment plus accrued interest. The check did not include the $3 million Gray1 had spent in attorney's fees seeking to enforce the judgment. The check was accompanied by a letter indicating that the judgment was "fully satisfied" by the check and directing Gray1 to file a full satisfaction of judgment. Rather than depositing the check immediately, the attorney filed a motion for attorney's fees. After the motion was filed, Gray1 deposited the check, which cleared.

The court held that the motion was untimely because relevant state law requires such a motion to be filed before the judgment has been fully satisfied. Gray1 responded that the judgment was not fully satisfied until the check cleared.

    a.   Why will Gray1 lose this argument?

    b.   How does the cashier's check meet the requirements of the accord-and satisfaction doctrine you have studied?

CHAPTER 10

PAYMENTS BEYOND ARTICLES 3 AND 4

■ ■ ■

This chapter presents several means of payment outside of Articles 3 and 4. Federal law governs some forms of payment presented in this chapter—such as credit cards and electronic fund transfers (including debit-card transactions). Other Articles of the UCC address others; for example, wholesale funds transfers fall within Article 4A, and documentary transactions implicate Articles 5 and 7. Finally, contract law covers a third group of payments, such as virtual currency and some mobile payments. This chapter introduces each of these, and also briefly discusses non-bank financial services.

A. CREDIT CARDS

1. CONSUMERS AND CREDIT CARDS

The Truth in Lending Act (TILA), together with the contract between the cardholder and the credit-card issuer, covers credit cards. TILA is Title I of the Consumer Credit Protection Act, **15 U.S.C. §§ 1601** *et seq.* Although these materials focus on TILA's credit-card provisions, TILA also covers an array of other consumer credit transactions. Regulation Z, found in **12 CFR 1026**, implements TILA. TILA became effective on July 1, 1969, and both TILA and Regulation Z have been amended many times since then to address emerging issues in consumer credit. For example, the Credit Card Accountability Responsibility and Disclosure Act of 2009 (Credit CARD Act) increased the notice a consumer must receive before the interest rate on his or her credit card account is raised. Regulation Z was also amended following the 2008 Higher Education Opportunity Act (HEOA) to add disclosure requirements for private educational lenders. The Helping Families Save Their Homes Act of 2009 amended TILA to require that consumers be notified within a certain period after their mortgage loan is sold or transferred. Regulation Z also governs the contents of the so-called "Schumer box," named after Senator Charles Schumer of New York, which highlights certain rates, fees, terms, and conditions of a credit card agreement. A sample Schumer box from Regulation Z, Appendix G-10B, appears below.

411

G-10(B) Applications and Solicitations Sample (Credit Cards)

Interest Rates and Interest Charges	
Annual Percentage Rate (APR) for Purchases	**8.99%** to **19.99%** when you open your account, based on your creditworthiness. After that, your APR will vary with the market based on the Prime Rate.
APR for Balance Transfers	15.99% This APR will vary with the market based on the Prime Rate.
APR for Cash Advances	21.99% This APR will vary with the market based on the Prime Rate.
Penalty APR and When it Applies	28.99% This APR may be applied to your account if you: 1) Make a late payment; 2) Go over your credit limit twice in a six-month period; 3) Make a payment that is returned; or 4) Do any of the above on another account that you have with us. **How Long Will the Penalty APR Apply?:** If your APRs are increased for any of these reasons, the Penalty APR will apply until you make six consecutive minimum payments when due and do not exceed your credit limit during that time period.
How to Avoid Paying Interest on Purchases	Your due date is at least <u>25 days</u> after the close of each billing cycle. We will not charge you interest <u>on purchases</u> if you pay your entire balance by the due date each month.
Minimum Interest Charge	If you are charged interest, the charge will be no less than $1.50.
For Credit Card Tips from the Federal Reserve Board	To learn more about factors to consider when applying for or using a credit card, visit the website of the Federal Reserve Board at **http://www.federalreserve.gov/creditcard**.

Fees	
Annual Fee	None
Transaction Fees	
• Balance Transfer	Either **$5** or **3%** of the amount of each transfer, whichever is greater (maximum fee: $100).
• Cash Advance	Either **$5** or **3%** of the amount of each cash advance, whichever is greater.
• Foreign Transaction	**2%** of each transaction in U.S. dollars.
Penalty Fees	
• Late Payment	**$29** if balance is less than or equal to $1,000; **$35** if balance is more than $1,000
• Over-the-Credit Limit	**$29**
• Returned Payment	**$35**
Other Fees	
• Required Account Protector Plan	**$0.79** per $100 of balance at the end of each statement period. See back for details.

How We Will Calculate Your Balance: We use a method called "average daily balance (including new purchases)."

Ratner v. Chemical Bank New York Trust Co., 329 F. Supp. 270, 273 (S.D.N.Y. 1971), describes TILA's scope and purpose in general terms:

> [TILA] imposes an array of disclosure requirements to further the objective of "truth in lending"—"so that the consumer will be able to compare more readily the various credit terms available to him and avoid the uninformed use of credit." Among other things, the creditor under an open-end plan, before opening an account, must disclose to the prospective obligor, "to the extent applicable," the conditions for imposing finance charges, the length of any freeride

period, the method of determining finance charges, the periodic rate for computing finance charges, and "the corresponding nominal annual percentage rate determined by multiplying the periodic rate by the number of periods in a year."

TILA rights may accrue before the cardholder's application for credit has been approved. In *Bryson v. Bank of New York*, 584 F. Supp. 1306, 1316 (S.D.N.Y. 1984), the court addressed when these rights first arise:

> [T]he Act was designed to facilitate informed shopping for credit as well as informed purchase of credit. Toward that end, it requires disclosure before, as well as when, credit is extended. Accordingly, the time of attachment of a right of action under the Act should be fixed with a view toward protecting the interests of those shopping for credit as well as those actually purchasing credit. Imposing the requirement that a binding contract be created on both sides before a right of action attaches would needlessly limit the plaintiff class while inhibiting enforcement of the former purpose. A more appropriate time of attachment is that point at which the consumer, on the basis of the information his "comparison shopping" has generated, makes a choice and commits himself or herself to the purchase of credit, without regard for the degree of commitment of the lender. This marks the end of the consumer's shopping. It is at this time that the consumer becomes vulnerable to actual damage from the lender's inadequate or deceptive disclosures, for at this time he or she can be contractually bound to the terms of the lending contract at the option of the lender. The rule insures that all plaintiffs are seriously-intentioned consumers of credit, for it requires them to incur some risk in return for a right of action under the Act. At the same time, it prevents the lender from binding his potential debtors with inadequate disclosure and then selecting as customers those whom he thinks are least likely to pursue their rights under the Act. Instead, it impresses upon the lender the importance of full compliance with the Act before the customer is committed.

Thus, a cardholder's TILA rights arise when the cardholder applies for credit rather than when the issuer approves the application.

As the title "Consumer Credit Protection Act" suggests, TILA generally covers consumer, rather than business, transactions. Some TILA provisions relating to the issuance or unauthorized or fraudulent use of credit cards do, however, apply to businesses.

2. UNAUTHORIZED USE OF CREDIT CARDS

The portion of TILA relating to unauthorized credit-card use, **15 U.S.C. § 1643**, provides powerful protection for consumers. The cardholder will not be liable for any purchases an unauthorized user makes after the cardholder has notified the issuer that the card was lost or stolen. In addition, the cardholder may be liable only up to $50 for charges incurred prior to such notification. As a practical matter, issuers often offer "Zero Liability" for unauthorized use, thus declining the up to $50 to which they would otherwise be entitled. This policy encourages credit-card use and also motivates issuers to contact cardholders whenever the issuer suspects fraud or abuse.

Although Section 1643 covers businesses as a default rule, a business providing cards from the same issuer to ten or more employees may, pursuant to **15 U.S.C. § 1645**, agree to lesser protection against unauthorized use. Even so, each individual employee's liability will be limited in accordance with **15 U.S.C. § 1643**.

The credit-card contract, interpreted in the light of state agency law, determines whether a given use was authorized. The cardholder is not required to prove that use of the card was unauthorized; instead, the issuer must prove authorization. Normally, the issuer relies on broad contractual language defining "authorized use." As an example of such language, Chase Bank USA provided the following excerpt from one of its credit-card agreements in pleadings it filed in the case of *Siler v. Chase Bank USA*, No. 08CV00130, 2009 WL 7817476 (N.D. W.Va Jan. 27, 2009):

> **Others Using Your Account**—You promise to pay for all purchases and advances made by anyone you authorize to use your account, whether or not you notify us that they will be using it. If someone else is authorized to use your account and you want to end that person's privilege, you must let us know in writing, and if he or she has a Card, you must return that Card cut in half with your written notice.

The following case illustrates express, implied, and apparent authority, as they relate to credit-card use. In reading this case, note how the court uses Article 4's Bank Statement Rule by analogy. This case also serves to introduce the concept of "an accepted credit card." **15 U.S.C. § 1602(m)** defines the term as follows:

> The term "accepted credit card" means any credit card which the cardholder has requested and received or has signed or has used, or authorized another to use, for the purpose of obtaining money, property, labor, or services on credit.

EDWARD J. MINSKOFF V. AMERICAN EXPRESS TRAVEL RELATED SERVICES CO., INC.

98 F.3d 703 (2d Cir. 1996)

MAHONEY, J.

* * *

Background

Minskoff is the president and chief executive officer of Equities, a real estate holding and management firm. In 1988, Equities opened an American Express corporate card account (the "Corporate Account") for which one charge card was issued in Minskoff's name. Minskoff also maintained a personal American Express account, which was established in 1963.

In October 1991, Equities hired Susan Schrader Blumenfeld to serve as its assistant to the president/office manager. Blumenfeld was responsible for both the personal and business affairs of Minskoff, and her duties included screening Minskoff's mail, reviewing vendor invoices and credit card statements (including statements for the Corporate Account), and forwarding such invoices and statements to Equities' bookkeepers for payment. Prior to Blumenfeld's employment with Equities, Minskoff personally reviewed all Corporate Account statements; after hiring Blumenfeld, he no longer reviewed any of these statements.

In March 1992, defendant-appellee American Express received an application for an additional credit card to issue from the Corporate Account in Blumenfeld's name. The application had been pre-addressed by American Express and mailed to Minskoff at his business address. It had been completed and submitted by Blumenfeld without the knowledge or acquiescence of Equities or Minskoff. American Express issued the supplemental card and mailed it to Equities' business address. From April 1992 to March 1993, Blumenfeld charged a total of $28,213.88 on that card.

During this period, American Express sent twelve monthly billing statements for the Corporate Account to Equities' business address. Each statement listed both Blumenfeld and Minskoff as cardholders on the Corporate Account, and separately itemized Corporate Account charges for Minskoff and Blumenfeld. These twelve statements show a total of $28,213.88 in charges attributed to Blumenfeld and $23,099.37 in charges attributed to Minskoff, for a total of $51,313.25. Between April 1992 and March 1993, American Express received twelve checks, drawn on accounts maintained by Minskoff or Equities at Manufacturers Hanover Trust ("MHT"), in payment of these charges, with each check made payable to American Express and bearing Equities' Corporate Account number. Minskoff did not review any statements or cancelled checks received during 1992 and 1993 from either his personal account with MHT or the Equities account with MHT.

In July 1992, American Express sent Minskoff an unsolicited invitation to apply for a platinum card. Blumenfeld accepted the invitation on behalf of Minskoff, again without the knowledge or acquiescence of either Minskoff or Equities. Blumenfeld also submitted a request for a supplemental card to issue from this new account (the "Platinum Account") in her name. When platinum cards arrived in both Minskoff's and Blumenfeld's names, Blumenfeld gave Minskoff his card, claiming that it was an unsolicited upgrade of his American Express card privileges. Minskoff proceeded to use his platinum card for occasional purchases, and Blumenfeld charged approximately $300,000 to the Platinum Account between July 1992 and November 1993.

Between August 1992 and November 1993, American Express mailed sixteen Platinum Account monthly billing statements to Equities' business address. Each statement named Blumenfeld and Minskoff as cardholders and itemized charges for each separately. These statements attributed a total of $250,394.44 in charges to Blumenfeld and $10,497.31 to Minskoff, for a total of $260,891.75. These bills were paid in full with checks drawn on the MHT accounts, made payable to American Express, and bearing the Platinum Account number.

In November 1993, Equities' controller, Steven Marks, informed Minskoff that MHT had called to inquire about a check made payable to American Express for approximately $41,000 that had been written on Equities' MHT account. Minskoff stopped payment on the check, initiated an internal investigation of Equities' accounts that revealed the full extent of Blumenfeld's fraudulent activities, and gave notice to American Express of Blumenfeld's unauthorized charges to the Platinum and Corporate Accounts. Blumenfeld subsequently stated in an affidavit that she had forged approximately sixty checks drawn on Equities' MHT account and Minskoff's personal MHT account, including at least twenty payments to American Express for charges to the Platinum and Corporate Accounts. Although some of these checks were used to pay legitimate obligations of plaintiffs-appellants, an accounting analysis attributed losses totaling $412,684.06 to Blumenfeld's theft. In January 1994, Blumenfeld agreed to repay $250,000 to Minskoff and Equities in return for their promise not to institute legal action against her.

Plaintiffs-appellants initiated this action in the United States District Court for the Southern District of New York on February 15, 1994. As previously noted, they sought (1) to recover $276,334.06 that had been paid to American Express in satisfaction of unauthorized charges by Blumenfeld, and (2) a declaration that they were not liable for the outstanding balances on the Platinum Account. The district court, however, dismissed their complaint and awarded American Express $51,657.71 on its counterclaim for that balance. The district court reasoned that the $50 limit on a cardholder's liability for the unauthorized use of the cardholder's credit card specified in **15 U.S.C. § 1643(a)(1)(B)** . . . did not apply to plaintiffs-appellants because their negligence in failing to examine credit card statements that would have revealed Blumenfeld's fraudulent charges "resulted in an appearance of authority [to use the cards] in Blumenfeld."

This appeal followed.

Discussion

* * *

Plaintiffs-appellants contend that because Blumenfeld obtained the platinum and corporate credit cards through forgery and fraud, her use of the cards is *per se* unauthorized under section 1643 . . . and plaintiffs-appellants' liability is therefore limited to $50 by section **1643(a)(1)(B)**. Section 1643 applies, however, only in the case of an "unauthorized use" of a credit card. *See* § **1643(a)(1)**, **(d)**. The term "unauthorized use" is defined as "a use of a credit card by a person other than the cardholder who does not have actual, implied, or apparent authority for such use and from which the cardholder receives no benefit." [**15 U.S.C. § 1602(p)**]. In determining whether a use is unauthorized, "Congress apparently contemplated, and courts have accepted, primary reliance on background principles of agency law in determining the liability of cardholders for charges incurred by third-party card bearers." *Towers World Airways v. PHH Aviation Systems*, 933 F.2d 174, 176–77 (2d Cir.), *cert. denied*, 502 U.S. 823, 112 S.Ct. 87, 116 L.Ed.2d 59 (1991).

Under general principles of agency, the authority of an agent "is the power of the agent to do an act or to conduct a transaction on account of the principal which, with respect to the principal, he is privileged to do because of the principal's manifestations to him." *Restatement (Second) of Agency* (the "*Restatement*") § 7 cmt. a (1958). Such authority may be express or implied, but in either case it exists only where the agent may reasonably infer from the words or conduct of the principal that the principal has consented to the agent's performance of a particular act. *See id.* cmt. b.

Apparent authority is "entirely distinct from authority, either express or implied," *id.* § 8 cmt. a, and arises from the "written or spoken words or any other conduct of the principal which, reasonably interpreted, causes [a] third person to believe that the principal consents to have [an] act done on his behalf by the person purporting to act for him," *Id.* § 27. Apparent authority, then, is normally created through the words and conduct of the principal as they are interpreted by a third party, and cannot be established by the actions or representations of the agent.

The existence of apparent authority is normally a question of fact, and therefore inappropriate for resolution on a motion for summary judgment. However, a principal may be estopped from denying apparent authority if

(1) the principal's intentional or negligent acts, including acts of omission, created an appearance of authority in the agent, (2) on which a third party reasonably and in good faith relied, and (3) such reliance resulted in a detrimental change in position on the part of the third party.

Viewing the facts in the light most favorable to plaintiffs-appellants, it is clear that Blumenfeld acted without actual or implied authority when she forged the platinum card acceptance form and supplemental card applications. Accordingly, plaintiff-appellants cannot be held accountable for Blumenfeld's initial possession of corporate and platinum cards.

    * * *

This result is consistent with the underlying policy of the TILA to protect credit card holders against losses due to theft or fraudulent use of credit cards on the theory that the card issuer is in the better position to prevent such losses. We accordingly disagree with the decision of the district court insofar as it imposed upon plaintiffs-appellants the entire burden of the unauthorized charges made by Blumenfeld to the Corporate and Platinum Accounts.

However, while we accept the proposition that the *acquisition* of a credit card through fraud or theft cannot be said to occur under the apparent authority of the cardholder, [this holding does not] preclude a finding of apparent authority for the subsequent *use* of a credit card so obtained. Under the rule urged by plaintiffs-appellants, a cardholder could disregard both credit card and bank statements indefinitely, or even fail to act upon a discovery that an employee had fraudulently obtained and was fraudulently using a credit card, and still limit his liability for an employee's fraudulent purchases to $50. Nothing in the TILA suggests that Congress intended to sanction intentional or negligent conduct by the cardholder that furthers the fraud or theft of an unauthorized card user. We therefore agree with the district court to the extent that it decided that the negligent acts or omissions of a cardholder may create apparent authority to use the card in a person who obtained the card through theft or fraud. Apparent authority created through the cardholder's negligence does not, however, retroactively authorize charges incurred prior to the negligent acts that created the apparent authority of the user.

Applying these principles to the case at hand, we address the district court's conclusion that plaintiffs-appellants' failure to examine credit card and bank statements amounts to negligence which created an appearance of authority in Blumenfeld to use the card. Under New York law, consumers are obligated to "exercise reasonable care and promptness to examine [bank] statement[s] . . . to discover [any] unauthorized signature or any alteration." N.Y.U.C.C. § 4–406(1) [UCC **4–406(a)**]. This provision is derived from a common law obligation to examine bank statements and report forgeries or alterations, and it is based upon a determination that "the depositor [is] in the better position to discover an alteration of the check or forgery of his or her own signature." *Woods v. MONY Legacy Life Ins. Co.*, 84 N.Y.2d 280, 284, 617 N.Y.S.2d 452, 453, 641 N.E.2d 1070, 1071 (1994) (extending application of N.Y.U.C.C. § **4–406** to brokerage accounts).

This policy is no less applicable to credit card holders than it is to bank depositors. Once a cardholder has established a credit card account, and provided that the card issuer is in compliance with the billing statement disclosure requirements of **15 U.S.C. § 1637**, the cardholder is in a superior position to determine whether the charges reflected on his regular billing statements are legitimate. A cardholder's failure to examine credit card statements that would reveal fraudulent use of the card constitutes a negligent omission that creates apparent authority for charges that would otherwise be considered unauthorized under the TILA.

It is undisputed that between April 1992 and November 1993, American Express mailed to Equities' business address at least twenty-eight monthly billing statements documenting charges made to the Platinum and Corporate Accounts. Each of those statements clearly lists Blumenfeld as a cardholder, and each specifically itemizes those charges attributable to her credit card. During that same period, MHT mailed to Equities' business address numerous bank statements showing that checks made payable to American Express had been drawn on Equities' business account and Minskoff's personal account to pay these American Express charges. Minskoff concedes that he failed to examine any of these statements until November 1993, and no other employee or agent of Equities (other than Blumenfeld) became aware of the disputed monthly payments to American Express prior to the inquiry by Bankers Trust in November 1993. These omissions on the part of plaintiffs-appellants created apparent authority for Blumenfeld's continuing use of the cards, especially because it enabled Blumenfeld to pay all of the American Express statements with forged checks, thereby fortifying American Express' continuing impression that nothing was amiss with the Corporate and Platinum Accounts.

Plaintiffs-appellants argue that summary judgment is inappropriate because they exercised reasonable care in the hiring and supervision of Blumenfeld and in the implementation and administration of internal accounting procedures designed to detect and prevent fraud. In this case, however, while American Express concedes that Equities employed bookkeepers who were responsible, *inter alia*, for reviewing credit card statements and arranging for their payment, as well as reviewing bank statements and cancelled checks, the inadequate manner in which these procedures were performed from April 1992 to November 1993 enabled Blumenfeld to acquire unauthorized American Express credit cards, run up more than $300,000 in invalid American Express charges, and pay for them with approximately twenty forged checks drawn on Equities' MHT account and Minskoff's personal MHT account, without detection.

A cursory review of any of the American Express statements would have disclosed charges by Blumenfeld made with an unauthorized credit card. A review of any MHT statement would have disclosed one or more payments to American Express (or, if the cancelled checks had previously been removed by Blumenfeld, charges that could not be matched to cancelled checks) generally in amounts far exceeding Minskoff's habitual American Express charges. We are not dealing in this case with an occasional transgression buried in a welter of financial detail. In our view, once a cardholder receives a statement that reasonably puts him on notice that one or more fraudulent charges have been made, he cannot thereafter claim lack of knowledge. The district court was justified in determining that no reasonable jury could conclude that this standard had been satisfied as to plaintiffs-appellants on the record presented in this case, warranting summary judgment in favor of American Express to the extent that we have previously indicated.

* * *

In the *Minskoff* case, because Blumenfeld obtained the additional credit cards without cardholder Minskoff's consent, the cards were not "accepted credit cards." Even so, the court held that Minskoff should have discovered Blumenfeld's fraud after he received the first statement from American Express. Thus, although Blumenfeld lacked authority to obtain the cards, Minskoff's actions in failing to review the statements and discover her fraud operated to create apparent authority.

One spouse's unwanted use of the other spouse's separate credit card is another fairly common problem potentially implicating **15 U.S.C. § 1643**. Courts take varying approaches to the issue of when such use is legally unauthorized. *Society National Bank v. Kienzle*, 463 N.E.2d 1261 (Ohio. App. 1983), illustrates one approach. In that case, the court held that "a husband is not answerable for the acts of his wife unless the wife acts as his agent or he subsequently ratifies her acts." Because "there was no evidence introduced that defendant's wife acted as his agent, or that he ratified her conduct," the husband was not liable for his estranged wife's shopping spree with his separate credit card. In so holding, the court noted that the husband notified the credit card issuer immediately upon discovering her use of the card. Other courts take a different approach, focusing on whether the cardholder benefited from the purchase, rather than authorization or ratification.

When a cardholder's friend—rather than a spouse—uses his or her credit card, the court's analysis may be different. In *Universal Bank v. McCafferty*, 624 N.E.2d 358, 360 (Ohio App. 1993), the court considered a dispute arising from James McCafferty's decision to apply for a Universal Bank credit card, which he subsequently received. His wife, concerned about the large number of cards the family already had, returned the card to the bank. McCafferty telephoned Universal Bank and asked that the card be reissued to a different address, where a friend lived. The bank assented, sending the card and PIN to the friend's address. The friend used the card for purchases and cash advances totaling around $3,800, without notifying McCafferty or reimbursing him for the charges. Universal Bank sued McCafferty. In finding the charges unauthorized and McCafferty's liability thus limited to $50, the court held as follows:

> Universal contends that McCafferty and his friend had an agency relationship based on apparent authority. Apparent authority is not established by the conduct of the agent, but by acts of the principal which cloak the agent with apparent power to bind the principal. Universal claims that McCafferty's act of requesting that the credit card be sent to his friend's address clothed his friend with apparent authority. We disagree. While McCafferty authorized Universal to send the card to his friend's address, that did not authorize use of the card by the addressee. The mere authorization to mail a credit card to a certain address cannot be expanded to encompass the apparent authorization to charge on that credit card.

In the following section, we move from unauthorized use into another kind of issue that can arise with credit-card use—disputes regarding the quality of the goods or services received.

3. CREDIT-CARD DISPUTE RESOLUTION

TILA provides protection to consumer cardholders who are dissatisfied with goods or services purchased with a credit card and are unsuccessful in resolving the dispute directly with the seller. **15 U.S.C. § 1666i** is the portion of the Act addressing dispute resolution. A number of credit-card issuers have posted the following language on-line providing an overview of consumer dispute resolution rights:

Your Rights if You're Dissatisfied with Your Credit Card Purchases:

If you are dissatisfied with the goods or services that you have purchased with your credit card, and you have tried in good faith to correct the problem with the merchant, you may have the right not to pay the remaining amount due on the purchase. To use this right, all of the following must be true:

1. The purchase must have been made in your home state or within 100 miles of your current mailing address, and the purchase price must have been more than $50. (Note: Neither of

these is necessary if your purchase was based on an advertisement we mailed to you, or if we own the company that sold you the goods or services.)

2.   You must have used your credit card for the purchase. Purchases made with cash advances from an ATM or with an Account check do not qualify.

3.   You must not yet have fully paid for the purchase.

If all of the criteria above are met and you are still dissatisfied with the purchase, contact us in writing at the address for billing inquiries and correspondence shown on the front of your statement. While we investigate, [you need not pay] the disputed amount. . . . After we finish our investigation, we will tell you our decision. At that point, if we think you owe an amount and you do not pay, we may report you as delinquent.

TILA's dispute-resolution feature encourages cardholders to use credit cards for large, important, or risky purchases. This protection, however, is available only when the cardholder has already tried, and failed, to obtain a reasonable resolution from the seller. As *Izraelewitz v. Manufacturers Hanover Trust Co.*, 465 N.Y.S. 2d 486, 487–88 (1983), shows, whether the merchant has acted reasonably is a fact-specific inquiry. George Izraelewitz ordered electronic diagrams from Don Britton Enterprises, a Hawaiian company that also sold rooftop-mounted listening devices and other surveillance- and counter-surveillance equipment. He then tried to return the merchandise. As a part of this process, Izraelewitz contacted Manufacturers Hanover Trust Company, his credit-card issuer, indicating the diagrams were unsuitable for his needs. He provided Manufacturers Hanover with a receipt showing he had returned the merchandise. The issuer credited his account and waived the finance charges for the purchase. Manufacturers Hanover then charged the purchase price back to the merchant. The merchant refused the charge-back, citing its strict "no refund policy" and emphasizing that Izraelewitz had admitted he was aware of the policy. The merchant produced evidence that Izraelewitz had acted dishonestly: he attempted to ensure the return would be accepted by labeling the package without a return address, repacking the merchandise, and delivering the returned package through indirect means rather than shipping it directly to the company. The merchant also indicated the diagrams appeared to have been photocopied. The issuer then informed Izraelewitz that it would redebit his account and, when he objected, the entire cycle of charge-back and refusal was repeated.

In finding the "no refund" policy was not unreasonable and that TILA's dispute-resolution process was therefore unavailable to Izraelewitz, the court held as follows:

"No Refund" policies, per se, are not unconscionable or offensive to public policy in any manner. [The] Truth in Lending Law "(n)either requires refunds for returns nor does it prohibit refunds in kind." Bank-merchant agreements, however, usually do contain a requirement that the merchant establish a fair policy for exchange and return of merchandise.

To establish the fairness in Don Britton's policy, the strength of the reasons behind the policy and the measures taken to inform the consumer of it must necessarily be considered. Don Britton's rationale for its policy is compelling. It contends that printing is a very small part of its business, which is selling original designs, and "once a customer has seen the designs, he possesses what we have to sell." Britton's policy is clearly written in its catalog directly on the page which explains how to order merchandise. To compensate for not having a refund policy, which would be impractical considering the nature of the product, Britton offers well-advertised backup plans with free engineering assistance and an exchange procedure, as well, if [the] original plans are beyond the customer's capabilities.

Thus, the merchant can resist a charge-back resulting from a cardholder's exercise of TILA rights and may prevail if the issuer determines the merchant is in the right.

4. ACCOUNT CANCELLATION
AND BILLING ERRORS

In addition to the disputes that can arise between cardholders and merchants, cardholders sometimes sue issuers for wrongful account cancellation or billing errors. In *Novack v. Cities Service Oil Co.*, 374 A.2d 89, 91–2 (N.J. Super 1977), the court considered a cardholder's claims of defamation and breach of contract based on alleged wrongful cancellation. The facts of the case are as follows:

Plaintiff applied for and obtained a Cities Service [Oil Company] credit card in September 1972. Included with the card, when mailed to plaintiff, was a pamphlet describing generally the terms of the account. One such term was that the account could be cancelled at any time and that, upon written request, the card was to be returned to Cities Service. On February 4, 1974, plaintiff's account had a substantial balance which was then more than 40 days past due. On that same date, defendant mailed a notice to the operator of one of its service stations which plaintiff had used on a regular basis. The notice informed the operator that plaintiff's card was no longer to be honored and that a reward would be paid for its return.

The operator seized the card, and the cardholder brought suit. In rejecting the cardholder's contract claim, the court held as follows:

> The issuance of a credit card is but an offer to extend a line of open-account credit. It is unilateral and supported by no consideration. The offer may be withdrawn at any time, without prior notice, for any reason or, indeed, for no reason at all, and its withdrawal breaches no duty—for there is no duty to continue it— and violates no rights. Acceptance or use of the card by the offeree makes a contract between the parties according to its terms, but we have seen none which prevents a termination of the arrangement at any time by either party. As a rule, there is no requirement of prior notice for termination by the issuer. A request to the person holding the card that it be surrendered upon termination of the extension of credit by the issuer is reasonable, and if he has the card it should be surrendered.

> * * *

> Basically, . . . a credit card is nothing more than an indication to sellers of commodities that the person who has received a credit card from the issuer thereof has a satisfactory credit rating and that if credit is extended, the issuer of the credit card will pay (or see to it that the seller of the commodity receives payment) for the merchandise delivered.

Although issuers generally have the right to cancel an account, in some cases they will be liable for wrongful cancellation. In *Gray v. American Express Co.*, 743 F.2d 10, 13–9 (D.C. Cir. 1984), the court addressed the following facts:

> [Oscar] Gray had been a[n American Express] cardholder since 1964. In 1981, following some complicated billings arising out of deferred travel charges incurred by Gray, disputes arose about the amount due American Express. After considerable correspondence, . . . American Express decided to cancel Gray's card. No notification of this cancellation was communicated to Gray until the night of April 8, 1982, when he offered his American Express card to pay for a wedding-anniversary dinner he and his wife already had consumed in a Washington restaurant. The restaurant informed Gray that American Express had refused to accept the charges for the meal and had instructed the restaurant to confiscate and destroy his card. Gray spoke to the American Express employee on the telephone at the restaurant who informed him, "Your account is cancelled as of now."

Mr. Gray sued under the Fair Credit Billing Act, **15 U.S.C. §§ 1666** *et seq.*, which is part of TILA, alleging American Express had handled the billing dispute improperly because it cancelled the account. In allowing the case to proceed past summary judgment, the court held as follows:

> [The] Fair Credit Billing Act seeks to prescribe an orderly procedure for identifying and resolving disputes between a cardholder and a card issuer as to the amount due at any given time. . . .
>
> If the [cardholder] believes that the statement contains a billing error, . . . he then may send the creditor a written notice setting forth that belief, indicating the amount of the error and the reasons supporting his belief that it is an error. If the creditor receives this notice within 60 days of transmitting the statement of account, [the Act] imposes two separate obligations upon the creditor. Within 30 days, it must send a written acknowledgment that it has received the notice. And, within 90 days or two complete billing cycles, whichever is shorter, the creditor must investigate the matter and either make appropriate corrections in the [cardholder's] account or send a written explanation of its belief that the original statement sent to the [cardholder] was correct. The creditor must send its explanation before making any attempt to collect the disputed amount.
>
> A creditor that fails to comply with [the Act] forfeits its right to collect the first $50 of the disputed amount including finance charges. In addition, [the Act] provides that, pursuant to regulations of the Federal Reserve Board, a creditor operating an "open-end consumer credit plan" may not restrict or close an account due to a [cardholder's] failure to pay a disputed amount until the creditor has sent the written explanation required by [the Act].

* * *

> . . . American Express . . . urges that, even if the Act is otherwise pertinent, Gray was bound by the terms of the Cardmember Agreement, which empowered American Express to cancel the credit card without notice and without cause.

The contract between Gray and American Express provides:

> [W]e can revoke your right to use [the card] at any time. We can do this with or without cause and without giving you notice.

American Express seems to argue that . . . it can exercise its right to cancellation for cause unrelated to the disputed amount, or for *no* cause, thus bringing itself out from under the statute. At the very least, the argument is audacious. American Express would restrict the efficacy of the statute to those situations where the parties had not agreed to a "without cause, without notice" cancellation clause, or to those cases where the cardholder can prove that the sole reason for cancellation was the amount in dispute. We doubt that Congress painted with such a faint brush.

. . . Within the limits of state and federal statutes, credit cards can still be cancelled without cause and without notice. But the cancellation can affect only transactions which have not occurred before the cancellation is communicated to the cardholder. In practical terms, American Express will have to make an effort to communicate its cancellation decision to the cardholder. The effort may be as informal as a phone call or a telegram. . . .

. . . If a cardholder seeks to use his American Express card to buy a car, for example, we think that a communication, through the car dealer, that the card has been cancelled prior to title passing to the cardholder may effect notice in reasonable fashion. But where the meal has been consumed, or the hotel room has been slept in, or the service rendered, the communication through the merchant comes too late to void the credit for that transaction.

Even contracts of adhesion are contracts. To allow cancellation without any communication of the decision is to turn the contract into a snare and deceit.

In a case like this one, in which the cardholder is in a billing dispute with the issuer, the issuer is well advised to make sure it can clearly establish that the card is being cancelled for reasons other than the cardholder's refusal to pay disputed charges.

5. DISCLOSURES AND RESPONSIBLE USE OF CREDIT

Even prior to the Financial Crisis of 2008, there were efforts to encourage responsible use of consumer credit, through enhanced disclosures and other mechanisms. The Bankruptcy Abuse Prevention and Consumer Protection Act of 2005 (BAPCPA), which became federal law on April 20, 2005, includes the following language:

ENHANCED DISCLOSURES UNDER AN OPEN END CREDIT PLAN.

(a) MINIMUM PAYMENT DISCLOSURES.—Section 127 (b) of the Truth in Lending Act (**15 U.S.C. 1637(b)**) is amended by adding at the end the following:

"(11) (A) In the case of an open end credit plan that requires a minimum monthly payment of not more than 4 percent of the balance on which finance charges are accruing, the following statement, located on the front of the billing statement, disclosed clearly and conspicuously: 'Minimum Payment Warning: Making only the minimum payment will increase the interest you pay and the time it takes to repay your balance. For example, making only the typical 2% minimum monthly payment on a balance of $1,000 at an interest rate of 17% would take 88 months to repay the balance in full. For an estimate of the time it would take to repay your balance, making only minimum payments, call this toll-free number: _____.' (the blank space to be filled in by the creditor)."

In addition, in January 2003, the U.S. Office of the Comptroller of the Currency issued new guidelines with respect to minimum monthly credit-card payments. Following this guidance, issuers raised the minimum monthly credit-card payment from 2% to 4%. This step was designed to encourage responsible use of consumer credit, but also caused difficulty for consumers who could barely afford a 2% minimum payment.

6. MERCHANTS AND CREDIT CARDS

Merchants and credit-card companies have ongoing relationships, just as cardholders and card issuers do. Customers may use credit cards only when purchasing goods or services from merchants equipped to accept the card tendered. The merchant must have pre-established banking and contractual relationships that allow it to accept whatever card the customer tenders, whether it be Visa, MasterCard, American Express, Discover, or some other card.

MasterCard describes its payment process on its website as follows:

Step 1: The customer pays with MasterCard

The customer purchases goods/services from a merchant.

Step 2: The payment is authenticated

The merchant point-of-sale system captures the customer's account information and securely sends it to the acquirer.

Step 3: The transaction is submitted

The merchant acquirer asks MasterCard to get an authorization from the customer's issuing bank.

Step 4: Authorization is requested

MasterCard submits the transaction to the issuer for authorization.

Step 5: Authorization response

The issuing bank authorizes the transaction and routes the response back to the merchant.

Step 6: Merchant payment

The issuing bank routes the payment to the merchant's acquirer who deposits the payment into the merchant's account.

To explain some of the terms used above, the acquirer is also known as a "merchant bank." This is the bank that works with the merchant to fulfill the payment transaction. The customer's issuing bank is the entity that issued the card to the customer. Typically, the name of the customer's issuing bank appears on the card. MasterCard describes itself as "neither an issuer nor an acquirer" and states, "Our role is to provide the technology and the network that power transactions."

When cardholders invoke the dispute-resolution process described earlier in this section, the merchant's account will be "charged back" if it is determined that the cardholder was justified in disputing the charge. High levels of charge-backs—which can result from a customer's unauthorized use of a card, a merchant's failure to obtain the cardholder's signature on the credit slip, a merchant's acceptance of an expired card, or processing errors, as well as disputes regarding the goods or services delivered—can lead to cancellation of the merchant's account.

B. ELECTRONIC FUND TRANSFERS

The Electronic Fund Transfers Act (EFTA), **15 U.S.C. §§ 1693** *et seq.*, is part of the Consumer Credit Protection Act, **15 U.S.C. §§ 1601** *et seq.* EFTA, enacted in 1978, governs a wide array of transactions. Examples include direct deposit, ATM withdrawals, debit transactions (either on-line or in-person), online bill payment in which your bank transfers funds electronically on your behalf, recurring pre-authorized bill payments, and conversion of a check into an electronic payment at the point of sale (ECK). The reason EFTA, rather than UCC Articles 3 and 4, covers ECK is that the check in an ECK transaction never enters the Article 4 check-collection system, but instead serves as a source document for an electronic transfer.

Regulation E, **12 CFR Part 205**, was written to effectuate EFTA. EFTA governs only retail (i.e. consumer) transactions; wholesale (i.e. business) transactions are within Article 4A, presented later in this chapter.

EFTA mandates periodic account statements, as well as certain disclosures, error resolution processes, and protections against unauthorized use. Although Regulation E normally requires a receipt with detailed transaction information to be issued for each transaction, transactions of $15 or less are now exempted. Regulation E has also been amended to address overdrafts. Banks can no longer charge overdraft fees for ATM and one-time debit-card purchases, unless the consumer has either opted in or affirmatively consented to having overdraft services provided in these transactions. Otherwise, the bank must decline the transaction.

EFTA's protection for unauthorized use is much more limited than TILA's. Consider the following language from GTE Financial Credit Union's Debit MasterCard agreement, which reflects the pertinent provisions of **15 U.S.C. § 1693g**:

> Tell us AT ONCE if you believe your card has been lost or stolen or if you believe someone has used your card or PIN or otherwise accessed your accounts without your authority. Telephoning is the best way of keeping your possible losses down. You could lose all the money in your account (plus your maximum overdraft line of credit). If a transaction was made with your card or card number without your permission, your liability for an unauthorized transaction is determined as follows. If you tell us within two business days after you learn of the loss or theft of your card, you can lose no more than $50 if someone used your card without your permission. If you do NOT tell us within the two business days and we can prove we could have stopped someone from using your card without your permission if you had told us, you could lose as much as $500. Also, if your statement shows transfers that you did not make, tell us AT ONCE. If you do not tell us within 60 days after the statement was mailed to you, you may not get back any money lost after the 60 days if we can prove that we could have stopped someone from making the transfers if you had told us in time.

Other issuers use identical or near-identical language. Thus, unlike TILA, under which consumer liability for unauthorized use is capped at $50 as a matter of federal law, consumer liability under EFTA is, under some circumstances, unlimited. In addition, EFTA does not include a dispute-resolution provision like TILA's for consumers who are disappointed with the quality of goods or services received from a seller.

Like TILA, EFTA handles account errors separately from allegations of unauthorized use. When a customer alleges that an electronic-fund-transfer error has occurred, **15 U.S.C. § 1693f** requires the bank that made the transfer to investigate the allegations and report the outcome to the consumer. In *Bisbey v. D.C. National Bank*, 793 F.2d 315, 317 (D.C. Cir. 1986), the court considered a suit based on a bank's alleged failure to follow-up on its investigation by providing its customer with notice of the outcome. The bank conducted an investigation and concluded no error had occurred, but notified its customer of these results only telephonically, rather than in writing. In finding that the customer had stated a cause of action under EFTA, the court held as follows:

> This section imposed a duty upon the Bank to "deliver or mail" the results of its investigation to [its customer who had requested the

transfer] and to advise her of her right to request reproductions of all documents which it relied upon to conclude that no error occurred. The oral notice given to appellant was insufficient.

Even so, because the court found the customer had suffered no damage due to the bank's failure of notice, it awarded only nominal damages.

Unauthorized withdrawals from automated teller machines can raise issues of customers' and banks' shared liability analogous to those presented in Chapter 8. The following case shows how one court resolved the issue and illustrates the potential for significant consumer loss under **15 U.S.C. § 1693g**.

KRUSER V. BANK OF AMERICA NT & SA

230 Cal. App. 3d 741 (Cal. App. 1991)

STONE, J.

Appellants Lawrence Kruser and Georgene Kruser filed a complaint against Bank of America, claiming damages for unauthorized electronic withdrawals from their account by someone using Mr. Kruser's "Versatel" [ATM] card. The trial court entered summary judgment in favor of the Bank because it determined appellants had failed to comply with the notice-and-reporting requirements of the Electronic Fund Transfer Act.

. . . The Krusers maintained a joint checking account with the Bank, and the Bank issued each of them a "Versatel" card and separate personal identification numbers which would allow access to funds in their account from automatic teller machines. . . .

The Krusers believed Mr. Kruser's card had been destroyed in September 1986. The December 1986 account statement mailed to the Krusers by the bank reflected a $20 unauthorized withdrawal of funds by someone using Mr. Kruser's card at an automatic teller machine. The Krusers reported this unauthorized transaction to the Bank when they discovered it in August or September 1987.

* * *

In September 1987, the Krusers received bank statements for July and August 1987 which reflected 47 unauthorized withdrawals, totaling $9,020, made from an automatic teller machine, again by someone using Mr. Kruser's card. They notified the bank of these withdrawals within a few days of receiving the statements. The Bank refused to credit the Krusers' account with the amount of the unauthorized withdrawals.

* * *

The ultimate issue we address is whether, as a matter of law, the failure to report the unauthorized $20 withdrawal which appeared on the

December 1986 statement barred appellants from recovery for the losses incurred in July and August 1987. . . .

* * *

The trial court concluded the Bank was entitled to judgment as a matter of law because the unauthorized withdrawals of July and August 1987 occurred more than 60 days after appellants received a statement which reflected an unauthorized transfer in December 1986. . . .

Appellants contend the December withdrawal of $20 was so isolated in time and minimal in amount that it cannot be considered in connection with the July and August withdrawals. . . . They argue that, if a consumer receives a bank statement which reflects an unauthorized minimal electronic transfer and fails to report the transaction to the bank within 60 days of transmission of the bank statement, unauthorized transfers many years later, perhaps totaling thousands of dollars, would remain the responsibility of the consumer.

The result appellants fear is avoided by the requirement that the bank establish the subsequent unauthorized transfers could have been prevented had the consumer notified the bank of the first unauthorized transfer. Here, although the unauthorized transfer of $20 occurred approximately seven months before the unauthorized transfers totaling $9,020, it is undisputed that all transfers were made by someone using Mr. Kruser's card which the Krusers believed had been destroyed prior to December 1986. According to the declaration of Yvonne Maloon, the Bank's Versatel risk manager, the Bank could have and would have cancelled Mr. Kruser's card had it been timely notified of the December unauthorized transfer. In that event, Mr. Kruser's card could not have been used to accomplish the unauthorized transactions in July and August. . . .

* * *

[N]othing in the record reflects any extenuating circumstances which would have prevented Mr. Kruser from reviewing the bank statements. The understanding he had with Mrs. Kruser that she would review the bank statements did not excuse him from his obligation to notify the bank of any unauthorized electronic transfers.

Appellants cite no authority which supports their claim that the consumer must not only receive the statement provided by the bank, but must acquire actual knowledge of an unauthorized transfer from the statement. Such a construction of the law would reward consumers who choose to remain ignorant of the nature of transactions on their account by purposely failing to review periodic statements. Consumers must play an active and responsible role in protecting against losses which might result from unauthorized transfers. A banking institution cannot know of an unauthorized electronic transfer unless the consumer reports it.

The Bank has established that the losses incurred in July and August 1987 as a result of the unauthorized electronic transfers by someone using Mr. Kruser's Versatel card could have been prevented had appellants reported the unauthorized use of Mr. Kruser's card as reflected on the December 1986 statement. The Bank is entitled to judgment as a matter of law.

———————

If the July and August unauthorized withdrawals had involved different means of fraud (i.e. hacking into the bank's computer system) rather than using the same means as the December transaction, then the bank could not have shown that timely reporting of the December transaction would have prevented the July and August transactions. Even so, this case serves as a reminder that EFTA provides significantly less protection than TILA against unauthorized use.

In the next section, we move from the "retail" transfers covered by EFTA into the "wholesale" transfers covered by UCC Article 4A.

C. WHOLESALE FUNDS TRANSFERS

Looking purely at dollar value, wholesale funds transfers (commonly called "wholesale wire transfers") are the means by which the vast majority of US payments are made. The term "wholesale funds transfers" refers to large-value transfers between banks, either on their own behalf or on behalf of customers. The Uniform Law Commission has estimated the average wholesale funds transfer at five million dollars. Domestically, the two primary systems for wholesale wire transfers are Fedwire, which is the Federal Reserve Wire Network, and CHIPS, the Clearing House Interbank Payments System. The Federal Financial Institutions Examination Council (FFIEC) Bank Secrecy Act/Anti-Money Laundering InfoBase describes these transactions as follows:

> The bulk of the dollar value of these payments is originated electronically to make large value, time-critical payments, such as the settlement of interbank purchases and sales of federal funds, settlement of foreign exchange transactions, disbursement or repayment of loans; settlement of real estate transactions or other financial market transactions; and purchasing, selling, or financing securities transactions. Fedwire and CHIPS participants facilitate these transactions on their behalf and on behalf of their customers, including nonbank financial institutions, commercial businesses, and correspondent banks that do not have direct access.

Article 4A covers wholesale funds transfers. As **4A–108** states, any electronic-fund transfer within the scope of EFTA is outside Article 4A.

However, EFTA's "retail" transfers are batched into Article 4A wholesale transfers.

A funds transfer may consist of one or more payment orders. The "originator," as that term is defined in **4A–104(c)**, begins the funds-transfer process by initiating a payment order for the purpose of making payment to the beneficiary of the order. Depending on the structure of the transaction, there may be an intermediary bank involved, in addition to the originator's bank and the beneficiary's bank.

FFIEC describes the process by which transfers are made:

> Structurally, there are two components to funds transfers: the instructions, which contain information on the sender and receiver of the funds, and the actual movement or transfer of funds. The instructions may be sent in a variety of ways, including by electronic access to networks operated by the Fedwire or CHIPS payment systems; by access to financial telecommunications systems, such as Society for Worldwide Interbank Financial Telecommunication (SWIFT); or e-mail, facsimile, telephone, or telex. Fedwire and CHIPS are used to facilitate U.S. dollar transfers between two domestic endpoints or the U.S. dollar segment of international transactions. SWIFT is an international messaging service that is used to transmit payment instructions for the vast majority of international interbank transactions, which can be denominated in numerous currencies.

[handwritten margin note: CONSUMER AS DEFINED IN EFTA]

Article 4A contains a number of provisions that are analogous to Articles 3 and 4. For example, just as Article 4 recognizes the common-law right of set-off, **4A–502(c)** allows a beneficiary's bank to set off an incoming funds transfer against an obligation the beneficiary owes to the bank. Likewise, just as Chapter 8 included an example of a bank altering the "properly payable" rule to place liability on a customer that refused to implement the bank's recommended "Positive Pay" practices, **4A–202(c)** allows a bank to escape liability for a transfer its customer claimed was unauthorized, after the customer refused to adopt a security procedure the bank offered. **4A–505** is analogous to Article 4's bank statement rule: Under **4A–505**, a customer loses the right to object to completion of any payment order debited from its account if it has not notified its bank within one year after receiving notification that the payment order was made.

[handwritten margin note: – NOT REVERSIBLE AS A MATTER OF LAW – NO DISPUTE RESOLUTION MEASURE – NO STRUCTURAL PROTECTIONS]

The following case shows how consequential damages are calculated under Article 4A, by way of analogy to the famous contracts case, *Hadley v. Baxendale*. As you read this case, note how the court uses familiar concepts to make Article 4A more approachable.

EVRA CORP. V. SWISS BANK CORP.

673 F.2d 951, 34 U.C.C. Rep. Serv. 227 (7th Cir. 1982)

POSNER, J.

The question—one of first impression—in this diversity case is the extent of a bank's liability for failure to make a transfer of funds when requested by wire to do so. The essential facts are undisputed. In 1972, Hyman-Michaels Company, a large Chicago dealer in scrap metal, entered into a two-year contract to supply steel scrap to a Brazilian corporation. Hyman-Michaels chartered a ship, the Pandora, to carry the scrap to Brazil. The charter was for one year, with an option to extend the charter for a second year; specified a fixed daily rate of pay for the hire of the ship during both the initial and the option period, payable semi-monthly "in advance"; and provided that, if payment was not made on time, the Pandora's owner could cancel the charter. Payment was to be made by deposit to the owner's account in the Banque de Paris et des Pays-Bas (Suisse) in Geneva, Switzerland.

The usual method by which Hyman-Michaels, in Chicago, got the payments to the Banque de Paris in Geneva was to request the Continental Illinois National Bank and Trust Company of Chicago, where it had an account, to make a wire transfer of funds. Continental would debit Hyman-Michaels' account by the amount of the payment and then send a telex to its London office for retransmission to its correspondent bank in Geneva—Swiss Bank Corporation—asking Swiss Bank to deposit this amount in the Banque de Paris account of the Pandora's owner. The transaction was completed by the crediting of Swiss Bank's account at Continental by the same amount.

When Hyman-Michaels chartered the Pandora in June 1972, market charter rates were very low, and it was these rates that were fixed in the charter for its entire term—two years if Hyman-Michaels exercised its option. Shortly after the agreement was signed, however, charter rates began to climb and, by October 1972, they were much higher than they had been in June. The Pandora's owners were eager to get out of the charter if they could. At the end of October, they thought they had found a way, for the payment that was due in the Banque de Paris on October 26 had not arrived by October 30, and on that day the Pandora's owner notified Hyman-Michaels that it was canceling the charter because of the breach of the payment term. Hyman-Michaels had mailed a check for the October 26 installment to the Banque de Paris rather than use the wire-transfer method of payment. It had done this in order to have the use of its money for the period that it would take the check to clear, about two weeks. But the check had not been mailed in Chicago until October 25, and of course did not reach Geneva on the twenty-sixth.

When Hyman-Michaels received notification that the charter was being cancelled, it immediately wired payment to the Banque de Paris, but the Pandora's owner refused to accept it and insisted that the charter was indeed cancelled. The matter was referred to arbitration in accordance with the charter. On December 5, 1972, the arbitration panel ruled in favor of Hyman-Michaels. The panel noted that previous arbitration panels had "shown varying degrees of latitude to Charterers"; "In all cases, a pattern of obligation on Owners' part to protest, complain, or warn of intended withdrawal was expressed as an essential prerequisite to withdrawal, in spite of the clear wording of the operative clause. No such advance notice was given by Owners of M/V Pandora." One of the three members of the panel dissented; he thought the Pandora's owner was entitled to cancel.

Hyman-Michaels went back to making the charter payments by wire transfer. On the morning of April 25, 1973, it telephoned Continental Bank and requested it to transfer $27,000 to the Banque de Paris account of the Pandora's owner in payment for the charter hire period from April 27 to May 11, 1973. Since the charter provided for payment "in advance," this payment arguably was due by the close of business on April 26. The requested telex went out to Continental's London office on the afternoon of April 25, which was nighttime in England. Early the next morning, a telex operator in Continental's London office dialed, as Continental's Chicago office had instructed him to do, Swiss Bank's general telex number, which rings in the bank's cable department. But that number was busy and, after trying unsuccessfully for an hour to engage it, the Continental telex operator dialed another number, that of a machine in Swiss Bank's foreign-exchange department which he had used in the past when the general number was engaged. We know this machine received the telexed message, because it signaled the sending machine at both the beginning and end of the transmission that the telex was being received. Yet Swiss Bank failed to comply with the payment order, and no transfer of funds was made to the account of the Pandora's owner in the Banque de Paris.

No one knows exactly what went wrong. One possibility is that the receiving telex machine had simply run out of paper, in which event it would not print the message although it had received it. Another is that whoever took the message out of the machine after it was printed failed to deliver it to the banking department. Unlike the machine in the cable department that the Continental telex operator had originally tried to reach, the machines in the foreign-exchange department were operated by junior foreign-exchange dealers rather than by professional telex operators, although Swiss Bank knew that messages intended for other departments were sometimes diverted to the telex machines in the foreign-exchange department.

At 8:30 a.m. the next day, April 27, Hyman-Michaels in Chicago received a telex from the Pandora's owner stating that the charter was cancelled because payment for the April 27—May 11 charter period had not been made. Hyman-Michaels called over to Continental and told them to keep trying to effect payment through Swiss Bank even if the Pandora's owner rejected it. This instruction was confirmed in a letter to Continental dated April 28, in which Hyman-Michaels stated: "please instruct your London branch to advise their correspondents to persist in attempting to make this payment. This should be done even in the face of a rejection on the part of Banque de Paris to receive this payment. It is paramount, in order to strengthen our position in an arbitration, that these funds continue to be readily available." Hyman-Michaels did not attempt to wire the money directly to the Banque de Paris as it had done on the occasion of its previous default. Days passed while the missing telex message was hunted unsuccessfully. Finally, Swiss Bank suggested to Continental that it retransmit the telex message to the machine in the cable department, and this was done on May 1. The next day, Swiss Bank attempted to deposit the $27,000 in the account of the Pandora's owner at the Banque de Paris, but the payment was refused.

Again the arbitrators were convened and rendered a decision. In it, they ruled that Hyman-Michaels had been "blameless" up until the morning of April 27, when it first learned that the Banque de Paris had not received payment on April 26, but that, "being faced with this situation," Hyman-Michaels had "failed to do everything in (its) power to remedy it. The action taken was immediate but did not prove to be adequate, in that (Continental) Bank and its correspondent required some 5/6 days to trace and effect the lost instruction to remit. (Hyman-Michaels) could have ordered an immediate duplicate payment—or even sent a Banker's check by hand or special messengers, so that the funds could have reached owner's Bank, not later than April 28th." By failing to do any of these things, Hyman-Michaels had "created the opening" that the Pandora's owner was seeking in order to be able to cancel the charter. It had "acted imprudently." The arbitration panel concluded, reluctantly but unanimously, that this time the Pandora's owner was entitled to cancel the agreement. The arbitration decision was confirmed by a federal district court in New York.

Hyman-Michaels then brought this diversity action against Swiss Bank, seeking to recover its expenses in the second arbitration proceeding plus the profits that it lost because of the cancellation of the charter. The contract by which Hyman-Michaels had agreed to ship scrap steel to Brazil had been terminated by the buyer in March 1973, and Hyman-Michaels had promptly subchartered the Pandora at market rates, which by April 1973 were double the rates fixed in the charter. Its lost profits are based on the difference between the charter and subcharter rates.

The case comes to us on Swiss Bank's appeal from the judgment in favor of Hyman-Michaels. . . .

* * *

When a bank fails to make a requested transfer of funds, this can cause two kinds of loss. First, the funds themselves or interest on them may be lost, and of course the fee paid for the transfer, having bought nothing, becomes a loss item. These are "direct" (sometimes called "general") damages. Hyman-Michaels is not seeking any direct damages in this case and apparently sustained none. It did not lose any part of the $27,000; although its account with Continental Bank was debited by this amount prematurely, it was not an interest-bearing account, so Hyman-Michaels lost no interest; and Hyman-Michaels paid no fee either to Continental or to Swiss Bank for the aborted transfer. A second type of loss, which either the payor or the payee may suffer, is a dislocation in one's business triggered by the failure to pay. Swiss Bank's failure to transfer funds to the Banque de Paris when requested to do so by Continental Bank set off a chain reaction which resulted in an arbitration proceeding that was costly to Hyman-Michaels and in the cancellation of a highly profitable contract. It is those costs and lost profits—"consequential" or, as they are sometimes called, "special" damages—that Hyman-Michaels seeks in this lawsuit, and recovered below. It is conceded that, if Hyman-Michaels was entitled to consequential damages, the district court measured them correctly. The only issue is whether it was entitled to consequential damages.

. . . *Hadley v. Baxendale*, 9 Ex. 341, 156 Eng. Rep. 145 (1854), is the leading common-law case on liability for consequential damages caused by failure or delay in carrying out a commercial undertaking. The engine shaft in plaintiffs' corn mill had broken, and they hired the defendants, a common carrier, to transport the shaft to the manufacturer, who was to make a new one using the broken shaft as a model. The carrier failed to deliver the shaft within the time promised. With the engine shaft out of service the mill was shut down. The plaintiffs sued the defendants for the lost profits of the mill during the additional period that it was shut down because of the defendants' breach of their promise. The court held that the lost profits were not a proper item of damages, because "in the great multitude of cases of millers sending off broken shafts to third persons by a carrier under ordinary circumstances, such consequences (the stoppage of the mill and resulting loss of profits) would not, in all probability, have occurred; and these special circumstances were here never communicated by the plaintiffs to the defendants." 9 Ex. at 356, 156 Eng. Rep. at 151.

The rule of *Hadley v. Baxendale*—that consequential damages will not be awarded unless the defendant was put on notice of the special circumstances giving rise to them—has been applied in many Illinois cases, and *Hadley* cited approvingly. *See, e.g., Siegel v. Western Union Telephone Co.*, 37 N.E.2d 868, 871 (1941). In *Siegel*, the plaintiff had delivered $200 to Western Union with instructions to transmit it to a friend of the plaintiff's. The money was to be bet (legally) on a horse, but this was not disclosed in the instructions. Western Union misdirected the money order, and it did not reach the friend until several hours after the race had taken place. The horse that the plaintiff had intended to bet on won and would have paid $1,650 on the plaintiff's $200 bet if the bet had been placed. He sued Western Union for his $1,450 lost profit, but the court held that, under the rule of *Hadley v. Baxendale*, Western Union was not liable, because it "had no notice or knowledge of the purpose for which the money was being transmitted." 37 N.E.2d at 871.

The present case is similar, though Swiss Bank knew more than Western Union knew in *Siegel*; it knew or should have known, from Continental Bank's previous telexes, that Hyman-Michaels was paying the Pandora Shipping Company for the hire of a motor vessel named Pandora. But it did not know when payment was due, what the terms of the charter were, or that they had turned out to be extremely favorable to Hyman-Michaels. And it did not know that Hyman-Michaels knew the Pandora's owner would try to cancel the charter, and probably would succeed, if Hyman-Michaels was ever again late in making payment, or that despite this peril Hyman-Michaels would not try to pay until the last possible moment and, in the event of a delay in transmission, would not do everything in its power to minimize the consequences of the delay. Electronic-funds transfers are not so unusual as to automatically place a bank on notice of extraordinary consequences if such a transfer goes awry. Swiss Bank did not have enough information to infer that, if it lost a $27,000 payment order, it would face a liability in excess of $2 million.

* * *

Siegel, we conclude, is authority for holding that Swiss Bank is not liable for the consequences of negligently failing to transfer Hyman-Michaels' funds to Banque de Paris; reason for such a holding is found in the animating principle of *Hadley v. Baxendale*, which is that the costs of the untoward consequence of a course of dealings should be borne by that party who was able to avert the consequence at least cost and failed to do so. In *Hadley*, the untoward consequence was the shutting down of the mill. The carrier could have avoided it by delivering the engine shaft on time. But the mill owners, as the court noted, could have avoided it simply by having a spare shaft. Prudence required that they have a spare shaft anyway, since a replacement could not be obtained at once even if there was no undue delay in carting the broken shaft to and the replacement shaft from the manufacturer. The court refused to imply a duty on the part of the carrier to guarantee the mill owners against the consequences of their own lack of prudence, though of course, if the parties had stipulated for such a guarantee, the court would have enforced it. The notice requirement of *Hadley v. Baxendale* is designed to assure that such an improbable guarantee really is intended.

This case is much the same, though it arises in a tort—rather than a contract—setting. Hyman-Michaels showed a lack of prudence throughout. It was imprudent for it to mail in Chicago a letter that, unless received the next day in Geneva, would put Hyman-Michaels in breach of a contract that was very profitable to it and that the other party to the contract had every interest in canceling. It was imprudent thereafter for Hyman-Michaels, having narrowly avoided cancellation and having (in the words of its appeal brief in this court) been "put . . . on notice that the payment provision of the Charter would be strictly enforced thereafter," to wait till arguably the last day before payment was due to instruct its bank to transfer the necessary funds overseas. And it was imprudent in the last degree for Hyman-Michaels, when it received notice of cancellation on the last possible day payment was due, to fail to pull out all the stops to get payment to the Banque de Paris on that day, and instead to dither while Continental and Swiss Bank wasted five days looking for the lost telex message. Judging from the obvious reluctance with which the arbitration panel finally decided to allow the Pandora's owner to cancel the charter, it might have made all the difference if Hyman-Michaels had gotten payment to the Banque de Paris by April 27 or even by Monday, April 30, rather than allowed things to slide until May 2.

This is not to condone the sloppy handling of incoming telex messages in Swiss Bank's foreign department. But Hyman-Michaels is a sophisticated business enterprise. It knew or should have known that even the Swiss are not infallible; that messages sometimes get lost or delayed in transit among three banks, two of them located 5,000 miles apart, even when all the banks are using reasonable care; and that therefore it should take its own precautions against the consequences—best known to itself—of a mishap that might not be due to anyone's negligence.

We are not the first to remark on the affinity between the rule of *Hadley v. Baxendale* and the doctrine, which is one of tort as well as contract law and is a settled part of the common law of Illinois, of avoidable consequences. If you are hurt in an automobile accident and unreasonably fail to seek medical treatment, the injurer, even if negligent, will not be held liable for the aggravation of the injury due to your own unreasonable behavior after the accident. If in addition you failed to fasten your seat belt, you may be barred from collecting the tort damages that would have been prevented if you had done so. Hyman-Michaels' behavior in steering close to the wind prior to April 27 was like not fastening one's seat belt; its failure on April 27 to wire a duplicate payment immediately after disaster struck was like refusing to seek medical attention after a serious accident. The seat-belt cases show that the doctrine of avoidable consequences applies whether the tort victim acts imprudently before or after the tort is committed. Hyman-Michaels did both.

The rule of *Hadley v. Baxendale* links up with tort concepts in another way. The rule is sometimes stated in the form that only foreseeable damages are recoverable in a breach of contract action. So expressed, it corresponds to the tort principle that limits liability to the foreseeable consequence of the defendant's carelessness. The amount of care that a person ought to take is a function of the probability and magnitude of the harm that may occur if he does not take care. If he does not know what that probability and magnitude are, he cannot determine how much care to take. That would be Swiss Bank's dilemma if it were liable for consequential damages from failing to carry out payment orders in a timely fashion. To estimate the extent of its probable liability in order to know how many and how elaborate fail-safe features to install in its telex rooms or how much insurance to buy against the inevitable failures, Swiss Bank would have to collect reams of information about firms that are not even its regular customers. It had no banking relationship with Hyman-Michaels. It did not know or have reason to know how at once precious and fragile Hyman-Michaels' contract with the Pandora's owner was. These were circumstances too remote from Swiss Bank's practical range of knowledge to have affected its decisions as to who should man the telex machines in the foreign department or whether it should have more intelligent machines or should install more machines in the cable department, any more than the falling of a platform scale because a conductor jostled a passenger who was carrying fireworks was a prospect that could have influenced the amount of care taken by the Long Island Railroad. *See Palsgraf v. Long Island Railroad*, 248 N.Y. 339, 162 N.E. 99 (1928).

In short, Swiss Bank was not required in the absence of a contractual undertaking to take precautions or insure against a harm that it could not measure but that was known with precision to Hyman-Michaels, which could by the exercise of common prudence have averted it completely. . . .

* * *

The legal principles that we have said are applicable to this case were not applied below. Although the district judge's opinion is not entirely clear, he apparently thought the rule of *Hadley v. Baxendale* inapplicable and the imprudence of Hyman-Michaels irrelevant. He did state that the damages to Hyman-Michaels were foreseeable because "a major international bank" should know that a failure to act promptly on a telexed request to transfer funds could cause substantial damage; but *Siegel* . . . make[s] clear that that kind of general foreseeability, which is present in virtually every case, does not justify an award of consequential damages.

We could remand for new findings based on the proper legal standard, but it is unnecessary to do so. The undisputed facts, recited in this opinion, show as a matter of law that Hyman-Michaels is not entitled to recover consequential damages from Swiss Bank.

Hyman-Michaels should have taken greater care to protect its valuable contractual relationship, not waiting until the last moment to send payment overseas. One basis of the court's opinion seems to be the belief that other parties ought not be required to treat the contract as being more precious than Hyman-Michaels itself did.

Also note that the bank did not get a windfall here. The bank did not retain any benefit from the transaction. Instead, the bank is simply not being forced to bear the burden of losses the court believes it had no reason to anticipate.

Notably, the *Evra* case involved a transfer of funds that implicated international commerce. Another, more complex means of effectuating payment internationally is through a letter of credit as part of a documentary sales transaction, as described in the next section.

D. DOCUMENTARY SALES

This section introduces letters of credit and documents of title, and shows how the two are often used together in a transaction called a documentary sale to maximize the security of parties—such as buyers and sellers—who may be located far from one another and may not be willing to rely upon one another's creditworthiness. The following language from *Bank of Cochin Ltd. v. Manufacturers Hanover Trust Co.*, 612 F. Supp. 1533, 1537 (S.D.N.Y. 1985) describes a letter-of-credit transaction:

> A letter of credit is a financing mechanism designed to allocate commercial credit risks whereby a bank or other issuer pays an amount of money to a beneficiary upon presentment of documents complying with specified conditions set forth in the letter. The beneficiary, typically the seller of goods to a buyer-customer, uses the letter to substitute the credit of the issuer for the credit of its customer. The customer applies for the letter of credit, specifies the terms of the letter and promises to reimburse the issuer upon honor of the beneficiary's draft. The letter of credit is thus an engagement by the issuer to the beneficiary to cover the customer's agreement to pay money under the customer-beneficiary contract. The reliability and fluidity of the letter of credit are maintained because the issuing bank is concerned exclusively with the documents, not the performance obligations created by the customer-beneficiary contract. . . .

These materials employ the common convention of referring to a letter of credit as a "credit." When a credit is part of what is called a documentary sale, both parties are protected. The seller, when it ships the goods, knows it will get paid. It can be sure of this because a credit is not just the buyer's personal promise to pay; it is the bank's direct obligation to pay on the buyer's behalf. At the same time, the buyer can be assured, if the credit has been thoughtfully constructed, that the goods shipped will comply with the terms of the parties' contract. This is because the credit will also include a list of legally significant documents, chosen by the buyer, that the seller must present to the bank before the seller will get paid.

The buyer can list as many documents as it wants in the credit, and the buyer and its attorney should have a thorough conversation about what the buyer wants to include. If the list is unreasonable, however, the seller will refuse the buyer's terms. Documents commonly specified in a credit include the following:

- A signed commercial invoice. This document serves to confirm that the goods conform with the buyer's purchase order. If the purchase order specifies yarn that is 75% Extrafine Merino Wool/ 20% Silk/ 5% Cashmere, the invoice should indicate the same.

- A bill of lading or other document of title. A bill of lading has several functions, one of which is to document that the goods have been delivered to a carrier.

- A certificate of origin. If the buyer's purchase order had, for example, specified "Copper River King Salmon," the buyer might require a certificate of origin confirming that the fish being shipped came from Alaska's Copper River.

- A certificate of inspection. If the buyer's purchase order had specified maple syrup of "Grade A: Dark Color and Robust Flavor," she might want an independent inspector to attest to the grade of the syrup rather than simply accepting the seller's representation. A certificate of inspection would accomplish this.

- A marine insurance policy. If the goods are being shipped and the seller has agreed to obtain insurance, the buyer might require the seller to supply the insurance policy to the bank as a condition of payment.

- A draft on the credit. This can be thought of as a formal demand for payment under the credit. The beneficiary would present the draft along with all of the documents specified under the credit.

The following graphic shows a typical documentary sale. Note how many Articles of the UCC can be implicated in a single transaction: Assuming that the buyer and seller are both U.S. parties, the sale of goods between the buyer and seller will be governed by Article 2 or, if the goods were leased, Article 2A. If this is a "standby" credit (further explained below) to be drawn upon only in the event of default, payment might be expected from the buyer in the form of an Article 3 draft or note or an Article 4A wholesale funds transfer, with this credit serving only as a back-up means of payment. If payment were made by check or other item collected through a bank, Article 4 would govern the collection process. Article 5 governs the credit itself, and Article 7 covers the bill of lading, which is a document of title representing the right to the goods. Article 9 would govern any security interest the seller retained in the goods. "L/C." in this chart, is the letter of credit.

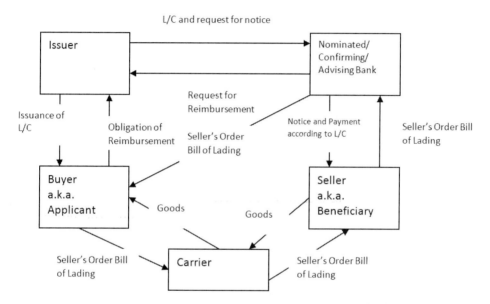

The first step, after the buyer and seller conclude their contract, is that the buyer must open a letter of credit with the issuer. In the application process, the buyer will identify the documents he or she would like to require the seller, as beneficiary, to produce.

After the application is completed and accepted, the bank will issue a credit. The issuer might communicate the credit to another bank near the beneficiary, with which the issuer has a contractual relationship. Depending on the exact relationship between the two banks, this second bank might be termed a nominated bank, confirming bank, or advising bank.

The following language is from a commercial credit in the case entitled *Banco Nacional de Desarrollo v. Mellon Bank, N.A.*, 726 F.2d 87 (3d Cir. 1984). The term "commercial credit" distinguishes this from a "standby" credit. Thus, this credit is the intended means of payment for the transaction, rather than a back-up to be used only in the event of default. In reading this language, note the particular documents this applicant has required the beneficiary to produce, and think about why each document might have been chosen. Also note that Mellon Bank has designated Banco

Nacional de Desarrolla, a Nicaraguan bank, as "advising bank." As the name suggests, the Nicaraguan bank will advise the beneficiary, also located in Nicaragua, that the credit has been issued. The advising bank will also authenticate the credit, which serves to avoid fraud.

Mellon Bank N.A.
Documentary Letter of Credit
Irrevocable

Place of issue: Pittsburgh, Pennsylvania.
Date of issue: August 7, 1980.
Letter of Credit Number: of issuing bank 47728.
Advising Bank: Banco Nacional de Desarrolla.
Applicant: I.B.P. Corporation.
Beneficiary: Empresa Nicaraguensa de la Carne, Encar.
Amount: U.S. $98,000.00 (ABOUT).
Expiry: Date August 31, 1980 in Nicaragua for negotiation.

We hereby issue this documentary letter of credit which is available against beneficiary's draft at SIGHT FOR 100% INVOICE VALUE drawn on Mellon Bank N.A. bearing the clause: "Drawn on documentary letter of credit No. 47728" accompanied by the following documents:

Signed Commercial Invoice in quadruplicate including statement that all cartons are marked with U.S.D.A. approved markings and that the product is free of any chemicals, additives, and pesticides, and conforms to all regulations of the USDA and country of origin and stating that the original Nicaraguan Meat Inspection Certificate has been airmailed to the broker at the port of discharge.

Special Customs Invoice 5515 in duplicate.

Packing List in duplicate.

One copy Nicaraguan Veterinary [sic] Meat Inspection Certificate.

Copy of your cable addressed to Gurrentz International Corporation dated not later than one week after date of the on board Bill of Lading stating this Letter of Credit Number, quantity, product, name of carrying vessel, and port of discharge.

2/3 set clean on board ocean Bills of Lading plus one non-negotiable copy consigned to order and blank endorsed evidencing refrigerated shipment from Nicaragua to Los Angeles, CA dated not later than August 21, 1980.

Copy of beneficiary's cable addressed to I.B.P. Corporation dated no later than one week after date of the on board Bill of Lading stating Letter of Credit Number 47728, quantity, product, name of carrying vessel and port of discharge.

One copy Ministry of Secursos Naturales Nicaragua Meat Inspection Certificate, purporting to cover Fresh frozen boneless beef packed in polylined fiber carton solid packed in even weight 60 # cartons. Approx 1200 carton min 90% C.L. chucks at 1.18 FOB and approx. 124 ctns. 100% lean product at 1.75 FOB Nicaragua.

Shipment from Nicaragua to Los Angeles, CA. Partial shipments are not permitted. Transshipments are not permitted.

* * *

We hereby engage with the bona fide holders of all drafts drawn and/or documents presented under and in compliance with the terms of this letter of credit that such drafts and/or documents will be duly honored upon presentation to us. The amount of each drawing must be endorsed on the reverse side of this letter of credit by the negotiating bank.

Indications of the advising bank: This is an irrevocable letter of credit of the above-mentioned issuing bank and is transmitted to you without any responsibility or engagement on our part.

Unlike a commercial letter of credit, which is the intended means of payment for the transaction, a standby letter of credit is drawn upon only in a situation of default. This is thus a much simpler document that does not include a lengthy recitation of documents to be produced for payment. The following language, taken from the disputed letter of credit in *Intraworld Industries, Inc. v. Girard Trust Bank*, 336 A.2d 316 (Pa. 1975), shows how a standby credit might read. This credit was used to provide assurance that Intraworld Industries, Inc. would pay Paulette Cymbalista, the lessor of certain hotel property, all rental amounts due. In this transaction, Intraworld is the applicant and Cymbalista is the beneficiary.

IRREVOCABLE LETTER OF CREDIT NO. 35798

Date: September 5, 1972
Amount: $100,000.00
Beneficiary: Paulette Cymbalista
C/o Carlton Hotel
St. Moritz, Switzerland
For account of: Intraworld Industries, Inc.
116 South Main Street
Wilkes Barre, PA 18701

Madam:

You are hereby authorized to draw on us at sight the sum of One Hundred Thousand and 00/100 Dollars United States Currency ($100,000.00) due on November 10, 1973 under a lease, a copy of which is attached to both Beneficiary's copy and Bank's copy of this letter of credit as Exhibit 1, available by your draft for said amount, accompanied by:

1.   Simple receipt for amount drawn.

2.   A signed statement of the drawer of the draft to the effect that the drawer is the lessor under said lease and that the lessee thereunder has not paid the installment of rent due under said lease on November 10, 1973, within 10 days after said installment was due and payable.

This credit expires on November 30, 1973.

Drafts under this credit must contain the clause "drawn under Credit No. 35798 of Girard Trust Bank, dated September 5, 1972.'"

Girard Trust Bank hereby agrees with the drawers, [i]ndorsers and bona fide owners of the bills drawn strictly in compliance with the terms of this credit that the same will be duly honored upon presentation.

Except so far as otherwise expressly stated, this credit is subject to the Uniform Customs and Practices for Documentary Credits (1962 revision), International Chamber of Commerce Brochure No. 222.

Now that you have seen samples of some of the documents involved in a documentary transaction, we will examine the legal standards to be applied to such a transaction.

1. THE LEGAL FRAMEWORK FOR A DOCUMENTARY TRANSACTION

In addition to UCC Article 5, practitioners in this area need to be familiar with the Uniform Customs and Practice for Documentary Credits, known as the UCP, promulgated by the International Chamber of Commerce. In fact, you might notice that the standby credit above includes a reference to the 1962 version of the UCP. The current version of the UCP, published in 2007, is known as "UCP 600," in recognition of the fact that it is the ICC's 600th publication. The UCP is a body of private commercial rules that parties commonly incorporate by reference into their documentary transactions. As an indication of how influential the UCP rules are, **5–116(c)** provides that Article 5 generally defers to the UCP in the event of conflict. As **5–103** Comment 2 indicates, the UCP rules are particularly important in determining compliance with the performance standards for issuers set forth in **5–108**.

Some provisions of Article 5 have analogues in Articles 3 or 4. For example, **5–108(g)**'s direction to disregard any nondocumentary conditions can be compared to the Article 3 concept of a negotiable instrument as a courier without luggage. Other matters, however, are handled differently. For example, as **5–108** Comment 7 indicates, "The issuer's obligation to honor [a conforming presentment] runs not only to the beneficiary, but also to the applicant." The reason for this rule is that "[i]t is possible that an applicant who has made a favorable contract with the beneficiary will be injured by the issuer's wrongful dishonor." Under Article 3, by contrast, a drawee faces liability for wrongful dishonor only to the drawer. An Article 3 holder—unlike the Article 5 beneficiary—has no cause of action for wrongful dishonor.

Under **5–108(b)**, an issuer has a reasonable time, not to exceed seven days, to examine the presented documents for compliance with the credit and determine whether to pay the beneficiary. As Comment 2 indicates, "the seven-day period is not a safe harbor"; a court may find an issuer should have acted sooner.

5–104 states only two formal requirements for a letter of credit, as contrasted with the seven requirements of an Article 3 negotiable instrument. A credit must be (1) a "record" that is (2) "authenticated." The use of the words "record" and "authenticated," which are broader than their Article 3 counterparts "writing" and "signature," indicate that electronic letters of credit are permissible. **5–104** Comment 1 explains the requirements—and some typical items often included:

> Neither Section **5–104** nor the definition of letter of credit in Section **5–102(a)(10)** requires inclusion of all of the terms that are normally in a letter of credit in order for an undertaking to be recognized as a letter of credit under Article 5. For example, a letter of credit will typically specify the amount available, the expiration date, the place where presentation should be made, and the documents that must be presented to entitle a person to honor. Undertakings that have the formalities required by Section **5–104** and meet the conditions specified in **5–102(a)(10)** will be recognized as letters of credit even though they omit one or more of the items usually contained in a letter of credit.

Each bank involved in the transaction typically charges a service fee. As **5–106** indicates, credits are presumptively irrevocable and expire one year after issuance, except "perpetual" credits, which expire five years after issuance. The credit can, of course, also state a fixed expiration period. Both of the credits presented in the materials above are irrevocable.

2.　THE DOCTRINE OF STRICT COMPLIANCE

5–108(a) sets forth the "strict compliance" test that an issuer must follow in determining whether to make payment pursuant to a letter of credit upon the beneficiary's presentation of documents. The same standard applies to a bank that agrees to confirm a credit issued by another bank. As Comment 1 states, the standard is more stringent than "substantial compliance," but stops short of "slavish conformity to the terms of the letter of credit."

The following case describes those kinds of nonconformities that will—and will not—justify dishonor according to the UCP. Both the UCC and the UCP require that an issuer or confirmer provide proper notice of any nonconformity in the documents presented, and this case illustrates that requirement. Because this case was decided before the UCP 600 was adopted in 2007, it refers to the prior version, UCP 500.

VOEST-ALPINE TRADING USA CORP. V. BANK OF CHINA
167 F. Supp. 2d 940, 46 U.C.C. Rep. Serv. 2d 808 (S.D. Tex. 2000)

GILMORE, J.

On June 23, 1995, Plaintiff Voest-Alpine Trading USA Corporation [Voest-Alpine] entered into a contract with Jiangyin Foreign Trade Corporation [JFTC] to sell JFTC 1,000 metric tons of styrene monomer at a total price of $1.2 million. To finance the transaction, JFTC applied for a letter of credit through Defendant Bank of China. The letter of credit provided for payment to Voest-Alpine once the goods had been shipped to Zhangjiagang, China and Voest-Alpine had presented the requisite paperwork to the Bank of China as described in the letter of credit. The letter of credit was issued by the Bank of China on July 6, 1995, and assigned the number LC9521033/95. In addition to numerous other typographical errors, Voest-Alpine's name was listed as "Voest-Alpine USA Trading Corp." instead of "Voest-Alpine Trading USA Corp" with the "Trading USA" portion inverted. The destination port was also misspelled in one place as "Zhangjiagng," missing the third "a." The letter of credit did indicate, however, that the transaction would be subject to the 1993 Uniform Customs and Practice, International Chamber of Commerce Publication Number 500.

By the time the product was ready to ship, the market price of styrene monomer had dropped significantly from the original contract price between Voest-Alpine and JFTC. Although JFTC asked for a price concession in light of the decrease in market price, Voest-Alpine declined and, through its agents, shipped the styrene monomer on July 18, 1995. All required inspection and documentation was completed. On August 1, 1995, Voest-Alpine presented the documents specified in the letter of credit to Texas Commerce Bank, the presenting bank. Texas Commerce Bank found discrepancies between the presentation documents and the letter of credit, which it related to Voest-Alpine. Because Voest-Alpine did not believe that any of the noted discrepancies would warrant refusal to pay, it instructed Texas Commerce Bank to forward the presentation documents to the Bank of China.

Texas Commerce Bank sent the documents via DHL courier to the Bank of China on August 3, 1995. According to the letter of credit, Voest-Alpine, the beneficiary, was required to present the documents within fifteen days of the shipping date, by August 2, 1995. As the documents were presented on August 1, 1995, they were presented timely under the letter of credit. Bank of China received the documents on August 9, 1995.

On August 11, 1995, the Bank of China sent a telex to Texas Commerce Bank, informing them of seven alleged discrepancies between the letter of credit and the documents Voest-Alpine presented, six of which are the subject of this action. The Bank of China claimed that 1) the beneficiary's name differed from the name listed in the letter of credit, as noted by the presenting bank; 2) Voest-Alpine had submitted bills of lading marked "duplicate" and "triplicate" instead of "original"; 3) the invoice, packing list and the certificate of origin were not marked "original"; 4) the date of the survey report was later than that of the bill of lading; 5) the letter-of-credit number in the beneficiary's certified copy of the fax was incorrect, as noted by the presenting bank; and 6) the destination was not listed correctly in the certificate of origin and the beneficiary's certificate, as noted by the presenting bank. The telex further stated, "We are contacting the applicant of the relative discrepancy [sic]. Holding documents at your risks and disposal."

On August 15, Texas Commerce Bank faxed the Bank of China, stating that the discrepancies were not an adequate basis to refuse to pay the letter of credit and requested that the bank honor the letter of credit and pay Voest-Alpine accordingly. The telex identified Voest-Alpine as the beneficiary in the transaction. Voest-Alpine also contacted JFTC directly in an effort to secure a waiver of the discrepancies but was unsuccessful.

On August 19, 1995, the Bank of China sent another telex to Texas Commerce Bank further explaining what it believed to be discrepancies between the letter of credit and the documentation presented by Voest-Alpine according to the UCP 500. In relevant part, the telex provided:

> You cannot say [the discrepancies] are of no consequence. The fact is that our bank must examine all documents stipulated in the credit with reasonable care, to ascertain whether or not they appear, on their face, to be incompliance [sic] with the terms and conditions of the credit. According to Article 13 of UCP 500. An irrevocable credit constitutes a definite undertaking of the issuing bank, providing that the stipulated documents are complied with the terms and conditions of the credit according to Article UCP 500. Now the discrepant documents may have us refuse to take up the documents according to article 14(B) of UCP 500.

The Bank of China returned the documents to Voest-Alpine and did not honor the letter of credit.

* * *

... The current statutory law requires an issuer to honor a presentation that, as determined by standard practice of financial institutions that regularly issue letters of credit, "appears on its face strictly to comply with the terms and conditions of the letter of credit." Determination of what constitutes standard practice of financial institutions is a "matter of interpretation for the court."

* * *

In this case, the parties expressly adopted the UCP 500 as the governing authority in the letter of credit. Where parties explicitly refer to the UCP 500 in their contracts, the UCP has been interpreted to apply to the transaction. Accordingly, the Court will look to the UCP for guidance in analyzing whether the actions of the Bank of China were in conformity with "standard practice" of financial institutions.

The Bank of China claims that its August 11, 1995, telex to Texas Commerce Bank constituted notice of refusal under the UCP 500 because it contained the required elements listed in Article 14(d). Voest-Alpine argues that the telex did not constitute notice of refusal because there is no clear statement of refusal and because the portion of the telex that indicated that the Bank of China was contacting JFTC to seek a waiver rendered the communication ambiguous.

Article 14(d) of the UCP 500 provides:

i.   If the Issuing Bank . . . decides to refuse the [presentation] documents, it must give notice to that effect by telecommunication or, if that is not possible, by other expeditious means, without delay but no later than the close of the seventh banking day following the day of receipt of the documents. Such notice shall be given to the bank from which it received the documents, or to the Beneficiary, if it received the documents directly from him.

ii.   Such notice must state all discrepancies in respect of which the bank refuses the documents and must also state whether it is holding the documents at the disposal of, or is returning them to, the presenter.

According to Article 14(d), if the issuing bank elects not to honor the presentation documents, it must provide a notice of refusal within seven banking days of receipt of the documents and the notice must contain any and all discrepancies and state the disposition of the rejected documents. The section requires that if a bank wishes to reject a presentation of documents, it "*must give notice to that effect*." (emphasis supplied).

Here, the Bank of China's notice is deficient because nowhere does it state that it is actually rejecting the documents or refusing to honor the letter of credit or any words to that effect. While it is true that, under the UCP 500, the notice must contain a list of discrepancies and the disposition of the documents and the Bank of China's telex of August 11, 1995, does indeed contain these elements, this only addresses the requirements of Article 14(d)(ii). A notice of refusal, by its own terms must actually convey refusal, as specified in Article 14(d)(i). This omission is only compounded by the statement that the Bank of China would contact the applicant to determine if it would waive the discrepancies. . . . [T]his additional piece of information holds open the possibility of acceptance upon waiver of the discrepancies by JFTC and indicates that the Bank of China has not refused the documents.

In the August 19, 1995, telex, the Bank of China stated, "*Now* the discrepant documents *may have us refuse* to take up the documents according to article 14(B) of UCP 500" (emphasis supplied). This is the bank's first mention of refusal, and it is tentative at best. The use of "now" further indicates that the documents were not previously refused in the August 11, 1995, telex. Even if this second telex was sent as a notice of refusal, it came too late. The Court finds that the evidence establishes that the telex was sent on August 19, 1995. Seven banking days, the refusal period allotted by the UCP 500 Article 14(d), would have expired on August 18, 1995.

Accordingly, the Court finds that the Bank of China did not provide a notice of refusal within seven banking days of receipt of the presentation documents as required by Article 14(d) of the UCP 500. The Bank of China's failure to formally refuse the documents before the deadline precludes the bank from claiming that the documents are not in compliance with the terms and conditions of the credit, according to Article 14(e) of the UCP 500. Although the Court could properly conclude its analysis here, the Court will analyze the discrepancies listed by the Bank of China in the August 11, 1995, telex.

Voest-Alpine claims that the six remaining discrepancies cited by the Bank of China are mere technicalities and typographical errors that do not warrant the rejection of the documents. Voest-Alpine argues for a "functional standard" of compliance, contending that if the whole of the documents obviously relate to the transaction covered by the credit, the issuing bank must honor the letter of credit. The Bank of China argues that the discrepancies were significant and that if the documents contain discrepancies on their face, it is justified in rejecting them and is not required to look beyond the papers themselves.

Section 13(a) of the UCP 500 provides:

> Banks must examine all documents stipulated in the Credit with reasonable care, to ascertain whether or not they appear, on their face, to be in compliance with the terms and conditions of the Credit. Compliance of the stipulated documents on their face with the terms and conditions of the Credit shall be determined by international standard banking practice as reflected in these Articles. Documents which appear on their face to be inconsistent with one another will be considered as not appearing on their face to be in compliance with the terms and conditions of the Credit.

The UCP 500 does not provide guidance on what inconsistencies would justify a conclusion on the part of a bank that the documents are not in compliance with the terms and conditions of the letter of credit or what discrepancies are not a reasonable basis for such a conclusion. The UCP 500 does not mandate that the documents be a mirror image of the requirements or use the term "strict compliance."

The Court notes the wide range of interpretations on what standard banks should employ in examining letter-of-credit document presentations for compliance. Even where courts claim to uphold strict compliance, the standard is hardly uniform. The first and most restrictive approach is to require that the presentation documents be a mirror image of the requirements.

Second, there are also cases claiming to follow the strict-compliance standard but support[ing] rejection only where the discrepancies are such that would create risks for the issuer if the bank were to accept the presentation documents. A third standard, without much support in case law, is to analyze the documents for risk to the applicant.

The mirror-image approach is problematic because it absolves the bank reviewing the documents of any responsibility to use common sense to determine if the documents, on their face, are related to the transaction or even to review an entire document in the context of the others presented to the bank. On the other hand, the second and third approaches employ a determination-of-harm standard that is too unwieldy. Such an analysis would improperly require the bank to evaluate risks that it might suffer or that might be suffered by the applicant and could undermine the independence of the three contracts that underlie the letter-of-credit payment scheme by forcing the bank to look beyond the face of the presentation documents.

The Court finds that a moderate, more appropriate standard lies within the UCP 500 itself and the opinions issued by the International Chamber of Commerce Banking Commission. One of the Banking Commission opinions defined the term "consistency" between the letter of credit and the documents presented to the issuing bank as used in Article 13(a) of the UCP to mean that "the whole of the documents must obviously relate to the same transaction, that is to say, that each should bear a relation (link) with the others on its face. . . ." The Banking Commission rejected the notion that "all of the documents should be *exactly* consistent in their wording."

A common sense, case-by-case approach would permit minor deviations of a typographical nature because such a letter-for-letter correspondence between the letter of credit and the presentation documents is virtually impossible. While the end result of such an analysis may bear a strong resemblance to the relaxed strict-compliance standard, the actual calculus used by the issuing bank is not the risk it or the applicant faces, but rather, whether the documents bear a rational link to one another. In this way, the issuing bank is required to examine a particular document in light of all documents presented and use common sense but is not required to evaluate risks or go beyond the face of the documents. The Court finds that, in this case, the Bank of China's listed discrepancies should be analyzed under this standard by determining whether the whole of the documents obviously relate to the transaction on their face.

First, the Bank of China claimed that the beneficiary's name in the presentation documents, Voest-Alpine *Trading USA,* differed from the letter of credit, which listed the beneficiary as Voest-Alpine *USA Trading.* While it is true that the letter of credit inverted Voest-Alpine's geographic locator, all the documents Voest-Alpine presented that obviously related to this transaction placed the geographic locator behind "Trading," not in front of it. Furthermore, the addresses corresponded to that listed in the letter of credit and Texas Commerce Bank's cover letter to the Bank of China identified Voest-Alpine Trading USA as the beneficiary in the transaction with JFTC. The letter of credit with the inverted name bore obvious links to the documents presented by Voest-Alpine Trading USA. This is in contrast to a misspelling or outright omission. In contrast with these cases, the inversion of the geographic locator here does not signify a different corporate entity. . . .

Second, the Bank of China pointed out that the set of originals of the bill of lading should have all been stamped "original" rather than "original," "duplicate," and "triplicate." It should be noted that neither the letter of credit nor any provision in the UCP 500 requires such stamping. [Moreover, it] is clear from the face of the documents that these documents are three originals rather than one original and two copies. The documents have signatures in blue ink, vary slightly, bear original stamps oriented differently on each page, and clearly state on their face that the preparer made three original bills. Further, one possible definition of duplicate is "[t]o make or execute again" and one definition of triplicate is "[o]ne of a set of three identical things." *Webster's II New Riverside University Dictionary* 410, 1237 (1994). While the "duplicate" and "triplicate" stamps may have been confusing, stamps do not make obviously original documents into copies.

Third, the Bank of China claimed that the failure to stamp the packing list documents as "original" was a discrepancy. Again, these documents are clearly originals on their face, as they have three slightly differing signatures in blue ink. There was no requirement in the letter of credit or the UCP 500 that original documents be marked as such. . . . The failure to mark obvious originals is not a discrepancy.

Fourth, the Bank of China argues that the date of the survey report is after the bill of lading and is therefore discrepant. A careful examination of the survey report reveals that the survey took place "immediately before/after loading" and that the sample of cargo "to be loaded" was taken. The plain language of the report reveals that the report may have been issued after the bill of lading but the survey itself was conducted before the ship departed. The date does not pose a discrepancy.

Fifth, the Bank of China claims that the letter-of-credit number listed in the beneficiary's certified copy of fax is wrong. The letter-of-credit number was listed as "LC95231033/95" on the copy of fax instead of "LC9521033/95" as in the letter of credit itself, adding an extra "3" after "LC952." However, adding the letter-of-credit number to this document was gratuitous and, in the numerous other places in the documents that the letter of credit was referenced by number, it was incorrect only in one place. Moreover, the seven other pieces of information contained in the document were correct. The document checker could have easily looked to any other document to verify the letter-of-credit number, or looked to the balance of the information within the document and found that the document as a whole bears an obvious relationship to the transaction. Madame Gao, the document checker who reviewed Voest-Alpine's presentation documents for the Bank of China, testified that she did not look beyond the face of this particular document in assessing the discrepancy. The cover letter from Texas Commerce Bank, for example, had the correct number.

Finally, the Bank of China claims that the wrong destination is listed in the certificate of origin and the beneficiary's certificate. The certificate of origin spelled Zhangjiagang as "Zhangjiagng" missing an "a" as it is misspelled once in the letter of credit, making it consistent. The beneficiary's certificate, however, spelled it "Zhanjiagng," missing a "g" in addition to the "a", a third spelling that did not appear in the letter of credit. Madame Gao first considered the discrepancy a "misspelling" rather than an indication of the wrong port, according to her notes. There is no port in China called "Zhangjiagng" or "Zhanjiagng." "Gng" is a combination of letters not found in Romanized Chinese, whereas "gang" means "port" in Chinese. The other information contained in the document was correct, such as the letter of credit number and the contract number, and even contained the distinctive phrase "by courie lukdt within 3 days after shipment," presumably meaning by courier within three days after shipment, as in the letter of credit. The document as a whole bears an obvious relationship with the transaction. The misspelling of the destination is not a basis for dishonor of the letter of credit where the rest of the document has demonstrated linkage to the transaction on its face.

Based on the foregoing, the Court finds in favor of the plaintiff, Voest-Alpine.

This court used a fact-specific approach to the question of how closely the documents must conform to the credit. The court noted that the UCP does not use the term "strict compliance" and further observed that "such a letter-for-letter correspondence between the credit and the presentation documents is virtually impossible." The court limited its holding, however, by indicating that the issuer "is not required to evaluate risks or go beyond the face of the documents." Setting aside the fact that the documents actually conformed with the credit, the Bank of China should have used clearer language of refusal in its communications with Texas Commerce Bank and should have ensured that its communication was made during the UCP refusal period.

Numerous cases have explored the concept of strict compliance under the UCC. In *Middlesex Bank & Trust Co. v. Mark Equipment Corp.*, 56 U.C.C. Rep. Serv. 2d 443 (Mass. Super. 2005), the court found that a bank acted properly in making payment even though the beneficiary presented documents erroneously referencing the issuance date of a previous, expired credit, rather than the issuance date of the then-current credit under which it was seeking payment. Because the beneficiary was not required to reference the issuance date at all, the court found no reason for the bank to dishonor the presentation. In so holding, the court stated, "[t]he strict compliance rule . . . is not absolute, as a bank may not reject a demand for payment on the basis of a hypertechnical reading of a letter of credit. Rather, a variance between documents specified and documents submitted is not fatal if there is no possibility that the documents could mislead the paying bank to its detriment."

By contrast, in *Courtaulds N.A., Inc. v. North Carolina National Bank*, 528 F.2d 802, 805–06 (4th Cir. 1975), where a credit required "a 'commercial invoice in triplicate stating (inter alia) that it covers 100% acrylic yarn,'" an invoice indicating the goods consisted of "imported acrylic yarn" did not satisfy the "strict compliance" test. The court noted that the issuer had contacted the applicant to ask whether it would waive the discrepancies, and the applicant would not do so. The court explained as follows:

> [T]he drawee bank is not to be embroiled in disputes between the buyer and the seller, the beneficiary of the credit. The drawee is involved only with documents, not with merchandise. Its involvement is altogether separate and apart from the transaction between the buyer and seller; its duties and liability are governed exclusively by the terms of the letter, not the terms of the parties' contract with one another. Moreover, as the predominant authorities unequivocally declare, the beneficiary must meet the terms of the credit—and precisely—if it is to exact performance of the issuer. Failing such compliance, there can be no recovery from the drawee.

The court used Article 4 language ("drawee bank") to describe the issuer. The court also rejected the beneficiary's argument that the issuer should have looked beyond the language of the invoices and noticed that the packing slips used the correct language: "100% acrylic yarn." In approving the issuer's conduct, the court held as follows:

> This is not a pharisaical or doctrinaire persistence in the principle, but is altogether realistic in the environs of this case; it is plainly the fair and equitable measure. (The defect in description was not superficial, but occurred in the statement of the quality of the yarn, not a frivolous concern.) The obligation of the drawee bank was graven in the credit. Indeed, there could be no departure from its words. [The issuer] was not expected to scrutinize the collateral papers, such as the packing lists. Nor was it permitted to read into the instrument the contemplation or intention of the seller and buyer.

This section has explored a bank's duties in examining the documents as presented by the beneficiary pursuant to a credit. The following section discusses what could be considered the flip side of this duty—that is, the bank's obligation *not* to look *beyond* the documents.

3.   THE INDEPENDENCE PRINCIPLE

5–103(d) and Comment 1, together with **5–108(f)(1)**, set forth the "independence principle" alluded to in the *Courtaulds* excerpt above. The independence principle allows the credit to substitute the issuer's economic reputation for that of the applicant, by providing that the issuer will not look beyond the credit documents to determine whether payment is due to the beneficiary. This principle is sometimes called "payment against documents."

The following case explains the independence principle and its importance to the efficacy of letter-of-credit transactions. The case also sets forth the limited exception for certain kinds of fraud that may vitiate an issuer's payment obligations. In reading this case, note how the circumstances invoking the fraud exception resemble those under which Article 4 allows reversal of final payment.

MENNEN V. J.P. MORGAN & CO., INC.
689 N.E.2d 869, 34 UCC Rep. Serv. 2d 162 (N.Y. 1997)

BELLACOSA, J.

* * *

This case arises from a 1991 stock buy-out of Mennen Medical, Inc., in which plaintiffs were major shareholders. Plaintiffs sold their shares to a group of investors including an entity named Odyssey Partners, L.P. To

[handwritten note in left margin: WORK IS WINDOWLESS ROOM.]

finance the transaction, Mennen executed and delivered a five-year promissory note to each plaintiff. The notes were identical except for the names of the shareholders and the amount of the note. Each note called for five equal annual payments of principal commencing September 1991, with monthly interest payments the first year, followed by annual interest payments on subsequent anniversary dates. The notes also contained an acceleration clause to cover defaults.

To secure the notes for payment to bought-out shareholders, Mennen obtained standby irrevocable letters of credit from defendant Morgan Guaranty Trust Company. Each letter of credit is identical in form except for the named beneficiary and face amounts. The letters of credit provide for payment within 10 days after presentation of a draft accompanied by a notarized statement that the draw represents an unpaid note installment or that the outstanding balance is due as a consequence of default. The letters of credit also include a standard merger clause to the effect that they reflect the full contractual undertaking and that "such undertaking shall not in any way be modified, amplified or amended by reference to any document, instrument, agreement or note referred to herein and any such reference shall not be deemed to be incorporated herein by reference to any such document, instrument, agreement or note." The letters of credit also expressly provide that they are subject to the Uniform Customs and Practice for Documentary Credits.

Mennen Medical, the obligor, timely paid the first two installments due under the promissory notes. Eventually, Odyssey took financial control of the group of investors who had purchased the Mennen stock. Prior to the third due payment, Odyssey defaulted on its obligations, and plaintiffs accelerated the notes and drew upon the maximum payment provided under the letters of credit.

Morgan promptly paid the respective draws to the beneficiaries of the letters of credit. Several months later, however, Morgan concluded that the amounts it had paid exceeded the amounts due under the promissory notes themselves. Morgan demanded reimbursement from plaintiffs for the alleged overpayments totaling approximately $230,000. Morgan alleged misstatements of the amounts declared to have been owing in the notarized draw statements. The beneficiaries retorted that the "overpayments" represented a premium above the face amounts of the notes, orally negotiated at the time of the purchase. They added that the premiums were designed to compensate them for increased tax liabilities upon acceleration and for the loss of future interest.

Notably, Morgan had contractually relinquished the right to seek reimbursement from its customer Odyssey through a defeasance agreement between those two parties. Under the defeasance device, Morgan, in exchange for an up-front, lump-sum payment, released Odyssey from any subsequent obligation to reimburse Morgan for any amounts Morgan paid to the beneficiaries pursuant to the letters of credit.

The beneficiaries preemptively sued for a declaration that their draws under the letters of credit were correct in amount and that Morgan enjoyed no separate rights over against them. Morgan counterclaimed for alleged overpayments under theories of money had and received, breach of contract, payment by mistake, unjust enrichment, negligent misrepresentation, and fraud. It moved for summary judgment, and plaintiffs cross-moved for similar relief and for dismissal of the counterclaims.

[The Supreme Court and Appellate Division held against Morgan.]

On this appeal, appellant Morgan argues that it should be entitled to recover overpayments made to plaintiffs . . . , notwithstanding that plaintiffs' allegedly false documentation facially complied with the terms of the instrument. Morgan contends that it did not learn until after making payments that the documents fraudulently (as it perceives and alleges the circumstance) specified the amounts owing and, as such, it should be permitted to assert a claim against the payee beneficiaries subsequent to satisfaction pursuant to the letters of credit.

* * *

Letters of credit typically involve three separate contractual relationships and undertakings: the underlying contract between the customer and the beneficiary; the agreement between the bank and its customer, by which the letter of credit is issued in exchange for the customer's promise to reimburse the bank; and, the letter of credit itself, which represents the financial institution's commitment to honor drafts presented by the intended beneficiary upon compliance with the terms and conditions specified in the instrument.

"[A] fundamental principle governing these transactions is the doctrine of independent contracts," which "provides that the issuing bank's obligation to honor drafts drawn on a letter of credit by the beneficiary is separate and independent from any obligation of its customer to the beneficiary under the . . . contract and separate as well from any obligation of the issuer to its customer under their agreement." *First Commercial Bank v Gotham Originals*, 64 NY2d 287, 294 (1985). "Stated another way, this principle stands for 'the fundamental proposition . . . that all parties [to a letter of credit transaction] *deal in documents rather than with the facts the documents purport to reflect.*'" *Id.* at 294 [emphasis added]). Therefore, "the issuer's obligation to pay is fixed upon presentation of the drafts and the documents specified in the letter of credit. It is not required to resolve disputes or questions of fact concerning the underlying transaction." *Id.* at 295.

The twist presented by this case requires the Court to determine first whether an issuer has violated this principle when it promptly pays a draw and only subsequently challenges the validity of the documentation on fraud grounds. A leading authority on the letters of credit type negotiable instruments has stated that "[i]n the event the documents comply on their face with the terms of the credit, the issuer should have a cause of action against the beneficiary if the issuer honors the conforming demand and then learns that, for some reason, the documents do not comply." Dolan, *Letters of Credit: Commercial and Standby Credits* ¶ 9.04, at 9–48 [2d ed]. Therefore, the issuer's initial, timely payment sufficiently satisfies the independence principle and, "[a]fter payment . . . the independence principle should not bar the issuer's claim against a beneficiary." (*Id.* at 9–48).

This is so because the independence doctrine realistically reflects "[t]he exigencies of credit law," which necessitate that the issuer honor presentations that comply on their face without looking beneath the documents. *Id.* . . . The underlying purpose of the rule, however, should not "permit a beneficiary to say, after payment, that [its] false, fraudulent, or inaccurate documents satisfied the conditions of the credit." *Id.*

The above precedents and authorities persuade us that Morgan, by timely paying the letters of credit upon presentation, did not violate the independence principle. The underlying purpose of the doctrine to insure that promptness of payment was and is fulfilled by requiring the issuer to pay up front, even though it would also recognize the issuer subsequently pursuing recovery against a beneficiary based on alleged fraud.

We, thus, conclude that the Appellate Division's holding that the independence principle was violated by Morgan in the instant case is not well founded. . . .

From the Uniform Commercial Code, we note a "limited exception" to the independence principle. Under the general rule, an issuer must honor a draft which complies with the terms of the relevant letter of credit, regardless of whether the documents conform to the underlying contract between the customer and the beneficiary. When a required document, however, does not conform to the necessary warranties, is forged or fraudulent, or there is fraud in the transaction, an issuer may properly refuse to honor a draft drawn under a letter of credit even though the documents presented appear on their face to comply with the terms of the letter of credit.

* * *

[That portion of the court's opinion relating to the application of UCP principles and affirming the lower court's holding against Morgan on grounds not relevant to this textbook's coverage has been omitted, as has Justice Titone's dissent.]

Following this case, and applying **5–109** Comment 1, fraud must be "material" to vitiate the issuer's obligation to pay under a credit. The bank's conduct in this case did not violate the independence principle: The bank paid according to the credit because the documents initially appeared on their face to satisfy the strict-compliance standard, but then sought to recover the funds when it had time to do a more thorough investigation. Not allowing an issuer to do this would put it in the untenable position of (1) trying to conduct a full investigation of fraud during the very short period of time in which it is simply charged with the task of comparing the presented documents with the letter of credit and determining facial compliance, or (2) allowing a fraudfeasor to escape liability for its fraud, so long as the fraud could not easily be discovered during the very short inspection period.

4. DOCUMENTS OF TITLE

A document of title, as defined in **1–201(b)(16)**, is one of the documents the applicant should require the beneficiary to produce to receive payment under a commercial credit. UCC Article 7 covers documents of title. **7–101**'s Official Comment describes some history behind Article 7 and how it can be understood in conjunction with other bodies of law—such as tort law and other state, federal, and international law—that may also apply to a transaction involving a document of title.

While a credit ensures payment will be made when the appropriate documents proving entitlement to payment are produced, a document of title controls the right to the goods themselves. Documents of title can be either negotiable or non-negotiable. *Bank of New York v. Amoco Oil Co.*, 35 F.3d 643 (2d Cir. 1994) involved a negotiable document of title. Amoco Oil Company leased platinum from Drexel Burnham Lambert Trading Corporation. The platinum was combined with aluminum and used to create catalysts for the gasoline-refining process. After each catalyst was used for about six months, it was returned to Drexel Burnham, where the platinum was separated from the aluminum and prepared for re-use. The following language from the parties' "holding certificate," which functioned as a document of title, memorialized the transaction:

This is to certify that as of [date], we are holding for the account or order of:

Drexel Burnham Lambert Trading Corporation
60 Broad Street
New York, New York 10004

The following material: [number of] troy ounces of platinum sponge metal 99.95% catalytic grade.

This material is free of all liens and encumbrances.

Material is to be released on surrender of this Certificate properly [i]ndorsed.

Company Name: Amoco Oil Company

By:		[Signature]

Date:		[Date]

The use of the language "for the account or order," which resembles the "magic words" of negotiability introduced in Chapter 6, contemplates that Drexel could sell the platinum while Amoco held it pursuant to the lease. Amoco must surrender the platinum to anyone who presents the certificate, properly indorsed.

There are two major types of documents of title: bills of lading and warehouse receipts. A bill of lading is a document of title issued by a carrier evidencing the carrier's receipt of goods for the purpose of shipment. "Bill of lading" is defined in **1–201(b)(6)**. A warehouse receipt, defined in **1–201(b)(42)**, is a document of title issued by a warehouse that has accepted goods for storage. The "holding certificate" presented above is somewhat similar to a warehouse receipt. As the court held in that case, "The only relevant difference between the two situations is that the warehouseman is paid for storing the goods for a time, while the lessee pays for the use of the goods for a time." Note the structure of Article 7: Parts 1, 4, 5, 6, and 7 apply equally to warehouse receipts and bills of lading, while Parts 2 and 3 address only warehouse receipts and bills of lading, respectively.

Here is how a bill of lading works as part of a documentary transaction: The carrier issues the bill of lading to the seller when it receives the goods. When the seller receives the bill of lading, it takes this document, together with any others specified in the credit, and makes presentment to the issuing or confirming bank, which examines the documents and, if they conform with the terms of the credit, pays the seller. The applicant must reimburse the issuer for payment, and, if a confirming bank is involved, the issuer must reimburse the confirming bank. In the meantime, the bill of lading is sent to the buyer, which presents it to the carrier in return for the goods.

As **1–201** Comment 16 indicates, documents of title may be electronic or tangible. In addition, as mentioned above, documents of title may be negotiable or non-negotiable. The standards for negotiability under Article 7 are different from Article 3. Under **7–104**, the only formal requirement for negotiability is the use of the right wording—"to bearer" or "to the order of a named person."

Much of the vocabulary is the same for warehouse receipts and bills of lading; there are, however, some differences. For example, **7–102(a)(3)** and **(4)** provide that the person delivering goods to a carrier is called the consignor, and the person to whom the goods are to be delivered is called a consignee. The Code provides no corresponding labels for the person delivering goods to a warehouse and the person to whom the warehouse is to release the goods; instead, drawing from the definition of "delivery order" in **7–102(a)(5)**, these parties are commonly called the deliveror and deliveree.

Both warehouses and carriers have a nondelegable duty of care with regard to the goods accepted for storage or carriage; these duties are provided in **7–204** and **7–309**, respectively. In addition, as **7–403** states, both are obliged to "deliver the goods to a person entitled under a document of title." "Person entitled under the document" is defined in **7–102(a)(9)** as either the holder of a negotiable document of title or the person designated in a non-negotiable document of title. This language, of course, sounds very similar to Article 3's "person entitled to enforce an instrument."

As **7–501(a)** provides, a document of title may pass through the hands of a wrongdoer and end up in the hands of an innocent party who has purchased it "in good faith, without notice of any defense or claim to it on the part of any person, and for value." If (1) the document of title is negotiable, and (2) the document of title has been transferred in such a way as to constitute "due negotiation" rather than a simple assignment, then (3) the innocent party may enforce the instrument as a "holder by due negotiation." **7–501** Comment 1 explains how this would work, as well as the policy behind this rule. This concept, of course, is very similar to Article 3's "holder in due course." A document of title payable "to bearer" is negotiated by mere transfer of possession, while a document of title payable "to the order of a named person" must be indorsed and delivered for negotiation to take place. Again, this is very similar to how Article 3 handles negotiation of bearer paper and order paper, respectively.

Documents of title play a key role in the documentary transactions outlined above, by controlling delivery of the goods just as the letter of credit controls payment for the goods.

Whereas this section has dealt with payment mechanisms used primarily by sophisticated businesses with substantial banking relationships, the following section addresses payments that occur outside the banking system.

E. NON-BANK FINANCIAL SERVICES

In 2015, 7.0 percent of U.S. households were "unbanked," meaning that no one in the household had a checking or savings account. An additional 19.9 percent of U.S. households were "underbanked" in 2015, meaning that the household had an account at an insured institution but also obtained financial services and products outside of the banking system. A household was categorized as underbanked if it had a checking or savings account and used one of the following products or services from an alternative financial services (AFS) provider in the past 12 months: money orders, check cashing, international remittances, payday loans, refund anticipation loans, rent-to-own services, pawn shop loans, or auto title loans.

Unbanked or underbanked individuals often use non-bank financial services such as those listed above. The following information was taken from a 2015 Federal Deposit Insurance Corporation (FDIC) national survey of unbanked and underbanked households.

- Approximately 9.0 million U.S. households, made up of 15.6 million adults and 7.6 million children, were unbanked in 2015.

- Approximately 24.5 million U.S. households, composed of 51.1 million adults and 16.3 million children, were underbanked in 2015.

- The underbanked rate was essentially unchanged from 2013.

- 68.0 percent of households in 2015 were "fully banked," meaning the household had a bank account and did not use AFS in the past 12 months. This was a 1.0 percentage point increase from the fully banked rate in 2013.

The FDIC reports several reasons why people are underbanked or unbanked:

- The most commonly cited reason was "Do not have enough money to keep in an account." An estimated 57.4 percent of unbanked households cited this as a reason and 37.8 percent cited it as the main reason.

- Other commonly cited reasons were "Avoiding a bank gives more privacy," "Don't trust banks," "Bank account fees are too high," and "Bank account fees are unpredictable." Of these, the most cited main reasons were "Don't trust banks" (10.9 percent) and "Bank account fees are too high" (9.4 percent).

- A higher proportion of unbanked households that previously had an account cited high or unpredictable fees as reasons for not having an account (33.8 and 31.5 percent, respectively), compared to those that never had an account (23.1 and 17.7 percent, respectively).

The survey also explored a variety of methods unbanked and underbanked persons use outside of the banking system to pay bills and receive income.

- To pay bills, 62.3 percent used cash, 35.5 percent used nonbank money orders, and 18.2 percent used prepaid cards in a typical month. The most prevalent method of receiving income among unbanked households was by paper check or money order. Among the 42.1 percent of unbanked households that received income in this way, roughly 45 percent (or 19.1 percent of all unbanked households) went to a place other than a bank to cash the check or money order.

- Underbanked households, on the other hand, used banks extensively to pay bills and receive income in a typical month. The key difference between underbanked and fully banked households is that, in addition to bank methods, underbanked households also widely used other methods, particularly for paying bills.

- Electronic payment from a bank account was the most used method of paying bills among both underbanked (62.3 percent) and fully banked (70.4 percent) households. Relative to the fully banked, use of personal checks was lower among underbanked households, and use of bank debit cards was higher. Direct deposit into a bank account was by far the most used method of receiving income, both for underbanked (82.0 percent) and fully banked (87.9 percent) households.

- 27.7 percent of underbanked households paid bills using cash in a typical month, and 25.6 percent used nonbank money orders.

- Overall, nearly half (44.9 percent) of underbanked households exclusively used banks to pay bills and receive income in a typical month.

Mobile payments are an increasingly popular form of payment used by consumers both with and without traditional banking relationships. This form of payment is explored in the following section.

F. MOBILE PAYMENTS

There is no body of governing law unique to mobile payments (m-payments). Instead, the key to identifying what law governs a mobile payment is to look at how the payment is funded. This factor will control the analysis, regardless of whether the m-payment is made by app, near-field communication (NFC), or other technology.

Consider the following three examples:

First, if you go to Starbucks and pay for your coffee through an app linked directly to your bank account, EFTA governs this transaction because EFTA governs ACH transfers from a bank account. If the app is linked to your credit card instead of your bank account, TILA governs the transaction because the credit card is the funding source.

Second, if you send money to a friend via the mobile app for Dwolla, a non-bank payment provider, identifying the governing law is more complicated. To see how this works, let's break down the transaction.

To use Dwolla, you start by creating an account. To fund the account, you authorize Dwolla to initiate an ACH debit from your financial institution. Because EFTA governs ACH transfers from bank accounts, EFTA covers the transaction to fund your account.

Once you have funded the account, rights within Dwolla are governed by the common law of contracts. Thus, the transaction whereby one Dwolla user transfers money to another is purely contractual. Because no regulations protect the funds held in a Dwolla account, it may be wise not to keep more than a nominal amount of money in such an account.

A person receiving such funds can either pay another Dwolla user or move the funds to his or her bank by authorizing Dwolla to send an ACH credit to his or her bank account. Again, the ACH transfer is an EFTA transaction, while transferring funds to another Dwolla user is governed by contract law.

So, in sum—EFTA covers transactions funding the account from a bank or sending funds out of the account to a bank; transfers within Dwolla are purely contractual.

Dwolla does not promise that its service will be available or error-free. A state attorney general or the Consumer Financial Protection Bureau (CFPB) might step in if the situation were extreme, but otherwise the consumer's rights are limited to those Dwolla provides under contract law. Venmo, PayPal, and SquareCash are all similar.

As a third and final example, if you download digital content (a ringtone, a song, etc.) on your phone, another body of law entirely might be involved. This is because you might have direct-to-carrier billing if your mobile carrier permits such billing.

Direct-to-carrier billing is governed by contract law as regulated by the Federal Trade Commission (FTC) and, to some extent, the Federal Communications Commission (FCC). Even though this is a retail money transfer, it is not governed by EFTA because mobile carriers are not banks.

Knowing what law governs a mobile payment allows a consumer to make choices regarding whether to use mobile payments and, if so, which platforms to use.

One final form of emerging payment is virtual currency, the most popular form of which is bitcoin. The final section of this chapter examines this form of payment.

G. VIRTUAL CURRENCY

Although the terms "virtual currency," "cryptocurrency," and "bitcoin" are sometimes used interchangeably, they are distinct. Virtual currency (VC) is a digital representation of value that is broader than just bitcoin. VC is purely electronic and intangible. Examples of VC include loyalty points and airline miles, as well as bitcoin. These examples all have in common the fact that they are not denominated in legal tender such as dollars, but instead might be described in points, miles, or other units of value, and can be converted to real world goods, services, and money. Cryptocurrency is a subset of virtual currency that is decentralized and uses cryptography technology as part of the validation process. Bitcoin is a virtual currency that is also a cryptocurrency. It is sometimes said that there is no bitcoin; there are only bitcoin transactions.

Although VC is clearly a means of payment, VC is not considered "money" in the generally understood meaning of the word. Money is a store of value, a medium of exchange, and a unit of account. Money is usually also treated as currency, or legal tender. Consider the dollar: The dollar is legal tender because everyone in the US recognizes it as a unit of exchange and can count on it being accepted as a means of payment. According to the International Monetary Fund, VC is too volatile to be a reliable store of value, too small and too limited to serve as a medium of exchange, and not generally used as an independent unit of account. Instead, when VC is used, it is used to pay for items that are priced in local currency (such as the dollar) rather than having originally been priced in VC.

The following describes how a bitcoin transaction works:

(1)   First, you have to create a Wallet.

(2)   Then, you purchase bitcoin on an exchange, acquire some in return for goods or services you have given, or earn some by volunteering your computer as part of the "mining" verification process described below.

(3)   Then, you go to buy something from some seller who accepts bitcoin.

(4)   The seller creates a bitcoin address and asks you to send payment to it.

   a.   This creates a private key (known only to the seller) and a public key (available to you and anyone else). This is a cryptographic pair.

   b.   Note that, just as a seller does not need to know your identity if you pay cash, you do not need to disclose your real identity to the seller and can remain anonymous.

(5) You instruct your Wallet to transfer bitcoin to the seller's bitcoin address. This is called the transaction message.

(6) Your Wallet will electronically "sign" the transaction request with the private key of the address from which you are transferring the bitcoin. (This is called the private key). Your public key is available to anyone for signature verification.

(7) Your transaction is broadcast to the Bitcoin network and will be verified presently. Bitcoin has been successfully transferred from your address to the seller's address.

To engage in a VC transaction, there is no need for a banking account—only a VC Wallet, which is a free app. Access to technology such as a smart phone is, however, necessary. The decentralized aspect of VC makes it potentially attractive to both unbanked persons and people living in countries with underdeveloped banking systems, but the volatility of the VC market is problematic.

The Blockchain is a distributed ledger of all bitcoin transactions that have ever occurred. To understand what the term "distributed ledger" means, it is helpful to contrast a typical banking transaction. When payment is made via a check, the drawee/payor bank is solely responsible for validating the transaction and posting the transaction to the drawer's account. This is a wholly centralized model because only the bank holds the ledger where the transactions are recorded. With the distributed ledger system, there are multiple copies of the ledger. More than one entity validates the transactions, with the theory being that it is easier to trick one entity than several. They each validate the transaction and achieve consensus as to its validity. No single entity can manipulate the ledger and, if one copy is compromised, there are many more.

"Mining" is the process of settling and validating bitcoin transactions. It has two outputs—(1) the settlement of the transaction and (2) generating new bitcoin. Anyone can engage in mining. To participate, you download special software (and generally also purchase special hardware that is proven to be efficient with mining). Miners bundle transactions in a block and (using their computers) solve very difficult mathematical problems called "Proof of Work" problems. When enough computational effort is devoted to the block, the transactions are verified and additional bitcoin is generated.

Bitcoin has some very attractive features, but also raises some concerns. The rather quick nature of the transfers is attractive for remittances. Migrant remittances have been very important in developing countries, but also generate high fees (about 7.7 percent on average) for a typical remittance of about $200. By contrast, the cost associated with a bitcoin transaction is typically about 1 percent. There are no centrally set fees; instead, the parties to a bitcoin transaction negotiate the fee that will be charged.

VC is seen as more of a risk for money laundering, tax evasion, terrorist financing, and fraud than other means of payment. Anonymity is the greatest concern. VC transactions are described as pseudo-anonymous; they can be traced back to a VC address but not to a real world identity. As a result, VC has sometimes been used for so-called Dark Web transactions in illegal goods. One marketplace where these transactions occurred was called Silk Road, which US authorities closed down in 2013.

VCs have been hard to regulate thus far, for several reasons. First, it is difficult to gather data because of the quasi-anonymous nature of VC transactions. Second, there is much debate as to whether the regulations that have been proposed thus far should govern all VC, all cryptocurrency, or just bitcoin. Third, the cross-border nature of the transactions means that no single jurisdiction can effectively control VC. The decentralized nature of VC also makes it hard to get all of the key players in the room or to regulate them.

Chapter Conclusion: As you leave this chapter, you should be comfortable knowing when you might advise a potential client to use a credit card, "retail" electronic fund transfer, letter of credit (as part of a documentary sales transaction), or wholesale funds transfer as a means of payment. You should also be aware of the existence of non-bank financial services and newer means of payment such as m-payments and virtual currency. With each of these means of payment, you should be aware of the basic legal framework, whether within the UCC, federal law, or ordinary contract law.

PROBLEMS

1.   Towers World Airways, Inc. had a credit card issued by PHH Aviation Systems. Towers leased a corporate jet from PHH and employed a company called World Jet Corporation to maintain the aircraft. Towers appointed Fred Jay Schley, an employee of World Jet, as chief pilot for the aircraft and allowed him to use the PHH credit card only to purchase fuel for non-chartered flights. In contravention of the parties' agreement, Schley used the PHH credit card to purchase about $89,000 in fuel for chartered flights.

a.   Was Schley's use of the card "authorized" within the meaning of 15 U.S.C. § 1643? Why or why not?

b.   How, if at all, could Towers have avoided the unwanted charges?

2.   Minot Builders Supply Association was listed as the cardholder on an Amoco Torch Club credit card. However, Minot never signed, used, or authorized use of this credit card. Instead, a Mr. Smith obtained the card without Minot's approval. Smith fraudulently used the card for three years, thereby embezzling money from Minot. During this period of time, Minot

always paid the monthly statement from Amoco when it arrived. Minot employed accountants to identify fraud during annual audits, but the audits did not reveal Smith's fraud.

   a. Was the Torch Club card an accepted credit card within the meaning of the Truth in Lending Act? Which TILA section did you use to reach your answer?

   b. Did Smith at any time acquire authority to use the card? If so, how?

   c. What, if any, consideration should the court give to the fact that outside auditors did not identify Smith's fraud?

   3. Daniel Calvin and Karen Horton lived together in a romantic relationship in New Jersey from January through March 1987. In March, Calvin stole Horton's car, created a fraudulent bill of sale showing he owned it, and left for Mississippi. He returned later that month, and the two continued to cohabitate, although their personal relationship did not continue. While Calvin was in Mississippi, Horton discovered he had stolen a gasoline credit card and a briefcase from her and had obtained a sum of money from her by misrepresentation. She cooperated with authorities in a criminal prosecution to which he later pled guilty.

In August, Horton realized her American Express card was missing when she sought to use it to pay for gasoline. The station attendant told her he had seen Calvin with the card earlier in the day. Horton immediately called American Express and reported the card missing. By that time, Calvin had used the card to purchase merchandise costing approximately $5,250. Approximately $925 was spent at Blaisdell Lumber Company during seven separate transactions. On at least one occasion, an unidentified female accompanied Calvin. Neither Calvin nor his companion were asked for identification. Calvin signed each charge slip in his own name.

Assume Horton and Calvin were still cohabitating at the time of the August purchases, and Horton denied knowing of the purchases.

   a. Were the Blaisdell Lumber Company purchases authorized?

   b. How, if at all, would your answer change if Horton and Calvin were married?

   4. Assume that you have used your credit card to pay for expensive car repairs which, you discover the following day, were not performed correctly.

   a. Whom should you contact first – your credit card issuer or the person who repaired your car? Why?

   b. What facts should you gather and be prepared to demonstrate before initiating a dispute with the credit card issuer?

   c. Assume that you are enormously protective of your excellent credit rating and always pay your balance in full every month. What, if anything, should you do differently this time, and why?

d.   Consider the transaction from the perspective of the person who repaired your car. Assume that being able to accept credit cards is very important to him or her, because credit-card payments account for more than 75% of the repair shop's income. How might this fact create an incentive for the repairperson to be reasonable in responding to your concerns about the quality of service performed?

e.   Now assume that you took a cash advance from your credit card to pay for the car repairs, since the person who repaired your car did not accept credit cards, but insisted instead on cash. Looking at the sample "Schumer" box that appeared earlier in this chapter, how much would this cash advance cost you, for a $2,000 car repair? If you were unable to pay the balance in full when the statement arrived, how might you figure out how much the repair would cost you if you paid only the 4% minimum payment on this card?

5.   Glen Wood was an executive vice president of SAR Manufacturing Company. He checked into a Holiday Inn in Phenix City, Alabama on business on February 1, 1972, and, pursuant to an arrangement between Gulf Oil Company and Holiday Inn Hotels & Resorts, tendered his Gulf credit card as payment for his room. The desk attendant made an imprint of the card and returned it to him.

As part of its normal practices, Gulf evaluated Wood's account regularly and provided information regarding the account to National Data Corporation. As part of this same process, Holiday Inn was authorized to contact National Data Corporation to inquire about the creditworthiness of Wood or any other Gulf cardholder. Gulf's credit manager had reviewed Wood's credit account on January 17, 1972, and had become concerned about the account, although payment was current at the time. The credit manager's concern related to the increasing charges being made in relation to Wood's income. Gulf therefore directed National Data Corporation to give the following message to any person seeking credit approval on Wood's account: "Pick up travel card. Do not extend further credit. Send card to billing office for reward."

During the middle of the night, after Wood had checked in, Phenix City Holiday Inn night auditor Jessie Goynes contacted National Data Corporation for an authorization on Wood's account and received the message Gulf had directed National Data Corporation to give. Accordingly, Goynes telephoned Wood's room around 5:00 a.m. and advised him that he needed to make another imprint of the card, since the first one was not readable. Wood assented, and Goynes came to the room to get the card. When the card had not been returned within half an hour, Wood became concerned that Goynes had stolen it. He dressed, went to the hotel's front desk, and was informed that Goynes had seized the card "upon the authority of National Data." Goynes demanded payment in cash and refused Wood's request to call Gulf.

When Wood returned home, he contacted Gulf to complain about its refusal to authorize the room charge. Gulf confirmed his account was current and immediately reinstated his charging privileges. Three days later, while

Wood was relating the story to a friend, still angry about the events, he suffered a heart attack.

    a.   Do these facts support a cause of action for wrongful cancellation?

    b.   If you represented Gulf, how would you advise it to handle matters like this one in the future, and why?

    6.   Consider the following description of a fraudulent scheme involving automated teller machines:

A customer enters the automated-teller-machine area for the purpose of using a machine for the transaction of business with the bank. At the time that he enters, a person is using the customer-service telephone located between the two automated teller machines and appears to be telling customer service that one of the machines is malfunctioning. This person is the perpetrator of the scam, and his conversation with customer service is only simulated. He observes the customer press his personal identification code into one of the two machines. Having learned the code, the perpetrator then tells the customer that customer service has advised him to ask the customer to insert his [ATM card] into the allegedly malfunctioning machine to check whether it will work with a card other than the perpetrator's. When a good-Samaritan customer accedes to the request, the other machine is activated. The perpetrator then presses a code into the machine, which the customer does not realize is his own code which the perpetrator has just observed. After continuing the simulated conversation on the telephone, the perpetrator advises the customer that customer service has asked if he would try his [ATM card] in the allegedly malfunctioning machine once more. A second insertion of the card permits cash to be released by the machine, and if the customer does as requested, the thief has effectuated a cash withdrawal from the unwary customer's account.

    a.   Look carefully at 15 U.S.C. § 1693a(12). Was this an unauthorized electronic fund transfer? Why or why not?

    7.   Dorothy Judd and her husband had a joint checking account with Citibank and were each issued an automated teller card. Each was responsible for choosing a PIN that would be known only to him or her and could not be retrieved by any third person, not even a bank representative. On February 26, 1980, between 2:13 and 2:14 p.m. and on March 28, 1980, between 2:30 and 2:32 p.m., funds totaling $800 were withdrawn from the Judd account, by automated-teller-machine transactions.

Mrs. Judd sought to recover those funds from Citibank, claiming neither she nor her husband, nor any person authorized by either, had withdrawn the funds. She produced a letter from her employer showing she had been at work when both withdrawals were made. She testified that she had never written down her personal identification number or shared the number with any person. Citibank, which produced computer records showing the withdrawals, responded that one of the Judds, or some person authorized by one of them, must have completed the transactions.

a. Look carefully at 15 U.S.C. § 1693g. Which party has the burden of proof in this matter?

b. Based only on the facts that appear above, has that party carried its burden? Why or why not?

8. On December 1, 1988, June Elga Wachter entered a branch of Denver National Bank and presented $153.42 in cash, which was used to effectuate a wire transfer of $143.42 to a recipient in California and to pay a $10 wire-transfer fee. Bank personnel initiated the transfer and provided Ms. Wachter with confirmation of the transaction.

a. Look carefully at 15 U.S.C. § 1693a(7). Is this an electronic fund transfer?

b. If the court were to determine that this was not an electronic fund transfer, what body of law would govern this transfer, and why?

9. The following paragraphs from a court's opinion describe the logistics of an Article 4A wholesale funds transfer using CHIPS.

Once the programming of the computer has been completed, the send form is sent to the appropriate area at the sending bank for approval. When a determination is made at the sending bank to make the payment, the form is returned to one of the computer-terminal operators, reinserted in the computer, and the release key is depressed. At that moment, the central computer at the Clearing House causes a credit ticket to be printed automatically at the terminal of the receiving bank and a debit ticket to be printed at the terminal of the sending bank. Further, the central computer automatically makes a permanent record of the transaction and debits the Clearing House account of the sending bank and credits the Clearing House account of the receiving bank. . . .

The funds received by a receiving bank for the account of one of its customers via the receipt of a CHIPS credit message are made available to the customer and can be drawn upon by the customer in the discharge of its obligations that same day, as soon as the receiving bank is aware of the fact that the funds have been received.

a. How does this excerpt help to explain the widespread use of wholesale funds transfers for large, time-critical payments?

b. How would you compare the availability of funds for a wholesale funds transfer with what you learned in Chapter 8 about Regulation CC?

10. Mr. Zhou was the victim of a fraud scheme specifically targeting attorneys. Under this scheme, a fake new client delivered a counterfeit cashier's check, which Zhou deposited. That same day, the fake client requested that Zhou make an emergency wire transfer to an account in Japan held by a third party. The amount of the wire transfer was about $10,000 less than the check, which was almost $300,000. A teller at Zhou's bank advised

Zhou that the money was available and "the funds were good." The check was subsequently returned as counterfeit, and Zhou's bank reversed the provisional credit.

 a.   You have previously learned that Articles 3 and 4 do not provide any relief to Zhou, notwithstanding the teller's advice, which may have misled him. Since this case involves an Article 4A wire transfer, does 4A–204 or 4A–205 provide any relief? Why or why not?

11.   After reading the *Voest-Alpine* case, what is the probable outcome in each of the following cases? You may assume that the issuer of each credit has refused to pay, and the beneficiary has sued.

 a.   A standby letter of credit was given to ensure performance of a construction project according to a contract the applicant had made with the beneficiary, a county in Florida. The letter of credit required presentation of a certificate by the County's Public Works Director declaring the applicant to be in default under the contract, as a precondition to payment. In seeking payment pursuant to the letter of credit, the County presented two documents: (1) an internal office memorandum from the Director requesting that another county official seek payment pursuant to the letter of credit because the applicant-contractor had defaulted, and (2) a certificate by the Director's subordinate declaring the applicant to be in default.   *No*

 b.   A letter of credit required the production of originals of all documents, to trigger payment. Because the original of one document could not be located, a "true copy" was produced.   *Yes*

 c.   A commercial letter of credit was issued at the request of an applicant named Mohammed Sofan, a resident of the Yemen Arab Republic, to facilitate his purchase of two prefabricated houses from a seller in the U.S., Dessaleng Beyene. The letter of credit required the beneficiary, Beyene, to submit, among other documents, a bill of lading to provide Mr. Sofan with assurance that he would receive the houses. The bill of lading Beyene presented identified the purchaser as "Mr. Mohammed Soran" and indicated that Mr. "Soran" was to be notified upon the goods' arrival in Yemen.   *No*

 d.   Change the applicant's name in "c" above to "Mohammed Smith" and assume the bill of lading bears the incorrectly spelled name "Mohammed Smithh."   *Yes*

12.   A successful businessperson has decided to purchase a McLaren P1 automobile valued at more than $1.3 million. The vehicle is being shipped from Surrey, England, where it was built, to Florida, where she lives. This individual is a sophisticated consumer of automobiles but has never purchased a McLaren, and she does not know the seller. She is trying to decide how to deliver the funds.

a. Assume that the seller has requested payment with bitcoin. If you represented the buyer, what concerns would you raise with respect to this form of payment?

b. Now assume that the buyer and seller have agreed to a documentary sales transaction including both a bill of lading and a letter of credit. What are some of the documents the buyer should require the seller to produce, in order to obtain payment under the credit?

c. If the buyer believes she may want to sell the McLaren while it is in transit from England to the United States, how might this affect the kind of document of title she should request, and why?

13. Assume you have a younger sibling who uses cash and nonbank money orders to pay most of her bills. She has a bank account, but her bank charges high transaction fees, so she looks for other alternatives whenever possible. You have learned that she has accumulated about $500 in a Venmo account, which represents her entire savings.

a. What, if any, concerns do you have?

b. What recommendations could you make?

CHAPTER 11

AN INTRODUCTION TO SECURED TRANSACTIONS

■ ■ ■

The remaining chapters in this book cover the law of secured transactions. Article 9 of the UCC governs secured transactions in personal property, but our discussions in this part of the book will include some other state debtor-creditor law as well as federal law. Because one of the key benefits of secured status is protection in bankruptcy, these chapters will introduce some federal law in the form of the Bankruptcy Code, which you will find in Title 11 of the United States Code.

Although you may not be familiar with the term "secured transaction," your Property professor probably introduced you to the concept. A mortgage on real estate is a secured transaction. A simplified explanation is this: any time a borrower gives a lender an interest in a specific asset (collateral) to provide additional assurance (security) that borrower will pay the loan, the borrower and lender have created a secured transaction. There's more to it than that, of course, as the next few chapters will explain. You should keep in mind, however, that Article 9 of the UCC governs secured transactions in personal property. That means all assets except real estate, but as you will see sometimes the line between personal and real property is blurry. Although these chapters do not discuss mortgage law, if you know something about mortgage law, you know something about the law of secured transactions under Article 9.

The following chapters roughly trace the timeline of a secured transaction. They will introduce a lot of new terminology. The law of secured transactions falls into the broad category of debtor-creditor law so two terms that you will see over and over again are "secured party" and "debtor." In plain English, the secured party is the lender or other person who has extended credit (although one that has done what is necessary to obtain a security interest in property). Although often we think of the debtor as the borrower or other person who owes money this is not always the case in Article 9. Article 9 governs transactions of all sizes and varying levels of complexity, and sometimes the borrower is not the party who gives collateral for the loan. Article 9 therefore distinguishes between the person who owes the money, or "obligor" (**9–102(a)(59)**) and the person who owns the collateral, or "debtor" (**9–102(a)(28)**). We will explore that distinction later in these materials. The UCC does not use the word "lender;" instead, it defines "creditor" in Article 1 (**1–201(b)(13)**). A secured party is one type of creditor. The chapters that follow will introduce you to other types of creditors.

Chapter 11 introduces the scope of Article 9 and the advantages of being a secured party. In this chapter, you will learn that Article 9 sweeps some transactions that are not labeled as loans within its scope. It is critically important to know which transactions are governed by Article 9, because if the transaction is governed by Article 9 but not properly documented, a creditor that thought it had retained an interest in property to ensure payment may find that it has no interest in the debtor's property at all.

Chapter 12 will explain how a creditor can obtain the status of a secured party. Chapter 12 will also introduce the various types of collateral, because collateral descriptions are key to the proper creation of a security interest. In Chapter 12, you will learn about the security agreement and the requisites for attachment. You will also learn that once a security interest has attached, the secured creditor has enforcement (foreclosure) rights. That's because a security agreement is a contract, and once the debtor has agreed that the secured party has an interest in its property in exchange for an extension of credit, the secured party has the right to seize and sell that property to satisfy its claims against the debtor. But that interest will not have priority against everyone else in the world until it is perfected.

Chapter 13 discusses default. These materials explore the concept of default and the secured creditor's remedies upon default. Article 9 of the UCC permits a creditor to use self-help to obtain collateral after default—in other words, a creditor can recover collateral without resort to the courts. This chapter will discuss the limitations on that right, and will also discuss the secured creditor's right to recover intangible assets after default.

Chapter 14 discusses perfection of security interests. Perfection is (usually) the act by which a secured creditor gives notice to the entire world of its security interest. When a creditor perfects its security interest, it establishes its priority in relation to other entities that might claim an interest in the collateral. Chapter 14 will introduce the various ways of perfecting a security interest in collateral, and explains how various events, including the passage of time, can affect the secured creditor's perfected status.

Chapter 15 examines priorities. There are several parties who may claim an interest in an asset that is encumbered by a security interest. These parties include other creditors, buyers, and, if the owner of the collateral files for bankruptcy, the trustee in bankruptcy. Because perfection is critical to a creditor's status in bankruptcy, this chapter will introduce some key bankruptcy rules.

A. TYPES OF CREDITORS

The world runs on credit. No matter your stage in life, you are no doubt familiar with the concept of credit. You likely have one or more credit cards, you may have taken out a student loan; perhaps you have financed the purchase of a car or even a home. Below is a brief description of the terminology used to distinguish among the various types of debtor-creditor relationships.

1. UNSECURED CREDITORS: NO INTEREST IN PROPERTY

Credit card obligations are a typical example of unsecured debt—the issuer extends credit for each purchase or cash advance, but the card holder does not grant the issuer any right in specific property to back up the card holder's promise to repay the debt. Student loans work the same way—the borrower signs a binding promise to pay, but the lender has no rights in any of the borrower's property at the outset of the relationship. Credit card lenders and student loan lenders are two examples of voluntary unsecured creditors because their relationships with their borrowers are created by contract.

Unsecured creditors can also be involuntary. A tort victim is an unsecured creditor of the person who harmed him. As soon as someone is hit by a car, that person is a creditor of the driver that hit him.

The most important point about unsecured creditors for the purpose of these materials is that an unsecured creditor does not bargain for any rights in any of its debtor's property at the beginning of the debtor-creditor relationship.

2. SECURED CREDITORS: CONSENSUAL INTEREST IN PROPERTY

As you have learned in the other sections of this book, one of the most important things to learn about a code is its scope. This chapter will concentrate on the scope of Article 9, but the first important point is that Article 9 applies to "a transaction, regardless of its form, that creates a *security interest* in *personal* property or fixtures by *contract*." **9–109(a)(1)**. What does that mean? See the definition of "security interest" in **1–201(b)(35)**.

A security interest is a type of lien. You can find a good definition of "lien" in the Bankruptcy Code. *See* **11 U.S.C. § 101(37)**,[1] which defines lien as a "charge against or interest in property to secure payment of a debt or performance of an obligation." Liens can be consensual or non-consensual.

---

[1] We will discuss several Bankruptcy Code sections in the next few chapters of this book. All of those sections are in Title 11 of the United States Code. In this book, we will designate Bankruptcy Code sections as "BC [number]"

A security interest is a type of consensual lien. A real property mortgage creates a security interest, but it is not an Article 9 security interest. There are two important things to remember about an Article 9 security interest. The first is that it is created by contract. In other words, it is a consensual lien, as opposed to a judicial lien. The second is that it attaches to personal, not real, property.

There are two important aspects of a security interest. The first is the *remedy* aspect. A secured creditor (whether an Article 9 secured party or a mortgage creditor) bargains for the right to seize and sell its debtor's property if that debtor does not pay its loan or otherwise defaults on its agreement with the secured creditor. You will study that process in detail in Chapter 13, but for a preview, look at **9–601, 9–609, 9–610**. The second is the *priority* aspect. Priority status is usually tied to public notice of the interest. We will cover priority and how a secured creditor obtains priority in later chapters.

3. LIEN CREDITORS

Later in these materials, you will see references to "lien creditors," but it is worth introducing you to those creditors now. *See* **9–102(a)(52)**. According to that definition, a lien creditor is a creditor who has obtained its lien by "attachment, levy or the like." The definition then adds parties to whom the UCC grants the same status as a lien creditor, notably the trustee in bankruptcy.

The terms "attachment and levy" refer to post judgment remedies. This is the key distinction between lien creditors and secured creditors. Secured creditors have the right to seize and sell certain property of the debtor upon the debtor's default. That right is created by contract at the outset of the transaction. Other creditors have no right to do so unless they first obtain a judgment in court against the debtor. As discussed above, unsecured creditors can be either voluntary (credit card issuers, for example) or involuntary (such as tort creditors). The voluntariness in that distinction refers to the beginning of the relationship between the debtor and the creditor. A credit card company intends to become a creditor; a tort victim does not. Whether the beginning of the relationship is voluntary or involuntary, the unsecured creditor must first obtain a judgment in court against its non-paying (or otherwise defaulting) debtor in order to get any kind of interest in the debtor's property. The lien, therefore, is involuntary.

After the court renders the judgment, the creditor has a right to proceed against the debtor's property but does not yet have any rights in specific property. The judgment transforms the creditor into a judgment creditor, but does not grant any property rights to that creditor. The post judgment procedure differs in terminology from state to state, so what follows is a basic framework that will give you some guidance so that you know what to look for in your own state law.

After obtaining a judgment, the creditor has the right to obtain an interest in assets of the debtor but does not yet have that interest. The judgment creditor is, however, entitled to a writ of execution, in which it directs the sheriff to seize property of the debtor. Statutes specify the types of asset that creditors can reach by a writ of execution. Some assets, such as bank accounts and other debts owing to the debtor, cannot be reached by a writ of execution, but the judgment creditor can reach those assets by using a writ of garnishment.

When the sheriff seizes the debtor's property, either by garnishment or execution, the creditor becomes a "lien creditor." *See* **9–102(a)(52)**. The sheriff will then sell the property at auction and deliver the proceeds to the creditor or if the sheriff is in possession of garnished funds, the sheriff will turn the funds over to the creditor. The foregoing is a general view of the process—your state might use different terminology. For an example of this process, see Pa. R.C.P. Rules 3101 *et seq.*

Sometimes you will see these creditors referred to as "judgment lien creditors" or "involuntary lien creditors." It is important to remember that these creditors do not obtain their property interests (liens) by contract. Some of you may find the following chart helpful:

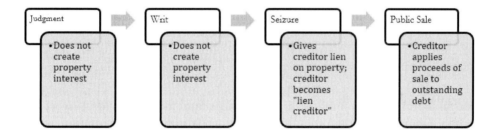

As you will learn in Chapter 13, the process for secured creditors will be different, and often will involve neither the courts nor the sheriff.

B. A VERY LITTLE BIT OF ARTICLE 9 HISTORY

The great contribution of Article 9 when it was first proposed in the 1950s was that it unified and simplified the business of lending secured by personal property, thus facilitating loans to small and medium-sized businesses that did not have the traditional collateral of real property, investment securities, and heavy machinery. Prior to the enactment of Article 9 a patchwork of statutes distinguished by type of property and type of loan governed this type of lending.

Article 9 has been revised several times, most recently in 1998 (with a uniform effective date of July 1, 2001) and 2010 (with a uniform effective date of July 1, 2013). The 1998 revisions were extensive, expanding the scope of Article 9 and changing the filing rules. Be careful when you come across cases decided before the 1998 revisions went into effect, because some of today's rules are quite different. The other thing to keep in mind about the 1998 Amendments is that they substantially "complexified" the material. Article 9 is still a statute that unifies the various types of personal property secured lending under one statutory umbrella. But it is now written in such a way to ensure that some types of extremely complex transactions are under that umbrella. As a result, your professor may skip over large swaths of Article 9. That's okay, because once you master the concept of a personal property secured transaction and the structure of Article 9, you should be able to tackle more complex transactions in practice.

The 2010 revisions were more modest, but they contain important rules governing the sufficiency of an individual debtor's name on a financing statement. Again, older cases may not be very helpful to you if you have a problem involving an incorrect name for an individual debtor. More on this later.

C. THE IMPORTANCE OF SECURED STATUS IN BANKRUPTCY

You will see bankruptcy concepts sprinkled through the remaining chapters of this book. Many of the opinions that you will study in this section of the book were written by bankruptcy judges to resolve disputes during a bankruptcy case. As a result, it is impossible to master the law of secured transactions without knowing a little bit about bankruptcy law.

The vast majority of debtors pay their debts when due, so most debtors and secured creditors do not fight with each other. When a debtor owes money to many entities and can't pay, the debtor might choose to file for bankruptcy. Bankruptcy is a federal process designed to resolve the financial distress of a debtor. That process begins when the debtor, or in rare cases, creditors of the debtor, file a petition in a bankruptcy court, a federal court. A bankruptcy judge manages the process. You will find the statute governing bankruptcy in **11 U.S.C. §§ 101** *et seq.* Bankruptcy is designed as a collective proceeding, and one feature of that collective proceeding is that unsecured creditors of the debtor share the debtor's property *pro rata.* A secured creditor, however, bargains at the outset of its transaction for a better bankruptcy deal—it gets paid the value of its security interest before any unsecured creditors are paid. This is the case both in a liquidation bankruptcy (under chapter 7 of the Bankruptcy Code) and in a reorganization or repayment bankruptcy (under chapters 11 and 13 of the Bankruptcy Code).

How does this work? Let's take the most straightforward type of bankruptcy, the Chapter 7 case. Although we start here, keep in mind that one must know the basic Chapter 7 principles in order to master the more complex bankruptcy problems. The debtor's bankruptcy filing creates an "estate," which consists of all "legal and equitable interests of the debtor in property" at the time that the bankruptcy petition is filed. **BC 541(a)(1).** A bankruptcy trustee is appointed in every chapter 7 case by the United States Trustee, an employee of the Department of Justice who oversees bankruptcy cases. In a chapter 7, the trustee sells the estate property to satisfy the debts outstanding at the time the petition is filed. The Bankruptcy Code prioritizes among unsecured claims (**BC 507(a)**), and you'll learn about priority claims in your Bankruptcy course. For the purpose of this course we'll assume that all unsecured claims are general non-priority unsecured claims. Because debtors who resort to chapter 7 will not have enough assets to satisfy all of their debts, those unsecured claims will be paid *pro rata* from the proceeds of sale of the estate property. In other words, if the debtor has five creditors, each of whom has a $1000 claim, but there is only $1000 in the bankruptcy estate, each creditor will receive $200, or 20 cents on the dollar (**BC 726(b)**). The remaining $800 that the debtor owes to each creditor will be *discharged*, meaning that the creditor is barred from ever trying to recover that money from the debtor (**BC 524(a)**).

The above analysis applies only to unsecured creditors. Take another look at **BC 541**. Only the debtor's interest in property goes into the estate. If the debtor's property is subject to a security interest, the secured creditor's interest does not go into the estate. The practical implication of that is that a creditor is paid in full to the extent of its secured claim before any unsecured creditors are paid.

One important section of the Bankruptcy Code that applies to both secured and unsecured creditors is **BC 362(a)**, which imposes an automatic stay on myriad actions against the debtor, the debtor's property, and property of the estate. The automatic stay arises at the moment that the debtor's bankruptcy petition is filed. Keep in mind that bankruptcy is intended to be a collective proceeding, and although secured creditors bargain for better rights in bankruptcy, even they are stayed from creating, perfecting, and enforcing their interests in property after a bankruptcy petition is filed. They will get their special rights, but they will have to wait for them.

Here is a fairly simple example, with reference to the governing Bankruptcy Code language. Sport-e Bikes, a manufacturer of electric-assist bicycles, files for bankruptcy. While things were going well for Sport-e Bikes, it obtained a $100,000 loan from Lakeside Bank. Lakeside Bank took a security interest in the equipment that Sport-e Bikes uses to make bicycles. The security interest was properly documented at the time that Sport-e Bikes filed for bankruptcy. At the time of filing, the equipment was worth $110,000 and Sport-e Bikes owed Lakeside Bank $90,000.

Lakeside Bank will have a $90,000 secured claim in the Sport-e Bikes bankruptcy. How do we know that? *See* **BC 506(a)**. This section tells us that "an allowed claim of a creditor, *secured by property in which the estate has an interest . . .* is a *secured claim* to the extent of the *value* of *such creditor's interest* in the *estate's interest* in such property." All of the debtor's interests in property go into the estate, so the estate has an interest in the equipment. The value of Lakeside's interest is $90,000 (the amount it is owed) and the value of the estate's interest is $110,000 (the value of the asset). In **Problem 7** you will work on more complicated variations of this problem.

The trustee is the representative of the estate. **BC 323.** Therefore, it is the trustee's job to maximize the estate for the benefit of the unsecured creditors. One way to maximize the estate is to search for security interests that may not be correctly documented. In many cases, no one looks at the loan documents after the closing takes place. The exception is when something goes wrong—if the debtor fails to pay or perhaps worse, files for bankruptcy, the secured creditor will want to make sure that the loan was properly documented in the first place.

Although you'll learn exactly how a trustee can challenge security interests in Chapter 17 of these materials, it is enough to know right now that a secured creditor that doesn't properly create and perfect its security interest will end up unsecured for bankruptcy purposes.

There is one other bankruptcy player to introduce at this point—the Debtor in Possession, or "DIP." When a business entity files to reorganize under chapter 11 of the Bankruptcy Code, corporate management remains in place to shepherd the company through bankruptcy. The management becomes the Debtor in Possession and obtains the powers of the trustee in bankruptcy. You will see the DIP as a party in several of the cases that you will read in this chapter and those that follow.

D. THE SCOPE OF ARTICLE 9

The foregoing discussion leads us to our first important Article 9 scope lesson. Take another look at **9–109(a)(1)**: Article 9 of the UCC governs a transaction, *regardless of its form* that creates a security interest in personal property by contract. First, Article 9 includes transactions creating security interests by contract. The language "by contract" indicates these are consensual transactions. We will take up the requirements for that contract in Chapter 12 of this book. Most liens arising by statute or operation of other law are outside Article 9, with the exception of agricultural liens, which are expressly included. *See* **9–109(a)(2)**. The scope section includes two other transactions in its coverage: the consignment and the sale of certain payment rights. In addition, if a transaction looks a lot like a secured transaction, it is a secured transaction, regardless of how the parties label the transaction. We will take up this last point first.

Before we dive into scope, a quick note on why it is so important. Disputes over property that may or may not be collateral for a loan come up primarily in two contexts. The first involves questions of default and foreclosure, which are usually decided in state court. If a transaction is subject to Article 9, the secured creditor has the repossession and foreclosure rights provided in Part 6 of Article 9 (**9–601** *et seq.*) We will cover those rights in more detail in Chapter 13 of this book. The second context involves priority disputes, which are often resolved in bankruptcy court. In order to have priority over other creditors, buyers, and the trustee in bankruptcy, the secured party must comply with Article 9's perfection requirements, which often, but not always, involve filing a notice in a public place (usually the Secretary of State's office in the debtor's location, but there are different rules for specified types of collateral, notably motor vehicles). If a transaction is subject to Article 9 but the secured party (or lessor or consignor, as we will see below) failed to properly document and publicize its interest, the secured party could end up getting a fraction of what it is owed.

1. THE "TYPICAL" ARTICLE 9 TRANSACTION

Before we discuss transactions that might not look like Article 9 transactions but nevertheless fall within Article 9's scope, let's talk about a "typical" Article 9 transaction. Some might say that there's no such thing as typical, but let's use a small business as an example. Our hypothetical small businessperson, Bridget Burton, is a firm believer in using business to serve the public good. She also loves chocolate. She is leaving her job as a lawyer to start a small-batch chocolate company that will use only sustainably-grown cocoa beans from companies that have a mission of empowering local populations. She has named her new company Bean-to-Bar-by-Bridget (BBB). To keep things simple, let's assume that Bridget owns BBB as a sole proprietor.

Now she needs to buy the machinery to roast, winnow, grind, and ultimately mold the product into chocolate bars. Bridget will be buying all of the necessary equipment from Cocoa Connections for $30,000. She wants to preserve as much cash as possible for her new business, so she would like to finance her purchase.

Bridget has applied for a loan from Community Bank, a local bank with which she has a good relationship. After considering her financial statements and her business plan, Community Bank has decided to provide Bridget with a loan for $27,000 and it has requested that Bridget grant it an interest in the purchased machinery as collateral for the loan. Community Bank and Bridget are entering into a secured transaction. The three key documents that Community Bank and Bridget will execute are the following:

(1) A Promissory Note in which Bridget will promise to pay Community Bank $27,000 plus the agreed upon rate of interest according to the payment schedule in the Note;

(2) A Security Agreement in which Bridget will grant to Community Bank a security interest in the machines as security for repayment of the loan

(3) A Financing Statement that Community Bank will file in a public place to give the world notice that Community Bank is claiming an interest in the equipment.

It's possible that Cocoa Connections would agree to finance Bridget's purchase of the equipment. In that scenario, Bridget would have no need to borrow money from Community Bank and Cocoa Connections and Bridget would execute the same three documents.

The above transaction creates a type of security interest that sometimes receives special treatment under the UCC, a purchase-money security interest. Simply put, a purchase money loan is one that enables a debtor to purchase the property that it is going to give as collateral for the loan. The security interest is called a purchase-money security interest, or PMSI. The example above illustrates the two types of purchase-money security interests: the one given to the third party (Community Bank) that advances funds to buy the collateral, and the one given to a seller (Cocoa Connections) that finances the purchase of the collateral.

We gave you the simple definition first so that you have some basis for understanding the language in **9–103**, the section that defines "purchase-money security interest." Although that definition might look daunting to you, let's break it into little bits. The best place to start is the definition of "purchase-money obligation" in **9–103(a)(2)**. Read that definition carefully and you'll see that it describes both types of transactions described above. "An obligation of an obligor incurred as all or part of the price of the collateral" describes Bridget's transaction with Cocoa Connections if Cocoa Connections agrees to finance the purchase; "an obligation incurred . . . for value given to acquire rights in . . . the collateral if the value is so used" describes Bridget's transaction with Community Bank. The last six words *"if the value is so used"* are key. If Bridget pays for her machines with money from her checking account and uses the Community Bank funds to pay her rent and utilities, Community Bank still has a security interest in the machines, but it is not a PMSI.

Below, we discuss leases as secured transactions. Note the similarities and differences between these lease transactions and the purchase-money secured transaction just described.

2. LEASES AS ARTICLE 9
SECURITY INTERESTS

We introduced you to the "lease/disguised sale" distinction in Chapter 1. Here, we revisit **1–203** and focus on its relationship to the law of secured transactions.

Imagine that you want a car. The most important thing for you is to have a car to drive, and you think that you will keep the car for four or five years. If that's how often you replace your car, you might think of leasing the car rather than buying it. If you bought the car, you would probably borrow money to do so, and the lender would want an interest in your car as collateral. You would make monthly payments to the lender over a period of time, perhaps four or five years. As an individual, the most important thing to you might be the amount of your monthly payment, and if that's the case, a lease might be more attractive to you than a purchase.

Businesses also often consider whether to lease or purchase property. In the Bean-to-Bar-by-Bridget transaction outlined above, Bridget could have decided to lease the chocolate making equipment from Cocoa Connections. Leasing property can preserve cash because buying involves a larger initial cash outlay. If the equipment that a business needs is likely to be replaced with more technologically advanced equipment in a short period of time, leasing will give the company the flexibility to update the equipment as needed. And as is the case with almost all transactional design decisions, taxes are a big consideration. Lease payments are deductible by a business, while the purchase price of an item may be deducted over a number of years according to a depreciation schedule.

Sometimes leases look so much like secured transactions that the law treats them as secured transactions. You have already learned the rules in **1–203**, but they are worth revisiting now so that you can appreciate both the similarities between leases and sales combined with a security interest as well as the distinction that the law makes between the two types of transactions. In order to understand the test in **1–203**, it is necessary to remember the key economic considerations behind leases and sales. Remember your Property course? When you studied estates in land and future interests, you learned that a leasehold is the right to possess property for a period of time and that the holder of the fee simple (or any greater estate) is entitled to get that property back at the end of the lease term. In the real estate context, this is not difficult to understand—land lasts forever. Personal property does not, however. Under the **1–203** test, if there's a good chance that the lessor will get the goods back with some useful life remaining in them, the transaction creates a lease. If there is not, the transaction creates a sale combined with a security interest.

Go back to Chapter 1 and re-read *In re Purdy*. This time, try to figure out why the lease/sale distinction was so important to the parties. The fact pattern anticipates the material that you will learn in a later chapter, but for now it is sufficient to know that priorities among secured parties are based on the rule of "first in time, first in right."

Sometimes the terminology in the lease/sale cases is a little confusing. Keep in mind that the entire **1–203** test is an "economic realities" test. Part of that economic realities test is the "bright line" test in **1–203(b)**. The bright line test can tell you one thing—that the lease agreement creates a secured transaction. It does *not* tell you that the arrangement creates a lease. As the court in *Purdy* notes, an agreement can "fail" the "bright line" test, but still be deemed a secured transaction because of other factors.

There are two parts to the bright line test. The first relates to the lessee's termination right. If the lessee cannot terminate the lease during its term, then the lease creates a secured transaction if one of the four factors in **1–203(b)(1)–(4)** exists. Think about the significance of termination to this test. A true lessee can return the leased goods to the lessor. A buyer cannot just give goods back to a seller. Each one of the factors listed in **1–203(b)(1)–(4)** indicates that it is highly unlikely that the "lessor" will receive anything of value at the end of the lease. In *Purdy,* the fact in question was the economic life of the goods. If there is no termination option and the lease term is equal to or longer than the remaining economic life of the goods, there will be nothing left for the lessor at the end of the term.

The three remaining factors similarly indicate that the purported lessor is unlikely to receive anything of value at the end of the purported lessee's use of the goods. For example, if the agreement requires the lessee either to purchase the goods or to renew the lease for the remaining economic life of the goods, the agreement creates a secured transaction if the lessee cannot terminate the agreement. *See* **1–203(b)(2)**. Last, if the lessee who lacks the right to terminate can either buy the goods for no or nominal additional consideration or renew the lease for the remaining economic life of the goods for no or nominal additional consideration, the agreement creates a secured transaction. *See* **1–203(b)(3), (4)**.

The next case addresses the concept of "nominal consideration," a concept that vexes both lawyers and law students.

IN RE ECCO DRILLING CO, LTD.

390 B.R. 221 (Bankr. E.D. Tex. 2008)

PARKER, J.

This matter is before the Court upon the Motion to Determine Characterization of Leases filed by Ecco Drilling Company, Ltd., the debtor in the above-referenced chapter 11 bankruptcy case. Ecco seeks a determination that its agreements executed in 2006 with [DB Zwirn

Special Opportunities Fund L.P. ("Zwirn")] are not finance leases as they purport to be, but are rather disguised secured transactions.

* * *

[In 2006, Ecco was having trouble obtaining traditional financing to expand its oil and gas drilling business. It was able to enter into a purported finance lease with Zwirn's predecessor in interest. Under the lease, Ecco would acquire rigs and rig components at periodic intervals. The lease did not permit Ecco to terminate its payment obligations prior to the end of the lease term. It contained a purchase option that allowed Ecco to buy the leased equipment at the end of the lease term for an amount equal to 15% of the greater of a) the value of such equipment or b) 40% of the going concern value of Ecco as determined by a third party appraiser.]

* * *

Collectively under the agreements, Ecco was obligated to tender to Zwirn forty-eight (48) monthly payments of $ 1,167,617.51, for a total of $ 56,045,640.48—constituting an approximate 14% return component added to the $ 42.3 million advanced by Zwirn. However, other than the initial payment in November 2006, Ecco made no payments on the leases to Zwirn. Under the threat of foreclosure by Zwirn, Ecco voluntarily filed for bankruptcy relief under chapter 11 of the Bankruptcy Code on November 23, 2007

* * *

In examining the economic structure of a purported leasing transaction, particularly with the growing use of financing leases, we are essentially searching for economic realities. In theory, those realities would seem easy to identify:

In a true lease, the economics are that the lessor has a realistic expectation of having the goods returned to it and having a residual value that it can then realize in those goods. So the key is whether or not the transaction in and of itself contemplates almost inevitably giving ultimate control and ownership for the life of the product to the lessee or giving an economically viable product back to the lessor at the end of the lease. Raymond T. Nimmer, *U.C.C. Article 2A: The New Face of Leasing,* 3 DEPAUL BUS. & COMM. L.J. 559, 565 (2005). In other words, is the transaction structured in such a way that the lessor has an objectively reasonable economic expectation that the goods will come back to it at the end of the lease term?

* * *

In this particular dispute, the parties agree that the referenced documents do not permit Ecco to terminate its payment obligations under the lease prior to the expiration of the lease term. Thus, the first prong of the bright-line test is satisfied. There is also no dispute that the remaining economic life of the rigs (20 to 30 years) extends much further than the four-year lease term provided in the agreements. The parties further agree that Ecco is not bound under the agreements to renew the lease or to exercise any purchase option. In fact, Ecco possesses no option to renew the lease agreement at all. Thus, the only circumstance available to trigger a *per se* finding of a security interest under [**1–203**] is whether the consideration to be paid under the purchase option granted to Ecco under the agreements was a nominal amount.

But what is "nominal" consideration? Zwirn contends that an option price measured in terms of millions of dollars could never be characterized as nominal. However, it is widely recognized that the term "is used in its relative, rather than absolute sense" and that "courts have had to devise tests to determine whether consideration of a significant amount can be relatively nominal under the circumstances and thus evidence of a disguised security interest." *WorldCom, Inc. v. Gen. Elec. Global Asset Mgmt. Serv. (In re WorldCom, Inc.)*, 339 B.R. 56, 62 (Bankr. S.D.N.Y. 2006) "Consideration may be sizeable yet still be nominal." In re *APB Online*, 259 B.R. 812, 818 (Bankr. S.D.N.Y. 2001). [**1–203**] offers merely the parameters of the spectrum of nominality. On one end, consideration is nominal if it is for less than the lessee's reasonably predictable cost of performing if the option is not exercised. On the other end, consideration is *not* nominal if the purchase option price is based on the fair market value of the property. However, parties rarely litigate those extremes and the statute offers little assistance for evaluating the nominality issue under more median circumstances. Thus, courts must necessarily revert to earlier common law tests in evaluating whether an option is nominal under the economic realities presented by each particular case.

Courts have utilized various comparisons in attempting to discern the relative nominality of a purchase option amount. Comparisons of the option price are made to the original purchase price, to the total lease payments, and, ultimately, courts simply try to make sense out of the economic circumstances. "No matter how the option amount is expressed, if the only sensible course of action is to exercise the option, then it is one intended for security." Richard L. Barnes, *Distinguishing Sales and Leases: A Primer on the Scope and Purpose of UCC Article 2A*, 25 U. MEM. L. REV. 873, 885 (1995) and cases cited therein [summarizing that "the option price is nominal if the sensible lessee would in effect have no choice and, in making the only sensible choice, would cut off the lessor's reversionary interest."].

Execution of a document in this type of dispute creates either a lease or a security interest. "Nominality, therefore, must be determined by considering the parties' *prediction* of concluding value at signing, not by considering the actual value at the conclusion of the term." 4 JAMES J. WHITE AND ROBERT S. SUMMERS, UNIFORM COMMERCIAL CODE § 30–3 at p. 32 (5th ed. 2002). "Transactions are not true leases where the parties anticipate, *at the outset of the transaction,* that the option will be irresistible in the sense that the option price is extremely low in comparison to the fair market value of the property." Edwin E. Huddleson, *Old Wine in New Bottles: UCC Article 2A-Leases,* 39 ALA. L. REV. 615, 633 (1988)(emphasis added). Thus, it is the value anticipated by the parties at the time the agreements were executed that determines whether the option price is nominal.

Ecco's representative, Bill Roberts, testified that he thought that the value of the equipment at the end of the contract term would be approximately the acquisition cost (less interest)—$ 42.5 million—and he estimated at that time that Ecco's EBITDA could be approximately $ 22 million. Though he believed that the eventual purchase option would be based upon 15% of the fair market value of the equipment (thereby resulting in an anticipated $ 6.375 million option price), there was never any doubt in his mind that the purchase option would be exercised and that, if the transaction resulted in Ecco's acquisition of six operating drilling rigs, the option price would be "a bargain" no matter which formula was used or what set of projected numbers was applied. In his words, "we would have never paid the principal and the interest and then walked away."

Conversely, the evidence establishes that Zwirn expected the purchase option to be exercised as well. It did no independent valuation regarding the anticipated fair market value of the equipment or the projected going concern value of Ecco at the end of the contract term. To the extent it was concerned at all about those issues, it simply relied upon Ecco's projections. The evidence establishes that Zwirn's focus instead was upon evaluating its exposure during the contract term and maximizing its anticipated return at the conclusion of the contract term. Zwirn operatives consistently evaluated this transaction in these terms. Those attenuated from the negotiations were surprised to learn that the stream of lease payments would fully amortize the debt at 14% and expressed disbelief that Ecco had agreed to pay a 15% purchase option in addition to the fully amortized debt. The purchase option was essentially viewed by Zwirn as a premium, which at one point was expected to raise its return on investment to the range of 19%. The evidence reflects that Zwirn was constantly evaluating its "exit point" and those evaluations never contemplated or evaluated the reacquisition of the equipment as a component.

No projection or contingency is ever made regarding the return of the equipment. No mention is ever made of any expectant value of returned equipment at the end of the contract term. Though Zwirn's representative, Todd Dittman, testified at the hearing that he "had no idea" at the time as to whether Ecco would exercise the purchase option and sought to highlight reasons which might have precluded the actual exercise of the purchase option by Ecco, he had honestly conceded at a deposition three weeks earlier that, "It looked to us as if it could have been a very attractive economic option for them." Despite its contemporary pleas to the contrary, Zwirn's actions at the time of the transaction fail to reveal any effort to plan, provide or protect any entrepreneurial stake or other residual interest which it supposedly held in the goods.

White and Summers suggest that the issue of nominality under [1–203] "is merely a proxy for the questions: Is the option price so low that the lessee will certainly exercise it and will, in all probable circumstances, leave no meaningful reversion for the lessor?" Under the circumstances presented in this case, the Court finds that the answer lies in the affirmative.

Many consequences flow from the recharacterization of a lease as a secured transaction. As you learned in Chapter 1, Article 2A of the UCC governs leases. A recharacterized lease is a seller financed sale—in other words, the lessor is considered a seller who has retained an interest in the goods sold as security for payment of the purchase price. Articles 2 and 9 of the UCC govern such a transaction. A true lessor its contractual remedies when its lessee fails to pay, which allow it to recover the leased property from the lessee. If the agreement creates an Article 9 security interest instead, the "lessor," who is now a secured party, must comply with the rules of Article 9 in order to recover the property. The case below illustrates.

GENERAL CAPITAL CORP. v. FPL SERVICE CORP.

986 F.Supp.2d 1029 (N.D. Iowa 2013)

BENNETT, J.

MEMORANDUM OPINION AND ORDER REGARDING PLAINTIFF'S MOTION FOR SUMMARY JUDGMENT

In late October and early November of 2012, Hurricane Sandy devastated the East Coast, causing 186 deaths and billions of dollars in damage to the states, businesses, and homes caught in its path. The defendant, FPL Services Corporation (FPL), was one of the businesses destroyed by the storm. In particular, flood waters from Hurricane Sandy destroyed two of FPL's industrial copiers, which it leased from the plaintiff, General Electric Capital Corporation (GECC). Because the copiers were destroyed, FPL stopped making lease payments to GECC. GECC repossessed and resold the copiers, and now seeks damages, claiming that FPL breached the parties' lease contract. FPL claims, among other things, that Hurricane Sandy excuses FPL from performing.

This case is now before me on GECC's motion for summary judgment. In its motion, GECC claims that FPL is liable under the parties' contract despite Hurricane Sandy, and requests $258,424.39, plus attorney's fees and costs. For the reasons discussed below, GECC's motion is granted as to FPL's liability, but I will defer ruling on the issue of damages until after the parties submit additional evidence as discussed below.

* * *

This case is about the enforceability of a contract between GECC and FPL. GECC is a Delaware corporation that does business in Iowa. FPL is a New York direct-marketing corporation located near the southern shore of Long Island, in Oceanside, New York. On June 14, 2011, GECC and FPL entered into a contract, which is entitled "Lease Agreement."[2] Under the contract, GECC agreed to provide FPL with two Ricoh Pro C901 copiers (the copiers), and related equipment. In return, FPL agreed to make 60 rental payments of $6,229.30 to GECC. For over a year, the parties performed under the contract without incident. But, in late October of 2012, Hurricane Sandy struck Long Island, destroying nearly all of FPL's equipment, including the two copiers it leased from GECC.

After the hurricane, FPL stopped making its rental payments. To this day, FPL has made only 19 of the 60 payments it agreed to make. In addition to FPL's rental payments, the parties' contract describes FPL's options if the copiers were to be damaged:

> If any item of Equipment is . . . damaged, [FPL] will (and Rental Payments will continue to accrue without abatement until [FPL]), at [FPL's] option and cost, either (a) repair the item or replace the item with a comparable item reasonably acceptable to [GECC], or (b) pay [GECC] a sum equal to (1) all Rental Payments and other amounts then due and payable under the Lease, and (2) the present value of (i) all Rental Payments to become due during the remainder of the Lease term, and (ii) the Purchase Option amount set forth in this Lease, each discounted at . . . (y) the lease charge rate (as determined pursuant to Section 16) if this Lease provides for A dollar Purchase Option . . . [GECC] will then transfer to [FPL] all [of GECC's] rights, title, and interest in the Equipment "AS-IS, WHERE IS" WITHOUT ANY REPRESENTATION OR WARRANTY WHATSOEVER, Insurance proceeds will be applied toward repair or replacement of the Equipment or payment hereunder, as applicable.

Though the copiers were damaged after Hurricane Sandy, FPL never paid to replace or repair them, nor did it pay GECC a sum equal to its then-due rental payments plus the present value of its future rental payments.

In January of 2013, GECC repossessed one of the copiers from FPL. The repossession cost GECC $600. On February 28, 2013, GECC sent FPL

---

[2] The parties dispute whether the contract is actually a lease, or is, instead, a secured transaction. Thus, I will refer to the agreement generally as "the parties' contract."

a "Notification of Disposition" letter, stating that "one or more events of default have occurred under the Loan Agreement," and that GECC intended to "sell the Collateral privately sometime after 10:00 am on March 11, 2013". The letter defines the "Collateral" as "the equipment described on the attachment." The attachment to the letter only describes one of the two copiers GECC leased to FPL. FPL never responded to GECC's letter.

On May 6, 2013, GECC's law firm sent a letter to FPL demanding "immediate payment of the entire outstanding balance due on the Lease . . . together with interest and other charges". On May 13, 2013, FPL's attorney wrote a reply letter to GECC's attorney disputing GECC's demand and stating that "[t]he other [copier] is still available should [GECC] wish to take it". On June 5, 2013, GECC repossessed the second copier. After repossessing the copiers, GECC resold them in June and July of 2013 with the help of Remarketing Solutions International, Inc. (Remarketing), a third-party remarketer that resells equipment like the copiers.

* * *

C. Disposition of Collateral

FPL alternatively argues that there is a genuine issue of material fact as to how GECC disposed of the two copiers after repossessing them. Specifically, FPL argues (1) that the parties' contract is a secured transaction governed by Article 9 of Iowa's Uniform Commercial Code (UCC), and (2) that, under Article 9, GECC failed to show that it properly disposed of the repossessed copiers. GECC argues that the parties' contract is an Article [2A] lease, not an Article 9 secured transaction, and, thus, GECC need not comply with Article 9's disposition requirements. But, even if Article 9 applies, GECC argues that FPL waived its rights under Article 9, and that, in any event, GECC complied with Article 9's requirements. I will address these arguments in turn.

1. Is this a lease or a secured transaction?

GECC's obligations to FPL in disposing of the two copiers depend, in large part, on whether the parties' contract is a lease or a secured transaction. If it is a lease, Article [2A] applies; if it is a secured transaction, Article 9 applies. FPL argues that Article 9 applies and that GECC failed to comply with it when it resold the copiers. In particular, FPL suggests that GECC cannot show that it resold the copiers in a commercially reasonable manner, and that GECC did not properly notify FPL of the resale, as is required under Article 9. *See* [9–610(b)] (requiring a commercially reasonable disposition); [9–611] (requiring notice of disposition). GECC argues that the parties' contract is a lease and, thus, GECC need not comply with these Article 9 requirements, which only apply to secured transactions. [9–109] (providing that Article 9 applies to secured transactions); [2A–103(1)(j)] (providing that a lease cannot be a secured transaction).

GECC relies on language in the parties' contract describing the agreement as a lease. The contract reads: "This lease constitutes a 'finance lease' as defined in Article 2A of the Uniform Commercial Code". Based on this clause, GECC argues that FPL voluntarily agreed that its contract with GECC was a lease, and that FPL cannot now claim that Article 9 applies.

Whether a contract constitutes a lease or a security agreement, however, does not depend on whether the parties call it a "lease" or a "security agreement." Rather, the nature of a contract depends "objectively on the economic reality of the transaction." *C&J Vantage Leasing Co. v. Wolfe,* 795 N.W.2d 65, 76 (Iowa 2011). More specifically,

> [w]hether an agreement creates a security interest depends not on whether the parties intend that the law *characterize* the transaction as a security interest but rather on whether the transaction falls within the definition of "security interest" in Section 1–201. Thus, an agreement that the parties characterize as a "lease" of goods may be a "security agreement," notwithstanding the parties' stated intention that the law treat the transaction as a lease and not as a secured transaction.

[9–102 cmt. 3(b)]. Parties may, however, agree to treat a general lease as a more specific "finance lease." *See* **[2A–103 cmt. g]** ("If a transaction does not qualify as a finance lease, the parties may achieve the same result by agreement. . . ."); *but see id.* ("For a transaction to qualify as a finance lease it must first qualify as a lease."). Parties may not agree to treat a secured transaction as a lease. *See Wolfe,* 795 N.W.2d at 76 ("[W]hile Lake MacBride and Frontier could have agreed to treat a lease as a finance lease, they could not agree to treat a sale with a security interest as a lease.").

"[T]o determine whether the lease agreement is properly considered a finance lease or a secured transaction, we must first consider whether the agreement retained or created a security interest." *Id.* at 74. "If so, the agreement cannot qualify as a lease or a finance lease because an agreement retaining or creating a security interest is specifically excluded from the definition of a lease." *Id.* (citing **2A–103(1)(j)**). **[1–203]** governs whether a contract in the form of a lease actually creates a lease or a security interest. It provides:

> A transaction in the form of a lease creates a security interest if the consideration that the lessee is to pay the lessor for the right to possession and use of the goods is an obligation for the term of the lease and is not subject to termination by the lessee, and:
>
> a.   the original term of the lease is equal to or greater than the remaining economic life of the goods;

    b.   the lessee is bound to renew the lease for the remaining economic life of the goods or is bound to become the owner of the goods;

    c.   the lessee has an option to renew the lease for the remaining economic life of the goods for no additional consideration or for nominal additional consideration upon compliance with the lease agreement; or

    d.   the lessee has an option to become the owner of the goods for no additional consideration or for nominal additional consideration upon compliance with the lease agreement.

[1–203(b)] By its text, [1–203(b)] creates a two-part, bright-line test. Under the test, the contract in this case creates a security interest, not a lease, "if it: (1) prohibits [FPL] from terminating the obligation to pay [GECC] for the right to possess and use the [copiers], and (2) meets one of the four independent criteria listed in [1–203(b)(1)–(4)]." *Wolfe,* 795 N.W.2d at 74 (citations omitted).

The contract at issue here satisfies [1–203(b)]'s two-part test. First, it prohibits FPL from terminating its obligation to pay GECC for the copiers when it states that "[FPL's] payment obligations hereunder are absolute and unconditional and are not subject to cancellation, abatement, reduction, recoupment, defense or setoff for any reason whatsoever". Second, it meets one of the four independent criteria—namely, subpart [(4)]—because it gives FPL the option to own the copiers for nominal consideration—$1.00—if it complies with the agreement. Specifically, the first page of the contract provides an "End of Lease Purchase Option" of "$1.00 Purchase Out" (docket no. 9–3, at 5). Later, the contract states that, "[i]f this lease provides for a Dollar Purchase Option and [FPL is] not in default, [GECC] will release any security interest we have in the Equipment at the end of the Lease Term" and that, "[u]pon payment of the applicable amount, [GECC] will transfer the Equipment to [FPL] 'as is, where is' . . . ." Because the contract here satisfies [1–203(b)], it constitutes a secured transaction, rather than a lease, regardless of the language used in the contract.

Moreover, after GECC repossessed the copiers, it sent FPL a "Notification of Disposition of Collateral" letter, which makes clear that the parties' contract was a secured transaction. The letter describes the parties' agreement using mostly secured-transaction terms. For instance, GECC describes itself as the "Secured Party" and FPL as the "Debtor." GECC notes that it has a "security interest" in "collateral" equipment—*i.e.,* the copiers. And, while the parties' contract is titled "Lease Agreement," GECC's notification letter calls it a "Loan and Security Agreement." These descriptions bolster what the application of [1–203(b)] confirms—that the parties' contract created a security interest in favor of GECC.

Because the parties' contract is a secured transaction, Article 9 applies. Thus, I will address below whether GECC complied with Article 9's requirements for disposing of the repossessed copiers.

In the case above, the dispute was between the two parties to the transaction and the application of Article 9's remedy provisions was at issue. We'll save the rest of the story for Chapter 13 of this book, but know that an Article 9 secured party has the right to obtain and sell the collateral in order to satisfy the outstanding loan due to it. If the secured party does not follow Article 9's requirements in doing so, it may not be entitled to pursue the debtor for the full amount owed.

The characterization of a transaction has important bankruptcy consequences. In the *Ecco Drilling* case above, the debtor wanted the court to declare that the transaction that was called a lease was in fact a secured transaction. Why would a debtor want such a characterization? In Chapter 1, you read an excerpt from *In re Bailey,* (Bankr. W.D. Ark 2005). Because you hadn't learned much about bankruptcy at that point, we left out the part of the opinion that explained why there was a dispute about the characterization of the transaction. Here's the beginning and end of that opinion. Lafayette is the party that thought it was a lessor.

On May 7, 2004, Keith and Karrie Bailey ("Debtors"), filed a voluntary petition for relief under the provisions of chapter 13 of the United States Bankruptcy Code. On November 16, 2004, Lafayette Investments, Inc. ("Lafayette") filed an objection to confirmation as well as several other pleadings.

* * *

Lafayette objects to confirmation on the single ground that it is not a secured creditor, but rather the lessor of two pieces of equipment pursuant to valid leases and that the Debtors must treat its claim in accordance with **11 U.S.C. § 365** as an unexpired lease.

The Debtors' first plan was filed on May 7, 2004, and it treated Lafayette's two claims as secured, one in the amount of $ 22,300.00 secured by collateral valued at $ 18,000.00 and the other in the amount of $ 20,800.00 secured by collateral valued at $ 18,000.00. The 60-month plan proposed identical payments for each claim in the amount of $ 357.00 per month with interest accruing at the rate of 7% per annum. The plan further proposed that Lafayette retain its lien and be paid over the life of the plan the value of its collateral or the amount of its claim, whichever is less.

* * *

If the transaction is construed as a sale of personal property and is secured by a perfected security interest in the property, the Debtor must propose to treat Lafayette's claim as provided in **section 1325(a)(4)** and **(5)** of the Bankruptcy Code. If the transaction is a true lease and the Debtor desires to keep the property, then the Debtor must assume the lease, cure all defaults, and perform the lease according to its terms in compliance with **sections 1322(b)(7)** and **365** of the Bankruptcy Code.

* * *

For the reasons stated, the Court finds that under Missouri law the agreement between Lafayette and the Debtor was a sale for security and the objection to confirmation is overruled, the motion to assume or reject the unexpired lease is denied, and the motion for relief from stay is denied.

In re Bailey was a Chapter 13 bankruptcy case. Chapter 13 allows individual debtors to keep their property and pay their creditors a portion of their claims over a three- to five-year period according to a plan that must be approved by the court. Creditors have the opportunity to challenge that plan, which is what Lafayette was doing in *Bailey*.

If a transaction creates a true lease, the lessee can keep the leased property in bankruptcy only if it pays all lease obligations in full. **BC 365.** If the lessee does not do so, the lessor is entitled to the property. If a transaction is recharacterized as a secured transaction, the "lessor" is worse off because if the property is worth less than the amount outstanding on the lease obligation (now a loan), the lessor is entitled only to the value of the property plus a portion of the remainder (now an unsecured deficiency claim). **BC 506.** And the "lessor" (now a secured party) will not even be considered a secured party if it has not complied with Article 9 by giving public notice of its interest. **BC 544.**

3. CONSIGNMENTS AS ARTICLE 9 SECURITY INTERESTS

Article 9 also sweeps some consignments into its scope. In a typical consignment arrangement, a consignor (the original owner) delivers goods to a consignee/seller for ultimate sale to a buyer. The consignor intends to remain the owner until the ultimate buyer purchases the goods. In debtor-creditor terms, the consignor wants to make sure that the goods never become subject to the claims of the consignee's creditors. As you will learn later in these materials, creditors need to know who "owns" what—that's why we have recording and filing systems. As the case below illustrates, if a consignment is governed by Article 9 and the consignor does not comply with Article 9, that consignor may lose its goods to the consignee's creditors.

IN RE G.S. DISTRIBUTION, INC.
331 B.R. 552 (Bankr. S.D.N.Y. 2005)

GROPPER, J.

Before the Court [is a motion] filed by G.S. Distribution, Inc. (the "Debtor") to authorize private sales of certain jewelry in its possession. . . . The Court denies the Debtor's motion for authority to conduct private sales of the jewelry. . . .

The Debtor is a New York corporation that leased and operated a retail jewelry store on Madison Avenue from August 6, 2003 until the spring of 2005. The Debtor is owned indirectly by Giuseppe Scavetta, who formed it for the purpose of marketing high-quality jewelry in the United States.

* * *

[T]he Debtor entered into an exclusive distribution contract, dated September 9, 2004 (the "Contract"), with Repossi Diffusion S.A.M. ("Ripossi"), a designer and manufacturer of high-end jewelry formed as a limited liability company under the laws of the Principality of Monaco. Pursuant to the Contract, the Debtor would import, distribute and sell in the United States jewelry manufactured by Repossi under the Repossi trademark and as a Repossi boutique. Although the Contract is in English, it apparently was drafted in Europe by representatives of Scavetta and of Repossi's principal, a well-known jewelry designer, Alberto Repossi. The Contract provides generally for sales of jewelry by Repossi to the Debtor and sets forth terms of price and various obligations. Schedule 4 to the Contract also spells out the terms of a different relationship pursuant to which, by mutual agreement, Repossi would provide jewelry to the Debtor on a consignment basis subject to certain specific terms and conditions. Schedule 4 provides in pertinent part, in somewhat broken English:

> Upon mutual agreement collection, Repossi Diffusion shall make available Repossi Jewelry to [G.S. Distribution] on a consignment basis subject to the terms and conditions of this Article. Such consignment of Repossi Jewelry is expected to be made for sales promotion to important customers, private visits, exhibitions, and show cases.

At the hearing, Scavetta testified that Repossi provided the jewelry now in the Debtor's possession—and the subject of the present motions— pursuant to Schedule 4 to the Contract.

The Contract also authorized the Debtor to use the Repossi trademark in promoting and selling the jewelry, requiring the Debtor to adhere to certain marketing guidelines, including refitting the Debtor's boutique under the Repossi name. The parties do not dispute that the Debtor's boutique on Madison Avenue was devoted entirely to the sale of Repossi jewelry.

Pursuant to the Contract, Repossi provided to the Debtor jewelry that is currently in the Debtor's possession and that has a wholesale value of over $ 5 million.

* * *

The record is not altogether clear regarding the amount of Repossi jewelry sold between September 9, 2004, when the Contract went into effect, and April 18, 2005, when Repossi obtained a preliminary injunction from the District Court, as further described below, prohibiting further sale of the jewelry.[2] Scavetta testified without documentary support that the Debtor sold a total of $ 500,000 worth of Repossi jewelry: approximately $ 300,000 worth at the boutique on Madison Avenue ($ 200,000 from September, 2004 through mid-March, 2005, and $ 100,000 from mid-March, 2005 to the grant of the injunction in April, 2005) and approximately $ 200,000 through Saks Fifth Avenue, Inc. ("Saks"). With regard to the sale process, Scavetta testified that the Debtor would inform Repossi when a piece of jewelry was sold, after which Repossi would issue an invoice to the Debtor for the wholesale purchase price.

It is undisputed that the Debtor never paid Repossi for any of the invoiced jewelry. In an effort to recover the jewelry, or the value thereof, Repossi filed an action against the Debtor in the District Court on March 15, 2005, claiming (i) breach of contract, (ii) conversion and (iii) trademark infringement. In response, the Debtor counterclaimed for damages for Repossi's alleged breach of the Contract by selling its jewelry directly to customers in the United States, its alleged improper appropriation of publicity that the Debtor had paid for, and its alleged violation of New York State franchise law. In support of its counterclaim based on breach of the franchise laws, the Debtor took the position in the District Court that the Contract was illegal and unenforceable.

Repossi moved for a preliminary injunction to prohibit the Debtor from continuing to sell Repossi jewelry or use the Repossi trademark. After two hearings, District Judge Chin granted Repossi's motion, finding that even under the Debtor's theory of the case, the Contract was "void and unenforceable." Under the terms of the injunction, the Debtor was enjoined from (i) holding itself out as a Repossi store, (ii) using the Repossi trademark in connection with any goods and services, (iii) selling or lending jewelry received from Repossi, and (iv) moving such jewelry or its proceeds out of the State of New York. Judge Chin also ordered the Debtor to close its store located on Madison Avenue as a Repossi store and to permit a Repossi representative to conduct an inventory of the jewelry and retrieve any Repossi jewelry the Debtor had loaned to third parties.

---

[2] The record is also silent as to whether this jewelry was consigned and the basis on which this jewelry was imported into the United States. It is clear that the Debtor had possession of substantial amounts of Repossi jewelry in addition to the $ 5 million of consigned jewelry still in its custody.

On the basis of the Debtor's alleged failure to comply with the order of the District Court, Repossi requested permission from Judge Chin to move for summary judgment and for contempt sanctions. On June 10, 2005, Judge Chin gave Repossi permission to file its motion.

Eleven days later, on June 21, 2005, the Debtor filed for bankruptcy relief under Chapter 11 of the United States Bankruptcy Code. The Debtor's schedules show Repossi as the primary creditor with a claim of approximately $ 5,000,000. The only other substantial creditor currently is Scavetta, who asserts a claim of $ 1,452,000. The remainder of the debt is minimal, amounting to approximately $ 25,000.

* * *

Thereafter, under the supervision of this Court, the jewelry was placed in a vault in New York, where it is currently located.

Discussion

* * *

II. The Debtor's Rights in the Jewelry

As stated above, Scavetta testified that the Repossi jewelry now in its possession was provided to the Debtor under a consignment arrangement pursuant to Schedule 4 to the Contract. The Debtor claims that this arrangement provided it, on the bankruptcy filing, with certain rights in the jewelry, and that as a debtor in possession it takes these rights for the benefit of the Debtor's creditors, including Scavetta, whether or not Repossi consents. As discussed below, the Debtor's rights as a debtor in possession do not appear, on the record to date, to overcome Repossi's rights as owner of the jewelry.

A. Uniform Commercial Code

Property acquired under a consignment arrangement, even if not paid for, may be subject to claims of the consignee's creditors, and a debtor in possession may be entitled to exercise these rights under the Uniform Commercial Code ("U.C.C.") for the benefit of the estate and its other creditors. See *In re Morgansen's Ltd.,* 302 B.R. 784 (Bankr. E.D.N.Y. 2003); *In re Valley Media, Inc.,* 279 B.R. 105 (Bankr. D. Del. 2002). Article 9 of the U.C.C. applies to a "consignment," **9–109(a)(4)**, and in determining the Debtor's rights to the jewelry, the starting point of the analysis is **9–102(a)(20)** as adopted in New York. **9–102(a)(20)** defines "consignment" as:

> a transaction, regardless of its form, in which a person delivers goods to a merchant for the purpose of sale and:
>
> (A) the merchant:
>
> > (i) deals in goods of that kind under a name other than the name of the person making delivery;

    (ii) is not an auctioneer; and

    (iii) is not generally known by its creditors to be substantially engaged in selling the goods of others;

  (B) with respect to each delivery, the aggregate value of the goods is $ 1,000 or more at the time of delivery;

  (C) the goods are not consumer goods immediately before delivery; and

  (D) the transaction does not create a security interest that secures an obligation.

If a transaction is a consignment under **9–102(a)(20)**, the consignor must ordinarily file a financing statement in order to protect its interest in the property from the claims of a bankruptcy trustee or debtor in possession acting on behalf of the estate's creditors under the "strong arm powers" of § 544 of the Bankruptcy Code. See *Morgansen's*, 302 B.R. at 787. A transaction must satisfy each element of the definition to be considered a consignment under **9–102(a)(20)**, and the burden of proof falls on the party claiming applicability of the section. *Id.* The Debtor has the burden of proof because it asserts that the transfer of jewelry was a consignment under **9–102(a)(20)**.

Repossi asserts that the consignment provided in the Contract is not subject to the U.C.C. because, referring to subsection (A)(i), the Debtor was not a merchant dealing in goods delivered to it for the purpose of sale "under a name other than the name of the person making delivery." This subsection is designed to carry out one of the purposes of making consignments subject to Article 9, which is to ensure that a consignee's general creditors are put on notice of the consignor's interest in the consigned property, and "to protect general creditors of the consignee from claims of consignors that have undisclosed consignment arrangements with the consignee that create secret liens on the inventory." *Valley Media,* 279 B.R. at 121. Where a consignee operates only under the name of the consignor, the U.C.C. assumes that the consignee's general creditors will be on notice of the consignment and will not be misled into believing that the merchant has ownership of the inventory in its possession. *Id.* at 123.

It is undisputed that during the term of the Contract the Debtor held itself out to be a merchant only of Repossi jewelry. Since the Debtor dealt only in Repossi goods and did not sell any other jewelry, it did not deal in goods under "a name other than the name of the person making delivery." The arrangement accordingly would not be a consignment for purposes of application of Article 9.

The Debtor argues nevertheless that the goods were provided by "Repossi Diffusion S.A.M.," a corporate seller with a name distinct from "Repossi" or "Repossi Joallier," as used by the Debtor in operating its business. However, the Debtor's argument exalts form over substance and ignores the purpose of the statute, which is to protect creditors from being "misled by the apparent ownership of goods held by a consignee." *Newhall v. Haines,* 10 B.R. 1019, 1022 (D. Mon. 1981) (discussing statutory predecessor to **9–102(a)(20)**).

The Debtor argues that the provisions of the statute relevant to the use of a name have been construed strictly, citing *In re Wicaco Machine Corp.,* 49 B.R. 340 (E.D. Pa. 1984), and *Mann v. Clark Oil & Refining Corp.,* 302 F. Supp. 1376 (E.D. Mo. 1969). These cases, which dealt with the predecessor to **9–102(a)(20)**, held that a consignor could avoid application of the statute only where its business was "completely enveloped" in or was "completely identified" with the business of the consignee, and that the statute would apply where the consignee sold goods of suppliers other than the consignor, or where it made known its separate identity. *Wicaco,* 49 B.R. at 343; *Mann,* 302 F. Supp. at 1380. The relationship between the Debtor and Repossi comes within the framework of complete envelopment or identification. The Debtor held itself out to the public as a Repossi store and has not provided evidence of any outward indication to suggest that it was an entity separate from Repossi or that it dealt in goods other than those delivered by Repossi. Moreover, as Repossi argues, the only substantial creditor who could benefit from a finding that Article 9 applies is Scavetta, and he certainly knew the facts.

Because the consignment arrangement falls outside the definition of consignment in **9–102(a)(20)**, the analysis must proceed to **2–326** to determine the respective rights of the Debtor (acting for its general creditors) and Repossi.

———————

In this case, the court did not find a consignment as defined in Article 9, so the court had to go back to Article 2 to determine the rights of the consignee and consignor.

4. REAL ESTATE RELATED COLLATERAL

We'll discuss the exceptions from Article 9's coverage below. The big one, however, is "the creation of an interest in or lien on real property." **9–109(d)(11).** It is important to distinguish between interests in real estate and interests in personal property that are related to real estate. There are many "real estate related" assets that are in fact personal property. Sometimes, it is not clear whether an asset is Article 9 collateral or not.

a. Fixtures

The first type of real estate related collateral that is within Article 9 is the fixture. Let's go one more time to **9–109(a)(1)**, which tells us that Article 9 applies to "a transaction, regardless of its form, that creates a security interest in personal property *or fixtures* by contract. A fixture is both real and personal property, a characterization that will be important when we discuss priorities. Although Article 9 defines "fixtures," *see* **9–102(a)(41)**, the definition points you to the real estate law of the relevant state. The excerpt below from *In re Onyan*, 163 B.R. 21 (Bankr. N.D.N.Y. 1993) provides a typical definition and analysis of whether a good is a fixture:

> While the test for determining whether an article has become a fixture has been stated in numerous ways, its requisites are as follows: (1) annexation to the realty; (2) adaptability of the affixed article to the use of the freehold, and (3) the intention of the party making the annexation is to make the article a permanent accession to the freehold. Applying these factors, the bankruptcy court in *Matter of Fink*, 4 B.R. 741 (Bankr. W.D.N.Y. 1980), concluded that a mobile home had become a fixture after finding, *inter alia*, that it was installed on land which the debtor had contracted to purchase, that as a part of the installation the debtor had added a crawl space, installed a septic system, and ran water and electricity into the home thereby making it ready for permanent occupancy. In that case the debtor was found to have resided in the mobile home since its installation.
>
> In the instant case, the Court similarly concludes that the mobile home was installed as a permanent accession to the Debtor's real property. Here, the Debtor testified that despite having lived in the home for a period of up to three weeks without running water, indoor plumbing or electricity, he admitted that it was never his intention to reside there for any significant period of time without these "modern conveniences," and that his short stay there under these circumstances was merely a temporary expedient until the necessary installations and hook-ups could be provided. As admitted by the Debtor under cross-examination, these items included the digging of a well, the installation of a water pump and a septic system, and the hook up of electricity.

Knowing whether property falls into the fixture category is important for transaction planning purposes. Before taking an item as collateral, the potential lender needs to know that no one else has a security interest in it. To do that, the lender needs to know which records to search (more on this in Chapter 14). And once the lender has decided to take that collateral for a loan, the lender needs to know where to publicize its interest (again, more in Chapter 14). If an item is a fixture, notice of a prior interest could potentially be in two places: the land records (usually the county recorder of deeds) and the personal property records (usually the Secretary of State's office). You will learn more about this point in a later chapter.

b. Personal Property Interests in Real Property

Sometimes a right that looks a lot like a right in real estate is in fact personal property for Article 9 purposes. One example is a partnership interest. Even if the sole asset of a partnership is real estate, the interest of a partner in that partnership is personal property. In order to reach that conclusion, you need to know something about both partnership law and the UCC. Consider the following reasoning from *Magers v. Thomas (In re Vannoy),* 176 B.R. 758 (Bankr. M.D.N.C. 1994). In that case, the court had to decide whether a mortgage (deed of trust in North Carolina) encumbered a debtor's interest in a partnership that owned the real estate.

> Turning to Vannoy's partnership interest, the extent of his rights as a partner and the nature of those rights are defined by statute. The "property rights" of a partner are described in G.S. § 59–54 as follows: (1) his right in specific partnership property; (2) his interest in the partnership; and (3) his right to participate in the management.

> The court will consider the effect of the deed of trust upon each of these partnership rights in the order which they are listed in the statute. First, did the deed of trust encumber or transfer Vannoy's right in specific partnership property, i.e., in the real property owned by the partnership? The starting point for answering this question is G.S. § 59–55 [North Carolina's law governing partnerships] which describes the nature of a partner's right in specific partnership property. Under this statute a partner is co-owner with his partners of specific partnership property holding such co-ownership as a tenant in partnership. This statute specifically provides that a partner's right in specific partnership property is not subject to attachment or execution, except on a claim against the partnership. The extent to which a partner may transfer or assign his interest in specific partnership property is controlled and limited by subparagraph (2) of G.S. § 59–55, which provides:

>> "A partner's right in specific partnership property is not assignable except in connection with the assignment of rights of all the partners in the same property."

> The effect of this provision is to invalidate or render void an assignment by a partner of his interest in specific partnership property if such assignment is not joined in by the other partners. The applicable rule is stated in 59 Am Jur 2d Partnership § 405:

>> "The Uniform Partnership Act provides that one of the incidents of a tenancy in partnership is that a partner's right in specific partnership property is not assignable except in connection with the assignment of rights of all the partners

in the same property. A partner's assignment of specific partnership property contrary to this general rule is void, except as to assignments made prior to the adoption of the Uniform Partnership Act, since the Act does not apply retroactively."

* * *

In the present case, the facts are that the other partners were informed that Vannoy was borrowing $107,500.00 from the defendant and that Vannoy intended to give the defendant a deed of trust on his interest in the apartments. The evidence also showed that the other partners approved of the transaction, including the execution of the deed of trust by Vannoy. However, the other partners were not asked to assign, convey or encumber their interest in the apartments and did not do so. Therefore, it cannot be said that Vannoy assigned or transferred his tenancy in partnership in the apartments "in connection with the assignment of rights of all the partners" in the apartments. The purported assignment therefore did not comply with the requirement of G.S. § 59–55(2) and his tenancy in partnership in the apartments was not assigned nor encumbered by the deed of trust from the debtors.

In order to determine whether the deed of trust encumbered Mr. Vannoy's "interest in the partnership", the second of his partnership rights under G.S. § 59–54, reference must be had to G.S. § 59–56 which provides:

"A partner's interest in the partnership is his share of the profits and surplus, and the same is personal property."

Did the deed of trust create a lien upon or encumber this "personal property" of Vannoy? The language of the deed of trust itself probably requires a negative answer to this question, since the deed of trust, by its terms, does not purport to transfer any interest other than an interest in real property. However, even if the deed of trust could be read as intended to create a security interest in Vannoy's partnership interest, it did not do so. The fact that the partnership interest is personal property brings into play [9–109(a)(1)] which makes Article 9 of the Uniform Commercial Code applicable to "any transaction (regardless of its form) which is intended to create a security interest in personal property or fixtures including . . . general intangibles. . . created by contract including . . . trust deed. . . ." Since a partner's interest in a partnership is personal property (i.e., a general intangible), a transaction intended to create a security interest in a partnership interest therefore must comply with the requirements of Article 9, including the requirement for filing financing statements.

The last of Mr. Vannoy's rights under G.S. § 59–54 is his right to participate in the management of the partnership. Under partnership law, this right is not transferable by a partner to an outsider. In that regard, G.S. § 59–57 specifically provides that a conveyance by a partner of his interest in the partnership does not "entitle the assignee, during the continuance of the partnership, to interfere in the management or administration of the partnership business or affairs. . . ." However, even if such interest were transferable, it would be personal property within the meaning of **[9–102]** and, as a result, no security interest could be perfected without complying with the requirements of the Uniform Commercial Code as discussed in the preceding paragraph. Therefore, even if the deed of trust had been intended to create a security interest in Vannoy's right to participate in the management of the partnership, the deed of trust was ineffective in doing so.

Mortgage paper is another trap for the unwary in Article 9. A home lender may sell its promissory notes and mortgages in order to get more money in make new loans. A sale of a promissory note is an Article 9 secured transaction under **9–109(a)(3)**. A home lender may also give its lender a security interest in its notes and mortgages in return for a loan. Does the fact that the notes are secured by real estate mortgages take the transaction out of Article 9? No, it doesn't. *See* **9–109(b)**. "The mortgage follows the note" is an important statement in finance law. A note is personal property, an "instrument" for Article 9 purposes. **9–102(a)(47)**. The fact that it is secured by a real property mortgage does not change that characterization.

5. SALES OF SOME TYPES OF PAYMENT RIGHTS AS SECURITY INTERESTS

As noted above, Article 9 also sweeps some sales within its scope. *See* **9–109(a)(3)**. This section introduces some new terminology: accounts (**9–102(a)(2)**), chattel paper (**9–102(a)(11)**), and payment intangibles (**9–102(a)(61)**), and reintroduces you to promissory notes (**9–102(a)(65)**), which you learned about in the Payment Systems part of this book. Why would Article 9 include sales of these assets? And what does it mean for Article 9 to include sales?

One way a business can raise money is to sell its accounts receivable (or, in Article 9 parlance, its "accounts"). Such a sale does not look all that different from a loan secured by an interest in such accounts as collateral. Rather than forcing parties to distinguish between a sale of accounts and a loan secured by accounts, the drafters of Article 9 chose to include sales within its scope. As a result, a purchaser of accounts must comply with the rules of Article 9 in order to have an interest in the accounts good against the world.

Chattel paper is similar to an account. The idea of chattel paper is difficult to understand at first, so consider the purchase of your first car. Most young people do not have the cash available to buy a new car outright. When Graduate goes to a Toyota dealer to purchase a new Prius, the dealer offers financing through its affiliated financial institution, Toyota Credit. The financing deal, as explained just above, will be a secured transaction—Graduate will give Toyota a promissory note promising to pay the purchase price, and a security agreement giving Toyota Credit an interest in the car to secure the promise to repay.

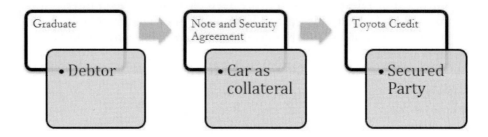

Put yourselves in Toyota Credit's shoes for a moment. At this point in time, Toyota Credit is holding on to a valuable asset—a right to repayment and a property interest to secure that right. In Toyota Credit's hands, this valuable asset is called chattel paper.

Toyota of course needs money to acquire more cars to sell. It can use the chattel paper as collateral to borrow money from Finance Co. to buy new cars, or sell the chattel paper to Finance Co. to get money to buy new cars. Either way, the transaction will be an Article 9 transaction.

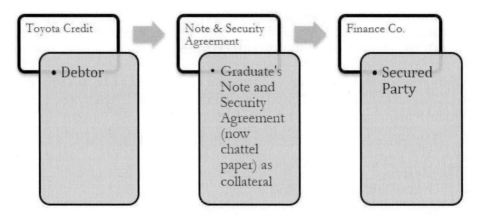

Or,

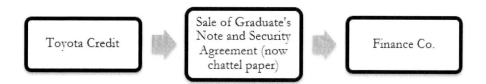

In the cases in this chapter, you saw several traps for the unwary lawyer or businessperson who is not familiar with the scope of Article 9. In the *Ecco Drilling* case, you saw someone who thought it had leased property when in fact it had sold it. The *G.S. Distributors* case showed you a fight over which body of law governed a consignment arrangement.

In the next chapter, you will see how parties can create an enforceable security interest. That will not be a problematic step for the unintentional secured parties described above. As you will learn in the next chapter, the lease or consignment agreement likely contains the few required elements of a security agreement and the other requisites of attachment will also likely be met. Perfection will be a problem however, and in order for the secured creditor to retain a property interest good against the entire world, it must perfect its interest.

6. EXCLUSIONS FROM ARTICLE 9 COVERAGE

As important as the inclusions are the exclusions. Article 9 does not govern all security interests, even if those interests are in personal property. We have already talked about the real property exclusion. The remainder of the exclusions are listed in **9–109(d)**. Keep in mind that parties *can* create a security interest in excluded property, but that interest will be governed by law other than Article 9. An easy way to remember this point is to consider real estate. Landowners grant security interests in real estate all the time, but those interests are called mortgages (or in some states, deeds of trust) and they are governed by state mortgage law, not by Article 9.

The real estate exclusion avoids duplication. The law of real estate mortgages and the systems for recording interests in real estate were in existence well before Article 9, so there was no reason to sweep real estate into Article 9. Other exclusions exist because of public policy. Two examples of that are the wage claim exclusion in **9–102(d)(3)** and the tort claim exclusion in **9–102(d)(12)**. Be careful about tort claims—a tort claim that falls within the definition of "commercial tort claim" (**9–102(a)(13)**) is Article 9 collateral.

It is always important to remember that you need to be familiar with the version of Article 9 that governs your transaction. Many states have amended § 9–109 to exclude additional transactions from the scope of Article 9. For example, California exempts from Article 9 security interests granted by governmental units. CAL. U. COMM. CODE § 9109(d)(17). Again, that does not mean that a governmental unit cannot grant a security interest, it means that other state law will govern such an interest.

Chapter Conclusion: At the end of this chapter, you should be familiar with the basic form of secured transaction and the scope of Article 9 as well as the concept of a purchase-money security interest. You should recognize that some transactions are the functional equivalent of secured transactions and that Article 9 treats them as such. You should also know that some secured transactions are excluded from the scope of Article 9. Going forward, you should keep in mind that if a transaction is an Article 9 secured transaction, either because the parties designate it as such or the law deems it as such, the secured party will have to comply with the rules that you will learn in subsequent chapters in order to have a legally recognized interest in the property given as collateral.

PROBLEMS

1.   Allison recently graduated from college and moved to a new city to take a job with a start-up company. Relying on her new employer's promise of a large salary, she spent $5,000 on her First Bank credit card to furnish her rental apartment. After six months the company crashed, and Allison is trying to make ends meet as a barista in a local coffee shop. Now she has maxed out her credit cards and has skipped several payments. First Bank is threatening to sue her.

    a.   Allison wants to know if the bank can seize her furniture to satisfy the debt. Can it? What does the bank need to do to obtain rights in the furniture? Look up the procedure in the state of your choice.

    b.   Assume that instead of charging the furniture on a credit card, Allison borrowed the money from her friend Ben. Ben asked Allison to sign an IOU promising to pay the $5,000 and a short document that said "Security Agreement" at the top describing the furniture. Allison signed both. Again, Allison has not yet paid. Does Ben have the right to Allison's furniture? What additional facts do you need to answer the question? See 9–203, 9–609.

2.   StartUp Public Relations, LLC (SUPR) helps emerging companies with their publicity. SUPR has entered into a lease agreement with Office Equipment, Inc., to lease a copier. If SUPR had purchased the copier outright it would have cost $5000. Because the copier incorporates a lot of new technology, it has an expected useful life of five years.

Which of the following leases will be subject to Article 9? For each hypothetical, please identify any additional facts that you would need to give a definitive answer.

(1) The lease is a three-year lease and SUPR has agreed to make payments of $150 a month. SUPR can terminate the lease at any time for a $100 early termination fee. At the end of the three-year term, SUPR can purchase the copier for $1000.

(2) Same facts as (1) but SUPR is responsible for maintaining insurance on the copier.

(3) Same facts as (1) but SUPR cannot terminate the lease during the term.

(4) Same facts as (3) but SUPR can purchase the copier at the end of the term for $50.

(5) Same facts as (3) but the lease term is five years.

3. You are the lawyer for Robot Concierge Leasing (RCL), the first leasing company to specialize in robots for the hospitality industry. RCL will be leasing robots to hotels throughout the United States and its primary concern is that it will get the robots, or their value, if any of its customers files for bankruptcy. Today, RCL has reason to believe that with regular maintenance and software updates, a robot concierge has a five-year useful life. RCL intends to lease them to customers for three years with a purchase option. Because robots are so new, no one really knows what they might be worth in three years. Your client insists that the leases not be terminable during the initial three-year lease term and wants you to make sure that upon a payment default, RCL will be able to recover the robots.

 a. RCL wants some guidance in coming up with a price for a purchase option. You are not the number cruncher, but you need to advise your client on what it needs to consider in developing an option price. What is on your list?

 b. Is there anything else that you should do for your client? See 9–505(b).

 c. Sweet Dreams Hotel Corp. entered into a three-year lease for 100 robot concierges. Two years into the term, it turned out that the robots were in fact useless after two years. Does this fact change the characterization of the transaction?

4. Central Financial Corp. (Central) is considering making a loan to Test Prep Partners (TPP), a company that runs prep courses for standardized tests such as the SAT and the LSAT. The loan will be secured by various items of property located in TPP facilities around the country.

 a. You are a new associate at the law firm that represents Central, and your supervising partner has given you the following list of collateral and wants to know what collateral on the list would be considered a fixture. 9–102(a)(41); Official Comment 3 to 9–334.

(1)   Desks and chairs in the TPP classrooms. The desks are attached to the floors of the buildings by heavy-duty screws. The chairs are not attached.

(2)   The Smart Board equipment in the TPP classrooms. The equipment consists of a projector attached to the ceiling and a whiteboard attached to the wall.

(3)   The stained glass window in the TPP headquarters building. The window was recently installed and was made by a famous modern artist.

(4)   A replica of the Rodin sculpture "The Thinker," which sits in the lobby of the TPP headquarters building. The sculpture is not attached to the floor, but it is too heavy to move without special machinery.

b.   Central is also going to ask for a personal guarantee from Dalia Martin, the founding partner of TPP. Dalia is an entrepreneur who invested in hotels before founding TPP. Dalia is giving as collateral for the guarantee her partnership interest in Center City Partners, a partnership that owns one asset, the Center City Luxury Hotel. Is the partnership interest Article 9 collateral?

5.   Extreme Sporting Goods ("ESG") has just filed for bankruptcy. One of its suppliers, Super Sneakers, has been providing sneakers to ESG under a consignment arrangement. Super Sneakers' supply contract with ESG provides that the sneakers are sold on consignment and Super Sneakers will remain the owner of the sneakers, even after delivery to ESG. The agreement obligates ESG to pay Super Sneakers for the sneakers when the sneakers are sold. You have been appointed as bankruptcy trustee in the ESG case. You have searched the relevant public records, and you have found no notice of any interest of Super Sneakers in the ESG inventory. At the time of filing, ESG owes Super Sneakers $30,000 and there is enough in the estate to pay all unsecured creditors 10% of their claims. ESG is holding $30,000 worth of sneakers.

How much will Super Sneakers receive in the ESG bankruptcy? What other information do you need to formulate your answer? See 9–102(a)(20); 9–109(a).

6.   Bridget Burton from Bean-to-Bar-by-Bridget is ready to expand her business. To do so, she is borrowing $100,000 from First Bank. First Bank has asked for an interest in the following rights as collateral for the loan.

(1)   The half interest in Bayview Farm that Bridget owns with her brother David. They own the farm as tenants in common.

(2)   Bridget's checking account at Community Bank.

(3) Bridget's products liability claim against Cocoa Connections. Cocoa Connections manufactured the roasting machine in her shop. The machine exploded and caused substantial damage to the building.

Are the interests covered by Article 9? Why or why not?

7.   Review the Sport-e Bikes example on pp. 481–482. Now assume that when Sport-e Bikes filed for bankruptcy, it owed Lakeside Bank $90,000, but the equipment that it gave as collateral for the loan was worth only $70,000.

    a.   How many claims does Lakeside Bank have in the Sport-e Bikes bankruptcy and how do you describe those claims?

    b.   If there is enough in the bankruptcy estate to pay 20% of non-priority unsecured claims, what will be the total amount of Lakeside Bank's payout?

CHAPTER 12

CREATION OF A SECURITY INTEREST

∎ ∎ ∎

Now that you know which transactions are subject to Article 9, it's time to learn how to create a security interest. In this chapter, you will learn how to create an enforceable security interest and what that security interest covers.

A. THE REQUISITES FOR ATTACHMENT

Article 9 describes the process of creating a security interest in a roundabout way. *See* **9–203(a)**, **(b)**. It tells us that a security interest *attaches* when it becomes enforceable and that it becomes *enforceable* when three requirements are met. A security interest becomes enforceable when 1) "value has been given;" 2) the debtor has "rights in the collateral;" and 3) there is either a written security agreement between the parties or the secured party possesses the collateral "pursuant to agreement."

In the last chapter, you learned that a security interest gives its holder a specific set of remedies and a specific type of priority. A secured party obtains its remedy rights upon attachment of its security interest. This is an important point to remember because in Chapter 14, you will learn about perfection of security interests, which gives the secured party its priority. Once a security interest has attached, the secured party is entitled to all of the rights granted in Part 6 of Article 9 upon the debtor's default.

Let's look at the three requirements for attachment in detail.

1. Value: **9–203(b)(1)** tells us that the first requirement for attachment is that "value has been given." That might seem a bit confusing, and it doesn't say to whom for what. You have already learned, however, that a security interest is given by a debtor to secure payment or performance of an obligation. Value, therefore, is the value given by the secured creditor to the debtor (or obligor) in exchange for the security interest.

As always, pay attention to the definitions. The UCC defines "value" in **1–204**. Value includes any consideration sufficient to support a simple contract. It also includes a binding commitment to make a loan as well as a pre-existing claim. Keep in mind that debtors and creditors will not often (if ever) fight about whether value has been given—if the secured party did not give value, it has not lost anything if the debtor defaults.

2.   *Rights in the Collateral:* The second requirement is that the debtor has rights in the collateral or the power to transfer rights in the collateral to a secured party (**9–203(b)(2)**). Remember that a security interest is a property interest, and you cannot convey a property interest that you don't have (or that you don't have the right to transfer). This is another expression of the rule *nemo dat quod non habet*, or you can't give what you don't have.

In many cases, it will be easy to determine that the debtor does indeed have rights in the collateral that can be transferred to a secured party. For example, a clothing manufacturer might want to give the sewing machines it owns as collateral for a loan. Ownership rights are certainly transferable rights in collateral. But there are a number of assets that are undoubtedly valuable to a debtor and that are in fact transferred often but are, either by statute or by contract, designated as non-transferable. Liquor licenses are a good example—they are issued by a state agency, and the state agency considers the license to be a grant of a revocable privilege. Because states limit the number of licenses that they issue the right to acquire one can be worth a lot of money. Different states approach the rights embodied in a liquor license in different ways.

Consider Pennsylvania's liquor license statute 47 P.S. § 4–468:

§ 4–468. Licenses not assignable; transfers

(a)

(1)   Licenses issued under this article may not be assigned.

. . .

(b.1) In the event that any person to whom a license shall have been issued under the provisions of this article shall become insolvent, make an assignment for the benefit of creditors, become bankrupt by either voluntary or involuntary action, the license of such person shall be immediately placed in safekeeping with the board for the balance of the term of the license and for an additional period of one year upon application to the board by the trustee, receiver, or assignee. The trustee, receiver, or assignee shall have, during said period of safekeeping, the same rights, benefits and obligations as to the license as the person to whom the license had been issued, including the right to transfer the license subject to the approval of the board. The license shall continue as a personal privilege granted by the board and nothing herein shall constitute the license as property. . . . .

(d)   The license shall constitute a privilege between the board and the licensee. As between the licensee and third parties, the license shall constitute property.

The statute reproduced above recognizes that the holder of a government issued license has two types of relationships with respect to such a license: a relationship with the issuing agency and a relationship with the rest of the world. The statute above characterizes the former as a privilege and the latter as property.

Liquor licenses are just one example. Broadcast licenses issued by a federal government agency provide another. In addition, sometimes non-assignable rights are created by contract. For example, a hotel chain will enter into franchise agreements with hotel owners to use to chain's brand. The chain is concerned about the value of its brand, so it wants to enter into agreements only with people that it has vetted and approved to use the brand. The brand will constitute a large part of the hotel's value, and its creditors will want a way to realize that value.

In the 1998 amendments to Article 9, the drafters intended to capture the value of some non-assignable rights for secured creditors. *See* **9–406(c)–(j)**; **9–408**. These sections codify the distinction that the Pennsylvania statute reproduced above codifies. Article 9 invalidates contractual and statutory prohibitions on transfer to the extent that those prohibitions would prevent the creation of a security interest. A secured party that obtains such a security interest cannot enforce it however. What good is such a security interest then? Read Official Comments 7 and 8 to **9–408**. Despite the attempt of the drafters of Article 9 to propertize and thus potentially turn into collateral everything of value to a debtor, some courts continue to hold that a non-assignable right is not a property right at all.

IN RE CIRCLE 10 REST., LLC

519 B.R. 95 (Bankr. D. N.J. 2014)

GAMBARDELLA, J.

Before the Court is Trustee's Motion to Reclassify Alleged Secured Claim of RELM, LLC to a general unsecured claim.[1]

* * *

1.   Factual Background

Prior to its bankruptcy filing Debtor had operated a restaurant under the name Margarita's in Livingston, New Jersey. On May 23, 2012, Debtor and its princip[al]s, Matthew Stadtmauer and Neal Erman, executed a Loan Agreement, Time Note and Unlimited Guaranty, with Northern Bank and Trust Company ("Northern Bank") for a $375,000 loan. On the same day, Debtor entered into a Loan and Security Agreement with Northern

---

[1]   The New Jersey Division of Alcoholic Beverage Control (the "ABC") filed a Motion to Intervene in the instant matter. At the May 22, 2014 hearing, this Court heard and granted ABC's Motion to Intervene. The order was entered on May 22, 2014.

Bank which granted Northern Bank a security interest in all of Debtor's rights to all of its personal property, present and after-acquired, explicitly including accounts, chattel paper, goods, inventory, equipment, instruments, documents, and general intangibles. On May 22, 2013, Northern Bank assigned to RELM, LLC ("RELM") all its rights and obligations in the loan note, guaranty, and security agreement. Id. On June 13, 2013, RELM filed a proof of claim in the amount of $378,779.59, asserting a secured claim based on its rights as Northern Bank's assignee.

* * *

On March 8, 2013, Debtor filed a voluntary petition for relief under chapter 7 of the Bankruptcy Code. On March 11, 2013, Jay L. Lubetkin was appointed as Chapter 7 Trustee by the Office of the United States Trustee.

* * *

The Liquor License was independently appraised at the request of the Trustee by A. Atkins Appraisal Corp. for $400,000.

By prior Application to the Court, the Chapter 7 Trustee sought Bankruptcy Court approval of the sale of the Liquor License to Onyx Equities III, LLC ("Onyx") for a purchase price of $500,000. Pursuant to bidding procedures approved by the Court, an auction for the purchase of the Liquor License premised upon Onyx's stalking horse bid took place before the Court and ultimately, Onyx submitted the highest and best offer of $835,000 for the purchase of the Liquor License.

* * *

The Trustee's sale of the liquor license has been consummated and the trustee is holding the net proceeds thereof.

Trustee's Motion to Reclassify Alleged Secured Claim of RELM, LLC

On February 27, 2014, the Trustee filed the instant Motion to Reclassify Alleged Secured Claim of RELM, LLC. Trustee asserts that the Liquor License is Debtor's only asset that has more than *de minimus* value and that the only other asset in the bankruptcy estate is Trustee's right to bring avoidance actions. Therefore, Trustee contends these are the only sources of funds for distribution to creditors.

First, Trustee argues that RELM's security interest never attached to the Liquor License. Trustee first concedes that RELM had made a prima facie demonstration that it holds a security interest in all of Debtor's personal property. However, Trustee contends that under New Jersey's Alcoholic Beverage Control Act (the "ABC Act"), liquor licenses cannot be deemed property subject to pledge, lien or any other transfer except for payment of taxes, and therefore, security interests cannot attach to liquor licenses or any proceeds arising from their sale. (citing N.J.S.A. § 33:1–26; In re Chris-Don, Inc. (Chris-Don II), 367 F. Supp. 2d 696, 701 (D.N.J. 2005)). Trustee asserts that this is because "liquor licenses do not constitute property to which security interests can attach." (citing Chris-Don II, 367 F. Supp. 2d at 701). Moreover, Trustee asserts that the "liquor license [. . .] is not deemed to be property of the Debtor under New Jersey law." (citing N.J.S.A § 33:1–26).

* * *

Next, RELM argues that this Court already determined that the Liquor License was "property," either implicitly or explicitly, in authorizing the sale of the liquor license under [**BC § 363**] since that provision only allows the trustee to sell "property of the estate." RELM continued that **BC § 541(a)** specifically provides that "property of the estate" must be "property." RELM asserts that whether something is "property" for the purposes of **BC § 541** must be determined by state law under *Butner v. United States*, 440 U.S. 48, 54, 99 S. Ct. 914, 59 L. Ed. 2d 136 (1979). RELM contends then that Trustee must have taken the position, and this Court must have found, that Debtor's Liquor License constituted "property" under New Jersey law in order for the sale to go forward.

RELM continues that in light of that conclusion, the Court's determination that the Liquor License was "property" is law of the case and cannot be reconsidered in connection with the instant motion. Further, and similarly, RELM asserts that the doctrine of judicial estoppel bars Trustee from now asserting that the Liquor License is not property.

RELM concludes that if this Court were to adopt the District Court's reasoning in Chris-Don II, it would be undermining its own order approving the settlement that authorized the sale of the Liquor License and perhaps undoing the protections afforded to the buyer. In addition, RELM asserts that this Court would be establishing precedent that would hamper the ability of trustees to sell liquor licenses, often the only property of value available for distribution to creditors.

* * *

Analysis

I.   RELM's Lien Does Not Attach to the Proceeds of the Sale of the Liquor License

Because RELM does not argue that its lien attaches to any avoidance actions Trustee may have, the only issue is whether RELM's lien attaches to the proceeds of the sale of the Liquor License such that it has a secured claim in those proceeds.

Whether Debtor's Liquor License was properly considered "property of the estate" that could be sold in Debtor's bankruptcy proceeding is a question of federal bankruptcy law. Under **BC § 541**, the scope of the bankruptcy estate is broad and includes "all legal or equitable interests of the debtor in property as of the commencement of the case."

* * *

This Court has no difficulty finding here that Trustee had an interest in Debtor's Liquor License that could properly be transferred and sold in this bankruptcy proceeding pursuant to **BC § 363**. The Court notes the broad scope of property of the bankruptcy estate under the Bankruptcy Code.

* * *

On the other hand, the question of whether Debtor's Liquor License or the proceeds resulting from its sale are subject to RELM's lien is one of New Jersey state law.

At the outset, this Court rejects RELM's argument that the fact that the Liquor License was sold under **BC § 363** establishes a "law of the case" such that judicial estoppel would bar Trustee's and the State's argument that the Liquor License is not "property" subject to lien or attachment under New Jersey state law.

* * *

In order for [**9–408**] to apply, RELM argues that the Liquor License is a general intangible, security interests in which are governed by Revised Article 9. However, Revised Article 9's definition of "general intangible" begins with "any personal property [. . .]." [**9–102(a)(42)**] Therefore, the Liquor License would have to be "personal property" to be a general intangible in which RELM could have a security interest.

As noted previously, Comment 3 to [**9–408**] explains that "[n]either this section nor any other provision of this Article determines whether a debtor has a property interest." Instead, "[o]ther law determines whether a debtor has a property interest ("Rights in the collateral") and the nature of that interest." N.J.S.A. § 33:1–26 is that "other law" in this case, and it unambiguously establishes that liquor licenses and the rights thereunder are not property subject to lien or attachment with limited exceptions under New Jersey law. The New Jersey Supreme Court has likewise interpreted N.J.S.A. § 33:1–26 to say that liquor licenses, although transferable, are not property. See *Kalogeras v. 239 Broad Ave.*, LLC, 202 N.J. 349, 360, 362, 997 A.2d 943 (2010); *The Boss Co. v. Bd. of Comm'rs of the City of Atlantic City*, 40 N.J. 379, 387, 192 A.2d 584 (1963). Therefore, because the Liquor License was not personal property of Debtor, by definition, it could not be a general intangible. See [**9–102(a)(42)**.]

For these reasons, this Court finds that the Liquor License falls outside the scope of Revised Article 9. Moreover, this Court finds that [**9–408**]'s anti-alienation provision does not repeal this clear statutory mandate. Nor will this Court find repeal by implication. Repeals by implication are not favored and will not be presumed unless the intention of the legislature to repeal is clear and manifest. *Nat'l Ass'n of Home Builders v. Defenders of Wildlife*, 551 U.S. 644, 662, 127 S. Ct. 2518, 168 L. Ed. 2d 467 (2007); *In re Brown*, 505 B.R. 638, 648 (E.D. Pa. 2014).

Thus, the plain language of N.J.S.A. § 33:1–26 controls this analysis. N.J.S.A. § 33:1–26 unambiguously provides that:

Under no circumstances [. . .] shall a license, or rights thereunder, be deemed property, subject to inheritance, sale, pledge, lien, levy, attachment, execution, seizure for debts, or any other transfer or disposition whatsoever, [other than for certain state tax liens and related obligations], except to the extent expressly provided by this chapter.

N.J.S.A. § 33:1–26. This is consistent with the long line of New Jersey case law that has recognized that "a liquor license, although transferable, is still to be considered a temporary permit or privilege, and not property, as it always has been even before our legislature so declared by statute, and this consideration is to continue to govern the relationship between state and local government and the licensee." *Kalogeras*, 202 N.J. at 362; *Boss Co.*, 40 N.J. at 387; *see Sea Girt Rest. & Tavern Owners Ass'n v. Bor. of Sea Girt*, 625 F. Supp. 1482, 1486 (D.N.J. 1986) aff'd, 802 F.2d 448 (3d Cir. 1986) *aff'd sub nom. Appeal of Avon Hotel Corp.*, 802 F.2d 445 (3d Cir. 1986) ("This clear legislative pronouncement that liquor licenses are not property has been consistently supported by case law, all of the cases holding that a license to sell intoxicating liquor is not a contract nor is it a property right. Rather, it is a temporary permit or privilege to pursue an occupation which otherwise is illegal.")

Next, this Court finds that the right to the proceeds from the sale of a liquor license is also governed by N.J.S.A. § 33:1–26 such that the proceeds are not property subject to lien or attachment. In In re Main St. Beverage Corp., 232 B.R. 303, 310 (D.N.J. 1998), the U.S. District Court for the District of New Jersey held that a private creditor had no valid security interest in the right to receive payment from the proceeds of the sale of the debtor's liquor license. The private creditor had loaned over $2.5 million to the debtor. As security for the loan, the debtor granted the private creditor a first priority security interest in, among other assets, its right to payment of all proceeds arising from the sale or disposition of the debtor's interest in a liquor license. . . After filing for Chapter 11, the debtor defaulted under its confirmed plan, and the bankruptcy court ordered that the liquor license be sold at public auction and confirmed the sale.

* * *

The court observed that perhaps a licensee should be able to utilize the economic value of his liquor license in a way that does not interfere with the regulatory agency's control over the license as a matter of commercial law. However, the court stated that "that is a matter for the state legislature, which may choose to redefine the nature of a liquor license under state law" as the Pennsylvania legislature did. *Main St. Beverage*, 232 B.R. at 310, citing *In re Walkers Mill Inn, Inc.*, 117 B.R. 197, 199 (Bankr. W.D. Pa. 1990) and the July 1, 1987 amendment of 47 Pa. Cons. Stat. Ann. § 4–468(d)). The court determined that "until such time as the

New Jersey legislature follows suit, this court must decline [creditor's] invitation to recognize a new exception to N.J.S.A. 33:1–26." Id. For those reasons, the court held that the private creditor had no valid security interest in the right to receive payment of the sale proceeds of the debtor's liquor license and that the bankruptcy court's conclusion to the contrary was erroneous. Id.

RELM argues that Revised Article 9 was the New Jersey legislature's response to Main Street Beverage. However, in enacting Revised Article 9, the New Jersey legislature did not "redefine the nature of a liquor license under state law" as Main Street Beverage suggested it would be necessary to allow a licensee to grant security interests in the economic value of its liquor license. That would have required amending N.J.S.A. 33:1–26, which defined the nature of a liquor license under New Jersey law as not property when Main Street Beverage was decided and so defines it today. *Compare In re Ciprian Ltd.*, 473 B.R. 669, 673 (Bankr. W.D. Pa. 2012) ("Although previously identified as a privilege, the Pennsylvania Liquor Code now characterizes a liquor license as 'a privilege between the board and the licensee. As between the licensee and third parties, the license shall constitute property.' 47 P.S. § 4–468(d). Therefore, as the license constitutes property, a security interest can be created.")

Keep in mind that as state law, Article 9 can invalidate only transfer restrictions created under state law. As noted above, some valuable license rights are created by federal law. In deciding that a creditor of a broadcasting company had a valid security interest in the proceeds of a broadcast license issued by the Federal Communications Commission, the court in *In re Tracy Broadcasting Corp.*, 696 F. 3d 1051 (10th Cir. 2012) had this to say:

A. Private Interests in Broadcast Licenses

Section 301 of the [Federal Communications Act (FCA)] "provide[s] for the use of [radio] channels, but not the ownership thereof, by persons for limited periods of time, under licenses granted by Federal authority." 47 U.S.C. § 301. In furtherance of that end it states that "no such license shall be construed to create any right, beyond the terms, conditions, and periods of the license." Id. Similarly, § 304 states:

> No station license shall be granted by the Commission until the applicant therefor shall have waived any claim to the use of any particular frequency or of the electromagnetic spectrum as against the regulatory power of the United States because of the previous use of the same, whether by license or otherwise.

Of particular relevance, § 310 limits the transfer of rights in a license:

> No . . . license, or any rights thereunder, shall be transferred, assigned, or disposed of in any manner, voluntarily or involuntarily, directly or indirectly, or by transfer of control of any corporation holding such permit or license, to any person except upon application to the Commission and upon finding by the Commission that the public interest, convenience, and necessity will be served thereby.

Id. § 310(d).

We begin our analysis by reviewing the FCC's view of what these provisions, and the purposes of the FCA as a whole, say about the rights of license holders to grant security interests. We will then defer to that interpretation under the doctrine of *Chevron, U.S.A., Inc. v. Natural Resources Defense Council, Inc.*, 467 U.S. 837, 842–44 (1984).

The FCC has consistently declared that a licensee cannot give a private party a lien on its license that would enable the lienholder to foreclose on the lien and obtain the licensee's rights without FCC approval. See In re *Walter O Cheskey*, 9 FCC Rcd. 986, 987 ¶ 8 (Mobile Servs. Div. 1994) ("The Commission has a policy against a licensee giving a security interest in a license. The reason for the policy is that the Commission's statutory mandate requires it to approve the qualifications of every applicant for a license. 47 U.S.C. § 310(d). If a security interest holder were to foreclose on the collateral license, by operation of law, the license could transfer hands without the prior approval of the Commission." (citation omitted)), *aff'd, In re Walter O'Cheskey*, 13 FCC Rcd. 10656 (1998). On the other hand, for some time the FCC has said that "[a] security interest in the proceeds of the sale of the license does not violate Commission policy." *Walter O Cheskey*, 9 FCC Rcd. at 987 ¶ 7, aff'd, *In re Walter O'Cheskey*, 13 FCC Rcd. at 10659–60. It has explained:

> [G]iving a security interest in the proceeds of the sale of a license does not raise the same concerns [as granting a lien that would allow the lienholder to obtain the license upon the debtor's default without FCC approval]. When a licensee gives a security interest in the proceeds of the sale of the system, including the license, the licensee's creditor has rights with respect to the money or other assets the licensee receives in exchange for the system and license. The creditor has no rights over the license itself, nor can it take any action under its security interest until there has been a transfer which yields proceeds subject to the security interest. Thus,

when the creditor exercises his security interest, the licensee will no longer be holding the license.

In re Walter O Cheskey, 9 FCC Rcd. at 987 ¶¶ 8, 9 (citations omitted). The FCC has emphasized that permitting such security interests will improve licensees' access to capital. See Facilitating the Provision of Spectrum-Based Services, 69 Fed. Reg. 75,144, 75,151 (Dec. 15, 2004) (codified at 47 C.F.R. pts. 1, 22, 24, 27 & 90). As for the prohibition on granting a security interest in the license itself, the FCC has "not yet taken a position on whether its policy . . . is statutorily mandated or solely dictated by regulatory policy." Id. (internal quotation marks omitted).

Courts and commentators have referred to the licensee's present interest in the right to the proceeds of a future sale of the license as a private right or interest, or an economic right. See MLQ Investors, L.P. v. Pac. Quadracasting, Inc., 146 F.3d 746, 749 (9th Cir. 1998); In re Ridgely Commc'ns, Inc., 139 B.R. 374, 379 (Bankr. D. Md. 1992); David Isenberg & Michael Reisz, Toward a Compromise on Collateralizing Loans to Broadcasters, 45 Fed. Comm. L.J. 541, 546, 557 (1993). These terms are appropriate because they contrast the right of the licensee to make money on a license (or at least recoup all or part of the licensee's investment in the license) with what the government controls—the use of the electromagnetic-wave spectrum. Under §§ 301 and 304 of the FCA, a licensee has no ownership rights in a channel of radio transmission or a frequency of the electromagnetic spectrum; the use of the channel (or frequency) is within the regulatory power of the FCC. The FCC's task is to ensure that the spectrum is used in the public interest. But the FCA does not prohibit a licensee from making money from its license—say, when a licensee sells a license (albeit only with FCC approval) and realizes a profit because of the value of listener loyalty to the frequency used by the licensee. In other words, the FCA does not prohibit private interests or rights in value created by the licensee's use of the airwaves. See In re Appls. of Various Subsidiaries & Affiliates of Geotek Commc'ns, 15 FCC Rcd. 790, 799 & n.49 (2000) (In approving assignment of licenses to creditors of bankrupt licensee, the Chief, Wireless Telecommunications Bureau, notes that "the vast majority of wireless licensees operate for-profit ventures using their licenses, and maximizing profits and returns are, no doubt, a high-ranking objective of these operators," and "find[s] that the Creditors' desire to maximize the return on their investment and their intention to assign the licenses to [another private party] are not in and of themselves inconsistent with their ability or intention to fulfill their responsibilities as licensees.").

It is important to understand precisely what rights are recognized by the FCC's policy. The FCC recognizes that one of the rights acquired by a licensee when it obtains a license is the right to receive money from a future transferee of the license. This right has value upon acquisition of the license, regardless of whether a prospective purchaser is in sight. And the FCC permits the licensee to grant a security interest in that right. Although the FCC speaks in terms of a "security interest in the proceeds of the sale of the license," In re Walter O Cheskey, 9 FCC Rcd. at 987 ¶ 7, the security interest is more precisely described as one in the licensee's right to the proceeds of a license sale and in the proceeds of that right (which are simply the sale proceeds). If the security interest were only in the sale proceeds, it could not attach before those proceeds existed (that is, before the sale was consummated), giving the holder of the security interest no priority over other creditors if the sale occurred after the licensee declared bankruptcy. A security interest of that sort would be of little value to a creditor and would hardly increase the licensee's access to capital. The security interest can, however, attach as soon as the licensee acquires the license if the security interest is in the right to receive proceeds from any future sale, a right that exists as soon as the licensee acquires the license. The FCC apparently uses the terminology "security interest in the proceeds of the sale" merely to emphasize that the secured party cannot realize any money on its security interest until the license has been transferred and that it has no right to use the license's broadcasting privilege.

3. *The Security Agreement Requirement:* This is a deceptively simple requirement, yet one that people sometimes get wrong. There are four ways to satisfy the security agreement requirement, but they fall into two categories: 1) the non-possessory security interest plus "written" security agreement category (**9–203(b)(3)(A)**); and 2) the "possessory" security interest category (**9–203(b)(3)(B)**, **(C)**, **(D)**). You'll soon see below why we put both "written" and "possessory" in quotation marks.

Consider possessory security interests first. **9–203(b)(3)(B)** tells us that the security agreement requirement is satisfied when the collateral is not a certificated security and is in the possession of the secured party pursuant to the debtor's security agreement. Note that there's nothing that says that the security agreement must be written, signed, or authenticated. You might have learned in your first year Property course that occupation of real estate gives notice to the world of an interest in that real estate. A similar rule, one based on possession, holds for personal property. As a result, possession is one way to create (and perfect) a security interest, and when a creditor has physical possession of collateral, we have pretty good evidence that the creditor has some property interest in it. When a creditor is holding collateral, therefore, the debtor need only agree to the possession and the additional evidentiary kick of a written agreement or authenticated record is not necessary. Most security interests in tangible personal property are non-possessory because the debtor needs the property in its business (or for his or her personal use).

Like so much of Article 9, **9–203(b)(3)** introduces new terms of art. With respect to "possessory" security interests, these terms of art reflect the diverse characteristics of personal property. When the collateral is a "certificated security in registered form," an oral agreement satisfies the security agreement requirement if the collateral is "delivered" to the secured party. Article 8 of the U.C.C. governs transfers of investment securities, so delivery, as defined in **8–301**, plus agreement satisfies the security agreement requirement of **9–203(b)(3)(C)**. A detailed discussion of Article 8 is beyond the scope of this book—we mention it just so that you know it's there in case you ever have a deal in which investment securities are collateral. Subpart (D) introduces the concept of "control" for some types of collateral. Control is also a concept borrowed from Article 8, and its inclusion in Article 9 recognizes the fact that not all personal property has a physical form. One example is a bank account (a "deposit account" in Article 9 parlance—**9–102(a)(29)**). An asset that does not have a physical form cannot be manually possessed (in other words, you cannot hold it in your hands), but there are ways that a secured creditor might be able to assert dominion over it in such a way to exclude access by others. Sections **9–104 through 9–107** define control for assets such as bank accounts. We will discuss control in more depth in Chapter 14, when we discuss perfection of security interests.

Most security interests are non-possessory. In order for a non-possessory security interest to attach, there must be an authenticated security agreement. Let's look at the "written" security agreement requirement in **9–203(b)(3)(A)**: The debtor must 1) authenticate, 2) a security agreement that 3) provides a description of the collateral.

What does authenticate mean? *See* **9–102(a)(7)**. "Authenticate" is the term that has replaced "sign" in Article 9 in order to accommodate electronic documentation. This definition was added when Article 9 was revised in the late 1990s, a period when lawyers were busily figuring out how to apply existing laws to rapidly developing electronic technologies. The term includes sign as we commonly understood that term in the 90s, but it was also designed to encompass methods of adopting information that is not written on paper and signed in ink.

What is a "security agreement?" At the very least, the writing must indicate that the debtor has agreed to give the secured property an interest in property as collateral for an obligation. The operative language in a security agreement might look something like this:

> The Grantor hereby grants to the Secured Party, to secure the prompt payment and performance in full of all of the Obligations

when due, a security interest in all of the Grantor's right, title and interest in, to and under the following properties, assets and rights, and in all similar properties, assets and rights that the Grantor is deemed by law to have rights in or the power to convey rights in, in each case wherever located, whether now owned or hereafter acquired or arising and whether governed by Article 9 of the UCC or other law (the "Collateral"): [description follows]

FORMS UNDER ARTICLE 9 OF THE UCC, THIRD EDITION (CINDY J. CHERNUCHIN, ED. 2016)

In the above excerpt, there is no question that the debtor is giving the secured party a security interest in its property and that the granting clause is evidence of an "agreement." Security agreements often contain terms like "grant," "pledge," and "assign," although courts routinely hold that no "magic words" are necessary to create a security interest. (More on that a little later. If you are drafting a security agreement, include the magic words).

The granting clause above is part of a model security agreement for a commercial transaction. In it, the borrower is giving a "blanket lien" on all of its personal property. Following is the collateral description:

(i)   all accounts (including health-care-insurance receivables);

(ii)   all chattel paper (whether tangible or electronic);

(iii)   all Commercial Tort Claims [include a specific description of Commercial Tort Claims existing at execution of this Agreement];

(iv)   all Deposit Accounts;

(v)   all documents (including electronic documents);

(vi)   all general intangibles (including payment intangibles and software);

(vii)   all goods (including inventory, equipment and any accessions thereto and all consigned goods);

(viii) all instruments (including promissory notes);

(ix)   all investment property and all other financial assets;

(x)   all letter of credit rights (whether or not the letter of credit is evidenced by writing);

(xi)   all money;

(xii)   [deleted by author];

(xiii) all insurance and insurance claims;

(xiv)   [deleted by author];

(xv) all other personal and fixture property of every kind and nature;

(xvi) all supporting obligations; and

(xvii) all products and proceeds arising from or relating to any of the foregoing.

The first basic rule about collateral descriptions is that the description must *reasonably identify* what is described. *See* **9–108(a)**. The section then provides a non-exclusive list of examples of reasonable descriptions. This security agreement describes the collateral by UCC type. *See* **9–108(c)**; **9–102(a)** and Official Comment.

The description above might seem broad to you, but remember, the idea is to grant a security interest in all of the debtor's assets. Why doesn't the agreement just say that? There are some limits on how broadly a security agreement can describe collateral. *See* **9–108(c)**. A supergeneric description in a security agreement will be ineffective as a collateral description. In addition, Article 9 requires a more exact description of some types of collateral. *See* **9–108(e)** and Official Comment 5. That's why the clause above requires additional information with respect to "commercial tort claims."

A description by Article 9 category will also be insufficient if the description is of "all consumer goods." Although Article 9 is not a consumer protection statute, you will see some provisions that are protective of consumer debtors. Disputes often arise about the level of precision needed for a description of consumer goods. Some of these disputes involve retailers who intend that all items bought with the retailer's charge card be covered by a security interest granted in the card application. Courts are split on how exact such a collateral description must be. Consider the following two excerpts.

IN RE CUNNINGHAM

489 B.R. 602 (Bankr. D. Kan. 2013)

BERGER, J.

Prior to the filing of the bankruptcy petition, Debtors purchased personal property in the form of consumer goods ("Consumer Goods") from Best Buy, N.A., a national retailer of consumer electronics and related products and services. Some of Debtors' purchases were made on credit provided by Capital One. In their brief, the Debtors concede that they purchased on the Capital One account "two ipods, a camera, a computer, and other micellaneous [sic]. . . ."

The items were purchased in 12 separate consumer transactions and are consumer goods. Three documents are pertinent to the Court's analysis. These documents are attached as exhibits to Capital One's brief in opposition to the Motion. In a footnote to its brief, Capital One describes these documents as follows:

> Exhibit C [credit application] is the application signed by Debtor, which states, "you grant the Bank a purchase money security interest in the goods purchased on your Account." Furthermore, the application states in that same section that the cardholder, here the Debtors, agree to the terms and conditions of the Cardholder Agreement (attached as Exhibit D is the Cardholder Agreement). It states in paragraph 17 of the Cardholder Agreement entitled "Security," "you grant us a purchase money security interest in the goods purchased with your Card.". [sic] Therefore, clearly the requisite language for Debtors to grant Secured Creditor [Capital One] a purchase money security interest exists.

Exhibit C, the "Application," is coincidental to Debtors' first purchase and is dated January 16, 2010. It appears that it was signed by both Debtors. The Application provided to the Court is a single-sided page. The Application contains the language recited above by Capital One; it is buried in a 16-line paragraph in a small font. This Court found it necessary to use a magnifying glass to find and read the language. The language appears in the ninth and tenth lines of the paragraph. With the assistance of a magnifying glass, the Court also was able to find buried in the sixth line of this Application paragraph that the Debtors agreed to the terms and conditions of the Cardholder Agreement. The Application indicates that the Cardholder Agreement would be sent to the Debtors after the Application and initial purchase of consumer products on January 16, 2010. The Cardholder Agreement is not signed. Buried in 41 numbered paragraphs in small print in the Cardholder Agreement is language that refers to Debtors granting to Capital One "a purchase money security interest in the goods purchased with your Card." Exhibit B to Capital One's brief in opposition is comprised of 12 Best Buy receipts ("Receipts"), all but one of which were signed by one of the Debtors. The Receipts contain basic information, such as the location of the Best Buy store, a brief description of items purchased and the price of these items, and the date and time of the sale. The Receipts also state "Payment Type: BBY CARD/HSBC." . . .

* * *

There is no reference on the Receipts to security interests, purchase money or otherwise, retained by anyone. The Receipts also do not contain a reference to the Application or the Cardholder Agreement.

<u>Analysis</u>

Debtors request a determination by this Court that Capital One does not hold a security interest, purchase money or otherwise, in the Consumer Goods purchased by Debtors at Best Buy.

* * *

With respect to the sufficiency of the collateral description for consumer transactions contained in a security agreement, it has been observed:

> Revised Article 9 continues the requirement that a security agreement or financing statement contain a description of the collateral that reasonably identifies the collateral. The use of categories or types of collateral defined under the UCC (i.e., inventory) is still permitted. However, in consumer transactions and a limited number of other situations, a description by type or class of collateral is ineffective as to after-acquired property. Note that Revised Article 9 permits "supergeneric" descriptions in the financing statement such as "all assets" or "all personal property" but not in the security agreement.

Property "type" descriptions of collateral are not sufficient for consumer goods. The essence of the Debtors' argument is that the description of the Consumer Goods in which Capital One asserts a security interest is insufficient as it only refers to the type of collateral, and Capital One therefore does not have a security interest in the Consumer Goods. Debtors argue that any security interest that Capital One may have never attached to the Consumer Goods because an insufficient description is fatal to the attachment of Capital One's security interest to the Consumer Goods. In response, Capital One argues that the description is sufficient if one combines the language contained in the Application, the Receipts, and the Cardholder Agreement. The issue before the Court is whether the description is sufficient as required by [9–108(e)(2)] to allow attachment and enforceability under [9–203(b)(3)(A)]. Aside from an insufficient description of the collateral, Debtors do not argue that Capital One did not comply with the other prerequisites of a security interest with respect to enforceability and attachment.

      * * *

A case not cited by the parties that is somewhat instructive is *In re McLeod*, 245 B.R. 518 (Bankr. E.D. Mich. 2000). Citing to the Michigan version of the U.C.C., the court observed: "Attachment of a security interest occurs when (1) debtor has signed a security agreement which contains a description of the collateral; (2) Value has been given; and (3) The debtor has rights in the collateral." The description of the collateral is sufficient "if it reasonably identifies what is described." Under Michigan law, a retail charge agreement was considered signed and accepted by the buyer if the charge account were used by the applicant. In McLeod, the debtor or his wife signed each of the sales slips. "The sales slips identified the item(s) purchased, incorporated the SearsCharge Agreement, and granted Defendant [Sears] a security interest." The *McLeod* court ultimately found that Sears enjoyed a purchase money security interest in the consumer goods purchased on the retail charge account. This "composite-document theory" has found a home with other courts. The deciding factor that underpins these decisions is that the Sears sales slips contained simple and clear purchase money security interest language. Courts have treated the Sears sales slips as security agreements when "(1) the sales slip incorporates a long-form security agreement by reference, (2) the retailer is prepared to present evidence of its general documentation practices, and (3) the sales slip contains solid 'granting' language and a transaction-specific description of the merchandise.

The difference between *McLeod* . . . and the case *sub judice* is that the receipts signed by debtors in those cases specifically stated that Sears retained a purchase money security interest in the goods that were purchased in the transaction. Michigan law cited in *McLeod* also provided that a retail customer assumed and agreed to the terms of the credit agreement upon use of the account. In the case *sub judice*, the Capital One Receipts do not contain a reference to a purchase money security interest or any other security interest. The only caution contained on the Capital One Receipts refers to the return and refund policies printed on the back of the Receipts and posted in the store. There is no reference to the Cardholder Agreement or the original Application on the Receipts. In McLeod, Sears was both the seller and the lienholder; in contrast, in the case sub judice, Best Buy is listed at the top of the Receipts, and the only reference to Capital One's predecessor-in-interest HSBC is: "Payment Type: BBY CARD/HSBC." Capital One's argument is that the description of the Consumer Goods is sufficient when one considers the three documents as a single security agreement. Remove any one of these legs and its argument, as with the metaphorical table, does not stand.

Is it enough to string together a signed Application that has buried within it purchase money security interest language; a Cardholder Agreement that was not signed by the Debtors that was mailed to them after the Application and buried within which is also purchase money security interest language; and 12 Receipts which, except for one, were signed but did not contain a reference to a security interest, the Application or the Cardholder Agreement? The answer is no: An enforceable security agreement has never existed between these parties as to the Consumer Goods.

So in Kansas Best Buy (or more precisely, Capital One) loses, right? Not so fast—a month later a judge on the same court published the following:

IN RE MURPHY

80 U.C.C. Rep. Serv. 2d (Callaghan) 764 (Bankr. D. Kan. 2013)

SOMERS, J.

* * *

Debtor contends that describing the collateral as "goods purchased on your Account" does not comply with **[9–108]**. The argument is that since the sale was a consumer transaction, subsection (e)(2) applies and was violated because it prohibits description by type of collateral and, in the Debtor's view, "goods purchased" is a type of collateral. Debtor contends that the security agreement must describe the specific goods purchased, such as TV or VCR.

Debtor's proposed construction of **[9–108(e)(2)]** is not correct. The "description by type" not permitted for consumer goods is the "types" of collateral defined in the UCC, such as accounts, chattel paper, consumer goods, deposit accounts equipment, general intangibles, and so forth. "Goods purchased on your Account" is not a "type of collateral defined in the uniform commercial code." The purpose of the collateral description in the security agreement is to define the security interest as between the parties; unlike a financing statement, the purpose of a security agreement is not to give notice to third parties. The description "goods purchased on your Account" adequately defines the collateral between the Debtor and the holder of the account.

This case is nearly identical to *In re Ziluck*, 139 B.R. 44 (S.D. Fla. 1992), which held debtors consumer goods purchased using a Radio Shack credit card were subject to security interests granted by the Radio Shack Account and Security Agreement signed by the debtor describing the collateral as "all merchandise charged to your Account." The court rejected the debtor's argument that the description of the collateral was insufficient, finding that it "reasonably identifies the property subject to the security interest—namely any property purchased with the subject credit card." *Ziluck* is identified as correctly decided in Barkley Clark's treatise on Article 9, which states, "it is always possible for the issuer [of a credit card] to retain a security interest in items purchased with the credit card, so long as the credit card application includes security agreement language."[8]

Research conducted before the hearing revealed one case reaching a contrary result, *In re Shirel*, 251 B.R. 157 (Bankr. W.D. Okla. 2000). In that case, the Bankruptcy Judge held that the description of collateral as "all merchandise purchased with the credit card" in a credit card form from an appliance center was insufficient for a security interest to attach to a refrigerator purchased using the card. I believe he erroneously found the

---

[8]   Barkley Clark and Barbara Clark, *The Law of Secured Transactions under the Uniform Commercial Code* ¶ 12.02[1] (A.S. Pratt 2012).

purpose of the security agreement was to give notice to third parties of the items which are subject to the security interest. Inquiry notice to third parities is the function of a financing statement, which is not required for a PMSI in consumer goods. When evaluating the sufficiency of the description, the *Shirel* court then focused only on the phrase "all merchandise," ignoring the phrase "purchased with the credit card," and found the phrase "all merchandise" imprecise. The *Ziluck* case was cited in a footnote as reaching a contrary result, but it was rejected since it was not decided under Oklahoma law or by the Tenth Circuit.

. . . [T]he *Cunningham* decision also reaches a contrary result. Although the facts in *Cunningham*, 489 B.R. 602 are indistinguishable from those in this case and the issue presented was identical, analysis focused upon construction of the three documents involved in each sale transaction, rather than on the UCC requirements for description of collateral. The Court concluded that "[a]n enforceable security agreement has never existed between these parties as to the" consumer goods purchased from Best Buy because "[t]he type of collateral referenced in the 'goods purchased on your Account' contained in the original Application is not sufficiently descriptive to allow attachment and enforceability under [9–108(e)] and [9–203(b)(3)(A)]." This Court respectfully disagrees. As discussed above, it is my conclusion that the description of the goods in the Application and the Cardholder Agreement is sufficient under [9–108(e)] and the security interest therefore attached under [9–203(b)(3)(A)].

CONCLUSION.

For the foregoing reasons, the Court denies the portion of Debtor's Motion seeking a determination that Capital One's security interest did not attach to the consumer goods purchased with Debtor's Best Buy credit card.

Note that the judge in *Cunningham* focused on the prohibition against descriptions by type when the collateral is consumer goods and the judge in *Murphy* focused on the difference between the contractual function of a security agreement and the notice function of a financing statement. Official Comment 5 to **9–108** suggests that the prohibition on some broad collateral descriptions serves a signaling function: we do not want debtors inadvertently encumbering some types of property.

B. SCOPE OF A SECURITY AGREEMENT

Although the requirements for a security agreement are minimal, the words used in a security agreement collateral description pack a lot of meaning. You will see that a security agreement can grant the secured party an interest in property that the debtor owns at the time it signs the security agreement as well as property that the debtor acquires in the future.

1. AFTER-ACQUIRED PROPERTY

Moving back to the security agreement granting clause on page 523, you see that the borrower grants an interest in assets "now owned or hereafter acquired." Article 9 permits such a grant, again with some limitations. *See* 9–204. Pause for a moment to consider a debtor's ability to grant a security interest in something it does not yet own. This is counter to the well-established property principle of *nemo dat quod non habet*. The history of the after-acquired property clause goes back to the days of the great expansion of the railroads in the 1800s. Loan to build the railroads were secured by the assets—rails, ties, locomotives—that made up the railroads. The lenders expected to acquire an interest in these items as the railroads were built, and it would have been too time-consuming (and expensive) to execute new documents each time the borrower acquired a new asset. Hence, the after-acquired property clause was born. See Russell A. Hakes, According Purchase Money Status Proper Priority, 72 OR. L. REV. 323, 329–334 (1993).

Parties to secured transactions expect that some types of collateral will turn over frequently. For example, if you walked into a Best Buy or any other electronics store yesterday, you saw many televisions, speakers, cameras, and other items for purchase. If you walk into the same Best Buy store tomorrow, you will probably see the same product mix, but if Best Buy is a successful retailer, some of the items you saw yesterday will have been sold, and new items will be on the shelves. Any lender financing Best Buy's inventory will expect this turnover. Courts honor this expectation by holding that some collateral descriptions, standing alone, include after acquired property. Accounts and inventory are the two collateral descriptions that, without more, include after-acquired inventory and accounts. Sometimes parties try to argue that other property is so similar to inventory and accounts that a description by type of that category, without more, includes after-acquired property. Usually, they lose.

ROBERT BOGETTI & SONS V. BANK
OF AMERICA NT & SA

162 B.R. 289 (Bankr. E.D. Cal. 1993)

HEDRICK, JR., J.

This matter comes before the court on complaint of debtor Robert Bogetti & Sons (the "Partnership") against Bank of America ("Bank") to determine the extent, validity, and priority of lien claimed by Bank.

[Background: The debtor ("Partnership") was engaged in farming operations. Its primary operations were growing beans on thirteen parcels of land located in two California counties. The Partnership borrowed money from Bank of America ("Bank") and executed a security agreement in favor of Bank, granting a security interest in, among other things, "All farm products of whatsoever kind or nature, including all crops now growing or hereafter to be grown or timber to be cut on that certain real property described below; and also including all livestock and supplies used or produced in farming operations." The security agreements referenced five parcels of land with legal descriptions attached as exhibits A through E. When the Partnership filed for bankruptcy, it listed as its assets beans and proceeds from the sale of beans from all thirteen parcels farmed by the Partnership.]

* * *

1991 Bean Crop from Eight Parcels not Described in the Security Agreements.

Bank concedes that attachment or perfection of a security interest in growing crops or crops to be grown requires descriptions of the real property to be attached to the security agreement. Bank also concedes that when the August 1991 security agreement was executed, all of the Partnership's 1991 crop was yet to be harvested. Notwithstanding, Bank contends to have a security interest in the entire 1991 crop based on having rights to "after-acquired farm products." Bank asserts that when the 1991 crop was severed from the ground in the harvest, it became "farm product" and Bank's security interest attached.

Bank urges this court to determine its security interest in after-acquired farm products based on two grounds. . . . Bank argues that the granting language in the security agreements should be construed to include after-acquired farm products because they referenced "all farm products of whatsoever kind or nature."

* * *

b.   "All farm products" language.

[Section **9–204**] provides that a security agreement may provide for a security interest in after-acquired collateral. Unless specifically provided for, however, a security interest attaches only to the collateral described and in existence at the time the security agreement is executed.

As discussed above, the security agreements did not include a clause describing after-acquired farm products. Nevertheless, Bank contends the language of the security agreements providing for a grant of a security interest in "all farm products of whatsoever kind or nature" created a security agreement in after-acquired farm products. Bank relies on a well-developed line of authority that where a security agreement provides for a security interest in "all inventory" or "all accounts" or similar broad language, the security interest includes after-acquired inventory and accounts.

Bank has, however, cited no case extending this line of authority beyond inventory and accounts receivable. As emphasized recently by the Ninth Circuit in *Stoumbos v. Kilimnik,* 988 F.2d 949 (9th Cir. 1993), this line of authority is based on the assumption that the parties realize that inventory and accounts receivable are in a constant state of turnover and "no creditor could reasonably agree to be secured by collateral that would vanish in a short time in the normal course of business." *Id.* at 955. In *Stoumbos,* the court refused to extend this line of authority to a security interest in "equipment" which it determined was not a category of goods subject to constant turnover.

"Farm products" is a broad subcategory of goods which includes crops, livestock, and supplies used or produced in farming operations. [**9–102(a)(34)**]. Although there are conceivably some items included in "farm products" that may, like inventory or accounts receivable, "vanish" and be replaced in a short period of time in the normal course of business, such turnover has not been shown by Bank to be so constant that a creditor would reasonably expect to secured by after-acquired farm products. Indeed, some farm products, such as livestock, may remain in the farmer's possession for substantial periods without replacement. Accordingly, the court is not willing to extend the line of authority cited by Bank to include "farm products."

Based on the foregoing, Bank has no security interest in the 1991 bean crop or crop proceeds from the eight parcels not identified in the security agreements.

———————————

It's easy enough to add an after-acquired property clause. If you're a lender and you intend to your security interest to extend to after-acquired property, include the clause.

There are two types of collateral for which an after-acquired property clause will not be effective. *See* **9–204(b)**. One is a commercial tort claim. You already saw above that a security agreement cannot describe a commercial tort claim by type. Instead, the security agreement must describe the claim with some specificity. A debtor can't describe a not-yet-in existence claim with specificity. The second is consumer goods unless the debtor acquires rights in the goods within 10 days after the secured party gives value. This is yet another place in Article 9 where you will see a different rule for consumer transactions. The exception to the general rule that an after-acquired property clause does not reach consumer goods accounts for revolving loans, such as secured credit cards.

2. PROCEEDS

The model granting clause on p. 523 combined with the collateral description on p. 524 grants the secured party not only a security interest in the listed assets, but also in the "proceeds and products thereof." What are proceeds and products and why would a secured party want an interest in them? *See* **9–102(a)(64)**. Proceeds are anything that the debtor receives in exchange for collateral, so if the collateral is a car, whatever the debtor receives when she sells the car constitutes proceeds. The definition is far more expansive than that, however. The term includes any value collected on or distributed on account of collateral (such as dividends on investment property collateral), claims arising out of the loss of collateral, and insurance payable on account of the loss of collateral. The term also includes the cryptic "rights arising out of collateral," a term which has been the subject of some litigation.

You will not find a definition of "products" in the UCC. The term "product" in commercial finance means an agricultural product (cows produce milk) or the product of a manufacturing process (a bunch of two by fours produce a shed). Proceeds and products are both value-tracing concepts. A secured party is a lender and its ultimate goal is to get paid. As a result, it is primarily concerned that it will receive the value of the collateral if anything goes wrong with the deal.

Why did the drafter of the granting clause above include a statement that the security interest extends to "proceeds and products?" *See* **9–315(a)(2)**. Note that a security agreement automatically extends to identifiable proceeds of collateral. It does not extend to products of collateral unless the security agreement expressly says that it does.

When are proceeds identifiable? Sometimes it is easy to identify proceeds. Suppose that the debtor, Kevin, owns a Toyota Prius that he bought with a loan from Auto Finance. Auto Finance has a security interest in the car. Kevin is moving to New York City, where he will not need a car, so he has decided to sell his car to his friend Catherine. When Catherine hands over her $8,000 check for the Prius, the check is identifiable proceeds of the car and Auto Finance has a security interest in it. (Auto Finance will also keep a security interest in the car if it has not consented to the sale, **9–315(a)(1)** something that we will explore in more detail in Chapter 15). A problem may arise, however, when Kevin deposits the check into his bank account. Once funds are deposited into a bank account, they are commingled with the other funds in the account. In order to identify the funds, parties resort to various common law tracing rules.

One such rule is the "lowest intermediate balance rule." The theory behind that rule is that a debtor spends its own unencumbered funds before it spends funds encumbered by a security interest. When an account contains both proceeds and other money, the lowest intermediate balance rule assumes that the account holder spends the "other money" first. Once the debtor starts spending encumbered funds (the proceeds) they're gone and can't be replenished. You will apply the lowest intermediate balance rule in **Problem 4**. The term "lowest intermediate balance" means that the "identifiable" proceeds are the lowest balance in the bank account between the time that the debtor deposits the proceeds and the time that the test is applied.

The lowest intermediate balance rule is just one of several tracing rules. The court in *GE Business Lighting Group v. Halmar Distributors, Inc. (In re Halmar Distributors, Inc.)*, 232 B.R. 18 (Bankr. D. Mass. 1999) explained another:

> GE has the burden of identifying the proceeds from the sale of its collateral. *See S.N.A. Nut Co. v. Tulare Nut. Co.* (In re *S.N.A. Nut Co.*), 204 B.R. 537, 542 (Bankr. N.D. Ill. 1997) (secured party has the burden of identifying commingled proceeds); *State Nat'l Bank of Platteville v. Cullen* (In re *Cullen*), 71 B.R. 274, 280 (Bankr. W.D. Wis. 1987) (same). "To do this, the secured party must 'trace' the claimed proceeds back to the original collateral; in other words, the secured party must establish that the alleged [identifiable] proceeds 'arose directly from the sale or other disposition of the collateral and that these proceeds [could] not have arisen from any other source.'" In re *Oriental Rug Warehouse Club, Inc.*, 205 B.R. 407 (Bankr. D. Minn. 1997). "The goal of 'tracing' is to establish what portion of a commingled account constitutes proceeds of the collateral." *Farmers and Merchants Nat'l Bank, Fairview v. Sooner Cooperative, Inc.*, 766 P.2d 325, 329 (Okla. 1988); *see also Connecticut Gen. Life Ins., Co. v. Universal Ins. Co.*, 838 F.2d 612, 620 (1st Cir. 1988) (The point of tracing is to follow the particular entrusted assets, not simply to identify some assets).

> In factually traceable situations, where accurate business records have been maintained, tracing proceeds into and out of an account can be reasonably simple. *See Gen. Motors Acceptance Corp. v. Taft* (In re *Dexter Buick-GMC Truck Co.*), 2 B.R. 242, 245–46 (Bankr. D.R.I. 1980) (evidence consisting of cash receipt journals, sales invoices, and bank statements of deposits demonstrated which portion of the funds constituted proceeds of the collateral). Where, however, deposited proceeds have completely lost their transactional identity, courts have relied upon artificial tracing methods developed in the law of trusts. *C.O. Funk & Son*, 431 N.E.2d at 372 (noting that section **1–103** specifically directs that the UCC be supplemented by principles of law and equity); *see also Brown & Williamson Tobacco Corp. v. First Nat'l Bank of Blue Island*, 504 F.2d 998 (7th Cir. 1974); *Universal C.I.T. Credit*

Corp. v. Farmers Bank of Portageville, 358 F. Supp. 317 (E.D. Mo. 1973); *Ex parte Alabama Mobile Homes, Inc.*, 468 So. 2d 156 (Ala. 1985).

GE asserts that, relying on both factual evidence and trust tracing principles, it can sustain its burden of proving which funds in the Bank's commingled collection constitute identifiable proceeds from the sale of Ralar's wiring devices. To accomplish this feat, GE has attempted to demonstrate what percentage of the original wiring device inventory belonged to Ralar and then apply that percentage to the total amount of proceeds received by the Bank from the sale of both Debtors' wiring devices. The following is a more detailed account of the tracing method utilized by GE.

To determine what percentage of the total wiring device inventory belonged to Ralar, GE first calculated how much of the original wiring device inventory belonged to Ralar before it was commingled. GE and the Bank agree that, as of July 3, 1989, Halmar was in possession of wiring devices valued at $ 406,512.00 (at cost) and Ralar of $ 56,656.00 (at cost). GE then contends that, on or after July 3, 1989, GE shipped Halmar an additional $ 108,355.35 (at cost) of wiring device inventory and shipped Ralar an additional $ 3,828.12 (at cost) of such inventory. In total then, according to GE, on and after July 3, 1989, Halmar possessed $ 514,867.35 (at cost) worth of the wiring device inventory and Ralar owned $ 60,484.12 (at cost) of the wiring device inventory.

* * *

From this evidence, GE calculates that Ralar possessed 10.512552% of the entire GE wiring device inventory held by the Debtors. In other words, out of the Debtors' entire wiring device inventory valued at $ 575,351.47, Halmar's pro-rata share of the inventory was 89.487448% ("89.4%") or $ 514,867.35 and Ralar's pro-rata share was 10.512552% ("10.5%") or $ 60,484.12.

GE next concludes that if Ralar owned 10.5% of the inventory, GE should entitled to 10.5% of the proceeds collected by the Bank during the period in which Ralar wiring devices were sold. According to GE, the Bank collected $ 781,831.35 in proceeds from the sale of GE wiring devices between July 3, 1989 and May 31, 1990. GE derives that sum by claiming that the Bank collected $ 335,594.95 from July 3, 1989 through September 14, 1989; $ 237,431.00 from September 15, 1989 through April 30, 1990; and an additional $ 208,805.40 after May, 1990. GE therefore contends that it is entitled to $ 82,190.42, being 10.5% of the collections of $ 781,831.35.

Having set out GE's tracing method, this Court must now evaluate it. If GE cannot sufficiently identify the proceeds of the sale of Ralar wiring devices and/or cannot prove that the Bank received these funds, its claim must fail and its security interest found invalid. *See Hollins & Arrousez Electric & Engineering Co. v. Moore,* 31 F.2d 50, 51 (9th Cir. 1929) (citing *First Nat'l Bank of Princeton v. Littlefield,* 226 U.S. 110, 57 L. Ed. 145, 33 S. Ct. 78 (1912)) ("The burden of proof is upon the one claiming [a right to the commingled (account)] and if he is unable to identify the funds as representing the proceeds of his property, his claim must fail.").

At the outset, this Court notes that "adherence to specific equitable principles, including rules concerning tracing analysis are 'subject to the equitable discretion of the court.'" *United States v. Durham,* 86 F.3d 70, 72 (5th Cir. 1996) (quoting *Quinn v. Montrose State Bank (In re Intermountain Porta Storage, Inc.),* 74 B.R. 1011, 1016 (D.C. Colo. 1987)). This Court further recognizes the need to construe the UCC liberally so as to promote its underlying policy of simplifying and modernizing commercial transactions. Mass. Gen. Laws Ann. ch. 106A, § 1–102.

Proration is a viable form of tracing where there are two or more secured creditors with an interest in commingled proceeds. *Gen. Motors Acceptance Corp. v. Norstar Bank, N.A.,* 141 Misc. 2d 349, 355, 532 N.Y.S.2d 685 (N.Y. Sup. Ct. 1988). Employing this approach, a court may consider identifiable proceeds as a pro-rata share of the commingled account, the share being determined by the percentage of collateral owned by the secured creditor before the proceeds were commingled. See *Bombardier Capital, Inc. v. Key Bank of Maine,* 639 A.2d 1065 (Me. 1994) (recognition of two secured creditors interests required prorating the account balance); *Mid-States Sales Co., Inc. v. Mountain Empire Dairymen's Assoc., Inc.,* 741 P.2d 342 (Colo. Ct. App. 1987) (secured creditor which has a security interest in fifty-two percent of the debtor's inventory had a fifty-two percent interest in total proceeds); *Ford Motor Credit Co. v. Troy Bank & Trust Co.;* 76 B.R. 836 (M.D. Ala. 1986) (debtor's bank account should be divided pro-rata between the two secured creditors); In re *Koch,* 54 B.R. 26 (Bankr. W.D. Wis. 1985) (same). "This accounting method has been universally accepted in . . . other jurisdictions that have interpreted section 9–306(2) . . . there is no compelling reason to reject it." *Norstar Bank,* 141 Misc. 2d at 355.

Based on the foregoing, this Court finds that the pro-rata method of tracing used by GE is an acceptable means to identify the proceeds of its collateral.

3. PROCEEDS AND AFTER-ACQUIRED PROPERTY DISTINGUISHED

Sometimes proceeds and after-acquired property look like the same thing. And often debtors use proceeds to buy more property that then becomes collateral for their loans. If a retailer sells inventory and receives cash in exchange for the inventory, it is likely that the retailer will use the cash to purchase new inventory. The proceeds of the proceeds are proceeds and thus collateral. *See* **9–102(a)(12)**, **(64)**.

The difference between the two is important for several reasons. As discussed above, a security agreement that is silent as to proceeds extends to proceeds; a security interest that is silent as to after-acquired property does not extend to after-acquired property except with respect to inventory and accounts. There is also a key difference in bankruptcy. Once a debtor files for bankruptcy, the floating lien stops floating. That means that an after-acquired property clause stops operating at the moment a bankruptcy petition is filed. *See* **BC 552**. If the "after-acquired" property is proceeds, that rule does not apply. As a result, the secured creditor's lien will attach to post-bankruptcy proceeds but not to non-proceeds after-acquired property.

IN RE WALLMAN

71 B.R. 125 (Bankr. D. S.D. 1987)

ECKER, J.

This matter is before the Court on a motion for contempt and sanctions filed on behalf of Willard Willis Wallman ("debtor") by Attorney J. Bruce Blake on January 26, 1987. Debtor substantively alleges that: 1) **Bankruptcy Code Section 552** extinguishes a creditor's otherwise properly perfected prepetition future crop security interest (after-acquired property clause in security agreement) on any crops which have been planted by the debtor postpetition; and 2) Because the creditor has no lien in the postpetition crops, it, therefore, has no lien in the proceeds resulting from the sale thereof.

* * *

BACKGROUND

Debtor filed for relief under Chapter 11 of the Bankruptcy Code on January 20, 1983. He operates a crop farming business in Beadle County, South Dakota.

Approximately one year prior to filing for relief, in exchange for a [Farmers Home Administration (FmHA)] loan, the debtor both executed a promissory note and entered into a security agreement. Among other things, the debtor granted the FmHA a security interest in:

"All crops, annual and perennial, and other plant products now planted, growing or grown, or *which are hereafter planted or otherwise become growing crops or other plant products . . . .*"

Both parties agreed that the FmHA properly perfected its security interest in the debtor's future crops.

* * *

In 1986, the debtor, still in the process of reorganizing, planted and, thereafter, harvested a wheat crop. On November 15, 1986, the debtor delivered a portion of this crop to the Yale Elevator and received a check in the sum of $9,983 payable to himself and the FmHA. FmHA insists that it has a lien interest in the proceeds from the sale of his 1986 crop.

ISSUES

The principal issues raised are:

1) Whether **Bankruptcy Code Section 552** extinguishes a creditor's otherwise perfected prepetition future crop security interest on crops which have been planted postpetition; and

2) If so, whether a creditor may properly claim a lien in the proceeds resulting from the sale of crops planted postpetition under **Bankruptcy Code Subsection 552(b)**.

LAW

A. First Issue

As to the first issue, the Court holds that **Bankruptcy Code Section 552** extinguishes a creditor's otherwise properly perfected prepetition future crop security interest on crops which have been planted postpetition. This is based on the following discussion.

With certain exceptions, **Bankruptcy Code Subsection 552(a)** clearly provides that property acquired by the debtor or the bankruptcy estate *after* the filing of the petition is *not* subject to any lien resulting from an after-acquired property clause in a security agreement entered into *before* the filing of the petition. **11 U.S.C. § 552(a)**. The legislative history of **section 552** states this proposition as follows:

> Under the Uniform Commercial Code, Article 9 [**9–204**], creditors may take security interests in after-acquired property. This section governs the effect of such a prepetition security interest in postpetition property . . . .
>
> As a general rule, if a security agreement is entered into before the [bankruptcy] case, then property that the estate acquires is not subject to the security interest created by the security agreement. . . .

House Rep. No. 595, 95th Cong., 1st Sess. 376–77 (1977).

Within given limits, **Bankruptcy Code Subsection 552(b)**, however, excepts certain lien interests from the effect of subsection (a). *See* **11 U.S.C. § 552(b)**. Among other things, "proceeds" are generally excepted under this provision. *Id.*

Offering no authority or argument other than noting its security agreement's after-acquired property interest clause, the FmHA simply insists that its lien attaches to the proceeds of the debtor's 1986 wheat crop. The Court is unsure as to exactly what the FmHA's argument is.

[S]everal courts, in some form, have addressed the issue of whether Bankruptcy Code Section 552 extinguishes a creditor's otherwise properly perfected prepetition future crop security interest on crops which have been planted postpetition and have unanimously held that the prepetition lien does not attach to postpetition planted crops. *See In re Drewes,* 68 B.R. 153, 155 (Bkrtcy. N.D. Iowa 1986); *In re Randall,* 58 B.R. 289, 290 (Bkrtcy. C.D. Ill. 1986); *In re Lorenz,* 57 B.R. 734, 736 (Bkrtcy. N.D. Ill. 1986); *In re Hugo,* 50 B.R. 963, 967 (Bkrtcy. E.D. Mich. 1985); *In re Hamilton,* 18 B.R. 868, 871 (Bkrtcy. D. Colo. 1982).

In the instant case, it is undisputed that the debtor planted the crops postpetition (more than three years after filing). Thus, the issue raised is precisely the question addressed by this Court in *In re Sheehan,* 38 B.R. 859 (Bankr. D.S.D. 1984). Based on the foregoing, this Court affirms its holding in *In re Sheehan* and, therefore, holds that the FmHA's lien did not attach to the debtor's 1986 wheat crop.

B.   Second Issue

As to the second issue, because the Court has previously found that the FmHA's lien did not attach to the debtor's 1986 wheat crop, the Court, therefore, holds that, under **Bankruptcy Code Subsection 552(b)** or otherwise, its lien does not attach to the $9,983 check which is proceeds resulting from the sale thereof. This is based on the following discussion.

The "proceeds" exception in subsection (b) *only* refers to proceeds generated by prepetition collateral, *not* proceeds of after-acquired property. **11 U.S.C. § 552(b).** Proceeds of collateral may be held to be secured by a prepetition security interest only if the collateral which produces the proceeds was acquired by the debtor prepetition. *Id.* What this means is if FmHA's lien did not attach to the debtor's postpetition planted wheat crop, it certainly does not attach to the proceeds resulting from the sale thereof. To hold otherwise would allow reattachment of the already eliminated lien in every case in which the debtor sells the property. Based on the foregoing, the Court holds that the FmHA's lien does not attach to the $9,983 check issued by Yale Elevator to the debtor in exchange for delivery of part of his 1986 wheat crop.

4. FUTURE ADVANCES

9–204 also allows a security agreement to extend to future advances of value made by the secured party. **9–204(c).** Sometimes the secured party disburses all of the loan proceeds at once, for example, when it is financing the purchase of a car. Other times, however, the parties contemplate that the borrower will be taking out the money in installments. A revolving line of credit, which works a bit like your credit card, is an example. Even if the secured party intends to disburse all of the loan proceeds at once, it will want to have a future advance clause in its security agreement. If a secured party has to purchase insurance on the collateral because the debtor has let its insurance lapse the secured party is going to want that advance secured by the collateral.

C. WHEN THE BANKRUPTCY TRUSTEE KNOCKS ON YOUR DOOR AND YOU DON'T HAVE A SECURITY AGREEMENT

Even though the requirements for creating a security agreement are minimal, some people get them wrong. Failure to create an effective security agreement is fatal to the creditor's secured status. Often, no one catches that mistake until the borrower files for bankruptcy. Then there's a scramble to try and prove the existence of a security agreement.

COVEY V. MORTON COMMUNITY BANK (IN RE SABOL)
337 B.R. 195 (Bankr. C.D. Ill. 2006)

PERKINS, J.

This adversary proceeding is before the Court, after trial, on the complaint by Charles E. Covey, as Trustee of the Chapter 7 estate ("TRUSTEE"), to determine the validity of a security interest held by Morton Community Bank ("BANK") in several items of sound equipment owned by Michael S. Sabol, one of the Debtors ("DEBTOR"). The matter was taken under advisement by the Court and the parties have submitted briefs. The main issue is whether the ***Composite Document Rule*** can rescue the BANK from the absence of a ***security agreement***.

The following facts are not in dispute. On May 25, 2002, the DEBTOR, doing business in the recording industry as Sound Farm Productions, completed an application for a Small Business Administration (SBA) guaranteed loan to expand his business, requesting approval of a loan from the BANK, as Lender, in the principal amount of $ 58,000. The BANK'S application for the SBA guarantee, comprised of a separate page completed and signed by its loan officers dated June 3, 2002, contains a section entitled "Loan Terms," which includes a subsection for collateral, requesting information as to description, market value and existing liens.

Among the assets listed on the application were assets the DEBTOR presently owned and pledged to BankPlus, in addition to two items he intended to acquire using a portion of the proceeds of the loan.

On July 5, 2002, the DEBTOR executed an SBA form promissory note in the principal amount of $ 58,000 payable to the BANK. In addition to the note, the DEBTOR signed another document, in letter format, which provided:

> In consideration for Morton Community Bank granting a loan to Michael S. Sabol DBA Sound Farm Productions, the undersigned does hereby authorize Morton Community Bank to execute, file and record all financing statements, amendments, termination statements and all other statements authorized by Article 9 of the Illinois Uniform Commercial Code, as to any security interest in the loan or refinancing presently sought by the undersigned, as well as all loans, refinancing or workouts hereafter granted by Morton Community Bank to Michael S. Sabol DBA Sound Farm Productions.

On July 18, 2002, the BANK filed a standard form Uniform Commercial Code (UCC) financing statement, covering inventory, accounts receivable and equipment. The financing statement was not signed by the DEBTOR. No separate document entitled "***Security Agreement***" was signed by the DEBTOR.

Although he initially dealt with loan officer Will Thomas, the DEBTOR testified that when he went to the BANK to sign the loan documents, a different loan officer handled the closing. He did not recall any discussion about a ***security agreement*** or a security interest. The DEBTOR testified that he signed the documents in order to comply with the BANK'S requirements to obtain the loan. The proceeds of the loan were used for operating capital and to purchase additional equipment. The DEBTOR spent less than $ 20,000 for equipment, which he began to purchase shortly after he received the loan.

The DEBTOR and his wife, Rhonda K. Sabol, filed a joint petition for bankruptcy under Chapter 7 on February 14, 2005. They listed Morton Community Bank as a secured creditor, holding a security interest in "tools" valued at $ 12,410, with a total claim of $ 35,792.91. The DEBTOR filed an intent to surrender the "tools" to the BANK. The BANK filed a proof of claim, asserting a secured claim in the amount of $ 36,967.34. Contending that the BANK'S purported security interest never attached to the equipment, the TRUSTEE filed a report of possible assets, disclosing that he intended to administer the sound equipment as assets of the bankruptcy estate and brought this adversary complaint to determine the validity of the BANK'S lien.

At the trial, the DEBTOR testified concerning the loan transaction. The only other witness was Josh Graber, a representative of the BANK. Although Graber was employed by the BANK at the time the loan was made, he was not involved in the making of the loan to the DEBTOR. He testified that no ***security agreement*** was prepared for the loan in question, although the BANK typically used one for secured loans.

The TRUSTEE contends that the BANK does not have a valid purchase money security interest under Article 9 of the UCC, because there is no separate document captioned "***Security Agreement***" or any language in any other document explicitly granting a security interest. The BANK, relying on the "***Composite Document Rule***," contends that the loan application, the promissory note, the authorization and the financing statement, taken together, establish an agreement to create a ***security agreement***.

ANALYSIS

Generally, state law determines the nature and extent of the property rights in the debtor's assets. *See, e.g., Butner v. U.S.,* 440 U.S. 48, 54, 99 S. Ct. 914, 59 L. Ed. 2d 136 (1979). Under Illinois law, which governs the issue of whether the parties have entered into a valid ***security agreement***, a nonpossessory security interest does not attach and is not enforceable unless the debtor has authenticated a ***security agreement*** that contains a description of the collateral, value has been given, and the debtor has rights in the collateral. **[9–203(b)(3)(A)]**. A "***security agreement***" is defined as "an agreement that creates or provides for a security interest." **[9–102(a)(74)]**. A "security interest" is an interest in personal property or fixtures which secures payment or performance of an obligation. **[1–201(b)(35)]**. The requirement of a written ***security agreement*** is said to serve two purposes: the first being evidentiary in that it eliminates disputes as to what items are secured and the second in the nature of a statute of frauds, by precluding the enforcement of claims based only on an oral representation. *In re Outboard Marine Corp.,* 300 B.R. 308 (Bankr.N.D.Ill. 2003); *In re Owensboro Canning Co., Inc.,* 82 B.R. 450 (W.D.Ky. 1988); *In re Data Entry Service Corp.,* 81 B.R. 467 (Bankr.N.D.Ill. 1988). No particular words of grant or "magic words" are required to be included in a ***security agreement*** to create a security interest. *In re Krause,* 114 B.R. 582, 593 (Bankr.N.D.Ind. 1988). Notwithstanding the lenity of the ***Composite Document Rule***, there must be some language reflecting the debtor's intent to grant a security interest. Accordingly, a financing statement which does not contain any grant language by the debtor creating a security interest in the described collateral, but merely identifies the collateral, cannot substitute for a ***security agreement***.

Notwithstanding the statutory requirement of a signed or authenticated ***security agreement*** that describes the collateral, some courts have adopted a liberal view of what suffices to meet that requirement. Under the "***Composite Document Rule***," two or more documents in combination may qualify as a ***security agreement***. *In re Numeric Corp.*, 485 F.2d 1328, 1331 (1st Cir. 1973) (separate formal document entitled "***security agreement***" is not always necessary to satisfy the signed writing requirement of § 9–203). Whether and to what extent the ***Composite Document Rule*** applies is a question of state law. *Matter of Bollinger Corp.*, 614 F.2d 924 (3rd Çir. 1980) (Pennsylvania law). The Seventh Circuit Court of Appeals has affirmed a district court's holding that all of the documents constituting a transaction may be considered when analyzing whether an assignment, absolute on its face, was, in fact, intended as a ***security agreement***. *Wambach v. Randall*, 484 F.2d 572 (7th Cir. 1973).

Illinois law governs this dispute. The Illinois Supreme Court has not addressed whether the ***Composite Document Rule*** may be used to satisfy the ***security agreement*** requirement of **9–203(b)(3)(A)**. The only Illinois Appellate Court decision addressing the Rule is *Sears, Roebuck & Co. v. Conry*, 321 Ill.App.3d 997 (Ill.App. 3 Dist. 2001), a case in which a Sears credit card purchase was at issue. After having earlier opened the account by signing a credit card application that contained a ***security agreement***, the customer made credit card purchases and signed sales tickets describing the merchandise and containing language granting Sears a purchase money security interest in the purchased goods.[4] The form of ***security agreement*** was periodically updated by Sears by sending the cardholder the new form with no signature required. On the issue of whether Sears proved that it retained a purchase money security interest in the goods listed on the sales receipts, the court held as follows:

> In the instant case, the defendants signed Sears credit card sales receipts incorporating a ***security agreement*** by reference and granting Sears a security interest in the items purchased. By analogy with the cases cited above, the signed Sears credit card receipts satisfied the Illinois statutory requirement of a signed ***security agreement***.

Since the sales receipts, by themselves, satisfied the requirements of **9–203** of a signed writing describing the collateral and granting a security interest therein, *Conry* is not a true composite document case and, in this Court's view, has no application to the issue at bar. It thus appears that no Illinois court has approved or disapproved of the use of the ***Composite Document Rule***.

The pre-UCC era of chattel mortgages, and the technical and sometimes complex requirements associated therewith, fostered common law exceptions in the name of equity and pragmatism. Beginning in 1962,

---

[4]   Immediately above the customer's signature on the sales receipts was printed: "Purchased under my Sears account and ***security agreement***, incorporated by reference. I grant Sears a security interest in this merchandise until paid, unless prohibited by law." 321 Ill.App.3d at 999.

however, the UCC ushered in a new, simplified regime for documenting and perfecting secured transactions. Because the UCC reduces to an absolute minimum the formal requirements for the creation of a security interest, the need for those equitable exceptions no longer exists. In the interests of certainty and maintaining some identifiable standard, it is important to enforce the minimal formal requirements set forth in Article 9 of the UCC. Thus, an argument can be made that strict rather than liberal interpretation of the UCC documentation requirements is more consistent with the overall purpose of the UCC to create certainty and reliability in commercial transactions. Other courts have applied the **_Composite Document Rule_** narrowly. *See, In re Dean & Jean Fashions, Inc.*, 329 F.Supp. 663 (W.D.Okla. 1971).

The BANK relies upon the DEBTOR'S testimony that he understood that by signing the loan documents that he was granting the BANK a security interest in the equipment that he was going to purchase, as reflected in his treatment of the BANK as a secured creditor in his bankruptcy schedules. The BANK also relies on the itemization of collateral on the loan application, the provision in the note regarding the BANK'S rights in "collateral" and its rights upon default, the debtor's authorization and the description of the collateral in the financing statement. The BANK'S reliance on the listing of collateral under the description of loan terms on its application for the SBA guarantee reveals nothing about the DEBTOR'S intent to grant a security interest. The application consists of two separate portions: one completed by the DEBTOR and one completed by the BANK. The listing of the collateral appears on the BANK'S portion of the document. That page was completed by officers of the BANK and is dated one week after the DEBTOR'S signature on his application for the loan.

The BANK points to the provisions of the note which describe, generically, the BANK'S rights in collateral and upon default. The note defines "Collateral" as "any property taken as security for payment of this Note." Upon default, the note authorizes the BANK to "take possession of any Collateral" and to "sell, lease, or otherwise dispose of any Collateral." The note also provides that the BANK may: "bid on or buy the Collateral at its sale;" "preserve or dispose of the Collateral;" "compromise, release, renew, extend or substitute any of the Collateral;" and "take any action necessary to protect the Collateral." The note does not identify the collateral. In fact, the note itself contemplates a separate **_security agreement_**. Under the heading of general provisions, the note provides that "Borrower must sign all documents necessary at any time to comply with the Loan Documents and to enable Lender to acquire, perfect, or maintain Lender's liens on Collateral."

The DEBTOR'S authorization for the BANK to file a financing statement is equally inefficacious. It authorizes that filing "as to any security interest in the loan . . . presently sought by the [DEBTOR]." *In re Numeric Corp.,* 485 F.2d 1328 (1st Cir. 1973), relied on by the BANK, is distinguishable. In *Numeric,* although the parties had not signed a formal ***security agreement***, the board of directors of the debtor authorized the preparation of a UCC financing statement to cover the creditor's security interest in certain equipment described in a bill of sale.[6] Finding that the directors' resolution established "an agreement in fact" by the parties to create a security interest, the court held that the resolution, taken with the financing statement's itemization of the collateral, constituted a ***security agreement***.

The BANK also relies on its UCC–1 financing statement. The financing statement, as permitted by the Revised UCC, was not signed by the DEBTOR. The financing statement was not filed by the BANK until July 18, 2001, almost two weeks after the loan was closed. No one from the BANK testified that the financing statement was presented to the DEBTOR at the time that he signed the document authorizing its filing. The DEBTOR'S testimony that a security interest was not discussed contradicts any suggestion that the financing statement was presented to the DEBTOR at or prior to the loan closing. This Court will not presume that a financing statement, not shown to be contemporaneous, has any part to play in the ***Composite Document Rule***.

In re Data Entry Service Corp., supra, a case involving an SBA loan, relied on by the BANK, is factually distinguishable. In that case, in addition to the note, the debtor signed a Loan Agreement which listed as collateral, first liens on machinery, equipment, furniture and fixtures, inventory, accounts and general intangibles. Directly above the debtor's signature, at the end of the document, the Agreement provided that the debtor agreed to the conditions imposed. In addition, two financing statements describing the collateral were filed with the Secretary of State, each signed by the debtor. The court determined that the Loan Agreement, by itself or in conjunction with the signed financing statements, was sufficient to create a security interest in favor of the SBA.

A similar result was reached in *In re Maddox*, 92 B.R. 707 (Bankr.W.D.Tex. 1988), another SBA-guaranteed loan case. As in *Data Entry,* the debtor had signed a loan agreement which identified collateral under "Terms of the Loan" as a "first lien on all equipment, inventory and accounts receivable." The court's decision in *In re Tracy's Flowers and Gifts,*

---

[6]   The resolution in *Numeric* provided:

That the Clerk of the corporation prepare standard form, Uniform Commercial Code financing statements on behalf of the corporation as debtor, to Russell Blank, as the secured party, in such manner and form as to cover Russell Blank's security interest in the property of this corporation as set forth in a Bill of Sale dated March 2, 1962, from said Russell Blank to the corporation, and as hereafter acquired, and as evidence of his security interest in the same.

485 F.2d at 1329.

Inc., 264 B.R. 1 (Bankr.W.D.Ark. 2001), highlights the weakness of the BANK'S position. Recognizing that a "bare bones" financing statement, standing alone, cannot double as a "***security agreement***," the court held that the following additional language included in the creditor's UCC–1, qualified as a ***security agreement***:

> This note is secured by all accounts, inventory and equipment now owned or hereafter acquired by [the debtor] . . . . The loan secured by this lien was made under [a SBA] nationwide program. . . .

264 B.R. at 2.

Whether considered alone or in combination, this Court finds that there is not sufficient evidence of the DEBTOR'S intent to create a security interest in the documents relied on by the BANK. No language conveying a security interest to the BANK is found in any of the documents. There is no evidence that the DEBTOR read or reviewed, much less agreed to, the "loan terms" contained in the BANK'S application to the SBA. The financing statement, containing the only description of collateral, is not signed by the DEBTOR and, in all likelihood, was never seen by him. What is left? Only boilerplate references in the note to the BANK'S rights in "any collateral" and in the authorization to "any security interest."

Had the BANK'S application for SBA guarantee, which listed the collateral, been signed by the DEBTOR, the minimal requirements of **9–203** may well have been satisfied. But without a description of the collateral in a signed or authenticated document or in a separate document incorporated by reference into a signed or authenticated document, no security interest can be recognized. This Court is of the view that the ***Composite Document Rule*** is most appropriately used, if at all, to allow the debtor's intent to grant a security interest to be demonstrated by reference to the various loan documents where the debtor has signed or authenticated a document containing a description of the collateral that does not contain words of grant. The Rule should not be applied, however, to bypass the necessity of a signed or authenticated writing that describes the collateral, as that is the clearly stated minimum requirement of **9–203**.

Even though the BANK may have intended that there was to be a security interest, the Court does not view the result reached as unduly harsh. The primary purpose of Article 9 of the UCC was to create uniformity and certainty in commercial transactions. The steps required to be taken by secured parties to establish and protect their interests, having been reduced to a minimum, are simple and clearly laid out. It is not unreasonable to require that they be complied with.

The TRUSTEE objected to the BANK'S proof of claim filed as secured in the amount of $ 36,967.34 on the basis that the BANK had no valid security interest. Having now obtained that determination, the objection should be allowed, the BANK should be denied any secured claim, but should be allowed an unsecured claim in the amount stated in its claim.

————————

So what is the result for the creditor in the case above? This is a bankruptcy case, so if the collateral value was equal to or greater than the amount owed to the bank, the bank would have bee paid in full *if* the loan had been properly documented. In *Sabol,* the value of the collateral was $12,401 and the bank filed a proof of claim for $36,967.34. *See* **BC 501**. If the loan had been properly documented, the Bank's claim in bankruptcy would have been bifurcated into two claims, a secured claim in the amount of the collateral value, which would have been paid in full, and an unsecured claim for the remainder, which would have shared the value of available assets *pro rata* with the other unsecured claims. *See* **BC 502, 506**. Because the bank in *Sabol* did not properly document the loan and its composite document rule argument was unsuccessful, it was treated in bankruptcy as an unsecured creditor and thus likely received only a small portion of what it was owed before bankruptcy.

The idea behind the composite document rule is that in the absence of a signed security agreement, several documents taken together can satisfy the security agreement requirement for attachment. As you saw in *Sabol,* courts differ as to what is required. To make a successful argument based on the composite document rule, a creditor must show the debtor's signature, the debtor's intent to grant a security interest, and a collateral description. There must also be evidence that all of the documents were executed in connection with the same transaction.

As you digest the composite document rule, remember that the security agreement and the financing statement serve two different functions. As explained by the court in *Bank of America v. Outboard Marine Corp. (In re Outboard Marine Corp.),* 300 B.R. 308 (Bankr. N.D. Ill. 2003),

> The formal requirement that a security agreement must be in writing is in the nature of the statute of frauds. *Little v. County of Orange,* 31 N.C. App. 495, 229 S.E.2d 823, 825 (N.C. App. Ct. 1976) (citing **9–203**, Official Comment 5); *Harden v. Maroon (In re Murray Bros., Inc.),* 53 B.R. 281, 283 (Bankr. E.D.N.C. 1985). That is, the signed-writing requirement prevents the enforcement of claims based on entirely oral representations. *Blank v. Numeric Corp. (In re Numeric Corp.),* 485 F.2d 1328, 1331 (1st Cir. 1973) (citation omitted). " 'When bankruptcy occurs[,] the anti-fraud function of the written security agreement serves mostly to protect third-party creditors.' " *Murray Bros.,* 53 B.R. at 283, *quoting* J. White & R. Summers, *Handbook of the Law Under the Uniform Commercial Code,* § 23–3, at 903 (2d ed. 1980); [**9–203**],

Amended Official Comment 5. The security agreement also serves an evidentiary function in order to foreclose the possibility of disputes as to exactly which items of property are covered by a security interest. *Numeric*, 485 F.2d at 1331 (citation omitted); *Equibank v. H. L. Clement Co. (In re H. L. Clement Co.)*, 12 B.R. 165, 168 (Bankr. W.D. Penn. 1981) (citation omitted).

In contrast, a financing statement merely notifies the public that a security interest might exist in the listed collateral. *Bollinger*, 614 F.2d at 926; *Rice v. Citizens First Bank of Fordyce (In re Cheqnet Sys., Inc.)*, 227 B.R. 166, 169 (Bankr. E.D. Ark. 1998) (noting that the financing statement is "a mere notice document"); *H. L. Clement Co.*, 12 B.R. at 168 (citation omitted); *Zoltanski v. Prod. Credit Assoc. (In re Hite)*, 4 B.R. 547, 549 (Bankr. N.D. Ohio 1980) (citation omitted) (observing that "the policy behind the financing statement requirement is clearly that of notice filing."); *Mountain Farm Credit Serv. v. Purina Mills, Inc.*, 119 N.C. App. 508, 459 S.E.2d 75, 80 (N.C. App. Ct. 1995) (finding that a financing statement serves to "provide notice to third parties of the debtor-creditor relationship").

Before 2001, Article 9 required that a debtor sign a financing statement. Therefore, you will come across cases in which a secured party argued that a financing statement, standing alone, can serve as a security agreement. That argument does not work anymore because debtors so not sign financing statements. That is why there is another document in the *Sabol* case, an authorization to file a financing statement. *See* **9–509(a)**. More on this in Chapter 14.

Chapter Conclusion: After reading this chapter, you should understand that a security interest is enforceable once it has attached and you should be familiar with the requirements for attachment. You should also understand the requirements for a valid security agreement and the concepts of after-acquired property and proceeds.

PROBLEMS

1.   You are representing First Bank, which is making a loan to the sports media conglomerate All Sports Network ("ASN"). ASN has a broadcast license issued by the Federal Communications Commission. ASN also owns a bar/restaurant, the ASN Café, in San Diego, California. First Bank wants to know if it can get a security interest in the broadcast license and the liquor license, and also wants to know if it can foreclose on the licenses if ASN defaults on the loan. What information do you need about California law in order to answer your client's questions?

2.   WeSellItAll, Inc. is borrowing $5,000,000 from First Bank. It is signing a security agreement that contains the granting clause and collateral description on pp. 523–524. Please determine whether the following assets are

covered by the security agreement, and explain which definition applies to each asset. If the item falls into the category of "goods," please identify the subcategory of goods that best defines the item.

a. The desks, desk chairs, and computers located in the WeSellItAll headquarters.

b. The SuperErgo ergonomic desk chairs that WeSellItAll sells. There are 50 of them in the company's warehouse waiting for a buyer.

c. The paper and pens that the employees at the WeSellItAll headquarters use in their daily business.

d. WeSellItAll sold 25 Bluetooth speakers to the Mountaintop Resort and the Mountaintop Resort agreed to pay for them 30 days after delivery. Does First Bank have a security interest in this payment right? If so, which collateral category describes it?

e. The WeSellItAll trademark.

f. WeSellItAll sells snowmobiles and has a snowmobile financing program whereby it sells snowmobiles to customers on credit and retains a security interest in the sold snowmobile to secure the purchase price. Each time it sells a snowmobile, WeSellItAll receives a signed security agreement describing the snowmobile and a promissory note in which the buyer promises to pay the remainder of the purchase price. Does the agreement grant First Bank a security interest in these promissory notes and security agreements? Under which category of collateral?

g. WeSellItAll's checking account at Second Bank.

h. WeSellItAll took payment for a snowmobile by check. The check is now on the desk of the Chief Financial Officer.

i. WeSellItAll has sued its former insurance broker, Ally Assured, for professional negligence after WeSellItAll lost $1,000,000 worth of inventory in a fire in one of its warehouses. Because Ms. Assured failed to place insurance coverage on the building, WeSellItAll's insurance company denied coverage for the fire. Does the above description cover WeSellItAll's claim against Ms. Assured? If not, what should be added to the description?

Are you concerned at all about the effectiveness of description (xv): "all other personal and fixture property of every kind and nature?"

3. Daniela has filed for bankruptcy. You are representing BigBuy Electronics, which claims to have a purchase money security interest in her $3,000 stereo system. Daniela charged the system on her BigBuy Charge Card. She had opened her charge account by filling out a form on the BigBuy web site. Daniela was required to click her agreement to the BigBuy Credit Terms in order to open her account. The Credit Terms contain the following statement: "Cardholder hereby grants a security interest in all merchandise purchased with this card."

a.   How are you going to support your argument that BigBuy has a security interest in the stereo system?

b.   Take the Trustee in Bankruptcy's side. How are you going to support your argument that BigBuy has no interest in the stereo system?

c.   BigBuy's credit officer has asked you to help BigBuy avoid disputes like this in the future in the most cost-effective way possible. What can BigBuy do to ensure that its security interests survive the scrutiny of bankruptcy judges across the country?

4.   Imagine that Kevin in the example on p. 535 deposits Catherine's $8,000 check in his checking account at Riverside Bank. The checking account contained $3,000 on October 1, the date that Kevin deposited the check. Below are the transactions that Kevin entered into between October 1 and November 1, the date that Riverside Bank found out about the sale and sought the proceeds of the transaction.

10/1 balance	$3,000
10/1 deposit	$8,000
10/5 Mortgage payment	$2,000
10/15 Bicycle Purchase	$3,000
10/25 Deposit	$2,000

a.   Applying the lowest intermediate balance rule, how much of the funds in Kevin's Riverside Bank account can Auto Finance claim as proceeds?

b.   Kevin made his mortgage payment to Central Mortgage Co. Can Auto Finance pursue Central Mortgage Co. for the money? Can Auto Finance claim Kevin's new bicycle as proceeds? See 9–102(a)(12); 9–102(a)(64); 9–332.

5.   Your client Valley Bank is making a loan to Bike and Paddle World (BPW), a bicycle, kayak, and stand-up paddleboard dealer. Valley Bank's loan will be secured by all of BPW's inventory. You have read the tracing cases, and as someone who went to law school because you are bad at math, the cases make your head explode.

a.   Can you suggest a way to ensure that all of the money that BPW receives for its inventory remains identifiable proceeds?

b.   You have also required that BPW obtain insurance on all of its inventory. If BPW's inventory is destroyed in a fire, does your client have the right to the insurance proceeds? How can you make sure that your client gets the money from the insurance company?

6.   The court in *In re Wallman* criticized the secured creditor for making a weak argument that the proceeds of the 1986 wheat crop were proceeds to which its lien attached.

Imagine that you are the lawyer for the FmHA. How could you make a better argument that your security interest extended to those proceeds, even in bankruptcy? What facts would you need to show?

7.   Your client Commercial Bank made a $1,000,000 loan to Smart Home Goods, Inc., secured by the equipment it uses to manufacture kitchen appliances that are connected to the internet. Smart Home Goods, Inc. recently filed for bankruptcy after a series of scathing news articles alleging that the company misused customer data. In preparing to file Commercial Bank's proof of claim form, you have collected all of the documents that were signed and filed in connection with the loan. Here is what you have found: 1) a promissory note signed by the debtor that contains the statement "this Note is secured by the security interest in collateral described in the Security Agreement of even date herewith between Commercial Bank and Smart Home Goods, Inc.;" 2) an "Authorization to File Financing Statement" signed by the debtor which authorizes Commercial Bank to "file all necessary financing statements in connection with the loan to Smart Home Goods, Inc.;"; 3) a Security Agreement signed by the debtor in which the debtor "grants a security interest in the collateral described in Schedule A;" 4) a filed Financing Statement that describes the collateral as "equipment;" and 5) a corporate resolution by the board of directors of Smart Home Goods, Inc. that authorizes the corporation to obtain a secured loan from Commercial Bank secured by the equipment it uses to manufacture smart kitchen appliances. There was no Schedule A attached to the Security Agreement and you cannot find the schedule in your files.

Does your client have a secured claim in the Smart Home Goods bankruptcy?

CHAPTER 13

DEFAULT AND ENFORCEMENT OF SECURITY INTERESTS

■ ■ ■

Now that you know how to create a security interest, we move to default and enforcement. It is important to know that a security interest is enforceable upon attachment and that no public notice is required for enforceability. Public notice is necessary to establish priority, not effectiveness of a security interest.

You can find Article 9's enforcement rules in Part 6, **9–601** *et seq.* Read **9–601(a)**. Note that although default triggers the secured party's enforcement rights, you will not find a definition of default anywhere in the UCC. The first part of this chapter will therefore explore the concept of default.

The chart below outlines the process from default to foreclosure.

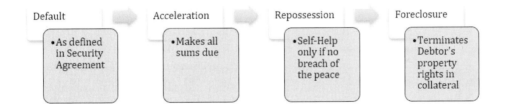

A. WHAT IS A DEFAULT?

Consider the following language from the ABA Model Security Agreement (Streamlined):

> **Events of Default.** Any of the following events or conditions will be an **"Event of Default"** hereunder: (a) Debtor fails to make any (i) scheduled principal or interest payment under the Note as and when due, or (ii) payment due under any Loan Document (other than the payments set forth in clause (i)) within 5 days after Debtor's receipt of written notice of nonpayment from Secured Party; (b) Debtor fails to *materially* perform any other *material* covenant in this Agreement or any other Loan Document and such failure continues uncured for 10 days after Debtor's receipt of written notice specifying such failure; (c) any representation or warranty made by Debtor in connection with this Agreement is

false or misleading in any material respect when made or deemed made; (d) Debtor shall become a debtor under applicable federal or state bankruptcy or insolvency laws, or a custodian (as defined in the Bankruptcy Code), receiver, receiver-manager, trustee or monitor is appointed for, or takes charge of, all or substantially all of the property of the Debtor; (e) Debtor suffers any appointment of any custodian, receiver, receiver-manager, trustee, monitor or the like for it or any substantial part of its property to continue undischarged or unstayed for a period of 60 days; (f) any event occurs that permits any of the Debtor's other creditors to accelerate the maturity of the Debtor's indebtedness in an amount in excess of [$] to such creditor; and (g) any of the Loan Documents ceases to be in full force and effect or the security interests granted pursuant to this Agreement cease to be valid, enforceable, perfected and first priority liens [*(subject to Permitted Liens)*] on the Collateral; then, the Secured Party may, without demand, notice or legal process of any kind, declare the Obligations [(including all accrued and unpaid interest thereon and all other amounts due hereunder [*and under the other Loan Documents)*] to be due and payable, whereupon the Obligations shall become, immediately due and payable; <u>provided</u>, <u>however</u>, that upon the occurrence of any Event of Default specified in clause (e) or (f) of this paragraph, the Obligations shall automatically become due and payable.

FORMS UNDER ARTICLE 9 OF THE UCC, THIRD EDITION (CINDY J. CHERNUCHIN, ED. 2016)

Note that although many people think of default to mean only non-payment, many other occurrences can also be defaults. You will understand why the parties (the secured party most likely) included some of the above occurrences in the definition of default after you have completed the chapters on perfection and priorities. We can place defaults into three general categories: occurrences that negatively affect the secured party's chances of repayment; occurrences that have a negative impact on the value of the collateral; and occurrences that impair the secured party's priority.

As you read the language quoted above, it may be obvious to you which defaults relate to the secured party's chances of repayment. Default (a) makes failure to pay the loan that is secured by the agreement a default (if the obligor has missed a payment the creditor's chances of repayment are certainly impaired). Defaults (d), (e), and (f) place the debtor in default when its financial condition significantly deteriorates.

Where do we find the other types of defaults? Take another look at default (b) above and then read the paragraph below from the same model document.

Debtor's Covenants. Until the Obligations have been paid in full, Debtor shall (a) keep the Collateral free from any effective liens, security interests, claims or encumbrances [*(other than Permitted Liens)*]; (b) to the extent deemed prudent business conduct (to be determined by Debtor in its reasonable discretion), maintain the Collateral in good order and repair; (c) [*other than to the extent reasonably likely to cause a material adverse effect,*] use the Collateral in accordance with all laws, regulations and orders, and safeguard and protect all Collateral; (d) [*other than in the ordinary course of business,*] [*other than as permitted by the Note*] [*other than sales or other dispositions of goods consistent with prudent business practices as determined by Debtor in good faith*] not sell, lease, license, transfer or dispose of any of the Collateral (except for sales or leases of inventory or licenses of general intangibles in the ordinary course of business); (e) promptly advise Secured Party of any event or circumstance that can reasonably be expected to have a material adverse effect on the Collateral; (f) to the extent not being contested by Debtor in good faith, pay when due all taxes and similar obligations that might result in a lien on the Collateral if not paid; (g) execute additional documents and take such other actions (at Debtor's expense) as Secured Party may reasonably request from time to time to implement or evidence the terms of this Agreement; (h) on or before the anniversary of the date hereof Debtor shall deliver to Secured Party an updated Perfection Certificate or confirmation that there has been no change in any such information since the later of (1) the date hereof or (2) the most recent anniversary of the date hereof; and (i) *promptly* notify Secured Party upon any change in the information set forth on the Perfection Certificate including (1) any change in Debtor's name, location or mailing address and (2) the acquisition of any commercial tort claim, letter-of-credit right, instrument, negotiable document, chattel paper, goods covered by certificate of title, intellectual property, investment property or deposit account, in case individually valued in excess of $[ ] or collectively valued in excess of $[ ], and promptly upon such change or acquisition, take all steps necessary, advisable or requested by Secured Party to create and/or preserve continuously the perfection and priority of Secured Party's security interests in the Collateral.

As you will learn in this chapter, when an obligor (who may or may not also be the Debtor, *see* **9–102(a)(28)**, **(59)**) defaults on its obligations to the Secured Party, the Secured Party has the right to sell the collateral to satisfy the debt owed to it. That's why the Debtor is in default if it sells the collateral without authorization or if it fails to keep the collateral in good repair. The above paragraph contains several references to a Perfection

Certificate. We'll talk about the information that a Debtor provides in that document in the next chapter. For now it is sufficient to know that in order to perfect a security interest the Secured Party must file a notice in a public place of its interest in the collateral. Article 9 contains requirements for the contents of that notice, and if the Secured Party does not comply with those requirements, the notice will be ineffective to give the Secured Party priority over other creditors, buyers, and the Trustee in Bankruptcy. As a result, if the Debtor moves or changes its name without telling the Secured Party, the Secured Party is at risk of losing its priority in the collateral.

Lenders can't think of everything so the UCC lends its imprimatur to the "deems itself insecure" clause. The default clause above does not have one; such a clause allows a secured party to accelerate the loan if it deems itself insecure in the possibility of repayment. *See* **1–309**. Note carefully what the "deems itself insecure" clause allows a secured party to do. The case excerpt below explains, and it also explains the parties' leeway in defining defaults:

CHORCHES V. OGDEN (IN RE BOLIN & CO., LLC)

437 B.R. 731 (D. Conn. 2010)

UNDERHILL, J.

This case arises from the bankruptcy of Bolin & Company, LLC ("Bolin"), a jewelry retailer in Greenwich, Connecticut. It concerns actions the defendant, Sally Ogden, took during the week of July 30, 2004 that the plaintiff claims to have precipitated Bolin's bankruptcy.

* * *

On April 30, 2007, the plaintiff, the Chapter 7 bankruptcy trustee for Bolin's estate commenced this lawsuit in the United States Bankruptcy Court for the District of Connecticut as an adversary proceeding against Ogden and Shannon Howey, a former Bolin employee.

* * *

1. *Bolin's history before July 26, 2004*

a. Bolin's origins

Andrea Ulanoff and her partner, Noah Citrin, opened Bolin in 2000 as a retail shop for antique, custom, and unusual or niche pieces of jewelry. Ulanoff, a former advertising and marketing professional, was to be responsible for the business and management sides of the store, and Citrin, a jeweler by trade, was to be responsible for the design and repair of the store's jewelry. In August 2000, Andrea Ulanoff registered Bolin as a Connecticut limited liability company in which she was the only principal.

* * *

From 2001 to 2002, Bolin's sales traced the arc of the national economy: business ground to a near halt following September 11, 2001—the store reported a net loss for 2001—and rebounded as the market recovered. Despite increasing sales in 2002, however, Bolin faced significant management problems. Ulanoff had trouble establishing relationships with jewelry vendors and adjusting to the business practices of the jewelry industry. Ulanoff also struggled to keep adequate records of the items she was receiving in inventory and the sales that Bolin was making. Although Bolin had an electronic inventory system for its jewelry, Ulanoff failed to update it consistently.

Finally, Bolin had significant cash-flow difficulties. Ulanoff often bought jewelry with a series of post-dated checks, each reflecting partial payment, for vendors to deposit over time once each check's date had passed. In effect, Ulanoff was buying jewelry on credit, and would pay vendors in installments after receiving their jewelry. Ulanoff's post-dated checks bounced frequently, however. Indeed, Bolin's habit of bouncing checks continued until it went out of business in 2004; Bolin bounced 660 checks, including paychecks to its employees, between April 2003 and July 2004, amassing more than $12,000 in overdraft fees.

* * *

Several parties won judgments for unpaid debts against Bolin between 2002 and 2004. The New York Times Company won a judgment of $6,400 against Bolin on October 18, 2002; Walter Bernd won a judgment of $3,535 against the store on October 21, 2003; Albert Tsang Jewelry Design Ltd. won a judgment of $18,112.39 against the store on June 28, 2004; and Wartski, Ltd. won a judgment of $13,092.44 on August 16, 2004. Besides those judgments, it was common for vendors to call Bolin to complain about not being paid. Joan Goss, another Bolin part-time worker, testified that she quit her job in February 2004 because she felt constantly harassed by phone calls from unhappy and unpaid vendors.

b. Sally Ogden's involvement in Bolin

Because of those problems, Ulanoff became interested in finding another principal for Bolin. That potential partner was Sally Ogden, the defendant in this case. Ogden, a Greenwich homemaker, had been a frequent customer at Bolin beginning in 2001. Ulanoff knew her from her visits to the store and from conversations they had while Ogden was shopping; the two developed a friendship based on their interactions in the store.

* * *

Ogden loaned $270,000 to Bolin in July 2002. That loan was to help Bolin with its business; Ogden did not intend it as an equity investment in Bolin.

* * *

In late 2002, Ogden's $270,000 loan to Bolin was memorialized in a promissory note and secured by a security agreement. The terms of the promissory note and security agreement differ in several ways. Most significantly for the purposes of this case are their terms concerning default and Ogden's rights to repayment. The promissory note permits Ogden to make a demand for repayment for the full sum whenever she wants. The note grants Bolin five days to repay; it is only after the five-day period has expired that Bolin defaults. The promissory note includes no prescription about how Ogden, as creditor, is to recover collateral in the event of Bolin's default. The security agreement, on the other hand, affords Ogden much greater rights with respect to demanding payment and remedying a default. First, the security agreement's definition of default is more inclusive than the promissory note. Under the promissory note's terms, default only occurs when Bolin, the debtor, fails to meet Ogden's demand for payment. But section 8 of the security agreement defines a default as occurring because of, *inter alia*, any of the following conditions:

> [F]ailure of any Obligor . . . to pay when due (whether by acceleration or otherwise), any amount payable on any of the obligations, . . . loss, theft, substantial damage, destruction, sale, or encumbrance to or of any of the Collateral, or the making of any levy, seizure, or attachment thereof or thereon . . . the entry of a judgment against any Obligor . . . [or] the dissolution, incompetence, consolidation, or reorganization of any obligor.

Section 9 of the security agreement then explains what Ogden, as the secured creditor, is entitled to do "[u]pon the occurrence of any such default" and, even in absence of an actual default by Bolin, "whenever Secured Party feels insecure for any reason whatsoever." In either of these events, the security agreement empowers Ogden to "declare all Obligations of each Debtor to Secured Party immediately due and payable without demand or notice of any kind." If a default occurs, Ogden has "the remedies of a secured party under the Uniform Commercial Code of Connecticut and any and all rights and remedies available to it under any other applicable law," and Bolin must, if Ogden so requests, "assemble the Collateral and made [sic] it available to Secured Party at a convenient place acceptable to Secured party."

Finally, section 9 of the security agreement states that "[i]n connection with the exercise of any rights available upon default, Secured Party or its agent may enter upon the premises of Debtor and Debtor expressly waives any and all claims for damage, trespass, or other injury occassioned thereby." As the secured creditor, Ogden is only obligated to give reasonable notice if she were to sell or otherwise dispose of the collateral she repossessed. The security agreement imposed no duty on Ogden to notify Bolin before repossessing collateral.

* * *

Santiago [the bookkeeper] faced problems collecting and entering data about Bolin's past cash sales from the store's receipts and account records. Although credit card transactions were well recorded, the cash transactions for jewelry often lacked documentation and did not correspond to credited and debited payments in the store's electronic inventory system. Santiago entered the data into his bookkeeping system by assuming that cash deposits in Bolin's accounts were payments from jewelry sales, and not loans. In the course of his investigation of Bolin's financial records, Santiago found many records that were unmarked or unexplained; those numbers were collected in a "garbage account" that Santiago created in the course of reviewing and entering the store's data. By the end of his accounting for 2003, there was well over $1 million in credited and debited entries in this garbage account. Santiago also observed that the credited sales totals he identified were greater than the sales totals identified in the electronic inventory system that Bolin had reported in its tax returns for 2000 and 2001; in other words, Bolin's accounting records revealed more cash coming into the store than did Bolin's electronic inventory system. Finally, he noted that Bolin regularly bounced checks and had liquidity problems.

In order to address the inconsistencies between Bolin's accounting and inventory data, Santiago recommended that Bolin take a physical inventory of its jewelry. In a fax sent to Ulanoff in November 2002, Santiago said that his bookkeeping would be "meaningless" without taking physical stock of the items in Bolin's possession. Santiago was never able to perform such an inventory, however. Ulanoff never made time for him to physically sort through the store's jewelry. Although she never gave Santiago a reason for why she did not want Bolin's jewelry to be properly inventoried, Santiago testified that she seemed reluctant to have a physical inventory taken.

After Santiago completed Bolin's electronic inventory system, Dubiago [the accountant] reviewed Bolin's financial records and produced Bolin's sales tax returns. Santiago informed Dubiago that the quality of the data was suspect, but was sufficiently credible to serve as the basis for the store's tax returns. In filing the tax returns, Dubiago, like Santiago, noticed glaring inconsistencies between Bolin's electronic inventory system and the store's accounting books. For instance, for the 2003 fiscal year, Dubiago found that there was $1,321,358.45 of debited store inventory in Bolin's electronic inventory system, but only $721,236.98 for debited entries in the company's accounting records. Dubiago had to adjust the sales tax return by more than $600,000 in order to bridge this gap in the amount of the store's claimed spending for the year.

By producing Bolin's tax returns, Dubiago learned that the store was failing.

* * *

c.   Bolin's pawning activity

Throughout its existence, Bolin had major problems with its cash flow. In order to increase Bolin's liquidity and free enough cash for payments owed to jewelers, the store's short-term expenses, and even their own compensation, Ulanoff and Citrin frequently pawned the store's jewelry, including its pieces held on consignment. Ulanoff believed that pawning inventory was a common business practice in the jewelry business. Furthermore, she claims that a number of her vendors were aware that she pawned jewelry in Bolin's possession in order to increase the store's cash flow, and that those vendors acquiesced in this practice. There is no other evidence to support those contentions, however. Bolin's pawning tended to increase in the summer, when sales were at their lowest; spikes in pawning activity also correlated with the periods when Ulanoff was unable to borrow funds from other sources.

By July 2004, Bolin was pawning consigned jewelry two to three times every week. Their pawnbrokers of choice were the Provident Loan Society ("Provident"), 48th Street Pawnbrokers ("48th Street"), and G. Modell, Incorporated ("Modell"), of all of which were based in New York City. Each time Ulanoff and Citrin pawned a piece of jewelry, they received a receipt that stated the item that had been pawned, the terms and conditions of its redemption, and the amount of time that Bolin had to redeem the item before the pawnbroker auctioned it. Those receipts are referred to as "pawn tickets." Shannon Howey was responsible for tracking and accounting for the jewels that were pawned and the cash that Bolin received as loans from pawnbrokers. Although Howey never testified at trial, the testimony of others, such as Nick Dubiago and Peter Santiago, suggests that Howey designated the cash loans as payments in the store's accounts, and thus treated the pawned jewelry as if it had been sold and not put up as collateral for loans. But Howey did not remove the pawned jewelry from the store's internal inventory system; according to Ulanoff, the inventory system did not include a field that permitted Howey to designate whether an item belonging to Bolin had been lent out of the store. That accounting explains why the credited payments in Santiago's bookkeeping system reflected greater payments than represented in the inventory system—in Bolin's accounting, the loans were treated as cash payments for pieces, while the electronic inventory system continued to treat the items as if they had not been sold but were in Bolin's possession. As a result, Bolin's accounts overstated the store's sales and understated its liabilities, and Bolin's inventories of the jewels in its possession were inaccurate.

* * *

2. *Bolin's closing*

On Friday, July 23, 2004, Andrea Ulanoff and Noah Citrin flew to Italy for a two-week vacation and to look for jewelry to buy for Bolin. That day, prior to leaving for Italy, Ulanoff was busy at the store contacting customers and vendors to pick up jewelry, and paying bills that were outstanding or coming due. Also in the store were [employees] Shannon Howey and Kathleen Raby.

* * *

On Wednesday, July 28, Ogden came to Bolin to collect jeweled clips that were being repaired by Citrin. Howey let her in and permitted her to search the store for the clips; Howey also looked for the clips but did not find them. Howey told Ogden that they may have fallen in the store's "black hole," a euphemism for being pawned. Howey then told Ogden about Ulanoff's pawning, the vendors who were calling about late payments, and the store's empty and overdrawn bank accounts. Ogden, who was already aware of Bolin's pawning habit, believed that Bolin's demise was imminent and became worried not only for her clips but for the security of her loan. At about 3:15 that afternoon, Ogden called [her attorney] Brian O'Connor at his office out of concern that Bolin was failing and that her loans were unprotected. O'Connor told Ogden that she was a secured creditor and had rights in the collateral, but cautioned that he had not reviewed her file recently and did not remember what her exact rights were. Following her call with O'Connor, Ogden asked Howey to pack the Bolin-owned jewelry. At Ogden's direction, Howey also went about creating an inventory of all of the store-owned jewelry she was packing. Ogden then left the store.

* * *

Brian O'Connor spoke with Ogden on July 30 to follow up on their discussion of the security of Ogden's loan to Bolin. O'Connor reported to Ogden what he found in conducting his UCC search and said that he had located a promissory note entitling her to collateral in the event of default. The promissory note he uncovered was for $500,000, and was not the correct, amended $270,000 note. He also advised her that the promissory note defined default as Bolin's failure to pay Ogden within five days of receiving notice that payment was due. O'Connor told Ogden that only after the five days had expired could she repossess collateral in order to secure her loan.

O'Connor counseled Ogden to be careful to take actions consistent with being Bolin's creditor, and not the store's manager or owner; furthermore, he advised Ogden not to remove anything from the store until the five-day waiting period had expired. O'Connor did not tell Ogden anything about returning items to vendors or creditors. He also said that if she repossessed any items from the store, she should take an independent inventory with a witness present.

* * *

At the end of the day of July 30, Howey and Ogden arranged the jewelry in the store that had not been claimed by or returned to vendors. Ogden asked Howey to separate the store-owned jewelry from the pieces Bolin held on consignment. Howey placed the jewelry she identified as store-owned in thirteen envelopes and inventoried them; together, the jewelry was worth $607,645.60 at cost. Neither Howey nor Ogden photographed this jewelry or took other steps to document it. Ogden also took the store's two computers and several books from the store's shelves. Ogden took the jewels and Bolin property to her Greenwich home and placed them in her bedroom, where she had left the pawn tickets the night before. She placed as many jewels as she could in her personal safe.

* * *

B.   Conclusions of Law

The Bankruptcy Trustee alleges the following causes of action against Sally Ogden: . . . wrongful repossession of Bolin's property in violation of the security agreement,[8]

* * *

2.   *Claims arising from Ogden's repossession of Bolin jewelry*

The Bankruptcy Trustee next alleges several causes of action against Sally Ogden for her taking possession of Bolin's jewelry during the week of July 26, 2004. Those causes of action are the Trustee's claims of trespass, conversion, wrongful repossession, and statutory theft. All of those claims are variations on the allegation that Ogden unlawfully entered Bolin's premises and took the store's property without permission. Trespass is a cause of action for Sally Ogden's unlawful entry on Bolin's premises; conversion is a cause of action for Ogden's unlawful possession of property that belonged to Bolin; wrongful repossession is a cause of action alleging that Ogden breached the terms of her security agreement with Bolin when she reclaimed her collateral;[13] and statutory theft is, essentially, conversion with an additional showing that Ogden's taking of possession was intentional or malicious. To all of those causes of action, Ogden pleads that Bolin defaulted on her security agreement and, therefore, she was within her rights, as prescribed in the same security agreement, to repossess Bolin's property as collateral.

---

    [8]   Count Seven of the Trustee's Complaint is designated as "Failure to Act in a Commercially Reasonable Manner" and not as wrongful repossession. The thrust of the claim, however, is that Ogden's actions during the week of July 26, 2004 exceeded what she was permitted to do under the Uniform Commercial Code of Connecticut and the private security agreement between her and Bolin. I am therefore considering it as one aspect of the Trustee's wrongful repossession liability theory. . .

    [13]   *See* [9–602] & [9–609] (permitting parties to a secured transaction to define secured party's rights upon default, including repossession of collateral).

Ogden held two instruments that protected her $270,000 loan to Bolin: a promissory note and a security agreement. The promissory note and security agreement entitled Ogden to different rights with respect to Bolin's default. The promissory note defined a default as Bolin's failure to repay Ogden's loan within five days of her demand, while the security agreement had a broader definition of circumstances amounting to default. The security agreement also granted Ogden a wider array of remedies in the event of Bolin's default, including repossession of collateral without a judicial proceeding. Ogden relies on the security agreement, and not the promissory note, to defend against the Trustee's claims relating to her repossession of Bolin property.

Secured transactions are governed by the Uniform Commercial Code ("UCC"), as adopted by the Connecticut legislature. That law gives leeway for parties to alter and vary their rights and responsibilities from what the UCC dictates for secured transactions. Parties to a security agreement are permitted to waive and vary the rules that the UCC sets with respect to default and repossession, unless those rules are mandatory. [9–602]; *see also* [1–302(a)] ("Except as otherwise provided . . . the effect of provisions of this title may be varied by agreement."). [9–602] lists a set of mandatory rules in the UCC that may not be waived or varied in a security agreement. Nonetheless, the parties to a security agreement may determine their own standards for measuring whether the rights and duties set forth by the mandatory rules have been satisfied, provided that those standards are not "manifestly unreasonable." [9–603(a)].[15] The upshot is that the security agreement is the primary source for adjudicating Ogden's and Bolin's rights with respect to Ogden's $270,000 loan. Only when a mandatory rule set forth in [9–602] applies does the UCC govern, and even then, the parties can determine by contract whether those rules have been satisfied.

Ogden makes two arguments for why the security agreement is a defense against the Trustee's conversion, wrongful repossession, trespass, and statutory theft claims. Ogden first argues that she was entitled to enter Bolin's premises and take the store's inventory into her possession under section 9 of the security agreement. That section states in relevant part, "whenever Secured Party feels insecure for any reason whatsoever, Secured Party may, at its option, declare all Obligations of each Debtor to Secured Party immediately due and payable without demand or notice of any kind and the same thereupon shall become due and payable." Ogden maintains section 9 of the security agreement vested her with rights to possess Bolin's collateral if she believed in good faith that her loan was at risk. Schedule A of the security agreement defines "collateral" as including Bolin's "inventory," a term referring broadly to "all goods, raw materials, work in process, finished goods, products, merchandise, and other tangible

---

[15]   The exception to that rule is whether repossession of collateral breaches the peace. Parties to a security agreement may not privately contract to determine whether the prohibition of breaching the peace has been met. [9–603(b)].

personal property now owned or hereafter acquired by Borrower and held for sale or lease or resale . . . or used or consumed in Borrower's business." Therefore, Ogden argues, all of the property she removed from the store— namely, jewelry, computers, and books—falls within the definition of property subject to repossession. In support, Ogden cites Connecticut law that permits a party to exercise an option to accelerate a counterparty's payment or performance when the party "in good faith believes that the prospect of payment or performance is impaired." [1–309]. Because Ogden had a good faith belief that her loan was insecure—on the basis of what she learned about Bolin's pawning activity and poor financial shape—she concludes that the security agreement entitled her to take Bolin's inventory.

This argument can be rejected without considering whether Ogden, in fact, had a good faith belief that her loan was at risk, a matter contested at trial. A plain reading of the security agreement shows that the "feels insecure" clause did not entitle Ogden to enter Bolin's premises and take the store's jewelry in her possession, but only permitted her to demand immediate payment on her loan. The security agreement permits Ogden to enter Bolin's premises and repossess the store's inventory only "[i]n connection with the exercise of any rights available upon default." As defined in section 8 of the security agreement, Ogden's feeling of insecurity does not constitute an event of default. Demanding payment, which Ogden was permitted to do because of her feeling of insecurity, is a predicate for default, and not a default in itself. Bolin would not default under the agreement's terms—and, by extension, Ogden would not be permitted to take any of Bolin's items—until the store failed to meet Ogden's accelerated payment date. Based on the terms of the promissory note and Ogden's demand letter left for Ulanoff, that would not have occurred until August 4, 2004, five days after July 30, 2004. Thus, the "feels insecure" clause of section 9 of the security agreement does not justify or otherwise serve as a defense for Ogden's conduct.

Ogden's second and more convincing argument is that Bolin defaulted on Ogden's loan by pawning jewelry and, as a result, the security agreement entitled her to enter the store and take possession of its inventory. Pawning, Ogden claims, encumbered the store's inventory and resulted in pawnbrokers obtaining liens against the collateral for Ogden's loan. Those encumbrances and liens qualified as default under section 8 of the security agreement (defining default as an "encumbrance to or of any of the Collateral, or the making of any levy, seizure, or attachment thereof or thereon". Ogden makes the same argument for the civil judgments that had been awarded against Bolin: because Bolin had several judgments against it, the store had defaulted under that section of the agreement.

Working from the premise that Bolin had defaulted, Ogden argues that the security agreement empowered her to take the store's inventory into her possession. Such self-help was authorized by the security agreement's terms: specifically, the agreement's reference to the "remedies of a secured party under the Uniform Commercial Code of Connecticut" in the event of a default. Under the UCC, a secured party, such as Sally Ogden, has the right "to take possession of the collateral . . . without judicial process" following a debtor's default, provided that the secured party's repossession "proceeds without breach of the peace." **[9–609(a) & (b)]**. Ogden claims that the security agreement, by its incorporation of the UCC and its self-help provisions, permitted her to enter Bolin's premises and take the store's inventory as collateral because of Bolin's pawning and the judgments entered against it.

The Trustee raises three challenges to this defense. First, the Trustee argues that there was no default. Although section 8 of the Security Agreement states that "encumbrance to or of any of the Collateral, or the making of any levy, seizure, or attachment thereof and thereon" and "the entry of a judgment against any Obligor" shall qualify as a default, the Trustee asserts that section 8 of the Agreement cannot mean what it literally says. Consider, for example, that the section defines a "sale . . . of any of the Collateral" as a form of default. Holding that any sale of Bolin-owned jewelry is a default would be unreasonable because it would deny Ulanoff the ability to operate her store. Ogden's purpose in making the loan was to help, not stymie, Bolin's retail business, and the meaning of what constitutes a default should be interpreted consistently with the parties' intent of assisting Bolin. *See Aruba Hotel Enters. N.V. v. Belfonti,* 611 F. Supp. 2d 203, 209 (D. Conn. 2009) (" 'A contract must be construed to effectuate the intent of the parties, which is determined from the language used interpreted in the light of the situation of the parties and the circumstances connected with the transaction.' " The Trustee argues that rendering any encumbrance or any civil judgment a default would be similarly unreasonable and should not establish Bolin's default of Ogden's loan.

The Uniform Commercial Code does not define the word default but, instead, leaves the meaning for the parties to decide in the terms of their security agreement. *Cofield v. Randolph County Comm'n,* 90 F.3d 468, 471 (11th Cir. 1996) (citing 4 James J. White & Robert S. Summers, Uniform Commercial Code § 34–2 (4th ed. 1995) ("White & Summers")). The security agreement's definition of default therefore governs this case. The Trustee is correct that the definition inscribed in a security agreement should not apply if that definition is unconscionable, was not made in good faith, or is otherwise unreasonable. *See* **[1–302(b)]** ("The obligations of good faith, diligence, reasonableness and care prescribed by this title may not be disclaimed by agreement."); 4 White & Summers, § 34–2 ("Apart from the modest limitations imposed by the unconscionability doctrine and the requirement of good faith, default is whatever the security agreement says it is." (quotation omitted)). But Bolin and Ogden's mutual definition of default as an encumbrance, such as a pawn lien on, or civil judgment against, the store's inventory is neither unconscionable nor unreasonable, and does not exhibit bad faith.

A definition of default that restricts Bolin's sale of jewelry in its normal course of business would be unreasonable and not permitted under the UCC because both parties anticipated that Bolin would use Ogden's loan for retail purposes. Even so, that does not compel the further conclusion that encumbrances and civil judgments are also unreasonable definitions of default. Unlike the case of defining default as the sale of jewelry, pawning items and being subject to civil judgments are not a reasonably expected part of a jewelry store's business. Ogden did not lend the store $270,000 with the anticipation that Ulanoff and Citrin would pawn jewelry in order to keep the business operating. Indeed, it seems quite reasonable for a lender to protect her loan by defining default in terms of actions against the debtor that threaten the collateral securing the loan or signal the debtor's imminent insolvency and inability to repay its debt. Defining default as encumbrance of the collateral or as civil judgments against the debtor therefore does not run afoul of the UCC.

———

The court concluded that the debtor was in default and then proceeded to discuss whether the creditor's actions in repossessing the jewelry breached the peace. We'll take up this second issue below.

In the case above, the court considered whether the debtor's actions constituted an enumerated default or whether such actions gave the creditor such a sense of insecurity that she was justified in calling the loan. The first important takeaway relates to the use of the "deems itself insecure clause" allowed by **1–309**. If the creditor believes in good faith that its chances of payment are impaired, then the creditor can accelerate the loan. When the creditor accelerates, it declares that all loan obligations are due and payable on a specified date. If the obligor/debtor does not pay on that date, then the secured party can exercise its Part 6 remedies.

The second important takeaway is that if the obligor/debtor has committed an act that constitutes an enumerated default, **1–309** is irrelevant. Does that mean that the secured party need not exercise good faith in calling the debtor in default? No, every obligation under the UCC carries with it an obligation of good faith pursuant to **1–304**. The excerpt below from *Regions Bank v. Thomas*, 422 S.W.3d 550 (Tenn. App. 2013) is helpful in explaining this point. The borrower, LGT Aviation, Inc., had failed to maintain insurance on the collateral as required by the loan agreement. It had, however, been making timely payments, and when the lender called the borrower in default for not maintaining insurance, the borrower called bad faith.

Although the case before us is distinguishable from *Lane v. John Deere Company,* 767 S.W.2d 138 (Tenn. 1989), which addressed acceleration under an "insecurity clause" and not for the failure to perform a contractual obligation, the court's analysis of the evidence relevant to good faith is instructive here. The *Lane* court cited numerous material factors relevant to the question of good faith, including the creditor's knowledge of the insecure circumstances at the time of contracting, *e.g., Clayton v. Crossroads Equipment Co.,* 655 P.2d 1125 (Utah 1982); his knowledge of facts that contradict the negative information acquired, *e.g., Eglin Federal Credit Union v. Curfman,* 386 So.2d 860 (Fla.App.1980); the nature and value of the collateral, *e.g., Jack M. Finley, Inc. v. Longview Bank & Trust,* 705 S.W.2d 206 (Tex.App.1985); . . . any deceit or outrageous conduct in the course of the whole transaction, including repossession, *e.g., Farmers & Merchants Bank of Centre v. Hancock,* 506 So. 2d 305 (Ala.1987); an abrupt departure from an established course of dealing, *e.g., Reid v. Key Bank of Southern Maine,* 821 F.2d 9 (1st Cir.1987); such circumstances relating only to the creditor as audits or personnel conflicts, *e.g., Farmers & Merchants Bank of Centre, supra*; erroneous assertion of default on some other ground, *e.g., Kupka v. Morey,* 541 P.2d 740 (Alaska 1975); the course of dealing between the parties, *e.g., Farmers & Merchants Bank of Centre, supra*; *Reid v. Key Bank, supra*; any oppressive use of his superior position, *e.g., Reid v. Key Bank, supra*; *Libby v. Twombly,* 213 Mont. 66, 689 P.2d 1226 (1984); any commercial advantage unrelated to the security of the debt, *e.g., State National Bank of El Paso v. Farah Mfg.,* 678 S.W.2d 661 (Tex.App.1984); gross negligence in record keeping, *McConnico v. Third National Bank,* 499 S.W.2d 874, 881 (Tenn.1973); prior assurances causing the other party to change position, *e.g., Libby v. Twombly, supra*; and a creditor's own conduct that contributes to the insecurity, *e.g., Kupka v. Morey, supra*.

Id. at 140–141.

* * *

As noted above, the documents executed by the parties clearly impose an obligation on LGT to maintain insurance on the aircraft. The promissory note defines default as, *inter alia,* "any 'Default' or Event of Default' [that] occurs under or with respect to any of the Security Documents or any other instrument or document executed in connection with this Note." The aircraft security agreement defines default as, *inter alia,* the "[f]ailure to maintain insurance against any of the hazards required to be insured against pursuant hereto, or cancellation of any policy providing for such insurance prior to payment of the [i]ndebtedness." The security agreement further provides that, upon the occurrence of any event of default that is not cured within 15 days of receipt of written notice of default, Regions shall have the right to, *inter alia*, declare the indebtedness due and payable in full and to take possession of the collateral and move, relocate, store, re-condition and sell the collateral. The evidence does not preponderate against the trial court's finding that Appellants breached the parties' agreement by failing to maintain a policy of insurance on the aircraft. The loan documents unambiguously imposed on Appellants an obligation to obtain and maintain insurance on the collateral, and provided that the failure to do so was an event of default. The failure to insure collateral as required by a loan agreement has been considered a default for which repossession may be a proper remedy. *McCall v. Owens,* 820 S.W.2d 748, 751 (Tenn. Ct. App. 1991). We affirm the trial court's finding that Appellants materially breached the loan agreement by failing to maintain insurance on the aircraft.

* * *

The duty of good faith . . . does not extend beyond the terms of the contract and the reasonable expectations of the parties under the contract. The obligation of good faith and fair dealing does not create additional contractual rights or obligations, and it cannot be used to avoid or alter the terms of an agreement. *Id.* (citations omitted).

Regions Bank v. Thomas, 422 S.W.3d 550 (Tenn. App. 2013)

That said, the role of good faith in calling defaults has spawned a genre of "lender liability" cases in which borrowers, often obligated on demand notes, have claimed that the secured party's actions in calling the loan resulted in the debtor's business failure. The excerpt below reviews some of the lender liability jurisprudence.

TRAVEL SERVS. NETWORK V. PRESIDENTIAL FIN. CORP.

959 F. Supp. 135 (D. Conn. 1997)

ARTERTON, J.

This action arises from a secured lending agreement between plaintiff Travel Services Network, Inc. ("TSN") and defendant Presidential Financial Corporation of Massachusetts ("Presidential"). TSN contends that Presidential, its creditor, is liable under various theories for nondisclosure, misrepresentation, and failure to fulfill contractual obligations. Presidential moves for summary judgment as to all of TSN's claims. For the reasons set forth below, Presidential's motion is GRANTED in part and DENIED in part.

Background

In April 1992, plaintiff TSN, a corporate entity established by Ronald Plasse ("Plasse") to acquire and operate travel agencies, entered into an agreement to purchase Kaplan Travel Bureau. In order to finance this transaction, which purportedly required a cash payment of $ 250,000 at closing, Plasse approached George Gochis ("Gochis") of Presidential.

On June 23, 1992, Presidential and TSN entered into a loan and security agreement by which Presidential agreed to provide financing to TSN based upon, and secured by, the accounts receivable from several of TSN's principal corporate customers. The loan agreement set a maximum limit on the advance funds that TSN could obtain from Presidential equal to 60% of TSN's select customer account receivables, or approximately $ 250,000. These funds were to be used by TSN for a revolving line of credit and to finance the purchase of Kaplan Travel, which was to occur on August 3, 1992.

By the terms of the Agreement, Presidential set forth several restrictions on its willingness to advance funds. First, Presidential required first-priority security interests in the receivables of TSN's select corporate customers. Second, Presidential required select customers of TSN to make payments due to TSN directly to Presidential. Third, Presidential insisted that it be given sole discretion over whether and when advances were made. In addition, pursuant to the Agreement, TSN was required to execute a Demand Promissory Note, in which TSN promised to pay on demand to Presidential the principal amount of $ 250,000 and any interest thereon. The Agreement also set forth several events that would constitute default by TSN. These events were as follows: if (1) any receivable was not paid in full within 91 days from the date that Presidential made an advance with respect thereto; (2) TSN became insolvent; (3) one of TSN's creditors took possession of collateral; or (4) Presidential deemed itself insecure.

With respect to the funds needed by TSN to purchase Kaplan Travel, Presidential and TSN entered into a separate Escrow Agreement on August 3, 1992. The Escrow Agreement established a special account allowing TSN to represent to Kaplan that the necessary funds would be available for the transaction. However, the Escrow Agreement did not provide for immediate disbursement of the funds, apparently giving Presidential time to determine whether TSN had acquired a collateral base sufficient to justify the advance of such funds. Notwithstanding the provisions of the Escrow Agreement, TSN maintains that Presidential made separate oral promises to advance $ 250,000 at the time of the closing of the Kaplan deal.

TSN purchased Kaplan Travel on August 3, 1992. Although the initial purchase agreement called for a cash payment of $ 250,000 to be made to Kaplan at the closing, no funds were released on that day. Plasse testified in his deposition that TSN and Kaplan agreed to postpone payment until a discrepancy between Kaplan's stated and actual receivables, which formed the basis of the purchase price, could be resolved. There is, however, no written record of this agreement to postpone.

On October 23, 1992, TSN and Presidential executed an amendment to the Escrow Agreement. This amendment stated, *inter alia*, that "no payments have been made by Presidential under the Escrow Agreement, nor was there any obligation upon Presidential to do so." At about the same time, Presidential began to advance funds to TSN under the Loan Agreement for the first time.

In late November or early December, TSN requested that its line of credit be increased from $ 250,000 to $ 500,000 in order to purchase Westport Travel Service. Presidential agreed, and TSN's advance rate was increased to 70% of receivables, or approximately $ 500,000. At this time, TSN executed a new promissory note for the increased amount. In December, 1992, using these funds, TSN successfully acquired Westport Travel.

In late December or early January, an internal auditor from Presidential visited TSN for the purpose of conducting a purportedly routine audit of TSN's books. This audit revealed problems with TSN's receivables. Due to errors by TSN's comptroller, who was later discharged, TSN had not received payment from its largest corporate customer for the month of November and, as a result, had insufficient funds to cover payments to its biggest creditor, Airlines Reporting Corporation ("ARC"). Based on this audit, Presidential advised TSN that it was going to restrict TSN's maximum line of credit to $ 275,000.

On January 15, 1993, ARC informed TSN by letter that $ 266,887.30 in checks drawn against TSN's account for payment had been dishonored and that TSN was in default of its agreement with the company. Because the default was never corrected, ARC later revoked the plates used by TSN to issue air travel tickets at TSN's Kaplan locations, which, TSN claims, resulted in negative publicity, damage to its reputation, and the loss of experienced employees. TSN did not notify Presidential of this default notice until late January or early February.

On February 19, 1993, Presidential formally notified TSN that TSN was also in default under the Loan Agreements. Presidential indicated that no further advances would be made until Presidential was satisfied that TSN could repay its outstanding ARC obligations. Three days later, TSN terminated its financing relationship with Presidential. As requested by TSN, Presidential repaid itself in full out of TSN's accounts receivable and forwarded all excess funds to TSN. On March 11, 1993, TSN entered into a new financing arrangement with Banker's Capital. The terms of this arrangement were apparently less favorable to TSN than the Loan Agreements with Presidential. TSN claims that it ceased to be profitable as a result of this new financing arrangement and subsequently went out of business.

Standard for Summary Judgment

In a motion for summary judgment, the moving party must initially demonstrate that there are no material facts in dispute and "all reasonable inferences and any ambiguities are drawn in favor of the non-moving party."

* * *

Discussion

TSN contends that Presidential caused its financial demise by refusing to provide the $ 250,000 necessary for the Kaplan closing, failing to advance funds in a timely manner in January and February of 1993, and failing to provide sufficient notice of its intent to terminate TSN's financing. TSN states these claims in terms of (1) breach of contract, (2) breach of an implied covenant of good faith and fair dealing, (3) breach of fiduciary duty, (4) negligent misrepresentation, (5) fraudulent misrepresentation and nondisclosure, and (6) violation of Connecticut's Unfair Trade Practices Act ("CUTPA"). Presidential moves for summary judgment as to all of plaintiff's claims.

* * *

Count Two (Breach of Implied Covenant of Good Faith and Fair Dealing)

In its second count, TSN claims that Presidential breached a covenant of good faith and fair dealing. Presidential does not dispute that such a covenant is implied in every contract, or that a breach of such a covenant is actionable. Rather, Presidential argues that it did nothing but exercise its express rights under the lending agreement and that, accordingly, it cannot be held liable for breach of the implied covenant. Presidential contends that, as a matter of law, a lender does not breach the implied covenant when it exercises its rights under a demand note and revolving credit agreement to refuse further extensions of credit and to demand payment on outstanding balances, regardless of the lender's good faith in so doing.

TSN responds that its claim encompasses not just the fact that Presidential terminated its financing, but also the *manner* in which Presidential exercised its rights. TSN contends that Presidential significantly slowed the speed with which funds were advanced on TSN's accounts receivable in January and February of 1993, while continuing to take in payments directly from TSN's chief customers. In consequence, TSN's outstanding debt was "virtually" erased in the space of a few weeks. TSN argues that, for all intents and purposes, Presidential called in its debt during that time, but without providing any formal notice to TSN so that TSN could arrange alternative financing. TSN further claims that

Presidential falsely denied its intentions in response to repeated direct inquiries during the January and February time period.

An examination of the lending agreements indicates that Presidential expressly reserved for itself the right to extend loans in its "sole discretion", TSN expressly waived "demand, presentment, notice, protest, and notice of dishonor", and TSN was obligated to "pay on demand" any balances due under the agreements. In light of these express contractual provisions, Presidential may not be held liable merely for slowing the rate at which it advanced money to TSN, reducing the outstanding balance of TSN's debt, or declining to advance additional funds after February 19, 1993. *See Shawmut Bank, N.A. v. Miller,* 415 Mass. 482, 614 N.E.2d 668, 669 (Mass. 1993) ("Good faith is not a necessary component of a holder's decision to collect the balance due on a demand note."); *Shawmut Bank, N.A. v. Wayman,* 34 Mass. App. Ct. 20, 606 N.E.2d 925, 928 (Mass. App. Ct. 1993) (holding that covenant of good faith and fair dealing does not require lender to provide notice concerning loans to individual who expressly waived notice in contract). However, TSN's claims appear less directed towards these actions per se, and more towards Presidential's failure to provide reasonable notice of its intentions and Presidential's deceptive responses to TSN's inquiries.

A.   Notice Claim

Although a lender does not violate the implied covenant of good faith and fair dealing merely by exercising express contractual rights, Massachusetts courts have left open the possibility that in certain circumstances lenders may violate the implied covenant by the *manner* with which they exercise express contractual rights. *See Miller,* 614 N.E.2d at 672 ("We, therefore, need not consider whether good faith is a necessary element of the setting of the terms of a demand for payment when dealing with a demand note . . . ."); *cf. Shawmut Bank v. Flynn,* 1993 WL 818771, *3 (Mass. Super.) (noting, but not addressing, argument that "*Miller* only establishes the irrelevancy of Shawmut's good or bad faith and motivation in its decision to demand payment on the loan, but that *Miller* does not immunize the plaintiff's conduct in demanding or collecting payment").

In arguing that a cause of action exists for Presidential's failure to provide "reasonable notice" of its intentions to deny further credit and call in outstanding balances, TSN relies principally on *K.M.C. Co., Inc. v. Irving Trust Co.,* 757 F.2d 752 (6th Cir. 1985), which involved a revolving credit agreement similar to that entered into by Presidential and TSN. Although the lender in *K.M.C.* contended that it had a contractual right to refuse to extend credit and to demand payment at its own discretion, the Sixth Circuit, applying New York law, found that these rights did not relieve the lender of an obligation to provide prior notice of its intent to cut off credit. The court observed:

As part of the procedure established for the operation of the financing agreement, the parties agreed in a supplementary letter that all receipts of K.M.C. would be deposited into a "blocked account" to which Irving would have sole access. Consequently, unless K.M.C. obtained alternative financing, a refusal by Irving to advance funds would leave K.M.C. without operating capital until it had paid down its loan. The record clearly established that a medium-sized company in the wholesale grocery business, such as K.M.C., could not operate without outside financing. Thus, the literal interpretation of the financing agreement urged upon us by Irving, as supplemented by the "blocked account" mechanism, would leave K.M.C.'s continued existence entirely at the whim or mercy of Irving, absent an obligation of good faith performance. Logically, at such times as Irving might wish to curtail financing to K.M.C., as was its right under the agreement, this obligation to act in good faith would require a period of notice to K.M.C. to allow it a reasonable opportunity to seek alternative financing, absent valid business reasons precluding Irving from doing so.

757 F.2d at 759.

Decided in 1985, *K.M.C.* has since been subjected to substantial criticism. *See, e.g., Kham & Nate's Shoes No. 2 v. First Bank,* 908 F.2d 1351, 1358 (7th Cir. 1990). Although Massachusetts courts do not appear to have addressed whether the *K.M.C.* cause of action is available under Massachusetts law, other state courts have consistently rejected the reasoning of *K.M.C.* or strictly limited the holding of *K.M.C.* to its facts. *See, e.g., Waller v. Maryland Nat'l Bank,* 95 Md. App. 197, 620 A.2d 381, 391 (Md. Ct. Spec. App. 1993); *Gaul v. Olympia Fitness Center, Inc.,* 88 Ohio App. 3d 310, 623 N.E.2d 1281, 1287 (Ohio Ct. App. 1993); *Southwest Savings & Loan Ass'n v. Sunamp Systems, Inc.,* 172 Ariz. 553, 838 P.2d 1314, 1322 (Ariz. Ct. App. 1992. Indeed, although *K.M.C.* purported to apply New York law, it is not clear that New York courts would recognize a cause of action in similar circumstances. *See Nat'l Westminster Bank v. Ross,* 130 B.R. 656, 680 (S.D.N.Y. 1991) (concluding that *K.M.C.* is inconsistent with *Murphy v. American Home Prods. Corp.,* 58 N.Y.2d 293, 448 N.E.2d 86, 461 N.Y.S.2d 232 (N.Y. 1983)).

Criticism of *K.M.C.* focusses on two aspects of the decision. First, the decision effectively overrode the express terms of the contractual arrangement between the parties. "Although courts often refer to the obligation of good faith that exists in every contractual relation, this is not an invitation to the court to decide whether one party ought to have exercised privileges expressly reserved in the document." *Kham & Nates Shoes,* 908 F.2d at 1357. Moreover, debtors are not necessarily benefited when courts constrain the ability of creditors to exercise contractual rights. If creditors are not permitted to bargain for the added protection of being to able to act without notice, then creditors will demand higher interest rates and faster repayment, or may decline to extend credit altogether.

Mark Snyderman, Note, *What's So Good About Good Faith?: The Good Faith Performance Obligation in Commercial Lending*, 55 U. Chi. L. Rev. 1335, 1350–51 (1988); *see Amoco Oil Co. v. Ashcraft,* 791 F.2d 519, 524 (7th Cir. 1986) ("The less protection [the creditor] has, the less willing it will be to extend credit").

Second, the court in *K.M.C.* found support for its conclusion in U.C.C. **[1–309]**, which states that "a term providing that one party . . . may accelerate payment or performance . . . 'at will' . . . shall be construed to mean that he shall have the power to do so only if he in good faith believes that the prospect of payment or performance is impaired." *See K.M.C.,* 757 F.2d at 760. However, the *K.M.C.* court failed to note that the official comment to **[1–309]** states, "Obviously this section has no application to demand instruments or obligations whose very nature permits call at any time with or without reason."

In light of the weight and persuasiveness of the case law criticizing *K.M.C.*, or questioning its general applicability, the Court concludes that the Massachusetts Supreme Judicial Court would either interpret *K.M.C.* quite narrowly or reject its reasoning altogether. Assuming the former, the Court notes several distinguishing features between *K.M.C.* and the present case. First, the parties in *K.M.C.* had a longer course of dealings with one another than TSN and Presidential. K.M.C. and Irving Trust entered into their financing agreement in 1979, and Irving Trust apparently advanced funds under the agreement without serious incident until the refusal on March 1, 1981, which gave rise to K.M.C.'s cause of action. By way of contrast, TSN and Presidential entered into their agreement in June of 1992; Presidential refused to advance funds under the agreement until October of that year; TSN's line of credit was doubled in December of 1992, but cut nearly in half the following month;[3] and financing was effectively terminated in February of 1993. TSN itself characterizes its "lending relationship" with Presidential as lasting only four months. Indeed, none of the evidence before the Court suggests that the relationship between TSN and Presidential was anything but short and tempestuous. TSN cannot claim, and does not appear to claim, that it was lulled into a belief that Presidential would provide advance notice of any change in TSN's status merely by virtue of the course of past dealings between the parties.

---

[3] Although the alleged notification of TSN in January of Presidential's intent to reduce TSN's credit line is not evidenced by writing, TSN does not appear to dispute that such notice was provided or that its credit line was so reduced. The present suit does not seem to challenge this reduction in TSN's credit line, but rather the alleged additional reductions that occurred *sub silencio* in January and February.

Whatever disclosure obligations may arise in the context of a long, stable relationship, such obligations are not necessarily present in this case.

K.M.C. is further distinguishable on other grounds. While the *K.M.C.* court found evidence that K.M.C.'s business was stable and that "March 1 was simply not that unusual a day in the history of the relationship between Irving and K.M.C.," 757 F.2d at 762, the undisputed evidence in this case is that ARC, TSN's most important creditor, provided notice to TSN that it was in default on its obligations on January 15, 1993, which default was not rectified prior to the termination of Presidential's financing; also in January, problems were becoming apparent with respect to the accounts receivable from Pfizer, one of TSN's most important customers; and, at about the same time, Presidential notified TSN that its credit line would be reduced from $ 500,000 to $ 275,000. In short, the Court would be hard pressed to conclude that the January-February time period at issue "was not that unusual a [time] in the history of" the financing arrangements between TSN and Presidential. Nor could the Court conclude that, absent affirmative misrepresentations by Presidential, TSN would have acted reasonably to assume that its financing arrangements with Presidential would go unchanged during the relevant time period.

Finally, the Court notes that circumstances in the *K.M.C.* case suggested a level of maliciousness on the part of the creditor that is not apparent in this case. Indeed, in *K.M.C.*, there was persuasive evidence that the creditor acted out of personal dislike for the debtor, 757 F.2d at 761, and that the creditor knew that its collateral was secure, but actually intended to "destroy" the debtor by terminating financing, *id.* at 762. The record in this case contains no comparable evidence.

In light of the important distinctions between the facts of this case and the facts of *K.M.C.*, as well as the likelihood that Massachusetts courts would at most interpret *K.M.C.* narrowly, the Court concludes that the provisions of the Loan Agreements and related documents, including the express waiver of notice, preclude a cause of action under the implied covenant of good faith and fair dealing for Presidential's alleged failure to provide TSN with advance notice of its intent to significantly restrict or terminate TSN's line of credit in January and February of 1993. Accordingly, Presidential is entitled to summary judgment on this issue.

B. Deception Claim

Although TSN may not proceed merely on the claim that Presidential failed to provide reasonable notice of its intent to terminate financing, TSN offers the additional claim, backed by affidavit, that Presidential falsely responded to direct inquiries that TSN's credit line was in no danger in January and February of 1993. Drawing all inferences in TSN's favor, as the Court must in a motion for summary judgment, the virtual elimination of TSN's outstanding balance during the January-February time period by process of delaying new advances, gives rise to an inference that Presidential intended to cut off or radically restrict TSN's financing *sub silencio*. Even if Presidential were under no obligation to give notice of its intentions, TSN argues that Presidential breached the implied covenant of good faith and fair dealing by falsely denying its intentions when directly asked.

TSN's claim of active deception clearly stands on firmer ground than its lack of notice claim. While TSN expressly waived notice in the lending agreements, Presidential has not identified any contractual basis for a right to respond falsely to direct inquiries. More generally, the Court can identify no tension between the bargained-for terms of the lending agreement and an implied covenant not to respond falsely to TSN's questions about its status. "When the contract is silent, principles of good faith . . . fill the gap." *Kham & Nates,* 908 F.2d at 1357. Here, the contract appears to be silent as to Presidential's rights and obligations in responding to TSN's inquiries.

In the present case, Presidential should have been particularly sensitive in its handling of TSN's inquiries in light of the waiver of notice: TSN had no means other than regular inquiries to obtain advance warning of trouble in its financing arrangements and of the potential need to seek alternative financing elsewhere. TSN does not argue that Presidential was obligated to respond to its inquiries, but maintains that when Presidential chose to respond, Presidential became obligated to respond honestly. The Court agrees that dishonesty in these circumstances would violate the implied covenant of good faith and fair dealing. *Cf. Wayman,* 606 N.E.2d at 928 (concluding that creditor entitled to summary judgment on good faith and fair dealing claim because debtor failed to offer evidence "of any misrepresentation or dishonest act"); *Flynn,* 1993 WL at *3 (holding that evidence of misrepresentations by creditor might support conclusion of bad faith, but concluding that any such misconduct was immaterial). Accordingly, Presidential's motion for summary judgment as to this claim is denied.

C.   Failure to Advance Funds Claim

TSN offers one final basis for its claim of breach of the implied covenant of good faith and fair dealing: Presidential's failure to adhere to its alleged oral promises to advance money at the time of the closing of the Kaplan deal. However, the Court has already held these alleged promises to be nonactionable as a matter of law by virtue of the subsequent Escrow Agreement.

———————

Remember that a security agreement is a contract, so the traditional defenses to contract enforcement apply. A secured transaction is a relationship, and sometimes a lender will accept late payments without objection. If a lender does so often enough and then sometime later calls a borrower in default for sending a late payment, the borrower might argue that the lender waived default. As a result, lenders will often add clauses to their loan documents specifying exactly how the lender can waive a default. The following excerpt, also from *Regions Bank v. Thomas*, explains:

> We next turn to Appellants' assertion that Regions waived breach of the obligation to maintain insurance where Regions accepted payments on the loan without objection, and that the breach was cured by Regions procurement of insurance. We begin our discussion of this issue by noting that Appellants did not specifically raise the defense of waiver in their answer or in their motion to alter or amend the judgment. Rather, the issue is tied to Appellants' assertion that Regions acted in bad faith by accepting installment payments while continuing to take actions to accelerate the loan and repossess the aircraft. We have long held that waiver is an intentional relinquishment of a known right and is a doctrine of very broad and general application. It concedes a right, but assumes a voluntary relinquishment of it. Our courts have held that there must be clear, unequivocal and decisive acts of the party of an act which shows determination not to have the benefit intended in order to constitute a waiver.
>
> *Collins v. Summers Hardware and Supply Co.,* 88 S.W.3d 192, 201–202 (Tenn. Ct. App. 2002).
>
> The promissory note executed by the parties in this case provides: "No waiver of any right or remedy by the Bank shall be effective unless made in writing and signed by the Bank." The loan agreement and security agreement contain similar provisions. The loan agreement further provides that "[n]o prior waiver by Lender, nor any course of dealing . . . shall constitute a waiver." The security agreement also provides that "[a]ny delay on the part of Bank in exercising any power, privilege or right shall not preclude other or further exercise thereof . . ."
>
> It is well-settled in Tennessee that, in general, acceleration clauses are valid and will be enforced by the courts according to their terms. *Lively v. Drake,* 629 S.W.2d 900, 902 (Tenn. 1982). In this case, the event of default was not the failure to pay amounts due, but the failure to maintain insurance on the aircraft. Regions accelerated the loan after Mr. Thomas repeatedly failed to respond to its inquires and demands, and did not waive any right in writing. The payment of monthly installments by LGT did not result in a cure of the event of default in this case, nor did Regions accept payments without objection. Rather, Regions continually

advised Mr. Thomas that the loan was in default for failure to maintain insurance. The evidence contained in the record demonstrates that Regions did not waive its rights under the contract, but repeatedly asserted that the loan was in default.

To demonstrate waiver by conduct, the proof must evidence some "absolute action or inaction inconsistent with the claim or right" waived. *Jenkins Subway, Inc. v. Jones,* 990 S.W.2d 713, 722–23 (Tenn. Ct. App. 1998). Nothing in the record indicates that Regions took any action to waive the contractual obligation of insurance, nor that its subsequent steps to secure insurance cured the default.

B. REMEDIES UPON DEFAULT

Once a default is established, the secured party's enforcement rights kick in. Article 9 gives the secured creditor the right to foreclose on collateral. **9–601(a).** Foreclosure is a concept you may already be familiar with, either from your first-year Property course or a real estate transactions course. There are a couple of things to remember about foreclosure. First, the term foreclosure is short for "foreclosure of the right of redemption." To get a sense of what this means, please read **9–623**. In a secured transaction, two parties have property rights in the collateral given for a loan. The secured party has a lien on the collateral, and the debtor has the right of redemption. That means that the debtor can, at any time, pay all amounts due on the loan and receive the collateral free of the lender's interest.

The second thing to remember is that foreclosure is one step in a process. The process starts with default and ends with a sale of the collateral and the proceeds being applied to the debt outstanding. Under Article 9, the secured party, not a public official (as is the case with mortgages in some states), conducts the foreclosure sale. The secured party therefore must obtain possession of the collateral.

Another point to remember is that remedies will depend on the type of collateral. A secured party can repossess an item with a physical form, such as a car or a piece of machinery. But what about a payment right? How do you repossess a payment right? And do you really have to sell a payment right? We'll address those questions after we talk about tangible collateral, but as a preview, Article 9 gives the secured party the right to "collect" payment rights after the debtor's default. **9–607.**

1. SELF-HELP REPOSSESSION

In order to sell the collateral to satisfy its claim against the debtor, the secured party must first obtain possession of the collateral. Article 9 is unique in American law in that it permits self-help. Consider what this means: a secured party can, after default, seize (or more likely, hire someone to seize) the collateral without going to court first. **9-609** permits a secured party to take possession of tangible collateral without judicial process if it can do so without a breach of the peace. Breach of the peace is another term not defined in the UCC and its parameters are left to case law. The only way to learn what actions constitute a breach of the peace is to consider the competing interests in the statute and to read a lot of cases addressing different factual scenarios. One court stated the objectives of **9-609** in this way:

> (1) to benefit creditors in permitting them to realize collateral without having to resort to judicial process; (2) to benefit debtors in general by making credit available at lower costs; and (3) to support a public policy discouraging extrajudicial acts by citizens when those acts are fraught with the likelihood of resulting violence. *Williams v. Ford Motor Credit Co.*, 674 F.2d 717, 719 n. 4 (8th Cir. 1982).

So what is a possible definition of breach of the peace? Courts tend to find a breach of the peace when violence appears likely. Courts often apply a definition such as the one stated in *Chrysler Credit Corp. v. Koontz*, 277 Ill. App. 3d 1078 (1996):

> the term "breach of the peace" connotes conduct which incites or is likely to incite immediate public turbulence, or which leads to or is likely to lead to an immediate loss of public order and tranquility. Violent conduct is not a necessary element. The probability of violence at the time of or immediately prior to the repossession is sufficient.

There is a voluminous body of breach of the peace case law. With the above definition and objectives in mind, consider whether the following actions by the parties result in a breach of the peace.

Strenuous objection to the repossession: Some courts hold that an unequivocal oral protest on the part of the debtor is not sufficient to cause a breach of the peace:

> Whether a given act provokes a breach of the peace depends upon the accompanying circumstances of each particular case. In this case, Koontz testified that he only yelled, "Don't take it," and that the repossessor made no verbal or physical response. He also testified that although he was close enough to the repossessor to run over and get into a fight, he elected not to because he was in his underwear. Furthermore, there was no evidence in the record that Koontz implied violence at the time of or immediately prior to the repossession by holding a weapon, clenching a fist, or even vehemently arguing toe-to-toe with the repossessor so that a reasonable repossessor would understand that violence was likely

to ensue if he continued with the vehicle repossession. We think that the evidence, viewed as a whole, could lead a reasonable fact finder to determine that the circumstances of the repossession did not amount to a breach of the peace.

We note that to rule otherwise would be to invite the ridiculous situation whereby a debtor could avoid a deficiency judgment by merely stepping out of his house and yelling once at a nonresponsive repossessor. Such a narrow definition of the conduct necessary to breach the peace would, we think, render the self-help repossession statute useless. Therefore, we reject Koontz's invitation to define "an unequivocal oral protest," without more, as a breach of the peace.

Chrysler Credit Corp. v. Koontz, 277 Ill. App. 3d 1078 (1996)

In a case in which the repossessors showed up at 5:00 in the morning and were confronted by the debtor, who was awakened by their actions, a court held differently:

In the case sub judice, defendants Anchor Bank, Omni and Carter contend there was no breach of the peace because Carter and his associates were polite, unabusive and unprofane at the time of repossession. Defendants Omni and Carter also argue that no breach of the peace occurred because plaintiff voluntarily relinquished her car-keys at the time of repossession. These arguments are without merit. It is not the function of this court (or the trial court) to resolve whether the acts of Carter and his associates constituted a breach of the peace. We review only the sufficiency of the evidence. *Hill v. Fed. Employees Credit Union,* 193 Ga. App. 44, 46 (2d) (386 S.E.2d 874). From this perspective, we find the circumstances of plaintiff's resistance to seizure of her automobile at the time of repossession sufficient to authorize a finding that Carter and his associates breached the peace while repossessing plaintiff's automobile. *Hopkins v. First Union Bank of Savannah,* 193 Ga. App. 109, 110, 387 S.E.2d 144 (1), supra. The fact that Carter and his associates may have been polite, unabusive and unprofane does not diminish the possibility that a jury may find that defendant Carter and his associates posed an intimidating presence during the early morning encounter with plaintiff and that their refusal to yield to plaintiff's resistance cultivated a hostile environment which could have led to a breach of the peace.

Fulton v. Anchor Sav. Bank, 452 S.E.2d 208 (Ga. Ct. App. Dec. 5, 1994)

When the debtor does more than scream, however, the result may be different:

While plaintiffs certainly played a role in any breach of the peace, Equitable's employees, despite the fact that plaintiffs jumped into the vehicle, raised the rear of the vehicle and actually towed the vehicle away from the driveway with two individuals in the vehicle and the doors open. All this was done while plaintiffs' family members and neighbors yelled at the agents to stop towing the vehicle. Equitable makes much of the fact that the plaintiffs themselves played a role in any breach by first jumping into the vehicle, but totally fails to address the fact that its own employees continued to tow the vehicle down the street *with the two women in the back*. In addition, they did so with a group of people yelling at them to stop. Finally, the police were called to the scene to restore order. Equitable has put forward no cases like this one where both parties contributed, in part, to the breach of the peace.

Smith v. AFS Acceptance, LLC, 2012 U.S. Dist. LEXIS 75976 (N.D. Ill. June 1, 2012)

Law enforcement involvement. Keep in mind that the term "self-help" means that the secured party is not involving state actors to carry out the repossession. When a creditor brought a sheriff in uniform to its "self-help" repossession, the court had this to say:

In the instant case, when the sheriff of Wallowa County, having no authority to do so, told the defendant Kessler, "We come over to pick up this tractor", he was acting *colore officii* [performing an act that his office gives him no authority to perform] and became a participant in the repossession, regardless of the fact that he did not physically take part in the retaking. Plaintiff contends that its sole purpose in having the sheriff present was to prevent anticipated violence. The effect, however, was to prevent the defendant Kessler from exercising his right to resist by all lawful and reasonable means a nonjudicial take-over. To put the stamp of approval upon this method of repossession would be to completely circumvent the purpose and intent of the statute.

Stone Mach. Co. v. Kessler, 1 Wn. App. 750 * (Wash. Ct. App. 1970)

It is important to consider why the police officer is at the scene, however.

The plaintiff claims that a breach of the peace occurred because Ogden created a chaotic scene when she entered the store the week of July 30, 2004 to prepare to and eventually take the store's inventory.

* * *

The plaintiff supports its chaotic-scene theory with testimony that at least one police officer was present at the store on July 30 to maintain order. Although the evidence is uncontradicted that a police officer was in the store at some point on July 30, the Trustee never established why that officer was present. The mere presence of a police officer while a repossession is taking place is not sufficient to establish a breach of the peace; rather, breach of the peace occurs when a police officer is present in order to assert his or her authority and compel a debtor to give a secured party possession of collateral. *In re MacLeod,* 118 B.R. at 2–3 (citing cases finding breach of the peace when police officers are present in order "to override the debtor's right to object"); *cf. United States v. Coleman,* 628 F.2d 961, 964 & n.1 (6th Cir. 1980) (distinguishing "mere acquiescence by the police 'to stand by in case of trouble' " from cases where unlawful repossession occurred when the police "affirmatively participat[ed]" in the taking of collateral from a debtor). There was no evidence that the officer was present to override a Bolin agent's attempt to keep the store's property from leaving the premises. Rather, it appears that the police officer was present in order to facilitate the Greenwich Police Department's own investigation of the store's unlawful activity and to ensure that vendors could search through Bolin's jewelry in an orderly fashion and immediately report lost items— neither of which would establish a breach of the peace. The Trustee did not provide enough evidence about the police officer's reason for appearing in the store to meet his burden that a breach of the peace took place.

Chorches v. Ogden (In re Bolin & Co., LLC), 437 B.R. 731 (D. Conn. 2010)

Entry onto and into the debtor's premises. Because of the high likelihood of violence, courts find that a repossession that involves entry into the debtor's home breaches the peace. In *General Electric Credit Corp. v. Timbrook,* 291 S.E. 2d 383 (W. Va. 1982), the collateral was a mobile home that served as the debtor's residence. The creditor's repossession agent broke the lock to the home to release a household pet and then removed the home from its cinder block foundation and took it to another state. In finding a breach of the peace, the court stated:

> We agree with those courts that have recognized breakings and unauthorized entries of debtors' dwellings to be breaches of the peace that deprive creditors or repossessors of self-help default remedies.

> A creditor has a legitimate interest in getting collateral from a defaulting debtor. That strong interest, however, must be balanced against a person's right to be free from invasions of his home.

General Elec. Credit Corp. v. Timbrook, 291 S.E.2d 383 (W. Va. 1982)

Note that the longer the distance between the repossession and the residence, the lower the likelihood that a breach of the peace has occurred. Courts have upheld repossessions from public streets, private parking lots, and driveways.

> See *Butler v. Ford Motor Credit Co.*, 829 F.2d 568 (5th Cir. 1987) (under Mississippi law, repossession of vehicle from debtor's open driveway was, as a matter of law, not a breach of the peace); *Oaklawn Bank v. Baldwin*, 289 Ark. 701, 709 S.W.2d 91, 92 (1986) (where creditor's agent repossessed vehicle from debtor's driveway without entering "any gates, doors or other barricades to reach the truck," no breach of the peace occurred); *Raffa v. Dania Bank*, 321 So. 2d 83, 85 (Fla. Dist. Ct. App. 1975) (where vehicle was parked partially under an enclosed carport in debtor's driveway, no breach of the peace occurred, it being "undisputed that no door, not even one to a garage, on the [debtor's] premises was opened, much less broken"); *Census Federal Credit Union v. Wann*, 403 N.E.2d 348, 351 (Ind. App. 1980) (repossession of vehicle from parking lot of apartment building where debtor lived did not constitute breach of the peace; although "secured party may not . . . break into or enter into homes or other buildings or enclosed spaces" it "may . . . take a chattel off a street, parking lot or unenclosed space").

Madden v. Deere Credit Services, Inc., 598 So. 2d 860 (Ala. 1992)

What about premises other than a home? Consider the following:

When the collateral is located inside a fence is otherwise enclosed, the secured creditor's privilege is considerably abridged. (See *Rogers* v. *Allis-Chalmers Credit Corp.* (8th Cir. 1982), 679 F.2d 138 (entry onto property of a third party through "at least one gate" to repossess machinery created issue of fact whether breach of peace occurred).) The creditor's privilege is most severely restricted when repossession can only be accomplished by the actual breaking or destruction of barriers designed to exclude trespassers. (See *Laurel Coal Co.* v. *Walter E. Heller & Co.* (W.D. Pa. 1982), 539 F. Supp. 1006 (creditor's "cutting a chain used to lock a fence which enclosed the [debtor's] property" to gain access to collateral constituted a breach of the peace within the meaning of the self-help repossession statute); *Bloomquist* v. *First National Bank* (Minn. App. 1985), 378 N.W.2d 81 (removing a cracked window pane to gain entry constituted a breach of the peace as a matter of law).) These cases implicitly acknowledge that the likelihood of a breach of the peace increases in proportion to the efforts of the debtor to prevent unauthorized intrusions and the creditor's conduct in defiance of those efforts. *Cf. Madden* v. *Deere Credit Services, Inc.* 598 So. 2d 860 (Ala. 1992).

Chrysler Credit Corp. v. Koontz, 277 Ill. App. 3d 1078 (1996)

Given the difficulty of defining breach of the peace, shouldn't parties just do so in their loan agreements? *See* **9–602, 9–603**. It is important to know these two sections as they provide some guidance as to what can be included in a security agreement. These two sections place important restrictions on the parties' freedom of contract.

What happens if the creditor cannot obtain the property without a chance of breaching the peace? The correct remedy in that case is replevin. Note that replevin replaces only the repossession part of the process; even if the creditor needs to resort to replevin to obtain the collateral, the creditor, not a public official, will conduct the sale of the collateral.

A creditor may also disable collateral under **9–609(a)(2)**, which allows a secured party to render equipment unusable and dispose of it on the debtor's premises. This is a useful remedy when the equipment is large and will be sold without moving it.

2.   SALE OF COLLATERAL

After the secured party obtains possession of the collateral, 9–610 governs. Note that 9–610(a) says that the secured party *may* sell, lease, or otherwise dispose of collateral. After we explore the rules governing foreclosure sales, we will see that a creditor may have the choice of retaining the collateral instead.

The idea behind a foreclosure sale is to bring in sufficient proceeds to pay the outstanding loan. In Property or Real Estate Transactions, you may have learned about a detailed statutory regime that dictates how property must be advertised for foreclosure, how notice of sale must be given, and where the property must be sold. When Article 9 governs the transaction, the code sets a standard of "commercial reasonableness." *See* **9–610**. Article 9 does not dictate a method of sale; a secured party can sell property by either a public or a private sale. What is the difference? *See* Official Comment 7 to **9–610**.

Before we get to the actual sale, let's talk about notice of sale. Read **9–611 through 9–614**. The debtor has the right to redeem its property from the secured party's lien either before the collateral is sold (public sale) or before the secured party has entered into a contract for its sale (private sale) (the section also refers to collection of the collateral and acceptance in lieu of foreclosure, which we will get to shortly) (**9–623**) so it is essential that the debtor receive notice in order to exercise this right. Several parties are entitled to notification of the sale, including other parties with security interests in the collateral. **9–611**.

Article 9 does not contain a strict timing rule for notice of sale. *See* **9–612**. Subsection (b) illustrates an important point and an important concept. The first is a qualifying statement that you will see in several sections of Article 9: "In a transaction other than a consumer transaction." This statement is the result of a "consumer compromise" during the Article 9 drafting process in the late 1990s. Remember two things about the UCC: it is not the law anywhere until it is approved by a state legislature, and generally, it applies to transactions of every size. Although Article 9 is not in any way a consumer protection statute, it contains many provision that have an impact on individuals who borrow money. During the drafting process in the 1990s, there were debates about the extent to which Article 9 should contain specific, more protective rules for individuals. To avoid protracted fights at the enactment stage, representatives of consumer interests agreed not to oppose the revisions at the state level if consumer transactions were carved out of certain Article 9 provisions. You will see the results of this compromise throughout these materials. For two views of this compromise, see Charles W. Mooney, Jr., *The Consumer Compromise in Revised U.C.C. Article 9: The Shame of it All,* 68 Ohio State L.J. 215 (2007) (written by one of the Reporters, who questioned the value of the compromise in the enactment process) and Jean Braucher, *Deadlock: Consumer Transactions Under Revised Article 9,* 73 Am. Bankr. L.J. 83 (1999) (explaining the substance of the compromise and urging the sponsoring bodies to find a better way to address consumer concerns in the future). As a result, although the 10-day safe harbor does not apply to consumer transactions, a court could find that 10 days is plenty of notice in a consumer transaction. The other important point to note is that not all states honored the consumer compromise in their enactments of Article 9. *See* Md. Code Ann. Com. Law § 9–626 (extending the reach of that section to consumer transactions).

The important concept illustrated by **9–612(b)** is that of a safe harbor. The general rule in **9–611** is that the secured party must send a "reasonable authenticated notification of disposition." The comment fleshes out this requirement by explaining that the notification must be reasonable as to "the manner in which it is sent, its timeliness, and its content." *See* **9–611** Official Comment 2. The code then provides a safe harbor in **9–612(b)**, which tells us that in transactions other than consumer transactions, "a notification sent after default and 10 days or more before the earliest time of disposition set forth in the notification is sent within a reasonable time before the disposition." This means that 10 days notice is good enough, but it does not mean that less than 10 days notice is not good enough. That's still a question of fact.

Is the secured party always required to give notice of sale to the debtor? No. **9–611(d)** excuses a secured party from the obligation to give notice in two scenarios: 1) when the collateral is perishable or threatens to decline speedily in value; and 2) when the collateral is of a type sold on a recognized market. In learning the rules governing disposition of collateral, it is always important to remember that in theory the rules are designed to encourage the secured party to seek the highest price possible for the collateral. It does no one any good to hold on to perishable collateral. Be careful, though, in finding that collateral is of a kind sold on a recognized market. A recognized market is one in which the assets sold are fungible and there are standardized price quotes, such as a stock market. *See* **9–627** Official Comment 4.

Now it's time for the sale. As noted above, the sale can be public or private, but all aspects of the sale must be commercially reasonable. Even the choice between a public and a private sale.

IN RE FRAZIER
93 B.R. 366 (Bankr. E.D. Tenn. 1988)

PAINE, J.

[In the excerpt below, the secured party had lent the debtor money to purchase an airplane to be used in the debtor's business. The bankruptcy court had granted the secured party relief from the automatic stay to sell the plane. The Chavers had guaranteed the loan; they now stand in the shoes of the secured party.

In Tennessee the disposition of collateral by a secured party must, in every aspect, including the method, manner, time, place and terms be "commercially reasonable". [**9–610(b)**]. The standard is further defined in [**9–627(b)**]:

> If the secured party either sells the collateral in the usual manner in any recognized market therefor or if he sells at the price current in such market at the time of his sale or if he has otherwise sold in conformity with reasonable commercial practices among dealers in the type of property sold he has sold in a commercially reasonable manner.

"Commercially reasonable" manner in Tennessee means disposition "in keeping with prevailing trade practices among reputable and responsible business and commercial enterprises engaged in the same or a similar business." *Mallicoat v. Volunteer Finance & Loan Corp.,* 57 Tenn. App. 106, 415 S.W.2d 347, 350 (1966). The term "commercially reasonable" by itself gives little guidance for the analysis of any particular case; this Court has previously identified those six (6) factors by which compliance with prevailing commercially reasonable practices may be measured. They are:

1. The type of collateral involved;
2. The condition of the collateral;
3. The number of bids solicited;
4. The time and place of sale;
5. The purchase price received or the terms of sale; and

6. Any special circumstances involved.

Pippin Way, Inc. v. Four Star Music Co., 2 Bankr. 454, 461 (M.D. Tenn. 1979).

In order to make the determination of commercial reasonableness, we must look to the facts and circumstances of the sale. Following repossession of the aircraft and the transfer of rights to the Chavers, the Lear jet was sold at a public sale. The aircraft, which sold to Frank Frazier's group for $ 850,000.00 in March, 1985, was sold in April, 1986 for $ 415,000.00. Although failure to procure the best price for collateral does not in and of itself make a sale commercially unreasonable, **[9–627(a)]**, and reasonableness is primarily assessed by the procedures employed, "a sufficient resale price is the logical focus of the protection given debtors. . . ." *Smith v. Daniels*, 634 S.W.2d 276, 278 (Tenn.App. 1982). The great disparity between the purchase price and the sale price of the collateral approximately one (1) year later raises the issue of whether the total circumstances demonstrate that the Chavers took all steps considered reasonable by prevailing practices to insure that the sale of the Lear jet would bring a fair price. *Smith v. Daniels,* 634 S.W.2d at 278. After reviewing the circumstances of the sale and the relevant legal factors, the Court determines that the Chavers have not met their burden for the following reasons.

Procedures employed to sell small jet aircraft are matters particularly within the knowledge of a small group of persons who are experts in the highly technical endeavor. The Chavers offered the testimony of two (2) experts, and Jamie, Inc. and Mrs. Frazier offered a third expert, Mr. Charles Mulle. After considering both the demeanor and the relative qualifications of these experts, the Court finds that Mr. Mulle was by far the pre-eminent expert. Mr. Mulle was a graduate of Riddle Aeronautic Institute where he received a Bachelor of Science Degree in Aeronautic sciences with a minor in aviation management. Prior to attending Riddle Aeronautic Institute, he served in Army aviation for four (4) years and assisted in the testing projects for certain military aircraft. He has served as a Canadian bush pilot, a corporate pilot, and since 1975 has been employed full time in the commercial aircraft leasing sales and management area. Since 1981 he has been the principal owner of Business Aircraft Leasing, Inc., a company which is solely involved in the buying, selling and leasing of corporate and commercial aircraft. In addition, Mr. Mulle had specific knowledge of the aircraft at issue in this case from the date it was initially ordered from the manufacturer. He had been responsible for leasing the aircraft and had subsequently sold the aircraft to Mr. Frazier, Conn-Aire, Inc. and Jamie, Inc. One of the Chavers' expert witnesses agreed that Mr. Mulle was a competent and knowledgeable person in the field of aircraft sales and procedures. The other expert witness offered by the Chavers advised the Court that he respected Mr.

Mulle's opinion and looked to him for information and advice. Mr. Mulle's experience was far in excess of that of the Chavers' experts.[1] Based on his experience, candor and qualifications, the Court finds Mr. Mulle highly credible and uniquely qualified to assist the Court in its determination.

The value of the aircraft at the time of its sale to Mr. Frazier, Conn-Aire and Jamie, Inc. was approximately $ 825,000.00 to $ 850,000.00, as established by the testimony of the banker who initially granted the loan to the Chavers. Mr. Mulle testified that the value was in that range and may have contained a premium of approximately $ 25,000.00 to $ 50,000.00 because the initial sale was one hundred percent (100%) financed.

1.   *The Hasty Sale Was Not Reasonable.*

The plaintiffs gained possession of the aircraft on May 2, 1986 and sold it at public auction on June 3, 1986. The Court finds the plaintiffs acted with unreasonable haste in their efforts to sell the aircraft, apparently in order to satisfy the time requirement imposed by the Bank.

The collateral at issue is a jet aircraft with a highly specialized and limited market. Under the circumstances of this case, the Court finds that the time permitted to advertise and market the plane to this select group of potential buyers was grossly inadequate. The Chavers could not satisfactorily explain their actions in April and May of 1986, but the following is clear from the record. First, the Chavers voluntarily observed the condition of selling the aircraft within sixty (60) days. Their principal advisor, who also testified at trial, was extremely inexperienced in the commercial sale of jet aircraft. The plaintiffs were aware that Mr. Mulle had worked on the aircraft previously and that he was available to assist them in the sale of the aircraft, yet neither the Chavers nor their advisors sought Mr. Mulle out for advice or aid. The plaintiffs' advisor knew of the proposed repossession on April 23, 1986 and that the custody of the aircraft would pass to the Chavers on May 2, 1986, but made no immediate recommendations as to the means of disposing of the aircraft. After "investigating options" for at least two (2) weeks, he and the Chavers made the initial decision to sell the aircraft at auction approximately three (3) weeks prior to the actual sale. All advertising for the sale was done from May 20, 1986 to May 29, 1986 and terminated within five (5) days of the sale.

The other expert witnesses, including the Chavers' own expert, believed greater time was needed to explore and reach the potential market. The Chavers' other expert witness testified that six (6) months to one (1) year was needed for the fair and proper sale of such an aircraft. Mr. Mulle considered ninety (90) days to be an appropriate, although

---

[1]   The Chavers' expert, who actually assisted them in devising a plan for the sale, testified that he had never conducted a retail sale of jet aircraft prior to the transaction in question.

minimum, time frame to judge the market and to make commercially reasonable efforts.

Regardless of the specific time requirements, which this Court does not determine, it is clear to the Court that the time requirement agreed to by the Bank and the Chavers was, in itself, unreasonable. The Court further finds that the Chavers sold an expensive and sophisticated jet aircraft in half the unreasonably brief time permitted by their agreement with the Bank and that this hasty sale was a significant cause of the low sale price. The Court further notes that the Chavers did not request an extension of the sale date requirement, that there were no adverse consequences to a delay of up to six (6) months based on the structure of the Chavers' loan with the Bank and that Mr. Chavers is a sophisticated and professional investor. Under these circumstances, the time allotted prior to the sale was inadequate and not commercially reasonable.

2.   *The Advertising Was Not Adequate.*

The Court considered substantial testimony concerning the adequacy of the advertising and further determines that the advertising was wholly inadequate for a commercially reasonable sale. *See Connex Press Inc. v. International Automotive, Inc.,* 436 F. Supp. 51, 55 (D.C. 1977) (Advertisements of airplane sale written so cautiously as "to in no way encourage buyer interest" and failure to contact dealer groups partial basis for finding sale unreasonable). Advertisements ran briefly in the Wall Street Journal and a trade publication known as Trade-A-Plane. The advertisements were described by Mr. Mulle as telegraphing a distress sale during "a brief flurry of advertising". Even one of the Chavers' experts felt that the use of the "as-is" phrase in the text of the advertising suggested a distress sale.

Mr. Mulle described a reasonable advertising protocol as follows. He testified first that in advertisements in the Wall Street Journal and Trade-A-Plane should be positive and run for an appropriate length of time. The Chavers' advertisements ran briefly and suggested a distress sale. He also testified that the potential market for jet aircraft was concentrated in corporations and professional aircraft brokers throughout the country. From this pool of qualified buyers the most likely prospects should have been determined; the particular needs of a buyer should have been addressed in a formal sales effort, including if necessary, taking the aircraft for a buyer to view. While the Chavers provided some information to those who responded to their advertisements, such information was described by Mr. Mulle as "laughable" and indicative of an amateur effort to sell the aircraft. The sales packet provided by the Chavers' advisor to potential buyers did not include a log book summary or copy of the log book, which even the Chavers' advisor admitted was important information to a potential buyer and would reflect the high degree of maintenance required by the Federal Aviation Authority for commercial and charter work.

3. *A "Distress Sale" Auction Was Not Reasonable.*

The method of sale is also an important factor. Under these circumstances, the Court finds that an initial effort to contact the fairly limited pool of qualified commercial buyers would have been in keeping with prevailing responsible practice, and not immediate resort to the public sale option, which in the words of even the Chavers' experts, is ordinarily a "last resort" method of sale. The Court finds the use of a public auction, under these circumstances, was not reasonable. It could be expected to draw only those it did—experienced wholesale aircraft dealers in an already small potential market looking for a distress type "deal". Potential retail buyers who would normally have concerns about the aircraft that could be addressed in the normal course of business were not identified and could not be reasonably presumed to attend an auction advertised in this manner within this time frame. This method of sale, while always a possibility, under these facts immediately telegraphed the message that this was a "fire sale". Under these circumstances, there was no reason initially to conduct such a distress disposal of the aircraft, and the Court finds it commercially unreasonable to have done so.

4. *Aircraft Maintenance Was Not Properly Addressed Prior to the Sale.*

A great deal of attention focused on the need for a "hot section inspection" on the aircraft. According to the rules and regulations of the Federal Aviation Authority, jet engines have to be inspected and, if necessary, overhauled. Estimates of the cost of performing this service were varied. From the testimony, it appears to the Court that the Chavers did not even consider whether this work should be accomplished and borne as a cost prior to sale, and if so, what effect it would have on resale value. The Court finds that under the circumstances, and in light of the condition of this particular airplane, a hot section inspection was an important and necessary step to prepare the plane for sale and failure of the Chavers to undertake the inspection seriously lessened their ability to obtain a fair price for the aircraft. The Chavers also failed to investigate paint options, possible financing options and a procedure for either undertaking or "capping" the hot section changes, which process likely would have allowed for recoupment of these charges upon sale. The failure to reasonably prepare the aircraft for sale, in the determination of this Court, constitutes a commercially unreasonable manner of sale.

5. *The Purchase Price Was Not Reasonable.*

The final factor is the purchase price obtained at the sale. Although this factor is not, by itself, determinative, it is a factor to consider. The proof in this case showed that even though the plane sold for $ 415,000.00, it was insured at that time for $ 700,000.00, as testified to by the bank officers. Even the Chavers' expert, Mr. Bunyan, was "surprised" that the plane sold for $ 415,000.00. Mr. Chavers testified that he thought the value of the plane was in the neighborhood of $ 700,000.00 when it was returned to him. Mr. Mulle testified that it was ludicrous to think that the fair market value of the plane could decrease by approximately one-half of its sale value a year earlier. The Court finds that the sale price corroborates Mr. Mulle's testimony that the Chavers failed to follow prevailing practices in responsible sales of this type: positive advertising, a more reasonable time frame for promotion and sale, more targeted yet wider dissemination of information about the aircraft, better information provided to prospective buyers, preparation of the aircraft for sale and a reasonable attempt to make a retail sale in the first instance. The Chavers' testimony demonstrates that of all these steps could have been accomplished, but were not even addressed.

The evidence shows that the low sale price cannot be explained by the condition of the aircraft upon foreclosure. During the fifteen (15) months between the sale and foreclosure the plane was used by Conn-Aire, Inc. for passenger and cargo flights. This use caused Conn-Aire to observe stricter standards than ordinarily imposed on a privately owned aircraft, to comply with Federal Aviation Authority regulations. Accordingly, even though the plane was used steadily by Conn-Aire, it was regularly maintained and inspected pursuant to those FAA standards. The condition of the plane was readily ascertainable from the aircraft maintenance log books which were available to interested buyers for the aircraft. The testimony indicates that even a small amount of money to refurbish the plane, and a thorough cleaning would have drastically affected its "eye appeal", and would have been part of a reasonable effort to dispose of the plane so as to obtain a fair price.

The excerpt above refers to the UCC's guidelines for determining whether a disposition was commercially reasonable. You will find these guidelines in **9–627(a)** and **(b)**. The fact that the secured party could have obtained a better price by disposing of the collateral by a different method does not *in itself* make a sale commercially unreasonable. That said, a debtor will argue that a sale was commercially unreasonable in order to reduce or eliminate its deficiency claim.

9–627(b) gives you three examples of a commercially reasonable sale. Two of them refer to a "recognized market." As we explained above, you should interpret that term narrowly. **9–627(b)(3)** sweeps more sales into the realm of commercial reasonableness, in that it tells you that a sale is made in a commercially reasonable manner if it is "in conformity with reasonable commercial practices among dealers in the type of property that was the subject of the disposition."

3. COLLECTING ACCOUNTS AND OTHER PAYMENT RIGHTS

In an earlier chapter, you learned that payment rights can serve as collateral. One benefit to a creditor of taking payment rights as collateral is that the creditor can notify the party obligated on those rights to pay the creditor directly after the debtor's default.

To understand the sections that govern collection of payment rights, you need to understand how Article 9 describes the parties to a secured transaction involving payment rights. Let's go back to the hypothetical Sport-e Bikes company from Chapter 11 of this book, but move the clock back to when it was a healthy company. Sport-e Bikes borrowed $100,000 from Riverside Bank secured by its accounts receivable. Sport-e Bikes sold electric-assist bikes to two companies, Mountain Adventures, a bike tour company, and Wheel World, a bike shop. It sold the bikes to both companies on 30-day credit, meaning that they had to pay Sport-e Bikes for the bikes within 30 days after receiving the bikes. The payment obligations are not evidenced by promissory notes or chattel paper, so are therefore accounts under **9–102(a)(2)**.

If Sport-e Bikes defaults on its obligation to pay Riverside Bank, **9–607** gives Riverside Bank the right to collect the accounts by notifying the "account debtors" to make payment to Riverside Bank. **9–404** and **9–406** limit the rights of Riverside Bank and give some protections to Mountain Adventures and Wheel World. In order to understand how they do so, you need to understand some of Article 9's labels.

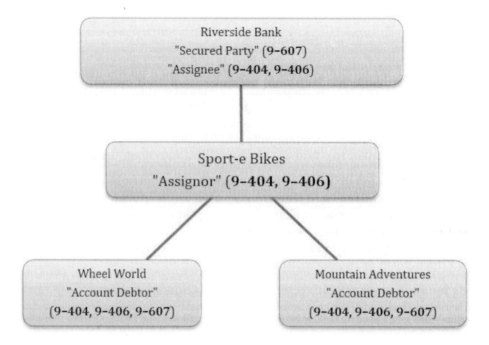

Note that there is a good chance that neither Wheel World nor Mountain Adventures has any idea that Sport-e Bikes has given its accounts as collateral to Riverside Bank. **9–406** tells us that an account debtor may discharge its obligation by paying the assignor only until it receives a notification from the assignee that the account has ben assigned and that payment is to be made to the assignee. What that means for Wheel World and Mountain Adventures is that if they pay Sport-e Bikes after getting a notice from Riverside Bank that complies with **9–406**, they may have to pay twice.

It is of course possible that one of the account debtors has a claim against Sport-e Bikes that would reduce its payment obligation. **9–404** covers that possibility and tells us that the assignee (Riverside Bank in our example) takes accounts subject to all of the terms of the agreement creating the account and all defenses or claims in recoupment that the account debtor has against the assignor.

You learned about claims in recoupment in the Payment Systems part of this book. A claim in recoupment arises when two parties to a transaction have claims against each other arising from the transaction. In the Sales part of this book you learned about warranties that attach to a sale of goods. If a seller sells goods to a buyer on credit, that seller has the right to be paid. If the goods breach one of the warranties in the contract, the buyer's claim for damages is a claim in recoupment.

4. AFTER SALE

What happens after sale? In a perfect world, the secured creditor will be paid in full. But the world is not perfect, and often there's a fight over the secured creditor's right to a deficiency. First, let's look at the governing statutory section—**9–615** (note that **9–608** provides the distribution rules when the secured party collects payment rights under **9–607**). This section tells us how the proceeds of any disposition must be distributed. First priority is always the reasonable expenses of sale. Attorney's fees in connection with the sale also get first priority, so long as they are reasonable and provided for by agreement. [Pro-tip—if you are drafting loan documents for a creditor, make sure that you include your fees]. Next comes the outstanding amount owed to the secured creditor conducting the foreclosure sale. Third priority is any subordinate secured creditor (you will learn about them when we cover priorities), but only if that secured creditor submits a demand for payment. Remember that subordinate secured creditors are entitled to notice of sale.

If there's money left over after all of those people are paid (there rarely is), then the surplus goes to the debtor. If there's not enough money to pay the foreclosing secured creditor, the debtor must pay the deficiency.

At this point, it is helpful to review two of the documents in a secured loan. The promissory note is the obligor's promise to pay, and it makes the obligor personally liable for the loan amount. The security agreement is the document that makes the collateral "liable" for the loan amount. If the sales proceeds of the collateral are not sufficient to satisfy the creditor, the creditor can pursue the obligor for the remaining outstanding loan obligation. That difference between the outstanding loan amount and the sales proceeds of the collateral is known as the "deficiency." When a creditor sells collateral in a commercially reasonable manner, the amount of the deficiency claim is the difference between the amount that the debtor owed to the creditor (the secured obligation, expenses, and attorney's fees) and the amount received from the sale of the collateral.

When debtors challenge sales based on a lack of commercial reasonableness, they are really challenging their liability for a deficiency. A creditor who sells collateral in a commercially unreasonable manner can see its deficiency reduced entirely or partially. The UCC explains this in a manner that most students (and attorneys) find somewhat confusing. *See* **9–626**. Before jumping into the language of **9–626**, it's important to know that before its adoption in the 1998 Amendments, courts took two approaches to reducing a deficiency judgment when a secured party sold collateral in a commercially unreasonable manner. Some courts eliminated the right to a deficiency entirely, applying a "absolute bar" rule. Others reduced it to an amount that the secured party would have received had it sold the collateral in a commercially reasonable manner.

9–626 takes the latter approach, applying a "rebuttable presumption" rule when the secured party fails to sell its collateral in a commercially reasonable manner. Note that **9–626** is another "consumer compromise" section. Therefore, the Official Text version of **9–626** *does not apply* to consumer transactions. We'll explore what that means shortly.

Under **9–626**, if the debtor claims that the sale was not commercially reasonable, the creditor has the burden of proving that it was. If it cannot do so, the rebuttable presumption kicks in. The presumption is that the value of the collateral was equal to the amount owed to the secured party. **9–626(a)(4).** It is up to the secured party to prove that the collateral was worth less than that sum. To overcome the presumption, the secured party must offer proof to the court of what the collateral would have sold for had the sale been conducted in a commercially reasonable manner. If it cannot do so, then the secured party loses its right to collect a deficiency. In the following case, the collateral at issue was a logging truck. The foreclosure sale brought $5,000, and the secured party claimed a deficiency of over $50,000. To prove the value of the truck, the secured party offered as its expert the truck's buyer, Mr. Ray:

> Even assuming *arguendo* that Ray had testified that he thought the truck was "worth" $5,000 to an eighteen-year veteran of the logging industry and that Ray's experience as a logger qualified him to provide expert testimony on the value of logging trucks, an

expert's testimony is meant to assist the finder of fact by providing the fact-finder insight into a topic about which the fact-finder lacks knowledge or experience. *State v. Allen*, 274 S.W.3d 514, 526 (Mo. App. W.D. 2008). Here, the fact-finder was the trial court, as this was a bench-tried case. The trial court received the benefit of hearing all of Ray's testimony. In so doing, the trial court was free to assess the weight to be given to Ray's "expert" testimony. *Whitnell v. State*, 129 S.W.3d 409, 413 (Mo. App. E.D. 2004) ("The extent of an expert's training or experience goes to the weight of his testimony. . . ."). " 'As the trier of fact, the trial court determines the credibility of witnesses and is free to believe or disbelieve all or part of the witnesses' testimony.' " *Zink v. State*, 278 S.W.3d 170, 192 (Mo. banc 2009) (quoting *Blue Ridge Bank & Trust Co. v. Hart*, 152 S.W.3d 420, 426 (Mo. App. W.D. 2005)). We defer to the trial court on credibility determinations even if the evidence could support a different conclusion. *McLain v. Johnson*, 885 S.W.2d 345, 348 (Mo. App. W.D. 1994). This is the case even where the testimony of a witness is not contradicted by other testimony as " 'it is well settled that the trial court is free to believe or disbelieve all, part or none of the evidence, including disbelieving evidence that is uncontroverted.' " *Simpson v. Simpson*, 295 S.W.3d 199, 204 (Mo. App. W.D. 2009) (quoting *Beery v. Shinkle*, 193 S.W.3d 435, 443 (Mo. App. W.D. 2006)); *see also Keen v. Campbell*, 249 S.W.3d 927, 931 (Mo. App. S.D. 2008).

Ray did not testify to the amount the logging truck would have sold for had the sale been in compliance with Article 9 of the Mo. UCC. Even had he done so in any capacity (expert or otherwise), the trial court was free to find that his testimony lacked credibility and was, instead, speculative and deserving of little or no weight on the topic. The Bank presented no other evidence of the logging truck's valuation. Conversely, Mr. Gerlt [the debtor] testified that the Bank's president, just one month prior to the repossession and sale of the logging truck, had approved a release of all collateral securing the Gerlts' $46,500 repayment obligation under the promissory note except for the logging truck. And, Mr. Gerlt testified that he had spent more than $5,000 on fourteen tires for the logging truck not long before the logging truck's eventual sale to Ray.

Exch. Bank of Mo. v. Gerlt, 367 S.W.3d 132 (Mo. Ct. App. 2012)

What happens in a consumer transaction? It depends. **9–626(b)** tells us that the exclusion of consumer transactions from **9–626** was "intended to leave to the court the determination of the proper rules in consumer transactions." Some courts, therefore, will apply the absolute bar rule to deny a deficiency to the creditor who sells collateral in a commercially unreasonable manner; others will apply the rebuttable presumption rule. Often, a court will do what courts in the same state did before the 1998 amendments as the court in the excerpt below did:

> Delaware adopted revised Article 9 on July 1, 2001. The former Article 9 did not directly address the consequence of a secured party's failure to comply with its provisions. Delaware case law, however, held that a failure to comply with the notice provisions of Article 9 created an absolute bar to the secured party recovering a deficiency. In a 1980 decision, this Court adopted the absolute bar rule in the context of deficient notice, for the policy reason that proper notice of the sale of collateral enables a debtor to ensure that the secured party follows procedures designed to yield the highest available sale price. Those same policy concerns are applicable in this case and under Article 9 in its current form, where the secured party has failed to establish that it sold the collateral in a commercially reasonable manner. We therefore hold that a secured party's failure to prove a commercially reasonable disposition of repossessed consumer goods will absolutely bar a recovery of any deficiency. Accordingly, the entry of a deficiency judgment in Onyx's favor (and its affirmance by the Superior Court) cannot stand.

Hicklin v. Onyx Acceptance Corp., 970 A.2d 244 (Del. 2009)

5. STRICT FORECLOSURE

Must a creditor sell the collateral? Note that **9–610** says that a secured party *may* dispose of the collateral. There are always costs involved in a sale, and as you saw just above, costs of sale receive first priority in payment. If there's not enough money after sale to pay the outstanding loan amount, the costs of sale increase the secured creditor's deficiency claim. Sometimes, a creditor might prefer to just keep the collateral without selling it. The UCC permits this if the creditor complies with the requirements of **9–620**.

The process of accepting the collateral in satisfaction of a debt is known as "strict foreclosure." To understand the requirements of **9–620** and how they apply in different situations, you need to keep some concepts in mind. First, the UCC distinguishes between acceptance of collateral in full satisfaction of a debt and acceptance of collateral in partial satisfaction of a debt. Acceptance in full satisfaction is less of a problem from a debtor's point of view—yes, the debtor loses the collateral, but it will not be liable for a deficiency. When a creditor accepts collateral in partial satisfaction of a debt, it can still claim a deficiency even though there has not been a sale to set the value of the collateral. Because there is no sale, the requirements for partial strict foreclosure are more stringent and partial strict foreclosure is not permitted at all in a consumer transaction. The foreclosing creditor must also send notice to other parties with an interest in the collateral pursuant to **9–621** and if any of those parties object to the strict foreclosure, the secured party must sell the collateral. A strict foreclosure leaves no surplus for subordinate creditors.

As in other places in Article 9, you also need to keep in mind the difference between a consumer transaction and a non-consumer transaction. Review the definition of consumer transaction in **9–102(a)(26)**. If the obligor in a consumer transaction has paid at least 60 of the price of the goods in a purchase-money transaction or 60% of the original loan amount in a mon-purchase-money transaction, the secured party must dispose of the goods. *See* **9–620(e)**. In other words, strict foreclosure is not allowed at all.

The following chart illustrates the important procedural differences between a partial strict foreclosure and a strict foreclosure in full satisfaction of a debt.

Acceptance in Partial Satisfaction of Debt	Acceptance in Full Satisfaction of Debt
Never in a consumer transaction **9–620(g)**	All transactions except for consumer goods transactions in which the debtor has paid at least 60 percent of the original obligation **9–620(e)**
Debtor must consent in a record authenticated after default **9–620(c)(1)**	Debtor is deemed to consent if it receives an unconditional proposal from secured party and does not object within 20 days after the proposal is sent **9–620(c)(2)**

If the secured party complies with all of the requirements of **9–620**, the debtor's rights in the collateral are terminated and the secured party becomes the owner of the collateral.

Chapter Conclusion: At the end of this chapter, you should understand the concept of default and that a default triggers the secured creditor's collection remedies under Part 6 of Article 9. You should also understand the remedies of sale, collection, and strict foreclosure and the distribution of the proceeds of any sale of the collateral. Last, you should understand the circumstances that may reduce or eliminate the secured party's right to a deficiency claim.

PROBLEMS

1.   One of your new clients is MegaFinance, a company that makes loans using an app-based lending platform. Describing itself as the "Uber of lending"

its goal is to make the loan process as easy as possible for both lenders and borrowers. MegaFinance makes secured loans to individuals and to small businesses.

The brains behind the operation is your college roommate Alexis Wilton, who believes that borrowers will gladly give up some of their legal protections for a lower interest rate and easier loan approval process. Alexis spent one year in law school before chasing the shiny lights of fintech, so she knows (or thinks she knows) about freedom of contract. To keep collection costs down, she *really* wants to avoid litigation. She has asked you to draft a security agreement that: 1) defines breach of the peace (in a way consistent with the policy behind forbidding self-help repossession that breaches the peace), 2) contains an agreement by the debtor that notice of a foreclosure sale sent seven or more days before the sale is sent within a reasonable time; and 3) contains an agreement by the debtor that in the event of a default, MegaFinance can keep any repossessed collateral in full satisfaction of the outstanding obligation.

Can you draft the agreement that Alexis wants? See 9–602, 9–603.

2.   You just received a phone call from your very agitated client Margie, who opened her restaurant, Burger Shack, in the Center City Outlet Mall last year. Her timing was not very good because the Center City Outlet Mall is struggling mightily. Burger Shack is getting great Yelp reviews, however, and business has picked up in the last month. You helped Margie when she borrowed $250,000 from Entrepreneurial Finance to start the business last year. Margie granted a security interest in all of the restaurant's inventory and equipment as security for the loan.

Margie has called you in a frenzy because two men from Entrepreneurial Finance's recovery department have just arrived at her restaurant claiming the right to take her kitchen equipment. When they entered the restaurant, they loudly told customers that they should not be eating at a "deadbeat restaurant." When a customer threw a plate of French fries at the repossessors, they called the police.

Margie told you that she was five days late making her last three payments, but each time, Entrepreneurial Finance accepted the payments without saying anything. She made next month's payment yesterday, a week early. Today the *Wall Street Journal* reported that Altitude Sports, a major tenant of the outlet mall, filed for bankruptcy and is closing its space in the Center City Outlet Mall.

   a.   The security agreement between Margie and Entrepreneurial Finance states that Margie is in default if she does not make her payments on the first of each month. It also says that Entrepreneurial Finance can accelerate payment if it deems itself insecure in its chances of repayment. Does Entrepreneurial Finance have any right to repossess Margie's equipment? Do you need any more facts to answer the question? If so, what questions do you have for Margie? What else do you need to look for in the security agreement?

b.   Regardless of your answers to the above questions, assume that the repo men from Entrepreneurial Finance have the right to be at the Burger Shack to repossess Margie's equipment. Did calling the police change that? Did the flying French fries change that?

c.   Suppose that Entrepreneurial Finance peaceably repossessed 100 pounds of ground beef from the Burger Shack. How much notice must Entrepreneurial Finance give Margie before selling the meat? Do you need to look at the security agreement for your answer?

3.   SuperShale Energy, Inc. has recently fallen on hard times. It had obtained a loan from Rockledge Finance, secured by its drilling equipment located on Windy Acres Farm, which sits atop a massive shale gas deposit. When SuperShale defaulted on its loan, it owed Rockledge Finance $1,000,000. On October 1, Rockledge peaceably disabled the equipment on Windy Acres Farm and on October 8 sent SuperShale notice that it would conduct a public sale of the collateral on Windy Acres Farm on October 19. Rockledge conducted no inspection of the equipment even though it had been idle since July. Rockledge advertised the sale in the *Potter County Times*, the newspaper of general circulation in the rural county in which Windy Acres Farm is located. The high bidder at the auction was the Renewables Forever Foundation, an environmental group backed by a reclusive tech billionaire who commissions artists to make massive public sculptures out of unused industrial equipment. Renewables Forever paid $300,000 for the equipment and Rockledge claims that SuperShale owes it $700,000 more dollars.

a.   SuperShale has come to you to challenge Rockledge's deficiency claim. What are your best arguments against Rockledge?

b.   Will SuperShale be liable for any deficiency? What information do you need to answer that question?

c.   Switch sides and advise Rockledge. What should it do to avoid problems like this in the future? Rockledge has several specialized lending divisions—it lends to radio stations, horse farms, and music companies. What should Rockledge do when it forecloses on collateral in those types of transactions?

4.   Now you are representing Entrepreneurial Finance Co., which made a $500,000 loan to Cocoa Connections secured by its accounts receivable. Cocoa Connections makes equipment that is used in the chocolate-making process. As the market for sustainably sourced bean-to-bar chocolates has grown, so has the number of Cocoa Connections' competitors. As a result, it has had to cut prices on its machines just to stay in business.

Cocoa Connections has just defaulted on its loan from Entrepreneurial Finance, and Jeremy Hill, the loan officer there, has asked you for your help in collecting the accounts.

a.   Draft a letter from Entrepreneurial Finance to the account debtors requesting payment directly to your client. What information do you need to write the letter?

b.   Switch sides and represent one of the account debtors, Chocolates by Christopher. Chocolates by Christopher owes Cocoa Connections $20,000 for a roasting machine that it recently bought. Christopher Blake, the President of Chocolates by Christopher, just received a letter from Entrepreneurial Finance requesting that it pay the $20,000 to Entrepreneurial Finance. Christopher just called you for advice on whether he should pay. He has never heard of Entrepreneurial Finance, and distrusts the letter because one of his best friends was recently taken in by an internet scam. What information should he request from Entrepreneurial Finance before making payment?

c.   Go back to representing Entrepreneurial Finance. You sent the letter that you drafted in part (a) of this problem by U.S. Mail to the account debtors on May 1. On May 8, you heard from two of the account debtors, Celestial Cacao and Revolution Chocolates. Celestial Cacao told you that it made payment in full to Cocoa Connections on May 2. Revolution Chocolates told you that it did indeed buy a roasting machine from Cocoa Connections, but when it arrived it did not work properly and as a result, Revolution Chocolates rejected the machine and is waiting for a new one. Must Celestial Cacao and Revolution Chocolates make payment to Entrepreneurial Finance?

5.   When things were going well in Janine's real estate business, she bought her dream car, a Mercedes convertible coupe. She uses the car only for personal purposes. She financed the purchase with a $60,000 secured loan from Wheels Finance. Recently, things have fallen apart for Janine in more ways than one. Her real estate business is in a slump, and she has separated from her husband and moved out of the house that they shared. She ended up missing two payments on her car loan and Wheels Finance repossessed the car from the parking lot adjacent to her office.

a.   Assume for the purpose of this part of the problem that Wheels Finance sold the car in a commercially reasonable sale. At the time that Wheels sold the car, Janine owed Wheels $50,000 in principal and interest on the loan plus $5,000 in collection and attorney fees as provided in the loan agreement. The car sold for $38,000, but according to the Kelly Blue Book, it was worth $45,000. How much can Wheels Finance collect from Janine as a deficiency claim?

b.   In an alternative universe, here is what happened when Wheels Finance foreclosed on Janine's car. On May 1, Wheels sent Janine a notification that it would sell the car at a public sale at the Wheels Finance headquarters on May 12. Wheels sent the notice to the home that Janine had shared with her husband. Her soon to be-ex-husband threw the letter in the trash and never told Janine about the letter. On May 11, Terry, an Executive Vice President of Wheels Finance, decided that she wanted the car for herself, so she bought the car from Wheels for $38,000 on May 11. The public sale never happened. The usual way for automobile finance companies to sell repossessed vehicles in the region in which Janine lives is to sell them at a weekly dealers-only auto auction.

As in Part (a) Janine owes Wheels a total of $55,000. How much can Wheels collect from Janine as a deficiency claim now? What other facts do you need to answer the question?

6.   The Kitchen Konnection sells high-end kitchen appliances. Its business has been booming with the popularity of HGTV. Last year it sold a $10,000 Viking stove on credit to Tim and Cecelia Moore and took back a purchase-money security interest in it. Tim and Cecelia had the stove installed in their home; they are caterers but they run most of their business out of a building about a mile away from their home.

Tim and Cecelia defaulted in their payments for the stove. The Kitchen Konnection would like to just keep the stove in satisfaction of the debt. The stove's value is roughly equal to the amount outstanding on the loan, and the Kitchen Konnection would like to use it for cooking demonstrations in its showroom.

Please tell the Kitchen Konnection whether it can keep the stove in satisfaction of Tim and Cecelia's debt, and if it can, please tell it what it has to do. If you need any more facts, please identify what those facts are.

7.   Smart Home, Inc. sells "smart" household appliances that are connected to the internet. A Smart Home refrigerator can sense when its owner is running low on groceries and order them for the owner. Smart Home, Inc. sold a smart refrigerator to Will and Marcy Fox for $6,000 and took back a security interest in it. The refrigerator is in Will and Marcy's home kitchen. The standard Smart Home Security Agreement states that upon default, Smart Home can remotely disable the refrigerator. Marcy has a medical condition that requires a lot of medication that she must keep refrigerated.

Last week Will and Marcy defaulted on their loan and Smart Home turned off the fridge. Did Smart Home do anything that is not permitted by Article 9 of the UCC?

CHAPTER 14

PERFECTING AND MAINTAINING THE PERFECTION OF SECURITY INTERESTS

■ ■ ■

Although attachment of a security interest gives a secured creditor the enforcement rights that you learned about in the last chapter, all secured parties must perfect their security interests to ensure that their rights to enforce have priority over all other parties who might claim an interest in the collateral. In Chapter 11 of this book, you learned that a security interest has a remedy aspect and a priority aspect. Attachment of a security interest gives a secured party its remedy rights; perfection gives a secured party its priority rights. The remaining two chapters will explain these priority rights.

A. WHAT IS PERFECTION?

The act of perfection tells the world that a secured party is claiming an interest in its collateral. It is critical to remember that perfection is not necessary for enforcement (unless the debtor is in bankruptcy, which we'll take up in the next chapter). Because perfection tells the world of the secured party's property interest, perfection is usually accomplished by the secured party taking some action to give the world notice of its interest. The vast majority of security interests are perfected by filing a financing statement in a public place. That is not the only method of perfection, however.

You can find the general perfection rules in Part 3 of Article 9, **9–301** *et seq.*

Let's start with the basic rule of **9–310(a)**, which tells us that "Except as otherwise provided in subsection (b) and Section 9–312(b), a financing statement must be filed to perfect all security interests and agricultural liens." In this chapter, we'll cover filing and the exceptions from the filing requirement. It's important to know the following about filing: (1) sometimes filing is the only method by which to perfect a security interest; (2) sometimes filing is one of two equally effective methods of perfecting a security interest; (3) sometimes filing is an effective, but less desirable method of perfecting a security interest; and (4) sometimes filing is ineffective to perfect a security interest. In order to know which of the above statements applies to your transaction, it is critical that you know how to classify your collateral. In this chapter, we will be doing a lot of collateral classification.

It is also important to remember that a security interest is not perfected unless it has first attached. **9–308**. This point will become important when we talk about priorities.

Collateral classification is critical to the perfection question. We can guarantee that at this moment, if we asked you how to perfect a security interest in an automobile or a chandelier, you could not answer the question. After you read these materials, you will be able to answer the question, but your first answer will have to be another question. That question will be: how do you classify the collateral?

B. PERFECTION BY FILING

Because filing is the most common way to perfect a security interest, perfection by filing is a good place to start. To understand how a secured party perfects its security interest in collateral by filing, you need to know two things: what to file and where to file.

The "what" is a financing statement. Article 9 contains a definition of financing statement in **9–102**, but we challenge you to tell us what a financing statement is based on that definition. More helpful, at least in the Official Text of the UCC, is **9–521**, which provides images of both the initial financing statement form (commonly known as a UCC–1) and the amendment form (commonly known as a UCC–3). You can find these forms on the web site of state Secretary of State's offices (giving away part of the answer to "where to file").

The "where" is (almost always) the Secretary of State's office in the state in which the debtor is located. The UCC gives you this answer in two pieces. Read **9–501(a)**. At first blush, you would think that UCC financing statements are filed in the county land records, the same place as a mortgage. **9–501(a)(1).** Some financing statements—those that cover real estate related collateral—are, and we'll cover those after we cover the basics. Most financing statements are filed in the office described in **9–501(a)(2)**, which contains two sets of brackets where the name of the office should be. In practice you will of course look at your state's enactment of the UCC to find out where to file. For your purposes in this course, you can fill the brackets with "the Secretary of State."[1]

The second piece is "which state?" For that answer, you go to **9–301(1)**, which tells you that "while a debtor is located in a jurisdiction, the local law of that jurisdiction governs perfection." When you combine this rule

---

[1]   In the overwhelming majority of states, financing statements are filed in the Secretary of State's office. There are exceptions however. For example, in Georgia, financing statements are filed in the office of "the clerk of the superior court of any county" in the state. *See* O.C.G.A. § 11–9–501(a)(2).

with **9–501**, you conclude that a secured party, in order to perfect its security interest in collateral, must file a financing statement in the Secretary of State's office in the state where the debtor is located. There is another set of rules by which you determine the debtor's location, so we'll save those for after we discuss the contents of a financing statement.

All of the filing rules that we discuss give information to two sets of people: the secured creditor looking to perfect its interest in the collateral and subsequent searchers who are looking to see if anyone is claiming an interest in the same collateral.

1. WHAT TO FILE

A financing statement must contain three pieces of information in order to be effective. **9–502.** Those three items are: 1) the debtor's name; 2) the secured party's name; and 3) an indication of the collateral. A financing statement missing any of these items of information is not effective against anyone, even if it somehow makes it onto the filing office's records.

What if the information is incorrect? Article 9 provides a rule for that as well. Under **9–506**, if any of the **9–502** information is incorrect, you need to ask two questions. First, is the mistake a minor error or omission? If the answer to that question is "yes," then you ask a further question: does the minor error or omission make the financing statement seriously misleading? Because the debtor's name is such an important piece of information, as you will learn below, the UCC contains a special rule for determining whether a mistake in the debtor's name renders a financing statement seriously misleading. **9–506(c).**

a. The Debtor's Name

The debtor's name is the most important item of information in a financing statement. Filing offices index financing statements according to the debtor's name, so subsequent searchers will not find a financing statement that contains an incorrect name for the debtor. Because the filing system exists to give notice of security interests, an "unfindable" financing statement will not give notice and will therefore be ineffective.

What is an unfindable financing statement for UCC purposes? **9–506** tells us that an incorrect debtor name renders a financing statement seriously misleading if a search of the UCC filing records under the debtor's correct name, using the filing office's standard search logic, would fail to reveal the financing statement. Filing office search logic differs from state to state. For example, some states use the Standard Search Logic Rules promulgated by the International Association of Commercial Administrators, which you can find on the IACA website, https:// www.iaca.org/secured-transactions/. Others do not. As a filer (meaning a secured party or its lawyer), it is critically important to make sure that the name is correct.

What is your name? Do you have an "official" name? Do you know what your landlord's name is? Perhaps you bought a sandwich from a local shop today. Do you know the name of that shop? If you think that these are trick questions, they are. Article 9 answers these questions in such a way that might surprise you.

In order to determine your debtor's name, you need to know what your debtor is. Read **9–503(a)**. The drafters of Article 9 strived for certainty in determine the name of the debtor, and therefore, if the debtor's name can be ascertained by looking at a specified public record or standard document, the name in that record or document must be used in the financing statement. Therefore, your answer to the question "what is the debtor's name?" will depend on whether the debtor is an individual, an organization (**1–201(b)(25)**), a registered organization (**9–102(a)(71)**), or a trust.

i.   *Individual Debtors*

The quest for certainty in providing a name for a debtor that is an individual drove the 2010 amendments to Article 9. The answer to the question "do you have an official name?" is "no" if you are a United States citizen. Before you protest and say, "but wait, I have a birth certificate," consider how many people you know are not known by the name that is shown on their birth certificates (for example, those who changed their name upon marriage). The drafting committee chose to give the states a choice in enacting a provision regarding an individual debtor's name in **9–503(a)(3)**. The two choices are the Alternative A "only if" rule, which states that a financing statement adequately provides the name of an individual debtor only if it provides the name indicated on the debtor's current driver's license, and the Alternative B "safe harbor" approach, under which the name on an individual's driver's license is sufficient, but so is the debtor's "individual name," and the debtor's surname and first personal name. Banks preferred Alternative A, so most states went along and adopted that alternative.

Some of the difficulties in determining an individual debtor's name are described in the excerpt below. Note that the reasoning below remains applicable in states that have adopted Alternative B to **9–503(a)(3)**.

CLARK V. DEERE & CO. (IN RE KINDERKNECHT)
309 B.R. 71 (10th Cir. B.A.P. 2004)

THURMAN.

* * *

I. Background

It is undisputed that the debtor's legal name is "Terrance Joseph Kinderknecht." In addition, it is undisputed that the debtor is informally known as "Terry."

The debtor granted Deere security interests in two farm implements. Deere promptly filed financing statements in the appropriate place, listing the debtor as "Terry J. Kinderknecht."

Subsequently, the debtor filed a Chapter 7 petition. His petition, while signed by "Terry Kinderknecht," is filed under his legal name, "Terrance J. Kinderknecht."

The trustee in the debtor's Chapter 7 case commenced an adversary proceeding against Deere, seeking to avoid its interests in the debtor's farm implements pursuant to *11 U.S.C. § 544(a)(1)*. According to the trustee, Deere's interests in the property were avoidable because they were not perfected under the Kansas Uniform Commercial Code inasmuch as its financing statements, listing the debtor by his nickname as opposed to his legal name, were "seriously misleading" and ineffective. Deere argued that providing the debtor's commonly used nickname in its financing statements was sufficient, and that its interests in the debtor's property were perfected under Kansas law. Cross motions for summary judgment were filed.

The bankruptcy court entered Judgment in favor of Deere, holding that Deere's interests in the debtor's property were not avoidable by the trustee under *§ 544(a)(1)*. In its Memorandum Opinion, *Clark v. Deere & Co. (In re Kinderknecht)*,[3] the bankruptcy court concluded that Deere's financing statements were sufficient to perfect its interests in the debtor's property even though Deere listed the debtor in its financing statements by the debtor's nickname.

The trustee timely appealed the bankruptcy court's Judgment to this Court. After the trustee's appeal was submitted, the Court granted the Secretary of State leave to appear and file a Brief as Amicus Curiae. Under Kansas law, the Secretary of State is charged with maintaining the data base used to track the filing of financing statements in Kansas, and with promulgating "standard search logic" for conducting searches of that data base. Like the trustee, the Secretary of State advocates reversal of the bankruptcy court's Judgment.

---

[3]   300 B.R. 47 (Bankr. D. Kan. 2003).

II. Discussion

The issue in this case is whether the bankruptcy court erred in concluding that Deere's interests in the debtor's property were perfected as of the petition date so as to make them immune from avoidance under _11 U.S.C. § 544(a)(1)_. We must determine, therefore, whether the bankruptcy court erred in holding that Deere's financing statements, listing the debtor by his nickname, were sufficient to perfect its interests in the debtor's property. . . . For the reasons stated below, we conclude that the bankruptcy court erred in holding that Deere's financing statements were sufficient and served to perfect its interests in the debtor's property. For a financing statement to be sufficient under Kansas law, the secured creditor must list an individual debtor by his or her legal name, not a nickname.

It is undisputed in this case that whether Deere's interests were perfected on the debtor's petition date depends on Kansas law. It is also undisputed that the applicable law is stated in Article 9 of the Kansas Uniform Commercial Code, as revised and adopted by the Kansas Legislature in 2000. The relevant portions of Revised Article 9, as adopted in Kansas, are as follows.

[**9–502(a)**] states that "a financing statement is sufficient only if it: (1) Provides the name of the debtor[.]" This requirement is to facilitate "a system of notice filing" under which security interest documents need not be filed, but rather only a single document notifying parties in interest that a creditor may have an interest in certain property owned by the named debtor. Because notice of a secured interest in property is accomplished by searching the debtor's name, the requirement that a financing statement provide the debtor's name is particularly important. Accordingly, pursuant to [**9–506(b)**], if a financing statement "fails sufficiently to provide the name of the debtor" it is "seriously misleading."

[The opinion then quotes the pre-2010 version of Article 9 which required that a financing statement provide the "individual name" of the debtor].

* * *

Although [the 1998 version of **9–503**] specifically sets parameters for listing a debtor's name in a financing statement when the debtor is an entity, it does not provide any detail as to the name that must be provided for an individual debtor—it simply states that the "name of the debtor" should be used. This could be construed, as it was by the bankruptcy court, as allowing a debtor to be listed in a financing statement by his or her commonly-used nickname. But, we do not agree with that interpretation because the purpose of [the 1998 version of **9–503**], as well as a reading of that section as a whole, leads us to conclude that an individual debtor's legal name must be used in the financing statement to make it sufficient under [**9–502(a)(1)**].

[The 1998 version of **9–503**] was enacted to clarify the sufficiency of a debtor's name in financing statements. The intent to clarify when a debtor's name is sufficient shows a desire to foreclose fact-intensive tests, such as those that existed under the former Article 9 of the UCC, inquiring into whether a person conducting a search would discover a filing under any given name. Requiring a financing statement to provide a debtor's legal name is a clear cut test that is in accord with that intent.

[The 1998 version of **9–503**] read as a whole, indicates that a legal name should be used for an individual debtor. In the case of debtor-entities, [the 1998 version of **9–503(a)**] states that legal names must be used to render them sufficient under [**9–502(a)**]. Trade names or other names may be listed, but it is insufficient to list a debtor by such names alone. A different standard should not apply to individual debtors. The more specific provisions applicable to entities, together with the importance of naming the debtor in the financing statement to facilitate the notice filing system and increase commercial certainty, indicates that an individual debtor must be listed on a financing statement by his or her legal name, not by a nickname.

Our conclusion that a legal name is necessary to sufficiently provide the name of an individual debtor . . . is also supported by four practical considerations. First, mandating the debtor's legal name sets a clear test so as simplify the drafting of financing statements. Second, setting a clear test simplifies the parameters of UCC searches. Persons searching UCC filings will know that they need the debtor's legal name to conduct a search, they will not be penalized if they do not know that a debtor has a nickname, and they will not have to guess any number of nicknames that could exist to conduct a search.[16] Third, requiring the debtor's legal name will avoid litigation as to the commonality or appropriateness of a debtor's nickname, and as to whether a reasonable searcher would have or should have known to use the name. Finally, obtaining a debtor's legal name is not difficult or burdensome for the creditor taking a secured interest in a debtor's property. Indeed, knowing the individual's legal name will assure the accuracy of any search that that creditor conducts prior to taking its secured interest in property.

* * *

By using the debtor's nickname in its financing statements, Deere failed to provide the name of the debtor within the meaning of [**9–503(a)**],

---

[16] We note that in the current case, Terrance and Terry are closely aligned; however we believe that it sets an unsatisfactory precedent to allow the use of nicknames in filing. *See* Harry C. Sigman, *The Filing System Under Revised Article 9*, 73 Am. Bankr. L. J. 61, 73 (1999) use of a legal name "does not burden searchers with the obligation to dream up every potential error and name variation and perform searches under all possibilities. Revised Article 9 allows a searcher to rely on a single search conducted under the correct name of the debtor and penalizes filers only for errors that result in the nondisclosure of the financing statement in a search under the correct name.").

and its financing statements are not sufficient under [9–502(a)]. Because the financing statements do not "sufficiently . . . provide the name of the debtor" under [9–503(a)], they are "seriously misleading" as a matter of law pursuant to [9–506(b)]. Furthermore, the undisputed facts in this case show that [9–506(c)] does not apply in this case. That section saves a financing statement from being "seriously misleading" if a search of UCC filings "under the debtor's correct name, using the filing office's standard search logic, . . . would disclose a financing statement that fails sufficiently to provide the name of the debtor" in accordance with [9–503(a)]. Included in the record before us are the results of a UCC search conducted by Deere's counsel in Kansas's official and unofficial UCC search systems. Under both systems, she found no matches for the debtor's legal name "Terrance," but numerous matches for his nickname "Terry" and the initial "T." Thus, a search of the debtor's "correct name" did not disclose a financing statement, and therefore, [9–506(c)] does not apply. The result of Deere's UCC searches underscores the need for a clear-cut method of searching a debtor's name in UCC filings. The logical starting point for a person searching records would be to use the debtor's legal name. When a UCC search of the debtor's legal name does not provide any matches, parties in interest should be able to presume that the debtor's property is not encumbered, and they should not be charged with guessing what to do next if the legal name search does not result in any matches. Deere's financing statements, being seriously misleading, do not perfect its interest in the debtor's property and, therefore, the bankruptcy court erred in refusing to avoid its interests as against the trustee as a hypothetical lien creditor under *11 U.S.C. § 544(a)(1)*.

III. Conclusion

For the reasons stated herein, the bankruptcy court's Judgment is REVERSED.

———————

Note that Alternative B says nothing about an individual debtor's "legal" name, so the *Kinderknecht* problem is alive in states that have adopted that alternative. Problem solved if a state adopted Alternative A, right? Maybe, but hold on until we get to the discussion of debtor name changes below. Also, keep in mind that Alternative A is unforgiving—the financing statement name must match the debtor's driver's license name and any misspelling will render the financing statement ineffective. One creditor of Ronald Markt Nay found that out the hard way when a bankruptcy court held that its financing statement listing "Ronald Mark Nay" as the debtor was ineffective. *See Mainsource Bank v. Leaf Capital Funding LLC (In re Nay)*, 563 B.R. 535 (Bankr. S.D. Ind. 2017).

ii. Entity Debtors

If the debtor is a business entity, the party filing the financing statement needs to verify the type of entity. If the entity is a "registered organization" the only permissible name is the name that appears on the entity's "public organic record." **9–102(a)(68)** defines public organic record as the record filed with the state to form the organization. If the entity is not a registered organization (a general partnership, for example), **9–503** requires only the debtor's name. Think about where you would find that name.

We asked you whether you know the name of the sandwich shop that sold you your lunch today. Although the answer might have seemed obvious to you, the name by which you know your sandwich shop may be its trade name, not its legal entity name. For example, the shop that you may know of as The Lunch Box from the sign outside of its shop may in fact be "Molly and Matthew's Lunch Box, LLC," on the documents its principals filed to form the limited liability company. "The Lunch Box," in that case, is the company's trade name. A trade name is not a correct entity name for filing purposes.

Usually the name of an entity shown on its public organic record includes a suffix such as LLC, Corp., Inc., or Ltd. Some search logic strips those endings as noise words. The excerpt below is from the Model Administrative Rules promulgated by the International Association of Commercial Administrators, a professional organization for government officials who administer filing systems. Note subsection (f) below, which provides some examples of how the model search logic works.

iii. IACA Model Administrative Rules

503 Search methodology. Search results are produced by the application of search logic to the name presented to the filing office. Human judgment does not play a role in determining the results of the search.

503.1   Standard search logic. The following rules describe the filing office's standard search logic and apply to all searches except for those where the search request specifies that a non-standard search logic be used:

* * *

503.1.2 No distinction is made between upper and lower case letters.

503.1.3 The following rules apply only to organization names:

(a) The character "&" (the ampersand) is deleted and replaced with the characters "and" each place it appears in the name.

(b) Punctuation marks and accents are disregarded. For the purposes of this rule, punctuation and accents include all characters other than the numerals 0 through 9 and the letters A through Z (in upper and lower case) of the English alphabet.

(c) The following words and abbreviations at the end of an organization name that indicate the existence or nature of the organization are "disregarded" to the extent practicable as determined by the filing office's programming of its UCC information management system:

[Insert the filing office's own "Ending Noise Words" list here.]

Alternative 1:   [The search logic will disregard all words, phrases or abbreviations from the preceding list beginning at the end of the name and working back until an unlisted word, phrase or abbreviation appears.]

Alternative 2:   [The search logic will disregard only the last word, phrase or abbreviation from the preceding list.]

(d) The word "the" at the beginning of an organization debtor name is disregarded.

(e)   All spaces are disregarded.

503.1.4 The following search rules apply to individual debtor names:

(a) Surname: The individual debtor surname on a filed record must exactly match the surname of the search request. The search logic does not provide equivalencies for the surname field, nor does the search logic disregard [spacing,] [punctuation,] titles, suffixes or ending noise words of any type if entered in the surname field.

* * *

(f)   Search Result Examples.

(1)   A search request for "John A. Smith" (first personal name and surname with an initial in the additional name(s)/initial(s) field) would cause the search to retrieve all filings against all individual debtors with (i) "John" or the initial "J" as to the first name, (ii) "Smith" as the surname, and (iii) no name or initial, the initial "A" or any name beginning with "A" in the additional name(s)/initials field.

(2) A search request for "J.A. Smith" (initial for first personal name, surname and an initial for the additional name(s)/initial(s) field), would retrieve all filings against individual debtors with (i) the initial "J" or any name

beginning with "J" as the first name, (ii) "Smith" as the last name, and (iii) no name or initial, the initial "A" or any name beginning with "A" in the additional name(s)/initial(s) field.

(3) A search request for "John Smith" (first personal name and surname with no designation in the additional name(s)/initial(s) field), would retrieve all filing against individual debtors with (i) "John" or the initial "J" as the first name, (ii) "Smith" as the last name and (iii) any entry or no entry in the additional name(s)/initial(s) field.

Keep in mind that the above rules are model rules, and therefore not universal. A creditor's best protection against idiosyncratic search logic rules is to get the name right in the first place.

OFFICIAL COMM. OF UNSECURED CREDITORS FOR TYRINGHAM HOLDINGS, INC. V. SUNA BROS., INC. (IN RE TYRINGHAM HOLDINGS, INC.)

354 B.R. 363 (Bankr. E.D. Va. 2006)

DOUGLAS, O. T., JR.

MEMORANDUM OPINION AND ORDER

Trial was held on November 13, 2006, on plaintiff's complaint to determine the validity, priority, or extent of a lien under a consignment held by defendant Suna Bros. Inc. The issue is whether Suna's financing statement was seriously misleading because it was not filed under the correct name of the debtor. For the reasons set forth below, the court finds that the financing statement is seriously misleading. Therefore, the defendant's lien is unperfected, and plaintiff may sell the collateral free and clear of any lien or interest of Suna.

Findings of Fact

Pursuant to a consignment agreement dated October 18, 2004, debtor Tyringham Holdings, Inc., held a number of pieces of jewelry inventory consigned to it by Suna. Suna held a security interest in the consigned inventory and attempted to perfect the security interest by filing a financing statement with the Virginia State Corporation Commission on June 10, 2005. The financing statement covered 65 pieces of jewelry totaling $ 310,925.00 worth of consigned inventory.

The financing statement was filed by Suna on June 10, 2005, and listed the debtor's name as "Tyringham Holdings." The debtor is a Virginia Corporation and is listed as "Tyringham Holdings, Inc." on the public records of the Virginia State Corporation Commission.

An official UCC search certified by the State Corporation Commission revealed a search conducted under the name "Tyringham Holdings, Inc.," which did not reveal the Suna financing statement.

<u>Discussion and Conclusions of Law</u>

Where a filed financing statement is required to perfect a security interest, it must substantially satisfy the requirements of a financing statement. Generally, the name of a corporate debtor, as indicated on the public record of the debtor's jurisdiction of organization, must be listed on the financing statement for it to be valid. **[9–503(a)(1)]**. Where the requirements are substantially satisfied, a financing statement "is effective, even if it has minor errors or omissions, unless the errors or omissions make the financing statement seriously misleading." **[9–506(a)]**. By law, "[e]xcept as otherwise provided in subsection (c), a financing statement that fails sufficiently to provide the name of the debtor in accordance with **[9–503(a)]** is seriously misleading." **[9–506(b)]**. There is no question in this case that the name of the debtor in the Suna financing statement, "Tyringham Holdings," was not the same corporate name as that on the public record for the state of Virginia, "Tyringham Holdings, Inc." Therefore, unless excepted by **[9–506(c)]**, the financing statement is seriously misleading and is ineffective to perfect Suna's security interest.

The exception in subsection (c) represents a shift between the previous version of Article 9 and Revised Article 9 in dealing with errors on financing statements. Prior to the revisions enacted in 2001, Virginia's version of Article 9 had no equivalent to subsections (b) and (c). Instead, the governing principle for financing statement sufficiency was a diligent searcher standard. Subsection (c) now provides a more concrete rule for determining if errors are seriously misleading, providing that:

If a search of the <u>records of the filing office</u> under the <u>debtor's correct name,</u> using the <u>filing office's standard search logic,</u> if any, would disclose a financing statement that fails sufficiently to provide the name of the debtor in accordance with **[9–503(a)]**, the name provided does not make the financing statement seriously misleading.

* * *

In the time period between filing of the financing statement and the trial in this Adversary Proceeding, a number of UCC searches were performed by private search companies such as Corporation Service Company, Access Information Services, Inc., and UCC Retrievals, Inc. Each of these searches disclosed the existence of the Suna financing statement. No evidence was presented as to the underlying methodology behind the Corporation Service Company or Access Information Services, Inc., searches. At trial, a witness for Suna testified that she had conducted the search by UCC Retrievals, Inc., under the name "Tyringham Holdings." Her search disclosed the existence of the Suna financing statement. Her rationale for searching under the name "Tyringham Holdings" rather than the correct "Tyringham Holdings, Inc.," was that she considered the term "Inc." to be a "noise word." Noise words for these purposes are words that are removed or ignored in the process of performing an electronic database search for financing statements. The witness classified "Inc." as a noise word because it is one of such words on a list promulgated by the International Association of Corporation Administrators (IACA). Other abbreviations on the IACA "noise word" list include "Corporation," "Corp," "Company," "Co," "Limited," and "Ltd."

Suna repeatedly emphasizes that these private searches used "standard search logic" to disclose the Suna financing statement. Suna would have this court readout the portion of the statute that specifies whose "standard search logic" is employed in the analysis. The relevant standard is clearly no longer the diligent searcher's standard search logic nor a private search organization's standard search logic, but it is instead the filing office's standard search logic.

The Virginia State Corporation Commission has promulgated filing rules in 5 Va. Admin. Code 5–30–70(E) (2006) that describe the standard search logic employed by the commission when conducting a search. Search results are produced by the application of standardized search logic to the name presented to the filing officer, along with several additional requirements, including the following subsection 4:

"Noise words" include, but are not limited to, "an," "and," "for," "of," and "the." The word "the" always will be disregarded and other noise words appearing anywhere except at the beginning of an organization name will be disregarded. Certain business words are modified to a standard abbreviation: company to "co," corporation to "corp," limited to "ltd," incorporated to "inc." The State Corporation Commission has not adopted the full list of noise words promulgated by the IACA.

* * *

Suna attempts to argue that the State Corporation Commission's search logic is faulty because it does not filter out "Inc." as a noise word, even though the IACA considers it as such. According to Plaintiff's witness, the State Corporation Commission is in the process of revising its list of noise words and changing the search logic to include terms such as "inc." However, the standard in place at all times relevant to this case did not include "Inc." as a noise word; at present, the underlying search engine code filters out only five articles as noise words. Suna makes much of the fact that noise words in the filing rules contained at 5 Va. Admin. Code 5–30–70(E)(4) "include, but are not limited to" the five articles filtered out by the search engine. Suna essentially argues that the search engine improperly employs the search methodology prescribed by the statute, because it in fact filters out <u>only</u> the five articles and thus is "limited to" those words only. Regardless of whether this argument makes logical sense, the court cannot conclude on the basis of the statutory language that "Inc." should be considered a noise word. The third sentence of subsection 4 says that "Certain business words are modified to a standard abbreviation . . . ," the last of which is "incorporated" to "inc." 5 Va. Admin.

Code 5–30–70(E)(4). If "inc" is a standard abbreviation, it cannot simultaneously be a disregarded noise word according to the State Corporation Commission's standard search logic as embodied by this statute and the search engine code utilizing it. As a result, it is clear that "Inc." is not a noise word for purposes of a Virginia UCC search, and the State Corporation Commission's search logic is functioning as it was presently intended to function in this respect.

None of the cases cited by Suna support its proposition that the language of [**9–503(c)**] does not mean what it says regarding the use of the <u>filing office's</u> standard search logic.

* * *

While application of the filing office's standard search logic may lead to situations where it appears that a relatively minor error in a financing statement leads to a security interest becoming unperfected, it is not that difficult to ensure that a financing statement is filed with the correct name of the debtor. Little more is asked of a creditor than to accurately record the debtor's name, and according to the statute, failure to perform this action clearly dooms the perfected status of a security interest.

The official search certified by the State Corporation Commission, under the correct name, "Tyringham Holdings, Inc.," fails to disclose the Suna financing statement. Thus, the only search which used the correct name under the standard search logic actually employed by the State Corporation Commission did not disclose the Suna financing statement. As a result, the court must conclude that the financing statement is seriously misleading and is insufficient to perfect Suna's security interest in the collateral. Therefore, Suna's security interest in the collateral is unperfected and the collateral may be sold free and clear of any lien held by Suna.

---

b. The Secured Party's Name

The second necessary item of information in a financing statement is the secured party's name. The rules governing the sufficiency of a secured party's name are not as strict as those governing the debtor's name. The purpose of requiring the secured party's name is so that others can communicate with the secured party. As a result, a trade name might be fine.

c. An Indication of the Collateral

In Chapter 12 we discussed collateral descriptions in depth. According to **9–504** a description that satisfies **9–108** will also be a sufficient collateral indication in a financing statement. **9–504** adds an additional sufficient indication—a financing statement can describe the collateral as "all of the debtor's assets."

d. Other Information

It's important to remember that a financing statement omitting any of the **9–502** information is ineffective, period. No competent lender would present for filing a financing statement that contained only those three pieces of information, however. That's because Article 9 requires several other items of information for filing, but tells you that in a complicated way. Here goes: **9–520** tells us that a filing office "shall refuse" a record ("record" is 21st century UCC-speak for "writing" and 'writing equivalents" **9–102(a)(70)**) for a reason set forth in **9–516(b)**, and "may refuse" a record only for such a reason. **9–516(b)** then provides three additional items that "must" be in a financing statement: the secured party's address, the debtor's address and an indication of whether the debtor's name is the name of an individual or an organization.

Sometimes a financing statement makes it onto the records missing some of the **9–516(b)** information, and sometimes a financing statement is rejected even though all of the necessary boxes are filled in. **9–520** and **9–338** tell us the effect of these scenarios.

Contents of Financing Statement	Accepted by Filing Office?	Effectiveness
Contains correct **9–502** and **9–516** information	Yes	Against everyone
Contains correct **9–502** and **9–516** information	No (wrongful rejection)	Against everyone *except* a purchaser **(1–201(b)(29), (30))** that gives value in reliance on the record's absence from the files **(9–516(d))**
Contains correct **9–502** information; missing **9–516** information	Yes	Against everyone
Contains correct **9–502** information; missing **9–516** information	No	Against no one **(9–516(b))** ("filing does not occur . . .")

Contains correct 9–502 information; wrong 9–516 information	Yes	Against everyone *except* secured parties and other purchasers who give value in reliance on the incorrect information as provided in 9–338
Contains correct 9–502 information; wrong 9–516 information	No (wrongful rejection)	Against everyone *except* a purchaser (1–201(b)(29), (30)) that gives value in reliance on the record's absence from the files (9–516(d))

e.   One Thing That Is Not Necessary: A Signature

Take another look at the form of financing statement in **9–521**. You'll note that there is no place for the debtor to sign the financing statement. That might seem odd to you at first; how can another person file a notice in a public record claiming an interest in the debtor's property if the debtor did not even sign the notice? How will anyone know that the notice is legitimate?

You are not the only one concerned about this. When the 1998 Amendments to Article 9 removed the requirement that a debtor sign a financing statement, government officials in several states expressed concern that financing statements could be used as tools of harassment against government officials by anti-government groups, prisoners, and others who might have a gripe (legitimate or not) with the government. These filings are not a joke, happened even when debtors were required to sign financing statements, and are unfortunately so common that several states have enacted non-uniform amendments to deal with them.

A signature is only one method of authorization, however. Article 9 requires that a financing statement be authorized by the debtor **9–510**. An unauthorized financing statement is an ineffective financing statement. So how does the debtor authorize a financing statement? In an authenticated record. An authenticated security agreement is authorization for the filing of a financing statement in connection with that agreement. **9–509(b)**. Keep in mind, though, that the UCC allows a secured party to pre-file a financing statement and as you will learn in the next chapter, it is often wise to do so. When the secured party files its financing statement before the debtor signs its security agreement, the secured party should obtain a signed (authenticated) authorization to file.

2. WHERE TO FILE

We introduced the "where" above. Now it's time to explore that concept in more depth. According to **9–301(1)**, the law of the debtor's location governs perfection of a security interest. Simple, right? Let's go back to the hypothetical sandwich shop at which you bought your hypothetical lunch. Do you know where it is located?

As was the case with the debtor's name, you cannot know the debtor's location until you know what the debtor is. *See* **9–307(b)–(f)**. **9–307(b)** tells you that an individual is located at her residence regardless of where she is doing business, an organization with only one place of business is located at its place of business and an organization with more than one place of business is located at its principal place of business. But wait, there's more! A substantial group of organizations is left out of **9–307(b)**. If your debtor is a registered organization (defined in **9–102(a)(71)**) **9–307(b)** does not apply at all. Instead, you go to **9–307(e)**, which tells you that a registered organization is located in its state of organization.

a. When Is the Secretary of State's Office Not the Right Place to Leave Your Notice?

While we're talking about place of filing, it's important to know that some security interests are not perfected by a filing in the Secretary of State's office. Below we'll talk about some security interests that are not perfected by filing at all, but here we're talking about laws that require a secured party to give public notice of its interest in an office other than the office of the Secretary of State.

i. *Fixtures*

In the first chapter of the secured transactions materials, we discussed fixtures, which are items of personal property that are so related to land that they convey with the real estate. **9–501** introduces you to a new term, a "fixture filing." For a filed financing statement to qualify as a fixture filing, it must satisfy two requirements: 1) it must contain the additional information set forth in **9–502(b)**; and 2) it must be filed in the land records in the county in which the real property is located. **9–501**. Note that requirement 2) does not depend on the legal form of the debtor. **9–301(3).**

Nowhere does Article 9 require that a secured party perfect its security interest in fixtures by filing a fixture filing. At this point, it is sufficient to know that a fixture filing is one of two methods by which to perfect a security interest in a fixture. As you will learn in the chapter on priorities, it is the better of the two methods.

ii. Perfection Governed by Other Law: 9–311

Article 9 recognizes that some federal laws establish systems for tracking security interests in certain types of collateral. Some state laws do so as well. **9–311** tells us that the filing of a financing statement is neither necessary nor effective to perfect a security interest that is governed by such other law. It also tells us that compliance with such a law is equivalent to filing under Article 9. **9–311(b).** That point is important because every time you see the word filing, you can include perfection pursuant to a law listed in **9–311**.

(a) Automobiles and Other Certificate of Title Property

Every U.S. state has a statute that requires that an owner of a motor vehicle obtain a certificate of title for that vehicle. Certificate of title statutes serve several purposes two of which are important for our discussion: they establish a reliable chain of title for vehicle so that a potential buyer knows that her seller is entitled to sell the vehicle, and they provide a method for perfecting a security interest in a motor vehicle. An example of a certificate of title statute is the Uniform Motor Vehicle Certificate of Title and Anti-Theft Act ("UMVCTA"), promulgated by the Uniform Law Commission. Although no state has enacted this uniform law, it contains many of the elements found in the various state laws.

As is the case with all statutes, scope is critical. The scope of UMVCTA mirrors the scope of the various state laws dealing with automobile certificates of title. The scope sections of UMVCTA are **§§ 2** and **4**. The section dealing with perfection of security interests is **§ 20**. Read those sections. Now do you understand that in order to know how to perfect a security interest in a car you need to know how it is used, which in turn determines collateral classification? Cars held as inventory do not need certificates of title. Cars that are going to be driven do.

You can safely assume that all states have laws that require certificates of title for cars and provide for a method of perfecting security interests with the Department of Motor Vehicles. Note that all other aspects of creating and enforcing security interests are governed by Article 9, it's just perfection that is governed by other law. Depending on your state, other items of personal property might be subject to certificate of title laws. The perfection of a security interest in boats is often, but not always, governed by a certificate of title law; some states have certificate of title laws that govern security interests in items such as snowmobiles and all-terrain vehicles.

(b) Intellectual Property

The method of perfecting a security interest in intellectual property depends on the type of intellectual property. If you have taken an intellectual property course, you know that we have federal laws governing copyrights, patents, and trademarks. The mere existence of a federal law, however, does not remove intellectual property from the purview of Article 9. You need to know what law other than Article 9 governs the transfer of rights in the intellectual property at issue, and then you need to know whether that law governs the transfer and recording of security interests in that intellectual property.

Before we look at federal law, into what collateral category would you place copyrights, patents, and trademarks? The answer to this question is important because it governs how a creditor can perfect its security interest. A patent, trademark or copyright would fall into the "general intangibles" category of collateral. Under Article 9, a secured party must file a financing statement in the correct Secretary of State's office in order to perfect its interest in a general intangible. Federal law might require a different result.

Copyrights: If you have taken a course in intellectual property law, you probably know that although federal law allows a copyright holder to register its copyright in the United States Copyright Office and that registration gives the holder a number of benefits, registration is permissive, not mandatory. When the secured party is taking a security interest in a copyright, whether that copyright is registered or not will govern the method of perfection. In a bankruptcy contest between a secured creditor who had perfected its interest in unregistered copyrights by a state UCC filing and a company that had bought the copyrights from the bankruptcy trustee, the court explained the distinction as follows:

> Our analysis begins with the Copyright Act of 1976. Under the Act, "copyright protection subsists . . . in original works of authorship fixed in any tangible medium of expression. . . ." While an owner must register his copyright as a condition of seeking certain infringement remedies, registration is permissive, not mandatory, and is not a condition for copyright protection. Likewise, the Copyright Act's provision for recording "transfers of copyright ownership" (the Act's term that includes security interests) is permissive, not mandatory: "Any transfer of copyright ownership or other document pertaining to copyright may be recorded in the Copyright Office. . . ." The Copyright Act's use of the word "mortgage" as one definition of a "transfer" is properly read to include security interests under Article 9 of the Uniform Commercial Code.

> Under the Copyright Act,

>> as between two conflicting transfers, the one executed first prevails if it is recorded, in the manner required to give constructive notice . . .within one month after its execution . . .or at any time before recordation . . .of the later transfer. Otherwise the later transfer prevails if recorded first in such

manner, and if taken in good faith, for valuable consideration
. . .and without notice of the earlier transfer.

The phrase "constructive notice" refers to another subsection
providing that recording gives constructive notice

but only if—

(1) the document, or material attached to it, specifically
identifies the work to which it pertains so that, after the
document is indexed by the Register of Copyrights, it would
be revealed by a reasonable search under the title or
registration number of the work; and

(2) registration has been made for the work.

A copyrighted work only gets a "title or registration number" that
would be revealed by a search if it's registered. Since an
unregistered work doesn't have a title or registration number that
would be "revealed by a reasonable search," recording a security
interest in an unregistered copyright in the Copyright Office
wouldn't give "constructive notice" under the Copyright Act, and,
because it wouldn't, it couldn't preserve a creditor's priority. There
just isn't any way for a secured creditor to preserve a priority in
an unregistered copyright by recording anything in the Copyright
Office. And the secured party can't get around this problem by
registering the copyright, because the secured party isn't the
owner of the copyright, and the Copyright Act states that only "the
owner of copyright . . .may obtain registration of the copyright
claim. . . ."

Aerocon argues that the Copyright Act's recordation and priority
scheme exclusively controls perfection and priority of security
interests in copyrights. First, Aerocon argues that state law, here
the California U.C.C., by its own terms "steps back" and defers to
the federal scheme.

* * *

A.   U.C.C. Step-Back Provisions

Article 9 of the Uniform Commercial Code, as adopted in
California, provides that unperfected creditors are subordinate to
perfected, and as between perfected security interests, the first
perfected interest prevails. The bank perfected first under state
law by filing a financing statement with the California Secretary
of State on existing and after-acquired copyrights. The U.C.C.
treats copyrights as "general intangibles." Security interests in
general intangibles are properly perfected under the U.C.C. by
state filings such as the one made by the bank in this case.

To avoid conflict with the federal law, the U.C.C. has two "step-back provisions," by which state law steps back and out of the way of conflicting federal law. The first, more general "step-back" provision says that Article 9 "does not apply . . . to a security interest subject to any statute of the United States to the extent that such statute governs the rights of parties to and third parties affected by transactions in particular types of property. . . ." As applied to copyrights, the relevant U.C.C. Official Comment makes it clear that this stepback clause does not exclude all security interests in copyrights from U.C.C. coverage, just those for which the federal Copyright Act "governs the rights" of relevant parties:

> Although the Federal Copyright Act contains provisions permitting the mortgage of a copyright and for the recording of an assignment of a copyright such a statute would not seem to contain sufficient provisions regulating the rights of the parties and third parties to exclude security interests in copyrights from the provisions of this Article.

The second step-back provision speaks directly to perfection of security interests. It exempts from U.C.C. filing requirements security interests in property "subject to . . . [a] statute . . . of the United States which provides for a national . . . registration . . . or which specifies a place of filing different from that specified in this division for filing of the security interest." Compliance with such a statute "is equivalent to the filing of a financing statement . . . and a security interest in property subject to the statute . . . can be perfected only by compliance therewith. . . ."

Under the U.C.C.'s two step-back provisions, there can be no question that, when a copyright has been registered, a security interest can be perfected only by recording the transfer in the Copyright Office. As the district court held in *National Peregrine, Inc. v. Capitol Federal Savings and Loan Ass'n (*In re *Peregrine Entertainment, Ltd.)*, 116 B.R. 194 (C.D. Cal. 1990), the Copyright Act satisfies the broad U.C.C. step-back provision by creating a priority scheme that "governs the rights of parties to and third parties affected by transactions" in registered copyrights and satisfies the narrow step-back provision by creating a single "national registration" for security interests in registered copyrights. Thus, under these step-back provisions, if a borrower's collateral is a registered copyright, the secured party cannot perfect by filing a financing statement under the U.C.C. in the appropriate state office, or alternatively by recording a transfer in the Copyright Office. For registered copyrights, the only proper place to file is the Copyright Office. We adopt *Peregrine's* holding to this effect.

However, the question posed by this case is whether the U.C.C. steps back as to unregistered copyrights. We, like the bankruptcy court in this case, conclude that it does not. As we've explained, there's no way for a secured creditor to perfect a security interest in unregistered copyrights by recording in the Copyright Office. The U.C.C.'s broader step-back provision says that the U.C.C. doesn't apply to a security interest "to the extent" that a federal statute governs the rights of the parties. The U.C.C. doesn't defer to the Copyright Act under this broad step-back provision because the Copyright Act doesn't provide for the rights of secured parties to unregistered copyrights; it only covers the rights of secured parties in *registered* copyrights. The U.C.C.'s narrow step-back provision says the U.C.C. doesn't apply if a federal statute "provides for a national . . . registration . . . or which specifies a place of filing different from that specified in this division for filing of the security interest." The U.C.C. doesn't defer to the Copyright Act under this narrow step-back provision because the Copyright Act doesn't provide a "national registration": unregistered copyrights don't have to be registered, and because unregistered copyrights don't have a registered name and number, under the Copyright Act there isn't any place to file anything regarding unregistered copyrights that makes any legal difference. So, as a matter of state law, the U.C.C. doesn't step back in deference to federal law, but governs perfection and priority of security interests in unregistered copyrights itself.

Aerocon Eng'g, Inc. v. Silicon Valley Bank (In re World Aux. Power Co.), 303 F.3d 1120 (9th Cir. 2002)

Trademarks: Trademarks are governed by the Lanham Act, 15 U.S.C. § 1051 *et seq.* In the following case, another bankruptcy dispute, the secured creditor had filed its UCC financing statement with the United States Patent and Trademark Office, but not with the Connecticut Secretary of State's Office. In ruling that such a filing was ineffective to perfect the creditor's security interest the court considered the language of the Lanham Act:

> The Lanham Act does not speak of security interests as such nor does it provide for the filing of notification of such interests. Section 1060 requires the recordation of assignments, without providing a definition of the word. The text of that section indicates that an assignee of a trademark must record its assignment if the assignee wants assurance that the assignment is not void as against a subsequent purchaser for value and without notice. 15 U.S.C. § 1060.

In stark contrast are the Federal Aviation Act ("FAA") and the Copyright Act. The FAA provides for recordation of "any conveyance which affects the title to, or any interest in, any civil aircraft . . . ." 49 U.S.C. § 44107 (1994). The Copyright Act specifically addresses the validity of security interests in copyrights. It provides that mortgages and hypothecations are transfers and establishes how they are validly made. It also contains a recordation scheme that requires the recording of copyright transfers at the Copyright Office in order to provide constructive notice of such transfers. 17 U.S.C. § 205 (1994). On the other hand, the Lanham Act contains no such similar provisions relating to mortgages, hypothecations or recordation schemes relating to the perfection of security interests.

Finally, in 1988 the United States Senate passed a bill that, among other things, would have (1) federalized the filing of documents relating to security interests in trademarks and (2) brought the recordation and priority of security interests in trademarks into conformity with the counterpart copyright provisions. S. 1883, 100th Cong. (1988). The portion of the bill related to security interests was not enacted, however, and thus, as one commentator notes, "the U.C.C. continues to control security interests in trademarks". Stuart M. Rilback, Intellectual Property Licenses: The Impact of Bankruptcy, 576 PLI/Pat 199, fn. 95 (1999).

3.   Case law

Case law addressing the issue at hand consistently supports the proposition that the Lanham Act does not pertain to security interests and that Article 9, therefore, continues to govern the perfection of such interests. *See In re Roman Cleanser Co.*, 43 B.R. 940 (Bankr. E.D. Mich. 1984), *aff'd* 802 F.2d 207 (6th Cir. 1986) (based solely on interpretation of Lanham Act).

In the *Roman Cleanser* case, a creditor moved to intervene in an adversary proceeding, contending that it had a security interest in trademarks which were sold by the trustee and as to which another creditor claimed ownership. The trustee argued that, in order to perfect a security interest in a federally registered trademark, a creditor must file a conditional assignment with the PTO, and because that creditor failed to do so, its security interest was unperfected.

The court found that the creditor had validly perfected his security interest by his U.C.C. filing. It held that a grant of a security interest could not be characterized as an "assignment" under the Lanham Act because (1) title to the collateral did not pass to the secured creditor and (2) a security interest is an agreement for a future assignment, not a present assignment of the mark or the goodwill associated with the mark. *In re Roman Cleanser*, 43 B.R. at 944. The court noted that

> the terms 'assignment' and 'security interest' are terms of art with distinct and different meanings. If Congress intended to provide a means for recording security interests in trademarks in addition to assignments, it would have been simple to so state.

Id. at 946.

The court pointed out that requiring federal filing of security interests would not further Congress's concern for protecting the public from the deceptive use of trademarks because a secured creditor has no right to use the mark absent debtor default. The court concluded that "since a security interest in a trademark is not equivalent to an assignment, the filing of a security interest is not covered by the Lanham Act" and the manner of perfecting a security interest in trademarks is governed by Article 9 of the U.C.C. *In re Roman Cleanser*, 43 B.R. at 944.

Courts which have subsequently dealt with the same issue have followed the logic and the holding of the Roman Cleanser court. See *In re TR-3 Industries*, 41 B.R. 128, 131 (Bankr. C.D. Cal. 1984) (HN9 the omission by Congress of a registration provision for security interests in trademarks was purposeful and the recordation provision of the Lanham Act does not preempt Article 9); *In re C.C. & Co., Inc.*, 86 B.R. 485, 487 (Bankr. E.D. Va. 1988) (Congress did not intend Lanham Act to provide method for perfection of security interest in trade names and lender had properly perfected its security interest in a trade name by filing financing statement under Virginia's U.C.C.); *In re Chattanooga Choo-Choo Co.*, 98 B.R. 792 (Bankr. E.D. Tenn. 1989) (Lanham Act provides only for registration of ownership, not notice of security interests, and therefore Article 9 governs perfection of a security interest in a trademark); *In re 199Z, Inc.*, 137 B.R. 778, (Bankr. C.D. Cal. 1992) (because Lanham Act refers only to assignments and not to "pledges, mortgages, or hypothecations of trademarks," a PTO filing did not perfect the creditor's security interest in a trademark).

4.   Policy Considerations

Finally, in terms of policy, it makes good sense to limit the application of **9–311(a)(1)** to those federal statutes which specifically and systematically provide for the filing of "all security interests" in a given form of property. A federal intellectual property registration or certificate of title, such as a certificate of federal trademark registration, reveals the name of the registrant and identifies the property but does not provide a list of lienholders. If national registration alone, without any federal system for the recordation of security interests, suffices to supplant U.C.C. requirements, the application of **9–311(a)(1)** would leave the holder of a security interest with no means of recording or perfecting that interest. Absent a reliable means of verifying the status of their collateral, secured lenders would be more reluctant to extend credit.

* * *

For the reasons stated in the Memorandum above, the determination of the Bankruptcy Court that: (1) the Lanham Act's registration provision does not preempt U.C.C. filing requirements for the perfection of a security interest in a trademark, and (2) Trimarchi failed to file in accordance with the U.C.C. and therefore did not perfect his security interest in the Trademark, are AFFIRMED.

Trimarchi & Personal Dating Servs. v. Together Dev. Corp., 255 B.R. 606 (D. Mass. Nov. 21, 2000)

Patents: The federal Patent Act, 35 U.S.C. § 1 *et seq.*, states that an "assignment, grant or conveyance" of a patent must be recorded in the U.S. Patent and Trademark Office in order to be effective against purchasers and mortgagees. So a secured party that files notice of a security interest in the U.S. Patent and Trademark Office beats a trustee in bankruptcy, right? Not so fast. Again, note how the court interprets the federal statute:

> The [Uniform] Commercial Code provides that the general rule for perfection of a security interest in a general intangible is by filing. There is an exception for "property subject to a statute, regulation, or treaty described in [**9–311**]." The referenced section provides that no filing is necessary to perfect a security interest in property subject to "a statute, regulation, or treaty of the United States whose requirements for a security interest's obtaining priority over the rights of a lien creditor with respect to the property preempt section [**9–310**]." I must determine if Federal legislation governing patents is such a superceding law.

> The applicable Federal law, substantively unchanged for over a century, provides that:

>> An assignment, grant or conveyance shall be void as against any subsequent purchaser or mortgagee for valuable consideration without notice unless it is recorded in the Patent and Trademark Office within three months from its date or prior to the date of such subsequent purchase or mortgage.

The Ninth Circuit addressed the question directly, applying California law, in *Moldo v. Matsco, Inc.* (In re *Cybernetic Services, Inc.*), 252 F. 3d 1039 (9th Cir. 2001), *cert. denied* 534 U.S. 1130 (2002). The issue was whether a chapter 7 trustee could prevail over a secured party which had perfected its interest in a patent under state law and not by filing with the USPTO. The trustee argued that the quoted Federal law supercedes Article 9 and that a security interest in a patent can only be perfected by filing with the USPTO.

In responding to the Trustee's position, the Ninth Circuit laid out the basics of preemption law:

> The Supremacy Clause invalidates state laws that interfere with, or any contrary to, federal law. Congress may preempt state law in several different ways. Congress may do so expressly (express preemption). Even in the absence of express preemptive text, Congress' intent to preempt an entire field of state law may be inferred where the scheme of federal regulation is sufficiently comprehensive to make reasonable the inference that Congress left no room for supplementary regulation (field preemption). State law also is preempted when compliance with both state and federal law is impossible, or if the operation of state law stands as an obstacle to the accomplishment and execution of the full purposes and objectives of Congress (conflict preemption). In all cases, congressional intent to preempt state law must be clear and manifest.

It narrowed the issue to this:

> If, as the Trustee argues, the Patent Act expressly delineates the place where a party must go to acquire notice and certainty about liens on patents, then a state law that requires the public to look elsewhere unquestionably would undercut the value of the Patent Act's recording scheme. If, on the other hand, § 261 does not cover liens on patents, then Article 9's filing requirements do not conflict with any policies inherent in the Patent Act's recording scheme.

The Ninth Circuit looked to the phrase in the statute "assignment, grant or conveyance," which has been in the act since 1870, to determine its scope. It concluded that the Patent Act requires parties to record with the USPTO only ownership interests in patents and does not preempt the Commercial Code as to the perfection of security interests:

> [T]he [Federal] statute's text, context, and structure, when read in the light of Supreme Court precedent, compel the

conclusion that HN6 a security interest in a patent that does not involve a transfer of the rights of ownership is a 'mere license' and is not an 'assignment, grant or conveyance" within the meaning of 35 U.S.C. § 261. And because § 261 provides that only an "assignment, grant or conveyance shall be void" as against subsequent purchasers and mortgagees, only transfers of ownership interests need to be recorded with the PTO.

I agree with and adopt that position . . . .

Braunstein v. Gateway Mgmt. Servs. (In re *Coldwave Sys., LLC*), 368 B.R. 91 (Bankr. D. Mass. 2007)

C. PERFECTION BY POSSESSION

As you may have already learned in law school (maybe when you talked about adverse possession in your Property course), possession of property gives notice to the entire world that the possessor may have some rights in the property possessed. Like perfection by filing, perfection by possession can be the only method by which a secured creditor can perfect a security interest or it can be one of two equally effective methods. For some types of collateral, perfection by possession is going to be the better way to perfect.

9–313 gives us the general rules regarding perfection by possession. There are several important points to note about this section. One is that it does not define possession. The second is that the secured party may perfect by a third party's possession. **9–313(c).**

In many cases, perfection by possession is equal in effectiveness to perfection by filing. This is the case for goods. Often, the debtor will need the goods to operate its business, so it will not give a lender possession of its goods. There may be some valuable collateral, however, that the debtor does not need to use. Suppose that the debtor is Big Corp. Big Corp. has several valuable paintings in one of its conference rooms. If Big Corp. grants a security interest in those paintings to Bank, Bank might prefer to perfect by possession. Although Bank may have a number of practical reasons for preferring possession, as a legal matter, possession and filing are equally effective methods of perfection.

That is not the case for certain payment rights, however. Payment rights such as negotiable instruments and chattel paper are ordinarily transferred in commerce by manual transfer plus an indorsement (as you learned in your payment systems materials). Because of this commercial reality, although **9–312** permits a secured party to perfect its interest in instruments and chattel paper by filing, perfection by possession is "better" than perfection by filing. **9–330.** We will take up these "non-temporal priorities in the next chapter.

For one type of collateral, possession is the *sole* method of perfection. That collateral is money. **9–312(b)(3).** The reason for this rule should make sense to you. Commerce would grind to a halt if we expected everyone who takes a cash payment to check for security interests in the cash.

D. PERFECTION BY CONTROL

We have up until now focused on the idea of perfection being some act that the secured party takes to give the world notice of interest in collateral. In some respects, perfection by control is consistent with this notion. In others, it is not.

The drafters of Article 9 borrowed the concept of control from Article 8. **9–314** tells us that a security interest in investment property, deposit accounts, letter of credit rights, electronic chattel paper, or electronic documents *may* be perfected by control. Note that for some of the above property (electronic chattel paper being a subset of chattel paper) a secured party may also perfect by filing. **9–312.** Again, non-temporal priorities will apply because of business realities, and we'll pick those up in the next chapter. The actions that constitute control depend on the type of collateral at issue, so it is important to understand all of the collateral definitions. **9–104 through 9–107** set forth the method of control for each type of collateral in which a secured party can perfect its interest by control.

It's worth highlighting electronic chattel paper **(9–102(a)(31))** as a collateral category. We saw chattel paper in Chapter 11 of this book. Electronic chattel paper emerged as a collateral category in the 1998 amendments to Article 9 at a time when lawyers were working hard to make sure that the law accommodated electronic methods of doing business. Then, as now, a secured party could perfect its interest in tangible chattel paper by taking possession of it. There really isn't a perfect analogue to possession in the electronic environment, however, in fact, one hallmark of the electronic environment is that it is simple to make a perfect copy of everything. **9–105** sets forth the method of control for electronic chattel paper in such as way that the industry can develop ways to ensure that the world can ascertain the one person to which collateral that is electronic chattel paper has been assigned. Today, many lawyers and business people believe that blockchain technology, the same technology that enables Bitcoin, holds some promise on this front.

For one type of collateral, the deposit account **(9–102(a)(29))** the secured party *must* perfect by control. Here is where perfection does not always equal notice. **9–104(a)** sets forth three methods by which a secured party can take control of a deposit account. Note that the agreement permitted by **9–104(a)(2)** need not be recorded in any public place.

One tricky point to keep in mind is that the rule that a security interest in a deposit account can be perfected only by control applies only when the secured party is taking the account as *original collateral*. We will see a different rule for proceeds later in this chapter.

E. AUTOMATIC PERFECTION

9–309 tells us that a secured party may perfect its interest in limited types of collateral automatically. Automatic perfection means that as soon as the security interest has attached under **9–203** it is perfected. For the purpose of a survey course in commercial law, the important type of automatically perfected security interest is the purchase-money security interest (**9–103**) in consumer goods (**9–102(a)(23)**). We introduced you to PMSIs in Chapter 11 of these materials. Here we discuss a special rule for a subset of PMSIs, the PMSI in consumer goods.

Automatic perfection means that the secured party need not give any public notice of its security interest in order to have priority over everyone else in the world. Why allow this for purchase-money security interests in consumer goods? Used consumer goods are not typically used as collateral, in fact, under the Federal Trade Commission Credit Practices Rule, a creditor that takes a nonpossessory security interest in certain used household goods commits an unfair trade practice. *See* 16 C.F.R. 444.2. Because many used consumer goods have little value, there will not be more than one creditor with a security interest in consumer goods and therefore no priority contest among such creditors.

There are a couple of things to keep in mind about automatic perfection of security interests in consumer goods. First, if the goods are subject to a certificate of title statute, the automatic perfection rule does not apply. *See* **9–309(a)(1)** (except as otherwise provided in **9–311(b)**). Therefore, if a creditor takes a security interest in a car that is a consumer good, it must perfect its security interest by complying with the applicable certificate of title statute. Again, it is important to know what items in your state are subject to certificate of title statutes.

Second, creditors taking purchase-money security interests in high-value consumer goods may want to file a financing statement even though it is not necessary to do so in order to perfect. You'll learn why in the next chapter when we discuss priorities between secured parties and buyers.

F. CHANGES

A loan transaction can be a long-term relationship between the debtor and the secured party. During the term of a loan, many things can happen: the debtor may change its name, it may change the way it uses the collateral, it may move, or it may sell the collateral. All of these changes will affect the notice function of a financing statement. Should the secured party be required to update the notice or should the potential buyer or subsequent lender be required to ask questions about where the property came from?

In the last chapter, we talked about a Perfection Certificate. Some lenders, particularly in large transactions, will require such a certificate to ensure that they have correct information about the debtor and the collateral. In the model agreement that we saw in the last chapter, the debtor was obligated to inform the secured party of any changes in the information that it provided in the Perfection Certificate. The material that we will cover below illustrates why.

Before buying or lending against property, the buyer or lender should do some "due diligence." Due diligence is a term that you will hear a lot in practice, but even if you have not yet heard it in law school, you know what it is. For example, we just discussed where a secured party must file a financing statement and that fact that a properly filed financing statement gives notice to the world of its contents. This is because a lender who makes a proper search of the records will find such a financing statement. You have already learned that possession of property gives notice of rights in that property. That is why due diligence should also involve a visual inspection of the property.

The material below gives some guidance as to the due diligence that a potential buyer or lender should undertake. You'll see that sometimes the burden is on the original secured party to update its notice to the world. In other instances, the law considers the original notice to be sufficient, even if it no longer gives adequate notice to the world of the security interest. In those latter cases, a potential buyer or subsequent lender needs to ask some questions before buying property or lending against it.

You have already learned about the contents of a UCC financing statement, still known to many as the UCC–1 even though the UCC does not use that moniker. Now we will talk about the use of the UCC Financing Statement Amendment, often referred to as the UCC–3.

1. LAPSE OF TIME

If you have ever done a real property title search, you know that the land records can contain documents that are decades, if not centuries, old. The same is not true for the UCC records. Under **9–515(a)**, a financing statement is effective for five years.

What if the loan term is longer than five years? This is one place where the UCC puts the burden on the secured party to keep tabs on its loans. If a secured party wants its financing statement to be effective for more than five years, it must file a continuation statement (**9–102(a)(27)**) within six months before the expiration date of the financing statement. If the secured party properly continues its filing, its new expiration date is five years from the date the continued financing statement would have lapsed. **9–515(e).**

Will a new UCC–1 suffice as a continuation, even if it is filed within the six month window? No. *See In re Hilyard Drilling Co.*, 840 F. 2d 596 (8th Cir. 1988) (holding that a new original financing statement does not satisfy the requirements for a continuation statement).

What if the secured party files its continuation statement before the six month window opens? Courts have something to say about that as well:

> [Article 9 of the UCC] provides, in effect, that if a security agreement which retains a security interest in collateral has been perfected by the filing of a financing statement, the statement lapses at the expiration of a five-year period unless a continuation statement is filed prior to the lapse. Further, if the security interest becomes unperfected by lapse, it is deemed to have become unperfected as against a person who became a purchaser before the lapse. To be timely, a continuation statement must be filed within six months prior to the expiration of the five-year period during which the original financing statement is effective. Only if the continuation statement is timely filed is the effectiveness of the original financing statement continued.

> Here, it is uncontroverted that appellant's continuation statement was filed with the clerk on April 10, 1987, which was six months and two days before the expiration of the financing statement's five-year effective period. Because the continuation statement was not filed within six months prior to the lapse of the financing statement's effective period, appellant's security interest in the rock truck became unperfected on October 12, 1987, which was five years after the date on which the financing statement was filed. [**9–515(a)**].

Banque Worms v. Davis Constr. Co., 831 S.W.2d 921 (Ky. Ct. App. 1992)

Ouch!

You may want to know exactly how to calculate the five-year period. Is the expiration date five years from the date of filing or five years minus one day from the date of filing? The answer depends not on the UCC, but on the applicable state's time computation statute. See below in which two creditors, the Bank of Holden and the Bank of Warrensburg, are fighting over priority:

> As detailed above, Warrensburg filed its original financing statement on January 30, 1992. Holden filed its financing statement on September 19, 1996. Warrensburg filed the pivotal continuation of its financing statement on January 30, 1997. Since Holden filed between Warrensburg's original filing and its continuation, Holden would establish a first priority interest in the cattle if Warrensburg did not timely file its continuation statement. This is so because an ineffective renewal loses priority

to an intervening filing. The question is whether or not Warrensburg's January 30, 1997, continuation statement filing effectively prevented Warrensburg's priority security interest from lapsing.

At issue is how to calculate the "five-year period" for purposes of Warrensburg's financing statement effectiveness. In order for its continuation statement to effectively prevent its priority interest from lapsing, Warrensburg must have filed within the six months *prior to the expiration of the five-year period.* The question is when the five-year period expired. Holden asserts the five-year period expired January 29, 1997. Warrensburg contends the five-year period expired January 30, 1997.

The parties arrive at different expiration dates due to their application of § 1.040, Missouri's time computation statute. Statute 1.040 reads, "the time within which an act is to be done shall be computed by excluding the first day and including the last. If the last day is Sunday it shall be excluded." Warrensburg contends § 1.040 is applicable to [9–515] and results in a January 30 expiration date. This is so because under § 1.040, the date of filing, January 30, 1992, would not be included in calculating the five-year period. *See Brickell v. Hopwood,* 729 S.W.2d 241, 242 (Mo. App. 1987) (Triggering event occurred January 27, 1976, and ten year statute of limitation applied. Under § 1.040, the last day on which to file petition was January 27, 1986). Holden asserts § 1.040 is inapplicable to [9–515] and therefore, the expiration date was January 29. Holden reaches this date by including the day of filing, January 30, 1992, in the five-year computation.

No Missouri court has taken up the issue of whether or nor § 1.040 applies to the Uniform Commercial Code (UCC) as adopted in this state. This court first notes the general applicability of § 1.040. In *Bambrick v. St. Louis,* 41 Mo. App. 648 (1890), the court construed the predecessor to § 1.040 and held, "this statute is intended to furnish a general rule, plain and comprehensible, for the computation of the time mentioned in *all statutes.*" (Emphasis added). The title to the statutory chapter in which § 1.040 is found is "Laws in Force and Construction of Statutes." *Friends of the City Market v. Old Town Redevelopment Corp.,* 714 S.W.2d 569, 574 (Mo. App. 1986). This again indicates a general applicability. From the face of things, there seems no reason why § 1.040 would not apply to [9–515], as it applies generally to all Missouri statutes.

With no guidance under the UCC as adopted, and with no common law directly on point, this court finds it necessary to look to the decisions of other courts. In *In re Gordon Square Pharmacy, Inc.,*

138 B.R. 533 (Bankr. N.D. Ohio, 1992), the U.S. Bankruptcy Court for the Northern District of Ohio took up the issue of when the "five-year" period expired considering Ohio's time computation statute. Ohio's computation statute reads, "the time within which an act is required by law to be done shall be computed by excluding the first and including the last day." This language is nearly identical to Missouri's § 1.040. The bankruptcy court determined that under Ohio's law, a continuation filed May 2, 1991, for a financing statement filed May 2, 1986, was timely. By the reasoning of that court, applying § 1.040 in the case at bar, Warrensburg's January 30 continuation statement filing would be timely.

In *SCT, U.S.A., Inc. v. Mitsui Manufacturers Bank,* 155 Cal. App. 3d 1059, 202 Cal. Rptr. 547 (Cal. App. 1984), the California Court of Appeals applied that state's civil code to the computation of the five-year period for financing statement effectiveness. The civil code required, "the time in which any act provided by law is to be done is computed by excluding the first day, and including the last. . ." The court held that a continuation statement filed January 25, 1982, timely prevented the lapse of a financing statement filed January 25, 1977. That court's application of its state computation statute also supports the application of § 1.040 in the case at bar and the timeliness of Warrensburg's January 30 continuation statement filing.

* * *

The trial court's ruling that § 1.040 is applicable to the UCC as adopted in the state of Missouri was not in error. Section 1.040 does apply to measure the computation of time under the UCC. Under § 1.040, the "five-year" effectiveness of Warrensburg's financing statement filed January 30, 1992, ran through January 30, 1997. Warrensburg's continuation statement filing on January 30, 1997, effectively prevented its priority interest in Borrowers' cattle from lapsing. Therefore, as first priority security holder, Warrensburg was entitled to the proceeds from the sale of the cattle.

Bank of Holden v. Bank of Warrensburg, 15 S.W.3d 758 (Mo. Ct. App. Apr. 18, 2000)

The above excerpt illustrates an important rule from **9–515(c)** regarding the effect of a lapse. If a financing statement lapses, the security interest is "deemed never to have been perfected as against a purchaser of the collateral for value." Remember that the definition of purchaser includes secured parties. If the Bank of Warrensburg had not timely continued its filing, the Bank of Holden, which filed its financing statement while the Bank of Warrensburg was perfected, would have jumped ahead of it. This rule applies only to purchasers for value, *not* to lien creditors or the trustee in bankruptcy.

2.   CHANGE IN USE OF THE COLLATERAL

Here, the UCC puts the burden on the searcher (subsequent lender or buyer) to find out how the collateral had been used in the past. You get this rule from **9–507(b)**, which tells you that except in the case of a debtor name change, if a financing statement becomes seriously misleading after it is filed, it remains effective.

3.   DEBTOR NAME CHANGE

9–507(c) tells us the effect of a debtor's name change on the perfection of a security interest in that debtor's collateral. The rules in **9–507(c)(1)** and **(2)** apply only if the debtor's name change makes the financing statement seriously misleading. If it does not, the secured party need not take any action to continue its perfection.

9–507(c) splits the due diligence burden between the secured party and subsequent searchers. If the debtor changes its name so that a financing statement filed against it becomes seriously misleading, the financing statement is effective to perfect a security interest in collateral acquired by the debtor before, or within four months after, the name change. This is one reason why secured parties ask, in their loan applications, for other names by which the borrower has been known.

If the security agreement extends to collateral acquired by the debtor after the four-month period, the policing burden shifts to the secured party. The financing statement containing a seriously misleading debtor name will not be effective to perfect a security interest in collateral acquired by the debtor after the four-month period unless the secured party files an amendment with the debtor's correct name.

Beware the traps for the unwary set by individual debtor names. In states that have enacted Alternative A to **9–503**, the debtor's name changes when the name on her driver's license changes.

4.   DEBTOR MOVE, A/K/A CHANGE
IN GOVERNING LAW

As we discussed above, the correct state in which to file a financing statement is the state in which the debtor is located. To find out the effect of a debtor move on the secured party's perfection, we go back to Part 3 of Article 9, specifically to **9–316**, which tells us the effect of a change in governing law.

9–316 places the policing burden on the secured party and gives it either four months or one year to file its financing statement in the new jurisdiction. The four-month rule of **9–316(a)(2)** is not the same four-month rule in **9–507**; if the secured party fails to reperfect in the new jurisdiction, it becomes unperfected with respect to all collateral. As is the case with secured parties that fail to continue their financing statements under **9–515**, a secured party that fails to timely file in the new governing jurisdiction loses its priority to a purchaser for value that purchases (or perfects its security interest) before lapse.

We characterize the one-year rule in **9–316(a)(3)** as a debtor move rule, but it is also a sale of the collateral rule. Here is why. Imagine that your debtor is the Fabulous Foods Corp., a Virginia corporation. The Board of Directors of Fabulous Foods believes that incorporation in Delaware would be advantageous to Fabulous Foods. A registered business entity does not just re-register in another state. Therefore, Fabulous Foods would accomplish its reincorporation by establishing a corporation in Delaware and then selling its assets to or merging with the Delaware entity. Either way, there's a transfer of Fabulous Foods' assets to another entity. That's where **9–316(a)(3)** comes in. If a secured party that filed a financing statement against Fabulous Foods' assets in Virginia does not re-file in Delaware within a year, it loses its perfection. As is the case with the four-month rule above, if it does not refile, it loses its priority to an intervening purchaser for value.

5. SALE OF THE COLLATERAL

a. Continuation of Perfection in Collateral Sold

When the debtor sells property subject to a security interest, **9–315(a)** protects the secured party in two ways. First, it provides that the security interest continues in the property sold, *unless* the secured party authorized the sale free of the security interest. Second, as we saw in Chapter 12, **9–315(a)** extends the secured party's security interest to any identifiable proceeds of the collateral. Below, we address the steps that the secured party must take to continue its perfection in the transferred property and the proceeds.

Let's start with property that the debtor sells collateral subject to a security interest. **9–507(a)** tells us that a financing statement remains effective with respect to collateral that the debtor sells or otherwise transfers. But that rule applies only if the collateral is transferred to a party located in the same state as the debtor. If the debtor sells the collateral to someone located in a different state, **9–316** controls.

9–508 governs sales of collateral to persons who become "new debtors" who are bound by the security agreement. Article 9 defines "debtor" as a person with an interest in the collateral. **9–102(a)(28).** Any person to whom collateral is sold is therefore a debtor. **9–508**, like **9–316(a)(3)** deals with changes in business entity structure. Throughout these materials, we have been discussing the hypothetical business Bean-to-Bar-by-Bridget.

When we first introduced BBB in Chapter 11 of this book, Bridget Burton was running her business as a sole proprietor.

Her first lender, Community Bank, correctly filed its financing statement naming Bridget Burton as the debtor. Bridget and her lawyer have decided that BBB would be better off as a limited liability company. To gain the advantages of an LLC, Bridget would have to transfer all of her business assets to the new entity. This is a sale of the collateral. Community Bank has no problem with this because Bridget's business has been successful, but it would want Bean-to-Bar-by-Bridget, LLC, to become bound by the security agreement. In order to maintain its perfection in BBB's collateral, Community Bank would have to comply with **9–508**, which sets forth the same four-month rule that we have already seen with respect to debtor name changes in **9–507(c)**.

b. Continuation of Perfection in Proceeds

To determine how to continue the perfection of a security interest in identifiable proceeds, you look to **9–315(c)** and **(d)**. Here, Article 9 once again splits the policing and due diligence burdens between the secured party and the subsequent searcher.

9–315(c) tells us that "a security interest in proceeds is a perfected security interest if the security interest in the original collateral was perfected." At first glance, this seems to say that a secured party need not do anything to continue its perfection in proceeds.

You don't have to read too far, however, to see that sometimes the secured party must take additional action. **9–315(d)** tells us that the perfected security interest becomes unperfected on the 21st day after the security interest attaches to the proceeds unless one of several conditions is met. This is why secured parties want to know about sales of collateral.

Let's look at the "no action required" rules first. **9–315(d)(2)** tells us that a secured party's perfection continues in "cash proceeds." This is one of the many times in this course when you need to treat learning UCC-peak like learning a foreign language. The term "cash proceeds," as defined in **9–102(a)(9)** encompasses more than cash. It also includes checks and deposit accounts. Earlier in this chapter, we explained that a secured party could perfect its security interest in deposit accounts as original collateral only by control. A secured party claiming a deposit account as identifiable proceeds can have a perfected security interest without control. secured party will not want to rest on this automatic continued perfection however. In the next chapter, we will discuss the non-temporal priorities that affect interests in deposit accounts. Security interests in checks, another type of cash proceeds, are also subject to non-temporal priorities that we will cover in the next chapter.

The "no action required" rule in **9–315(d)(1)** has three parts. In order for a secured party to remain continuously perfected in identifiable proceeds under this rule there must be a filed financing statement covering the original collateral, the proceeds must be property in which a secured party can perfect a security interest by filing in the same office, and the proceeds must not have been acquired with cash proceeds. A typical situation would be when a debtor sells inventory and the sale generates an account. If the secured party has filed a financing statement describing the inventory, its security interest will continue in the account proceeds without further action.

There's a third "no action" rule that is implicit in **9–315(d)(3)**. This subsection tells us that a security interest continues in proceeds if it is perfected when the security interest attaches to the proceeds or within 20 days thereafter. Suppose that the debtor, Hockey World, has granted a security interest in its inventory to Great Northern Bank. Great Northern Bank filed a financing statement in the proper place describing the collateral as "inventory." Hockey World sells some of its inventory for cash and then uses the cash to acquire new inventory. he security interest does not remain perfected under **9–315(d)(2)** because there is a cash interval— in other words, Hockey World acquired the proceeds with cash proceeds. Hockey World's financing statement describes the collateral as "inventory" however, therefore as soon as Hockey World acquires the inventory proceeds, its security interest in the proceeds is perfected.

In all other cases, the secured party must reperfect in the proceeds. It can do this by an amendment to the financing statement to add collateral if the proceeds are collateral in which a security interest can be perfected by filing.

G. TERMINATING A FINANCING STATEMENT

Sometimes a debtor will pay off a loan within the five-year period during which a financing statement is effective. Certainly the debtor will want the records cleared so that they don't show a security interest against its property. **9–513** provides for the filling of another financing statement amendment—the termination statement. You'll see in **9–513** separate rules for financing statements covering consumer goods and those covering other collateral. When the collateral is consumer goods, the secured party itself must file the termination statement within the time period designated in **9–513(b)**. In all other transactions, the secured party need not file a termination statement unless the debtor asks for it. In order for a termination statement to be effective to release collateral from the secured party's interest, the secured party must authorize its filing. **9–509(d)**.

What is authorization? See below for a case involving a mistake made by some very big players.

OFFICIAL COMM. OF UNSECURED CREDITORS OF MOTORS LIQUIDATION CO. v. JP MORGAN CHASE BANK, N.A. (IN RE MOTORS LIQUIDATION CO.)

777 F.3d 100 (2d Cir. 2015)

WINTER, R., WESLEY, R., AND CARNEY, S.

BACKGROUND

In October 2001, General Motors entered into a synthetic lease financing transaction (the "Synthetic Lease"), by which it obtained approximately $300 million in financing from a syndicate of lenders including JPMorgan Chase Bank, N.A. ("JPMorgan"). General Motors' obligation to repay the Synthetic Lease was secured by liens on twelve pieces of real estate. JPMorgan served as administrative agent for the Synthetic Lease and was identified on the UCC–1 financing statements as the secured party of record.

Five years later, General Motors entered into a separate term loan facility (the "Term Loan"). The Term Loan was entirely unrelated to the Synthetic Lease and provided General Motors with approximately $1.5 billion in financing from a different syndicate of lenders. To secure the loan, the lenders took security interests in a large number of General Motors' assets, including all of General Motors' equipment and fixtures at forty-two facilities throughout the United States. JPMorgan again served as administrative agent and secured party of record for the Term Loan and caused the filing of twenty-eight UCC–1 financing statements around the country to perfect the lenders' security interests in the collateral. One such financing statement, the "Main Term Loan UCC–1," was filed with the Delaware Secretary of State and bore file number "6416808 4." It "covered, among other things, all of the equipment and fixtures at 42 GM facilities, [and] was by far the most important" of the financing statements filed in connection with the Term Loan. *Official Comm. of Unsecured Creditors of Motors Liquidation Co. v. JPMorgan Chase Bank, N.A. (In re Motors Liquidation Co.)*, 486 B.R. 596, 603 n.6 (Bankr. S.D.N.Y. 2013).

In September 2008, as the Synthetic Lease was nearing maturity, General Motors contacted Mayer Brown LLP, its counsel responsible for the Synthetic Lease, and explained that it planned to repay the amount due. General Motors requested that Mayer Brown prepare the documents necessary for JPMorgan and the lenders to be repaid and to release the interests the lenders held in General Motors' property.

A Mayer Brown partner assigned the work to an associate and instructed him to prepare a closing checklist and drafts of the documents required to pay off the Synthetic Lease and to terminate the lenders' security interests in General Motors' property relating to the Synthetic Lease. One of the steps required to unwind the Synthetic Lease was to create a list of security interests held by General Motors' lenders that would need to be terminated. To prepare the list, the Mayer Brown associate asked a paralegal who was unfamiliar with the transaction or the purpose of the request to perform a search for UCC–1 financing statements that had been recorded against General Motors in Delaware. The paralegal's search identified three UCC–1s, numbered 2092532 5, 2092526 7, and 6416808 4. Neither the paralegal nor the associate realized that only the first two of the UCC–1s were related to the Synthetic Lease. The third, UCC–1 number 6416808 4, related instead to the Term Loan.

When Mayer Brown prepared a Closing Checklist of the actions required to unwind the Synthetic Lease, it identified the Main Term Loan UCC–1 for termination alongside the security interests that actually did need to be terminated. And when Mayer Brown prepared draft UCC–3 statements to terminate the three security interests identified in the Closing Checklist, it prepared a UCC–3 statement to terminate the Main Term Loan UCC–1 as well as those related to the Synthetic Lease.

No one at General Motors, Mayer Brown, JPMorgan, or its counsel, Simpson Thacher & Bartlett LLP, noticed the error, even though copies of the Closing Checklist and draft UCC–3 termination statements were sent to individuals at each organization for review. On October 30, 2008, General Motors repaid the amount due on the Synthetic Lease. All three UCC–3s were filed with the Delaware Secretary of State, including the UCC–3 that erroneously identified for termination the Main Term Loan UCC–1, which was entirely unrelated to the Synthetic Lease.

A.   General Motors' Chapter 11 Bankruptcy Filing

The mistake went unnoticed until General Motors' bankruptcy in 2009. After General Motors filed for chapter 11 reorganization, JPMorgan informed the Committee of Unsecured Creditors (the "Committee") that a UCC–3 termination statement relating to the Term Loan had been inadvertently filed in October 2008. JPMorgan explained that it had intended to terminate only liens related to the Synthetic Lease and stated that the filing was therefore unauthorized and ineffective.

* * *

B.   Prior Certification Opinion

On appeal to this Court, the parties offered competing interpretations of UCC **9–509(d)(1)**, which provides that a UCC–3 termination statement is effective only if "the secured party of record authorizes the filing." JPMorgan reasoned that it cannot have "authorize[d] the filing" of the UCC–3 that identified the Main Term Loan UCC–1 for termination because JPMorgan neither intended to terminate the security interest nor instructed anyone else to do so on its behalf. In response, the Committee contended that focusing on the parties' goal misses the point. It interpreted UCC **9–509(d)(1)** to require only that the secured lender authorize the act of filing a particular UCC–3 termination statement, not that the lender subjectively intend to terminate the particular security interest identified for termination on that UCC–3. The Committee further argued that even if JPMorgan never intentionally instructed anyone to terminate the Main Term Loan UCC–1, JPMorgan did literally "authorize[ ] the filing"—even if mistakenly—of a UCC–3 termination statement that had that effect.

In our prior certification opinion we recognized that this appeal presents two closely related questions. First, what precisely must a secured lender of record authorize for a UCC–3 termination statement to be effective: "Must the secured lender authorize the termination of the particular security interest that the UCC–3 identifies for termination, or is it enough that the secured lender authorize the act of filing a UCC–3 statement that has that effect?" *In re Motors Liquidation Co.*, 755 F.3d at 84. Second, "[d]id JPMorgan grant to Mayer Brown the relevant authority—that is, alternatively, authority either to terminate the Main Term Loan UCC–1 or to file the UCC–3 statement that identified that interest for termination?" *Id.*

Recognizing that the first question—what is it that the UCC requires a secured lender to authorize—seemed likely to recur and presented a significant issue of Delaware state law, we certified to the Delaware Supreme Court the following question:

> Under UCC Article 9, as adopted into Delaware law by Del. Code Ann. tit. 6, art. 9, for a UCC–3 termination statement to effectively extinguish the perfected nature of a UCC–1 financing statement, is it enough that the secured lender review and knowingly approve for filing a UCC–3 purporting to extinguish the perfected security interest, or must the secured lender intend to terminate the particular security interest that is listed on the UCC–3?

Id. at 86. The second question—whether JPMorgan granted the relevant authority—we reserved for ourselves, explaining that "[t]he Delaware Supreme Court's clarification as to the sense in which a secured party of record must authorize a UCC–3 filing will enable us to address . . . whether JPMorgan in fact provided that authorization." *Id.* at 86–87.

C.   The Delaware Supreme Court's Answer

In a speedy and thorough reply, the Delaware Supreme Court answered the certified question, explaining that if the secured party of record authorizes the filing of a UCC–3 termination statement, then that filing is effective regardless of whether the secured party subjectively intends or understands the effect of that filing:

> [F]or a termination statement to become effective under **9–509** and thus to have the effect specified in **9–513** of the Delaware UCC, it is enough that the secured party authorizes the filing to be made, which is all that **9–510** requires. The Delaware UCC

contains no requirement that a secured party that authorizes a filing subjectively intends or otherwise understands the effect of the plain terms of its own filing.

Official Comm. of Unsecured Creditors of Motors Liquidation Co., 2014 Del. LEXIS 491, 2014 WL 5305937, at *5. That conclusion, explained the court, follows both from the unambiguous terms of the UCC and from sound policy considerations:

> JPMorgan's argument that a filing is only effective if the authorizing party understands the filing's substantive terms and intends their effect is contrary to **9–509**, which only requires that "the secured party of record authorize[ ] the filing."
>
> * * *

Even if the statute were ambiguous, we would be reluctant to embrace JPMorgan's proposition. Before a secured party authorizes the filing of a termination statement, it ought to review the statement carefully and understand which security interests it is releasing and why. . . . If parties could be relieved from the legal consequences of their mistaken filings, they would have little incentive to ensure the accuracy of the information contained in their UCC filings.

2014 Del. LEXIS 491, [WL] at *3–4 (first alteration in original) (footnote omitted).

DISCUSSION

The Delaware Supreme Court has explained the sense in which a secured party must "authorize[ ] the filing" of a UCC–3 termination statement. What remains is to answer the question we reserved for ourselves in our prior certification opinion: Did JPMorgan authorize the filing of the UCC–3 termination statement that mistakenly identified for termination the Main Term Loan UCC–1?

In JPMorgan's view, it never instructed anyone to file the UCC–3 in question, and the termination statement was therefore unauthorized and ineffective. JPMorgan reasons that it authorized General Motors only to terminate security interests related to the Synthetic Lease; that it instructed Simpson Thacher and Mayer Brown only to take actions to accomplish that objective; and that therefore Mayer Brown must have exceeded the scope of its authority when it filed the UCC–3 purporting to terminate the Main Term Loan UCC–1.

JPMorgan's and General Motors' aims throughout the Synthetic Lease transaction were clear: General Motors would repay the Synthetic Lease, and JPMorgan would terminate its related UCC–1 security interests in General Motors' properties. The Synthetic Lease Termination Agreement provided that, upon General Motors' repayment of the amount due under the Synthetic Lease, General Motors would be authorized "to file a termination of any existing Financing Statement relating to the Properties [of the Synthetic Lease]." And, to represent its interests in the transaction, JPMorgan relied on Simpson Thacher, its counsel for matters related to the Synthetic Lease. No one at JPMorgan, Simpson Thacher, General Motors, or Mayer Brown took action intending to affect the Term Loan.

What JPMorgan intended to accomplish, however, is a distinct question from what actions it authorized to be taken on its behalf. Mayer Brown prepared a Closing Checklist, draft UCC–3 termination statements, and an Escrow Agreement, all aimed at unwinding the Synthetic Lease but tainted by one crucial error: The documents included a UCC–3 termination statement that erroneously identified for termination a security interest related not to the Synthetic Lease but to the Term Loan. The critical question in this case is whether JPMorgan "authorize[d] [Mayer Brown] to file" that termination statement.

After Mayer Brown prepared the Closing Checklist and draft UCC–3 termination statements, copies were sent for review to a Managing Director at JPMorgan who supervised the Synthetic Lease payoff and who had signed the Term Loan documents on JPMorgan's behalf. Mayer Brown also sent copies of the Closing Checklist and draft UCC–3 termination statements to JPMorgan's counsel, Simpson Thacher, to ensure that the parties to the transaction agreed as to the documents required to complete the Synthetic Lease payoff transaction. Neither directly nor through its counsel did JPMorgan express any concerns about the draft UCC–3 termination statements or about the Closing Checklist. A Simpson Thacher attorney responded simply as follows: "Nice job on the documents. My only comment, unless I am missing something, is that all references to JPMorgan Chase Bank, as Administrative Agent for the Investors should not include the reference 'for the Investors.' "

After preparing the closing documents and circulating them for review, Mayer Brown drafted an Escrow Agreement that instructed the parties' escrow agent how to proceed with the closing. Among other things, the Escrow Agreement specified that the parties would deliver to the escrow agent the set of three UCC–3 termination statements (individually identified by UCC–1 financing statement file number) that would be filed to terminate the security interests that General Motors' Synthetic Lease lenders held in its properties. The Escrow Agreement provided that once General Motors repaid the amount due on the Synthetic Lease, the escrow agent would forward copies of the UCC–3 termination statements to General Motors' counsel for filing. When Mayer Brown e-mailed a draft of the Escrow Agreement to JPMorgan's counsel for review, the same Simpson Thacher attorney responded that "it was fine" and signed the agreement.

From these facts it is clear that although JPMorgan never intended to terminate the Main Term Loan UCC–1, it authorized the filing of a UCC–

3 termination statement that had that effect. "Actual authority . . . is created by a principal's manifestation to an agent that, as reasonably understood by the agent, expresses the principal's assent that the agent take action on the principal's behalf." Restatement (Third) of Agency § 3.01 (2006); *accord Demarco v. Edens*, 390 F.2d 836, 844 (2d Cir. 1968). JPMorgan and Simpson Thacher's repeated manifestations to Mayer Brown show that JPMorgan and its counsel knew that, upon the closing of the Synthetic Lease transaction, Mayer Brown was going to file the termination statement that identified the Main Term Loan UCC–1 for termination and that JPMorgan reviewed and assented to the filing of that statement. Nothing more is needed.

———————

We transactional lawyers sometimes bemoan the fact that we don't have our own TV shows like the litigators do. The above excerpt may illustrate why. The truth is that most law practice does not involve flashy performance in court. Lawyers read, and they need to read carefully. The failure to do so in the transaction above led to an enormous financial loss.

Chapter Conclusion: At the end of this chapter, you should be familiar with the various methods by which a secured party can perfect its interest in collateral. You should understand that the method of perfection in an asset is going to depend on that asset's collateral classification under **9–102**. You should also know the filing rules and the fact that the type of debtor will dictate both the contents of the financing statement and where it is filed. Last, you should know the effect of changes such as the lapse of time and sale of the collateral on a secured party's perfection.

PROBLEMS

1.   Corinne Morrison left her job as a lawyer to become a baker and has started her own business, Corinne's Confections. You are a new lawyer representing Entrepreneurial Finance Co., which has agreed to make a loan to Corinne to expand her business. The loan will be secured by the baking equipment located in the Corinne's Confections workshop and bakery as well as the inventory and accounts receivable of the business, the "Corinne's Confections" trademark, and the copyright for the Confections by Corinne cookbook. It is your job to prepare the financing statement(s).

In a small world story, when you met Corinne at the loan closing you realized that you knew her in high school. At the time, you knew her as Cory Peters and if you remember correctly she decided that she liked the name Corinne after your French teacher "Frenchified" all of your names for class purposes. She told you that she recently married Matt Morrison.

a.   What questions do you need to ask Corinne and what documents do you need to see in order to make sure that you have the correct name for the debtor?

b. Corinne lives in Thurmont, Maryland and her workshop/bakery is located in Gettysburg, Pennsylvania. Where are you going to file the financing statement(s)? What information do you need from Corinne and what documents do you need to see in order to answer this question? How many financing statements do you need to file?

2. Brendan Rett is a State Representative well known for his outspoken position on the anti-government groups that proliferate in his state. He is leaving the legislature at the end of his current term and is starting an alpaca farm. He borrowed money from his sister-in-law Rosemarie King to start the farm. He signed a security agreement granting a security interest in all of his livestock and farm equipment Rosemarie prepared a financing statement containing all of the correct **9–502** and **9–516** information.

Martina Beck is the attorney at the Secretary of State's Office responsible for UCC filings. After attending a conference about fraudulent filings by anti-government groups, Martina directed all clerks at the Secretary of State's office to reject UCC filings against public officials if the secured party is an individual. Following Martina's direction, the Secretary of State's office rejected Rosemarie's financing statement.

a. At the moment that the Secretary of State's office rejects the filing, is Rosemarie a perfected secured creditor?

b. If Hillside Bank makes a loan to Brendan a week later and files an authorized "all assets" financing statement that the Secretary of State accepts, who as between Rosemarie and Hillside has priority, assuming that Rosemarie has not yet refiled?

c. Assume that there is no Hillside Bank loan. If Brendan files for bankruptcy a week after Rosemarie's financing statement is rejected and before she refiles, will Rosemarie's security interest have priority over the trustee in bankruptcy?

3. You are the new lawyer for Lakeside Bank and in reviewing some recent loan files, you came across some inconsistencies in debtor addresses. The two loans that concern you are one made to Kristen Adams and another made to Juliet Moringiello. In the Adams file, the driver's license copy that you have on file says that the debtor's address is 4421 Palm Way, St. Petersburg, Florida. The financing statement that Lakeside filed with the Florida Secretary of State's office lists her address as 1450 Harbor Drive, #4, Tampa, Florida. You have confirmed that the St. Petersburg address is the correct one.

The driver's license in the Moringiello file shows the debtor's address as 2142 North 25th Street, Camp Hill, PA. The financing statement filed with the Pennsylvania Secretary of State's office lists the debtor's address as 14 Cocoa Drive, Hershey, PA. The Camp Hill address is the correct one.

Neither one of these discrepancies involves a debtor move. Should you amend the financing statements? Does your client face any risks if you do not?

4. You ran across another problem file at Hillside Bank. Hillside made a loan to Yolande's Yoga Wear on October 21, 2012 secured by all of her

equipment and inventory. It filed a complete and accurate financing statement in the correct office on October 22, 2012.

It is October 24, 2017 and you do not see any continuation statement in the file.

    a.   Can you file a continuation statement today? If the filing office accepts a continuation statement, what effect will it have?

    b.   If you file a new financing statement today, what effect will it have?

    c.   A former employee obtained a judgment against Yolande's Yoga Wear and caused the sheriff to seize some of Yolande's inventory in execution of the judgment on October 15, 2017. Who has priority in the seized inventory?

5.   Hillside Bank just acquired North Star Bank, which operates primarily in the northern and western states. North Star has a niche business financing snowmobiles, and Hillside will be continuing that business. You have the task of developing perfection procedures for the snowmobile business. How will you perfect the following security interests?

    a.   A security interest in connection with a loan to Snowmobile World, a retailer that does business in several states. Snowmobile World is a Colorado corporation. The loan will be secured by Snowmobile World's inventory.

    b.   A security interest in connection with a loan to Northern Wyoming College. NWC is borrowing money to purchase a fleet of snowmobiles for its security guards.

    c.   Security interests in connection with loans to individuals who are buying snowmobiles.

    d.   What research would you need to do to give a correct answer to these questions?

6.   Hillside Bank made a loan last year to the Culinary Corner, a retailer of high-end kitchen appliances for home and restaurant use. The loan was secured by Culinary Corner's inventory, and Hillside filed an authorized financing statement describing the collateral as "inventory" in the correct office. The loan agreement permits sales of inventory in the ordinary course of business and states that a buyer in any such sale will take the inventory free from Hillside's security interest. Thirty days ago, the Culinary Corner entered into the following transactions:

    a.   The sale of a freezer to Tom's Taqueria. Tom's paid the $6,000 purchase price by check and Culinary Corner deposited the funds into its bank account at Southern Bank.

    b.   The sale of a Viking stove to Gabby and Ken Moore. Gabby and Ken paid the $8,000 purchase price with a check and Culinary Corner cashed the check so that it could pay Office World for new office furniture for the Culinary Corner showroom.

    c.   The sale of stoves and ovens to Lakeshore Junior College for its culinary arts program. The college has promised to pay for the ovens 60 days after delivery. The ovens were delivered to Lakeshore 28 days ago.

In which of the new property does Hillside Bank have a perfected security interest?

7.   The company formerly known as The Snack Foods Corporation is a food manufacturer that sells healthy and not-so-healthy snacks nationwide. Two years ago, Rockledge Finance made a loan to The Snack Foods Corporation secured by its inventory, equipment, and accounts receivable. The financing statement filed by Rockledge in the correct office describes the collateral as "inventory, equipment, and accounts receivable."

    a.   As part of its rebranding campaign, The Snack Foods Corporation changed its name five months ago to "Snack Company, Inc." The only financing statement filed in connection with the Rockledge loan is the one it filed two years ago. Does Rockledge need to do anything right now?

    b.   Rockledge wants to avoid perfection problems in the future, so it has sought your advice. Anna Gregory, one of the loan officers at Rockledge, told you that Snack Company is considering some other major changes. Snack Company is currently a Pennsylvania corporation with its headquarters in Philadelphia. Do you need to do anything to the financing statement if it moves its headquarters to Charlotte, North Carolina? What if it decides to reincorporate in North Carolina? If you need to take action, by when must you do so?

CHAPTER 15

PRIORITIES

■ ■ ■

The last chapter of these materials covers priority contests. The most important thing to do when you are faced with any priority contest is to classify your contestants. The category into which your parties fit will determine which section of Article 9 governs their contest. Here are the contests that we will discuss in this chapter:

Secured Party versus Lien Creditor

Secured Party versus Secured Party

Secured Party versus the Trustee in Bankruptcy

Secured Party versus Mortgagee

Secured Party versus Buyer

Within the category of "secured party," there are several other classifications. Secured parties can be perfected or unperfected. They can also be "purchase-money" secured parties. **9–103.** And there are some purchase-money secured parties, those who have security interests in inventory, who need to take additional steps to earn their status. That's a lot to keep in mind, but remember that knowing how to identify your parties is the first step in resolving every priority dispute.

Article 9's most basic priority rule is in **9–201(a)**, which tells us that "except as otherwise provided" in the UCC, a security agreement is "effective according to its terms between the parties, against purchasers of the collateral, and against creditors." You will find the exceptions in subpart 3 of part 3 of Article 9, or **9–317** to **9–342**.

Before jumping into the sections that govern each type of dispute, there are a few important things to remember. First, if a secured party is continuously perfected, it maintains its original priority date. In the last chapter, you learned of several reasons why a UCC filing might become ineffective, such as the passage of time, a name change, or a sale of the collateral. You also learned what a secured creditor must do to continue its perfection if one of those things happen. So long as there is no lapse in perfection, the secured party's priority date is its original priority date. Once there is a lapse, however, the clock starts running again.

Second, it is helpful to review the concept of priority. When one party has priority over another, that party is paid *in full* before the subordinate party can receive anything. In the world of secured transactions, there is no such thing as *pro rata* sharing (unless the secured parties themselves agree—**9–339** or the security interest is in commingled goods, a category that we will not cover—**9–336**). **9–615** sets forth Article 9's priorities.

A. SECURED PARTY VERSUS LIEN CREDITOR

We have been talking about bankruptcy a lot in these materials, and by now you understand that a creditor that properly creates and perfects a security interest in its debtor's property has a special status in bankruptcy. To appreciate why, it is first important to know how the UCC resolves a priority contest between a lien creditor and a secured party. Why? Two reasons, one in state law and the other in the Bankruptcy Code. **9–102(a)(52)** includes the trustee in bankruptcy in the definition of "lien creditor." And the Bankruptcy Code gives the trustee powers that are based on the rights of lien creditors under state law. **BC 544(a)(1).**

1. THE BASICS

So how does Article 9 resolve a contest between a lien creditor and a secured party? If you identify your contestants as "lien creditor" and "secured party" you go to **9–317**. The basic rule of **9–317** is that if a person becomes a lien creditor with respect to an item of property before a secured party perfects its security interest in the same item of property, the lien creditor wins. **9–317(a)(2)(A).** Like most of the rules that you will study in this chapter, this is a "first-in-time, first-in-right" rule. Any time you see such a rule, you need to ask, "first in time of what?"

9–317(a)(2) gives even some creditors who have not yet obtained security interests priority over lien creditors. Read **9–317(a)(2)(B)** and recall that there are three requirements for attachment of a security interest. **9–317(a)(2)(B)** gives priority to the creditor that has filed a financing statement and obtained a security agreement (or its equivalent) before the lien creditor obtains lien creditor status. Such a creditor has not yet perfected its interest; remember that under **9–203**, a secured party must give value and a debtor must have rights in the collateral in order for a security interest to attach. A security interest that has not attached cannot be perfected. **9–308(a).** The effect of **9–317(a)(2)(B)** is to protect secured parties who make future advances secured by the collateral at issue. *See* Official Comment 4 to **9–317**.

2. PURCHASE-MONEY SECURED PARTIES

9–317(e) has a special rule when the competing creditors are a lien creditor and a secured party who holds a PMSI. If such a secured party files its financing statement within 20 days after the debtor receives delivery of the collateral, it will have priority over a lien creditor who becomes a lien creditor between the date the security interest attaches and the date the secured party files its financing statement.

B. SECURED PARTY VERSUS SECURED PARTY

If both of the competing parties are secured parties, **9–322** resolves the dispute, unless one (or both) of the parties is a purchase-money secured party, in which case **9–324** controls. (If you are wondering how two parties can be purchase-money secured parties, keep reading). Within the category of secured party v. secured party, we have a few special contests in addition to contests involving purchase-money secured creditors. We will also address contests involving PMSIs in inventory, and non-temporal priorities involving payment rights, deposit accounts, and transferred collateral.

1. THE BASICS

9–322(a)(2) tells us that a perfected security interest takes priority over an unperfected security interest. This makes sense; all along we have been stressing that if a secured party wants priority over everyone else in the world, that secured party must perfect its security interest. As between two *unperfected* security interests, the first to attach takes priority.

When the competitors are two creditors with *perfected* security interests, **9–322(a)(1)** tells us that the first creditor to file or perfect wins. Why file or perfect? **9–502(d)** allows a creditor to "pre-file" or file its financing statement before it has entered into a security agreement. Why would a creditor do this? Remember that a secured party files its financing statement in a public place to give the world notice of its interest. Searchers (subsequent lenders and buyers) can then find the properly filed financing statement and learn that the debtor has granted a security interest in the listed property.

Let's go back to our new business from the beginning of the secured transactions materials, Bean-to-Bar-by-Bridget ("BBB"). This time, BBB is borrowing some money against its equipment that it already owns and its accounts receivable. Lakeside Bank has agreed to make the loan to BBB, and asked Bridget as part of the loan approval process whether BBB had given these assets to any other lender as collateral. Although Bridget truthfully answered "no," BBB is a new business and this is the first loan that Lakeside Bank is making to BBB, so it wants a little bit of extra protection. It might therefore obtain authorization from Bridget (let's assume that Bridget has the power to make such decisions for BBB) to file a financing statement before advancing the loan funds to BBB. It will then file and wait a week or two before doing a search. If the search reveals no creditors who filed before Lakeside Bank, the bank can be confident that it will have first priority in BBB's equipment and accounts. And it will also have set its priority date—the date of filing.

So what does the "file or perfect" language really mean? Remember that when the collateral is goods, filing and possession are equally effective means of perfecting a security interest. If SP 1 perfects by possession before SP 2 files its financing statement against an item of collateral, SP 1 will have priority.

2. PMSIs

Earlier in these materials, you learned that a borrower can give a security interest in after-acquired property. *See* **9–204**. Now that you have learned that the date of filing is the priority date, you know that a secured party can have a priority date that is set well before the debtor ever acquires the collateral.

Let's go back to the above hypothetical loan to Bean-to-Bar-by-Bridget. Imagine that the security agreement that BBB signed granted Lakeside Bank a security interest in all of its equipment "now owned and after-acquired." Lakeside filed its financing statement on June 1, 2016. A year later, BBB's business was growing, and it decided to buy a new roasting machine. Cocoa Connections, the manufacturer, agreed to finance the purchase of the machine, and because Cocoa Connections itself was expanding its business, it offered favorable financing terms to chocolatiers who purchased its machines. On June 1, 2017, BBB signed a security agreement in favor of Cocoa Connections for the $40,000 purchase price of the roasting machine and Cocoa Connections filed a financing statement in the proper place. BBB took delivery of the machine the following day.

If **9–322**'s first to file or perfect rule were the only rule governing competitions among secured parties, the Cocoa Connections security interest would be subordinate to that held by Lakeside Bank. Cocoa Connections might be less likely to offer financing if that were the case, and as a result, Cocoa Connections might sell fewer machines. Fortunately for Cocoa Connections and other sellers, **9–324** provides a special rule for PMSI creditors. This section gives priority to a PMSI creditor if that creditor perfects its interest either before the debtor receives possession of the collateral or within 20 days thereafter. **9–324(a).** As a result, if Cocoa Connections complies with **9–324(a)**, it will have priority in the roaster that it sold to BBB over Lakeside Bank.

3. PMSIs IN INVENTORY

Inventory financing poses special challenges. As discussed earlier in these materials, inventory constantly turns over. Therefore, the inventory on a successful retailer's shelves in June might be completely different from the inventory on those shelves the preceding March.

From the preceding discussion, you should understand that the scenario in which the special PMSI rule arises is the competition between the floating lien secured creditor (one who has a security interest that extends to after-acquired property, either through an after-acquired property clause or because the collateral is inventory or accounts) and the PMSI creditor. When a creditor finances the purchase of inventory, it expects its security interest to extend to after-acquired inventory. Imagine, then, if we applied the rule from **9–324(a)** to PMSIs in inventory. A secured party with a floating lien on all inventory could find its entire security interest subordinated to future PMSI creditors.

9–324(b) addresses this problem by giving a creditor with a PMSI in inventory priority over a prior creditor only if it 1) perfects its security interest in the financed inventory before the debtor receives possession of the inventory and 2) gives notice to that prior creditor. **9–324(b)** contains the requirements for such a notice, and says that the holder of the conflicting security interest (the floating lien secured creditor) must receive the notice within 5 years before the debtor receives possession of the inventory. **9–324(b)(3).** What this means is that a notice complying with **9–324(b)** is good for five years to give the PMSI creditor priority over the floating lien creditor.

What might a floating lien creditor do upon receiving such a notice? Remember that it will want to protect its interest in its collateral. Perhaps its debtor is in default if it grants such a PMSI interest; if so, the secured party will be on notice of the pending default when it receives such a notice. Or perhaps it will offer to finance the new inventory itself.

There's one more thing to know about PMSI priority in inventory. Usually, a secured party's priority in original collateral extends to proceeds of that collateral. That rule is limited when the PMSI priority is in inventory. *See* **9–324(b)**. A secured party with PMSI priority in inventory does not enjoy the same priority with respect to proceeds that are accounts or chattel paper. There's a good business reason for this, and it is explained well in Official Comment 8 to **9–324**.

4. NON-TEMPORAL PRIORITIES FOR CHATTEL PAPER AND INSTRUMENTS

We have already discussed some of the special rules for perfecting security interests in payment rights and deposit accounts. Now we turn to the answer to why perfection by possession is superior to perfection by filing when certain types of payment rights are involved.

Let's review some of the different types of payment rights. We have discussed accounts several times already in these materials. An account is a right to payment of a monetary obligation arising in all of the scenarios listed in **9–102(a)(2)**. Often the account is a right to payment for goods sold or services rendered, but the definition is much broader than that. It is important to remember what an account is not; it is not a right to payment evidenced by chattel paper or an instrument, and it is not a deposit account.

As you learned in the payment systems chapter of this book, some types of payment rights are commonly transferred by indorsement and manual delivery. The laws governing negotiable instruments give special rights to persons in physical possession of those instruments. Two such payment rights are instruments, **9–102(a)(47)**, and chattel paper, **9–102(a)(11)**. As we discussed in the last chapter, electronic chattel paper, **9–102(a)(31)**, is a subcategory of chattel paper. An instrument *must* be a writing. You have learned that the UCC and many other laws have replaced the word "writing" with "record" to facilitate electronic transactions. The law of negotiable instruments does not do so.

The last type of payment right that we'll highlight is the payment intangible, **9–102(a)(61)**. Be careful of this term—it is not as broad as it may seem initially. In order for a payment right to be a payment intangible, it must first be a general intangible. General intangible is a "catch-all" definition—an asset is a general intangible only if it does not fit within any other collateral category. Therefore, a payment intangible is a payment right that does not fit into any of the other payment right categories.

Now that we have classification issues out of the way, let's look at the non-temporal priorities. **9–330(d)** tells us that the purchaser of an instrument has priority over a security interest perfected by filing if the purchaser gives value and takes possession of the instrument in good faith and without *knowledge* that the purchase violates the rights of the secured party. We have talked about the difference between notice and knowledge several times already in this book; knowledge means actual knowledge. **1–202.** The mere existence of a properly filed financing statement does not impart knowledge that a purchase of an instrument violates the rights of the secured creditor that filed the financing statement. **9–330(f).**

9–330(a) and **(b)** contain similar non-temporal priority rules for chattel paper. The rules apply to both tangible and electronic chattel paper.

Both chattel paper and instruments are "reified" debts. In other words, the paper itself has value. Contrast this with the printout of an account receivable. Such a piece of paper has no value in itself. Sometimes it is difficult to determine whether a signed writing promising payment is an instrument; the definition of instrument in Article 9 includes the negotiable instruments that you learned about in the payment systems portion of this course as well as "any other writing that evidences the right to payment of a monetary obligation, is not itself a security agreement or a lease, and is of a type that in the ordinary course of business is transferred by delivery with any necessary indorsement or assignment." **9–102(a)(47).** Think about what a creditor should do to perfect its security interest in a writing that promises payment for goods or services and may or may not be an instrument.

Chattel paper may consist of more than one writing. Sometimes parties argue over which writings constitute chattel paper.

DeGiacomo v. Raymond C. Green, Inc.
(In re Inofin Inc.)

512 B.R. 19 (Bankr. D. Mass. 2014)

Feeney, J.

The issues presented in this adversary proceeding include whether [Raymond C. Green, Inc.] RCG established that it has a perfected security interest in Retail Installment Sales Contracts ("Installment Contracts") in its possession in light of an authenticated Security Agreement between Inofin's predecessor and RCG through which RCG obtained a security interest, ... in "all of the Debtor's rights in and to chattel paper . . . . and all motor vehicle installments sales contracts [sic] purchased by Debtor with the proceeds of loans from Secured Party and assigned and delivered to Secured Party."

* * *

B.   The Debtor's Business and Its Written Agreements with Dealers and RCG

Inofin was a licensed financial services company, specializing in purchasing and servicing sub-prime automobile loans. Used car dealers ("Dealers") in Massachusetts and other states up and down the Eastern Seaboard would sell vehicles to consumers for small cash down payments. The balance of the purchase price was financed by the Dealers using Installment Contracts. Each Installment Contract set forth the buyer's weekly payment obligations to the Dealer and also granted the Dealer a security interest in the vehicle. Pursuant to the Installment Contracts, the buyer of the automobile granted the Dealer a security interest "in the collateral and all parts or other goods put on the collateral," as well as "all money or goods received for the collateral and all insurance premiums, service and other contracts we finance."

The Dealers then sold and assigned the Installment Contracts to Inofin pursuant to a Seller Agreement." Each Installment Contract, such as the one introduced as an exhibit, was signed by the Dealer as Seller and Inofin and contains the following assignment clause:

> By Signing below the Dealer/Creditor accepts this Contract and Assigns it to Inofin Incorporated in accordance with the Assignment of Seller below.
>
> Stoughton Motor Mart, Inc.
>
> Dealership
>
> By: L. Jack Giandomenico Title: President Date: 8/23/2008
>
> **Assignment of Dealer:** For value received, Dealer hereby transfers and assigns to Inofin Incorporated ("Assignee") all of its rights, title and interest in this contract and the collateral. This

transfer and assignment is made pursuant to and is subject to an Agreement between the Dealer and the Assignee by which the Assignee has agreed to accept the transfer and assignment of contracts from Dealer. The Dealer understands that this contract is sold under the recourse provisions of the Agreement.

It is unclear which "Agreement" the Dealers and Inofin referenced in the Installment Contracts, as Inofin and the Dealers separately executed a "Seller Agreement" and a "Partial Purchase and Assignment" ("PPA"). The Seller Agreement was an agreement between Inofin, as Buyer, and the Dealer, as Seller, and pertained to all Installment Contracts assigned by the Dealer to Inofin. The consideration for the Seller Agreement was set forth as follows:

> In consideration for the purchase of the Contracts by INOFIN, Seller agrees to sell, assign, convey, transfer, and set over to INOFIN all of its right, title and interest in and to the Contracts and Contract Documents (as hereinafter defined) and all rights conferred thereunder. All Contracts, Contract Documents and assignments shall be in a manner and form acceptable to INOFIN. The term "Contract Documents" as used herein shall mean contracts of sale, installment contracts, security agreements, UCC filings, and all other documents or instruments evidencing, securing otherwise [sic] relating to the Contracts.
>
> * * *

Inofin and the Dealers (but not the motor vehicle buyers) also executed a PPA for each transaction, which included a VIN number and a reference to an Inofin Worksheet Number. Among other things, the PPA set forth Inofin's obligation to remit to the Dealers the balance of the weekly cash payments received by Inofin from the motor vehicle purchasers after Inofin had fully recovered the monies due it under the PPA. These payments to the Dealers are commonly referred to as the "dealer reserve," or "backend payments."

Specifically, in each PPA, the Dealer agreed to assign, transfer, set over and convey to Inofin all of its right, title and interest in a specific "security instrument," to be reassigned as provided in the agreement. That reassignment provision is as follows:

> **TERMINATION OF ASSIGNMENT:** This assignment shall terminate at such time as Buyer [Inofin] has received the Amount Purchased required under this Agreement, together with all other additional expenses for which Buyer is entitled to reimbursement or at any prior time as the Buyer, in its discretion, may determine. Upon such termination, Buyer shall reassign to Seller all Buyer's then remaining right, title and interest in the Security Instrument and shall execute such documents and instruments as

may be necessary to effect such reassignment and terminate Buyer's interest as a matter of record. Upon reassignment any [and] all liability of the Buyer, if any, in regard to the Security Instrument or in regard to obligations, if any owed to Seller shall cease. Seller may terminate the assignment at any time by paying to [B]uyer the amount due together with all other additional expenses for which buyer is entitled to be reimbursed. Buyer may terminate any residual interest that [S]eller may have in the security instrument, notwithstanding any term or provision to the contrary in this agreement, at any time sixty (60) days after a default has occurred on the security instrument.

* * *

MISCELLANEOUS: Seller further acknowledges that Buyer is purchasing an interest as defined in this agreement and specifically acknowledges that this is not a loan or loan type transaction. *This Agreement shall inure to the benefit of and be binding upon the heirs, successors, representatives and assigns of the parties hereto.* This Agreement shall not be modified except in writing signed by all parties hereto. In the event any term or provision of this Agreement is found to be unenforceable or unlawful for any reason, the remainder shall be carried into effect as though the unenforceable portion was stricken here from.

(emphasis supplied). Thus, RCG, as an assignee of Inofin, as set forth in detail below, is bound by the terms of the PPA. Kenneth Shilson, CPA ("Shilson"), RCG's expert witness, testified that the PPAs were typical documents found in subprime used car financing transactions.

RCG and Inofin . . . commenced their lending relationship in April of 1996. . . . Inofin obtained most of its capital for purchasing Installment Contracts from a large number of private lenders, including RCG, whose principal and owner is Raymond C. Green ("Green"). Inofin and RCG maintained a business relationship for almost 15 years until Inofin's bankruptcy.

* * *

[I]f the PPAs are part of the chattel paper, then RCG was required, as stated in the Loan Agreements, to have possession of the *original* PPAs to perfect its security interest in Installment Contracts [by possession].

2.   Arguments of the Parties

(a)   The Trustee's Arguments

The Trustee maintains that possession by RCG of the original PPAs was required based on the Trustee's view that they were the documents by which RCG acquired title to payment streams under the Installment Contracts. Accordingly, the Trustee asserts that because RCG only had copies of the PPAs, the Installment Contracts were not perfected, and, therefore, RCG had no rights to the Installment Contracts. The Trustee argues that the PPAs are the "operative document[s]" with respect to the Dealers' rights under the Installment Contracts and relies on the language at the end of each Installment Contract.[49]

He also points to the Loan Agreements which provided that "Lender agrees that if and to the extent that there is a difference between the Borrower's rights under any 'Partial Purchase and Assignment' and any 'Recourse Assignment' [the Allonge], the former shall control."

The Trustee argues the following:

In order to perfect its security interest in chattel paper by possession, a creditor must have possession **of** the original chattel paper described in its security agreement. See *In re Equitable Financial Management, Inc.,* 164 B.R. 53, 56 (Bankr. W.D. Pa. 1994). "A secured party fails to perfect by possession its security interest in [chattel paper] when it fails to exercise dominion and control over all chattel paper pertaining thereto." *Id.*; *see also In re Funding Systems Asset Management Corp.,* 111 B.R. 500 (Bankr. W.D. Pa. 1990).

Because the PPAs are integral to the purchase of the Installment Contracts by Inofin from Dealers, as Inofin was not purchasing the entire payment stream due under the Installment Contracts and because the assignment language contained at the conclusion of the Installment Contracts does not constitute an absolute assignment, the Trustee contends that, in the absence of possession of original PPAs, RCG could not perfect a security interest in the Installment Contracts by possession. The Trustee adds that RCG's failure to require Inofin to assign and deliver the original PPAs (despite the requirement to do so in the Loan Agreements) is "further evidence that RCG was not primarily relying on 'possession' to perfect its security interest."

(b) RCG's Arguments

RCG asserts that it did not need the original PPAs because the PPAs are not chattel paper, and that the PPAs did not limit the absolute nature of the Dealer's assignment of its lien in the vehicle to Inofin. According to RCG, the PPAs provided Inofin with no rights and only provided the Dealers with the right to compel the re-assignment of Installment Contracts after Inofin had collected the agreed upon "Amount Purchased." It diminishes the importance of the PPAs as "merely a side deal between the Dealer and Inofin," which did not affect RCG's right to pursue and obtain the payments due from consumers under the Installment Contracts

---

[49] The language is as follows:

. . . Dealer hereby transfers and assigns to Inofin . . . all of its rights, title and interest in the contract and the collateral. This transfer and assignment is made pursuant to and is subject to an Agreement between the Dealer and the Assignee by which the Assignee has agreed to accept the transfer and assignment of contracts from Dealer . . . .

or repossess vehicles in the event of default. RCG did not attempt to distinguish the **cases** cited by the Trustee with respect to the absence of original PPAs.

3.   Applicable Law and Analysis

Although the Loan Agreements provided that RCG was to receive original PPAs, RCG received only copies of the original documents. An issue arises as to whether the PPAs were part of the "record or records that evidence both a monetary obligation and a security interest in specific goods . . ." namely, chattel paper or the Installment Contracts. Certainly, the PPAs circumscribed Inofin's rights after payment of the "Amount Purchased" or net sum set forth in the PPAs. Moreover, the Dealers were provided with important rights under the PPAs. For example, the Dealers' assignment of the Installment Contracts terminated when Inofin received the Amount Purchased required under the Agreement, together with all other additional expenses for which Inofin might have been entitled. Upon such termination, Inofin, and thus RCG, as its assignee, was required to reassign to the Dealer all Inofin's remaining right, title and interest in particular Installment Contracts (and execute any necessary documents and instruments to effect the reassignment and termination of Inofin's interest as a matter of record). In addition, the Dealers could terminate the assignment at any time by paying Inofin the amount due together with all other additional expenses for which it was entitled to be reimbursed; Inofin also could terminate the assignment and any residual interest that the Dealers may have had in the Installment Contracts at any time sixty days after a default had occurred.

         * * *

RCG's statement that the PPAs provided Inofin with no rights, is inaccurate, as Inofin had rights against the Dealers pursuant to the PPAs, as evidenced by the PPA submitted as an exhibit, as Inofin bought, for example, the right to receive $14,016.00 from the Dealer with respect to the Installment Contract, which were assigned to RCG. The assignment set forth in the Installment Contract from the Dealer to Inofin was made subject to an "Agreement" between the Dealer and Inofin as assignee. Whether that is a reference to the Seller Agreement or the PPA, it is clear that Inofin had rights against the Dealer and vice-versa.

         * * *

Accordingly, the Court must consider the effect of RCG's failure to obtain the original PPAs.

Two decisions from the United States Bankruptcy Court for the Western District of Pennsylvania provide guidance on the issue of what constitutes chattel paper. In *Glosser v. Colonial Pacific Leasing Co. (In re Equitable Fin. Mgmt., Inc.)*, 164 B.R. 53 (Bankr. W.D. Pa. 1994), the Chapter 7 trustee sought, pursuant to *11 U.S.C. § 544(a)(1)*, to avoid the security interest of defendant Colonial Pacific Leasing Company ("CPL") in two equipment leases. According to the Chapter 7 trustee, CPL's security interest could be avoided pursuant to the holding in *Funding Sys. Asset Mgmt. Corp. v. Chem. Bus. Credit Corp. (In re Funding Sys. Asset Mgmt. Corp.)*, 111 B.R. 500 (Bankr. W.D. Pa. 1990), because the debtor possessed "duplicate originals" of the chattel paper evidencing CPL's security interest. CPL contended the trustee could not avoid its security interest because the documents the debtor possessed did not constitute "duplicate originals" of the chattel paper in its possession and that all chattel paper pertaining to the leases in question remained in its exclusive possession at all **relevant** times. *Equitable Fin. Mgmt., Inc.*, 164 B.R. at 54. The court framed the issue as whether or not the defendant's security interest was fully perfected as of the date of the filing of the petition by virtue of its possession of the chattel paper which the debtor had delivered to it. The bankruptcy court observed:

> A secured party fails to perfect by possession its security interest in a lease when it fails to exercise absolute dominion and control over all chattel paper pertaining thereto. Accordingly, CPL's security interest in the above leases is unperfected by possession only if an entity other than CPL had control and possession of chattel paper pertaining thereto.

In re Equitable Fin. Mgmt., Inc., 164 B.R. at 56. The court found the trustee's contention without merit because "[t]he lease agreements debtor possessed were merely preliminary versions and were not completed documents having any legal effect.

> * * *

The Court is hampered by the lack of evidence as to the significance of the PPAs. The Trustee submitted no evidence to establish that the PPA was, in fact the "operative document" as he contends, although Shilson testified that it was an important document in the "buy/here sell here" market.[50]

In other words, the Court cannot answer the question of whether Inofin could have procured funds by providing original PPAs as security for loans coupled with copies of Installment Contracts—the converse of what it did with RCG. It is unclear whether Inofin could in Wallerstein's words, "double hawk" the Installment Contracts by offering original PPAs and copies of Installment Contracts to other lenders in exchange for loans. The Trustee introduced no evidence that a lender in the business of financing Inofin's acquisition of Installment Contracts would lend money to Inofin without an original Installment Contract and titles with Inofin's name appearing as lienholder, if it were offered only a PPA and a copy of an

---

[50] He was not asked to elaborate on that testimony, and the Trustee's counsel conducted no cross-examination on that point.

Installment Contract and a certificate of title. In addition, the Trustee offered no detailed analysis with analogies of how the <u>Funding Systems Asset Management Corp.</u> case and the documents considered by the court should be applied to the documents used by Inofin and RCG.

Neither the Trustee nor RCG submitted evidence relative to how other creditors secured their interests in Installment Contracts purchased by Inofin. In the instant case, RCG maintains that possession of the Installment Contracts was sufficient and a copy of the PPA sufficed. Thus, the Court lacks evidence to determine the importance of the PPAs in the sub-prime automobile financing industry. The Trustee did not sustain his burden of showing that the PPAs were chattel paper which RCG was required to possess to have a perfected security interest. The Trustee failed to submit sufficient evidence for this Court to conclude that the absence of original PPAs would have the effect of defeating RCG's security interest in the Installment Contracts. Although RCG may not have had "control" over the PPAs, the lack of such control appears not to have conferred on Inofin an ability to "double hawk" Installment Contracts. The only evidence that exists was Shilson's testimony that the PPAs were "important" documents. That description is different from an essential one. Without expert testimony as to how the business of purchasing and servicing sub-prime loans is documented, the Court must conclude that the Trustee failed in his burden of establishing that the PPA was, as he asserts, the "operative document."

––––––––––––––––

In the above case, the trustee in bankruptcy was challenging the creditor's perfected status. As you saw, the argument was about possession. The full facts of the case were far more complicated that the excerpt above shows but it is sufficient for you to understand how the court determined the adequacy of the documents that the creditor possessed.

So what good does perfection by filing in instruments and chattel paper do if a purchaser that complies with **9–330** always wins, regardless of timing? A secured party that perfects in an instrument or chattel paper prevails over a lien creditor, including a trustee in bankruptcy. A purchaser, as defined in **1–201(b)(29)** and **(30)**, is a person that takes property in a voluntary transaction. Lien creditors do not receive their interests in voluntary transactions.

5. NON-TEMPORAL PRIORITIES FOR DEPOSIT ACCOUNTS

You have already learned that a secured party that takes a security interest in a deposit account as original collateral (**9–102(a)(29)**) can perfect that interest only by taking control of the deposit account. You also learned in the last chapter that a secured party's perfected security interest in collateral continues in proceeds that are identifiable cash proceeds (**9–315(d)(2)**) and that proceeds in a deposit account are cash proceeds. As a result, it is possible to have a security interest in a deposit account that is perfected by filing.

9–327 gives us the non-temporal priority rules governing security interests in deposit accounts. To understand the hierarchy set forth in **9–327** you must read this section together with **9–104**, which sets forth the methods of taking control of a deposit account.

9–327(1) tells us that control beats filing, period. The remainder of **9–327** sets forth a hierarchy of control methods. You will recall that a secured party is in control of a deposit account if it meets any one of the following requirements: 1) it is the bank at which the deposit account is maintained (**9–104(a)(1)**); 2) it enters into a "control agreement" with the debtor and the bank at which the deposit account is maintained in which the bank agrees to comply with the secured party's instructions regarding disposition of the funds in the deposit account (**9–104(a)(2)**); or 3) the secured party becomes the bank's customer with respect to the deposit account (**9–104(a)(3)**).

If more than one secured party has perfected its interest in a deposit account by control, the first party in time wins if they have both perfected by a control agreement (**9–327(2)**). If one secured party is the bank at which the deposit account is maintained and the other has perfected by a control agreement, the bank at which the deposit account is maintained wins (**9–327(3)**). The secured creditor with top priority is the one that perfects by becoming the bank's customer (**9–327(4)**).

What happens when the debtor uses money from the bank account to pay bills or buy items? First, remember that proceeds of proceeds are proceeds. You get this rule from two definitions in **9–102(a)**: the definition of collateral (**9–102(a)(12)**) and the definition of proceeds (**9–102(a)(64)**). If the proceeds are traceable to the original collateral, the secured party has a security interest in those proceeds.

Once funds leave the deposit account, however, the secured party loses its security interest in those funds. **9–332(b).** If the rule were otherwise, sellers of goods and services could not be confident that they could take payments without searching for security interests in the funds transferred. This rule does not apply if the transferee is acting in concert with the debtor in violating the secured party's rights.

C. SECURED PARTY VERSUS THE TRUSTEE IN BANKRUPTCY

As you learned in Chapter 13, the Trustee in Bankruptcy has the job of maximizing the estate for the unsecured creditors. The Bankruptcy Code gives the trustee the power to avoid security interests in **BC 544** and **BC**

547. The power granted by **BC 544** is called the "strong arm" power, a term not used in the Bankruptcy Code but known by all bankruptcy lawyers. The power granted by **BC 547** is the power to avoid preferential transfers. The strong arm power is easier to understand, so we'll start with that one.

1. THE STRONG-ARM POWER

BC 544(a)(1) tells us that the bankruptcy trustee has, at the commencement of the bankruptcy case, "the rights and powers of, or may avoid any transfer of property of the debtor ... that is voidable by ... a creditor that extends credit to the debtor at the time of the commencement of the case, and that obtains, at such time and with respect to such credit, a judicial lien on all property on which a creditor on a simple contract could have obtained such a judicial lien, whether or not such a creditor exists." The quoted language means that the bankruptcy trustee has the status of a hypothetical lien creditor that obtains and perfects its interest in the property in question at the moment the debtor files its bankruptcy petition.

The bankruptcy trustee has the status of a lien creditor, and to resolve a priority dispute between a lien creditor and a secured creditor, you go to **9–317**. As a result, the strong-arm power gives the bankruptcy trustee the power to avoid security interests that are unperfected at the moment of bankruptcy. Why doesn't **BC 544(a)(1)** just say that? Because an Article 9 secured creditor is only one of several types of competing creditors.

Learning the trustee's strong-arm power gives you an excellent opportunity to review everything you have learned in the secured transactions portion of this course. In determining priority between a trustee in bankruptcy, you need to remember the requirements for a valid security agreement, the perfection requirements, and the conditions under which perfection continues after some change such as the passage of time, change in use of the collateral or a move by the debtor to another state. The consequences of getting any of the attachment and perfection requirements wrong are drastic for the secured party. If the trustee can avoid the security interest, the secured party is treated as unsecured in the bankruptcy case and thus receives a *pro rata* share of its claim along with all of the other non-priority unsecured claimholders. The following two excerpts illustrate.

GOLD v. PASTERNACK
(IN RE HARVEY GOLDMAN & CO.)

455 B.R. 621 (Bankr. E.D. Mich. 2011)

SHEFFERLY, J.

The Plaintiff in this adversary proceeding is the Chapter 7 Trustee. The Trustee filed this adversary proceeding seeking various forms of relief against the Defendants. Count I of the Trustee's complaint seeks a determination under **§ 544** of the Bankruptcy Code that the Trustee is entitled to avoid a security interest claimed by the Defendants because the financing statement for that security interest was recorded under an assumed name of the Debtor, rather than under the corporate name of the Debtor. . . . For the reasons explained in this opinion, the Court grants the Trustee's motion for summary judgment on Count I.

* * *

Facts

The following facts are not in dispute. Harvey Goldman & Company ("Debtor") was formed as a Michigan corporation in 1947. The Debtor's articles of incorporation state that the name of the corporation is "Harvey Goldman & Company." Over the years, the Debtor has been involved in many aspects of buying and selling machinery and equipment. On June 7, 1991, the Debtor filed a certificate of assumed name with the State of Michigan that states that the "true name of the corporation" is "Harvey Goldman and Company," and further states that the "assumed name" under which the Debtor will transact business is "Worldwide Equipment Company." Paragraph 1 of the "Information and Instructions" on the certificate of assumed name states that the "certificate of assumed name is to be used by corporations . . . desiring to transact business under an assumed name other than the true name of the corporation . . . ."

On January 3, 2007, the Abraham and Geraldine Pasternak Irrevocable Living Trust ("Defendant") filed a UCC–1 financing statement ("Financing Statement") with the Michigan Secretary of State. The Financing Statement identifies the debtor's "exact full legal name" as "World Wide Equipment Co." The Financing Statement identifies the secured party's name as "Geraldine & Abraham Pasternak Trust." The Financing Statement also states that it covers "inventory in the amount of $650,000.00 to secure outstanding loan."

On July 14, 2010, an involuntary Chapter 7 petition was filed against the Debtor. An order for relief was subsequently entered. On May 9, 2011, the Trustee filed this adversary proceeding. On the same day, the Trustee filed an amended complaint. . . . Count I seeks a determination that the Financing Statement did not perfect any security interest in favor of the Defendant because the Financing Statement was not filed under the Debtor's corporate name, "Harvey Goldman & Company," as required by applicable Michigan law. The amended complaint alleges that because the Financing Statement was not filed under the corporate name of the Debtor, any security interest claimed by the Defendant is unperfected under applicable Michigan law and, therefore, the Trustee may use § 544(a) of the Bankruptcy Code to avoid any security interest claimed by the Defendant.

* * *

Discussion

Section **544(a)(1)** of the Bankruptcy Code provides:

(a) The trustee shall have, as of the commencement of the case, and without regard to any knowledge of the trustee or of any creditor, the rights and powers of, or may avoid any transfer of property of the debtor or any obligation incurred by the debtor that is voidable by—

> (1) a creditor that extends credit to the debtor at the time of the commencement of the case, and that obtains, at such time and with respect to such credit, a judicial lien on all property on which a creditor on a simple contract could have obtained such a judicial lien, whether or not such a creditor exists[.]

"The 'strong arm' clause of the Bankruptcy Code, 11 U.S.C. **§ 544(a)**, grants a bankruptcy trustee the power to avoid transfers of property that would be avoidable by certain hypothetical parties." *Simon v. Chase Manhattan Bank (*In re *Zaptocky)*, 250 F.3d 1020, 1023 (6th Cir. 2001). This section "allows the trustee to 'step into the shoes' of a creditor in order to nullify transfers voidable under state [law] for the benefit of all creditors." *Corzin v. Fordu* (In re *Fordu)*, 201 F.3d 693, 697 n.3 (6th Cir. 1999) (quotation marks and citation omitted). Under **§ 544(a)(1)**, "the trustee by law acquires all the rights under state law of a hypothetical creditor with a lien on all the property of the debtor . . . ." *LSA Leasing Corp. v. Phipps Constr. Co.*, 972 F.2d 347 (6th Cir. 1992).

In this case, the Trustee argues that the Defendant filed the Financing Statement under the wrong name. Instead of filing the Financing Statement under the Debtor's corporate name, "Harvey Goldman & Company," the Defendant filed the Financing Statement under the name "World Wide Equipment Co.," which is similar, although not identical, to the Debtor's registered assumed name of "Worldwide Equipment Company." According to the Trustee, a review of the Uniform Commercial Code ("UCC") provisions enacted in Michigan compels the conclusion that the Financing Statement is insufficient as a matter of law. The Trustee's motion for summary judgment is supported by a July 1, 2011 affidavit of Charles Taunt, who served as the interim trustee prior to the election of the permanent Trustee in this case. Taunt's affidavit explains that on or about November 29, 2010, while serving as the interim trustee, Taunt directed his staff to obtain a UCC and tax lien search from the office of the Michigan Secretary of State under the name "Harvey Goldman & Company." A copy of the search that was obtained by Taunt's staff is attached to his affidavit. That search did not reveal the Financing Statement because the Financing Statement was filed under the name "World Wide Equipment Co." and not under the Debtor's corporate name, "Harvey Goldman & Company." Therefore, the Trustee argues that the Financing Statement did not perfect any security interest held by the

Defendant, and a hypothetical judgment lien creditor in Michigan would have priority over an unperfected security interest held by the Defendant. As a result, the Trustee argues, any security interest held by the Defendant is avoidable under **§ 544(a)** of the Bankruptcy Code.

The Defendant does not dispute that the corporate name of the Debtor is "Harvey Goldman & Company." Instead, the Defendant argues that the Financing Statement is still sufficient to perfect a security interest in favor of the Defendant, since it was filed under an assumed name that the Debtor had registered in the public record. The Defendant does not dispute that the Financing Statement did not show up in the UCC and tax lien search obtained by Taunt from the office of the Michigan Secretary of State. However, the Defendant argues that this fact is irrelevant, because the Debtor did business under an assumed name, and because the Financing Statement would show up in a UCC and tax lien search under the assumed name of "Worldwide Equipment Company."

* * *

The Trustee and the Defendant do not dispute that a financing statement must be filed in order to perfect any security interest that the Defendant holds in the Debtor's inventory. Nor do they dispute that if the Debtor's security interest is unperfected under Michigan law, then the Trustee may avoid it under **§ 544(a)** of the Bankruptcy Code. The only dispute between the Trustee and the Defendant pertains to the sufficiency of the name of the Debtor on the Financing Statement. The resolution of that dispute turns on the application of the UCC as enacted in Michigan.

[9–502(1)] governs the contents of a financing statement. **[9–502(1)(a)]** states that a financing statement "is sufficient only" if it "provides the name of the debtor." **[9–503(1)]** sets forth the criteria to determine whether a financing statement sufficiently provides the name of a debtor. **[9–503(1)(a)]** states that "if the debtor is a registered organization" then the financing statement is only sufficient if it "provides the name of the debtor indicated on the public record of the debtor's jurisdiction of organization which shows the debtor to have been organized."

Application of **[9–502]** and **[9–503]** to this case is easy. The Debtor is a registered organization. It is a corporation organized by articles of incorporation filed in Michigan. The name of the Debtor indicated in the articles of incorporation and on the public record for the state of Michigan is "Harvey Goldman & Company." Therefore, "Harvey Goldman & Company" is the name of the Debtor for purposes of **[9–503(1)(a)]**. Because the Financing Statement does not sufficiently provide the name of the Debtor under **[9–503(1)(a)]**, the Trustee is correct that the Financing Statement is not sufficient under **[9–502(1)(a)]**.

The Defendant attempts to escape this result by making four arguments. First, the Defendant argues that the registration of an assumed name by the Debtor somehow made *that* assumed name the corporate name of the Debtor. It did not. The registration of an assumed name does not have the legal effect in Michigan of changing the Debtor's corporate name. See Mich. Comp. Laws Ann. § 450.1217(1) (providing under the Michigan Business Corporation Act that "a domestic or foreign corporation may transact business under any assumed name or names other than its corporate name by . . . filing a certificate stating the true name of the corporation and the assumed name under which the business is to be transacted") (emphasis added). The Debtor's true corporate name is that which is set forth in the articles of incorporation under which the Debtor was organized. In this case, the Debtor's true corporate name is "Harvey Goldman & Company." The Debtor's assumed name is a name "other than its corporate name." The Defendant cites no authority to support its contention that the assumed name somehow either changed or became the true corporate name of the Debtor.

Second, conceding that the Financing Statement does not contain the name "Harvey Goldman & Company," the Defendant next argues that this omission does not make the Financing Statement seriously misleading. The Defendant's argument is not persuasive. [**9–506(a)**] does provide that a financing statement that substantially satisfies the requirements regarding the contents of a financing statement is still effective even if it has minor errors or omissions "unless the errors or omissions make the financing statement seriously misleading." [**9–506(b)** and **(c)**] provide the Court with assistance in determining whether a financing statement that contains errors or omissions is seriously misleading. [**9–506(b)**] states that a financing statement that fails sufficiently to provide the name of the debtor in accordance with [**9–503(1)**] is "seriously misleading." Under that statutory provision, the Financing Statement is seriously misleading because it does not sufficiently provide the name of the Debtor in this case.

Nor does [**9–506(c)**] rescue the Defendant in this case. That statutory provision states that "[i]f a search of the records of the filing office under the debtor's correct name, using the filing office's standard search logic, if any, would disclose a financing statement that fails sufficiently to provide the name of the debtor in accordance with section **9–503(1)**, the name provided does not make the financing statement seriously misleading." In other words, even if a financing statement does not sufficiently provide the correct name of the debtor as required by [**9–503(1)(a)**], it can still be effective if a search of the records of the Michigan Secretary of State using that office's standard search logic would disclose the financing statement in question. But in this case, as shown by Taunt's affidavit, a search of the office of the Michigan Secretary of State under the Debtor's correct corporate name (i.e., "Harvey Goldman & Company") does not disclose the Financing Statement. The Defendant does not contest Taunt's affidavit.

Therefore, because the Financing Statement is not disclosed by a UCC and tax lien search under the correct name of the Debtor (i.e., "Harvey Goldman & Company"), the Financing Statement is seriously misleading.

Third, the Defendant tries to avoid this result by arguing that a search of the internet website of the Michigan Department of Licensing and Regulatory Affairs under the Debtor's corporate name of "Harvey Goldman & Company" would lead the searcher to the Debtor's assumed name and, conversely, a search of the same internet website under the Debtor's assumed name would lead the searcher to the Debtor's corporate name of "Harvey Goldman & Company." The Defendant asserts that the Debtor's assumed name is *a* name provided on *a* public record, and can be found by a search of the records of the Department of Licensing and Regulatory Affairs, which itself is a public record. Therefore, according to the Defendant, the savings clause under **[9–503]** for a financing statement with errors or omissions is applicable in this case. This argument is sophistry. While the Department of Licensing and Regulatory Affair's records is certainly a "public record" within the common, ordinary meaning of those words, the savings clause contained in **[9–503(3)]** requires "a search of the records of *the filing office* . . . using *the filing office's* standard search logic." **[9–506(3)]** (emphasis added). This means a search of the Michigan Secretary of State's records. The fact that the Defendant's search of another public record (i.e., the Department of Licensing and Regulatory Affairs) revealed a cross reference to both the Debtor's corporate name and to its assumed name does not qualify for the exception contained in **[9–506(3)]**.

The Defendant makes one last argument against granting Plaintiff's motion for summary judgment by identifying the following "issues of fact" to be resolved at trial: (1) the Debtor conducted business using the name "Worldwide Equipment Company"; (2) all checks were in that name; (3) all invoices and letterhead were in that name; (4) all signs were in that name; and (5) the financing statement has the proper tax identification number. Even assuming all of these alleged facts are true, it makes no difference. These are all unremarkable actions one would expect from a corporation doing business under an assumed name. They do not change the fact that the name of the Debtor appearing on the Financing Statement is not the correct corporate name but is instead an assumed name of the Debtor that makes the Financing Statement seriously misleading.

Conclusion

. . . The Financing Statement was not filed under the corporate name of the Debtor indicated on the public record of Michigan, the jurisdiction of organization of the Debtor. Instead, the Financing Statement was filed under a name that resembles, but is not identical to, an assumed name of the Debtor. That Financing Statement was not disclosed in the UCC search obtained in this case by the interim trustee from the office of the Michigan Secretary of State. The Financing Statement is insufficient because it does not provide the correct name of the Debtor. The errors and omissions contained in the Financing Statement, by using another name for the Debtor, make it seriously misleading. Under [9–317(a)(2)(A)], an unperfected security interest is subordinate to a lien creditor in Michigan. Therefore, under the strong arm clause of **§ 544(a)(1)** of the Bankruptcy Code, the Trustee in this case may avoid any security interest claimed by the Defendant, because the Financing Statement was ineffective to perfect any security interest claimed by the Defendant. The Court will enter a separate order granting the Trustee's motion for summary judgment.

The court said that complying with **9–502** and **9–503** is easy. The failure to do so in the case above was an expensive mistake.

2. THE POWER TO AVOID PREFERENTIAL TRANSFERS

The Bankruptcy Code gives the trustee in bankruptcy the power to avoid some security interests that are properly perfected under state law. This power, found in **BC 547(b)**, is known as the power to avoid preferential transfers (commonly known to bankruptcy lawyers as "preferences").

Before we jump into **BC 547** let's distinguish the factual scenarios that would lead you to apply the strong-arm rules from those that would lead you to apply the preferential transfer rules. You apply the strong-arm rules when you determine that the secured party does not have a perfected security interest on the date of the bankruptcy filing.

The preferential transfer rules are aimed at preventing one creditor from obtaining an advantage over others within 90 days before the debtor files for bankruptcy (one year if the creditor is an insider of the debtor). Suppose that Center City Bank made an unsecured loan to Unlimited, a clothing retailer. Center City Bank starts to hear rumors that Unlimited is circling the drain, so it asks Unlimited to provide some collateral for its loan. If Unlimited does so and files for bankruptcy within 90 days, Center City Bank has received a preferential transfer that the trustee in bankruptcy can avoid. This is one of the classic preferences; another is the late perfection of a security interest, as we will see below. The important point is that when you see some activity by a creditor to improve its position within 90 days before the filing of a bankruptcy petition, you may have a preferential transfer problem.

Let's look at the statute, **BC 547(b)**. The chart below explains the components. **BC 547(b)** allows the trustee to avoid:

Any transfer of an interest of the debtor in property	**BC 101(54)** defines transfer to include the creation of a lien (defined in **BC 101(36)**; includes security interest) as well as "each mode, direct or indirect, absolute of conditional, of disposing of or parting with . . . an interest in property."
To or for the benefit of a creditor	**BC 101(10)** defines creditor.
For or on account of an antecedent debt owed by the debtor before such transfer was made	The existence of a preexisting debt is key—policy behind power to avoid preferential transfers is to deter one creditor from jumping ahead of the others shortly before a debtor files for bankruptcy.
Made while the debtor was insolvent	**BC 101(32)** defines the condition in which a debtor's debts exceed its assets. **BC 547(f)** presumes that the debtor was insolvent during the 90-day period preceding bankruptcy.
Made on or within 90 days before the bankruptcy petition; made within one year before if the transferee is an insider	This 90-day period is known as the "preference period." **BC 101(31)** defines insider in terms of different types of debtors.
That enables the debtor to receive more than it would in a chapter 7 bankruptcy case had the transfer not been made	This is the essence of a preferential transfer, and you need to understand how secured and unsecured claims are treated in bankruptcy.

Let's focus on the last requirement for a preferential transfer. By definition, an insolvent debtor does not have sufficient assets to satisfy the claims against it. If a creditor is unsecured and its debtor is insolvent, that creditor will not be paid in full in a chapter 7 liquidation. That is why any time an unsecured creditor becomes secured within 90 days before its debtor's bankruptcy, it receives a preference. Late perfection is a little bit more complicated. When you learned about creating a security interest earlier in these materials, you learned that the property interest in collateral is transferred upon attachment of the security interest. The Bankruptcy Code changes that rule when a secured party perfects its security interest on account of an antecedent debt during the preference period. *See* **BC 547(e)(2)**.

The case below involves late perfection and an allegedly mistaken termination statement.

WARD V. BANK OF GRANITE
(IN RE HICKORY PRINTING GROUP, INC.)

479 B.R. 388 (Bankr. W.D. N.C. 2012)

WHITLEY, J.

In this action, Plaintiff James T. Ward, Sr. ("Plaintiff"), Chapter 7 Trustee for Debtor Hickory Printing Group, Inc. (the "Debtor"), seeks to avoid under a variety of theories a security interest held by Defendant Bank of Granite (the "Bank") in the Debtor's inventory and accounts receivable (the "Collateral"). The Trustee maintains that shortly before bankruptcy the Bank (1) re-perfected a security interest in the Debtor's inventory and accounts receivable. . . .

I.   Trustee's Position

In the current motion, the Trustee seeks partial summary judgment on Phase 1 issues. Specifically, he asks this Court to rule that:

a.   The Bank's original security interest in the Collateral was terminated by the Bank filing a Termination Statement on December 1, 2008.

b.   The Bank's subsequent filing of a Correction Statement on November 10, 2009, did not alter the effectiveness of the prior Termination Statement, and, as a matter of law, did not revive the Bank's perfected security interest; therefore, even after Bank of Granite filed its Correction Statement, its Lien remained unperfected.

c.   The Bank's filing of a New Financing Statement on May 27, 2010, re-perfected a security interest in the Debtor's property and was a transfer of the Debtor's property under the Code.

* * *

III. Holding

As a matter of law, the Bank's perfected Lien on the Collateral was terminated by its filing of a Termination Statement in December 2008. The subsequent filing of a Correction Statement by the Bank did not alter the effectiveness of the Termination Statement and was entirely ineffective in reversing the effect of the Termination Statement. Therefore, between December 1, 2008, and May 27, 2010—even after Bank of Granite filed its Correction Statement on November 10, 2009—its Lien remained unperfected. Because the Bank's Lien was unperfected as of May 27, 2010 (the date the Bank filed a new financing statement), that New Financing Statement constituted a transfer of an interest of the Debtor in property.

* * *

IV. Because the Bank's Lien was Unperfected after the Filing of the Correction Statement, the Filing of a New Financing Statement Constitutes a Transfer of an Interest of the Debtor in Property.

The Defendants deny that the filing of the New Financing Statement constituted a transfer of an interest of the Debtor in property. Their denial appears to be founded on the assertion that the Original Financing Statement had been reinstated by the filing of the Correction Statement. As demonstrated above, this contention is wrong as a matter of law. There is little question that, for bankruptcy purposes, the filing of the New Financing Statement constituted a transfer of an interest in property of the Debtor under the Code. See 11 U.S.C. §§ 547(e), 548(d). Accordingly, the Trustee is entitled to summary judgment as to that issue.

Under 11 U.S.C. § 547, the perfection of a security interest is a transfer subject to avoidance. See 11 U.S.C. § 101(54). A transfer, for purposes of bankruptcy law, is defined very broadly, and includes "the creation of a lien" as well as "each mode, direct or indirect, absolute or conditional, voluntary or involuntary, of disposing of or parting with property or an interest in property." 11 U.S.C. § 101(54)(A) & (D). It follows, therefore, that because the Original Financing Statement became ineffective upon filing of the Termination Statement and resulted in an unperfected Lien, the re-perfection of the Lien qualifies as a transfer under bankruptcy law. Taken to its logical conclusion, and one which is widely accepted, when a creditor re-perfects its security interest in a debtor's property after the original perfection has lapsed, the re-perfection of the security interest potentially constitutes a **preferential transfer** of property, avoidable under 11 U.S.C. § 547(b).

HN23 For the purposes of 11 U.S.C. § 547, a transfer is deemed made as of the date of the perfection of the security interest, and not on the date on which it was created except where perfection occurs within thirty days of creation. 11 U.S.C. § 547(e)(2)(B). When there is a gap in perfection, perfection is not continuous, and the date of perfection is the date of filing of the latter financing statement. [9–308] cmt. 4, example 1. Thus, the filing of the New Financing Statement does not relate back to the date of the filing of the Original Financing Statement. As stated in the Official Comment to 9–308, the "security interest would be vulnerable to any interests arising during the gap period which under Section 9–317 take priority over an unperfected security interest." 9–308 cmt. 4, example 1.

A transfer of interest of the Debtor in property took place on the date that the Lien was potentially re-perfected—the day the New Financing Statement was filed. See 11 U.S.C. § 547(e)(2)(B). Section 547(e)(1)(B) further defines the concept of perfection by stating that a "transfer of a fixture or property other than real property is perfected when a creditor on a simple contract cannot acquire a judicial lien that is superior to the interest of the transferee." 11 U.S.C. § 547(e)(1)(B). In order to determine when a creditor cannot acquire a judicial lien superior to the transferee's interest, a court must look to applicable state law. See Howard Thornton Ford, Inc. v. Fitzpatrick, 892 F.2d 1230, 1232 (5th Cir. 1990); Long v. Joe Romania Chevrolet, Inc., 175 B.R. 56, 60–61 (B.A.P. 9th Cir. 1994). North Carolina law is clear. [**9–317(a)(2)**] provides that a lien creditor has priority over an unperfected security interest.

Here, the Bank's Lien became unperfected as a consequence of its filing of the Termination Statement. It remained unperfected until the filing of the New Financing Statement, i.e., within the 90-day period preceding bankruptcy. Prior to the date of the New Financing Statement, any other creditor could have acquired a judicial lien superior to the Bank's interest. As a result, the filing of the New Financing Statement was a transfer of an interest of the Debtor in property because it constituted perfection of an unperfected security interest.

D. SECURED PARTY VERSUS MORTGAGEES

As you learned in Chapter 11 of this book, although people like to say that Article 9 of the UCC has nothing to do with real estate, there are many Article 9 security interests that affect interests in real estate. Earlier in these materials, we introduced fixtures and discussed perfection of security interests in fixtures. Here, we will talk about priority of those security interests.

A fixture is an item of personal property that is so closely related to real property that an interest in it arises under real estate law. If an item is a fixture, it is transferred with the real estate. To use a simple example, assume that Alexandra wants to install a central air conditioning system in her house. Central air conditioning systems are expensive, so she wants to finance the purchase of the system. Her house is already encumbered by a mortgage in favor of Island Bank. As soon as the air conditioning system is installed, it will also be encumbered by the mortgage. Can the seller take back a security interest in the air conditioning system that will be superior to Island Bank's mortgage?

You will have to apply the fixture priority rules when your two competitors for collateral are a mortgage creditor or a purchaser of real estate and a secured party with a security interest in the fixture. The fixture financier will want priority over the mortgage creditor so that it can remove the fixture from the real property upon the debtor's default. *See* **9–604(c)**. Even if the fixture creditor has priority and can remove the fixture, it must compensate the mortgage creditor for any damage that it does to the real property.

Article 9 sets forth the priority of security interests in fixtures in **9–334**. To understand the rules set forth in **9–334**, it is useful to keep the following points in mind. For example, every fixture falls into another UCC collateral category. The air conditioning system is consumer goods if it is installed in a residence and equipment if installed in an office. It is also a fixture. This is important because **9–334(e)** refers to security interests "perfected by any method permitted by this article." Any method means both fixture filing and "plain old UCC perfection."

"Fixture filing" is a term of art in Article 9. A fixture filing is filed in the same place as a deed or mortgage on real estate, usually the county land records. **9–501(a)(1)(B).** It also contains some additional information that is necessary in order to file a document in the land records, notably a description of the real estate. **9–502(b)(3).**

The second point to keep in mind always is the role of a "lien creditor." You'll see the lien creditor in **9–334(e)**. We have special rules for fixture filings because persons obtaining an interest in real estate always check the land records by doing a title search before they acquire their interests. But trustees in bankruptcy do not check the land records before acquiring their interests in real property. The rules in **9–334** accommodate that reality.

The following case illustrates the classic fixture fight between a secured creditor with an interest in personal property that is a fixture and a mortgage creditor.

IN RE SAND & SAGE FARM & RANCH
266 B.R. 507 (Bankr. D. Kan. 2001)

NUGENT, J.

This matter came before the Court on May 22, 2001 for evidentiary hearing on Debtors' Motion for Authority to Sell Property Free and Clear of Liens. Debtors, Sand & Sage Farm & Ranch, Inc. ("Sand & Sage"), and Randolf and Sandra Ardery, owners of Sand & Sage, filed Chapter 12 petitions on June 13, 2000. Pursuant to 11 U.S.C. **§ 363(c)(1)** and **(f)**, and Fed. R. Bankr. P. 6004, the Arderys seek to sell real and personal property located in Edwards County, Kansas, to Bohn Enterprises, L.P. ("Bohn") for $ 100,000.00. Ag Services of America ("Ag Services") objected to the proposed sale asserting a first and prior lien over Offerle National Bank, formerly Farmer's State Bank ("the Bank") in the irrigation system, pumps and grain bins. Ag Services claims a valid and perfected security interest in, inter alia, the Arderys' equipment. The Bank holds a recorded mortgage which encumbers the real estate to be sold, along with any buildings, improvements or fixtures thereon.

At issue is whether the center pivot irrigation system is a "fixture" or simply "equipment" as defined in case law and the Kansas Uniform Commercial Code. If the Court determines that the irrigation system is equipment, then Ag Services' lien prevails because the Bank does not have a lien in the Arderys' equipment. However, if the irrigation system is a fixture, then the Bank's lien on the Arderys' fixtures is superior to Ag Services' security interest.

Whether personal property annexed to real estate is a fixture depends on: (1) whether it is actually annexed to the real estate; (2) whether it is adapted to the use of the land; and (3) whether the parties to the transaction intended the personalty to be permanently annexed. *Peoples State Bank v. Clayton*, 2 Kan. App. 2d 438, 439, 580 P.2d 1375 (1978). Put another way,

> ". . . goods are 'fixtures' when affixing them to real estate so associates them with the real estate that, in the absence of any agreement or understanding with his vendor as to the goods, a purchaser of the real estate with knowledge of interest of others of record, or in possession, would reasonably consider the goods to have been purchased as part of the real estate."

[9–102(a)(41)]. Because the Court determines the center pivot system to be so associated with the realty as to be deemed a part of it, and therefore a fixture, the Bank's filed mortgage constitutes a prior perfected security interest in the same and Ag Services' objection is overruled.

> * * *

Ardery purchased the property from Kinsley Bank. In order to secure a purchase money loan to acquire the land, the Arderys granted a mortgage to Farmers State Bank which covered both the real estate as well as improvements and fixtures. By its terms, the mortgage conveyed a lien to Farmer's State Bank in the above-described real property,

> "together with all the right, title and interest of the Mortgagor in said property now owned or hereafter acquired *and all buildings, improvements, and fixtures of any type now or hereafter placed on said property* and all easements, rights, appurtenances, rents, royalties, oil and gas rights and profits, water, water rights, and water stock, and all fixtures on or hereafter attached to the foregoing described property, all of which including replacements and additions thereto, shall be deemed to be and remain part of the property covered by this Mortgage." (Emphasis added).

Pursuant to K.S.A. § 58–2221, Farmers State Bank recorded the mortgage in the office of the Register of Deeds of Edwards County on June 2, 1988. Offerle National Bank is the successor to Farmers State Bank and the current holder of the mortgage.

Eight years later, on January 4, 1996, the Arderys and Sand & Sage executed a security agreement granting Ag Services a security interest in their equipment as well as other farm-related assets. Ag Services filed a financing statement with the Kansas Secretary of State on January 17,

1996. Neither the security agreement nor the financing statement refers to fixtures.

The irrigation system in question is an eight-tower Zinmatic center pivot system which was attached to the land when Ardery purchased it in 1988. The irrigation system is comprised of an underground well and pump which is connected to a pipe which runs from the pump to the pivot where the water line is attached to a further system of pipes and sprinklers which are suspended from the towers, extending out over the crops in a circular fashion transmitting water for irrigation. Integral parts of the system are the engine and gearhead which are bolted aboveground to a concrete slab directly above the pump and well and are attached to the irrigation pipe. The irrigation system is neither easily removed from its present location nor easily transportable to another. Unlike some pivot systems, the towers of this system are not towable, meaning that they must be partially disassembled and transported one tower at a time because their tires are not positioned in a manner which would allow them to be towed on the road. Removal of the system would also require disassembly of the engine and removal of the gearhead.

Extraction of the down-hole pump which sits 120–130 feet below the ground would be expensive and would require the services of an oil service company or some other person owning pulling equipment. Mr. Ardery estimated that it would take two experienced men a full day to disassemble and move the entire irrigation system including the pipes, engine, pump and gearhead at a cost of approximately $ 2,500–3,000. The irrigation pipes are valued at $ 5,000, the engine at $ 1,000–1,200, the pump at $ 2,500, and the gearhead at $ 700–800, equaling a total maximum value of approximately $ 10,000. The irrigation system is in fair condition but is starting to show rust, and the only major upkeep to the system has been the purchase of a new 1997 Ford gas engine. Mr. Ardery was unable to testify about sales of irrigation systems in pieces rather than as a whole, although theoretically the Zinmatic irrigation components could be sold separately.

Ardery testified that he intended to purchase the irrigation system when he purchased the land from the Kinsley Bank. Both he and Bartlett, the Bank's president, testified that they intended the sprinkler system to be a part of what was encumbered by the Bank's mortgage. Ardery also intended to sell the irrigation system to Bohn. This farmland has always been irrigated, and would likely be worth less than one-half of its current value if not irrigated.

Mr. Bartlett, an experienced banker who has worked in Edwards County for a number of years and is familiar with irrigated land and with the Zinmatic system in question, also estimated the value of the irrigation system to be approximately $ 10,000. Bartlett's estimate was based on a recent inspection of the system. Bartlett's photographs of the system, introduced in evidence, illustrated the system's great age and fair to poor condition. While Bartlett agreed with Ardery's values with respect to the entire irrigation system, he contended that the moving costs might be as high as $ 4,500, thus resulting in a net value of $ 4,000–6,000.

It is the Bank's custom not to file a separate fixture filing with respect to collateral already affixed to real estate when the mortgage is executed. However, if the landowner improves the land and adds fixtures, the Bank then obtains a new security agreement and makes a fixture filing describing the newly-annexed property. Here, the irrigation system was annexed to the land and included in the Arderys' mortgage to the Bank. Presumably, the Bank made no further filings because the debtors did not improve or replace the system.

Bartlett agreed with Ardery that, without irrigation, the value of the eighty acres would be substantially lower.

* * *

This case presents two issues to the Court. To be determined first is the nature of the irrigation system itself: is it a "fixture" as that term is defined by case law, the Uniform Commercial Code, and the Bank's mortgage, or is it simply "equipment?" Once this issue is resolved, the Court turns its attention to an analysis of each creditor's security interest to determine the nature, extent and priority of each creditor's lien in the property.

As noted above, the Kansas Court of Appeals has set out a three-step judicial test for determining whether personalty attached to real estate is legally a fixture in *Peoples State Bank v. Clayton*, 2 Kan. App. 2d 438, 439, 580 P.2d 1375 (1978). Paraphrased, the steps are:

(i)   how firmly the goods are attached or the ease of their removal (annexation);

(ii) the relationship of the parties involved (intent); and

(iii) how operation of the goods is related to the use of the land (adaptation).

Of the three factors, intent is the controlling factor and is deduced largely from the property-owner's acts and the surrounding circumstances. *Dodge City Water & Light Co. v. Alfalfa Irrigation & Land Co.*, 64 Kan. 247, 67 P. 462 (1902); *Schwend v. Schwend*, 1999 MT 194, 983 P.2d 988, 991, 295 Mont. 384 (Mont. 1999) (quotation omitted).

* * *

Turning to the present case, the Court concludes that the irrigation system is a fixture. It is firmly attached to the realty. The irrigation pipes are connected to the center pivot which is bolted to a cement slab in the center of the irrigation property and connected to the underground well and pump by wires and pipes. Further, the system is not easily removable. The towers must be disassembled in sections and transported separately, and disassembly and removal of the engine, gearhead and pump would be time-consuming and require the assistance of experienced people. It would also be expensive, particularly in view of the fact that the system's likely value is not more than $ 10,000, and the cost of removal could reach $ 6,000.

The relationships between the parties involved in each transaction also suggest the shared intent that the irrigation system be a fixture. In 1988, the Kinsley Bank sold the land to Ardery with the irrigation system included. Ardery, in turn, mortgaged the land, and the fixtures, to the Bank. Banker Bartlett testified that he considered the conveyance of the mortgage to include the system as that was the Bank's custom and practice in Edwards County. Ardery and Bohn clearly intend the system to pass with the land in the sale now before the Court. Finally, Ag Service's security agreement contains a specific reference to an irrigation system other than that which is at issue here, but contains no reference whatever to this system. The debtor, his grantor, his lender, and his grantee, all share the intent that the system in question should pass with the land.

The irrigation system is suitably adapted to the land. There can be little dispute concerning the need for pivot irrigation in the semi-arid conditions of southwestern Kansas. All witnesses agreed, and it is well within this Court's common experience, that irrigated units of land are substantially more productive of crops than dryland acres. This alone demonstrates the relation between the operation of the goods and use of the land.

Finally, as suggested above, it is apparently not unreasonable for a western Kansas buyer to expect a center pivot system to be sold as part of a transaction involving arable ground. Both Ardery and Bartlett testified to as much and Ag Services offered no rebuttal testimony on that point.

Based on the forgoing, this Court concludes that the center pivot system is indeed a "fixture" as contemplated by both common law and the U.C.C.

* * *

Having determined that the irrigation system is a fixture as defined under the U.C.C. and common law, the Court must now determine the relative priority of the two creditors' interests in the system. Ag Services' security agreement grants it a security interest in all of the debtors' equipment and farm-related assets. Ag Services has filed a financing statement that describes, inter alia, all of the debtors' "equipment," whether now owned or hereafter acquired. Unfortunately, to claim an interest in this fixture, Ag Services needed to do more. Its security agreement omits any mention of the debtors' fixtures. [9–502(b)] provides that a financing statement covering a fixture must not only describe the fixture but also contain a legal description of the real estate concerned as well as the name of the record owner. While Ag Services' financing statement contains a legal description, it appears to pertain only to Ag Services' crop security interest. Nothing in either Ag Services' security agreement or financing statement alludes in any way to the pivot system or to fixtures.

The Bank's mortgage, on the other hand, contains a description of the realty, the name of the owner, and an express reference to fixtures. In particular, the mortgage refers to "all fixtures now or hereafter attached to the foregoing described property, all of which including replacements and additions thereto, shall be deemed to be and remain part of the property covered by the Mortgage." . . . . [N]othing in Article Nine ". . . prevents the creation of an encumbrance upon fixtures pursuant to real estate law." [**9–334(b)**]. This provision obviates the need for a separate security agreement.

Because the Bank has a valid and perfected encumbrance on the Arderys' fixtures by virtue of its mortgage, and Ag Services has neither a security agreement which refers to fixtures nor a financing statement formally sufficient as a fixture filing or filed as one, the Court finds that the Bank's interest in the center pivot irrigation system to be first and prior.

* * *

For the reasons stated above, the Court finds that the Arderys' center pivot irrigation system is a "fixture" as that term is defined under the Kansas Uniform Commercial Code and that Offerle National Bank holds a valid and perfected security interest in it. Ag Services of America's objection to the Arderys' Motion For Authority To Sell Property Free And Clear Of Liens is therefore OVERRULED.

The excerpt above illustrates the general rule of **9–334(c)**, which is that the interest of an encumbrancer (mortgagee) or non-debtor owner of real property takes priority over a security interest in fixtures *unless* one of the rules in **9–334(d)–(h)** provides otherwise. The fixture creditor would have lost in the above case even if it had filed a fixture filing—the mortgage was first in time. The chart below summarizes the rules that apply when a creditor with a security interest in fixtures is in a priority contest with a person with an interest in the land.

Fixture Secured Party v. Mortgagee	First-in-time, first-in-right, but fixture secured party wins *only* if it has filed a *fixture filing* before the mortgage is recorded **9–334(e)(1)**
PMSI in Fixture v. Mortgagee	PMSI wins even if financing statement is filed after mortgage is recorded *only if* PMSI creditor files a *fixture filing* before the goods become fixtures or within 20 days thereafter **9–334(d)**
Fixture Secured Party v. Lien Creditor/Trustee in Bankruptcy	Fixture secured party wins if its security interest is perfected by *any method* permitted by Article 9 **9–334(e)(2)**
Fixture Secured Party v. Fixture Secured Party	**9–334** is irrelevant; **9–322, 9–324** control.

The above chart illustrates that a fixture secured party can be a perfected secured party without filing a fixture filing. But if it wants priority over mortgage creditors and buyers of the real estate, it must make a fixture filing.

E. SECURED PARTY VERSUS BUYERS OF THE COLLATERAL

You learned in the last chapter that a security interest in collateral can survive a sale of that collateral, and the secured party's perfected status may survive as well. These rules set up our final competition for collateral—that between a buyer of the collateral and a party with a security interest in that collateral.

If a buyer of property buys that property subject to a security interest, the buyer is at risk of losing the property if the debtor does not pay its loan. The buyer cannot be personally liable for the debt, but the property remains liable. You find the rules regarding priorities between buyers and secured parties in **9–315** and **9–320**.

1. AUTHORIZED SALES

Sometimes the loan documents will tell you whether a buyer of collateral takes the collateral free of the secured party's interest. **9–315(a)(1)** tells us that a security interest in collateral continues notwithstanding sale *unless* "the secured party authorized the disposition free of the security interest."

As always, you need to read the agreement closely.

WAWEL SAVING BANK V. JERSEY TRACTOR TRAILER TRAINING, INC. (IN RE JERSEY TRACTOR TRAILER TRAINING INC.)

580 F.3d 147 (3d Cir. 2009)

BARRY, J.

This case arises out of the competing claims of Wawel Savings Bank ("Wawel") and Yale Factors LLC ("Yale") to the accounts receivable of debtor Jersey Tractor Trailer Training, Inc. ("JTTT"). Wawel entered into a loan agreement with JTTT and its president, William B. Oliver, for the principal amount of $ 315,000. In the corresponding security agreement, JTTT pledged all capital equipment and assets of the company as collateral, and Wawel perfected its security interest by filing Uniform Commercial Code Financing Statements ("UCC–1s") . . . . Approximately one year later, JTTT entered into a factoring agreement with Yale whereby JTTT agreed to sell the rights to its accounts receivable in return for, inter alia, a 61.5 percent up-front payment of the amount due on the particular account receivable. Yale subsequently filed a UCC–1 statement describing its lien on all present and after-acquired accounts receivable of JTTT.

On April 4, 2006, JTTT filed a voluntary petition for bankruptcy under Chapter 11 of the United States Bankruptcy Code, *see* 11 U.S.C. § 1101, *et seq.*, and on June 29, 2006, Wawel brought this action seeking declaratory relief that its lien on JTTT's accounts receivable had priority over Yale's lien; that it was entitled to the proceeds of JTTT's accounts receivable that had been held in escrow following a state action filed by Yale; and that it was entitled to JTTT's outstanding accounts receivable until its lien was satisfied. Because the parties did not dispute that Wawel had a "first in time" lien against JTTT's accounts receivable—and thus a senior security interest—the central issue was whether Yale could establish that it maintained a priority position as a matter of law. *See* **9–322(a)(1)** ("Except as otherwise provided . . . [c]onflicting perfected security interests . . . rank according to priority in time of filing or perfection."). More specifically, unless Yale could establish (a) that Wawel consented to the sale of JTTT's accounts receivable free of its security interest, *see* **9–315(a)(1)**. . . . then Wawel was entitled to the relief it sought.

* * *

A.   Consent to Sale & **9–315(a)(1)**

Yale's argument that Wawel waived its security interest in JTTT's accounts receivable relies on HN3 U.C.C. § **9–315(a)(1)**), which states that "a security interest . . . continues in collateral notwithstanding sale . . . or other disposition thereof *unless the secured party authorized the disposition free of the security interest* . . . ." (Emphasis added). The general rule, as the commentary notes, is "that a security interest survives the disposition of the collateral," and Yale must establish that JTTT's sale of its accounts receivable fits within the exception for "authorized disposition 'free of' the security interest." *Id.* at cmt. 2. The question we must answer is whether the Bankruptcy Court clearly erred in concluding that it did not do so.

Yale argues, first, that because the security agreement accompanying Wawel's loan to JTTT did not expressly prohibit the sale of collateral, Wawel waived its security interest. That argument is without merit, especially given that in its agreement with Wawel, JTTT represented that it "w[ould] not settle any account for less than its full value without your written permission," and that it would "collect all accounts until [told] otherwise." JTTT's sale of its accounts receivable, therefore, ran afoul of the security agreement.

Alternatively, Yale argues that Wawel, in its course of dealing, implicitly waived its security interest. That argument has two components: first, that the Bankruptcy Court clearly erred in finding that Wawel lacked knowledge of the factoring agreement until December 9, 2005; and, second, that Wawel approved of the agreement to the extent that it surrendered its security interest in JTTT's accounts receivable. We are receptive to Yale's position regarding knowledge. At least one of four officers at Wawel—each of whom, according to Ranzinger's testimony, had the authority to bind the bank—received notification (via phone, facsimile, or mail) of each of the 199 wire transfers from "Yale Factors NJ LLC" to JTTT. *Cf. NCP Litig. Trust v. KPMG LLP*, 901 A.2d 871, 879, 187 N.J. 353 (N.J. 2006) ("The imputation doctrine is derived from common law rules of agency . . . [and p]ursuant to those common law rules, a principal is deemed to know facts that are known to its agent"). We assume, therefore, for purposes of our analysis (and contrary to the Bankruptcy Court's factual determination), that Wawel was aware that JTTT was involved with a factor—and thus was selling its accounts receivable.

Even assuming that knowledge, however, there is a substantial difference between Wawel knowing of the sale of JTTT's accounts receivable, and Wawel authorizing the sale "free of its security interest." *See* **9–315(a)(1)**. Yale argues to the contrary, but relies exclusively on cases interpreting former U.C.C. § 9–306(2), which was replaced by revised **9–315(a)(1)** in New Jersey, effective July 1, 2001. . . . The two sections differ in one material respect. Former § 9–306(2) stated that "a security interest continues in collateral notwithstanding sale, exchange or other disposition thereof, *unless the disposition was authorized* by the secured party in the security agreement or otherwise . . ." (emphasis added), while revised **9–315(a)(1)** states: "a security interest . . . continues in collateral notwithstanding sale, lease, license, exchange, or other disposition thereof *unless the secured party authorized the disposition free of the security interest . . . .*" (emphasis added).

Consistent with revised **9–315(a)(1)**, we must determine whether there is any evidence to support Yale's contention that Wawel impliedly authorized the sale of JTTT's accounts receivable free and clear of its security interest. In so doing, we keep in mind that the theory underlying **9–315(a)(1)** "is that a security interest would be meaningless if the secured party could not reach the collateral in the hands of a third party . . . when the debtor disposes of it without authorization." William D. Hawkland, Frederick H. Miller & Neil B. Cohen, 9B *Hawkland U.C.C. Series* § 9–315:1 [Rev] (2008). Because **9–315(a)(1)** does not require a secured party to take action to preserve its security interest, inaction alone may not lead to a finding of implied authorization. Inaction, however, is all Yale can demonstrate—specifically that Wawel failed to stop the ongoing sales of JTTT's accounts receivable. Acts of "[i]mplied authorization . . . must unequivocally demonstrate an intent to waive the security interest," Lary Lawrence, 11 *Anderson U.C.C.* § 9–315:9 [Rev] at 439 (2007), and evidence of such unequivocal intent is absent here.

* * *

III. Conclusion

For the foregoing reasons, we will affirm the District Court's decision to the extent it affirms the Bankruptcy Court's determination that Wawel did not waive its security interest in JTTT's accounts receivable.

---

2. SALES TO BUYERS IN THE ORDINARY COURSE OF BUSINESS

Now that you are at the end of this course, you have probably figured out that all businesses borrow money. Does that mean that every time you buy something from Target or Bed Bath and Beyond you need to be worried that one of the store's creditors will show up at your door to seize your coffee maker if the retailer falls on hard times?

The ordinary course of business exception to the rule that a security interest survives sale can give you some comfort. **9–320(a)** tells us that a buyer in the ordinary course of business takes free of a security interest created by its seller, even if the security interest is perfected and even if the buyer knows of its existence.

The key to understanding the **9–320(a)** exception is understanding the definition of buyer in the ordinary course of business (BIOCOB). To qualify as a BIOCOB under **1–201(b)(9)**, a person must buy goods: 1) in good faith; 2) without *knowledge* that the sale violates the rights of another person in the goods; 3) from a person, other than a pawnbroker, in the business of selling goods of that kind. To determine whether a buyer is a BIOCOB, you focus on the seller's business.

Can everyone who obtains goods from a dealer in those goods rest easy that they have acquired those goods free from a security interest in those goods? No. To qualify as a BIOCOB, the sale to the buyer must be consistent with the usual or customary practices in the kind of business in which the seller is engaged or consistent with the seller's own usual or customary practices. In addition, a buyer who takes goods in total or partial satisfaction of a debt is not a BIOCOB. **1–201(b)(9).**

3. CONSUMER-TO-CONSUMER TRANSACTIONS

In the last chapter, we gave you a hint about this priority contest. Recall that a creditor with a PMSI in consumer goods has the benefit of automatic perfection of its security interest. **9–309(1).** Such a creditor's security interest is perfected upon attachment, and the creditor need not give any public notice of its interest. When we discussed that rule in the last chapter, we told you that sometimes a creditor with a PMSI in consumer goods might want to file a financing statement anyway. The reason is **9–320(b)**, the "consumer-to-consumer" exception to the rule that a security interest survives sale.

9–320(b) applies only when both the seller and buyer are consumers (you might want to think of the exception as a "garage sale exception"). **9–320(b)** tells us that a buyer of goods who buys goods for the buyer's personal, family, or household purposes can take free if she buys from a seller who used or bought the goods primarily for personal, family, or household purposes *if* the buyer buys 1) without *knowledge* of the security interest; 2) for value; and 3) before the filing of a financing statement covering the goods. It is this last condition that tells us that a PMSI creditor with a security interest in consumer goods might want to file a financing statement if the goods are worth a lot of money.

Chapter Conclusion: At the end of this chapter, you should be able to classify the contestants in priority fights and the section of Article 9 that applies to each such contest. You should be able to identify the different types of payment rights and understand the rules that award non-temporal priority to some secured parties and you should know when a secured party has to take additional action to remain perfected in proceeds of its original collateral. You should also have a basic understanding of the trustee in bankruptcy's strong-arm power and its power to avoid preferential transfers.

PROBLEMS

1. You are advising Startup Finance, which is making a loan to Catherine's Catering Co. The loan will be secured by a perfected security

interest in the company's equipment, inventory, and accounts. Sheila Gregory is in charge of food industry lending at Startup Finance, and she is concerned about losing her collateral if Catherine's collects its accounts and deposits the funds in a bank account. Does Sheila have anything to worry about? If so, can you give her some advice that will give Startup Finance more protection?

2. Pinnacle Lending makes loans to companies like Startup Finance in the last problem. The general counsel of Pinnacle just quit to pursue her dream of opening a yoga resort. You are the new general counsel.

When Pinnacle makes a loan to a finance company, it intends to obtain a perfected security interest in that company's instruments and chattel paper. It would like first priority status, but sometimes it takes collateral in which it knows that another lender has an interest. After reviewing Pinnacle's loan files, you have the following questions.

a. Last May, Pinnacle made a loan to First Capital, secured by promissory notes payable to First Capital. You have found in the files ten promissory notes that appear to be originals signed by the parties to whom First Capital made loans, and there is no financing statement on the records. You also found a complete and accurate Security Agreement signed by First Capital and correctly describing the collateral. In reviewing some of the correspondence for the First Capital loan, you saw an e-mail message from your predecessor expressing some concern that when First Capital makes loans, it asks the borrower to execute the note in triplicate. What should you do right away and why? Do you need any permission from First Capital to do what you need to do?

b. If First Capital files for bankruptcy before you have the chance to take any further action, what will be Pinnacle's status in the bankruptcy?

c. The second file that you reviewed was the Speedy Lending file. Pinnacle made a loan to Speedy in February, 2017, secured by Speedy's chattel paper. You do not see the chattel paper in the files, nor do you see a financing statement filed by Pinnacle. You do, however, see a financing statement filed by First Bank on May 1, 2017 filed in connection with a loan made by First Bank to Speedy on that date. You came across a letter in the files dated February 1, 2017 from Main Street Finance to Pinnacle Lending, acknowledging that Main Street Finance made a loan to Speedy Finance in December, 2015, secured by Speedy's chattel paper, and that Main Street will possess all chattel paper as security for its own loan and for Pinnacle Lending's loan. What are the relative priorities among Pinnacle Lending, First Bank, and Main Street Finance?

d. The last file you reviewed was a problem file. You learned this morning that one of Pinnacle's borrowers, Millennial Money, Inc., filed for bankruptcy. You reviewed the Millennial Money file, and although you found a complete and accurate Security Agreement granting a security interest in Millennial Money's instruments to Pinnacle, you found no instruments in the file and no one at the Pinnacle can find any instruments. You did, however, see that Pinnacle filed a financing statement describing the collateral as instruments in the correct office 14 months ago. What is Pinnacle's status in the Millennial Money bankruptcy?

3.   You are the trustee in bankruptcy for Mountain Adventures, Inc. Mountain Adventures filed for bankruptcy on May 1, 2017. Assume that it is now May 5, 2017. Which of the following security interests will you be able to avoid? All of the financing statements described below were filed in the Secretary of State's office in the state in which Mountain Adventures is incorporated.

   a.   Summit Bank made a loan to Mountain Adventures on November 1, 2016. On November 2, 2016 Summit filed a complete and accurate financing statement describing the collateral as equipment. The Security Agreement from Mountain Adventures to Summit describes the collateral as "the Collateral described in Exhibit A to this agreement." There is no Exhibit A attached to the agreement.

   b.   Is your answer to a. any different if the loan officer from Summit offers to provide the collateral description today?

   c.   Countryside Bank made a loan to Mountain Adventures on January 15, 2017 secured by its accounts receivable. Countryside filed its financing statement the next day. The financing statement names the secured party as "Countryside Bank," the debtor as "Mountain Adventures Corp.," and contains an incorrect address for Mountain Adventures.

   d.   Treetop Trails sold ziplining equipment to Mountain Adventures on October 1, 2016. Mountain Adventures paid a $5,000 down payment and signed a promissory note in favor of Treetop Trails for the remainder of the $50,000 purchase price. Treetop Trails retained a security interest in the ziplining equipment, which consists of pylons, staircases, and decks attached to the ground, cables, braking systems, and harnesses. The financing statement filed in the Secretary of State's office describes the collateral as "equipment" and does not contain a description of the real estate. The Security Agreement between Treetop Trails and Mountain Adventures is complete and accurate.

4.   Bankruptcy work is booming these days, especially in the retail sector. Athleisure World, Inc. also filed for bankruptcy on May 1, 2017. You are the trustee. In reviewing the Athleisure World matter, you find the following:

   (1)   Financing statement filed by State Bank against Athleisure World on April 2, 2017. The collateral is described as "accounts." State Bank made the loan in March, 2012, and filed a financing statement against Athleisure World on March 3, 2012. It

appears that the April 2, 2017 financing statement was filed in connection with the same loan.

(2)   Financing statement filed by Second Bank on March 5, 2017, secured by Athleisure World's "equipment." The security agreement between Second Bank and Athleisure World is dated January 15, 2017.

Athleisure World's bankruptcy will pay its general unsecured creditors 20% of their claims. Can you avoid either of the above security interests?

5.   Lulu Lemon, Inc. is a yoga wear manufacturer. Elizabeth Lemon, the company's CEO, wants to make absolutely sure that her company has a first-priority security interest when the company agrees to sell clothing on credit to retailers. Lulu Lemon is about to send a large shipment of clothing to the Namaste Threads chain of stores. In doing your due diligence, you found an "all assets" financing statement filed last year by Worldwide Credit against Namaste Threads. Can Lulu Lemon, Inc. obtain first priority in the clothing it is about to send to Namaste Threads?

6.   Home Lighting sells elaborate lighting systems, most of which are installed by individuals in large, expensive houses. It sells its lighting systems on credit, and when it sells a lighting system on credit, it requires the buyer to sign a security agreement granting it a security interest in the system.

   a.   Home Lighting wants to make sure that it has the right to rip out a lighting system if a buyer defaults on its obligation to pay for it. What must Home Lighting do to make sure that it has this right?

   b.   Home Lighting sold a lighting system to Jim and Annie on credit. Jim and Annie had the system installed in their home. Jim and Annie signed a security agreement in favor of Home Lighting describing the system. There is no financing statement on any records in connection with the sale to Jim and Annie. Jim and Annie filed for bankruptcy last week. What is the status of Home Lighting in Jim and Annie's bankruptcy?

7.   Waterside Finance Co. lent $500,000 to Bayview Boats, a boat retailer, secured by Bayview's inventory. Waterside properly created its security interest and perfected it by filing a financing statement in the Secretary of State's office. Waterside is concerned that Bayview is selling boats without using the proceeds to pay Waterside. You learned about the following transactions. What is Waterside's collateral after these transactions?

   a.   Bayview recently transferred a boat to its accountant, Lynne Jackson, in payment of an overdue bill.

   b.   Bayview sold a boat to Andrew Kiely. Andrew paid $30,000 in cash for the boat, which Bayview deposited into a bank account containing only boat proceeds. Bayview then used the money to pay back rent on one of its marina leases.

8. Two years ago, Bayview Boats in the above problem sold a boat for $30,000 to Luca Bell. Luca paid $3,000 down and financed the remainder of the purchase price through Bayview. Luca signed a security agreement in favor of Bayview granting a security interest in the boat. There is nothing on any public record that indicates that Bayview has a security interest in the boat. Luca uses the boat to go fishing with his family and friends.

   a. Does Bayview have a perfected security interest in the boat? What additional information do you need in order to answer that question?

   b. Assume that your answer to Part a. is yes. Luca is moving inland and sadly has no more need for a fishing boat. He sold the boat last week to his friend Anne-Marie for $15,000. If did not pay the $15,000 to Bayview, as required by his security agreement with Bayview, does Bayview have the right to recover the boat from Anne-Marie?

INDEX

References are to Pages

691